Automotive Brake Systems

Shop Manual

Fourth Edition

Chek-Chart

Jeffrey Rehkopf
Revision Author

James D. Halderman
Series Advisor

PEARSON
Prentice Hall

Upper Saddle River, New Jersey
Columbus, Ohio

Library of Congress Cataloging-in-Publication Data
Rehkopf, Jeffrey.
   Automotive brake systems. Shop manual / Jeffrey Rehkopf, revision author.—4th ed.
   p. cm.
   ISBN 0-13-048204-8
   1. Automobiles—Brakes—Maintenance and repair. I. Halderman, James D., 1943- Automobiles brake systems. II. Title.
   TL269.R442 2006
   629.2'46—dc22
                                                                                2005020690

Acquisitions Editor: Tim Peyton
Associate Editor: Jill Jones-Renger
Editorial Assistant: Nancy Kesterson
Production Coordination: Carlisle Publishers Services
Production Editor: Christine Buckendahl
Design Coordinator: Diane Ernsberger
Cover Designer: Jeff Vanik
Cover art: Corel
Production Manager: Deidra Schwartz
Marketing Manager: Ben Leonard
Senior Marketing Coordinator: Liz Farrell
Marketing Assistant: Les Roberts

This book was set in Times by Carlisle Communications, Ltd. It was printed and bound by Banta Book Group. The cover was printed by The Lehigh Press, Inc.

"Portions of materials contained herein have been reprinted with permission of General Motors Corporation, Service and Parts Operations" License Agreement #0510862.

Copyright © 2006 by Pearson Education, Inc., Upper Saddle River, New Jersey 07458. Pearson Prentice Hall. All rights reserved. Printed in the United States of America. This publication is protected by Copyright and permission should be obtained from the publisher prior to any prohibited reproduction, storage in a retrieval system, or transmission in any form or by any means, electronic, mechanical, photocopying, recording, or likewise. For information regarding permission(s), write to: Rights and Permissions Department.

Pearson Prentice Hall™ is a trademark of Pearson Education, Inc.
Pearson® is a registered trademark of Pearson plc
Prentice Hall® is a registered trademark of Pearson Education, Inc.

Pearson Education Ltd.
Pearson Education Singapore Pte. Ltd.
Pearson Education Canada, Ltd.
Pearson Education—Japan

Pearson Education Australia Pty. Limited
Pearson Education North Asia Ltd.
Pearson Educación de Mexico, S.A. de C.V.
Pearson Education Malaysia Pte. Ltd.

PEARSON
Prentice Hall

10 9 8 7 6 5 4 3 2
0-13-048204-8

Introduction

Automotive Brake Systems is part of the Chek-Chart automotive series. The entire series is job-oriented and is designed especially for students who intend to work in the automotive service profession. The package for each course consists of two volumes, a *Classroom Manual* and a *Shop Manual*.

This fourth edition of *Automotive Brake Systems* has been revised to include in-depth coverage of the latest developments in automotive braking systems. Students will be able to use the knowledge gained from these books and from the instructor to diagnose and repair automotive brake systems used on today's automobiles.

This package retains the traditional thoroughness and readability of the Chek-Chart automotive series. Furthermore, both the *Classroom Manual* and the *Shop Manual*, as well as the *Instructor's Manual*, have been greatly enhanced.

CLASSROOM MANUAL

New features in the *Classroom Manual* include:

- More than 60 new figures and photographs.
- Updated information on Federal regulations
- Updated information on brake fluids
- Expanded coverage of antilock brake systems (ABS)
- Introduction to advanced antilock brake functions, including traction control, stability control, and braking assist systems
- Introduction to new vehicle communication systems related to ABS

SHOP MANUAL

The chapters of the revised *Shop Manual* correlate closely with the *Classroom Manual*. There are over 130 new or revised illustrations. New features in the *Shop Manual* include:

- Addition of shop safety practices in Chapter 1
- Consolidate repair procedures for disc and drum brakes
- New photo sequences showing brake pad replacement on three common types of brake systems.
- New photo sequence on the use of the on-vehicle-lathe
- Update on the latest antilock brake systems and components.

INSTRUCTOR'S MANUAL

The *Instructor's Manual* includes task sheets that cover many of the NATEF tasks for *Automotive Brake Systems*. Instructors may reproduce these task sheets for use by the students in the lab or during an internship. The *Instructor's Manual* also includes a test bank and answers to end-of-chapter questions in the *Classroom Manual*.

The *Instructor's Resource* CD that accompanies the *Instructor's Manual* includes Microsoft® PowerPoint® presentations and photographs that appear in the *Classroom Manual* and *Shop Manual*. These high-resolution photographs are suitable for projection or reproduction.

Because of the comprehensive material, hundreds of high-quality illustrations, and inclusion of the latest automotive technology, these books will keep their value over the years. In fact, *Automotive Brake Systems* will form the core of the master technician's professional library.

How to Use This Book

WHY ARE THERE TWO MANUALS?

This two-volume text—*Automotive Brake Systems*—is unlike most other textbooks. It is actually two books, a *Classroom Manual* and a *Shop Manual* that should be used together. The *Classroom Manual* teaches you what you need to know about brake system theory and the braking systems on cars. The *Shop Manual* will show you how to repair and adjust complete systems, as well as individual components.

WHAT IS IN THESE MANUALS?

There are several aids in the *Classroom Manual* that will help you learn more.

- Each chapter is based on detailed learning objectives, which are listed in the beginning of each chapter.
- Each chapter is divided into self-contained sections for easier understanding and review. This organization clearly shows which parts make up which systems, and how various parts or systems that perform the same task differ or are the same.
- Most parts and processes are fully illustrated with drawings and photographs.
- A list of Key Terms is located at the beginning of each chapter. These are printed in **boldface type** in the text and are defined in a glossary at the end of the manual. Use these words to build the vocabulary needed to understand the text.
- Review Questions follow each chapter. Use them to test your knowledge of the material covered.
- A brief summary at the end of each chapter helps you review for exams.

The *Shop Manual* has detailed instructions on the test, service, and overhaul of automotive brake systems and their components. These are easy to understand and often include step-by-step explanations of the procedure. Key features of the *Shop Manual* include:

- Each chapter is based upon ASE/NATEF tasks, which are listed in the beginning of each chapter.
- Helpful information on the use and maintenance of shop tools and test equipment.
- Detailed safety precautions.
- Clear illustrations and diagrams to help you locate trouble spots while learning to read the service literature.
- Test procedures and troubleshooting hints that help you work better and faster.
- Repair tips used by professionals, presented clearly and accurately.

WHERE SHOULD I BEGIN?

If you already know something about automotive brake systems and know how to repair them, you will find that this book is a helpful review. If you are just starting in car repair, then the book will give you a solid foundation on which to develop professional-level skills.

Your instructor will design a course to take advantage of what you already know, and what facilities and equipment are available to work with. You may be asked to read certain chapters of this manual out of order. That is fine; the important thing is to fully understand each subject before you move on to the text. Study the vocabulary words, and use the review questions to help you comprehend the material.

While reading the *Classroom Manual*, refer to your *Shop Manual* and relate the descriptive text to the service procedures. When working on actual car brake systems, look back to the *Classroom Manual* to keep basic information fresh in your mind. Working on such a complicated modern brake system isn't always easy.

How to Use This Book

Take advantage of the information in the *Classroom Manual,* the procedures in the *Shop Manual,* and the knowledge of your instructor to help you.

Remember that the *Shop Manual* is a good book for work, not just a good workbook. Keep it on hand while you're working on a brake system. For ease of use, the *Shop Manual* will fold flat on the workbench or under the car, and it can withstand quite a bit of rough handling.

When you perform actual test and repair procedures, you need a complete and accurate source of manufacturer specifications and procedures for the specific vehicle. As the source for these specifications, most automotive repair shops have the annual service information (on paper, CD, or Internet formats) from the vehicle manufacturer or an independent guide.

Acknowledgments

In producing this series of textbooks for automotive technicians, Chek-Chart has drawn extensively on the technical and editorial knowledge of the vehicle manufacturers and their suppliers. Automotive design is a technical, fast-changing field, and Chek-Chart gratefully acknowledges the help of the following companies and organizations that provided help and information allowing us to present the most up-to-date text and illustrations possible. These companies and organizations are not responsible for any errors or omissions in the instructions or illustrations, or for changes in procedures or specifications made by the manufacturers or suppliers, contained in this book or any other Chek-Chart product:

- Ammco Tools, Inc.
- Audi of America, Inc.
- Bendix Aftermarket Brake Division, Allied Automotive
- Benwil Industries, Inc.
- Continental Teves, Inc.
- DaimlerChrysler
- DMC Technical Products/Diemolding Corporation
- Earl's Performance Products
- Easco/K-D Tools
- EIS Division, Parker Hannifin Corporation
- Failure Analysis Associates
- Ford Motor Company
- FMC Corporation, Automotive Service Equipment Division
- General Motors Corporation
- Goodyear Tire & Rubber Company
- Hako Minuteman
- Honda Motor Company, Inc.
- Kelsey-Hayes Group
- Kent-Moore Tool Group, Sealed Power Corporation
- MAC Tools, Inc.
- Mazda Motor Corporation
- Mercedes-Benz USA, Inc.
- Nissan Motors
- OTC Division, Sealed Power Corporation
- Porsche Cars North America
- Robert Bosch Corporation
- Snap-On Tools Corporation
- Stainless Steel Brakes Corporation
- Subaru of America, Inc.
- Sumitomo Corporation
- Toyota Motor Corporation
- The White Lung Association of New York

The comments, suggestions, and assistance of the following reviewers and technical consultants were invaluable:

Lance J. David, *College of Lake County*
James D. Halderman

The authors have made every effort to ensure that the material in this book is as accurate and up-to-date as possible. However, Chek-Chart, Prentice Hall, or any related companies are not responsible for mistakes or omissions, or for changes in procedures or specifications by the manufacturers or suppliers.

Contents

Chapter 1 — Safety, Shop Practices, Special Tools, Cleaners, and Lubricants 1
Objectives 1
Introduction 1
Safety in the Shop 2
Shop Practices 9
Tricks of the Trade 11
Cleaning Tools 12
Chemical Cleaners 15
Adjusting Tools 16
Special Wrenches 16
Tubing Tools 18
Assembly/Disassembly Tools 19
Measuring Tools 24
Cylinder and Caliper Refinishing Tools 29
Friction Component Refinishing Tools 30
Hydraulic Service Tools 32
Lubricants 33
Antilock Brake System Tools 35

Chapter 2 — Brake System Diagnosis 37
Objectives 37
Introduction 37
Talking to the Customer 38
Preliminary Checks 38
Brake System Road Testing 38
Road Test Procedure 39
Brake Inspection 42
Brake System Diagnostic Charts 44

Chapter 3 — Fluid-Related Brake Service 55
Objectives 55
Introduction 55
Fluid Level Checking 55
Brake Bleeding 59
Master Cylinder Bench Bleeding 60
Master Cylinder On-Vehicle Bleeding 63
Bleeding the Wheel Brakes 64
Fluid Changing 71
Recentering Pressure Differential Switches 72

Chapter 4 — Brake Line and Hose Service 75
Objectives 75
Introduction 75
Brake Line Inspection 75
Brake Hose Replacement 77
Brake Tubing Replacement 79
Brake Tubing Fabrication 79

Chapter 5 — Pedal Assembly and Master Cylinder Service 85
Objectives 85
Introduction 85
Brake Pedal Assembly Service 85
Master Cylinder Inspection and Testing 87
Master Cylinder Replacement 91
Master Cylinder Overhaul 92
Master Cylinder Overhaul Procedures 94

Chapter 6 — Hydraulic Valves and Electrical Component Service 101
Objectives 101
Introduction 101
Hydraulic Control Valve Service 101
Brake Electrical Component Tests 106
Stoplight Circuit Tests and Adjustments 107
Warning Light Circuit Tests 111
Failure Warning System Switch Tests 112

Chapter 7 — Drum Brake Service 115
Objectives 115
Introduction 115
Brake Drum Removal 116
Brake Inspection 119
Brake Adjusting 123
Brake Adjusting Procedure 124
Specific Brake Adjusters 124
Brake Shoe Replacement 127
Initial Brake Adjustment 132
Brake Shoe Burnish-in 133

Wheel Cylinder Service 133
   Shoe Replacement Procedures 139

Chapter 8 — Disc Brake Service 151
   Objectives 151
   Introduction 151
   Brake Pad Inspection 151
   Brake Pad Replacement 153
   Brake Pad Replacement Procedures 157
   Brake Pad Burnish-In 162
   Brake Caliper External Inspection 162
   Brake Caliper Overhaul 164
   Brake Caliper Piston Removal 165
   Brake Caliper Internal Inspection 169
   Brake Caliper Honing 169
   Brake Caliper Assembly 172
   Brake Caliper Overhaul Procedures 174

Chapter 9 — Brake Drum and Rotor Machining 197
   Objectives 197
   Introduction 197
   Drum and Rotor Service 197
   Visual Drum and Rotor Inspection 198
   Brake Drum Measurement 199
   Brake Rotor Measurement 201
   Drum Replacement 203
   Drum and Rotor Refinishing 204
   Brake Lathe Operation 204
   Turning a Brake Drum 209
   Rotor Turning Procedures 214
   Turning a Brake Rotor off the Vehicle 214
   Turning a Brake Rotor on the Vehicle 220
   Resurfacing a Brake Rotor 220

Chapter 10 — Parking Brake Service 221
   Objectives 221
   Introduction 221
   Parking Brake Testing 221
   Parking Brake Adjustment 225
   Parking Brake Shoe Adjustment 225
   Parking Brake Cable Adjustment 226
   Parking Brake Cable Replacement 228
   Parking Brake Shoe and Pad Service 231
   Automatic Release Systems 231

Chapter 11 — Power Brake Service 235
   Objectives 235
   Introduction 235
   Vacuum Booster Testing 236
   Vacuum Booster Output Pushrod Adjustment 238
   Vacuum Booster Replacement 240
   Hydro-Boost Testing 241
   Hydro-Boost Replacement 244
   Hydro-Boost Bleeding 245
   Powermaster Testing 245
   Powermaster Replacement 248
   Powermaster Fill and Bleed 249

Chapter 12 — Antilock Brake Basics 251
   Objectives 251
   Introduction 251
   Service Basics 251
   Onboard Diagnostics 257
   ABS Performance Checks, Precautions, and Procedures 258
   General Bleeding Procedures 264

Chapter 13 — ABS Diagnostic and Service Procedures 265
   Objectives 265
   Introduction 265
   Bendix Antilock Brake Systems 265
   Bosch Antilock Brake Systems 272
   Delphi Chassis (Delco) Antilock Brake Systems 284
   Kelsey-Hayes Antilock Brake Systems 289
   Nippondenso Antilock Brake Systems 298
   Sumitomo Antilock Brake Systems 299
   Teves Antilock Brake Systems 303
   Toyota Antilock Brake Systems 311

Chapter 14 — Brake-Related Suspension Service 315
   Objectives 315
   Introduction 315
   Types of Wheel Bearings 316
   Wheel Bearing Diagnosis 318
   Basic Wheel Bearing Service 320
   Adjustable Dual-Wheel Bearing Service 323
   Sealed Wheel Bearing Replacement 327
   Solid Axle Wheel Bearing Service 330
   Tire and Wheel Service 334
   Tire and Wheel Runout 336
   Chassis Service 338

1

Safety, Shop Practices, Special Tools, Cleaners, and Lubricants

OBJECTIVES

Upon completion and review of this chapter, you will be able to:

- List the required safety practices for the brake shop.
- Explain Right-To-Know requirements.
- List the correct shop practices.
- Describe the use of lifts, hoists, jacks, and safety stands.
- List and describe the use of brake cleaning tools.
- List and describe chemical cleaners.
- Explain the use of brake spoons and wire hooks.
- List and describe the use of special wrenches.
- List and describe the use of tubing tools.
- List and describe the use of assembly/disassembly tools.
- List and describe the use of measuring tools.
- List and describe the use of cylinder and caliper refinishing tools.
- List and describe the use of friction component refinishing tools.
- List and describe the use of hydraulic service tools.
- List and describe the use of brake lubricants.

INTRODUCTION

Automotive brake systems are basically easy to service and overhaul, once you understand their construction. If you have a good grasp of the fundamentals presented in the *Classroom Manual,* you will find brake system service to be easy, interesting, and satisfying.

This chapter begins with general and specific safety practices that are required in every vehicle repair shop. This includes personal safety, fire safety, and hazardous materials training and handling. This is followed by a number of recommended shop practices for brake repair. Among the most important of these are the procedures used to jack cars and properly support them before you begin work. If you always follow good shop practices, your work will be both easier and safer.

This chapter also covers the unique tools used by the brake technician. Like any specialized area of automotive repair, brake work requires certain special tools in addition to the normal assortment of basic hand tools. These include tools designed to clean, adjust, disassemble, assemble, and measure wheel friction assemblies. Special tools are also required to refinish the brake hydraulic and friction components, and to work with the seamless, doublewall, steel tubing used for brake lines.

Finally, this chapter covers the various chemicals used to clean brake parts, and the unique lubricants that smooth the operation of the brake system and extend component life. These cleaners and lubricants are necessary to do accurate and professional brake work.

SAFETY IN THE SHOP

Safety is vitally important, both to you and to the people who work around you. No repair job is worth a permanent, crippling injury, or the lost time and income resulting from a preventable accident. Even so, technicians who follow poor work practices take these risks regularly, even when the correct procedures require little or no extra time or effort. By following a few common sense safety practices, you can minimize your chances of being involved in an accident or of causing injury to others.

Personal Safety

Automotive brake repair requires the same attention to personal safety as does working on any other automotive system. Most safety practices are simple common sense:

- Tie back long hair, or contain it with a cap. Tuck in any loose clothing, and remove sweaters. Button loose sleeves, or better yet, wear short-sleeved shirts when you work.
- Remove any rings, watches, or jewelry before working on an electrical component, or any moving parts. A ring can weld itself to a battery terminal and become red hot in seconds, and a necklace can pull your face into a rotating engine fan.
- Wear closed leather shoes or boots with oil-resistant soles in the shop. Aside from the obvious hazards of dropping sharp and heavy objects on your feet, sandals and canvas shoes can't protect you from sharp metal chips, hot particles from grinders, or spills of caustic or toxic chemicals. Professionals often wear steel-toed shoes or boots whenever they work in the shop.
- Wear ear protection when working around impact wrenches and other noisy equipment to prevent hearing loss.

First-Aid Response

If someone becomes injured in the shop, his or her life can often hang in the balance depending on what you do next. Cool, leveled-headed thinking and common sense go a long way to prevent a relatively minor injury from becoming a severe or deadly one. Obtain first-aid training if possible.

Take time to know the location of the first-aid kit and the contents contained within. Report missing, damaged, or depleted first-aid kits to your supervisor.

The locations of emergency phones and first-aid procedures must be posted.

If someone is burned, cool the burn site immediately with cold running water. If someone is bleeding, try to stop the blood loss by applying direct pressure to the wound with a clean gauze or clean cloth. Elevate the wound if possible. Do not move someone with broken bones except to remove them from immediate danger only. In all cases, call 911.

Eye Protection

Eye protection is critically important when you are working with vehicle brakes. Your eyes can be permanently damaged when you work with stationary machine tools, power drills, or impact wrenches, and even when you are working under a car that has a dirt- and sand-encrusted engine compartment.

To meet OSHA requirements, eye and face protection must comply with the American National Standards Institute, ANSI Z87.1–1989 standard. Look for this to be marked on the equipment package before you buy it.

Make sure that you wear clean, approved safety glasses or goggles whenever necessary, figure 1-1. When you are working with stationary or handheld grinders, wearing a full-face shield along with safety glasses gives you better protection against flying abrasive particles, figure 1-2.

Memorize the location of the eyewash stations in your shop in case you get dirt or debris in your eyes.

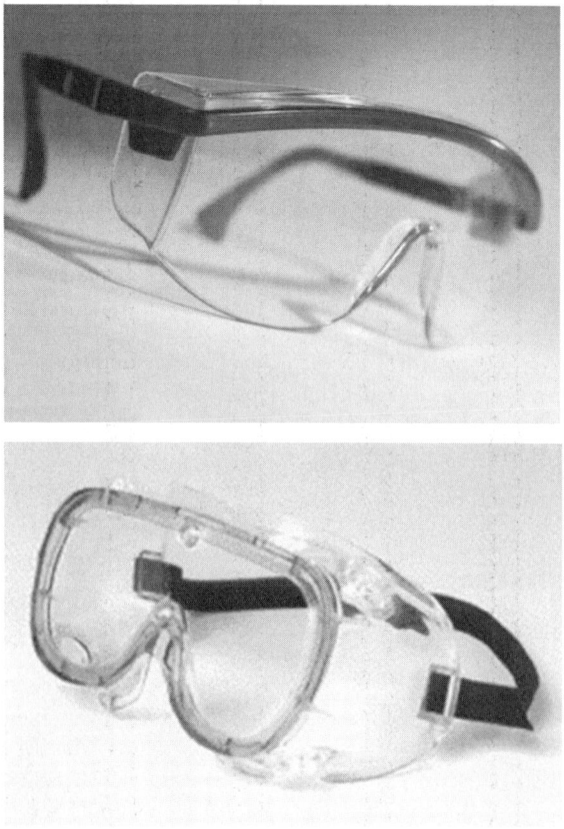

Figure 1-1. Always wear safety glasses or goggles when using any power or impact tools. (www.osha.gov)

Safety, Shop Practices, Special Tools, Cleaners, and Lubricants

Figure 1-2. A full-face shield along with safety glasses protects even better from chips and fragments from grinding wheels or brushes. (www.osha.gov)

Also, have adequate lighting in your work area to prevent eye strain. Extension lights should be protected by safety shields. For much more information on eye safety and industrial safety in general, go to www.osha.gov on the Internet and look at the e-Tools menu.

Know Your Shop

Take the time to become familiar with the shop in which you work:

- Know the location of the first-aid supplies and the nearest telephone in your shop. In an emergency, call 911.
- Know the location of the fire extinguishers in your shop and any nearby emergency fire alarm switches.
- Know the location of any specific emergency equipment in your shop such as eyewashers or emergency showers.
- Know the location of the emergency exits.
- Know the location of the fuse boxes and the master cut off switches.
- If your shop pipes in gas for oxyacetylene welding, know the location of the master cutoff valves.

Fire

Avoiding fire hazards is critical in the confined space of many repair shops:

- Remember that most cars have a fuel tank containing gasoline and highly explosive gasoline vapors. Make sure that any vehicles you work on are parked so that the fuel tank, lines, and filler necks aren't near any source of spark or flame.
- Do not smoke inside the shop, or while you are working. Flammable materials are always present in a repair shop, and you can easily avoid them by smoking outside or in another area.

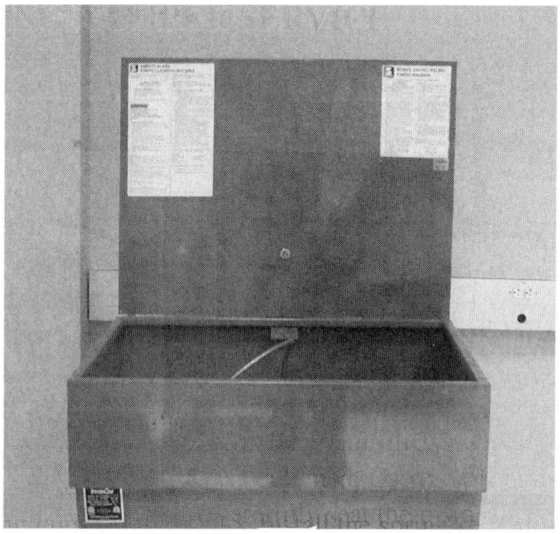

Figure 1-3. Keep the parts washer lid closed unless you are actually using it. This reduces fumes as well as the fire risk.

- Never use gasoline as a cleaning solvent.
- Dispose of oil-soaked rags in a metal container. This will contain the flames if the rags catch fire.
- Keep solvent containers, parts washers, and paint or oil containers closed. Parts washers often have a fusible link to close the lid if the solvent inside catches fire, figure 1-3, but avoiding the fire in the first place is much safer.

Fire Extinguishers

There are four classes of fire extinguishers. Each class should be used on specific fires only:

- Class A is designed for use on general combustibles, such as cloth, paper, and wood.
- Class B is designed for use on flammable liquids and greases, including gasoline, oil, thinners, and solvents.
- Class C is used on electrical fires.
- Class D is effective only on combustible metals, such as powdered aluminum, sodium, or magnesium.

Solvents and Chemicals

Most shops contain quantities of cleaning solvents, thinners, lubricants, paints, or other chemicals. These are often flammable, and/or poisonous.

- Keep any spray cans and solvents away from heat sources. Heat can pressurize the contents until the container explodes.
- Make sure your shop has adequate ventilation. If you have fume hoods or ventilating fans, make sure they work, and use them.
- Always read the instructions before using any new cleaning material.

- Use only the recommended solvents in parts washers. Using the wrong fluids can increase fire risks, expose you to toxic chemicals, and can even destroy the parts you want to clean.
- Do not splash cleaning solvents when putting parts into, or removing them from, a parts washer or cleaning tank. Be sure to wear eye protection.
- Use neoprene or butyl gloves and eye protection when working with chemicals, such as wire-brushing a solvent-soaked part.
- Use plastic or rubber aprons to protect your skin and clothing. Change any chemical-soaked clothing immediately.
- Clean up any spills right away, and wash any chemicals off your skin with soap and water or hand cleaner. Do not use gasoline, cleaning solvent, or thinner to clean your hands.
- Wash your hands after working with chemicals, especially before eating, drinking, smoking, or using the toilet.
- Dispose of all used chemicals properly. Remember that many cities and states have specific ordinances regulating disposal of hazardous wastes, and that most of the chemicals you use qualify as such. Call your local Fire Department for information on how to dispose of chemicals.

Carbon Monoxide Dangers

Carbon monoxide (CO) is a lethal gas that is both colorless and odorless. It is emitted from the exhaust pipe when the engine is running. Do not run the engine in a closed area or room. Instead, connect the vehicle's exhaust pipes to shop exhaust ducts, figure 1-4, or make sure there is sufficient ventilation to prevent the accumulation of poisonous exhaust gases. Symptoms of CO asphyxiation are headaches, tunnel vision, nausea, lethargy, red skin, and unconsciousness.

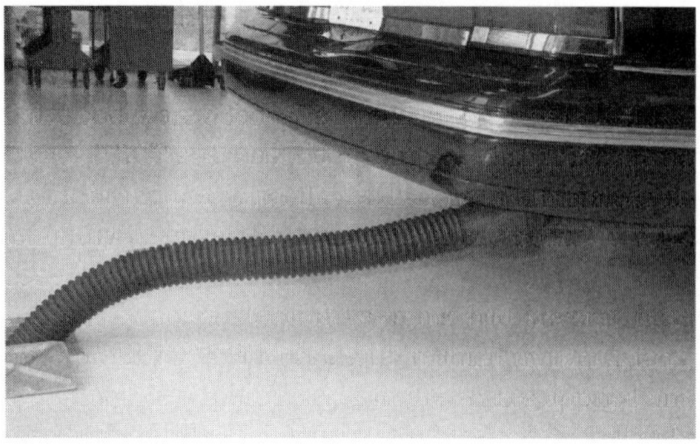

Figure 1-4. An exhaust hose and extractor must be used when running the engine in a closed area.

If someone is overcome by CO, get that person out to fresh air immediately and summon emergency medical assistance.

Chemical Exposure

Technicians are exposed to cleaners and solvents every day in an automotive repair shop. Therefore, many technicians wear disposable latex, nitrile (non-latex), or vinyl gloves while working. Gloves not only help to keep grease off of your hands, they also form an effective barrier against toxins.

Your hands are not the only contact point for chemical exposure. Inhalation of dust and contact through the face or bare arms are also potential sources. Think of your skin as a sponge that can absorb liquids it contacts. In addition, used lubricants contain trace amounts of any material they are exposed to, such as heavy metals and solvents. This includes any metals, plastics, composites, ceramics, rubbers, fibers, adhesives, sealers, or other fluids in the system. Be aware of what you are working with and protect yourself accordingly.

"Right To Know" Laws

Every shop employee is protected by "Right to Know" laws to ensure employers provide a safe working environment, training on how to properly dispose of hazardous materials, and familiarity with the types of chemicals used, in the workplace.

Employees must be trained annually about the nature of the hazardous materials present in the workplace, and the labeling of chemicals as described in a document called the Material Safety Data Sheet (MSDS), figure 1-5. New employees must be trained during their orientation before handling hazardous materials. Sources for safety and "Right to Know" training can be found on the Internet. Try the www.osha.gov site for training materials. For an online training program, go to www.sp2.org.

Hazardous Materials

Hazardous material is defined as a substance believed to pose a risk to health, safety, or property. The manufacturer must provide proper warning labels, including what hazard the substance poses and what protective equipment is necessary to handle each chemical. Most states require shop owners to:

- Train their employees about their right to know the nature of hazardous materials used in the workplace, the posting or availability of MSDSs, and protection equipment required to handle hazardous material.
- Train their employees on the procedures to follow in case of accidental spills or other special

Material Safety Data Sheet

Product Identification: LITE-DRI® absorbent #PLP201

Please Note: PIG® absorbent products must be disposed of in compliance with local, state and federal regulations. This product is considered non-hazardous in its purchased or unused state and requires no special disposal procedures.

I. Distributor's Identification

Distributed By: New Pig Corporation
Address: One Pork Avenue
Tipton, PA 16684-0304
Emergency Telephone Number: (800) 468-4647
Telephone Number for Information: (800) 468-4647
(Above numbers during the hours of 8 a.m. - 5 p.m. ET)
Date Prepared: 04-20-93 (3)

II. Ingredients/Identity Information

Component: 98.5% cellulose (CAS#: 65996-61-4)
Component: <1% Fiber Surface Modifier (CAS#: 577-11-7)
Component: <1% Treated Petroleum oil
NPCA-HMIS Health Index:
- Health: 0
- Flammability: 1
- Reactivity: 0
- Personal Protection: N/A

	OSHA	ACGIH	OTHER
Total Dust	15mg/m^3	10mg/m^3	N/A

III. Physical/Chemical Characteristics

Boiling Point: N/A
Vapor Pressure (mm Hg.): N/A
Vapor Density: N/A
Solubility in Water: Insoluble
Specific Gravity (H2O = 1): 1.3
Melting Point: N/A
Appearance and Odor: Light gray granules with no odor.

IV. Fire and Explosion Hazard Data

Flash Point: 451°F, Open cup
Flammable Limits: N/A **LEL:** N/A **UEL:** N/A
Extinguishing Media: In its purchased or unused form; water, chemical foam, dry chemical or CO_2. In its used form; that which is compatible to fluid absorbed.
Special Fire Fighting Procedures: In its purchased or unused form; N/A. In its used form; refer to fluid(s) MSDS(s), for LITE-DRI® absorbent does not render liquids non flammable, neutral or less hazardous.
Unusual Fire and Explosion Hazards: Refer to liquid(s) MSDS(s), for LITE-DRI® absorbent does not render liquids non flammable, neutral or less hazardous.
Hazardous Combustion Byproducts: Carbon Monoxide

V. Reactivity Data

Stability: Unstable _____ Stable _X_
Conditions to Avoid: N/A
Incompatibility (Materials to avoid): Product may be affected by acids and bases.
Hazardous Decomposition or Byproducts: N/A
Hazardous Polymerization: Will not occur.

VI. Health Hazard Data

Route(s) of Entry: Inhalation Possible Skin N/A
Ingestion Possible
Health Hazards (Acute and Chronic): N/A
Carcinogenicity: NTP N/A IARC N/A
OSHA Regulated N/A
Signs/Symptoms of Exposure: Breathing of excessive airborne dust may cause symptoms typical of nuisance dusts such as coughing, sneezing or minor respiratory irritation. Direct eye contact may cause minor physical irritation.
Medical Conditions Generally Aggravated by Exposure: N/A
Emergency and First Aid Procedures: If inhaled, get fresh air. In case of eye irritation, flush with plenty of water. Not considered harmful by ingestion.

VII. Precautions for Safe Handling and Use

Steps to Be Taken in Case Material Is Released or Spilled: In its purchased or unused form: Sweep or vacuum product and dispose of as a non-hazardous material.
Waste Disposal Method: In its purchased or unused form: No special precautions necessary. (Not classified as a hazard). In its used form: Dispose of all waste (based on the components of the fluid absorbed) according to federal, state, and local laws.
Precautions to Be Taken in Handling and Storing: N/A
Other Precautions: N/A (Refer to absorbed liquid(s) MSDS(s), for LITE-DRI® absorbent does not render liquids nonflammable, neutral, or less hazardous.)

VIII. Control Measures

Respiratory Protection: Should a spillage occur that creates excessive dust (See limitations specified in Section II) it may be advisable to use an approved dust mask.
Ventilation: Local Exhaust N/A Mechanical N/A
Special N/A Other N/A
Protective Gloves: N/A
Eye Protection: N/A
Other Protective Clothing or Equipment: N/A
Work/Hygienic Practices: N/A

Figure 1-5. A typical manufacturer safety data sheet.

handling concerns. Employees may be expected to use grease-sweep, broom, sand, shovels, etc., to clean or contain a spill.

- Label all hazardous materials to indicate their health, fire, and reactivity hazards. A list of all hazardous materials must be posted where the employee can read it.
- Keep documentation in the workplace on proof of training provided to the employee, as well as records of accidents or spills involving hazardous materials.
- Hold regular safety meetings to reinforce safe work habits in the shop.
- Designate an employee to be the emergency coordinator. It is that persons's responsibility to know when and what to report after a spill has occurred.

Hazardous Waste

Hazardous waste is defined as any used solid, liquid, or gaseous waste in its container that may cause illness, or pose a substantial present or future hazard to human health or the environment when improperly managed or disposed of.

From the moment you accumulate materials that meet the criteria in the following list, they become hazardous waste. Figure 1-6 is a typical example of a label you will find on a hazardous waste container. Waste substances are generally recycled, although some, such as gasoline, transmission and differential fluids, engine oils, and chemicals, must be disposed of in accordance with local and federal regulations. Many states limit the length of time these materials can remain in the shop before being properly disposed of. Date the material each time you put it in the recycle tank, figure 1-7.

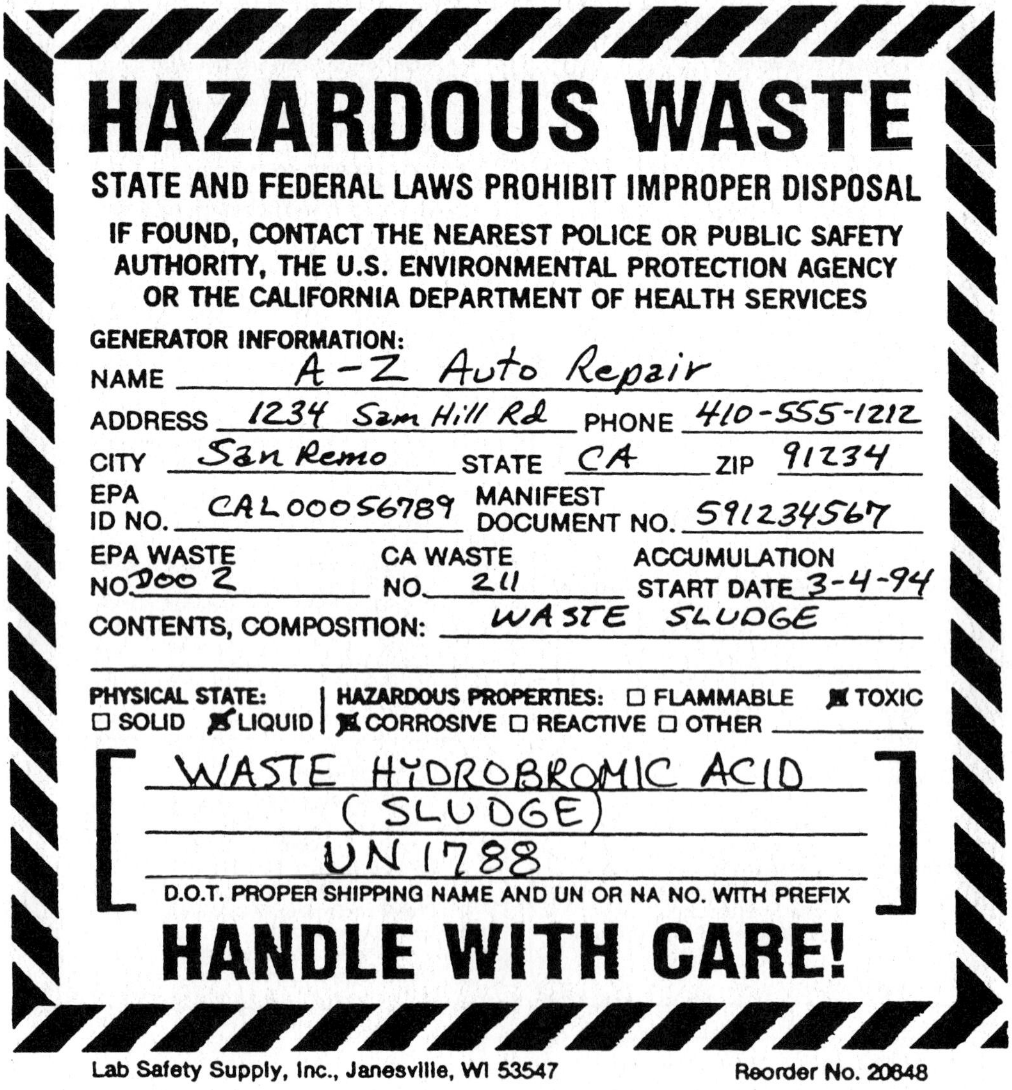

HAZARDOUS WASTE

STATE AND FEDERAL LAWS PROHIBIT IMPROPER DISPOSAL

IF FOUND, CONTACT THE NEAREST POLICE OR PUBLIC SAFETY AUTHORITY, THE U.S. ENVIRONMENTAL PROTECTION AGENCY OR THE CALIFORNIA DEPARTMENT OF HEALTH SERVICES

GENERATOR INFORMATION:
NAME A-Z Auto Repair
ADDRESS 1234 Sam Hill Rd PHONE 410-555-1212
CITY San Remo STATE CA ZIP 91234
EPA ID NO. CAL000567891 MANIFEST DOCUMENT NO. 591234567
EPA WASTE NO. D002 CA WASTE NO. 211 ACCUMULATION START DATE 3-4-94
CONTENTS, COMPOSITION: WASTE SLUDGE

PHYSICAL STATE: ☐ SOLID ☒ LIQUID | HAZARDOUS PROPERTIES: ☐ FLAMMABLE ☒ TOXIC ☒ CORROSIVE ☐ REACTIVE ☐ OTHER

WASTE HYDROBROMIC ACID
(SLUDGE)
UN 1788
D.O.T. PROPER SHIPPING NAME AND UN OR NA NO. WITH PREFIX

HANDLE WITH CARE!

Lab Safety Supply, Inc., Janesville, WI 53547 Reorder No. 20848

Figure 1-6. Look for a label such as this one on hazardous waste containers. (Courtesy of Lab Safety Supply, Inc.)

NOTICE
HAZARDOUS WASTE SATELLITE ACCUMULATION AREA

Legal Limit 55 Gallons/12 mo.

Responsible person: _____

<u>NO</u> MIXING, LEAVING OPEN, SMOKING, LONG-TERM STORAGE, OR UNAUTHORIZED USE ALLOWED

Accumulation Date: _____	Accumulation Date: _____
Accumulation Date: _____	Accumulation Date: _____
Accumulation Date: _____	Accumulation Date: _____
Accumulation Date: _____	Accumulation Date: _____
Accumulation Date: _____	Accumulation Date: _____
Accumulation Date: _____	Accumulation Date: _____
Accumulation Date:	Accumulation Date:

Figure 1-7. Many states limit how long hazardous waste may be stored.

Shop employees are required to know how to properly dispose of all used chemicals. Many states have specific ordinances regulating disposal of hazardous wastes, and many chemicals you use qualify as such. In addition to training, your shop is also required to provide documentation on how to properly dispose of hazardous waste. Call your local public health agency for additional information on how to dispose of chemicals. Hazardous waste includes both solids and liquids and is categorized in four ways:

- Ignitability. The liquid flash point (temperature at which liquid will ignite) is below 140°F (45.8°C) or if the solid will spontaneously ignite due to heat generated by a reaction of the materials.
- Corrosivity. The material burns the skin or dissolves metals.
- Reactivity. The materials reacts violently with water or other substances, or releases dangerous gases when exposed to low acid solutions, or generates toxic fumes, vapors, mists, or flammable gases.
- Toxicity. The material proves harmful to human health or the environment.

Every shop should obtain all the current applicable information regarding workplace safety and health, and the handling and disposal of hazardous materials, chemicals spills, and hazardous waste. Failure to comply can result in heavy fines or imprisonment.

Vehicle and Underhood Safety

Working with motor vehicles requires some specific safety practices:

- Do not drive a vehicle into or out of your shop area faster than 5 miles per hour.
- Before driving a vehicle into the shop, make sure that the brakes are able to bring the vehicle to a safe stop.
- Before starting an engine, be sure the parking brake is set, the drive wheels are blocked, and the transmission or transaxle is placed in Neutral (manual) or Park (automatic).
- Turn the engine off before working on components under the hood. If you must work with the engine running, be absolutely sure that neither you nor your tools can strike or brush against any moving parts.
- Keep your hands and other body parts away from hot exhaust components. Catalytic converters heat up quickly and retain their heat for a long time after the engine is shut off. If you must work with or around hot engine parts, wear special heat-resistant gloves. You can also obtain heat-resistant sleeves to protect your arms from heat.
- Remember that electric radiator fans can start at any time if the vehicle has been running recently, even if the ignition is off. Always disconnect the fan power lead before working near it.

Jump Start and Battery Safety

When jump-starting a car, observe a few simple precautions, such as avoiding arcing the terminals of a battery to see if it is charged. Wear your eye protection and be aware that there may be hydrogen gas fumes present under the hood, especially in the case of a malfunctioning charging system. Sparks produced when hooking up jumper cables can ignite the explosive hydrogen gas just as easily as can an open flame. On most batteries, the negative ground terminal is marked with a minus (−) sign and the positive or insulated terminal with a plus (+) sign. Do not rely on the color of the cable for identification.

Make sure you reconnect the battery cables to their proper terminals. Connecting the cables backwards will reverse the polarity, causing damage to vehicle electronic systems, the alternator, and other vehicle systems.

When jumping a vehicle with a booster battery, always make the final ground connection on the engine or chassis ground instead of on the battery ground itself. The electrical arc that occurs when this connection is made could cause an explosion if it occurs near the battery. This technique moves the spark away from the battery.

Electrical Safety

You will use many electric power tools while you are working on engines. In addition, today's vehicles are loaded with electrical and electronic control systems.

Shop Electrical Safety

- Make sure your hands, the floor, and your entire workspace are dry before you touch any electrical switches or plugs, or use any electrical equipment.
- Use correctly grounded three-prong sockets and extension cords to operate power tools. Some tools use only two-prong plugs. Make sure these are double-insulated.
- Don't use two-prong adapters to plug in a tool requiring a three-hole grounded socket. Use the correct socket instead.
- Keep electrical cords off the floor when not in use to prevent tripping. Tape the cords down if they are placed in high foot traffic areas.
- Don't overload any single circuit with electrical tools or fixtures.

Safety, Shop Practices, Special Tools, Cleaners, and Lubricants

Vehicle Electrical and Electronic Safety

- When working with or near air bag system connectors, sensors, or components, make sure the system is disabled according to manufacturer's instructions. This usually involves removing the air bag fuse and disconnecting the battery ground for at least 2 minutes.
- Keep flames and sparks away from batteries at all times. Batteries give off explosive hydrogen gas and, if ignited, can detonate like a bomb filled with sulfuric acid. Batteries being charged are especially dangerous.
- Disconnect the battery when working on or near electrical/electronic components. Do so by removing the battery ground cable. When installing a battery into a car, always connect the ground cable last.
- Never use the battery top as a tool tray. A wrench touching both battery terminals will melt, and can cause an explosion.
- Make sure the ignition switch is off when connecting or disconnecting the battery or any electronic control unit or computer.
- Many electronic modules under the hood and on the engine are sensitive to electrostatic discharge (ESD). Refer to manufacturer's instructions and be careful when probing electrical harnesses. Do not touch exposed terminals on modules; static electricity from your body can cause damage.

SHOP PRACTICES

The professional brake technician makes good shop practices a normal part of his or her on-the-job activities. Good shop practices are concerned primarily with three areas: convenience, safety, and cleanliness. Various recommended practices are listed below. As you read them, you may note that they are difficult to separate from each other—a clean, well-organized work area is also a safe one. The practices recommended below are both basic and common sense. This list is by no means complete; when you have finished reading it, see if you can think of other practices that will help you do a first-class job.

1. Organize your work area. This keeps unneeded movements to a minimum, which increases your efficiency and makes the repair procedure less tiring.
2. Keep your work bench clean and free of unnecessary tools, old parts, and other clutter. This provides more useful space to work in, and reduces the possibility of losing small parts.
3. Set aside enough bench space for any component overhauls that will be necessary.
4. Equip your bench with a container suitable for draining brake fluid from hydraulic system components. This makes it easier to keep the work area clean and free from brake fluid that can damage painted surfaces.
5. Keep all tools clean and dry. A clean tool will not slip off the part on which you are working or out of your hand.
6. Replace tools in their proper storage area after each use so you will always know exactly where they can be found when needed.
7. Keep a supply of clean shop towels near your work area to wipe up spills.
8. Keep the shop floor and your work area clean and free from brake dust and fluid. To prevent asbestos particles from getting into the air when cleaning, use a vacuum with a high efficiency particulate air (HEPA) filter or a wet cleaning system.
9. Brake cleaning fluid fumes can be harmful. Provide adequate ventilation regardless of the weather.
10. Shop lighting should be adequate to prevent eyestrain. When using extension lights, make sure the bulbs are covered with safety shields to prevent burns. Keep electrical cords off the floor to prevent tripping on them.
11. Keep your hands as clean and dry as possible. A certain amount of dirt and dust is normal during disassembly, but should be washed away before eating or using the restroom. Never handle clean parts with dirty hands during reassembly.
12. Do not smoke while working, especially when working near brake dust and cleaning fluids. Inhalation of these items can cause serious diseases, and cleaning fluid vapors may be volatile and can cause major injuries if ignited.
13. Have plastic bags or other suitable containers available for saving old parts to be returned to the customer. Never dispose of old parts until the repairs are finished and the customer has been given the option of taking the parts home.
14. Keep up-to-date shop manuals, technical service bulletins, and other specification sources available for use. Refer to them whenever you are uncertain; *never guess.*
15. Maintain a professional personal appearance in keeping with your responsibilities. Customers tend to judge between a "grease monkey" and a "technician" solely on looks. If you are dirtier than the car on which you are working, you will inspire little confidence in your ability.

Electronic Service Information

Because of their focus on a single vehicle line, manufacturers' service information is the most detailed source of engine specifications. Most manufacturers provide this information to their dealer network in electronic format or over the Internet, making the paper manual obsolete. Paper manuals generally cover only a single model year and are expensive, and you must usually buy new ones for each model, each year. The change to electronic format has made this information much more accessible to both the dealer technician and the aftermarket technician. There is usually a fee required to access the information.

Here are some sources of repair and technical information:

AC Delco	http://www.acdelcotechconnect.com
BMW	http://www.bmwtechinfo.com
International Automotive Technician Network	http://www.iatn.net
Mini	http://www.minitechinfo.com
DaimlerChrysler	http://www.techauthority.com
Ford	http://www.motorcraft.com
Honda	http://www.serviceexpress.honda.com
Mazda	http://www.mazdatechinfo.com
Mitsubishi	http://www.mitsubishitechinfo.com
Toyota	http://techinfo.toyota.com
Volkswagen	http://www.erwin.vw.com

Lifts and Hoists

The easiest way to service the wheel brakes is to raise the vehicle off the ground so the friction assemblies are at a convenient working height. A lift or hoist, figure 1-8, is the safest and most efficient way to do this. There are several types of single- and double-post hoists available, and most of them are suitable for brake service. Naturally, hoists that support the car under the wheels, like those commonly used for exhaust system service, cannot be used when servicing the wheel brakes.

When raising a car on a lift or a hoist, you must position the lifting pads *only* at the locations designated by the vehicle manufacturer for this purpose. These lifting points are shown in the owner's manual, shop manual, and certain aftermarket service publications, figure 1-9. Even very minor damage caused when the car is lifted in other locations can significantly weaken

Figure 1-8. Raising the vehicle on a lift makes it easier to service the wheel friction assemblies.

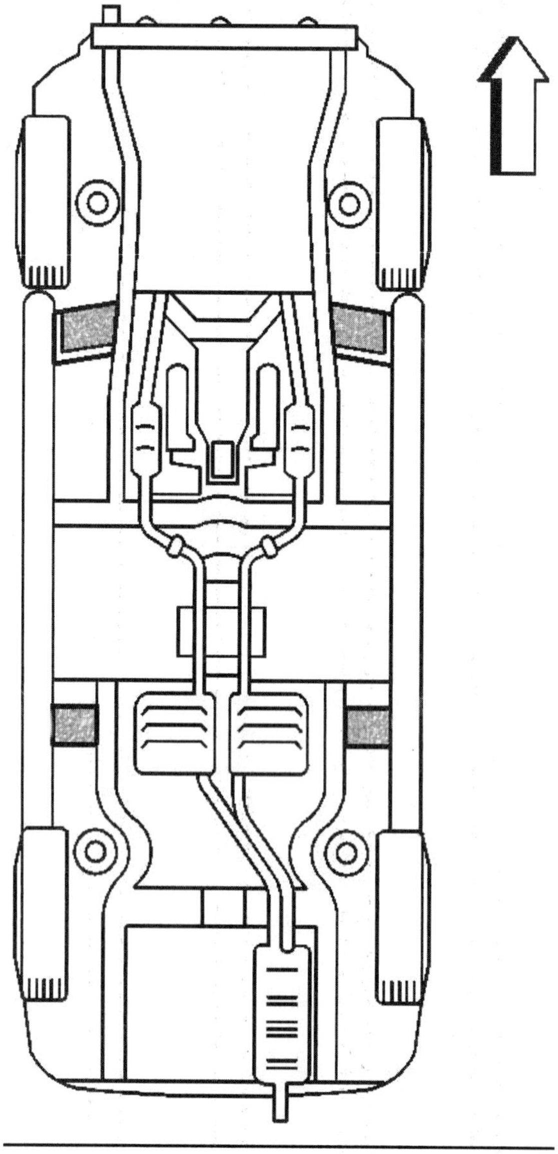

Figure 1-9. Vehicle lift points, shown in gray, are shown in the owner's manual and manufacturer's service information. (Courtesy of General Motors Corporation, Service and Parts Operations)

Safety, Shop Practices, Special Tools, Cleaners, and Lubricants

the body structure and reduce the crashworthiness of the vehicle; this is particularly true with unit-body cars.

Jacks and Jack Stands

When a hoist is unavailable, the car can be raised with a hydraulic floor jack and supported on jack stands, figure 1-10. Be sure to use a jack with adequate lifting capacity for the vehicle being serviced. Never use the jack that came with the car to lift or support the vehicle for brake service.

Compared to hoists, jacks and jack stands have a number of disadvantages. They limit the height to which the vehicle can be raised and force you to work in an awkward and uncomfortable position, which increases the amount of time the job will take. Jack stands are also more dangerous than hoists. If a stand is defective or extended beyond its safe working height, or if a careless person bumps into the car or stand, the vehicle can slip off and injure a person working underneath. Always check the stability of the stands before you begin work, figure 1-11.

TRICKS OF THE TRADE

There are no shortcuts in the proper diagnosis and repair of an automobile or light truck brake system. The safety concerns involved with vehicle brakes, and the legal liabilities that can result from improper repairs, make it foolish to do anything but a complete and professional repair in every case. However, even though factory shop manuals contain approved procedural sequences for every part of a particular job, no two brake technicians in the field approach a repair in exactly the same way. Experience has taught them different, and sometimes more efficient ways of doing the same job. These are often called "tricks of the trade."

The practices loosely defined by the expression "tricks of the trade" generally fall into two catagories, ways to organize the job, and alternative tools and procedures. Performing brake repairs in an organized manner requires less time and reduces the chances of mistakes. Every brake job can benefit from good organization. Alternative tools and procedures allow you to do some jobs without the special equipment that would otherwise be required, or allow you to save a great deal of time. However, you should never use an alternative tool or procedure if there is any chance it may cause damage or provide less than professional results.

There are literally hundreds of "tricks of the trade" and they cannot all be mentioned here. Some general examples are provided below to explain what we mean and to stimulate your thinking. Additional examples that apply to specific situations can be found throughout this text in the appropriate chapters.

Helpful Hints

1. When rebuilding hydraulic components, particularly master cylinders, it is often helpful to lay out the parts in the order they are removed, figure 1-12, or in the same sequence shown in an exploded drawing furnished by the factory. This helps prevent time-consuming mistakes when you overhaul a part with which you are unfamiliar.
2. When overhauling wheel friction assemblies with which you are unfamiliar, finish one wheel before starting on the other. It is easier to keep track of fewer parts, and you can use the other brake as a guide for reassembly. Taking apart the brakes at both wheels increases the possibility of mistakes.

Figure 1-10. A hydraulic floor jack can be used to lift the vehicle if a lift is not available.

Figure 1-11. Make sure that the jack stands are secure before you remove the wheels and begin work.

3. Other than removing frozen pistons from hydraulic components, do not force brake parts apart or together. Virtually all apart in a brake system can be disassembled or assembled with hand pressure and the appropriate tools. If you cannot separate or install a part without the use of force, something has been put together wrong.
4. Never wipe hydraulic parts with rags or shop towels. Lint and threads from rags and towels can collect on the parts. This debris will find its way into the hydraulic system and clog ports, causing seal leaks. Allow parts to air-dry, or dry them with clean, unlubricated compressed air after cleaning.
5. Lubricate all hydraulic pistons and seals with brake fluid or assembly lube before reassembly. This makes it easier to slide the parts together, helps prevent seal damage, and provides internal lubrication before the brake system is bled.
6. Certain brake repair operations are designed to be done with the aid of special tools available from the dealer. In many cases, aftermarket companies market similar tools for the same purpose. If you get stuck during a repair of an unfamiliar brake assembly, stop and consult a shop manual to determine if a special tool may be required. A number of common special tools are described in the following sections.

CLEANING TOOLS

Brake friction assemblies must be cleaned before a complete inspection or acceptable work can be performed. Road grime, wheel bearing grease, axle lubricants, brake fluid, and brake dust are some of the contaminants that collect on the brake assembly as a result of normal use or failures in the system. These contaminants disguise the condition of brake parts that may need to be replaced. And, if contaminants are not removed, they may lead to premature failure of new parts that are installed.

Another reason for cleaning the wheel friction assemblies is to avoid exposure to the asbestos fibers in brake dust and the health hazards they present. Special cleaning tools have been developed for this purpose. Under no conditions should an air hose be used to simply blow the brake dust off of a friction assembly into the shop air. The cleaning tools used to remove friction assembly contaminants and brake dust include:

- Brake vacuums
- Brake washers
- Brushes and scrapers
- Parts washers
- Air compressors.

Brake Vacuums

The special vacuums used to remove loose dust and dirt from the brake assembly are equipped with high efficiency particulate air (HEPA) filters designed to trap asbestos fibers. These fibers are small enough to pass through the conventional filters of general-use industrial vacuums, so a normal shop vacuum is *not* an acceptable substitute for a proper brake vacuum. Vacuums that collect asbestos fibers are also found on brake shoe arcing equipment.

The brake vacuum shown in figure 1-13 is typical of those on the market. A shroud fits over the friction assembly to prevent the escape of fibers during the cleaning process. A vacuum is attached to the shroud to create a low pressure area around the friction assembly. A compressed-air nozzle built into the shroud is then used to dislodge dust and other contaminants which are drawn into the vacuum and trapped for later disposal.

A consideration when using a vacuum enclosure brake cleaning system is the need for periodic filter changes. These systems have a gauge, figure 1-14, which indicates when the filter is clogged, requiring replacement. The used filters must be bagged, stored, and labeled as asbestos waste. Check with local environmental agencies for proper disposal procedures.

Brake Washers

An alternative to the brake vacuum is the brake washer, figure 1-15. A brake washer connects to a compressed air hose and sprays a low-pressure stream of cleaning solution onto the brake. The solution is a mixture of water and a non-petroleum-base solvent. Brake washers are very effective at removing loose dirt and dust from

Figure 1-12. When disassembling a component, such as a master cylinder, lay the parts out in the order in which they are removed.

Safety, Shop Practices, Special Tools, Cleaners, and Lubricants

Figure 1-13. A brake vacuum is a safe and efficient means to remove dust containing asbestos fibers from a friction assembly.

Figure 1-14. The brake vacuum may have a gauge that indicates when to change the filters.

Figure 1-15. A brake washer safely cleans the friction assembly and captures brake dust into the bottom container.

the friction assembly, and the cleaning solution traps asbestos fibers so that they do not become airborne and present a health hazard. Because they use a solvent cleaning solution, brake washers are also able to wash away brake fluid, grease, or axle lubricant that has leaked onto the brake.

These brake washers, also called aqueous brake washers, will require changing of the solvent and filters from time to time. This service may be included in the lease cost if the unit is leased from a local vendor. Having the vendor handle the waste disposal can help keep the brake repair shop in compliance with environmental regulations.

If using aerosol cans of brake cleaner to spot clean or dry brakes after washing, be sure to move the aqueous cleaner unit away from the brake area first. Aerosol brake cleaners contain chemicals that can contaminate the aqueous cleaning solution, causing it to be classified as hazardous waste. Just one drop of the aerosol brake cleaning solvent that drips into the washing solution is enough to make it a regulated hazardous waste. Use light compressed air pressure or evaporation to dry the brakes after washing.

Brushes and Scrapers

Once a brake vacuum or washer has been used to remove loose dust particles from a friction assembly, wire brushed and scrapers are often used to clean away baked-on contamination. To prevent dangerous asbestos particles from being released into the air, these tools should only be used when the part to be cleaned is wetted with brake cleaning solvent. A brush should *never* be used to remove asbestos dust from a dry friction assembly.

A wire brush, figure 1-16, consists of a wooden handle fitted with many stiff, mild-steel bristles. The bristles are able to clean hard-to-reach areas without damage to steel parts. Wire brushes should not be used on hydraulic cylinder bores or pistons, or on any aluminum part where the surface finish is important to proper brake operation.

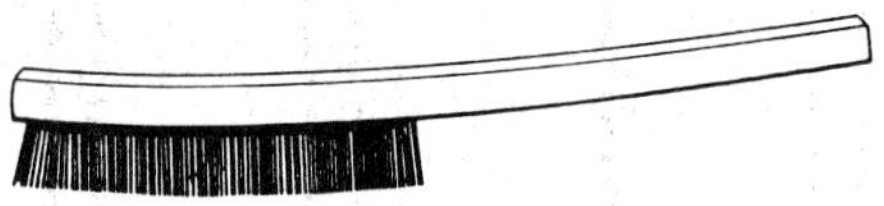

Figure 1-16. A wire brush used to clean brake friction assemblies.

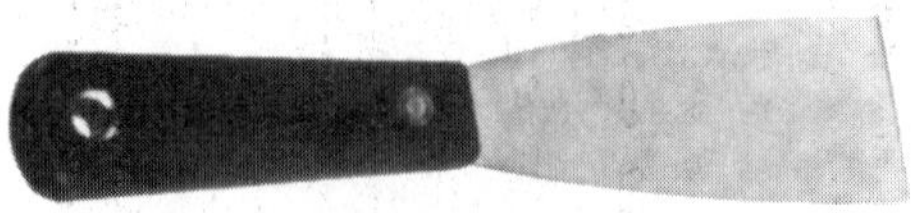

Figure 1-17. A scraper used to clean brake friction assemblies.

Figure 1-18. Parts washers have an electric pump that circulates a petroleum-base solvent.

Figure 1-19. An air compressor can be used to dry some brake system parts.

Scrapers, figure 1-17, consist of a thin, unsharpened, steel blade fitted to a handle. Scrapers will remove stubborn buildup, and are most effective when cleaning flat surfaces.

Parts Washers

Virtually all automotive shops where brake work is performed have a parts washer, figure 1-18. The typical parts washer has a steel tank to hold the parts to be cleaned and a hose and brush to direct a stream of solvent onto the parts in the tank. The solvent is circulated by a small electric pump and is filtered to remove larger particles of contamination.

Parts washers may use a petroleum-based solvent or a water-based (aqueous) solution for cleaning. Petroleum-based solvents are unsuitable for cleaning most brake parts due to the residue that remains after cleaning. Any solvent left in the hydraulic system will damage the rubber parts of the system. If petroleum-based solvents are used, the parts must be cleaned with soap and water or some other nonsolvent cleaner.

Aqueous parts cleaners are water-based solutions that, unlike petroleum-based solvents, are typically nonflammable and more environmentally friendly. Instead of dissolving grease and solids, aqueous cleaners rely on heat, agitation, and soap action to break dirt into smaller particles. Although they clean differently, aqueous cleaners perform as well as solvents. Hydraulic parts washed in this type of parts washer will not have any damaging solvent residue.

Air Compressors

An air compressor, figure 1-19, is a piece of equipment found in almost every automotive repair shop. Compressed air directed through a nozzle is a common method used to dry parts once they have been rinsed

Safety, Shop Practices, Special Tools, Cleaners, and Lubricants

after cleaning in a solvent tank or other type of parts cleaner. For brake work, this practice is unacceptable in many cases because compressed air is usually contaminated with water and oil. Water lowers the boiling point of brake fluid, and *any* petroleum-base fluid will attack the rubber seals in the brake hydraulic system.

There are several ways compressed air becomes contaminated. First, condensation collects in the air storage tank as a result of temperature and pressure changes. In addition, moisture can be condensed out of the atmosphere as the high-pressure air goes through a pressure drop leaving the tip of the air nozzle. Oil contamination can come from a couple of sources. A small amount of the lubricating oil in the compressor always leaks past the rings and into the air storage tank. Also, some compressor air outlets are fitted with automatic oilers that add oil to the airstream to keep impact wrenches and other pneumatic tools operating smoothly.

Whenever compressed air is used to dry parts of the brake system, you should be sure that the compressor has been serviced regularly and is not equipped with an automatic oiler. It is best to install a dehumidifier/filter unit to help ensure that the air supply is as free from contamination as possible.

CHEMICAL CLEANERS

Once the bulk of the dirt and grime is removed from a brake component, a final cleaning must be done to remove any trace of contamination; this is particularly true of hydraulic system parts. Final friction assembly cleaning, and all hydraulic component cleaning, must be done with a chemical cleaner that falls into one of three groups:

- Non-petroleum-base solvents
- Alcohol
- Detergents.

Non-Petroleum-Base Solvents

Petroleum- or oil-base solvents such as Stoddard solvent, kerosene, and gasoline cannot be used on most brake parts because they leave an oil film wherever they touch. Even if a film is not visible on the surface, oils from the solvents become trapped in the pores of the metal and emerge later to create problems in the brake system. Gasoline is highly flammable and its vapors are explosive; *never* use gasoline as a solvent to clean parts.

When hydraulic system parts that have been cleaned in petroleum-base solvents are reassembled, the oil film contaminates the brake fluid and causes the rubber seals and hoses in the system to shrink or swell. The results are fluid leaks, reduced strength, and possible brake system failure. The solvent film left on the friction surface of drums or rotors can reduce stopping ability when it contaminates the friction material on the brake shoes or pads.

Because conventional petroleum-base solvents are unsuitable for brake system service, non-petroleum-base solvents were developed. As discussed in the *Classroom Manual*, these solvents are made from chemicals like 1,1,1-trichlorethane, tetrachlorethane, and perchlorethylene or "perk." These solutions are powerful and effective in removing most dirt, grease, and carbon deposits, and they dry quickly without leaving harmful residue.

Perk-type solvents are available in bulk form or in convenient spray cans. The parts to be cleaned are either dipped in the bulk solvent, or sprayed with solvent from an aerosol can until all of the contaminants are removed. When a solvent spray is used to clean wheel friction assemblies that use asbestos-based friction materials, the runoff contains asbestos fibers and should be recovered in a catch basin and disposed of in a safe and approved manner.

If using aqueous cleaning systems, do not let the runoff from these solvents drip into the aqueous solution. This will contaminate the solution, resulting in a hazardous waste disposal problem.

Alcohol

Because of its chemical similarity to polyglycol brake fluid, denatured alcohol is another good cleaner for brake parts. Alcohol is not as powerful a solvent as perk-type cleaning solutions, but it is cheaper and also dries quickly without leaving harmful residue.

Denatured alcohol is also useful for flushing brake lines clean, and can be used as an assembly lubricant for hydraulic system components. In both these situations, however, it is essential that the alcohol be completely evaporated before the hydraulic system is sealed and filled with brake fluid. Alcohol has a very low boiling point that will significantly lower the brake fluid boiling point and lead to vapor lock if the two liquids are mixed.

Detergents

Mild dish-washing detergents are low cost alternatives to other types of brake cleaners in certain applications. Alcohol and other non-petroleum-base solvents evaporate readily and are used up quickly. For these reasons they tend to be fairly expensive. Mild detergents do a good job of removing the oily film from parts such as drums and rotors that have been cleaned with petroleum-base solvents.

ADJUSTING TOOLS

Drum brakes with manual adjusters can sometimes be adjusted using a standard screwdriver. However, special adjusting tools are available to make the job simpler and faster. These tools are also used to manually adjust drum brakes with automatic adjusters in certain situations. On some cars, a special tool is mandatory to adjust the brakes.

The two main types of brake adjusting tools are spoons and wire hooks, figure 1-20. Brake spoons are shaped to easily allow the technician to reach through a hole or slot in the backing plate or brake drum to engage the teeth on a starwheel adjuster and turn it. When the brakes on a vehicle with automatic starwheel adjusters are adjusted manually, a wire hook is used along with the brake spoon to hold the automatic adjuster lever away from the teeth of the starwheel. This allows the starwheel to be turned freely in both directions.

SPECIAL WRENCHES

Special wrenches used in brake service are designed to make certain jobs easier, to help avoid damaging special parts, or to tighten nuts and bolts to a specific degree of tightness. Their unique designs usually make these wrenches less suitable for general work, but perfect for their particular jobs. Special wrenches used in brake work include:

- Bleeder-screw wrenches
- Flare-nut wrenches
- Torque wrenches.

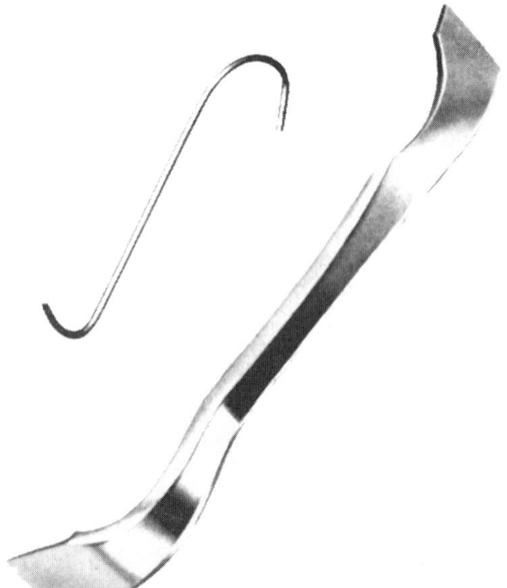

Bleeder-Screw Wrenches

Bleeder-screw wrenches, figure 1-21, are boxend wrenches with special offsets that make it easier for the technician to loosen and tighten hard-to-reach bleeder screws. The box ends of the wrench are hexagonal, or six-point, like the bleeder screw itself. This design makes a bleeder-screw wrench less likely than a twelve-point box wrench, or an open-end wrench, to round off the corners of the small hex on the bleeder screw.

Flare-Nut Wrenches

Flare-nut wrenches are used on brake tubing connections and fittings, figure 1-22; for this reason they are often called tubing wrenches. These tools are essentially box-end wrenches with one side of the box opening cut away so the wrench can be passed over the brake line.

Flare-nut wrenches are required because tubing fittings have relatively thin walls and can be easily dam-

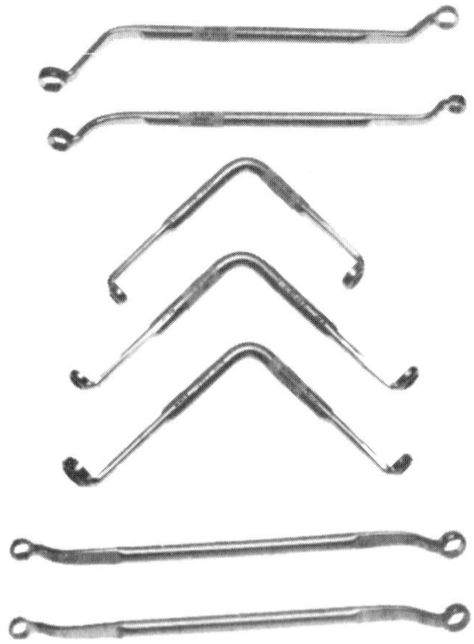

Figure 1-21. Bleeder-screw wrenches help prevent damage to the bleeder screw.

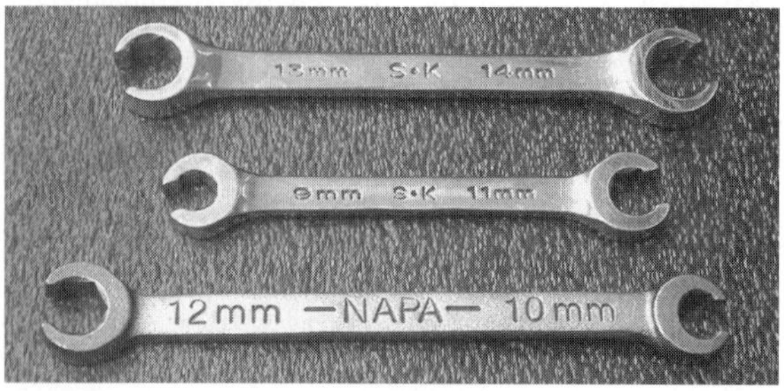

Figure 1-20. Brake spoons and wire hooks are used when rotating starwheel adjusting mechanisms.

Figure 1-22. Flare-nut or tubing wrenches.

Safety, Shop Practices, Special Tools, Cleaners, and Lubricants

aged if an open-end wrench is used on them; even a small amount of distortion can cause a tubing fitting to leak. Open-end wrenches place all of the turning torque on only two flats of a hexagonal tubing fitting. Flare-nut wrenches circle the fitting to apply the force evenly and prevent distortion.

Flare-nut wrenches are available with either six- or twelve-point openings. The six-point type applies force over a larger area of the fitting than a twelve-point design and is less likely to round the corners of the fitting. However, the twelve-point type is easier to use where space to turn the wrench is limited.

Torque Wrenches

In brake repair, it is often essential that a nut or bolt be tightened a specific amount. This is true of *all* fasteners, but it is particularly important for fasteners in critical applications such as caliper bridge bolts or mounting bolts and wheel lugnuts. On any part, tightening beyond the specifications, "for good measure," can stretch the fastener beyond its elastic limit, strip the threads, or distort the parts being fastened together. The end result is nut or bolt failure, or possibly fluid leaks.

To obtain proper fastener tightness, a special tool called a torque wrench is used. A torque wrench has a scale on it that indicates the amount of tightening force being applied to a nut or bolt. The scale may be graduated in inch-pounds, foot-pounds, Newton-meters, kilogram-meters, or a combination of these values depending on the wrench.

There are three basic types of torque wrenches: beam type, dial type, and micro-adjusting type, figure 1-23. With the beam-type wrench, a pointer indicates the torque on a scale near the handle. With the dial-type wrench, the torque is indicated by a needle and scale on a dial built into the wrench body. With the micro-adjusting-type wrench, the torque is preset by rotating the wrench handle until it aligns with a specific torque value marked on the body of the wrench; when the preset level of tightness is reached, the mechanism inside the wrench overcenters and produces a "click" that can be heard as well as felt through the wrench handle. For this reason, the micro-adjusting torque wrench is sometimes called a "click-type" torque wrench.

Torque Wrench Extensions

Torque wrenches can be used with various extensions and adapters that help get around obstructions or make it easier to use the wrench in tight quarters. Extensions on the handle end of the wrench do not affect the torque reading, although they make it easier to achieve because of the increased leverage. Extensions on the drive end of the wrench that increase the height of the wrench above the bolt or nut also will not affect the torque reading since the effective length of the wrench is not changed. However, adapters on the drive end of the wrench, figure 1-24, do increase the effective length of the wrench, and thus cause more torque to be applied to the fastener than is indicated by the scale on the wrench.

When using an adapter that lengthens the drive end of the wrench, the following formula is used to determine the proper wrench setting or reading for the torque required.

$$\frac{\text{wrench}}{\text{reading}} = \frac{\text{torque at fastener} \times \text{wrench length}}{\text{wrench length} + \text{adapter}}$$

For example, if a technician needs to tighten a bolt to 30 foot-pounds using a 16-inch torque wrench with a 4-inch adapter, the formula would read:

$$\frac{30 \times 16}{16 + 4} = \frac{480}{20} = 24$$

As the equation shows, the bolt will be torqued to 30 foot-pounds when the torque wrench scale shows 24 foot-pounds.

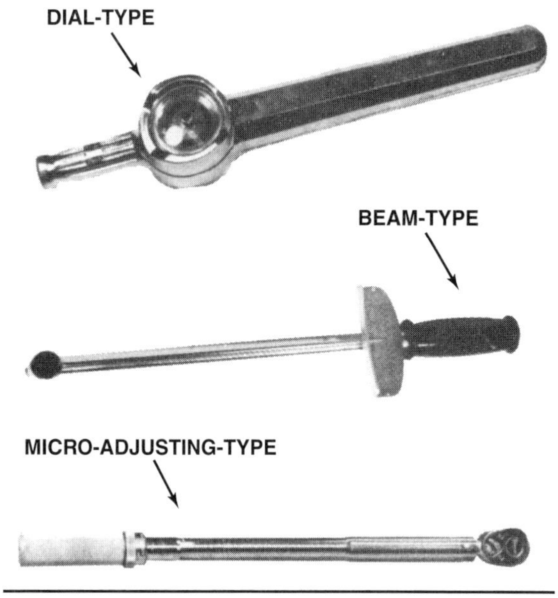

Figure 1-23. The three basic types of torque wrenches.

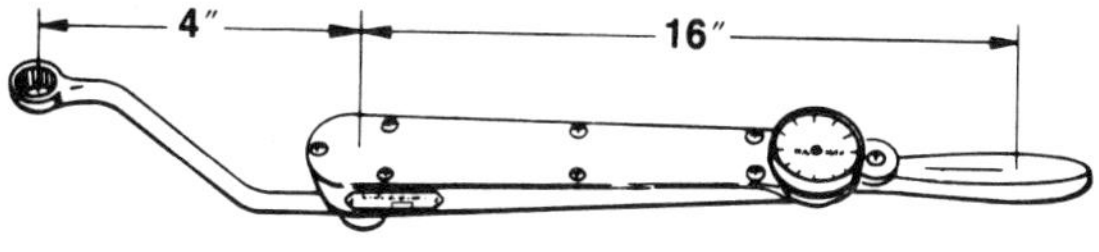

Figure 1-24. This adapter changes the effective length of the torque wrench.

TUBING TOOLS

Replacement steel brake lines are most often sold in fixed lengths and must be cut, bent, and flared to fit the individual application. These operations require three basic special tools:

- Tubing cutters
- Tubing benders
- Flaring tools.

Tubing Cutters

When a piece of brake line tubing is cut to length, the end must be left perfectly round and at a right angle to the body of the tubing so that fluid flow is not restricted and a good flare can be formed. This precision cut is achieved with a tubing cutter, figure 1-25, that supports the tubing on steel rollers perpendicular to a sharp, hardened cutting wheel. A screw forces the cutting wheel and tubing together, and the cutter is rotated around the tubing while the screw is slowly tightened until the cut is completed.

Many tubing cutters include a reamer bit used to remove flashing from the tubing bore after the cut is made. This prevents the flashing from breaking loose later and causing problems in the hydraulic system. Where the reamer is not a part of the tubing cutter, a similar separate tool must be used for the same purpose.

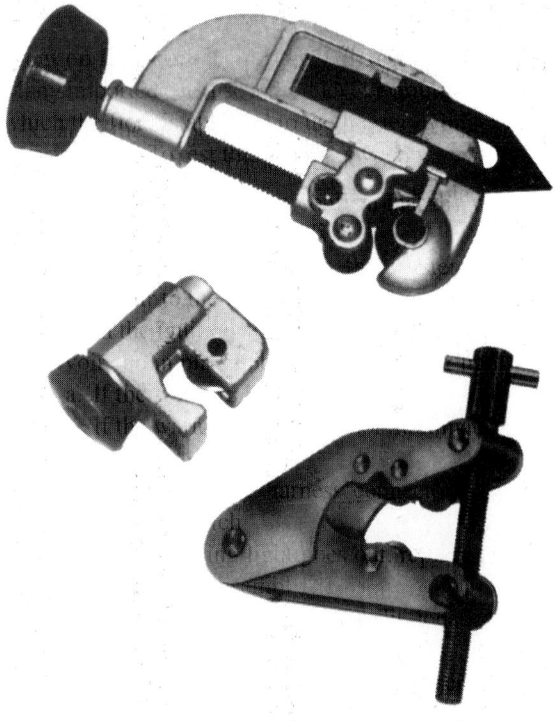

Tubing Benders

Although certain brands of brake tubing are designed to be bent by hand, most tubing must be bent with a special tubing bender that eliminates the chance of kinking and/or cracking the tubing. The two most common types of tubing benders are the lever type and the spring type.

Lever-type tubing benders, figure 1-26, use a pair of levers to form the tubing around a wheel or pulley that has grooves sized to match various tubing diameters. The walls of the grooves prevent distortion of the tubing that can cause a restriction in fluid flow. Some lever-type benders have interchangeable dies for different sizes of tubing, others have multiple grooves built into the tool itself. The lever-type bender has the advantage of being able to bend tubing whose ends are already flared.

Spring-type benders, figure 1-27, are tightly wound coil springs approximately 10 to 12 inches (254 to 305 mm) long. These springs have inside diameters from ⅛ to ⅜ inch to match the standard outside diameters of brake line tubing. To use a spring-type bender, the tub-

Figure 1-25. Typical brake tubing cutters.

Figure 1-26. Lever-type tubing benders are effective, but limited in the size of bend they can make.

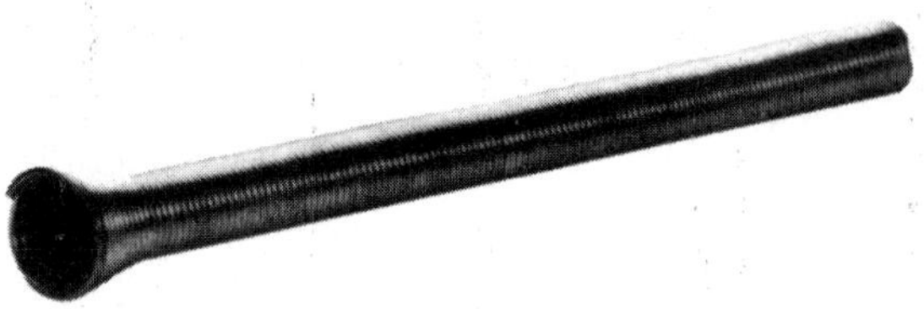

Figure 1-27. A spring-type tubing bender.

Safety, Shop Practices, Special Tools, Cleaners, and Lubricants

ing is slipped inside the spring and bent into shape by hand; the strength of the spring coils prevents the tubing from becoming distorted. Spring-type benders can be used in tighter quarters than lever-type designs, and they make it possible to bend smaller and more intricate shapes. Spring-type benders cannot be used on pre-flared tubing, however, because the spring will not fit over the flare.

Flaring Tools

There are two types of flaring tools, those for making the SAE double flares used in most brake systems, and those for making the ISO flares that are becoming more common on newer brake systems. The SAE flare is formed in a two-step process with a double flaring tool, figure 1-28. This type of tool usually comes in a kit that includes a holder to clamp the tubing firmly in position, a press to shape the tubing, and flare forming dies for various tubing sizes.

The ISO flare is formed in a single-step process which requires only a tubing holder and a forming die, figure 1-29. However, a separate tool is required for each size of tubing since there is no way to change the clamp and forming die to accommodate different diameters of tubing.

ASSEMBLY/DISASSEMBLY TOOLS

A wide variety of special tools are available to aid in the assembly and disassembly of brake friction assemblies. Some of these tools are specific to certain car models, but others are fairly universal in their application. These tools include:

- Holddown spring tools
- Return spring tools
- Wheel cylinder retainer removal tools
- Caliper piston removers
- Disc brake pad spreaders
- Wheel cylinder clamps
- Parking brake cable tools
- Dust boot tools
- Caliper piston seating tools
- Swaging removal tools.

Holddown Spring Tools

The pin-and-spring holddowns that secure some brake shoes to the backing plate can often be serviced by hand. However, a special tool is available to speed their installation or removal in difficult situations. The holddown spring tool, figure 1-30, basically consists of a handle and steel shaft similar to a screwdriver. On the end of the shaft is a basket-shaped serrated socket which grips the retaining spring washer so it can be pushed down, rotated, and released from the holddown pin.

Another type of holddown spring tool is used to remove and install one-piece "beehive" coil-spring-type

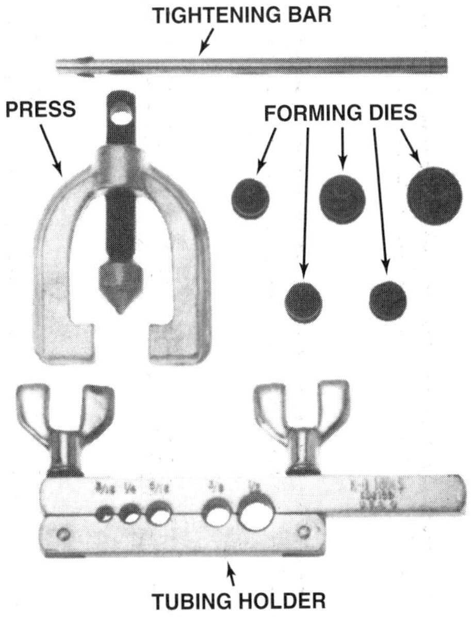

Figure 1-28. Double flaring tools have interchangeable forming dies for different tubing sizes.

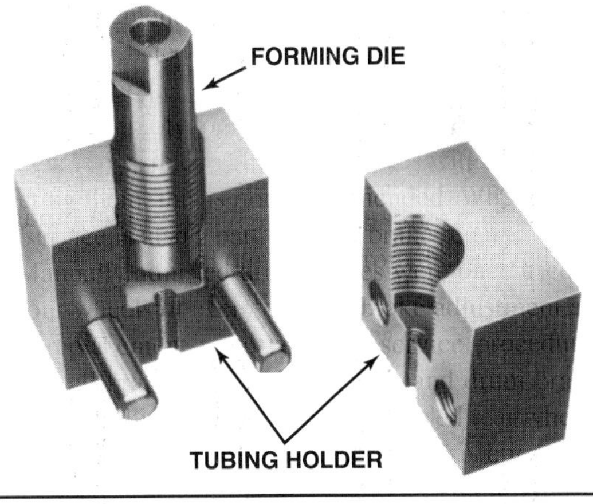

Figure 1-29. An ISO flaring tool for brake tubing.

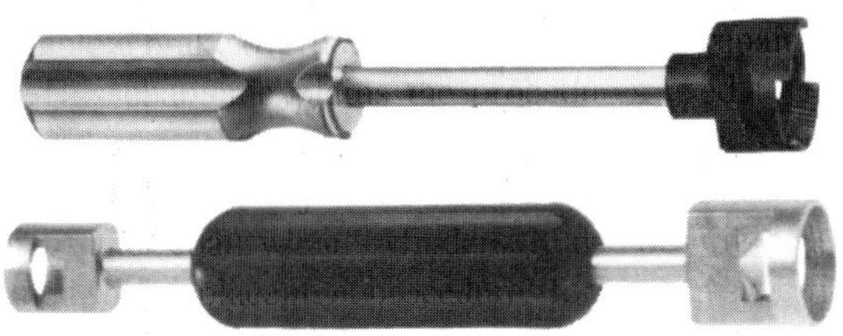

Figure 1-30. Typical holddown spring tools.

shoe holddowns. This tool consists of a handle and a straight shaft with a slot cut in the end. The shaft is inserted into the center of the holddown spring to engage the retaining hook, then the tool is depressed and rotated to release the holddown.

Return Spring Tools

Unlike holddown springs, brake shoe return springs are very strong; special removal and installation tools, figure 1-31, are mandatory to remove and install these springs. These tools usually have a special socket on one end and a cupped depression at the other, figure 1-31A. To remove a spring hooked over an anchor post, the socket end of the tool is placed over the post and rotated. A lip or protrusion on the rim of the socket opening then sweeps the return spring off of the anchor. To reinstall the spring, the cupped end of the tool is placed on the edge of the anchor post. The spring is then hooked over the tool shaft, and the tool is used to lever the spring into position on the post.

Another type of return spring tool, figure 1-31B is a special pliers used to remove and install springs that attach between two brake shoes. One end of the pliers rests against a rivet in the shoe lining, or on bonded linings, against the friction material itself. The other end of the pliers has a hook that grabs the end of the spring. As the pliers are tightened, the spring is pulled toward the lining table until it can be removed from, or hooked into, its mounting hole in the shoe web. Regular pliers should never be used on brake shoe return springs because they can nick or otherwise damage the springs and lead to premature failure.

Many newer General Motors cars have return springs that attach to metal hooks on the shoe anchor, rather than to a more conventional anchor post. The special spring installation and removal tool for these brakes, figure 1-31C, has a separate pivoting wire hook to make servicing of this design easier.

Wheel Cylinder Retainer Removal Tools

In addition to having different return spring attachments than other brakes, the rear wheel cylinders on some late-model General Motors cars are held to the backing plate with a unique spring-steel retainer clip. The clip is most easily removed and installed with a special retainer removal tool, figure 1-32. The tool fits inside the two retainer clip prongs, and expands them outward to release the clip from the wheel cylinder.

Caliper Piston Removal Tools

Rust and corrosion can make it very difficult to remove brake caliper pistons from their bores. In extreme cases, hundreds of pounds of force may be required. To make this job easier, two types of special caliper piston removal tools are available, mechanical and hydraulic.

The mechanical piston remover shown in figure 1-33A, is basically a pair of pliers with expanding jaws that have serrated teeth to grip the inside of the piston. Once the piston is grasped with this tool, it can be worked back and forth until it is free enough to be removed from the bore. A similar tool, figure 1-33B, is tightened against the inside of the piston with a long allen wrench. Generally, these types of removal tools will only work when the piston is slightly stuck in the caliper.

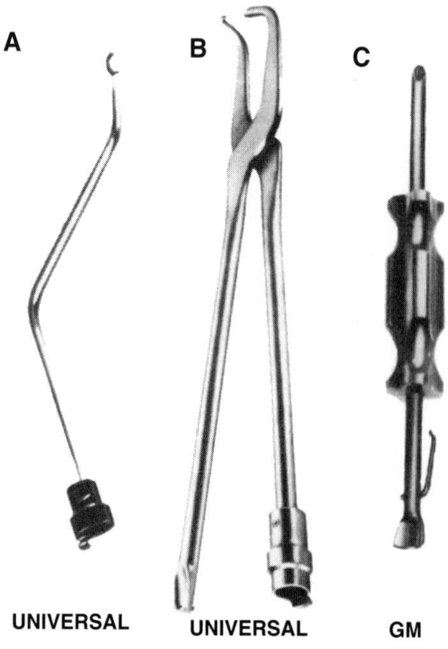

Figure 1-31. Brake return spring tools.

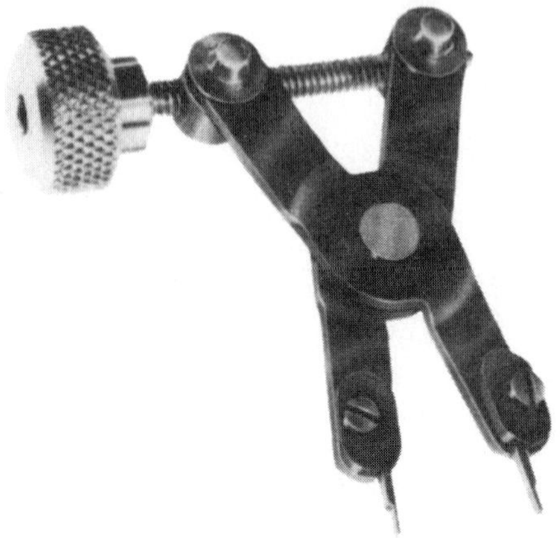

Figure 1-32. A GM wheel cylinder retainer clip tool.

Safety, Shop Practices, Special Tools, Cleaners, and Lubricants

In cases of severely frozen pistons, the best removal tool is a hydraulic caliper piston remover, figure 1-34. With the caliper off the car, a hydraulic line from a hand-operated master cylinder is connected to the fluid inlet. The hand lever is then pumped until sufficient hydraulic pressure is created to force the caliper piston from its bore. This type of tool can create more than 1,000 psi (6,900 kPa) of pressure to free frozen pistons. To prevent injury from brake fluid spray, always wear eye protection when using this type of piston removal tool.

Disc Brake Pad Spreaders

Disc brake pad spreaders, figure 1-35, are used when assembling early four-piston brake calipers equipped with piston return springs. After the brake pads are installed in the caliper, the spreader is used to hold them apart against piston return spring pressure while the caliper is installed over the brake rotor. The pad spreader in figure 1-35A is operated by rotating its handle to expand the scissor-like legs. The spreader in figure 1-35B operates by rotating a threaded bolt at one end of the tool to spread the arms at the opposite end.

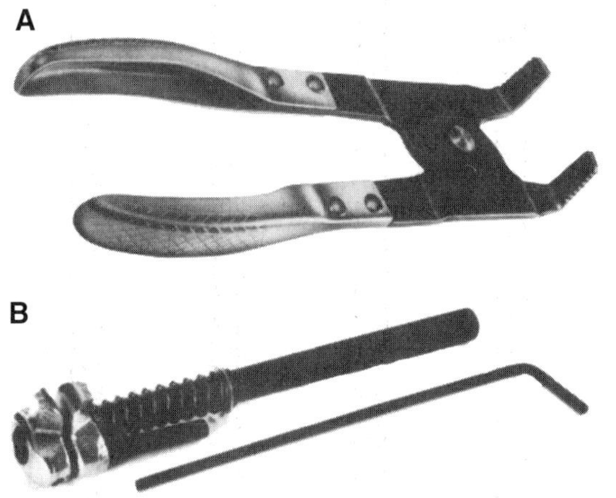

Wheel Cylinder Clamps

Wheel cylinder clamps, figure 1-36, are large spring-steel devices used to hold pistons in wheel cylinders bores against cup expander spring pressure. These clamps are used on brakes without piston stops to hold the wheel cylinders together during brake disassembly and assembly. The clamps prevent the wheel cylinder from coming apart unintentionally, and make it easier to install the brake shoes.

Parking Brake Cable Tool

A parking brake cable tool, figure 1-37, is used when assembling drum brake friction assemblies that have a parking brake cable that is retained by a spring built into the end of the cable. The end of the tool fits between the spring and the beaded cable end to provide a pliers action that compresses the spring, making it easier to attach the cable to the parking brake lever.

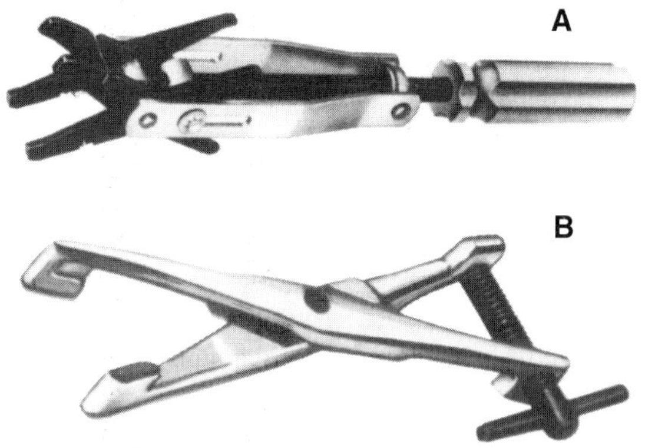

Figure 1-33. These special tools are used to remove brake caliper pistons.

Figure 1-34. Frozen pistons can be removed hydraulically using a caliper bench.

Figure 1-35. Disc brake pad spreaders.

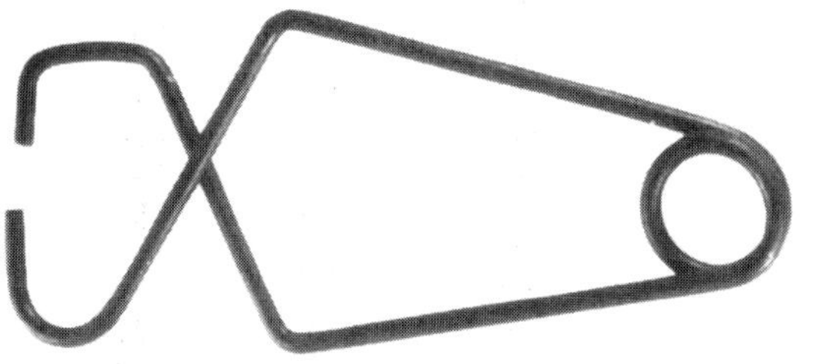

Figure 1-36. Wheel cylinder clamps hold the pistons in the cylinder bore during brake assembly.

Figure 1-37. A typical parking brake cable tool.

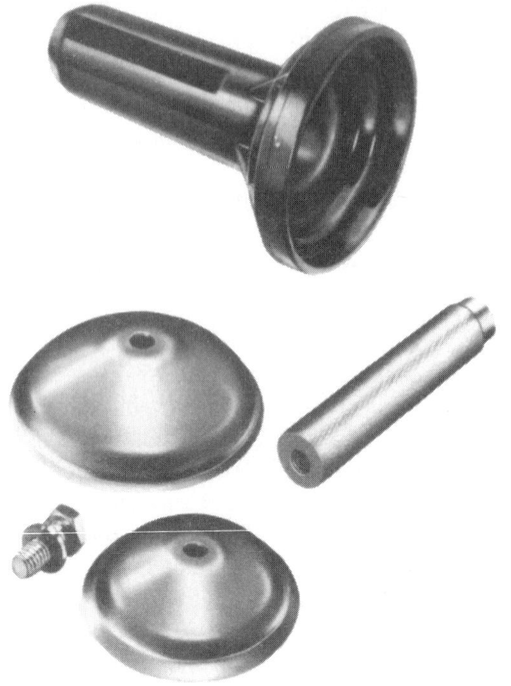

Figure 1-38. Caliper dust boot drivers.

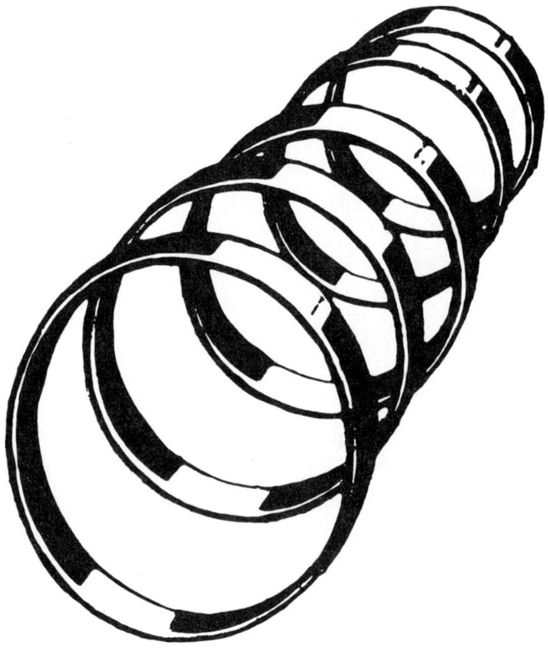

Figure 1-39. Dust boot installation rings.

Dust Boot Tools

Brake caliper dust boots attach tightly to the caliper piston and the caliper body to prevent contamination from entering between these two parts and causing rust, corrosion, or scuffing that can lead to fluid leaks and stuck pistons. Depending on the caliper and dust boot design, there are three particular special tools that may be required or helpful when assembling the caliper:

- Dust boot drivers
- Dust boot rings
- Dust boot pliers.

Dust Boot Drivers
Dust boot drivers, figure 1-38, are used when assembling calipers in which the outer edge of the dust boot contains a metal retaining ring that provides a press fit in the caliper body. These types of calipers are common on General Motors cars. The driver is centered on the outer circumference of the boot, then struck with a hammer; this provides equal pressure at all points and prevents distortion of the metal retaining ring.

Dust boot drivers are made in various sizes to match different diameter dust boots. Some drivers are one-piece plastic castings, but others have interchangeable metal drivers that attach to a common shaft.

Dust Boot Rings and Pliers
Dust boot rings and pliers, figures 1-39 and 1-40, are used to assemble calipers in which the dust boot installs into a groove in the caliper bore before the piston is installed. These types of calipers are common on Chrysler and Ford vehicles. The rings or pliers are used to expand the piston opening in the dust boot so the caliper piston can be installed through it.

Dust boot rings are usually made of plastic, and come in sets of five. Each ring has an inside diameter slightly larger than a common piston diameter. Dust boot pliers come in a single size that can be expanded or contracted as necessary. Because of this, a single pair of dust boot pliers can do the same job as a set of several size rings.

Caliper Piston Seating Tools

When disassembling disc brakes for service or pad replacement, it is necessary to push the caliper piston into the caliper bore. Seating the piston makes it easier to remove the caliper, particularly if the rotor has a deep ridge at its outer edge or if the rotor is deeply scored.

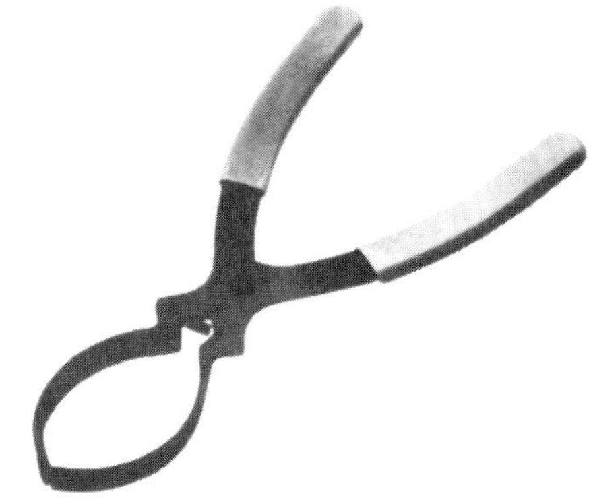

Safety, Shop Practices, Special Tools, Cleaners, and Lubricants

Figure 1-40. Dust boot installation pliers.

Figure 1-41. This tool can be used to seat the caliper piston into the caliper bore.

Figure 1-42. This tool kit is used to seat the caliper piston when changing brake pads on some rear disc brake calipers with integral parking brake actuators.

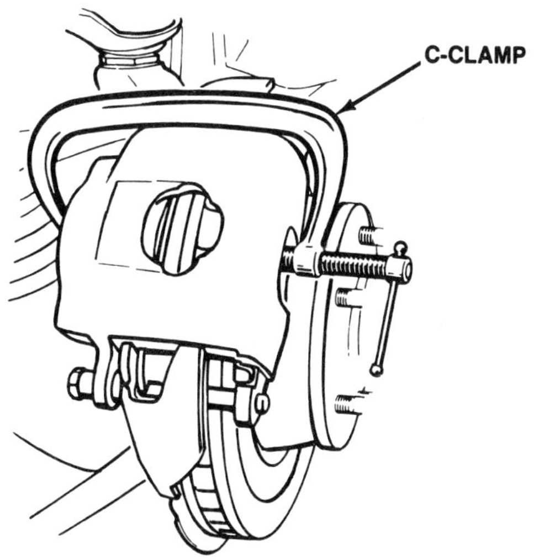

Figure 1-43. C-clamps can be used to bottom caliper pistons in their bores.

Seating Tools

Screw-type piston seating tools, figure 1-41, are placed between the caliper body and the caliper piston to push the piston into the bore. On rear disc calipers with integral parking brake actuators, it may be necessary to turn and push the piston at the same time. Figure 1-42 shows a kit that may be used on many types of rear calipers.

C-clamps

Large C-clamps, figure 1-43, are often used on single-piston calipers to seat the piston in the bore. When used for this purpose, the C-clamp is positioned across the caliper with its threaded rod pushing against the back of the outer brake pad. The rod is then carefully turned until the piston is fully seated.

Swaging Removal Tools

Swaging removal tools, figure 1-44, are required to remove brake drums that are swaged to the hub. The removal tool is placed over the stud and turned by a drill motor. The hardened cutting teeth of the tool then mill

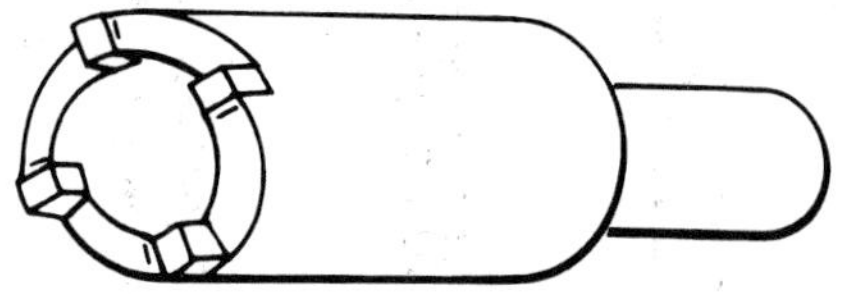

Figure 1-44. A swaging removal tool.

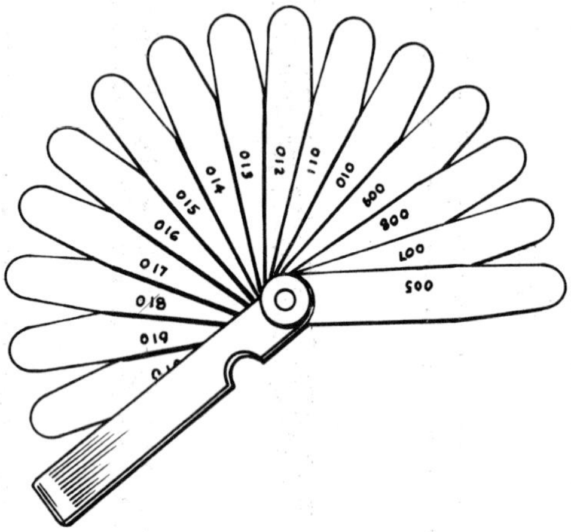

Figure 1-45. A typical set of feeler gauges.

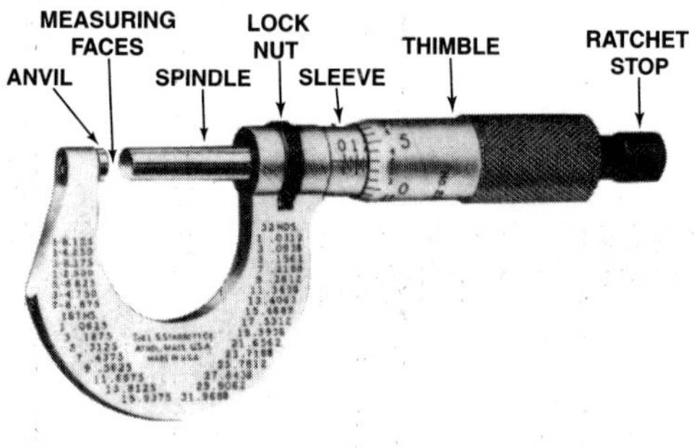

Figure 1-46. Outside micrometers are the type most often used in brake service.

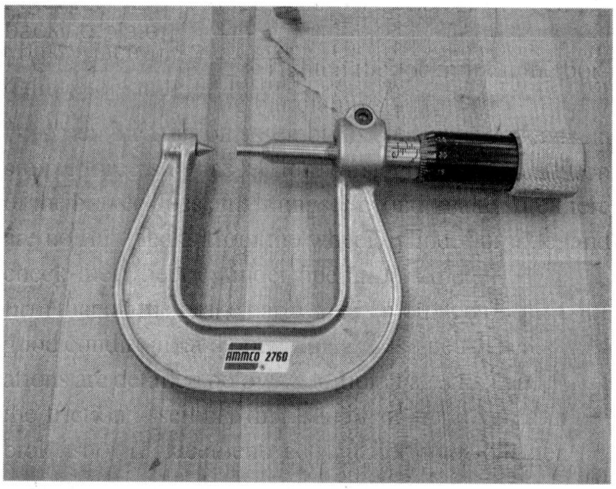

Figure 1-47. This brake rotor micrometer can measure any rotor thickness from 3/8 inch to 2 inches.

away the swaged metal from around the stud, allowing the drum and hub to be parted.

MEASURING TOOLS

In order to properly inspect and refinish certain brake parts, it is important to know their exact dimensions. In some cases, brake adjustment can also benefit from a precise knowledge of component size. Truly accurate measurement is only possible when done with proper measuring tools. Tools of this type used in brake service include:

- Feeler gauges
- Micrometers
- Dial indicators
- Shoe-setting calipers
- Drum micrometers
- Cylinder bore go/no-go gauges
- Pedal effort gauge
- Brake testing meters.

Feeler Gauges

Feeler gauges, figure 1-45, are thin, flat pieces of metal manufactured to a precise thickness. Gauges of various sizes are inserted into a gap to be measured until one that just fits is found. The thickness of the gauge then indicates the size of the gap.

Feeler gauges that conform to the English system of measurement commonly range in thickness from .001" to .025" in .001" increments. Metric feeler gauges typically range from 0.05 mm to 1.00 mm in 0.05-mm graduations. Thicker gauges of both types are available for special purposes, but in most instances, combinations of thinner gauges are stacked to obtain the desired measurement.

Micrometers

Micrometers are used to precisely measure the outside, inside, or depth of an object, opening, or depression. The micrometers used in automobile service are primarily outside micrometers that measure in thousandths of an inch or hundredths of a millimeter. An outside micrometer, figure 1-46, has a measuring range one inch less than its capacity. For example, a one-inch micrometer, the size typically used to measure the thickness of brake rotors, can measure objects from 0 to 1 inch in size.

Specialized micrometers are made specifically for measuring brake disc rotors, figure 1-47. The extra wide

Safety, Shop Practices, Special Tools, Cleaners, and Lubricants

Figure 1-48. A micrometer designed for brake work may have a pointed anvil.

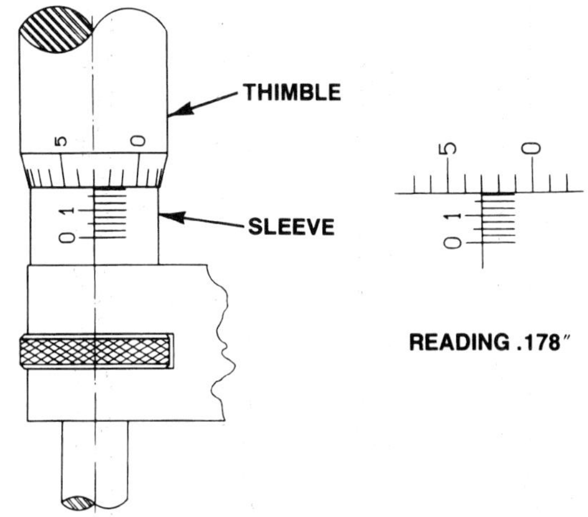

Figure 1-49. Reading the measurement on a standard micrometer.

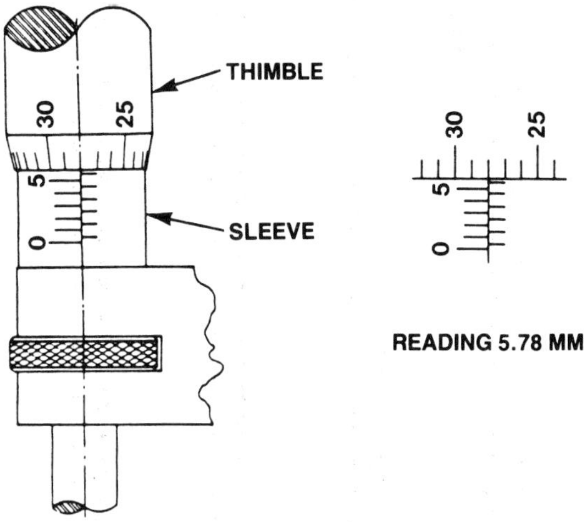

Figure 1-50. Reading the measurement on a metric micrometer.

jaws allow for a measurement range from 0 to 2 inches or 0 to 50 mm, covering most rotor sizes with just one tool. The extra large thimble and sleeve are also easier to read when compared to a standard micrometer.

Most outside micrometers have anvils and spindles with flat surfaces. However, those designed specially for measuring brake rotors have a pointed anvil, figure 1-48. This type of micrometer measures rotor thickness in the same manner as a standard micrometer, but the pointed anvil also permits measuring the depth of any scoring that may be present on the friction surfaces.

To use an outside micrometer, place the object to be measured between the anvil and spindle. Turn the thimble to move the spindle into contact with the object being measured until a slight amount of drag is felt when the micrometer is moved across the surface. Some micrometers, like the one shown in figure 1-46, have a ratchet built into them to provide the proper amount of drag; on these designs, turn the ratchet stop knob until you can feel it slip.

Once the proper tension is achieved, read the dimension of the object from the graduations on the sleeve and thimble. Each exposed line on the sleeve indicates .025″. Every fourth line of the sleeve is .100″, and is marked by a number to indicate this. Each revolution of the thimble moves the measuring face .025″, and the edge of the thimble is graduated with 25 lines, each representing .001″. Every fifth line on the thimble is marked with a number for easy identification.

To obtain the total reading, multiply the number of graduations exposed on the sleeve by .025″, then add that figure to the number of the graduation on the thimble that is aligned with the marker on the sleeve. In figure 1-49, there are seven graduations multiplied by .025″ giving .175″. The third graduation on the thimble is aligned with the mark on the sleeve giving .003″. Adding the two makes a total of .178″.

A metric micrometer, figure 1-50, is read in basically the same manner except for the difference in graduations. Each line on the top of the sleeve scale indicates 1 mm. Each line on the bottom of the sleeve scale indicates .5 mm. The lines on the thimble each indicate .01 mm. To obtain the reading shown, add the 5 mm indicated on the top sleeve scale and the .5 mm indicated on the bottom sleeve scale for a subtotal of 5.5 mm. To this, add the .28 mm indicated on the thimble scale, for a total of 5.78 mm.

Inside and depth micrometers are seldom used in brake service. Although they differ in their physical

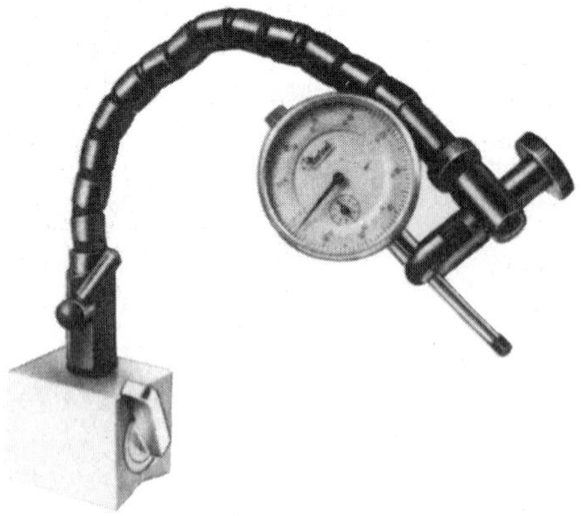

Figure 1-51. In brake service, dial indicators are used primarily to measure runout and out-of-round.

construction, the thimbles and sleeves of these micrometers operate, and are read, in the same way as those on outside micrometers.

Dial Indicators

Dial indicators, figure 1-51, measure the movement of a plunger and show the distance traveled on a dial. The measurement is generally calibrated in thousandths of an inch, or hundredths of a millimeter. Many kinds of holders, stands, and fixtures are available that allow the dial indicators to be used to measure a variety of components. In brake service, dial indicators are used primarily to measure rotor runout and brake drum out-of-round conditions. A dial indicator can also be used to check wheel bearing adjustment.

Shoe-Setting Calipers

Brake shoe-setting calipers, figure 1-52, are combination inside/outside measuring devices that consist of two interlocking pieces of steel that slide together and apart, and can be locked in position by tightening a knob. When new brake shoes are installed, the shoe-setting caliper is used to measure the inside diameter of the brake drum, and then locked in place. The opposite side of the caliper is then placed over the center of the brake shoes, allowing them to be quickly adjusted to the proper size to match the drum. The actual dimension of this measurement is not important for brake adjustment, so many shoe-setting calipers do not have inch or millimeter markings on them.

Drum Micrometer

A brake drum micrometer is used to quickly and easily measure the inside diameter of brake drums. The typi-

Figure 1-52. Shoe-setting calipers transfer the drum inside diameter measurement to the brake shoes.

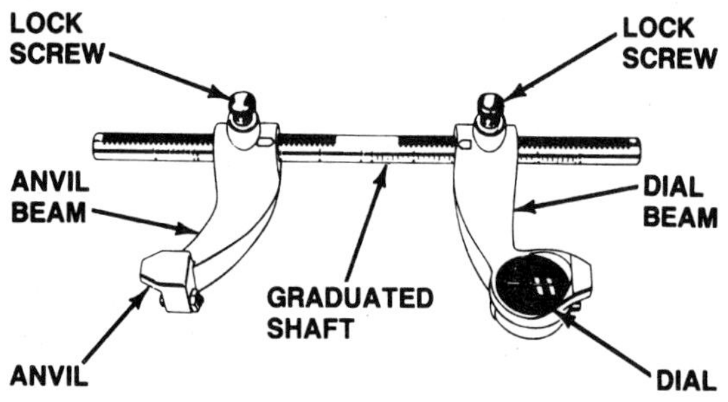

Figure 1-53. A typical brake drum micrometer.

cal drum micrometer, figure 1-53, consists of an anvil beam and a dial beam that are secured to a graduated shaft with lock screws. The shaft is marked in one-inch increments, and the lock screws for the beams fit into notches machined every .125″. The dial scale is graduated in .005″ increments.

To use a drum micrometer, loosen the lock screws and move the anvil and dial beams out along the shaft until they align with the graduations equivalent to the nominal size of the drum being measured. For example, to measure a drum with a standard inside diameter of 11.375 inches, figure 1-54, set one beam at the 11-inch marking on the shaft, and the other beam at the opposing 11-inch mark plus three .125″ graduations for a total of 11.375 inches.

Once the micrometer is set, place it inside the brake drum and hold the anvil steady against the friction surface. Slide the dial end of the micrometer back and

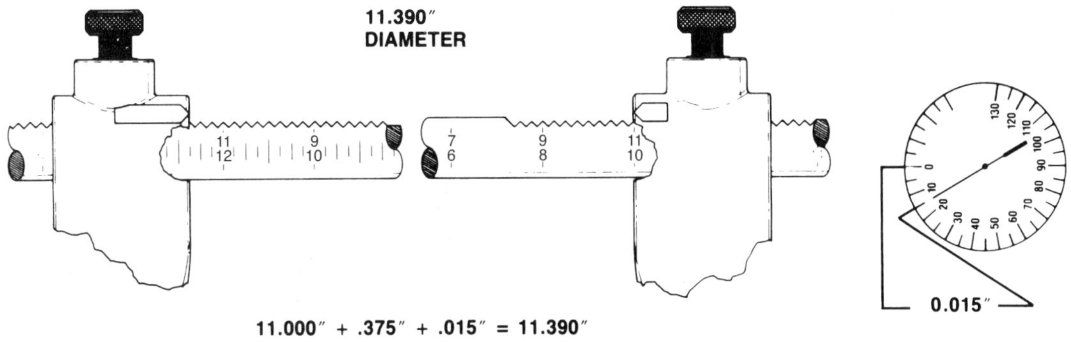

Figure 1-54. Reading the measurement on a standard brake drum micrometer.

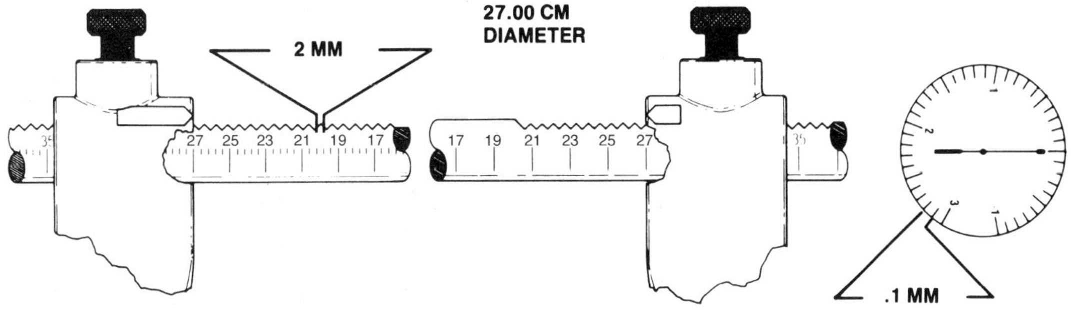

11.390" DIAMETER

11.000" + .375" + .015" = 11.390"

0.015"

Figure 1-55. Reading the measurement on a metric brake drum micrometer.

2 MM

27.00 CM DIAMETER

.1 MM

forth until the highest reading is obtained on the dial scale. In this case the dial reads .015" for a total drum diameter of 11.390 inches.

Drum micrometers graduated in metric measurements operate in much the same manner. The only exceptions are the dimension markings, figure 1-55. The shaft is marked in one-centimeter (cm) increments, and the lock screws for the two beams fit into notches machined every 2 mm. The dial scale is graduated in .1-mm increments.

Cylinder Bore Go/No-Go Gauges

Cylinder bore go/no-go gauges, figure 1-56, are used to quickly determine if a master cylinder or wheel cylinder bore is worn beyond service limits. If the bore of a hydraulic cylinder is too for oversize, the piston cup seals will not have adequate tension against the cylinder walls. This can cause the cylinder to leak fluid, enable air to enter the hydraulic system, or allow fluid under pressure to bypass the seals. A go/no-go gauge is generally used to check the size of the cylinder bore after honing to ensure that too much metal has not been removed.

A set of go/no-go gauges consists of a handle and various hardened steel plugs. The plugs are sized to match the diameters of typical cylinder bores, plus approximately .006 inch. To use the go/no-go gauge, select the size plug that corresponds to the nominal bore diameter and attach it to the handle. Attempt to insert the plug into the bore; if the plug fits, the bore is too far oversize and the master cylinder of wheel cylinder must be replaced.

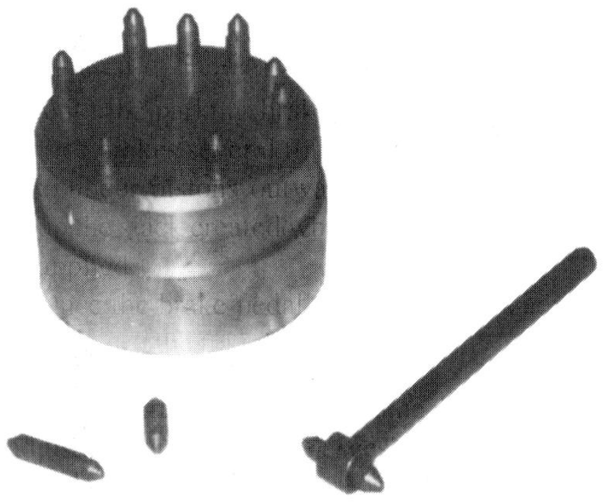

Figure 1-56. Hydraulic cylinder bore go/no-go gauges are used to check for wear.

Brake Pedal Effort Gauge

The brake pedal effort gauge, figure 1-57, measures the amount of force applied to the brake pedal by the operator's foot. Some manufacturers specify the use of this gauge when checking brake pedal travel or adjusting the parking brake. The pedal effort gauge is graduated in pounds or Newtons of force, and operates hydraulically through an attached pedal. The entire assembly is attached to a steel bracket that allows it to be installed over the vehicle brake pedal.

Brake Testing Meters

Equipment used to measure the performance of a vehicle braking system may be mechanical or electronic. This testing is required in some areas, usually for school buses and commercial vehicles. Brake testing meters can measure the vehicle's rate of deceleration, acceleration, and tendency to pull to either side.

Tapley Brake Testing Meter

The Tapley brake testing meter, figure 1-58, is a decelerometer used to test the efficiency of braking systems. It does this by measuring braking force in gravities of deceleration. One gravity (g), is an acceleration or deceleration that changes at the rate of 32 feet per second, per second. Braking force is shown on the Tapley meter scale as a percentage of 1 g. For example, ½ g of braking force would show on the Tapley meter scale as 50 percent braking efficiency.

When the Tapley meter was introduced many years ago, only racing cars could decelerate at a rate anywhere near 1 g. However, because of advances in brake systems, suspensions, and tires, most modern cars can approach this figure, and some high-performance models can brake even harder than 1 g! Nevertheless, 1 g deceleration is still the practical maximum for most vehicle brake systems, and a measurement based on that value is useful when evaluating a car's braking performance.

To measure braking efficiency, mount the Tapley meter in the car in a level position using a clamp or the available 14-pound (6.4 Kg) floor mounting block. The meter must be free to swing forward and back along the lengthwise axis of the vehicle. Drive the car at approximately 20 mph (32 kph) on a smooth, dry,

Figure 1-57. A pedal effort gauge indicates the amount of force applied to the brake pedal.

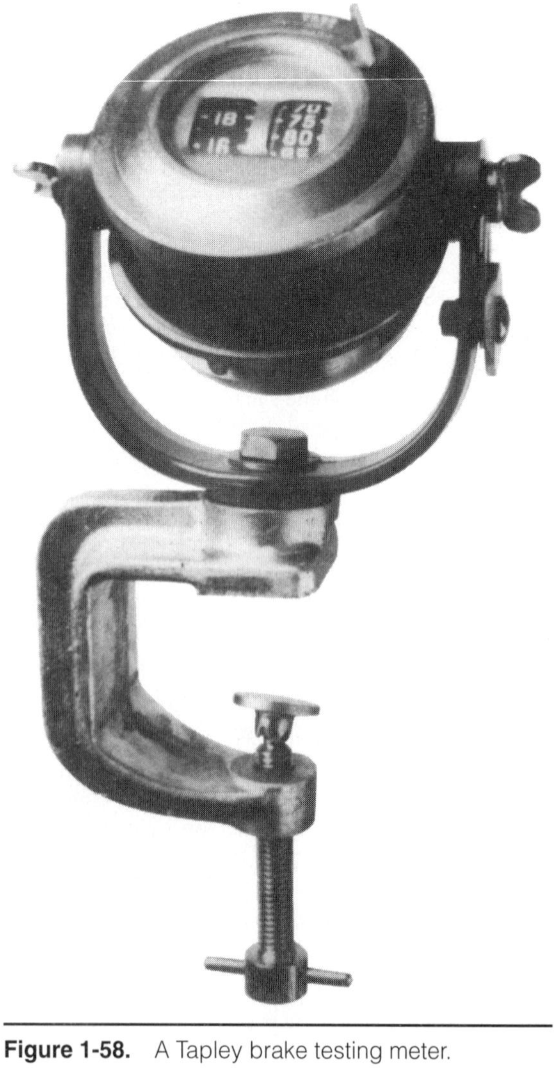

Figure 1-58. A Tapley brake testing meter.

Safety, Shop Practices, Special Tools, Cleaners, and Lubricants

level road and apply the brakes smoothly and as hard as possible without locking the wheels.

The meter will swing forward under deceleration, and a reading of the vehicle's braking efficiency will be displayed on the readout until the meter is reset.

Electronic Brake Testing Meter

The electronic brake testing meter, figure 1-59, is a portable device that can test and report on brake efficiency. Like the Tapley meter, it can measure deceleration and acceleration in gravities (g). In addition, the lateral accelerometer can detect if the vehicle pulls to the left or right when braking.

The meter is placed anywhere in the vehicle with a flat surface and zeroed out with the control buttons. The vehicle is driven to the specified speed and then the brakes are applied. Braking efficiency, brake pull, and many other measurements are recorded and placed into the device memory. The test results can be sent to a printer or computer for printing using a built-in infrared port or a cable, figure 1-60.

CYLINDER AND CALIPER REFINISHING TOOLS

In some cases, it may be necessary to rebuild a hydraulic component rather than replace it. It is usually better to replace a leaking component since it is very difficult for the technician to duplicate the smooth bore of a new part. This is especially true of aluminum cylinders with an anodized bore.

To provide a proper sealing surface and prevent piston seizure, the bores of master cylinders, wheel cylinders, and brake calipers must be free from rust and corrosion, and have the proper finish. If the bore surface has only minor damage, special tools can be used to refinish it. These tools include:

- Drill motors
- Stone hones
- Ball hones.

Drill Motors

Electric drill motors and pneumatic drill motors, figures 1-61 and 1-62, commonly called electric and air drills, are handheld motors with special clamps for holding other tools such as drill bits and hones. The clamp on a drill motor is called the chuck, and is tightened and loosened with a chuck key. The chuck key is the only tool that will properly tighten and loosen the chuck.

Hones

Cylinder hones, figure 1-63, are used to remove rust, corrosion, minor pits, and residue from the bores of master cylinders, wheel cylinders, and brake calipers. There are two basic types of cylinder hones, stone hones and ball hones.

```
          BrakeCheck
          ==========

   Serial No:    BRK00003
   S/W Version:  1.0.2

   Test Performed:
     21:25:45 20/12/2002

        Service Brake Test
        ==================
   Front-Back Acceleration
     Peak:            85 %g
     Average:         66 %g
   Left-Right Acceleration
     Peak:             2 %g
     Vehicle pulls: LEFT
   Test Speed:       41 km/h
   Stopping Dist:    9.8 m
   Brake Efficiency:  67 %

   Calibration Ok
     Due: 17/01/2004

   ........................
   Vehicle Registration

   ........................
   Inspector Name

   ........................
   Signature
```

Figure 1-59. An electronic brake testing meter. (Courtesy of Bowmonk, Ltd.)

Figure 1-60. Electronic brake testing meter printout. (Courtesy of Bowmonk, Ltd.)

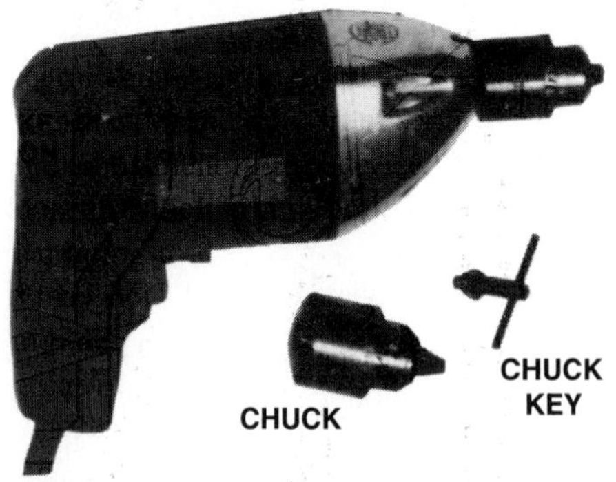

Figure 1-61. An electric drill motor, chuck, and chuck key.

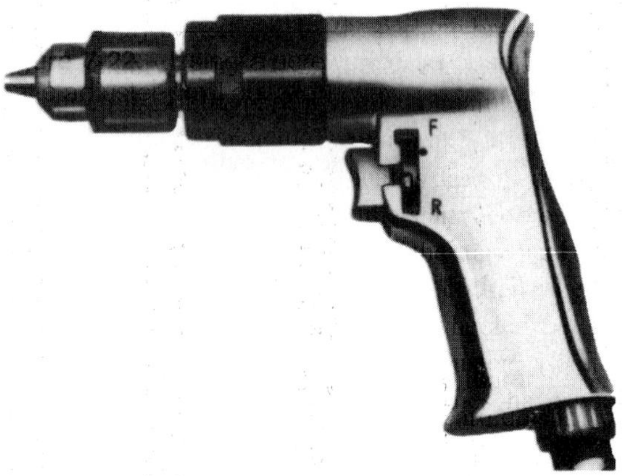

Figure 1-62. A pneumatic, or compressed-air-powered, drill motor.

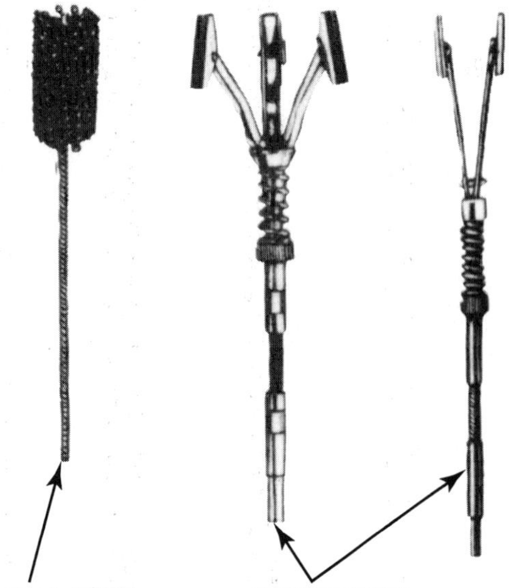

Figure 1-63. Typical brake cylinder hones.

Stone hones are available in both two-arm and three-arm models; the two-arm designs can fit into smaller bores than can the three-arm types. A replaceable abrasive stone is mounted to the end of each arm, and the arms are forced outward against the cylinder wall by spring pressure. The spring pressure is usually adjustable so the hone can apply proper tension to refinish a variety of bore diameters. The hone attaches to the drill motor through a flexible shaft that makes perfect alignment between the drill motor and the cylinder or caliper bore unnecessary.

Abrasive stones of various grits are available for master cylinder and wheel cylinder service. Medium-grit stones can be used to remove material rapidly, although care must be taken not to remove too much metal. Fine-grit stones are most common, and provide a smoother surface finish with less chance of honing the cylinder too far oversize. Coarse-grit stones are also available, but they are not recommended for master cylinder and wheel cylinder service. Coarse stones are normally used only to rapidly clean up the bores of brake calipers with fixed piston seals; the quality of the surface finish is less critical in these applications.

Ball hones consist of silicon carbide abrasive balls, with a medium-fine grit, attached to flexible metal bristles. The balls and bristles are connected to a flexible metal shaft that is inserted in the drill motor chuck. Ball hones are not adjustable but come a range of sizes to match different bore diameters. The nature of the abrasives on ball hones provides a better surface finish, and makes a ball hone less likely to remove excessive metal than a stone hone.

FRICTION COMPONENT REFINISHING TOOLS

The friction components of the brake system are the drums and rotors, and shoes and pads. A proper fit between these parts is essential for maximum braking power. The tools for refinishing friction components include:

- Brake lathes
- Drum grinders
- Rotor resurfacers.

Brake Lathes

As discussed in Chapter 11 of the *Classroom Manual*, brake lathes use an electric motor to turn a spindle that holds the drum or rotor to be machined. As the drum or rotor turns, a carbide steel tool bit, rigidly mounted on a boring bar, is passed over the friction surface to cut away a thin layer of metal and restore a smooth finish. Some lathes are designed to machine only drums,

Safety, Shop Practices, Special Tools, Cleaners, and Lubricants

figure 1-64, while others will machine only rotors, figure 1-65. Still others can be adapted to machine drums or rotors. A typical lathe used for passenger-car brake service can machine drums from 6 to 28 inches (152 to 711 mm) in diameter, and rotors as large as 13 inches (330 mm) in diameter.

Most brake lathes require that the rotor be removed from the car for machining. However, portable lathes are also available that machine the rotor while it is still in place, figure 1-66.

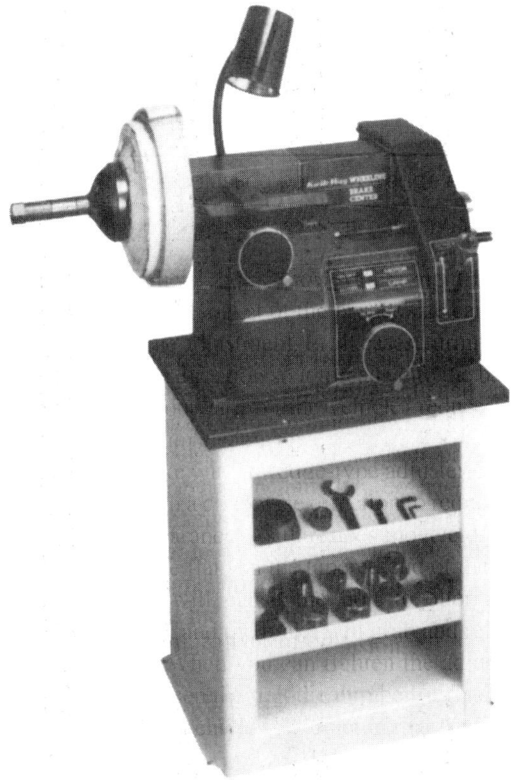

Drum Grinders

Drum grinders are attachments that mount to a brake lathe in place of the boring bar that holds the cutting tool bit. A drum grinder, figure 1-67, uses a stone grinding wheel to cut hard spots down flush with the drum friction surface.

Rotor Resurfacers

Rotor resurfacers, figure 1-68, use abrasive sanding discs to remove rust, corrosion, and lining deposits from the rotor, and give it a nondirectional surface finish. Rotor resurfacers remove only very small amounts of metal to correct for minor rotor damage and distortion.

Figure 1-64. A brake drum lathe.

Figure 1-65. A brake rotor lathe.

Figure 1-66. A portable brake lathe that machines rotors on the car.

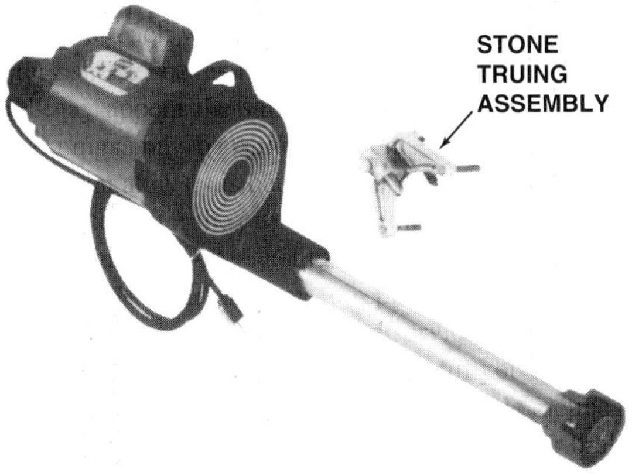

Figure 1-67. A drum grinding attachment for a brake lathe.

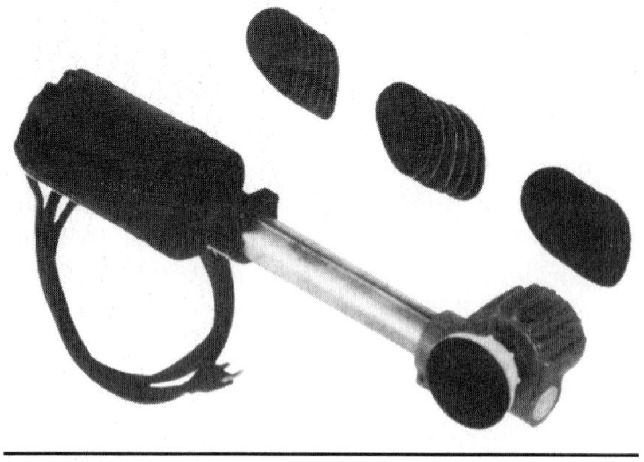

Figure 1-68. A rotor resurfacing attachment for a brake lathe.

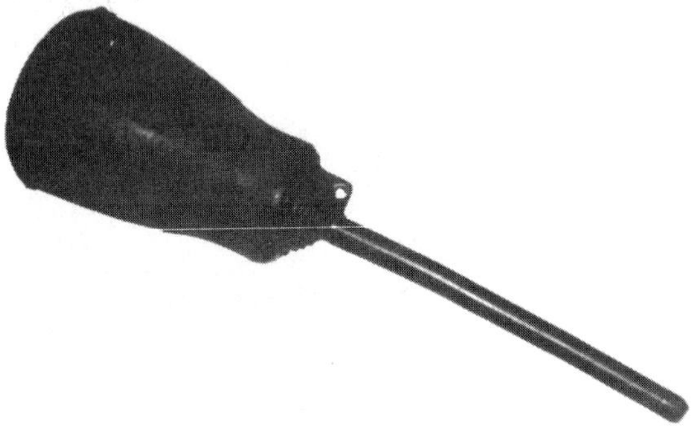

Figure 1-69. A brake fluid syringe.

HYDRAULIC SERVICE TOOLS

The brake hydraulic system contains the fluid that transmits application force to the wheel friction assemblies. Much of the service on this system involves maintaining the proper fluid level, and bleeding trapped air from the brake lines, cylinders, and calipers. The two most common tools used in hydraulic system service are the:

- Brake fluid syringe
- Pressure bleeder.

Brake Fluid Syringe

The brake fluid syringe, figure 1-69, is a simple device used to withdraw fluids from reservoirs. This type of syringe consists of a hollow plastic tube attached to a rubber bulb. To use this tool, compress the bulb, place the open end of the tube into the fluid, then release pressure on the bulb. As the bulb returns to its relaxed state, it will draw a quantity of the fluid into the syringe. Brake fluid syringes are primarily used during brake pad replacement to remove fluid from the master cylinder reservoir before the caliper pistons are bottomed. A syringe is also used to remove old fluid from the reservoir when the hydraulic system is flushed and new brake fluid is installed.

Pressure Bleeder

A pressure bleeder, figure 1-70, uses compressed air to force brake fluid through the hydraulic system. This enables the system to be quickly and easily purged of any air that may be trapped in it.

A pressure bleeder consists of a sealed tank fitted with an air inlet valve and a fluid outlet valve. The tank is filled with a supply of brake fluid, then pressurized to approximately 30 psi (200 kPa); a relief value prevents accidental overcharging. Some early, inexpensive pressure bleeders exposed the brake fluid directly to the air in the tank, but modern designs have a rubber diaphragm that separates the fluid from the air. This prevents the fluid from absorbing moisture out of the air which will greatly reduce its boiling point. It also prevents the fluid from becoming aerated which can make it impossible to properly bleed the brake system.

The pressurized brake fluid is routed from the tank through the fluid outlet valve into a rubber hose that ends in a quick release fitting. The fitting can be attached to a variety of adapters that fit various master cylinder fluid reservoirs, figure 1-71. To prevent injury

Figure 1-70. Pressure bleeders are used to rapidly purge air from the brake hydraulic system.

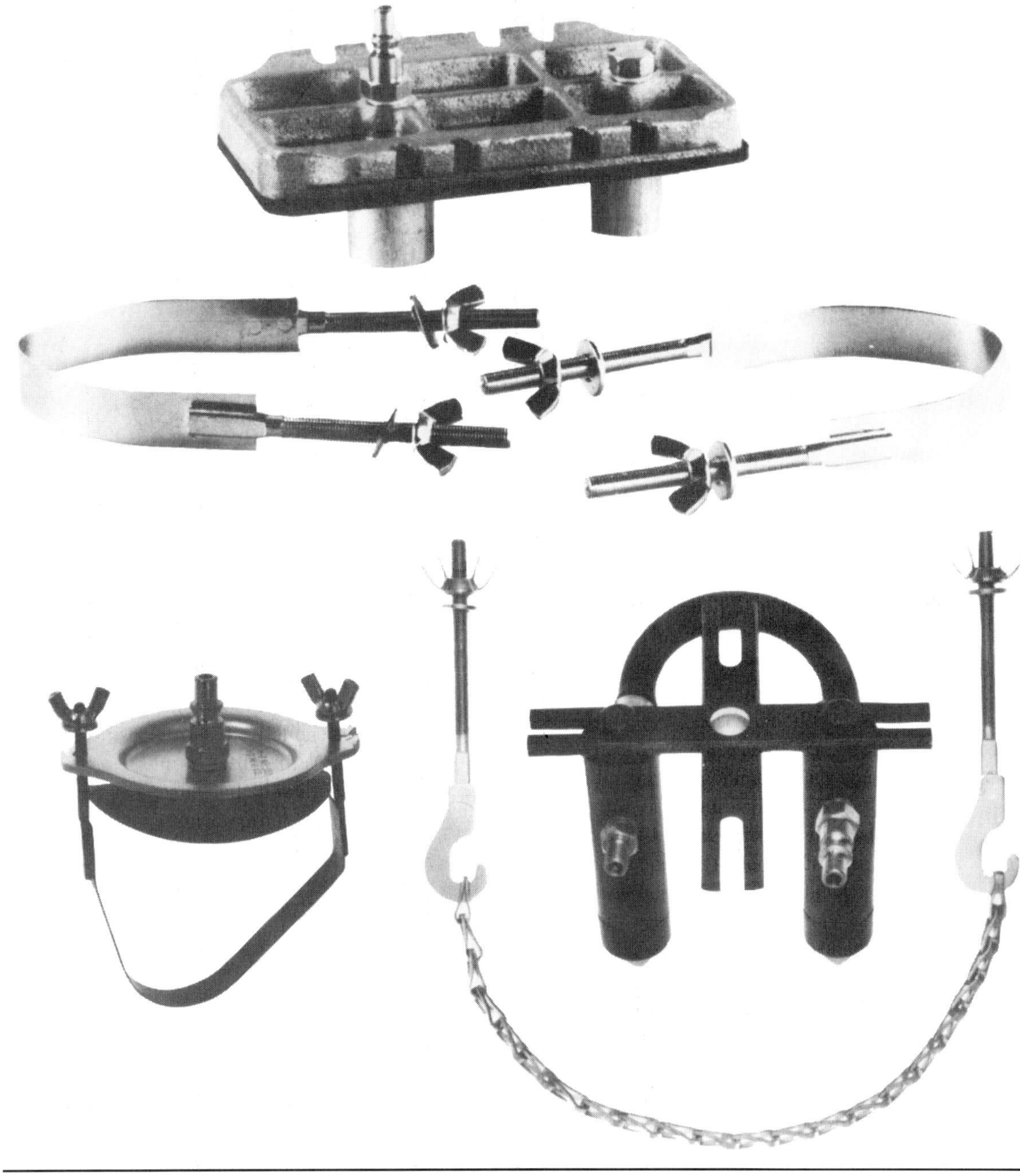

Safety, Shop Practices, Special Tools, Cleaners, and Lubricants

Figure 1-71. Typical master cylinder adapters for a pressure bleeder.

from brake fluid spray, always wear eye protection when connecting or disconnecting a pressure bleeder.

LUBRICANTS

A variety of lubricants are used in brake work to aid assembly, preserve parts from corrosion, and prevent mechanical seizure, figure 1-72. These lubricants include:

- Brake grease
- Assembly fluid
- Rubber grease.

Brake Grease

Special high-temperature brake grease has a melting point of over 500°F (260°C) and contains solid lubricants such as zinc oxide. Even at extreme temperatures where the grease melts and runs off, the solid lubricants remain to provide protection. Like any grease, brake grease is designed to provide lubrication for moving parts, and thus prevent rust, corrosion and seizure.

Many manufacturers are specifying silicone or synthetic brake grease for use on caliper slides and shoe

Figure 1-72. This lubricant is designed for use on brake parts such as the adjuster threads and backing plate.

backing plates. This grease has a temperature range of from −50°F to 570°F and resists melting and washout from water. Silicone and molybdenum disulfide are used, along with other ingredients, to make a long-lasting brake lubricant.

Brake grease is generally applied to the shoe support pads on the backing plates of drum brakes, and to the sliding surfaces of sliding brake calipers. Several manufactures also recommend that brake grease be applied to the locating pins, sleeves, and bushings of floating brake calipers.

Assembly Fluid

When brake system hydraulic components are rebuilt, some type of lubricant is needed to help ease pistons past fixed seals, or piston seals into bores. Alcohol can be used for this purpose, but it evaporates quickly and leaves no residual lubrication. Many technicians use brake fluid to smooth the assembly of hydraulic components because it is readily available. However, the best product for this purpose is one of the special assembly fluids designed for the job. Assembly fluids are very similar to brake fluid, except that they have a much higher viscosity; some types have a consistency close to that of grease. The higher viscosity of assembly fluids provides better lubrication because the fluid will remain where it is needed.

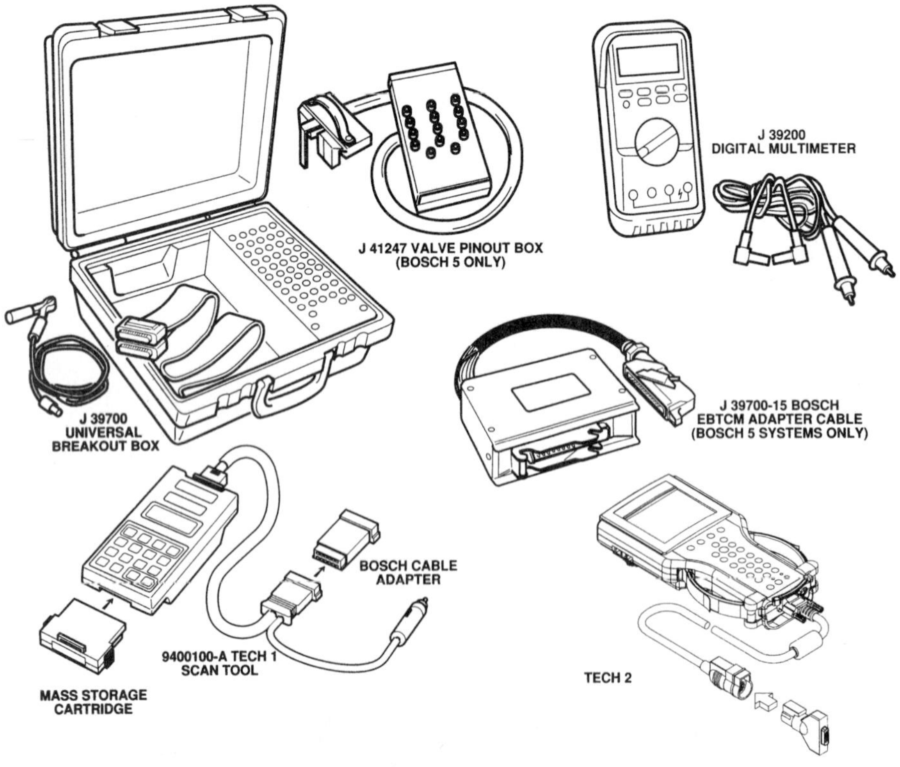

Figure 1-73. Special tools and equipment may be needed to properly service antilock brake systems. (Courtesy of General Motors Corporation, Service and Parts Operations)

Safety, Shop Practices, Special Tools, Cleaners, and Lubricants

Rubber Grease

Some manufacturers include a package of red or pink rubber grease in their master cylinder rebuild kits. These non-petroleum-base greases are intended to be packed into the master cylinder wiper boot where the pedal pushrod enters the cylinder. This provides lubrication between the boot and pushrod, and helps seal moisture away from the cylinder bore opening. A small amount of the grease between the pushrod and piston can also help prevent rust and corrosion. Rubber greases should never be mistaken for, or used in place of, brake assembly fluids.

ANTILOCK BRAKE SYSTEM TOOLS

Antilock brake systems may require the use of special tools or equipment, figure 1-73. Some equipment is specific to a particular antilock brake system (ABS), figure 1-74, while other tools can be used on many different systems.

The ABS technician needs to have at least a digital multimeter (DMM) and a diagnostic scan tool. The DMM is used to check wheel speed sensors, solenoids, and other ABS components. The scan tool is needed to retrieve diagnostic information from the ABS electronic control module. On some systems, the scan tool is required to bleed the brake system. Use of these tools is covered in Chapter 12 and Chapter 13.

Figure 1-74. These special testers are designed for use on specific antilock brake systems.

2
Brake System Diagnosis

OBJECTIVES

Upon completion and review of this chapter, you will be able to:

- Ask the correct questions of a customer.
- Road test a vehicle correctly.
- Test for driveline and brake vibration.
- Test braking power and stability.
- Troubleshoot brake pedal "feel."
- Troubleshoot the cause of some brake noises.
- Perform a complete brake inspection.

INTRODUCTION

The professional brake technician knows that the most efficient way to identify a brake problem is to follow a thorough and logical diagnosis procedure. This makes it quick and easy to locate the cause of the complaint, and ensures that any other potential problems are located and can be repaired *before* a failure occurs. For reasons of safety, not to mention legal liability, vehicle brakes should *always* be serviced as a complete system. Never repair a brake problem without inspecting the entire system, and never allow a car to leave your shop unless the brakes are working perfectly. If a car owner decides not to have needed brake work done, note that fact on the work order along with the recommended repairs, and have the customer initial it.

This chapter covers general diagnosis of the base brake system. Antilock brake system (ABS) diagnosis is covered in Chapter 12 and Chapter 13. When there is a concern about ABS operation or there are ABS warning lamps or diagnostic trouble codes stored, diagnosis always begins with a thorough inspection of the non-ABS components of the braking system. Any faults with this base brake system must be corrected before any further work is done on the ABS components.

Brake system diagnosis can be broken down into three steps. The first is to listen to the car owner's explanation of the problem, and ask questions to help isolate the defect. If the car can safely be driven, the second step is to perform a road test to check out the symptoms described by the car owner, and assess the overall performance of the brakes. The third and final step is to perform a complete brake system inspection to confirm your diagnosis and locate any additional problems.

The first three sections of this chapter discuss how to talk to the customer, perform the road test, and inspect the brake system. General guidelines are provided for each step, but it is not practical to list every detail of how these jobs are done. Professional brake system diagnosis requires a thorough knowledge of *all* the information in both volumes of this textbook set, as well as a certain "feel" for the job that only comes from experience. The concepts set forth in this chapter will serve as a framework on which you can build your own personal diagnosis procedure.

When you are just starting out in brake repair, you have only limited training and experience on which to base your diagnosis. And sometimes, even expert technicians are stumped by unusual or uncommon brake problems. In these situations, a diagnostic chart can be helpful in identifying possible causes of a brake problem. The final section of this chapter contains 26 diagnostic charts that describe typical brake system problems and their repair.

TALKING TO THE CUSTOMER

An important fact many technicians fail to realize is that brake repair is a business, not just a job. As in any successful business, the ultimate goal is not just to make a profit, but to satisfy the customer. While the actual repairs on the vehicle brake system are a part of achieving this goal, they are not the entire job. You must also treat customers with courtesy when they bring a car in for brake service, and pay attention to their description of the problem. This makes them feel they are receiving the service they pay for, and goes a long way toward ensuring repeat business for your shop.

When it comes to brake problem diagnosis, there is another good reason to pay attention to the customer. Although they may not realize it, car owners know a great deal about what is wrong with their cars. If you listen carefully to the customer's description of the problem, then ask specific questions about likely problem areas, you can substantially shorten your diagnosis time. For example, if a customer complains of poor stopping power, you may ask if there is a grinding noise from the wheels, indicating that the brake pads are worn to the backing plates. Another question might be whether the brake pedal must be applied with greater force than in the past, possibly indicating a problem with the power booster.

The exact questions you need to ask will vary with the problem. However, there are some general questions that can be useful in many circumstances, for example: what are the symptoms of the brake system problem? When did the problem first occur? Is the problem present at all times, or does it occur only in certain situations? Have there been any other events, such as an accident or recent repairs, that took place about the same time the brake problem appeared?

When asking these and other questions, remember that most customers are unfamiliar with the expressions used by technicians to describe brake problems. Terms such as fade, pull, lockup, and others may not have any meaning to the car owner. Make sure you fully understand the condition being described, and if necessary, take the customer along on the test drive to identify the symptom causing the complaint. Sometimes a brake "problem," such as the his of air entering a vacuum booster as the brakes are applied, is just a normal part of brake operation that the customer does not understand.

PRELIMINARY CHECKS

Diagnosis begins with a quick visual inspection. This may be done in the service lane or parking lot, before driving the vehicle. The following are easily checked:

- Brake fluid level—Check for low fluid level. This may indicate that the disc pads are worn or that there is a leak.
- External leaks—Look for leaks at brake line fittings, master cylinder, and other hydraulic components, including the ABS actuator.
- Parking brake operation—Operate the parking brake and note if it holds the vehicle as it should.
- Red brake warning light—The red brake warning light should be off, except when the parking brake is engaged. If the red warning light is on, either all the time or when pressing the brake pedal, the vehicle may not be safe to drive. Diagnose and repair before driving the vehicle.
- ABS warning light—The amber ABS warning light should stay on for a few seconds after the ignition is turned on and then go off. If the ABS light goes out and then comes back on, a problem with the ABS is indicated.
- Brake pedal check—Always check that the brake pedal does not sink partially or completely to the floor before driving the vehicle.

BRAKE SYSTEM ROAD TESTING

In some cases, a skilled technician can diagnose a brake problem simply by questioning the customer without ever looking at the car. He is able to do this because he has repaired many similar brake problems in the past, knows the symptoms for most common brake problems, and may have knowledge of unique problems that are specific to certain vehicles. In these situations, a road test may not be required, although a complete brake system inspection should still be done to confirm the diagnosis and locate any other potential problems.

Experience is not always enough, however, when you have to diagnose unusual brake system problems, multiple problems occurring at the same time, or problems that are interrelated with other vehicle systems. In these cases, a road test can help better identify the problem before the brake system is inspected. As al-

Brake System Diagnosis

Figure 2-1. A road suitable for a brake system road test.

ready mentioned, the road test allows you to confirm the symptoms described by the customer, but more importantly, it enables you to experience the condition first hand and determine if it is, in fact, a brake problem. Many tire, wheel, suspension, and driveline problems contribute to inefficient braking and display symptoms similar to those of brake problems.

To minimize the effect of the road surface on braking performance, a brake system road test should always be done on smooth, clean, dry, and level pavement, figure 2-1. Because braking force is limited by tire traction, a road that is bumpy, wet, greasy, or covered with loose dirt and leaves will not provide adequate traction for a proper road test. A road that is heavily crowned may cause the car to pull to one side. For safety, use a road that has only light traffic, and is safe for speeds up to 55 mph (88 kph).

ROAD TEST PROCEDURE

The road test focuses primarily on those symptoms that are best checked when the car is in motion. You use the road test to reduce the number of potential problem areas, then you use the more specific tests in the inspection procedure, and in later chapters of this *Shop Manual,* to isolate the exact problem. There are six basic areas you want to examine in a brake system road test:

- Driveline vibration
- Brake vibration
- Braking power
- Braking stability
- Brake pedal travel and feel
- Brake noise.

The procedure below describes how to isolate and identify brake problems related to these symptoms.

Before beginning the road test, make sure the tire pressures are set to the vehicle manufacturer's specifications. Check that the tire sizes are the same on each axle, and that all four tires are of the same construction. Both tires on each axle should have the same amount of tread wear, and you should inspect the tires for unusual wear patterns that may indicate a wheel alignment problem. Finally, take note of any obvious sagging of the suspension toward one corner, side, or end of the car. A problem in any of these areas will affect the car's braking behavior.

Driveline Vibration Test

The first part of the road test is a driveline vibration test. Driveline vibration is felt most strongly through the car body, and occurs regardless of whether the brakes are applied. To check for this condition, accelerate the car to 55 mph (88 kph), and coast down to 20 mph (30 kph) without using the brakes. Any vibrations that occur during this portion of the road test are most likely caused by bent, worn, or out-of-balance driveline parts; check for problems with the tires, wheels, axles, or driveshaft.

Brake Vibration Test

The second part of the road test is a brake vibration test. Brake vibration occurs *only* when the brakes are applied, and although it may shake the car body, it is usually felt most strongly through the brake pedal. To check for this condition, accelerate the car to 25 mph (40 kph), 40 mph (65 kph), and 55 mph (88 kph), and make stops with both light and heavy pedal pressure from each speed. Do not lock the wheels when making these stops. If you feel a body vibration or pedal pulsation when you apply the brakes, suspect distorted drums or rotors, or possibly loose wheel bearings.

Generally, front-brake vibration problems occur at speeds above 45 mph (70 kph), while rear-brake vibration problems occur below that speed. On cars where two of the service brake friction assemblies function as the parking brake, you can sometimes isolate a vibration by using the parking brake control to apply the brakes at only one axle. To do this, accelerate to speed, actuate the parking brake release lever or button to disengage the ratchet mechanism, figure 2-2, then slow the car using the parking brake. As the car decelerates, check for body vibration or a pulsation through the parking brake pedal, lever, or handle. Pulsations felt through the parking brake control are generally not as strong as those at the service brake pedal

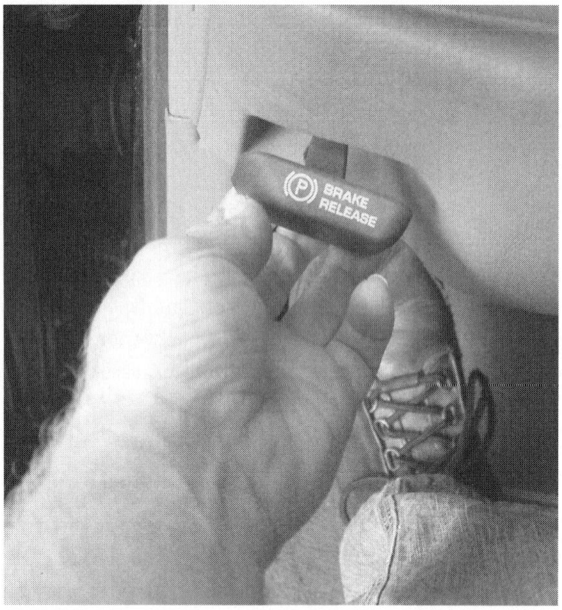

Figure 2-2. Deactivate the ratchet locking mechanism when using the parking brake to isolate a vibration.

because parking brake cable stretch absorbs some of the variation in force.

If a vibration disappears when the parking brake is used to slow the car, and no pulsation can be felt through the parking brake control, the wheel brakes not used for the parking brake are the source of the problem. If a vibration remains at the same intensity when the parking brake is used to slow the car, and a pulsation can be felt through the parking brake control, the problem is in the parking brake friction assemblies. If a vibration continues at a reduced level when the parking brake is used to slow the car, and some pulsation can be felt through the parking brake control, the problem is most likely being caused by the brakes at all four wheels.

Braking Power

When you apply the brakes at the different speeds described above, note the amount of braking power available. The stopping distance from each speed should be appropriate for the type of vehicle being tested. Experience will give you a better idea of how hard particular types of vehicles can stop, but as a general rule the larger and heavier a vehicle is, the longer its stopping distances will be.

In some cases, a deceleration measuring device like the Tapley meter described in Chapter 1 can be helpful in assessing braking power, figure 2-3. All brake systems should provide enough stopping power to lock the wheels; unless, of course, the car is equipped with

Figure 2-3. Using a Tapley meter to measure braking efficiency. (Courtesy of D. Evans Electrical, Ltd.)

anitlock brakes. If the stopping distances seem too long, or it is impossible to lock the wheels, suspect a problem with restricted brake lines, contaminated brake linings, or a defective power booster.

Don't overlook the parking brake when testing braking power; this system uses two of the service brakes on most cars, and can give you a good indication of the efficiency of those friction assemblies. Include a hill on your road test route, and apply the parking brake on the incline. The pedal, lever, or handle should apply smoothly without binding; if not, suspect cable problems. If more than two-thirds of the parking brake control travel is required to apply the brake, shoe and/or cable adjustments are called for. Finally, if the parking brake fails to hold the car in position on a good grade, inspect the friction assemblies for glazed linings or other problems that reduce braking power.

Braking Stability

As you apply the brakes at the different speeds described above, note the distribution of braking force to the wheels, and the overall stability of the vehicle. The car should stop smoothly with no tendency toward wheel lockup. During very heavy braking in ideal conditions, the front brakes should lock just before the rear brakes to ensure vehicle stability; however, not all

Brake System Diagnosis

brake systems behave in this manner when less than fully loaded.

If both brakes on the front or rear axle lock prematurely, suspect a problem with restricted brake lines, or the metering or proportioning valve. The master cylinder may also be at fault if the dual-circuit hydraulic system has a front/rear split. If only one wheel locks, the problem may be contaminated or misadjusted brake linings that are causing the friction assembly to grab. Sometimes, contaminated linings make a friction assembly slip, causing the brake in good condition on the opposite end of the axle to lock as more pedal pressure is applied to stop the car. You will determine the exact cause of the problem in the brake system inspection that follows the road test.

During the road test stops, the car should brake in a straight line with your hands resting lightly on the steering wheel. A side-to-side braking imbalance that is not severe enough to cause lockup will usually result in a pull to one side when you apply the brakes. The imbalance can be in the tires, wheels, or suspension just as easily as in the brake system. If your pre-road-test check did not indicate any unusual problems outside the brake system, suspect a restricted brake hose or a defective friction assembly with limited braking power. Once again, you will identify the precise cause of the problem in the brake system inspection that follows the road test.

Brake Pedal Travel and Feel Test

The travel and feel of the brake pedal while making the road test stops can tell you a great deal about the condition of the brake system, figure 2-4. In fact, almost every brake system problem eventually results in some type of pedal symptom. There are many possibilities, and these are all covered in the diagnostic charts at the end of the chapter. The most common symptoms and causes are described below.

A spongy pedal with longer than normal travel usually indicates a hydraulic problem, such as a fluid leak or air in the lines. Long pedal travel with a firm feel often indicates a mechanical problem such as a friction assembly in need of adjustment. However, if the brake pedal gradually sinks part way to the floor, then becomes firm, one circuit of the dual-circuit brake hydraulic system is probably at fault. If the pedal gradually sinks all the way to the floor, suspect a master cylinder that is bypassing internally. When excessive pedal pressure is required to stop the car, suspect a power booster problem, or defective wheel friction assemblies that are not providing full braking power.

Figure 2-4. An experienced foot on the brake pedal is an excellent diagnostic tool.

Brake Noise

Like pedal feel, brake noise is a significant aid in diagnosing brake problems. However, some noises are considered normal; certain semimetallic pads cause a slight grinding sound, and the high-temperature organic friction materials used on many European import cars have a normal tendency to squeal. Fixed calipers are often noisier than other designs because their solid mountings transmit vibration directly into the chassis; the more flexible mountings of floating and sliding calipers damp many vibrations that might otherwise cause noise.

Although many different problems cause brake noise, the sounds are often similar, and in some cases resemble the noise of normal brake operation. Only experience can teach you which sounds are normal and which are not, and which of several problems is the source of a specific noise. During the test drive, listen for noises when the brakes are both released and applied. Common noises and their sources are described below.

When the brakes are released, rattles and scrapes are the most common noises. A rattle at low speeds indicates excessive clearance between the brake pads and rotor caused by pads that are not securely mounted as a result of worn, damaged, or missing parts. On many newer disc brakes, a light scraping or "chirping" noise when the brakes are not applied is caused by the pad wear indicator rubbing against the rotor to signal the need for pad replacement, figure 2-5. A louder scraping noise can be caused by a bent splash shield rubbing a rotor, or a bent backing plate contacting a brake drum.

Another noise that may be heard when the brakes are not applied is the growing sound that signals a

Figure 2-5. Pad wear indicators are designed to create brake noise.

worn wheel bearing. To confirm this problem, swerve the car back and forth to alternately load and unload the bearings on opposite sides of the car. The noise from the bad bearing will increase with the load on that side of the car, and decrease as the load is reduced. See Chapter 14 for complete wheel bearing diagnosis procedures.

Noises that occur when the brakes are applied include scrapes, grinding, squeaks, squeals, snaps, clicks, and thumps. A scraping or grinding sound usually indicates worn out brake linings that have resulted in metal-to-metal contact between the pad backing plate and rotor, or shoe lining table and drum. Squeaks and squeals commonly occur when the brakes are applied, and most often result from problems with the lining friction material, or worn, damaged, and missing vibration damping or anti-rattle parts. A snap or click on brake application is usually caused by loose, worn, or broken mechanical parts, or an improper rotor or drum surface finish. A thumping sound when the brakes are applied is usually associated with a cracked brake drum, defective brake shoes, or weak brake shoe return springs. The exact cause will be determined during the brake system inspection that follows the road test.

BRAKE INSPECTION

After you have discussed the brake problem with the customer and road tested the vehicle, you should have a fairly good idea of where the problem lies. The final step in the diagnosis procedure is to perform a complete brake system inspection to confirm your suspicions and locate any additional brake components in need of repair. Perform the basic inspection procedure described below on any vehicle that comes into your shop for brake work. As with the road test, it is not possible to cover every detail of brake inspection in this section; detailed checks and tests for each component are described in later chapters on each part or system.

Preliminary Checks

If you were unable to road test the car, or a road test was unnecessary, perform the pre-road-test checks and inspections at this time. Make sure the tire pressures are set to the vehicle manufacturer's specifications. Check that the tire sizes are the same on each axle, and that all four tires are of the same construction. Both tires on each axle should have the same amount of tread wear, and you should inspect the tires for unusual wear patterns that may indicate a wheel alignment problem. Finally, take note of any obvious sagging of the suspension toward one corner, side, or end of the car. A problem in any of these areas will affect the car's braking behavior.

Brake Pedal Checks

The first step in the inspection is to sit in the driver's seat, apply the brake pedal, and listen for noise. A squeak as the pedal is applied or released is usually caused by a lack of lubrication. If the noise is from under the dash, lubricate the pedal linkage. If the noise is from the wheel brakes, the caliper floating or sliding parts, or the shoe support pads on the drum brake backing plates, are in need of lubrication. As you apply the brake pedal for this test, make sure there is the proper amount of freeplay.

Next, if the brake system is so equipped, test the vacuum power booster. With the engine off, apply the brake pedal repeatedly with medium pressure until the booster reserve is depleted. At least two brake applications should have a power-assisted feel before the pedal hardens noticeably. If the pedal feels hard immediately, or after only one brake application, a vacuum leak or low level of engine vacuum is indicated. To test booster function once the reserve is depleted, hold moderate pressure on the brake pedal and start the engine. If the booster is working properly, the pedal will drop slightly toward the floor. During this part of the inspection, have an assistant verify that the stoplights come on when you apply the brake pedal.

Fluid Checks

Next, check the brake fluid level in the master cylinder reservoir. A low level indicates that either the brake linings are worn or there is a leak in the hydraulic system. Dip a clean finger into the fluid and wipe it across the bottom of the reservoir. Withdraw your finger and

Brake System Diagnosis

Figure 2-6. The master cylinder fluid reservoir should be free of residue.

Figure 2-7. In-and-out movement indicates wheel bearing wear or misadjustment.

Figure 2-8. Mark the wheel and hub before removing the wheel so it can be reinstalled in its original position.

check it for signs of rust, corrosion, or other residue, figure 2-6. If there is any buildup, the hydraulic system should be flushed, and the wheel cylinders and brake calipers may need to be rebuilt or replaced. The master cylinder is at the top of the hydraulic system; any contamination there is always found in larger quantities at the lower ends of the system.

Inspect the brake lines from the master cylinder to the point where they disappear under the car. Look for leaks and corrosion along the lines and at their connections. Heavily rusted or corroded brake lines, and any line with a kink in it, must be replaced. Also inspect any hydraulic control valves located in the engine compartment. Check them for leaks, and make sure that any electrical switches they contain are properly connected to the vehicle wiring harness.

Friction Assembly Checks

Raise the vehicle on a lift, grasp the front tires at the top and bottom, then check for wheel bearing play by attempting to wobble the tires in and out, figure 2-7. You should feel little or no play. Experience will give you a better idea of how much play is acceptable; until then, you may want to use a dial indicator to check the bearing play as described in Chapter 14. More than a minimal amount of play indicates a need for bearing service.

Mark each wheel and one of its studs with chalk or a grease pencil so you can replace the wheels in their original positions, figure 2-8. This prevents problems if the wheels and tires have been balanced on the car. Remove the wheels from the car so you can inspect the brake friction assemblies.

On disc brakes, verify that the brake linings are at least $\frac{1}{32}$ inch (.030″ or .75 mm) above the pad backing plate or rivet heads, figure 2-9. Inspect the calipers for leaks, and make sure the mounting hardware is tight. The floating or sliding surfaces of the caliper should be properly lubricated and free of rust and corrosion. Inspect the rotors for scoring, cracks, heat checking, and hard spots. Measure the rotor thickness. And finally, inspect the brake hoses for swelling, leaks, cracks, or abrasions.

Remove the drums from drum brake friction assemblies and verify that brake shoe linings are at least $\frac{1}{32}$ inch (.030″ or 75 mm) above the lining table or rivet heads, figure 2-10. Pull back the wheel cylinder boots

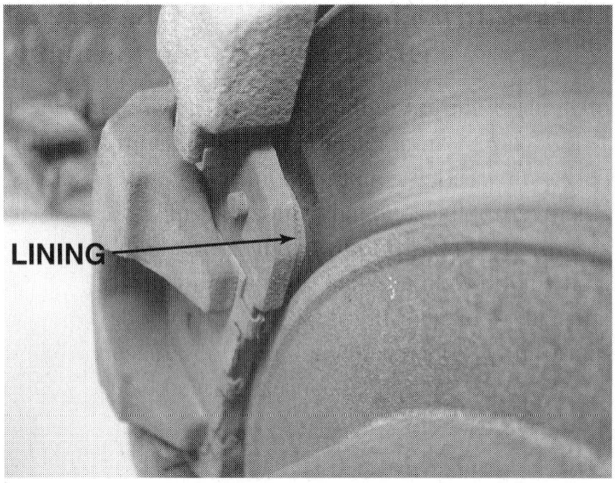

Figure 2-9. The disc brake pad lining should be at least 1/32 inch (.75 mm) thick. The pads on this vehicle need to be changed.

Figure 2-10. A tire tread depth gauge provides an easy way to measure brake shoe lining thickness. This lining is within specification.

and inspect for piston seal leakage; no more than a slight amount of dampness should be present. Inspect the drum friction surface for scoring, cracks, heat checking, or hard spots. Measure the drum diameter. And finally, inspect any brake hoses for swelling, leaks, cracks, or abrasions.

Continue your inspection of the brake lines under the car. Look for leaks along the lines and at the connections. Heavily rusted or corroded brake lines, and any line with a kink in it, must be replaced. While checking the fluid lines, inspect the parking brake cables for rust, corrosion, and fraying.

BRAKE SYSTEM DIAGNOSTIC CHARTS

The following diagnostic charts can help you determine the cause and cure of most brake problems. The charts are organized into four sections with a heading for each basic type of symptom: pedal, wheel brake, brake performance, and brake noise. Each symptom is then broken down into specific problems with a cause and a cure for each. On each chart, subheadings (All, Disc, and Drum) are used to indicate whether the problems listed apply to all brakes, only disc brakes, or only drum brakes.

SYMPTOM   CHART NUMBER

Pedal Symptoms:

Spongy Pedal	1
Excessive Pedal Travel	2
Sinking Brake Pedal	3
Pedal Vibration or Pulsation	4
Excessive Pedal Effort	5

Wheel Brake Symptoms:

One Brake Drags	6
Front Brakes Drag	7
Rear Brakes Drag	8
All Brakes Drag	9
One Brake Locks	10
Premature Front Brake Lockup	11
Premature Rear Brake Lockup	12
Uneven Lining Wear	13
Rapid Lining Wear	14

SYMPTOM   CHART NUMBER

Brake Performance Symptoms:

Pull During Braking	15
Brake Fade	16
Steering Wheel Shimmy	17
Grabbiness or Sensitivity	18
Chatter or Shudder	19
Unable to Fully Bleed System	20

Brake Noise:

Squeak on Application at Rest	21
Click or Snap on Application	22
Thump on Application	23
Squeal While Braking	24
Scraping or Grinding	25
Rattle When Brakes Unapplied	26

Brake System Diagnosis

I. PEDAL SYMPTOMS

1. Spongy Pedal—All

1. Air in hydraulic system
2. Weak brake hose expanding under pressure
3. Water-contaminated brake fluid (low boiling point)
4. Master cylinder leaking internally
5. Master cylinder mounting bolts loose
6. Cracked firewall or power booster housing

1. Bleed brake system
2. Replace hose
3. Flush brake hydraulic system
4. Rebuild or replace master cylinder
5. Tighten bolts
6. Repair or replace as needed

- **Spongy Pedal—Disc**

1. Caliper distortion from frozen piston (multipiston calipers)

Rebuild or replace caliper

- **Spongy Pedal—Drum**

1. Bent or warped brake shoes
2. Poor lining-to-drum contact
3. Thin or cracked brake drum
4. Faulty residual pressure check valve admitting air (if used)
5. Leaking wheel cylinder
6. Shoes not centered in drum (with adjustable anchors)
7. Bent or broken backing plate

1. Replace shoes in axle sets
2. Replace brake shoes
3. Replace drum
4. Replace check valve and bleed brakes
5. Rebuild or replace wheel cylinder
6. Adjust shoe anchors
7. Replace backing plate

2. Excessive Pedal Travel—All

1. Air in hydraulic system
2. Water-contaminated brake fluid (low boiling point)
3. Master cylinder pushrod adjustment incorrect
4. Brake booster output pushrod adjustment incorrect
5. Master cylinder bypassing internally
6. Pressure loss in one half of split hydraulic system
7. Fluid bypassing quick-take-up valve in master cylinder
8. Brake pedal bushings worn out

1. Bleed brake system
2. Flush brake hydraulic system
3. Adjust pushrod
4. Adjust pushrod
5. Rebuild or replace master cylinder
6. Repair leak in hydraulic system
7. Replace quick-take-up valve
8. Inspect, replace bushings

- **Excessive Pedal Travel—Disc**

1. Loose, broken, or worn caliper attachment
2. Excessive pad knockback from rotor runout
3. Damaged or worn caliper piston seals
4. Loose or worn wheel bearings
5. Warped or bent brake pad

1. Torque caliper mounting bolts to specifications or repair attachment
2. Turn or replace rotor
3. Rebuild or replace caliper
4. Service and adjust bearings
5. Replace pads in axle sets

- **Excessive Pedal Travel—Drum**

1. Excessive clearance between linings and drums
2. Automatic adjusters not working
3. Bent or warped brake shoes

1. Adjust brakes
2. Service adjusters
3. Replace shoes in axle sets

3. Sinking Brake Pedal—All

1. Hydraulic system leaking externally
2. Master cylinder leaking internally
3. Bleeder screw left open

1. Locate and repair leak
2. Rebuild or replace master cylinder
3. Close screw and bleed brake system

4. Brake Pedal Vibration or Pulsation—All

1. Loose or worn wheel bearings

1. Service and adjust bearings

- **Brake Pedal Vibration or Pulsation—Disc**

1. Excessive rotor thickness variation or lateral runout
2. Rust on rotor surface

1. Turn or replace rotor
2. Resurface rotor

- **Brake Pedal Vibration or Pulsation—Drum**

1. Drum out of round or eccentric
2. Drums machined incorrectly
3. Incorrect shoes (too wide for drum)

1. Turn or replace drum
2. Turn or replace drum
3. Replace shoes

5. Excessive Pedal Effort—All

1. Brake pedal linkage binding
2. Power booster failure

3. Friction material contaminated with grease

4. Glazed brake shoe or pad linings
5. Restricted brake lines
6. Frozen master cylinder piston
7. Center orifice in quick-take-up valve clogged

1. Lubricate, repair, or replace linkage
2. Repair vacuum, hydraulic, or electrical power supply to booster. Rebuild or replace booster if needed
3. Replace leaking grease seal or repair brake fluid or brake fluid leak. Replace brake shoes or pads in axle sets
4. Replace shoes or pads in axle sets
5. Repair or replace lines
6. Rebuild or replace master cylinder
7. Replace quick-take-up valve

- **Excessive Pedal Effort—Disc**

1. Frozen caliper pistons
2. Semimetallic brake pads used in system designed for organic friction materials
3. Rust-pitted discs/rotors

1. Rebuild or replace caliper
2. Install pads with organic-based linings

3. Replace rotors

- **Excessive Pedal Effort—Drum**

1. Reversed primary and secondary brake shoes
2. Frozen wheel cylinder pistons

1. Install shoes in proper locations—if badly worn, replace shoes in axle sets
2. Rebuild or replace wheel cylinder

Brake System Diagnosis 47

II. WHEEL BRAKE SYMPTOMS

6. One Brake Drags—All

1. Restricted brake line preventing fluid return
2. Loose or worn wheel bearings

1. Replace hose or tube
2. Service and adjust bearings

- **One Brake Drags—Disc**

1. Warped or bent brake pad
2. Sticking caliper piston
3. Swollen caliper piston seal
4. Rusted or frozen caliper slides

1. Replace pads in axle sets
2. Rebuild or replace caliper
3. Rebuild or replace caliper
4. Clean and lubricate caliper slides

- **One Brake Drags—Drum**

1. Brake adjustment too tight
2. Weak or broken shoe return spring
3. Shoes sticking on worn backing plate support pads
4. Warped or bent brake shoe
5. Sticking wheel cylinder piston
6. Adjustable shoe anchor loose

1. Adjust brakes
2. Replace springs in axle sets
3. File support pads smooth and lubricate with brake grease
4. Replace shoes in axle sets
5. Rebuild or replace wheel cylinder
6. Tighten anchor

7. Front Brakes Drag—Disc

1. Master cylinder faulty, compensating ports not open when pedal is released
2. Restricted brake line preventing fluid return
3. Defective metering valve

1. Replace master cylinder
2. Replace brake line
3. Replace metering valve

8. Rear Brakes Drag—All

1. Restricted brake line preventing fluid return
2. Improper parking brake cable or shoe adjustment
3. Sticking or frozen parking brake cables

1. Replace hose or tube
2. Adjust cable and/or shoes
3. Lubricate or replace cables

- **Rear Brakes Drag—Drum**

1. Automatic adjusters damaged
2. Brake adjustment too tight
3. Faulty proportioning vavle
4. Faulty master cylinder

1. Repair or replace adjusters
2. Adjust brakes
3. Replace proportioning valve
4. Replace master cylinder

9. All Brakes Drag—All

1. Brake pedal linkage binding
2. Master cylinder pushrod adjustment incorrect
3. Brake booster output pushrod adjustment incorrect
4. Weak brake pedal return spring
5. Sticking master cylinder pistons
6. Swollen rubber parts from contaminated brake fluid
7. Master cylinder compensating ports plugged

1. Lubricate or repair linkage
2. Adjust pushrod
3. Adjust pushrod
4. Replace spring
5. Rebuild or replace master cylinder
6. Replace all rubber parts, and flush brake hydraulic system
7. Rebuild or replace master cylinder

10. One Brake Locks—All

1. Worn or mismatched tires
2. Incorrect tire pressure
3. Failing wheel bearing
4. Improper size or type of brake lining
5. Brake linings contaminated by grease or brake fluid

1. Make sure the tires on each axle have the same construction, size, and treadwear
2. Adjust tire pressures to vehicle specifications
3. Replace and adjust bearing
4. Replace shoes or pads in axle sets
5. Replace grease seal or repair fluid leak; replace shoes or pads in axle sets

11. Premature Front Brake Lockup—Disc

1. Faulty metering valve allowing early application
2. Failure of master cylinder rear brake hydraulic circuit
3. Defective proportioning valve restricting fluid flow to rear brakes
4. Restricted brake line preventing fluid flow to rear brakes
5. ABS actuator fault

1. Replace valve
2. Rebuild or replace master cylinder
3. Replace proportioning valve
4. Replace hose or tube
5. Perform ABS diagnosis

12. Premature Rear Brake Lockup—All

1. Failure of master cylinder front brake hydraulic circuit
2. Restricted brake line preventing fluid flow to front brakes
3. Defective proportioning valve allowing excessive pressure to rear brakes
4. ABS Fault

1. Rebuild or replace master cylinder
2. Replace hose or tube
3. Replace proportioning vavle
4. Perform ABS diagnosis

- **Premature Rear Brake Lockup—Drum**

1. Defective proportioning valve allowing full pressure to rear brakes

1. Replace proportioning valve

13. Uneven Lining Wear—Disc

1. Sticking or binding caliper mount (floating and sliding calipers)
2. Sticking or frozen caliper pistons (fixed calipers)
3. Caliper loose on mount
4. Bent caliper mount
5. Damaged or improperly machined caliper body
6. Caliper not aligned over rotor (fixed calipers)

1. Replace mounting hardware and lubricate properly
2. Rebuild or replace caliper
3. Torque mounting bolts to specifications
4. Replace spindle or anchor plate
5. Replace caliper
6. Align caliper

- **Uneven Lining Wear—Drum**

1. Frozen wheel cylinder piston
2. Shoes reversed in dual servo brake
3. Shoes not centered in drum (with adjustable anchors)

1. Rebuild or replace wheel cylinder
2. Install shoes in correct positions
3. Adjust anchors

Brake System Diagnosis

14. Rapid Lining Wear—All

1. Incorrect type of brake linings
2. Inadequate type of brake linings (severe service) lining
3. Rough drum or rotor surface finish
4. Parking brake adjusted too tight
5. Master cylinder held in partially applied position

1. Replace with proper lining material
2. Upgrade to semimetallic or premium-quality
3. Resurface to proper finish
4. Adjust parking brake
5. Adjust brake pedal freeplay

III. BRAKE PERFORMANCE SYMPTOMS

15. Pull During Braking—All

1. Unequal tire pressure side-to-side
2. Uneven tire size or treadwear side to side
3. Restricted brake line on one side of vehicle
4. Brake linings contaminated with grease or brake fluid
5. Worn suspension parts
6. Incorrect wheel alignment
7. Water fade of brake linings

1. Equalize pressures
2. Install matched tires with equal treadwear
3. Replace hose or tube
4. Replace grease seal or repair fluid leak. Replace shoes or pads in axle sets
5. Replace as necessary
6. Align front end
7. Apply brakes gently to dry linings

- **Pull During Braking—Disc**

1. Unequal brake action side to side

1. Check for loose calipers; incorrect or broken parts; charred, glazed, contaminated, or worn pads; worn or damaged rotors; sticking caliper pistons; etc. Repair, replace, or adjust as necessary

- **Pull During Braking—Drum**

1. Unequal brake action side to side

1. Check for unequal brake adjustment; incorrect or broken parts; charred, glazed, contaminated, or worn linings; worn or damaged drums; sticking wheel cylinder pistons; weak return springs; loose backing plate; etc. Repair, replace, or adjust as necessary

16. Brake Fade—All

1. Excessive repeated use of brakes without adequate cool-down time
2. Water-contaminated brake fluid (low boiling point)
3. Low quality friction materials
4. Dragging brakes
5. Drums or rotors worn beyond discard dimension
6. Glazed brake linings

1. Stop vehicle and allow brakes to cool
2. Flush brake hydraulic system
3. Install premium brake shoes or pads in axle sets
4. See earlier chart
5. Replace drums or rotors
6. Replace shoes or pads in axle sets

- **Brake Fade—Drum**

1. Poor lining to drum contact

1. Replace shoes in axle sets

17. Steering Wheel Shimmy—All

1. Worn suspension and steering parts
2. Damaged or out-of-balance tires and wheels

1. Check and replace as needed
2. Check and replace as needed

- **Steering Wheel Shimmy—Disc**

1. Excessive rotor runout
2. Excessive rotor thickness variation

1. Replace or turn rotors
2. Replace or turn rotors

- **Steering Wheel Shimmy—Drum**

1. Drum out of round

1. Replace or turn drum

18. Grabbiness or Sensitivity—All

1. Incorrect size or type of brake linings
2. Brake linings contaminated with grease or brake fluid
3. Binding brake pedal linkage
4. Failing wheel bearings
5. Power booster malfunction

1. Replace shoes or pads in axle sets
2. Replace seal or repair fluid leak and replace shoes or pads in axle sets
3. Lubricate, repair, or replace linkage
4. Replace bearings
5. Repair or replace booster

- **Grabbiness or Sensitivity—Disc**

1. Caliper loose on mount
2. Defective metering valve allowing early application
3. Sticking or frozen caliper pistons

1. Torque mounting bolts to specifications
2. Replace valve
3. Rebuild or replace caliper

- **Grabbiness or Sensitivity—Drum**

1. Brake adjustment too tight
2. Brake adjustment too loose (dual-servo brakes)
3. Lining loose on brake shoe
4. Excessive debris in drums
5. Incorrect or warped brake shoes
6. Shoes not centered in drum (with adjustable anchors)
7. Backing plate loose
8. Scored or out-of-round drums
9. Improper lining-to-drum contact

1. Adjust brakes and repair automatic adjusters
2. Adjust brakes and repair automatic adjusters
3. Replace shoes in axle sets
4. Clean friction assembly
5. Install proper shoes in axle sets
6. Adjust anchors
7. Tighten mounting bolts
8. Replace or turn drums
9. Arc linings or replace brake shoes in axle sets

19. Chatters or Shudder—All

1. Bent axle or axle flange
2. Incorrect lug nut/bolt torque or tightening sequence
3. Normal during ABS braking

1. Replace axle
2. Torque lug nuts/bolts to specification in correct sequence
3. Check ABS operation

- **Chatter or Shudder—Drum**

1. Incorrect brake adjustment
2. Backing plate, wheel cylinders, or anchors loose
3. Weak or broken brake shoe return spring
4. Brake lining contaminated with grease or brake fluid
5. Twisted or warped brake shoe
6. Out-of-round or damaged brake drum

1. Adjust brakes and repair automatic adjusters
2. Tighten mounting bolts
3. Replace springs in axle sets
4. Replace seal or repair fluid leak and replace shoes in axle sets
5. Replace shoes in axle sets
6. Replace and/or turn drums

Brake System Diagnosis

20. Unable to Fully Bleed System—All

1. Restricted brake lines
2. Master cylinder ports plugged
3. Pressure differential switch not centered
4. ABS may require special procedure to bleed

1. Replace hoses or tubes
2. Rebuild or replace master cylinder
3. Locate and repair leak in hydraulic system
4. Check service information for ABS bleeding instructions

- **Unable to Fully Bleed System—Disc**

1. Metering valve not disarmed
2. Fluid transfer passage between caliper halves blocked (fixed calipers)

1. Disarm valve with proper tool
2. Rebuild or replace caliper

- **Unable to Fully Bleed System—Drum**

1. Load-sensing proportioning valve restricting fluid flow or rear wheels
2. Proportioning valve faulty or incorrectly adjusted.

1. Do not bleed with wheels hanging. Disconnect valve or support vehicle by the axle.
2. Replace or adjust proportioning valve

IV. BRAKE NOISE

21. Squeak on Application at Rest—All

1. Brake pedal linkage dry
2. Loose master cylinder or power booster mounting

Lubricate linkage
2. Tighten mounting bolts

- **Squeak on Application at Rest—Drum**

1. Backing plate shoe support pads dry
2. Cracked brake drum

1. Lubricate pads with brake grease
2. Replace and turn drum

22. Click or Snap on Application—All

1. 1. Loose or worn suspension parts

1. Tighten or replace as needed

- **Click or Snap on Application—Disc**

1. Loose or missing caliper mounting bolts
2. Spiral machining grooves on rotor friction surface
3. Worn brake pad backing plate creating excessive caliper end clearance
4. Pad hardware missing or incorrectly installed

1. Replace missing bolts and tighten to specifications
2. Resurface rotor
3. Replace pads in axle sets and check end clearance
4. Replace or correct hardware installation

- **Click or Snap on Application—Drum**

1. Excessive lining-to-drum clearance
2. Loose backing plate, wheel cylinder, or shoe anchor
3. Backing plate shoe support pads grooved
4. Spiral machining grooves on drum friction surface
5. Shoe holddown pin bent
6. Weak holddown spring
7. Bent or warped brake shoe
8. Cracked drum

1. Adjust brakes
2. Tighten loose parts
3. File pads smooth and lubricate
4. Resurface drum
5. Replace pin
6. Replace spring
7. Replace shoes in axle sets
8. Replace drum

23. Thump on Application—Drum

1. Cracked drum
2. Shoe return springs weak or of unequal tension

1. Replace drum
2. Replace springs in axle sets

24. Squeal While Braking—All

1. Glazed friction material
2. Incorrect type of friction material
3. Poor-quality brake linings
4. Front wheel bearings worn or loose

1. Replace shoes or pads in axle sets
2. Install linings with proper friction material
3. Install premium quality shoes or pads in axle sets
4. Replace and/or adjust bearings

- **Squeal While Braking—Disc**

1. Brake pad wear indicators contacting rotors
2. Anti-rattle clips, springs, or shims are weak, missing, or incorrectly installed
3. Outboard brake pad retaining tabs not clinched tightly against caliper
4. What bearings incorrectly adjusted
5. Caliper piston incorrectly positioned
6. Rotor surface incorrectly finished

1. Replace pads in axle sets
2. Replace or reposition anti-rattle parts
3. Bend tabs to secure pad in caliper
4. Check bearing adjustment
5. Rotate piston to correct position
6. Turn or replace rotor

- **Squeal While Braking—Drum**

1. Poor brake shoe lining-to-drum contact
2. Debris imbedded in brake lining
3. Drum silencer spring missing or weak
4. Riveted lining loose on brake shoe
5. Drum out-of-round
6. Weak or broken shoe holddown springs
7. Loose backing plate, wheel cylinder, or shoe anchor
8. Bent backing plate, brake shoes, or anchors
9. Wrong size or type of brake shoe
10. New linings installed in scored drum
11. Debris in brake drum

1. Arc or replace shoes
2. Replace shoes if debris cannot be removed
3. Fit new spring
4. Replace shoes in axle sets
5. Turn or replace drum
6. Replace springs in axle sets
7. Tighten loose parts
8. Replace defective parts
9. Install correct shoes in axle sets
10. Turn or replace drums
11. Clean out drum

25. Scraping or Grinding—All

1. Worn brake linings causing metal to metal contact
2. Debris imbedded in brake linings

1. Replace shoes or pads in axle sets and turn drums or rotors as needed
2. Replace shoes or pads in axle sets and turn drums or rotors as needed

- **Scraping or Grinding—Disc**

1. Rotor rubbing against dust shield or caliper
2. Caliper mounting bolts too long and contacting rotor

1. Inspect alignment of parts and repair or adjust as needed
2. Install mounting bolts of the correct length

- **Scraping or Grinding—Drum**

1. Rough drum surface
2. Brake shoe contacting drum web

1. Replace or turn drums
2. Correct shoe installation or install correct shoes

Brake System Diagnosis

26. Rattle When Brakes Unapplied — Disc

1. Excessive pad knockback from rotor runout
2. Anti-rattle clips, springs, or shims are weak, missing, or incorrectly installed

1. Replace or turn rotor
2. Replace or reposition anti-rattle parts

3
Fluid-Related Brake Service

OBJECTIVES

Upon completion and review of this chapter, you will be able to:

- Check the fluid levels in conventional brake systems as well as the Powermaster and Teves antilock system.
- Inspect brake fluid for contamination.
- Select the correct brake fluid for its intended purpose.
- Explain and follow the correct brake bleeding sequence.
- Bench bleed a master cylinder by the manual, basic reverse, or on-car methods.
- Bleed the wheel brakes by the manual, vacuum, gravity, or pressure methods.
- Override a metering valve.
- Perform surge bleeding.
- Perform a fluid change.
- Recenter the three types of pressure differential switches.

INTRODUCTION

Fluid-related service procedures are among the most basic, yet most important, brake system services. An adequate fluid reserve in the master cylinder reservoir, and a hydraulic system free of air and contamination, are critical to the performance and service life of the brake system. This chapter begins with simple fluid level checking procedures, then goes on to explain more involved fluid-related services such as brake bleeding, and brake fluid changing. The final section of the chapter explains how to reset the pressure differential switches used to trigger brake system warning lights.

FLUID LEVEL CHECKING

The brake fluid level in the master cylinder reservoir should be checked regularly as part of routine vehicle maintenance. Most manufacturers recommend that the fluid level be checked at least twice a year. A fluid level check should also be done both before and after any other brake work is performed. A low fluid level can allow air to enter the brake system; this causes an increase in brake pedal travel, and gives the pedal a spongy feel. If enough air enters the system, a total loss of braking power will result.

The most common reason for a low fluid level is normal brake pad wear that leaves the pistons in the brake calipers farther out in their bores. This is due to the self-adjusting action of the caliper piston; as the pad wears down, the piston moves out to maintain the designed pad-to-rotor clearance. Fluid from the master cylinder reservoir then flows to fill the space behind the piston and the fluid level drops. If the fluid level is low, be sure to check the brake pad thickness, in addition to checking for leaks.

Brake pad wear, and the accompanying fluid level drop, occurs relatively slowly over a period of months. A rapid and complete loss of brake fluid in the reservoir is usually a sign of a leak in the hydraulic system. The leak may be caused by something as simple as a loose brake line fitting, but it is more likely to be the result of a leaking hydraulic system component.

Brake Fluid Inspection

Whenever the brake fluid level is checked, the fluid should also be inspected for dirt, moisture, or oil contamination. Fluid in good condition appears relatively clear, with only a slight tint; the exact color depends on the type of fluid. A cloudy appearance indicates fluid contaminated by moisture, while a dark appearance indicates contamination from dirt, rust, corrosion, or brake dust. Oil contamination causes brake fluid to layer and separate because petroleum products are not compatible with polyglycol brake fluids. However, layering can also occur when silicone brake fluid is mixed with polyglycol fluid. The most common indications of oil-contaminated brake fluid are leaks caused by damage to the rubber seals and hoses in the hydraulic system.

If contamination is suspected, but the exact type is difficult to determine with the fluid in the reservoir, use a clean syringe to remove a sample of fluid in place it in a clear jar for closer examination, figure 3-1. Any visible contamination is sufficient reason to flush the system and install new fluid.

To check for oil, transmission fluid, or power steering fluid contamination, put a sample from the reservoir in a clean Styrofoam cup. Any petroleum product in the sample will dissolve the Styrofoam, leaving a ring around the cup, figure 3-2.

Brake Fluid Moisture Content

The moisture content of brake fluid can be determined in a number of ways. The most common methods use a brake fluid test strip kit or an electronic fluid tester.

The brake fluid test strip kit contains paper strips that are dipped into the fluid. A treated pad on the end of the strip changes color, depending on the moisture content of the fluid, figure 3-3. The color is then matched to a chart on the side of the kit container, indicating moisture content percentage.

The electronic fluid tester uses a small heating element that heats the fluid to the boiling point. The actual boiling point is then displayed on the digital screen, figure 3-4.

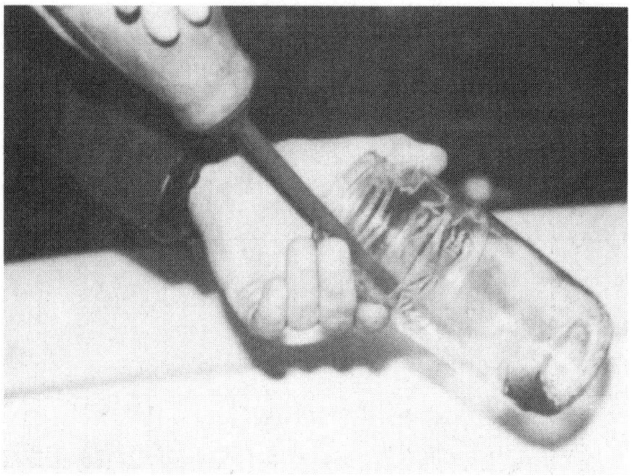

Figure 3-1. Checking a brake fluid sample for contamination.

Figure 3-2. Brake fluid that is contaminated with oil will leave a ring when left to stand in a Styrofoam coffee cup.

NOTE: These tests only indicate the condition of the fluid in the master cylinder. The condition of the fluid in the rest of the hydraulic system is unknown; it could be better or worse than the fluid in the reservoir. If there is any doubt, flush the system out and install new fluid.

Brake Fluid Selection

When you top up the brake fluid level, always use the correct type and DOT grade of brake fluid recommended by the vehicle manufacturer. Many cars use polyglycol type DOT 3 grade fluids; however, that is not always the correct choice. Ford Motor Company cars require a special DOT 3 fluid with an extremely high dry boiling point, and a number of imported cars

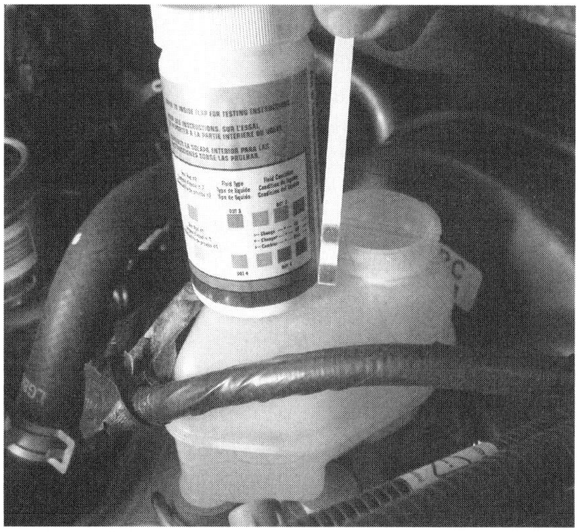

Fluid-Related Brake Service

Figure 3-3. Brake fluid test strips are dipped into the fluid and then matched to a color chart to indicate moisture content.

Figure 3-4. The electronic brake fluid tester indicates the boiling point of the fluid.

require DOT 4 fluid. The use of DOT 5 silicone fluid as original equipment is quite rare, as are brake systems that require Hydraulic System Mineral Oil (HSMO). Consult the owner's manual or shop manual if you have any question about the type of fluid that should be used in a specific brake system.

Using a lower *grade* of fluid than is recommended, for example putting DOT 3 fluid in a system designed for DOT 4 fluid, will lower the boiling point of the fluid, and thus the temperature at which the system will vapor lock. If the boiling point drops below the highest temperature a fluid may reach under extreme braking conditions, a loss of braking power, and possibly an accident, will occur.

Using the wrong *type* of brake fluid can also create problems. While the DOT grades of fluid are technically compatible, adding either DOT 3, 4, or 5.1 polyglycol fluid to a system filled with DOT 5 silicone fluid will reduce the boiling point. Since the two types do not mix, the heavier polyglycol fluid will sink to the lowest points in the system (the wheel cylinders and brake calipers) where any moisture it absorbs will lead to rust, corrosion, and leaks.

NOTE: Some manufacturers do not allow the mixing of different grades of polyglycol fluids. Certain components in the hydraulic system, especially ABS actuators, may be designed to use *only* one type of fluid. Check service information to be sure.

Another case where the wrong *type* of brake fluid will cause problems is if engine oil, HSMO, automatic transmission fluid, or any other petroleum-base product is used in a system designed for polyglycol fluid. Petroleum-base fluids cause the rubber parts in the system to soften and swell, resulting in fluid leaks, stuck pistons, and eventually, total hydraulic system failure. When this occurs, the entire system must be torn down, flushed of all contaminated fluid, and reassembled with all-new rubber parts. The same kind of damage will occur if polyglycol fluid is accidentally used in a system designed for Hydraulic System Mineral Oil (HSMO).

Polyglycol brake fluid used to top up a master cylinder should only be taken from a sealed container. If the container has been previously opened, it should have been stored for only a short time, and kept tightly capped in storage. Remember that polyglycol brake fluid is a powerful solvent that can cause injury and remove paint in seconds. Whenever you handle this type of fluid, wear safety glasses and take special care not to spill any on the vehicle finish.

If you should spill polyglycol brake fluid on a car's paint, do not attempt to wipe it off with a shop towel; this will only make the problem worse. Instead, immediately flush the area with large amounts of clean water. Once all traces of brake fluid are washed away, dry the area with a soft cloth. If the damage is not too great, you may be able to restore the finish with polishing compound and a good wax.

Specific Brake Fluid Level Checks

Checking the fluid level in most brake systems is a simple procedure. However, certain vehicles have brake systems with electrohydraulic power boosters that require special fluid level checking procedures. The following sections describe how to check the fluid levels in conventional brake systems, the GM Powermaster brake system, and two versions of the Teves antilock brake system.

Conventional Brake System Level Check

Brake system fluid reservoirs are made of plastic, or cast in metal as an integral part of the master cylinder body. Most translucent plastic reservoirs have marks or lines cast on the outside of them to indicate high and low fluid levels, figure 3-5. To check the level, simply sight through the reservoir. Some vehicles have opaque plastic reservoirs that are filled to a mark or plastic ring located inside the reservoir, figure 3-6. To check the fluid level in these master cylinders, remove the reservoir cover, or filler caps, to expose the markings.

The cover must also be removed to check the fluid level on a master cylinder with an integral metal reservoir. This type of reservoir is not marked to show the proper fluid level; instead, the maximum level is designed to be ¼ inch (6 mm) from the top, figure 3-7. To check and adjust the brake fluid to the proper level:

1. Wipe the fluid reservoir and cover clean.
2. Remove the reservoir cover and check the brake fluid level.
3. Add fluid to the reservoir, or draw fluid from it with a brake fluid syringe, to obtain the proper level.

Powermaster Brake System Level Check

The General Motors Powermaster brake system combines an electrohydraulic power booster and master cylinder into one unit. Because of this, the Powermaster fluid reservoir is divided into three chambers, figure 3-8. The left side of the reservoir has two small chambers that serve the master cylinder; the fluid level

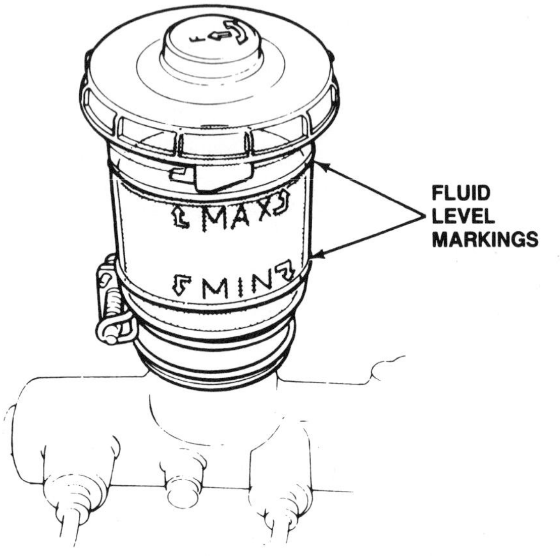

Figure 3-5. This translucent plastic reservoir has cast-in fluid level markings.

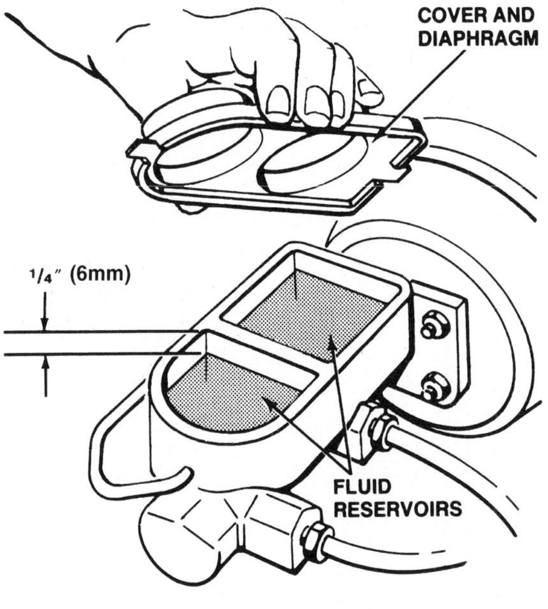

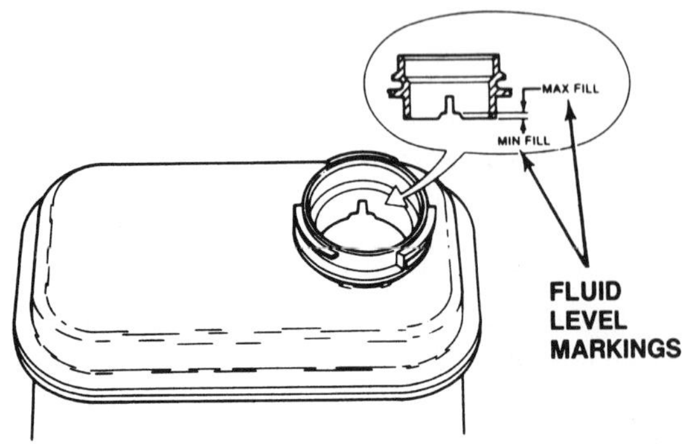

Figure 3-6. Opaque plastic reservoirs have internal fluid level markings.

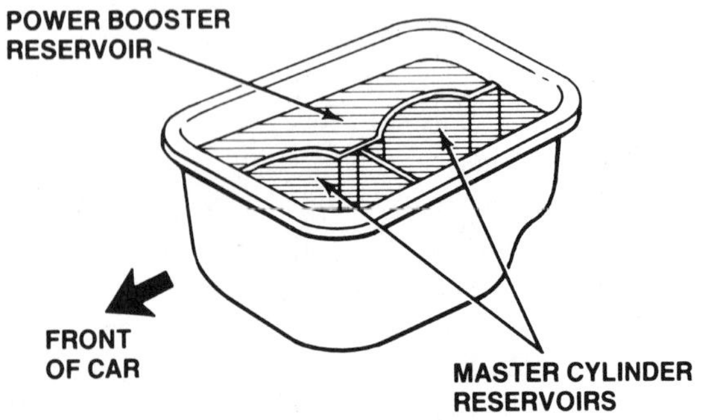

Figure 3-7. Unmarked master cylinders are typically filled to within ¼ inch (6 mm) of the top.

Figure 3-8. The GM Powermaster brake system fluid reservoir.

Fluid-Related Brake Service

in these chambers is checked in basically the same manner as described above. There are minimum and maximum level markings cast into the walls of the reservoir chambers, figure 3-9.

The right side of the reservoir has a single large chamber that serves the power booster accumulator. Checking the level in this side of the reservoir requires a special procedure. In normal operation with the accumulator charged, the fluid level is very low, barely covering the pump ports in the bottom of the reservoir. When checking the fluid level, the accumulator must be discharged. To do this:

1. Leave the reservoir cover in place and make sure the ignition switch is OFF.
2. Pump the brake pedal at least 10 times using approximately 50 pounds (110 kg) of force. Pedal feel will become noticeably harder when the accumulator is discharged.
3. Remove the reservoir cover and check the fluid level; it should be between the maximum and minimum level markings cast into the wall of the reservoir, figure 3-9.

General Motors states that only new DOT 3 brake fluid should be used when adjusting the fluid level in the Powermaster brake system. Silicone DOT 5 fluids are specifically *not* recommended. As discussed in the *Classroom Manual*, never transfer fluid from the power booster chamber of the reservoir to the master cylinder chambers; the power booster chamber is not sealed off from the atmosphere so its fluid is free to absorb moisture.

Teves Antilock Brake System Level Check

The Teves antilock brake system used by General Motors, Ford, and on some imports incorporates an electrohydraulic power booster that shares a single fluid reservoir with the master cylinder. However, differences in the fluid level markings on the reservoirs dictate a unique checking procedure for each manufacturer's unit. The Ford/Teves system is checked with the accumulator charged; the GM/Teves system, like the Powermaster, is checked with the accumulator discharged.

To check the brake fluid level in the Teves antilock system used by Ford:

1. Turn the ignition switch ON.
2. Pump the brake pedal until the hydraulic pump motor begins to run. When the pump stops, the accumulator is fully charged.
3. Check that the fluid level is even with the "MAX" marking cast into the reservoir body, figure 3-10. Use DOT 3 fluid that meets Ford specifications when adjusting the fluid level.

To check the hydraulic fluid level in the Teves antilock system used by General Motors and imports:

1. Turn the ignition switch OFF.
2. Pump the brake pedal a minimum of 20 times. Pedal feel will become noticeably harder when the accumulator is discharged.
3. Adjust the fluid level in the reservoir until it is even with the full mark cast into the reservoir body, figure 3-11.

BRAKE BLEEDING

Brake bleeding is a process that pushes new brake fluid through the brake system to force out contaminated fluid and trapped air. Air is present in the hydraulic system when the vehicle is first assembled, and enters the brake lines whenever the system is opened for service. Defective seals can also allow air to enter during normal brake operation.

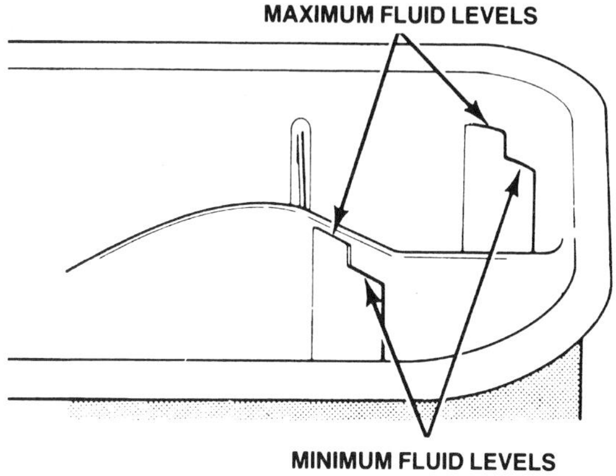

Figure 3-9. Powermaster reservoir fluid level markings.

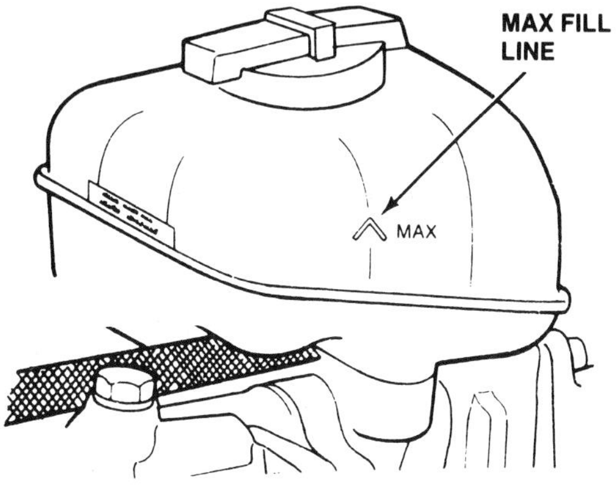

Figure 3-10. Check the fluid level in the Ford/Teves antilock system reservoir with the accumulator charged.

Figure 3-11. Check the fluid level in the GM/Teves antilock system reservoir with the accumulator discharged.

A system free of air has a high, firm brake pedal. A system with air trapped in it has a spongy, low, or bottoming brake pedal. The low pedal will rise and become somewhat firmer if it is pumped rapidly. However, when the pedal is released for even a short period of time, it falls to its initial level on the next stroke. An air-entrapment test can be used to help determine if there is air in the brake system:

1. Remove the master cylinder cover and adjust the brake fluid to the proper level. Replace the master cylinder cover but do not secure it in place.
2. Have an assistant pump the brakes rapidly 10 to 20 times, then hold the pedal down firmly.
3. Remove the master cylinder cover and have the assistant release the pedal quickly. If a squirt of brake fluid occurs above the surface in either reservoir, air is trapped in the system.

The air-entrapment test works because any air in the system is compressed when the brake pedal is pumped. When the pedal is released, the compressed air pushes the fluid back through the lines and the compensating ports. Note the side of the reservoir in which the squirt of brake fluid occurs; this indicates the side of the dual-circuit split brake system that contains the trapped air.

A low brake pedal caused by air trapped in the hydraulic system should not be confused with a low pedal resulting from drum brakes in need of adjustment. These problems have similar symptoms; however, when the brakes simply need adjusting, the pedal will firm up within one or two strokes, and will not have the spongy feel typical of trapped air.

Bleeding Sequences

Brake bleeding can sometimes be performed on only part of the brake hydraulic system. For example, as explained in the next section, master cylinders can be bled off the vehicle. In addition, if a single leaking wheel cylinder or brake caliper is replaced, it is often necessary to bleed only that portion of the hydraulic system. However, when the entire brake system is bled, the operation must be carried out in a specific order called a bleeding sequence.

Using the proper sequence allows the brakes to be bled most efficiently and with the least possible chance of air remaining trapped in the system. The correct bleeding sequence at the wheels varies from vehicle to vehicle depending on the design of the brake system; the overall bleeding sequence is usually:

- Master cylinder
- ABS hydraulic actuator, if equipped
- Combination valve
- Wheel cylinders and brake calipers
- Load-sensing proportioning valve.

ABS actuators, combination valves, and load-sensing proportioning valves are only bled when present in the system and equipped with bleeder screws.

Antilock brake systems may require special procedures when bleeding. It is common to use a scan tool, figure 3-12, to activate and move the solenoids in the actuator when bleeding. This is especially true when the ABS hydraulic actuator has been removed or replaced. These special procedures are discussed in Chapter 13.

Wheel bleeding sequences are covered in greater detail later in the chapter. Because the master cylinder is always bled first, the procedures used to do this job are described immediately below. Master cylinders can be bled off the car on the workbench, or while in position on the car.

MASTER CYLINDER BENCH BLEEDING

New or rebuilt master cylinders can be bled on the workbench before they are installed. Bench bleeding may be necessary if the master cylinder mounts in the car at an angle. Once installed, any air it contains rises to the high points in the cylinder and becomes trapped away from the fluid outlets or bleeder screws. There are three types of bench bleeding, manual bench bleeding, basic bench bleeding, and reverse bench bleeding.

Manual Bench Bleeding

Manual bench bleeding is just what its name implies—bleeding the master cylinder by hand. To do this, the

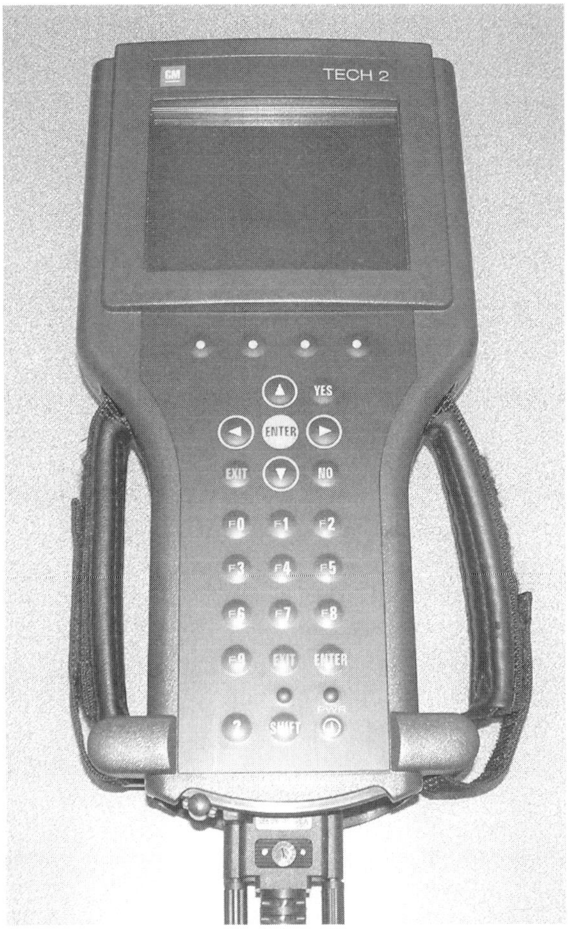

Fluid-Related Brake Service

Figure 3-12. A scan tool may be needed when bleeding brakes on ABS-equipped vehicles.

Figure 3-13. A master cylinder mounted on a vise for bench bleeding.

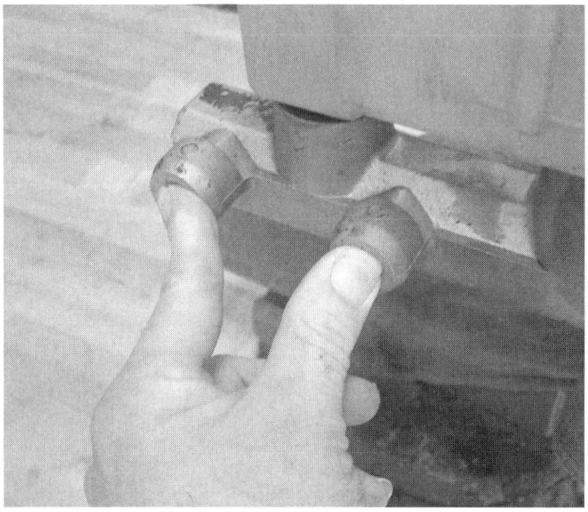

Figure 3-14. Manually bench bleeding a master cylinder.

pistons are bottomed in the cylinder bore and the fluid outlets are plugged. As the pistons are then released, a low pressure area is created in the cylinder bore, which allows atmospheric pressure to force fluid into the cylinder.

This procedure can be messy, and sometimes results in fluid spray, so have a suitable basin available to catch excess brake fluid. Also, wear safety glasses to protect your eyes, and take precautions to avoid getting fluid on painted surfaces. To bench bleed the master cylinder in this manner:

1. Clamp the master cylinder in a vise by its mounting flange so you have access to the fluid outlet ports, figure 3-13. Do not clamp on the master cylinder body or the bore may distort. If the vise has sharp teeth, use smooth-faced jaw protectors to prevent damage to the cylinder mounting flange.
2. Position the basin to catch any fluid leakage from the outlet ports, then fill the master cylinder reservoirs with new brake fluid of the proper type and grade.
3. Use the master cylinder pushrod, or other round-ended rod, to slowly stroke the master cylinder pistons inward until they both bottom.
4. Plug the fluid outlets with your fingertips, figure 3-14, then slowly allow both pistons to fully return on the back stroke. Remove your finger tips from the fluid outlets.
5. Repeat steps 3 and 4 until the fluid coming from the outlets is air free, and bubbles no longer emerge from the compensating and replenishing ports in the reservoir.
6. Plug the outlets while mounting the master cylinder on the vehicle.

Basic Bench Bleeding

Basic bench bleeding is the most common method used to bleed master cylinders. This procedure requires a vise and two short lengths of tubing. The bleeding tubes may be included with the new master cylinder. One end of each piece of tubing has a fitting that threads into a master cylinder outlet port; the other end twists around to route fluid from the port back into the reservoir. To bench bleed a master cylinder in this manner:

1. Clamp the master cylinder in a vise by its mounting flange so you have access to the fluid outlet ports, figure 3-13. Do not clamp on the master cylinder body or the bore may distort. If the vise has sharp teeth, use smooth-faced jaw protectors to prevent damage to the cylinder mounting flange.
2. Connect the lengths of special tubing to the outlet ports of the master cylinder, figure 3-15, and route the tubing ends back into the fluid reservoir.
3. Fill the reservoir with new brake fluid of the proper type and grade.
4. Use the master cylinder pushrod, or other round-ended rod, to slowly stroke the master cylinder pistons in and out. Be sure to bottom both pistons on the forward stroke, and allow both pistons to fully return on the back stroke. Continue until air bubbles no longer emerge from the tubing ends.
5. Stroke the pistons with short sharp movements of approximately ½ inch (13 mm) until bubbles no longer emerge from the tubing ends or the compensating and replenishing ports in the reservoir.
6. Remove the tubes and plug the outlets.

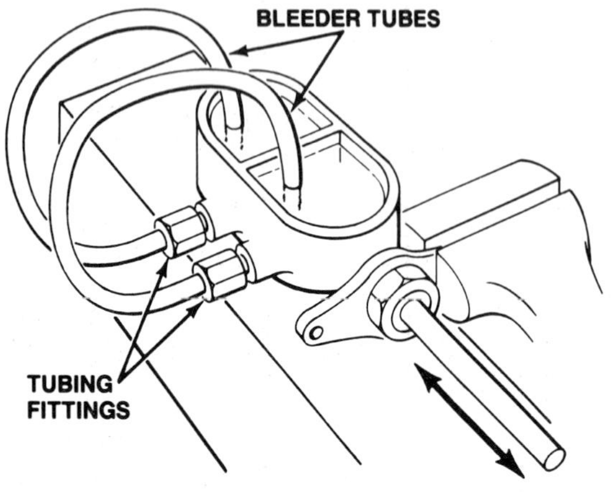

Reverse Bench Bleeding

Reverse bleeding does the same job as manual or basic bench bleeding. However, instead of stroking the pistons to move fluid through the master cylinder and force out the air, a special large plastic syringe is used to create a low-pressure area in the cylinder bore. This allows atmospheric pressure to force fluid through the cylinder and into the syringe. The same fluid (minus any trapped air) is then forced back through the cylinder in the opposite direction. To reverse bleed a master cylinder:

1. Clamp the master cylinder in a vise by its mounting flange so you have access to the fluid outlet ports, figure 3-13. Do not clamp on the master cylinder body or the bore may distort. If the vise has sharp teeth, use smooth-faced jaw protectors to prevent damage to the cylinder mounting flange.
2. Seal the fluid outlet ports using the plugs supplied with the syringe, then fill the reservoir half full of new brake fluid.
3. Fully depress the plunger of the syringe
4. Remove the plug from one of the fluid outlets and press the syringe firmly against the opening. Extend the plunger until the syringe is half full of fluid, figure 3-16.
5. Remove the syringe and temporarily block the fluid outlet. Point the tip of the syringe upward and slowly depress the plunger until all of the air is removed, figure 3-17.
6. Press the syringe to the same outlet and force the fluid back into the master cylinder by depressing the plunger, figure 3-18. Air bubbles will exit the compensating port and rise to the surface of the reservoir.
7. Repeat steps 3 through 6 until the air bubbles stop, then plug the fluid outlet. Repeat these same steps at the other fluid outlet or outlets.

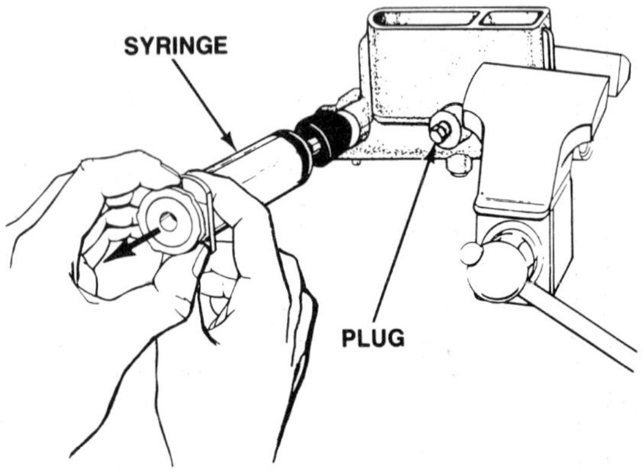

Figure 3-15. Bench bleeding tubes route fluid from the outlet ports back into the reservoir.

Figure 3-16. Extend the syringe plunger to draw brake fluid and air bubbles out of the master cylinder.

Fluid-Related Brake Service

8. Use the master cylinder pushrod, or other round-ended rod, to stroke the pistons with short sharp movements of approximately ½ inch (13 mm) until bubbles no longer emerge from the compensating and replenishing ports in the reservoir.

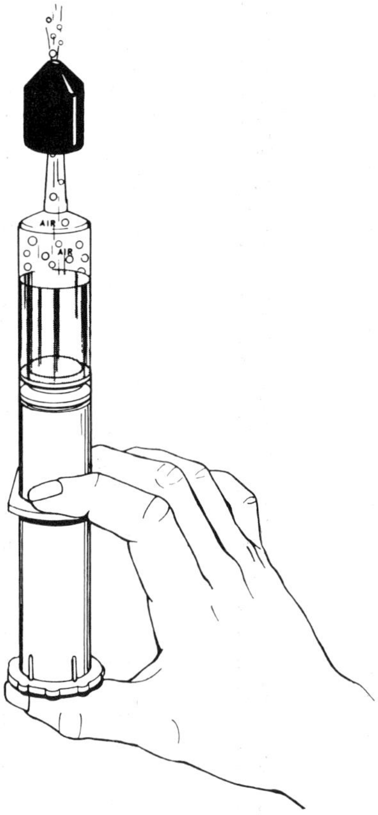

Figure 3-17. With the syringe in an upright position, slowly depress the plunger to expel any air.

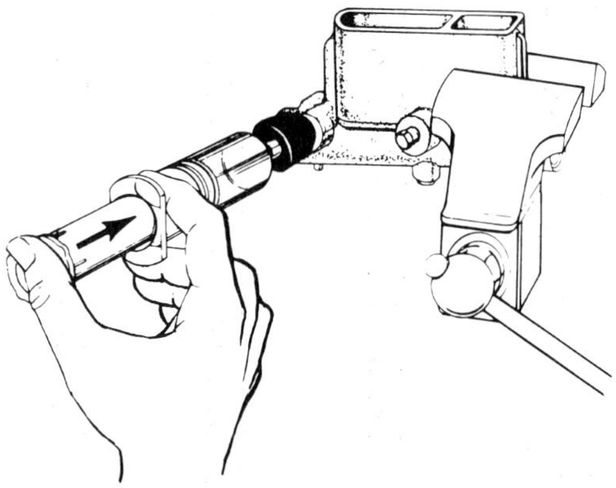

Figure 3-18. Force the air-free brake fluid back into the master cylinder to dislodge trapped air bubbles.

MASTER CYLINDER ON-VEHICLE BLEEDING

Bleeding the master cylinder on the vehicle purges any last bit of trapped air in it. On-vehicle bleeding is sometimes necessary to remove small pockets of air that can develop when the plugs are removed from the master cylinder fluid outlets and the hydraulic lines are connected. On-car bleeding is done after the master cylinder is bench bled, and prior to bleeding the rest of the hydraulic system.

The pressure used to move fluid through the master cylinder can come from either a pressure bleeder or force applied to the brake pedal. In both cases, brake fluid under pressure can spray from the fittings where the cylinder is bled. Always wear safety glasses or other eye protection when bleeding a master cylinder on the car. In addition, use a fender cover to prevent brake fluid spray from getting on the vehicle finish.

On-Vehicle Bleeding with Bleeder Screws

Some master cylinders that mount in a level position are designed to be bled on the vehicle and have bleeder screws for this purpose, figure 3-19. Bleeding a master cylinder with bleeder screws requires a bleeder wrench of the proper size, a length of clear plastic hose with an inside diameter small enough to fit snugly over the bleeder screws, and a jar partially filled with clean brake fluid. To bleed such a master cylinder:

1. Discharge the vacuum or hydraulic power booster (if equipped) by pumping the brake pedal with the ignition OFF until the pedal feels hard.

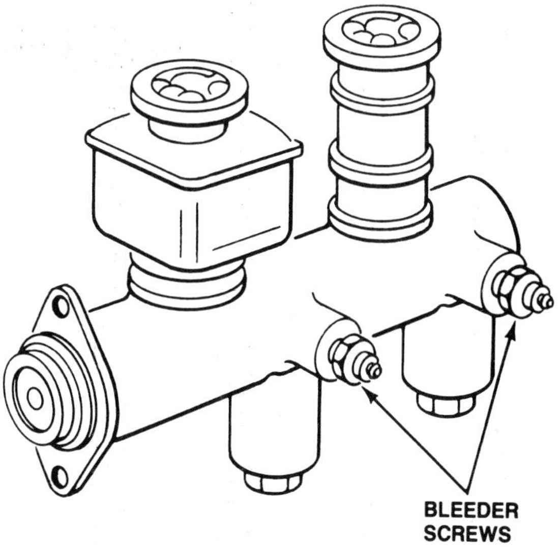

Figure 3-19. A master cylinder with bleeder screws.

2. Fill the master cylinder reservoir with new brake fluid, and make sure it remains at least half full throughout the bleeding procedure.
3. Connect the plastic hose to the forward bleeder screw and submerge the end of the hose in the jar of brake fluid.
4. Loosen the bleeder screw approximately one-half turn, and have your assistant slowly depress the brake pedal and hold it to the floor. Air bubbles leaving the bleeder screw will be visible in the hose to the jar.
5. Tighten the bleeder screw, then have your assistant slowly release the brake pedal.
6. Repeat steps 4 and 5 until no more air emerges from the bleeder screw. Transfer the plastic hose to the rear bleeder screw and repeat these same steps until the master cylinder is completely bled.

On-Vehicle Bleeding without Bleeder Screws

Most master cylinders do not have bleeder screws. Once they are bench bled and installed on the vehicle, any remaining air is bled from the brake line fittings at the fluid outlets. The majority of master cylinders have a single fitting for each hydraulic circuit; however, some newer designs have dual outlets for each circuit. On these newer designs, both fittings of a circuit must be opened when bleeding the master cylinder on the vehicle. This job requires a flare-nut wrench to loosen the tubing fittings, and a basin or rag to catch the fluid pumped out of the system. To bleed a master cylinder without bleeder screws:

1. Discharge the vacuum or hydraulic power booster (if equipped) by pumping the brake pedal with the ignition OFF until the pedal feels hard.
2. Fill the master cylinder reservoir with new brake fluid and make sure it remains at least half full throughout the bleeding procedure.
3. Loosen the forward brake tube fitting approximately one-half turn, and have your assistant slowly depress the brake pedal and hold it to the floor. Brake fluid and air bubbles will flow out from between the tubing and tubing fitting, figure 3-20. Hold a basin or rag under the fitting to catch the fluid released.
4. Tighten the tubing fitting, then have your assistant slowly release the brake pedal.
5. Repeat steps 3 and 4 until no more air bubles emerge from the fitting. Repeat these same steps at the rear tubing fitting until the master cylinder is completely bled.

Figure 3-20. Bleeding a master cylinder on the vehicle.

BLEEDING THE WHEEL BRAKES

When bleeding the wheel brakes, the proper bleeding sequence must be followed. Generally, the wheel cylinder or caliper farthest from the master cylinder is bled first, followed by the next closest cylinder or caliper, and so forth. On cars with front-rear split brake systems, the rear brakes are bled first, then the front brakes. On cars with diagonal-split brake systems, one rear brake is bled first, then the opposite front brake, then the other rear brake, and finally the remaining front brake. Not all manufacturers follow these sequences, however. Chrysler recommends that both rear brakes be bled first regardless of the hydraulic system split. Figure 3-21 shows bleeding sequences for most late-model cars and light trucks. The correct sequence for a specific model can also be found in published service information.

The many variations in brake hydraulic systems make some easier to bleed than others. In addition, certain brake systems respond better to one bleeding procedure than another. There are actually five methods that can be used to bleed the wheel brakes:

- Manual bleeding
- Vacuum bleeding
- Gravity bleeding
- Pressure bleeding
- Surge bleeding.

Manual Bleeding

Manual bleeding uses hydraulic pressure created by the master cylinder to pump fresh fluid through the

Fluid-Related Brake Service

DOMESTIC MODELS		
Daimler Chrysler		
1965-1987	All w/RWD (1)	RR-LR-RF-LF
1988-1992	Premier, Monaco (2)	RR-LR-RF-LF
1978-1994	All w/FWD	RR-LF-LR-RF
1995 & UP	Breeze, Neon, Stratus	LR-RF-RR-LF
1997 & UP	Concorde, Intrepid, LHS, New Yorker, Vision, 300M	RR-LR-RF-LF
1997 & UP	Avenger, Sebring, Talon	RR-LF-LR-RF
1995 & UP	PT Cruiser, Cirrus	LR-RF-RR-LF
Ford		
1978-1994	All w/FWD, no ABS	RR-LF-LR-RF
1965-1993	All w/RWD, no ABS (1)	RR-LR-RF-LF
1994-1997	Cougar, Thunderbird	RR-LF-LR-RF
1994 & UP	All others (3)	RR-LR-RF-LF
1995 & UP	Crown Victoria, Grand Marquis, Town Car (3)	RR-LR-RF-LF
1990-1994	Crown Victoria, Town Car	RR-LR-RF-LF
1988-1992	Cougar, Thunderbird, Mark VII, VIII	RF-LF-RR-LR
1995 & UP	Contour, Cougar, Mystique	LF-RR-RF-LR
1995 & UP	Continental, Escort, Sable, Taurus, Tracer (3)	RR-LR-RF-LF
1995-1997	Probe	RR-LF-LR-RF
1988-1989	Continental	RF-LF-RR-LR
1990-1994	Continental, Sable, Taurus	RR-LR-RF-LF
1995 & UP	Continental, Crown Victoria	RR-LR-LF-RF
1997 & UP	Escort, Tracer, Focus	RR-LR-RF-LF
General Motors		
1977- & UP	All w/RWD (1, 5)	RR-LR-RF-LF
1971 & UP	All w/FWD (5)	RR-LF-LR-RF
1965-1986	Corvette (4)	LR-RR-LF-RF
1987-1991	Corvette	RF-RR-LR-LF
1992-1998	Cavalier, Malibu, Corsica	RR-LR-RF-LF
1999 & UP	Cavalier, Malibu, Monte Carlo, Impala	LR-RF-LR-RF
1980-1985	Toronado, Regency 98	RR-LR-RF-LF
1989-1992	Cutlass Supreme	RF-RR-LR-LF
1993 & UP	Achevia, Ciera, Cutlass	RR-LR-RF-LF
1993 & UP	Alero, Cutlass Supreme, Intrigue	RF-LF-LR-RF
1995 & UP	Aurora	RR-LR-RF-LF
1986-1990	88, 98, Toronado	RF-LF-RR-LR
1991 & UP	88, 98	RR-LR-RF-LF
1998 & UP	Intrigue, Silhouette	RR-LF-RF-LR
1991 & UP	Grand Am, Sunbird, Sunfire, Bonneville	RR-LR-RF-LF
1989-1991	Grand Prix	RF-LF-RR-LR
1992-& UP	Grand Prix	RR-LR-RF-LF
1995-1999	Roadmaster, LeSabre, Park Ave., Riviera	LR-RR-LF-RF
1993-1996	Allante, Eldorado, Seville, Fleetwood, Deville	LF-RF-LR-RR
1997-2001	Catera	RR-LR-RF-LF
1997 & UP	Deville, Concours, Eldorado, Seville	RR-LR-RF-LF
1991 7 UP	Saturn	RR-LF-LR-RF
DOMESTIC LIGHT TRUCKS		
Daimler Chrysler		
1965-1994	All w/RWD (1)	RR-LR-RF-LF
1995 & UP	All w/RWD w/RWAL	LR-RR-RF-LF
1997 & UP	All w/RWD w/4WAL	RR-LR-RF-LF
1986 & UP	FWD/AWD Vans No ABS	RR-LR-RF-LF
1993-1994	FWD/AWD Vans w/ABS	RR-LF-LR-RF
1995 & UP	FWD/AWD Vans w/ABS	LF-RF-RR-LF
1978 & UP	Jeep, Wrangler, Cherokee	RR-LR-RF-LF
1990 & UP	Cherokee, Grand Cherokee	RR-LR-RF-LF
1994-1997	1500-3500, Dakota, B Van, w/ABS	LR-RR-RF-LF
1997 & UP	1500-3500, dakota, B Van, Durango	RR-LR-RF-LF
Ford		
1965 & UP	All w/RWD (3)	RR-LR-RF-LF
1993-1994	All w/FWD w/o ABS	RR-LR-RF-LF
1994 & UP	Villager, Windstar	LF-RF-LR-RR
General Motors		
1965 & UP	All w/RWD	RR-LR-RF-LF
1990-1992	All w/FWD no ABS	RR-LR-RF-LF
1993-1994	All w/FWD no ABS	RR-LF-LR-RF
1992-1996	All w/FWD w/ABS	RR-LR-RF-LF
1997 & UP	All w/FWD w/ABS	RR-LF-RR-LF
1998 & UP	Tracker	LR-RF-LF
IMPORT MODELS		
Acura		
1986-1989	All w/o ABS	LF-RR-RF-LR
1990-1996	All w/o ABS	RR-LF-LR-RF
1990-1996	Integra, Legend, Vigor	RR-LF-LR-RF
1997 & UP	Integra	LF-RR-RF-LR
1997 1998	2.2CL, 3.0CL	RR-LF-LR-RF
1995 & UP	2.5TL, 3.2TL, 2.2CL, 3.0CL, 3.5RL, MDX	LF-RR-RF-LR
1996 & UP	SLX	RR-LR-RF-LF
1991-2000	NSX	LR-RF-LR-RF
Alfa Romeo		
1965-1995	All w/RWD	RR-LR-RF-LF
1988-1995	All w/FWD	RR-LF-LR-RF
Audi		
1978-1992	All (6)	RR-LR-RF-LF
1990-1996	All w/ABS w/o TC	RR-RF-LR-LF

Figure 3-21A. Brake bleeding sequences for some popular vehicles.

brake system. In this procedure, one technician opens the bleeder screws while another applies the brake pedal; air, contamination, and old fluid is pushed out of the bleeder screws ahead of the new fluid.

It is extremely important when manually bleeding a brake system that the pedal be applied and released slowly and gently. Rapid pedal pumping can churn up the fluid and reduce the size of trapped air bubbles,

Year	Model	Sequence
1996 & UP	All w/ABS & TC	RR-LR-RF-LF

BMW

Year	Model	Sequence
1965-1985	All	RR-LR-RF-LF
1986-1992	All w/o ABS	RR-LR-RF-LF
1990-1994	7 Series w/ASC+T	RR-LR-LF-RF
1986 & UP	All	RR-LR-RF-LF

Chrysler/Eagle Imports

Year	Model	Sequence
1971-1989	All w/RWD	RR-LR-RF-LF
1979-1985	Champ	LR-RF-RR-LF
1979-1994	Colt, Vista, Colt/Summit (7)	LR-RF-RR-LF
1994-1996	Summit (7)	RR-LF-LR-RF
1995-1996	Summit Wagon (7)	LR-RF-RR-LF
1990-1998	Lazer, Talon, Stealth (7)	RR-LF-LR-RF

Ford Imports

Year	Model	Sequence
1988-1993	Festiva	RR-LF-LR-RF
1991-1994	Capri	RR-LF-LR-RF
1994-1997	Aspire	RR-LF-LR-RF

General Motors Imports

Year	Model	Sequence
1985-1997	LeMans, Metro, Nova	RR-LF-LR-RF
1989-1997	Prizm/Storm	RR-LR-RF-LF
1985-1989	Spectrum	LF-RR-RF-LR
1989-1993	Tracker	RF-LF-LR-LSPV
1994-1997	Tracker	RR-LR-RF-LF

Honda

Year	Model	Sequence
1975-1990	All	LF-RR-RF-LR
1990-1993	Accord	LR-RF-RR-LF
1994-1997	Accord	RR-LF-LR-RF
1990-1999	Civic	RR-LF-LR-RF
1995-1997	Odyssey, Passport	RR-LF-LR-RF
1998 & UP	Accord, CR-V, Odyssey, Prelude	LF-RF-RR-LR

Hyundai

Year	Model	Sequence
1986-1998	All	LR-RF-RR-LF
1999 & UP	All	RR-LF-LR-RF

Infiniti

Year	Model	Sequence
1990-1995	M30, Q45	LR-RR-LF-RF
1991-1993	G20 (8)	LR-RF-RR-LF
1994 & UP	J30, G20, I30 (8)	RR-LF-RR-RF
1996 & UP	Q45	LR-RR-RF-LF
1997 & UP	QX4 (8)	LSV-LR-RR-LF-RF

Isuzu

Year	Model	Sequence
1984-1991	Trooper, Amigo, Pickup, Impulse (7)	LR-RR-LF-RF
1990-1997	Pickup, Rodeo, Passport (7)	LR-RR-LF-RF
1992 & UP	Trooper, Trooper II (7)	RR-LR-RF-LF
1998 & UP	Rodeo, Passport	RR-LR-RF-LF

Lexus

Year	Model	Sequence
1990 & UP	All	RR-LR-RF-LF
1998 & UP	GS300, 400, 430, LX470	RF-LF-RR-LR

Mazda

Year	Model	Sequence
1986-1995	Pickup, MPV	LR-LF-RF
1980-1995	RX-7	RR-LR-RF-LF
1987-1992	626, MX-6, 323, 929	LR-RR-LF-RF
1990 & UP	All others	See note (9)

Mercedes-Benz

Year	Model	Sequence
1980 & UP	All	RR-LR-RF-LF

Mitsubishi

Year	Model	Sequence
1983-1989	Montero, Starion, Pickup	RR-LR-RF-LF
1983-1996	Cordia, Tredia, Galant, Mirage, Precis, Expo	LR-RF-RR-LF
1990 & UP	Eclipse, Diamante, 3000GT, Mirage, Galant (7)	RR-LF-LR-RF
1992-2000	Montero (7)	RR-LR-RF-LF

Nissan

Year	Model	Sequence
1980-1990	Pickup, Pathfinder	LR-RR-LF-RF
1980-1984	510, 210, 200SX, 280ZX, 810, Maxima, Sentra	RR-LR-RF-LF
1984-1990	Sentra, 310	LR-RF-RR-LF
1985-1994	Maxima, Stanza, Sentra (8)	LR-RF-RR-LF
1984-1989	200SX, 300 ZX	LR-RR-RF-LF
1990-1994	240SX, 300ZX (8)	LR-RR-LF-RF
1994 & UP	Altima, Sentra, 200SX, Maxima, Quest (8)	RR-LF-LR-RF
1996 & UP	Pathfinder, QX4, Frontier, Xterra (8)	LR-RR-LF-RF

Porsche

Year	Model	Sequence
1965-1992	All (10)	LR-RR-RF-LF
1993 & UP	All (10)	RR-LR-RF-LF

Saab

Year	Model	Sequence
1980-1993	900	LR-RF-RR-LF
1986-1997	9000 w/Mk IV ABS	RF-LR-RF-RR
1994 & UP	900, 9000	LF-RF-LR-RR
1994 & UP	9-3, 9-5	LF-RR-RF-LR

Subaru

Year	Model	Sequence
1990-1997	Impreza, Outback, Legacy, SVX	RF-LR-LF-RR
1997 & UP	Forester, Outback, Legacy	RF-LR-LF-RR
1990-1994	Loyale, XT, XT6	LF-RR-RF-LR

Suzuki

Year	Model	Sequence
1999 & UP	Vitara, Grand Vitara, XL-7	RF-LF-RR
1995 & UP	Swift, Esteem, Aerio	RR-LF-LR-RF
1986-1994	Samurai, Sidekick	RF-LF-RR
1995-1998	Sidekick	RF-LF-PV-RF

Figure 3-21B. Brake bleeding sequences for some popular vehicles.

making them more difficult to bleed from the system. There are, however, special situations where rapid pedal pumping is helpful in brake system bleeding. These are covered in the *Surge Bleeding* section later in the chapter.

When bleeding older or high-mileage vehicles, use a short pedal stroke to avoid possible damage to the master cylinder. If the master cylinder has not been replaced, such as when the system is being flushed or the fluid is being changed, take care when pumping the pedal. Un-

Fluid-Related Brake Service

Toyota		
1965 & UP	All	See note (9)
1996 & UP	4 Runner	RR-LR-RF-LF
1997 & UP	Avalon, Camry, Sienna, Solara	RR-LR-RF-LF
Volkswagen		
1980-1997	All w/o ABS	RR-LR-RF-LF
1985-1994	All w/ABS	LF-RF-RR-LR
1993 & UP	Beetle, Golf, Jetta, GTI	RR-LR-RF-LF
Volvo		
1975-1985	240,260,740,760	LF-RF-LR-RR
1986-1992	240	LF-RF-LR-RR
1986-1992	740, 760, 940, 960	RR-LR-RF-LF
1988-1997	All w/ABS	LR-RR-LF-RF
1997 & UP	V70, V70XC, XC70	LF-RF-LR-RR
1998 & UP	S60, S80	LF-RR-LR-RF

NOTES

1. Proportioning valve must be held open when pressure bleeding.
2. Rear wheels must be on the ground when bleeding.
3. Bleeding ABS requires the use of the New Generation Star (NGS) Scan Tool.
4. When bleeding, rear of vehicle must be lower than the front.
5. Vehicles equipped with quick take-up master cylinder, allow 15 seconds between pedal strokes.
6. Height-sensing brake pressure regulator lever must be pushed towards rear of vehicle before bleeding.
7. Engine must be running.
8. ABS actuator must be disconnected or battery must be disconnected.
9. Bleed starting with the longest brake line.
10. Use short pedal strokes on high-mileage vehicles to prevent damage to master cylinder primary cup.

Figure 3-21C. Brake bleeding sequences for some popular vehicles.

der normal conditions the piston seals only travel over a short part of the cylinder. This may allow debris or corrosion to form on part of the cylinder. If the pedal is then pushed all the way down when bleeding, the seals will travel over this area, possibly damaging the seal.

Manual bleeding requires an assistant to apply and release the brake pedal; a bleeder screw wrench; approximately two feet of clear, plastic hose with an inside diameter small enough to fit snugly over the bleeder screws; and a clear jar partially filled with clean brake fluid. To manually bleed the brake system:

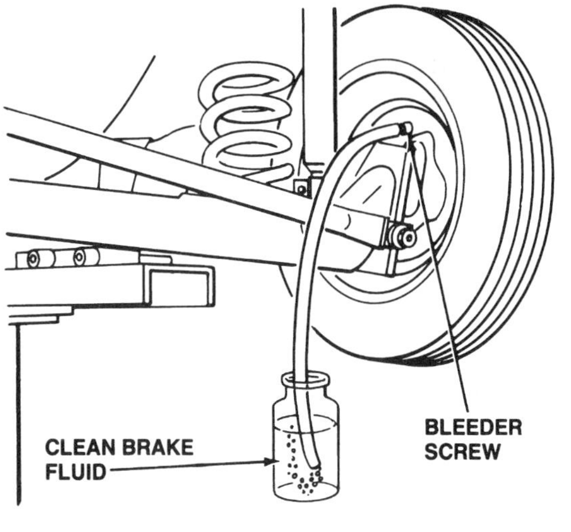

1. Discharge the vacuum or hydraulic power booster (if equipped) by pumping the brake pedal with the ignition OFF until the pedal feels hard.
2. Fill the master cylinder reservoir with new brake fluid and make sure it remains at least half full throughout the bleeding procedure.
3. Slip a clear plastic hose over the bleeder screw of the first wheel cylinder or caliper in the bleeding sequence, and submerge the end of the tube in the jar of brake fluid, figure 3-22.
4. Loosen the bleeder screw approximately one-half turn, and have your assistant slowly depress the brake pedal and hold it to the floor. Air bubbles leaving the bleeder screw will be visible in the hose to the jar.
5. Tighten the bleeder screw, then have your assistant slowly release the brake pedal.

Figure 3-22. When brakes are bled through clear tubing into a jar, air bubbles are easy to spot and fluid spills are prevented.

6. As the pedal is released, observe the fluid level in the reservoir. The level should drop slightly each time, as the fluid moves into the system through the replenishing ports. If the level does not drop, there may be a problem with the master cylinder or the wheel bleeder screw may be plugged up; repair before proceeding.
7. Repeat steps 4, 5, and 6 until no more air bubbles emerge from the bleeder.
8. Transfer the plastic hose to the bleeder screw of the next wheel cylinder or caliper in the bleeding sequence, and repeat steps 4 through 7. Continue around the car in the specified order until the brakes at all four wheels have been bled.

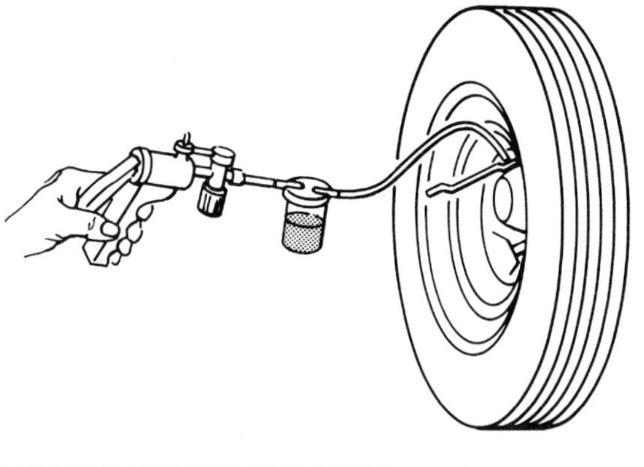

Figure 3-23. A vacuum bleeder attached to a bleeder screw.

Vacuum Bleeding

Vacuum bleeding uses a vacuum pump that attaches to the bleeder screw. The pump creates a low-pressure area at the bleeder screw that allows atmospheric pressure to force brake fluid through the system when the bleeder screw is opened. Vacuum bleeding requires only one technician.

NOTE: Vacuum bleeding may pull air from around the threads of the bleeder screw as well as from the hydraulic system. This will cause bubbles to appear in the bleeder tube, even though the hydraulic system may be free of air. Remove the bleeder screw and coat the threads with rubber grease to prevent this problem.

To vacuum bleed a brake system:

1. Fill the master cylinder reservoir with new brake fluid and make sure it remains at least half full throughout the bleeding procedure.
2. Attach the plastic tube from the vacuum bleeder to the bleeder screw of the first wheel cylinder or caliper in the bleeding sequence, figure 3-23. If necessary, use one of the adapters provided with the vacuum bleeding kit.
3. Squeeze the pump handle 10 to 15 times to create a partial vacuum in the catch bottle.
4. Loosen the bleeder screw approximately one-half turn. Brake fluid and air bubbles will flow into the bottle. When the fluid flow stops, tighten the bleeder screw.
5. Repeat steps 3 and 4 until no more air bubbles emerge from the bleeder.
6. Transfer the vacuum bleeder to the bleeder screw of the next wheel cylinder or caliper in the bleeding sequence, and repeat steps 3 and 4. Continue around the vehicle in the specified order until the brakes at all four wheels have been bled.

Gravity Bleeding

Gravity bleeding uses the force of gravity to pull new brake fluid through the hydraulic system. In this process, the bleeder screws at each wheel are opened one at a time, and the system is allowed to drain naturally until the fluid coming from the bleeder is free of air.

Gravity bleeding is a slow process that can take an hour or more. In addition, this procedure cannot be used on brake systems with residual pressure check valves because the valves restrict the fluid flow. The advantage of gravity bleeding is that it can be done by a single technician, who is freed to attend to other jobs while the brakes bleed. When other bleeding procedures fail, gravity bleeding can sometimes be effective on brake systems that agitate the fluid and trap small pockets of air.

Gravity bleeding requires a bleeder wrench, a length of plastic hose that fits snugly over the bleeder screw, and a jar to catch the dripping fluid. Unless a plastic hose is used to "start a siphon" at each bleeder screw, it is possible that air may enter the system rather than be bled from it. To gravity bleed the brake system:

1. Fill the master cylinder reservoir with new brake fluid. During the bleeding process, check the fluid level periodically to ensure that the reservoir remains at least half full.
2. Attach a length of plastic tubing to the bleeder screw, and place the end of the tube in the jar to catch the drainage.
3. Open the bleeder screw approximately one full turn and make sure that fluid begins to drain. Allow the system to drain until the fluid flowing from the bleeder screw is free of air bubbles.

Fluid-Related Brake Service

4. Close the bleeder screw and top up the fluid level in the master cylinder reservoir.
5. Transfer the hose to the bleeder screw of the next wheel cylinder or caliper in the bleeding sequence and repeat steps 3 and 4. Continue around the vehicle in the specified order until the brakes at all four wheels have been bled.

Pressure Bleeding

Pressure bleeding, sometimes called power bleeding, is the fastest, most efficient, and most common method used to bleed the brake hydraulic system. In this process, a pressure bleeder attached to the master cylinder forces brake fluid through the system under pressure to purge any trapped air. Pressure bleeding is done by one person; once the hydraulic system is pressurized, the technician simply opens the bleeder screws in the prescribed order and allows fluid to flow until it is free of air bubbles.

The tools required for pressure bleeding include a plastic hose and fluid catch jar as used in manual bleeding, as well as a pressure bleeder, a source of air pressure to charge the bleeder, and an adapter to attach the pressure bleeder to the master cylinder fluid reservoir. Cast-metal cylinders with integral reservoirs commonly use a flat, plate-type adapter that seals against the same surface as the reservoir cover, figure 3-24. Some plastic master cylinder reservoirs also use plate-type adapters, but others require adapters that seal against the bottom of the reservoir, figure 3-25. Pressure bleeder manufacturers offer many adapters to fit specific applications.

Metering Valve Override Tools

In addition to the tools described above, a metering valve override tool is required when pressure bleeding the front brakes of certain vehicles. The override tool is used to deactivate the metering valve because the operating pressure of power bleeders is within the range where the metering valve blocks fluid flow to the front brakes. Metering valves that require an override tool have a stem or button on one end that is either pushed in or pulled out to hold the valve open. The override tool performs this service.

To install the override tool used on General Motors vehicles, figure 3-26, loosen the combination valve mounting bolt and slip the slot in the tool under the bolt head. Push the end of the tool toward the valve body until it depresses the valve plunger, then tighten the mounting bolt to hold the tool in place.

Some full-size Ford vehicles manufactured after 1979 have a metering valve with a stem that must be pushed in to bleed the front brakes, much like the General Motors design. Ford does not offer a special tool for this purpose, however. Have an assistant manually override the valve when you bleed the front brakes on one of these vehicles.

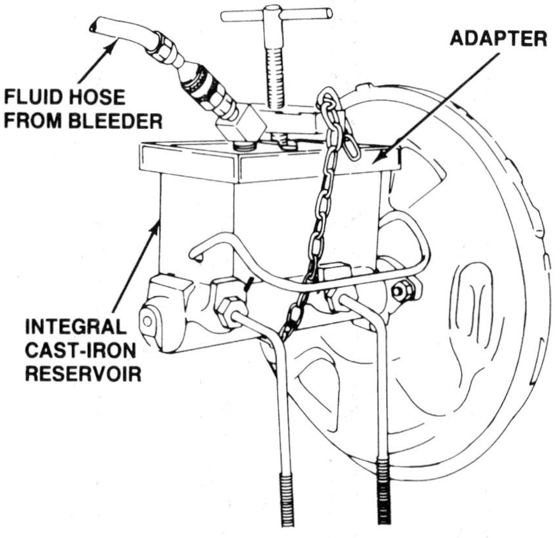

Figure 3-24. A pressure bleeder adapter for an integral master cylinder reservoir.

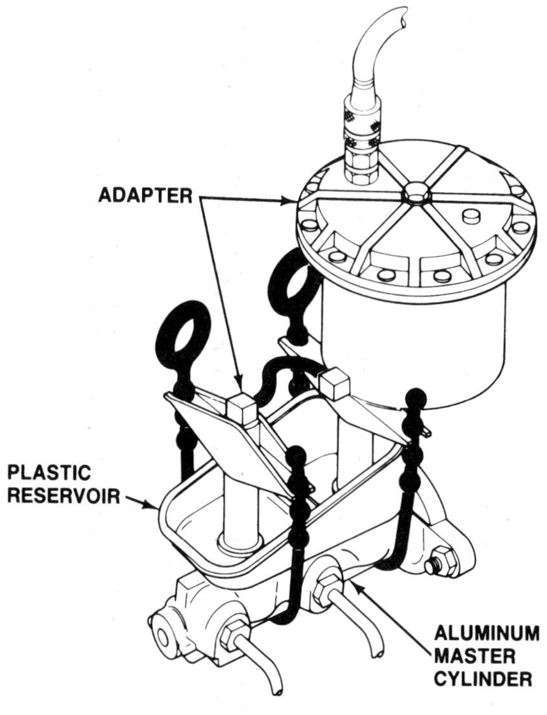

Figure 3-25. A pressure bleeder adapter for a plastic master cylinder reservoir.

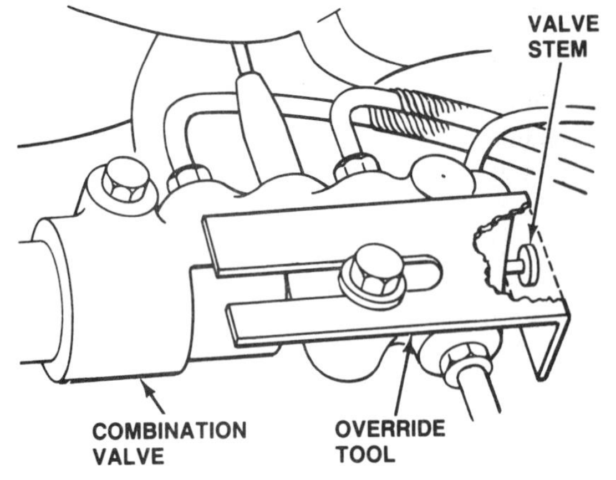

Figure 3-26. Installation of a General Motors metering valve override tool.

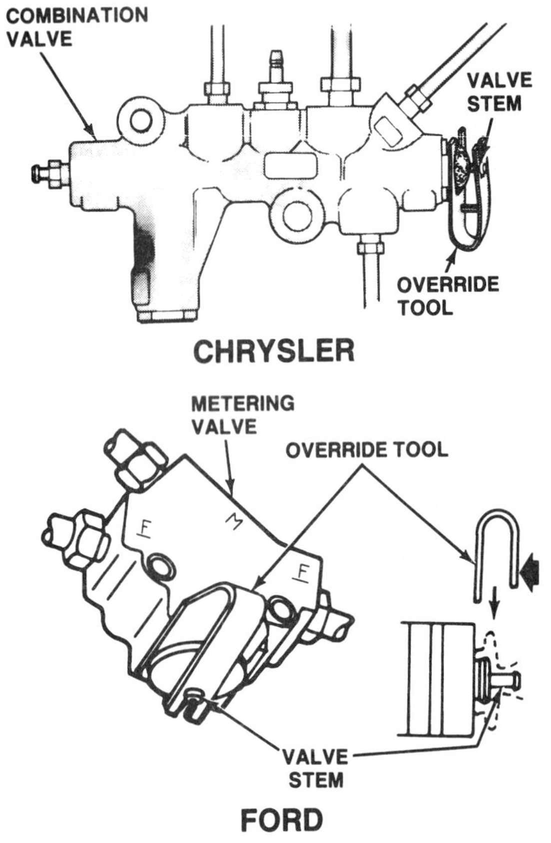

Figure 3-27. Installation of Chrysler and Ford metering valve override tools.

To install the override tool used on Chrysler and early Ford vehicles, figure 3-27, slip one fork of the tool under the rubber boot, and the other fork under the valve stem head. The spring tension of the tool holds the valve open, but allows the valve stem to move slightly when the system is pressurized. If the valve is held rigidly open, internal damage will result.

Pressure Bleeding Procedure

Just as in manual bleeding, it is important to follow the proper sequence when pressure bleeding a brake system. Some manufacturers recommend one sequence for manual bleeding, and another for pressure bleeding. To pressure bleed a brake system:

1. If it has not already been done, consult the equipment manufacturer's instructions and fill the pressure bleeder with the proper type of brake fluid.
2. Make sure the bleeder is properly sealed and the fluid supply valve is closed, then use compressed air to pressurize the bleeder until approximately 30 psi (207 kPa) is indicated on the bleeder gauge, figure 3-28.
3. If the vehicle is equipped with a metering valve, override it with the appropriate tool.
4. Clean the top of the master cylinder, then remove the master cylinder cover and clean around the gasket surface. Be careful not to allow any dirt to fall into the reservoir.
5. Fill the reservoir about half full with new brake fluid, then install the proper pressure bleeder adapter on the master cylinder.
6. Connect the pressure bleeder fluid supply hose to the adaptor making sure the hose fitting is securely engaged.
7. Open the fluid supply valve on the pressure bleeder to allow pressurized brake fluid to enter the system. Check carefully for fluid leaks that can damage the vehicle finish.
8. Slip the plastic hose over the bleeder screw of the first wheel cylinder or caliper to be bled, and submerge the end of the tube in the jar of brake fluid.
9. Open the bleeder screw approximately one-half turn, and let the fluid run until air bubbles no longer emerge from the tube. Close the bleeder screw.
10. Transfer the plastic hose to the bleeder screw of the next wheel cylinder or caliper in the bleeding sequence, and repeat steps 9 and 10. Continue around the car in the specified order until the brakes at all four wheels have been bled.
11. Remove the metering valve override tool.
12. Close the fluid supply valve on the pressure bleeder.
13. Wrap the end of the fluid supply hose in a shop towel, and disconnect it from the master cylinder adapter, figure 3-29. Do not spill any brake fluid on the vehicle finish.
14. Remove the master cylinder adapter, adjust the fluid level to the full point, and install the fluid reservoir cover.

Fluid-Related Brake Service

Figure 3-28. Compressed air is used to charge the pressure bleeder.

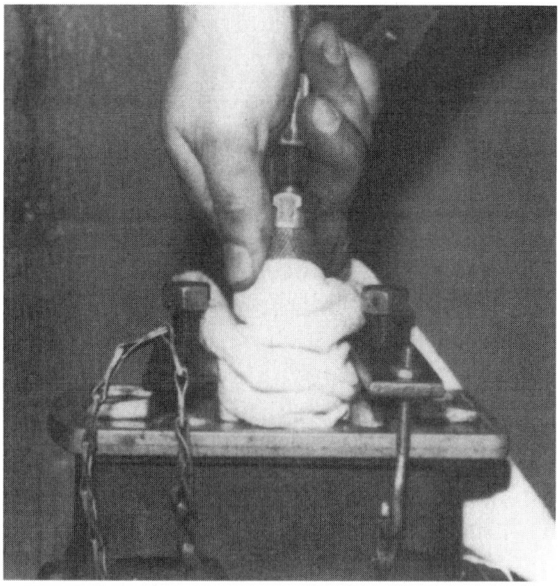

Figure 3-29. When you disconnect the pressure bleeder hose fitting, wrap it in a shop towel to catch any fluid spray.

Surge Bleeding

Surge bleeding is a supplemental bleeding method used to help remove air bubbles that resist other bleeding processes. In surge bleeding the brake pedal is pumped rapidly to create turbulence in the hydraulic system. This agitation helps dislodge air bubbles that cling to the pores of rough castings, or become trapped at high points or turns in the brake lines. Surge bleeding is *not* recommended for systems filled with silicone DOT 5 brake fluids. These fluids tend to trap tiny air bubbles that are very difficult to bleed from the hydraulic system; the added agitation of surge bleeding only makes the problem worse.

Surge bleeding requires an assistant to pump the brake pedal, a bleeder screw wrench, approximately two feet of clear, plastic hose with an inside diameter small enough to fit snugly over the bleeder screw, and a jar partially filled with clean brake fluid. To surge bleed a brake system:

1. Slip the plastic hose over the bleeder screw of the wheel cylinder or caliper to be bled and submerge the end of the tube in the jar of brake fluid.
2. Open the bleeder screw approximately one-half turn.
3. With the bleeder *open*, have your assistant rapidly pump the brake pedal several times. Air bubbles should come out with the brake fluid.
4. While your assistant holds the brake pedal to the floor, close the bleeder screw.
5. Repeat steps 2 through 4 at each bleeder screw in the recommended order.
6. Re-bleed the system using one of the four other methods described above.

FLUID CHANGING

In addition to removing air, brake systems need to be bled in order to clean out old and/or contaminated fluid. This process is called fluid changing or flushing. The hygroscopic (water attracting) nature of most brake fluid makes it necessary to flush the brake system periodically because moisture in the fluid drastically lowers its boiling point, water also causes rust and corrosion of system components that can lead to brake failure. To avoid these problems, brake fluid should be changed according to manufactures recommendations.

Brake fluid changing or flushing is done by bleeding the system until all of the old fluid is purged from the system. Because fluid changing requires the ability to flush out contamination and move a great deal of fluid, the best method to use is pressure bleeding. Other acceptable choices are manual bleeding and vacuum bleeding. Gravity bleeding is *not* recommended for fluid changing because it is slow, and without significant pressure behind the fluid flow, there is no guarantee that contamination will be completely flushed from the system.

To change a vehicle's brake fluid, first use a syringe to remove all of the old brake fluid from the master cylinder reservoir. Fill the reservoir with new fluid, then follow the procedures outlined earlier in the chapter for the chosen method of bleeding. Continue to bleed at each wheel until the fluid that emerges from the bleeder screw is free of any discoloration and contamination.

RECENTERING PRESSURE DIFFERENTIAL SWITCHES

After the brake system has been bled, the pressure differential switch may have to be recentered to turn off the warning light. The reason is that opening a bleeder screw creates a pressure differential between the circuits of the hydraulic system. The switch "sees" this difference as a leak or partial system failure. The piston inside the switch body then moves to one side and completes the warning light circuit.

If the warning light remains on after bleeding, make sure the parking brake is off and the master cylinder reservoir is full of fluid before you assume that the pressure differential switch needs to be recentered. The monitor switches for these parts often share the same warning light as the pressure differential switch, and may be the reason the light is on! There are three types of pressure differential switches; each type requires a different recentering procedure.

Single-Piston Switch without Centering Springs

Some older Ford Motor Company cars and light trucks have a single-piston pressure differential switch without centering springs, figure 3-30A. A similar switch is used on some imports. Recentering this type of switch requires an assistant and a bleeder wrench. To recenter the switch:

1. Turn the ignition switch ON. The warning light will come on because the piston has raised the switch plunger to complete the circuit.
2. Determine if the brake hydraulic system of the car you are working on is split diagonally or front to rear, then open a bleeder screw in the circuit of the system opposite that which was last bled.
3. Have your assistant slowly push on the brake pedal until the warning light goes out.
4. Close the bleeder screw.

Very little pedal pressure or movement is required for this procedure. If too much is applied, the piston will overcenter and re-illuminate the warning light. Should that happen, open a bleeder screw in the opposite side of the hydraulic system. It is often easier and more accurate to depress the brake pedal by hand when centering the switch in this manner.

Single-Piston Switch with Centering Springs

Most domestic and import cars manufactured after 1970 have a single-piston pressure differential switch equipped with centering springs, figure 3-30B. This type of switch illuminates the warning light only when the brakes are applied and a pressure difference exists between the two circuits of the brake system. The switch recenters itself automatically when the brakes are released, unless the piston sticks in position against the terminal stud. If the warning light remains lit after the brake system has been repaired:

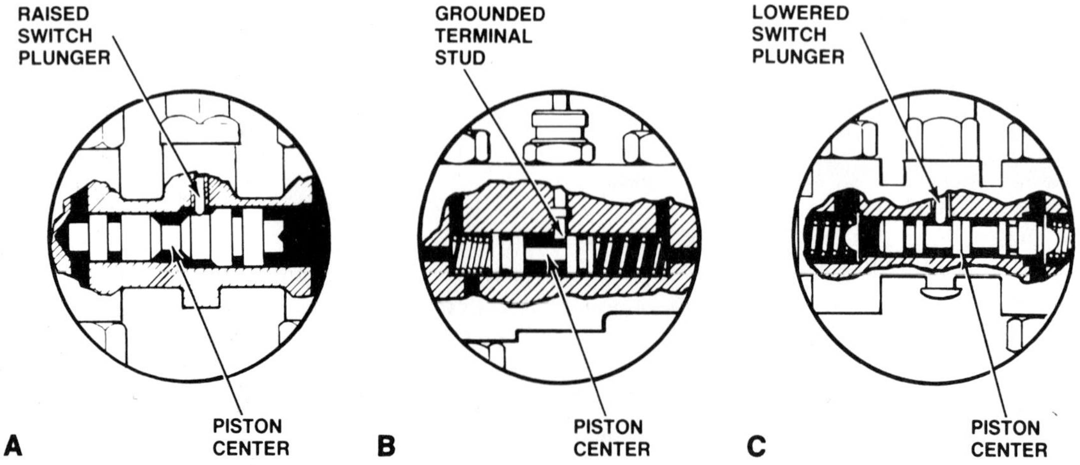

Figure 3-30. Pressure differential switch pistons must be centered to turn off the brake system warning light.

Fluid-Related Brake Service

1. Turn the ignition switch ON. The warning light will illuminate.
2. Apply the brake pedal with moderate-to-hard force. Hydraulic pressure will free the stuck piston and the centering springs will position it properly in the bore. The warning light will then go out.

If the warning light remains lit, and the parking brake or fluid level switches are not at fault, you can attempt to free the piston by using the centering procedure given above for switches without centering springs. If this does not free the piston, replace the pressure differential switch.

Two-Piston Switch with Centering Springs

A few domestic cars built before 1971, and some imports, have a two-piston pressure differential switch with centering springs, figure 3-30C. This type of switch locks the warning light on until it is recentered. To do this:

1. Turn the ignition switch ON. The warning light will illuminate because piston movement has allowed the switch plunger to extend and complete the circuit.
2. Unscrew the switch plunger assembly from the switch body, and apply the brake pedal with medium to hard force. The centering springs will then recenter the piston.
3. Reinstall the switch plunger assembly in the switch body.

If the warning light remains lit, and the parking brake or fluid level switches are not at fault, you can attempt to free the piston by using the centering procedure given above for switches without centering springs. If this does not free the piston, replace the pressure differential switch.

4
Brake Line and Hose Service

OBJECTIVES

Upon completion and review of this chapter, you will be able to:

- Inspect brake hoses and tubing and recognize problems with these parts.
- Replace a brake hose.
- Recognize the proper use of hose retaining clips and nuts.
- Understand the proper use and replacement of hose sealing washers.
- Replace a section of brake tubing.
- Fabricate an SAE tubing double flare.
- Fabricate an ISO tubing "bubble" flare.

INTRODUCTION

Brake lines distribute pressurized brake fluid from the master cylinder to the hydraulic components at the wheel friction assemblies. Any brake line failure will cause at least one of the two brake system hydraulic circuits to fail as well. This chapter covers the inspection, replacement, and fabrication of brake lines and hoses.

BRAKE LINE INSPECTION

Brake lines, both reinforced rubber hoses and double-wall steel tubing, are relatively trouble free. However, each can suffer wear and deterioration from a number of factors including ozone in the air, contaminants in the brake fluid, debris thrown up by the tires, abrasion from contact with suspension and steering components, and stress created in an accident. Damaged brake lines can fail at any moment and cause a serious accident.

Because of the wear and deterioration that take place, brake lines should be checked periodically for damage and leaks. Most manufacturers recommend that brake hoses be inspected twice a year, or any time the brakes are serviced. Steel brake tubing should be inspected yearly, or any time the brakes are serviced. Brake lines that are not in perfect condition must be replaced.

Brake Hose Inspection

Rubber brake hoses suffer damage both from within and without. On the inside of the hose, contaminated brake fluid attacks the rubber lining and causes it to swell, restricting fluid flow. Hoses softened by contaminated fluid also expand under pressure, causing a spongy brake pedal and increased pedal travel. And if a brake caliper is allowed to hang by the hose, the inner hose lining may be torn, creating a flap that blocks the flow of fluid to or from the friction assembly, figure 4-1.

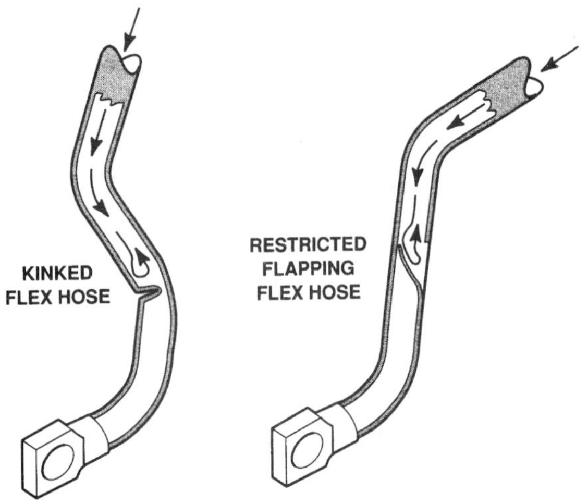

Figure 4-1. Brake hoses may fail due to excessive bending or a torn inner liner. (Courtesy of General Motors Corporation, Service and Parts Operations)

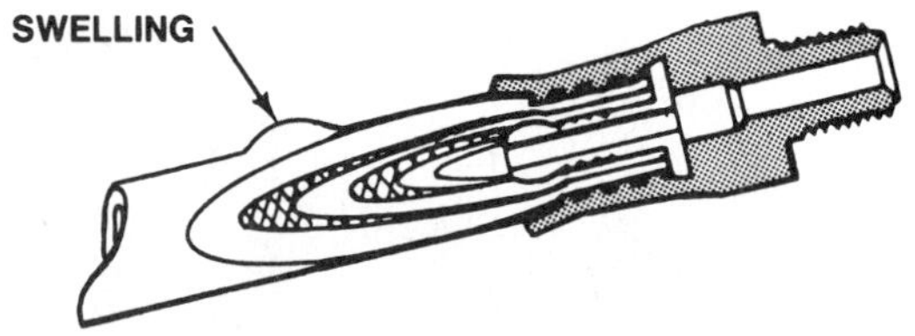

Figure 4-2. A swollen or blistered hose usually has an internal leak.

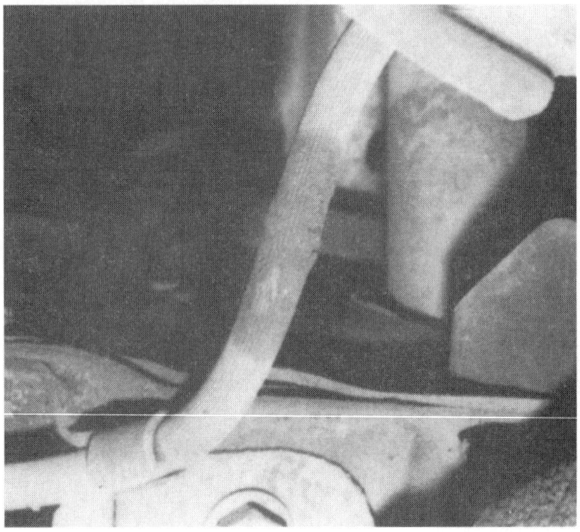

Figure 4-3. Fluid leaks often appear as a dark stain on the hose.

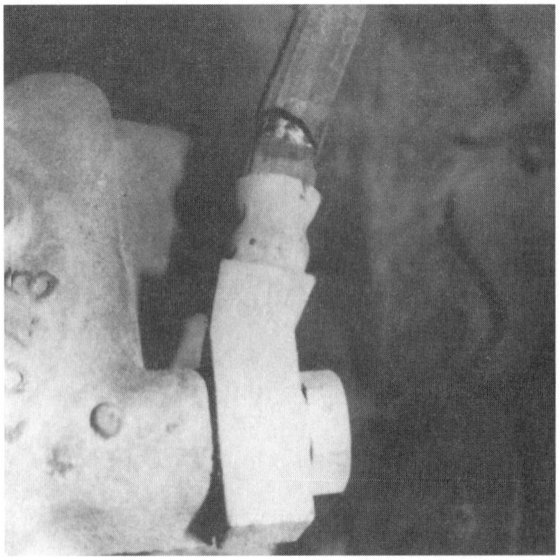

Figure 4-4. Cracked and weathered brake hoses are weakened and must be replaced.

On the outside of the hose, ozone in the atmosphere attacks the rubber in the hose outer casing, causing it to age and become brittle. Cracks then develop that eventually become leaks. The other main external wear problem is abrasion from contact with suspension and steering parts, as well as debris thrown up by the tires. An improperly routed hose or a hose that is too long and rubs against part of the suspension will quickly be worn through, creating a leak. Nonstandard parts such as wide wheels and tires can also rub against the hoses and cause abrasions. A hose that is too short can be stretched or pulled apart during steering or suspension movement.

Most cars have three or four brake hoses. All cars have a hose at each front wheel, and cars with independent rear suspension also have a hose at each rear wheel. Cars with a live rear axle generally have a single rear hose between the axle and the chassis. Visually inspect the brake hoses for swelling, blisters, leaks, stains, cracks, and abrasions. Swelling and blisters, figure 4-2, are signs of internal fluid leakage that has penetrated to the outer hose covering. Obvious leaks, or stains from leaks, figure 4-3, may appear on the surface of the hose and around the fittings on the hose ends. Cracks can appear anywhere on the hose, figure 4-4, as can signs of abrasion, figure 4-5. Finally, check the hose mounting hardware and locating brackets for damage and tightness.

Brake Tubing Inspection

Steel brake tubing is naturally more durable than rubber brake hoses, and usually requires less service. Tubing does, however, suffer from rust and corrosion, cracking, and impact damage. Rust and corrosion, figure 4-6, are caused by water trapped around the brake lines, and the damage is accelerated by salt and other chemicals used to melt ice and snow. Once the

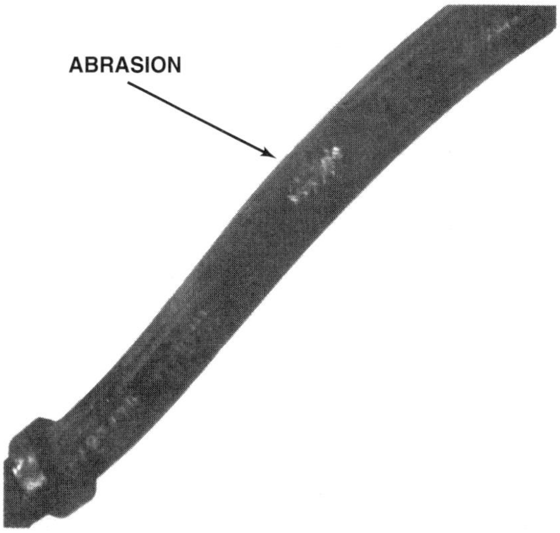

Brake Line and Hose Service

Figure 4-5. Abrasions result when the hose is improperly routed, or the wrong length for the application.

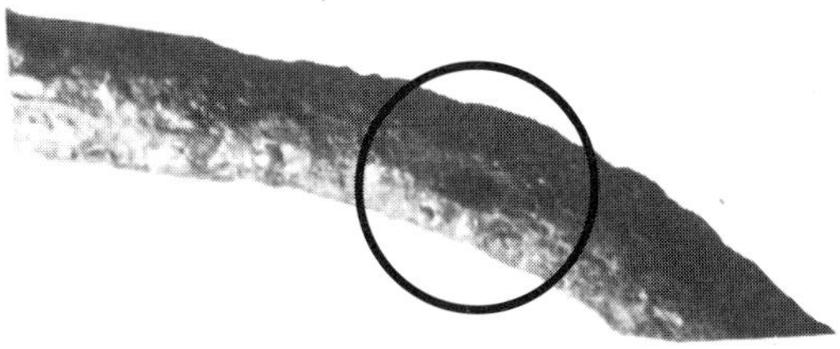

Figure 4-6. Rust and corrosion on brake tubing are most likely along frame rails or around mounting clips.

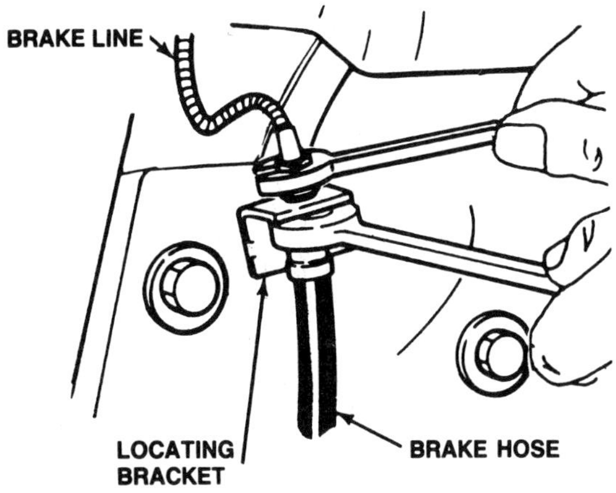

Figure 4-7. Disconnect the female end of a brake hose first.

problem becomes severe, rusted and corroded tubing will rupture from hydraulic pressure.

Another problem with steel tubing is that it fractures from vibration if not mounted securely. Loose tubing can also snag on objects the vehicle passes over and be ripped away, and unsecured tubing may come into contact with the exhaust system, heating the brake fluid and potentially causing vapor lock.

Impact damage of the brake tubing, mainly dented and restricted tubing, can be caused by debris thrown up by the tires. However, the most common causes of this type of damage are careless attachment of towing hooks, and improper floor jack and hoist positioning.

To inspect the brake lines, begin where they attach to the master cylinder and follow them along their paths to the wheels. Look for rust and corrosion along the frame rails, at the mounting clips, or any place where water, dirt, and road salt accumulate. Make sure the tubing is properly fastened to the chassis; cracks caused by vibration will be indicated by obvious fluid leaks. Physical damage is most likely in the areas directly behind the wheels, or where the tubing crosses below an axle or frame member.

BRAKE HOSE REPLACEMENT

Brake hoses that fail an inspection are replaced with a new hose. Replacement is the only common form of service because the tools necessary to fabricate new brake hoses are not commonly available in the field.

Hose Removal

Many front brake hoses, and rear hoses on cars with independent rear suspensions, have a male fitting on one end and a female fitting on the other; these fittings are swaged or crimped onto the hose and do not turn. With this type of hose, the female end must be disconnected first. Other brake hoses have a banjo fitting in place of the male hose end fitting. With this type of hose, it does not matter which end is disconnected first. To remove a brake hose:

1. Clean any dirt from around the fittings at the ends of the hose to prevent it from entering the hydraulic system.
2. Locate the fitting where the steel brake tubing attaches to the female end of the hose. Loosen the tubing nut with a flare-nut wrench, figure 4-7, and unscrew it from the hose. Although the hose fitting is usually prevented from rotating by its locating bracket, it is best to always use a second wrench on the fitting to make sure it does not twist and cause damage to the hose or bracket.
3. Remove the hose retaining clip with a pair of pliers, figure 4-8, and separate the hose from the locating bracket.
4. Detach the hose from any other locating devices.
5. Use a flare-nut wrench to disconnect the other end of the hose from the wheel cylinder or caliper. On hoses with male fittings, figure 4-9, simply loosen the fitting and unscrew the hose

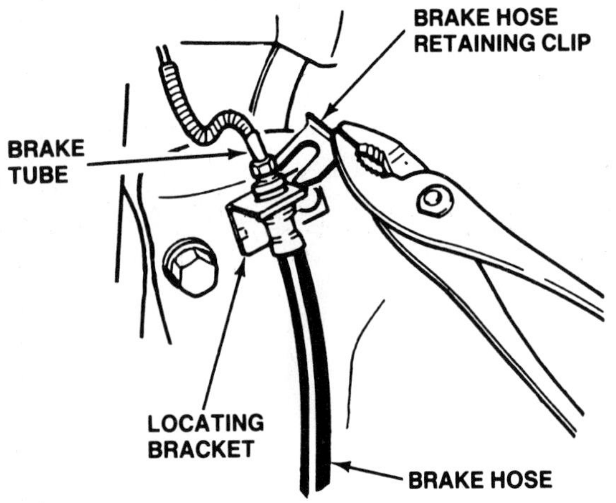

Figure 4-8. A retaining clip secures the brake hose in the locating bracket.

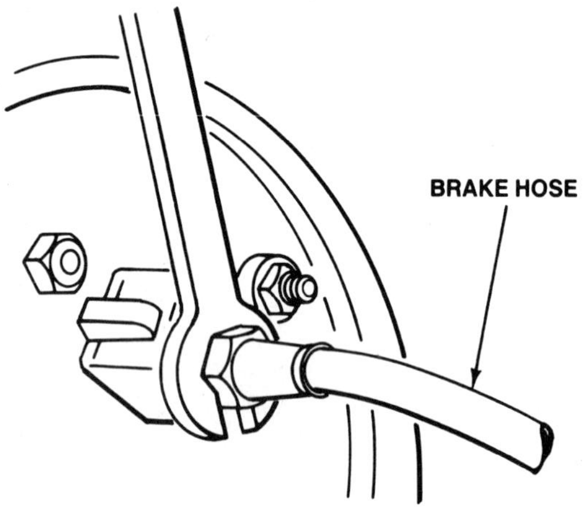

Figure 4-9. Disconnect male hose fittings with a flare-nut wrench.

Figure 4-10. Remove the hollow bolt to disconnect a hose with a banjo fitting.

from the caliper. On hoses with banjo fittings, figure 4-10, remove the hollow bolt from the center of the fitting, taking care not to lose the sealing rings on each side of the fitting.

Some rear hoses on cars with live axles have two female ends; in this case, either end can be disconnected first. Use one flare-nut wrench to prevent the hose from twisting, and a second to loosen the tubing nut on the steel brake line. Repeat for the other end of the hose.

Hose Installation

Before you install a new front brake hose, make sure it is the proper part for that side of the car; left- and right-side hoses are not always interchangeable. The new hose must also be the proper length, and when the original equipment hose has special armoring and bracket fittings, the replacement part must have them as well.

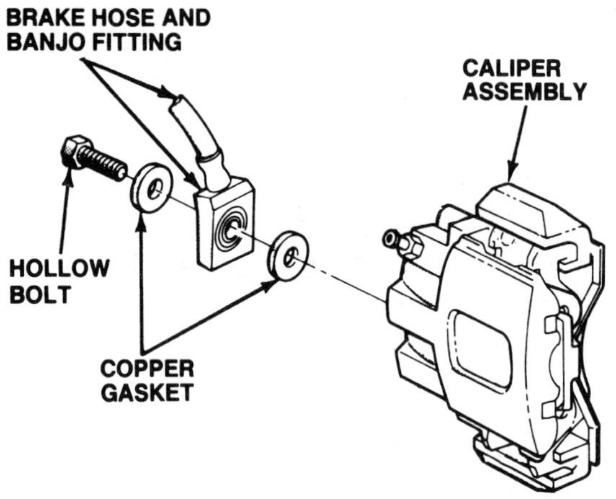

During installation, carefully route the new hose in the original location. Make sure the hose maintains a distance of at least ¾ inch (20 mm) from all steering and suspension parts throughout the full range of their movement so there is no danger of the hose being chafed. Never route brake hoses near exhaust systems where heat will harm the rubber casing or increase brake fluid temperatures. If copper sealing gaskets are used at either of the hose fittings, use only new parts when installing the hose. Copper gaskets take a set when they are first used, and reusing an old one may cause a leak. To install a brake hose:

1. If the hose has a male end, thread it into the wheel cylinder or brake caliper; use a new copper gasket where required. Tighten the fitting to the proper torque.
2. If the hose has a banjo fitting, place the hollow bolt through the fitting and thread it into the caliper; use a new copper gasket on each side of the fitting. If the fitting mounts to the caliper in only one position, tighten it to the proper torque. If the position can vary, leave the fitting slightly loose at this time.
3. Route the hose through any locating devices.
4. Place the open end of the hose through the locating bracket, and start the threads of the steel brake line tubing nut into the female fitting.
5. Observe the colored stripe or raised rib on the hose outer casing, figure 4-11; position the hose so that it is not twisted.
6. Hold the female hose fitting in position with a flare-nut wrench, and tighten the tubing nut with a second wrench.

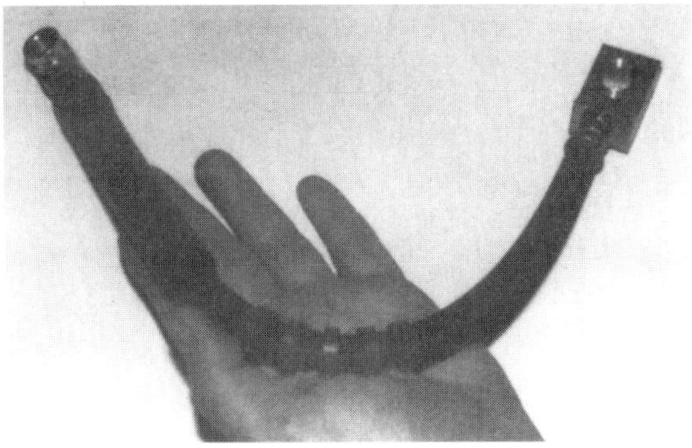

Brake Line and Hose Service

Figure 4-11. Observe the colored stripe or raised rib on the outer casing to prevent twisting a hose when installing it.

7. Again check that the hose is not twisted and that it does not contact any suspension or steering parts. If necessary, loosen the tubing nut, reposition the hose, and retighten the connection.
8. Install the retaining clip to secure the tubing and brake hose to the locating bracket.
9. If the banjo fitting was left loose in step 2, position it so that the hose clears all obstacles, then tighten the fitting to the proper torque.

When a hose is equipped with two female ends, one end is assembled and tightened, then the other. Start the tubing nut on the steel brake line into one end of the hose, and use a pair of flare-nut wrenches to tighten the connection. Observe the colored stripe or raised rib on the outer casing, and position the hose so that it is not twisted. Start the tubing nut of the other steel brake line into the open end of the hose, then use one flare-nut wrench to prevent the hose fitting from turning, and a second wrench to tighten the tubing nut into the fitting.

BRAKE TUBING REPLACEMENT

Brake tubing service consists of two operations, replacement and fabrication. In some cases, replacement tubing that is pre-bent and flared can be purchased for a specific application; this type of tubing is generally available only from the vehicle manufacturer. Most of the time, the technician in the field fabricates replacement tubing from straight tubing stock.

Brake tubing is held in place by clips bolted to the chassis at various points along the line, figure 4-12. To replace a section of tubing, you need flare-nut wrenches to loosen the fittings at both ends of the line, and suitable sockets, wrenches, or screwdrivers to remove the retaining clip bolts or screws. To remove a section of brake tubing:

1. Clean any dirt from around the tubing fittings.
2. Disconnect the fittings at each end of the tubing with a flare-nut wrench. Use a second wrench where two brake lines connect to prevent twisting the tubing or brake hoses.
3. Unbolt or unscrew the mounting clips from the chassis, and detach the brake line.
4. Remove the mounting clips for use on the new replacement tubing. If the new section of tubing must be fabricated, save the old tubing to use as a bending guide.

To install a section of brake tubing:

1. Attach the mounting clips to the new tubing.
2. Position the tubing in place, and loosely install the retaining clip bolts or screws.
3. Connect the fittings at both ends of the tubing, and tighten them with the appropriate flare-nut wrenches.
4. Tighten the retaining clip bolts or screws.

BRAKE TUBING FABRICATION

As mentioned earlier, most sections of brake tubing replaced in the field are fabricated from straight tubing stock. To minimize the chance of leaks and ensure the strongest possible repair, a single length of tubing should be used to connect two hydraulic components wherever possible. Sometimes, when a brake line is extra long or routed through a hard-to-reach area, the only practical repair is to splice two lengths of tubing together. This should only be done using connectors that seal with flare fittings; *never* use spherical sleeve compression fittings to splice brake tubing.

Brake lines should be fabricated only from special double-walled steel tubing designed for brake system services. *Never* use copper or aluminum tubing for brake lines because these materials do not have sufficient burst strength or resistance to corrosion. The replacement tubing should also be armored if the original equipment tube had this feature.

Sections of straight tubing stock come in a variety of lengths, and the ends are usually fitted with tubing nuts and formed into SAE or ISO flares, figure 4-13. Occasionally, a piece of replacement tubing will be exactly the right length for the job, and its fittings and flares will match those of the original tubing. In these cases, the only fabrication needed is to bend the new tubing to the appropriate shape. More often, however, you will have to select a length of tubing slightly longer than required, then remove one or both fittings to adjust the length of the tubing, install a different

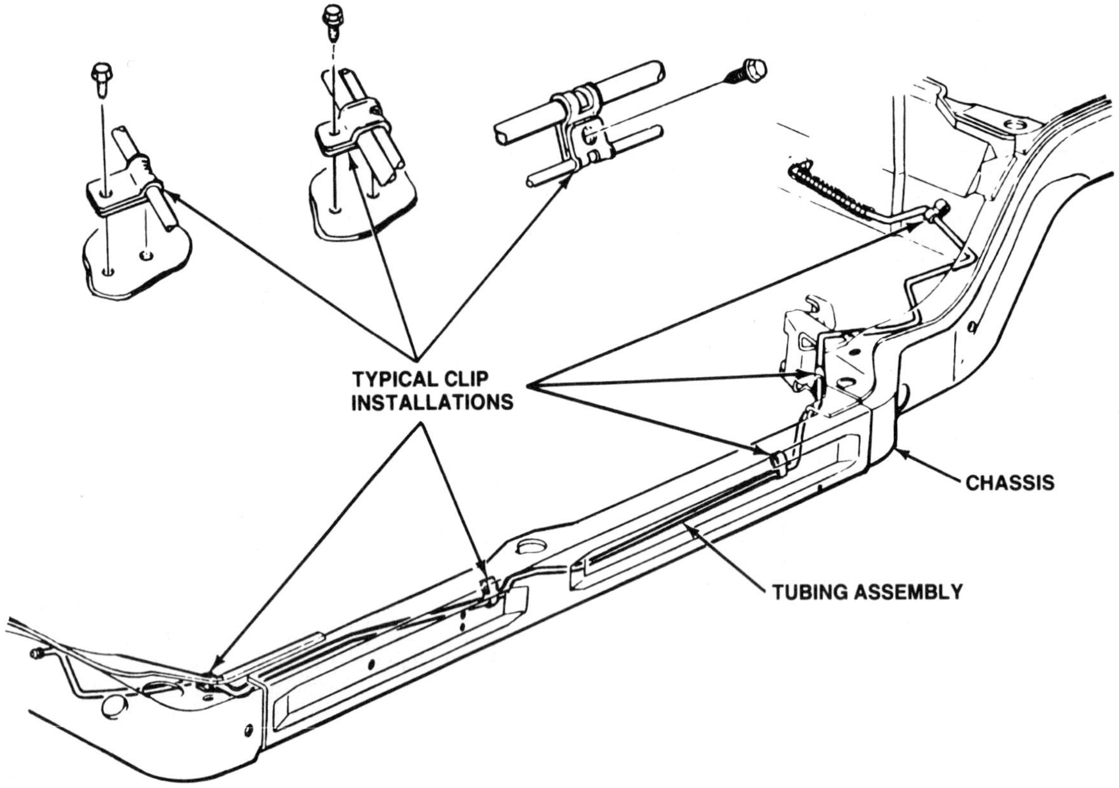

Figure 4-12. Brake tubing is attached to the chassis with special mounting clips.

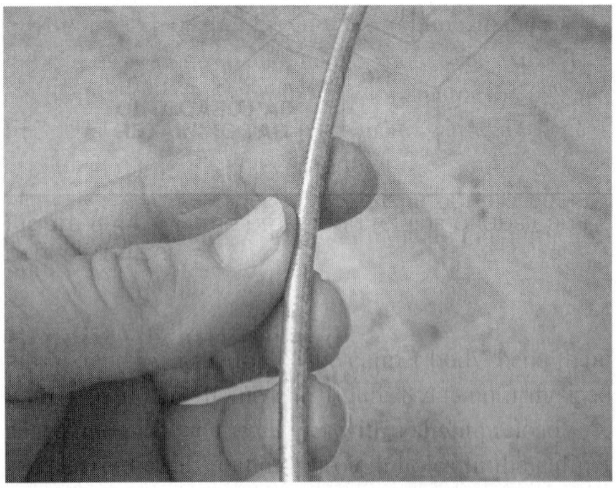

Figure 4-13. Pre-made brake lines can be purchased and then bent to fit the vehicle.

type of tubing nut, or form a different type of flare. As a result, brake tubing fabrication consists of three operations, those used to cut, bend, and flare the tubing.

Tubing Cutting

Brake tubing must be cut when a damaged section is removed from the vehicle, or when a piece of replacement tubing is trimmed to the proper length. When tubing is cut on the car, the cut is usually made in a location that allows good access. This makes the job easier, and also simplifies the flaring operation that will be required later. When cutting a length of new replacement tubing, measure the old piece as accurately as possible, then add approximately one-eighth inch (3 mm) for each flare that needs to be formed.

Brake tubing should never be cut with a hacksaw; the uneven pressure the blade exerts will distort the tubing shape and leave a ragged edge that cannot be properly flared. Metal chips and flashing are also likely to be left in the line where they can later come loose and cause problems in the hydraulic system. Always cut tubing with one of the many special tools made for this purpose. To cut a piece brake tubing:

1. Determine the exact length of replacement tubing needed, and mark the straight tubing stock at that point.
2. Position the tubing cutter so that the cutting wheel is directly over the mark, figure 4-14. Tighten the knob on the cutter until the cutting wheel makes firm, but not tight, contact with the tubing.
3. Rotate the cutter around the tube while slowly tightening the knob to maintain cutting wheel

Brake Line and Hose Service

Figure 4-14. A special tubing cutter is required to accurately cut brake tubing.

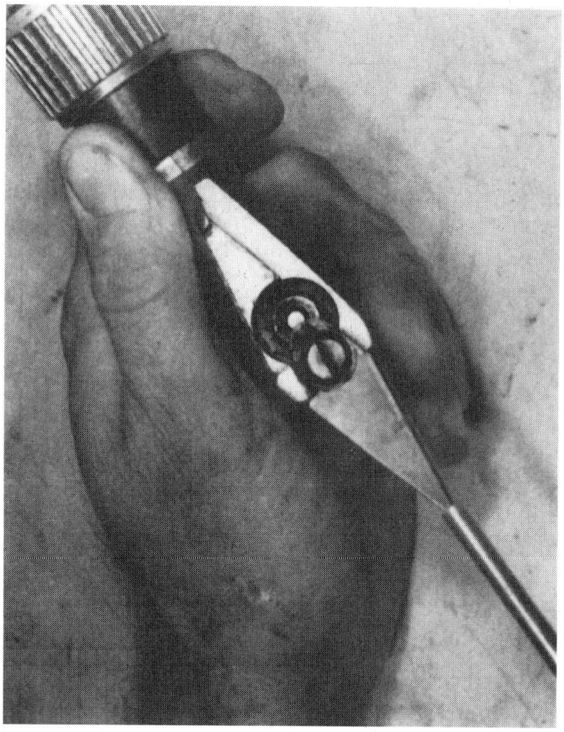

Figure 4-15. Ream the cut end of the tubing with a de-burring tool before flaring.

pressure against the tubing. Continue until the tube is severed.

4. Use the de-burring tool on the cutter, or a similar separate tool, to ream the inner bore of the tube and remove any metal flashing, figure 4-15.
5. Blow through the tubing with compressed air to remove any loose metal particles.

Tubing Bending

Once a section of replacement tubing has been cut to the proper length, it can be bent to the proper shape. Unless it is specifically designed to be bent by hand, brake tubing must be bent with the proper bending tool or it will be distorted and kink. A kink creates a weak spot, and the tubing may eventually crack at that location. Kinks also restrict the flow of brake fluid through the tubing.

If a spring-type bender is used, the brake tubing must be bent while at least one end remains unflared. Slide the coiled spring over the unflared end of the tubing to the location where the bend must be made. Using the original section of tubing as a guide, carefully bend the replacement part to the proper shape, figure 4-16.

If a lever-type bender is used, the tubing can be bent either before or after flaring. Slip the tubing into the bender until the location where the bend is to be made is at the fulcrum point. Using the original section of

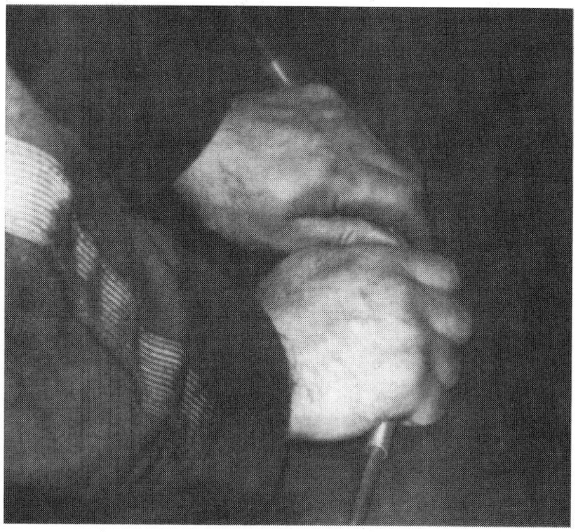

Figure 4-16. Forming brake tubing with a spring-type bending tool.

tubing as a guide, carefully exert force on the bender levers to form the replacement tubing into the desired shape, figure 4-17.

Tubing Flaring

Once the cutting and bending operations are completed, flares must be formed on any unfinished tubing

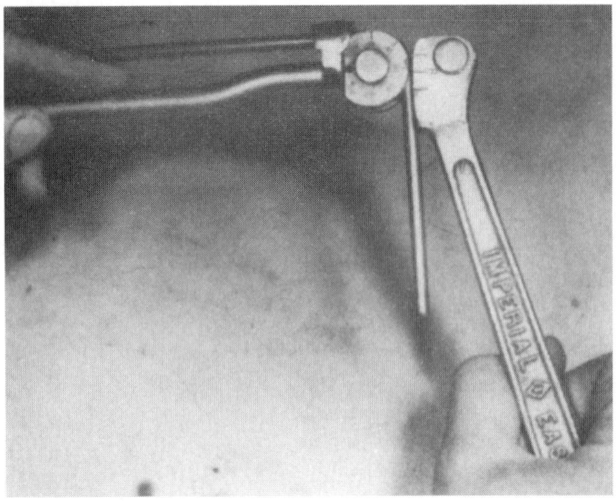

Figure 4-17. Forming brake tubing with a lever-type bending tool.

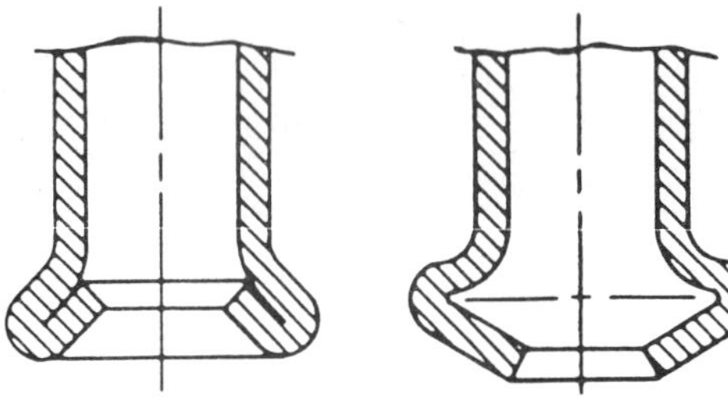

Figure 4-18. SAE and ISO flares are not interchangeable, and require different tools to form.

Figure 4-19. Install the tubing to the proper height in the tubing holder.

Figure 4-20. The first step in forming an SAE double flare.

ends. Brake tubing is flared with either the SAE double flare or the ISO "bubble" flare, figure 4-18. These flares, and their fittings, are not interchangeable and cannot be mixed. Make sure you form the proper type of flare for the application.

A different special tool is required to form each of the types of flare. The procedures for using these tools are described below. Before forming any type of flare, make sure you install the tubing nut onto the tubing with the threaded portion facing the end of the tubing.

Forming SAE flares

The SAE double flare is formed in a two-step process:

1. Select the forming die from the flaring kit that corresponds to the diameter of the tubing to be flared.
2. Make sure the tubing nut is installed onto the tube, then clamp the tubing in the appropriate hole of the tubing holder. The end of the tube should protrude from the tapered side of the hole, and should extend above the holder surface a distance equal to the height of the first ring on the forming die, figure 4-19.
3. Install the forming die onto the tubing by placing the die pin into the tubing bore.
4. Position the press over the forming die on the tubing holder, and turn the threaded rod of the press until the cone-shaped anvil contacts the die. Continue to tighten the rod until the forming die bottoms on the tubing holder, figure 4-20.
5. Loosen the press and remove the forming die. The end of the tubing should appear as shown in figure 4-21A.

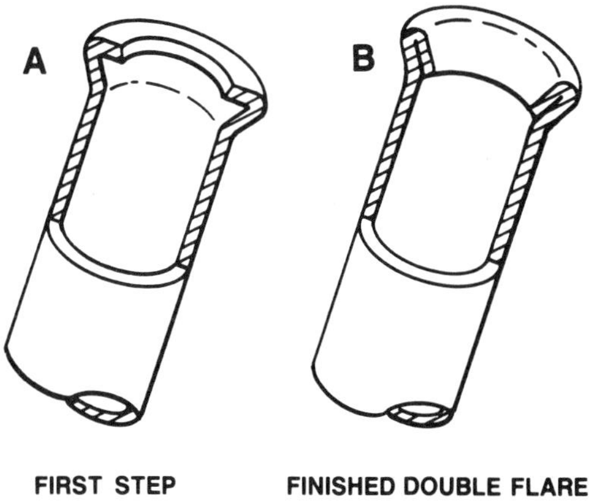

Brake Line and Hose Service

Figure 4-21. The SAE double flare is formed in two steps.

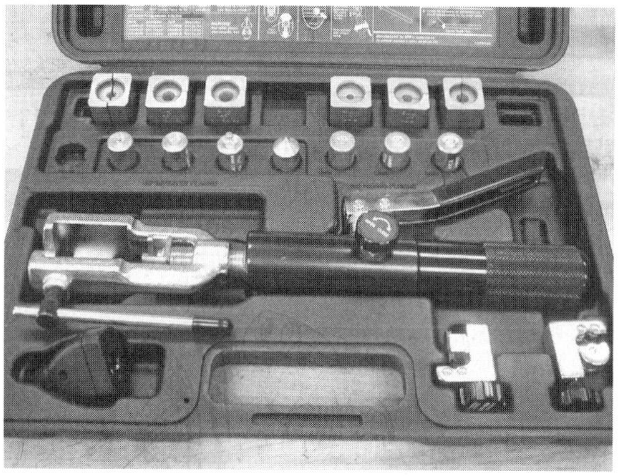

Figure 4-23. This flaring kit features a hydraulic press and can form SAE and ISO flares.

Figure 4-22. The second step in forming an SAE double flare.

Figure 4-24. Cut the tubing with the tubing cutter.

6. Re-tighten the threaded rod of the press to force the cone-shaped anvil into the tube, figure 4-22. Apply light to medium pressure until the lip formed in the first step is in full contact with the inner surface of the tubing.
7. Loosen and remove the press. The end of the tubing should appear as shown in figure 4-21B. If the flare does not have the correct shape, or any cracks are visible, you must cut off the end of the tubing and form a new flare.

Forming ISO Flares

The ISO flare is made in a one-step process using a special flare tool kit, figure 4-23. To form an ISO flare:

1. Cleanly cut the tubing with the tubing cutter, figure 4-24. De-burr the inside and outside of the cut tubing with the de-burring tool.
2. Select the correct forming mandrel, figure 4-25.
3. Set the forming mandrel into the tool. Select the proper size split die and clamp it around the tubing in the tool. The tubing should protrude flush with the split die, figure 4-26.
4. Screw the pump/handle and mandrel into the tubing and die until it seats snugly, figure 4-27.
5. Close the release valve on the tool pump and pump the handle until resistance is felt, figure 4-28.
6. Release the pump valve and unscrew the handle. Loosen the clamping handle and remove the tubing from the die, figure 4-29. The completed ISO flare should be shaped like that shown in figure 4-30. If the flare does not have the correct shape, or any cracks are visible, the flare must be cut off and reformed.

Figure 4-25. Select the proper size forming mandrel.

Figure 4-26. Place the mandrel into the tool and clamp the tubing in the split die.

Figure 4-27. Thread the tool handle in until the mandrel seats into the tubing and die.

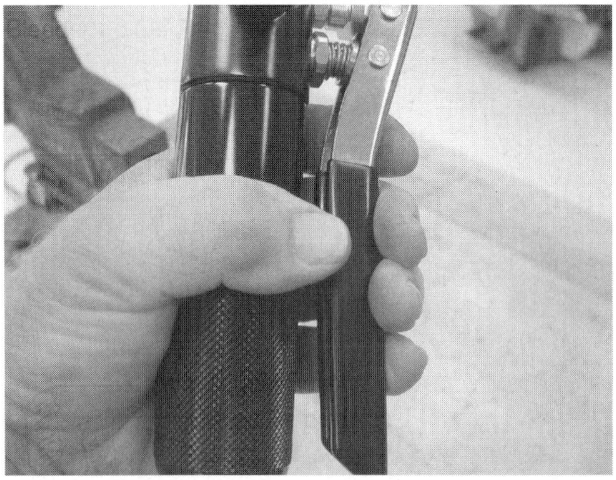

Figure 4-28. Close the tool valve and pump the handle until the mandrel seats in the die.

Figure 4-29. The strong hydraulic pump forms the ISO flare.

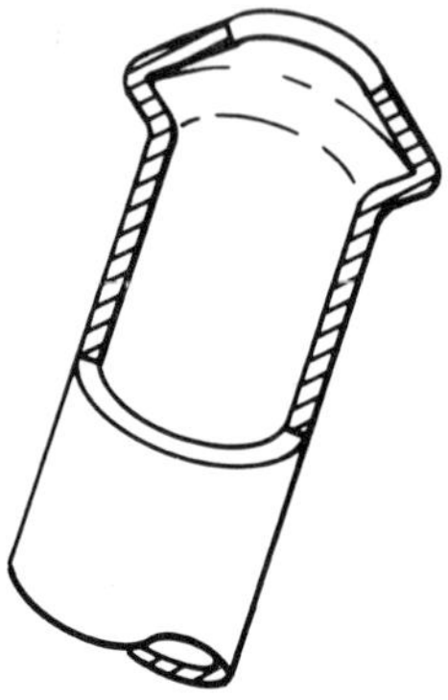

Figure 4-30. A properly formed ISO flare.

84

5
Pedal Assembly and Master Cylinder Service

OBJECTIVES

Upon completion and review of this chapter, you will be able to:

- Inspect a pedal linkage.
- Adjust pedal freeplay.
- Replace a brake pedal.
- Inspect a master cylinder.
- Perform the quick-take-up valve test.
- Perform the master cylinder compensating port test.
- Perform the master cylinder external leak test.
- Perform the master cylinder internal leak test.
- Remove and replace a master cylinder.
- Overhaul a master cylinder.

INTRODUCTION

The functions of the brake pedal assembly and master cylinder are fundamental to the proper operation of the brake system. The pedal assembly transmits and increases the mechanical force applied by the driver to the brake pedal. The master cylinder converts that force into hydraulic pressure that is routed to the wheel friction assemblies. The calipers and wheel cylinders convert that pressure back into mechanical force that is used to apply the brake pads and shoes, creating the friction required to stop the car.

An improperly adjusted brake pedal either increases pedal freeplay, or holds the master cylinder in a partially applied position. In the former situation, the brake pedal reserve is reduced; in the latter case, the brakes will initially drag, and can eventually lock completely. A leaking master cylinder can greatly reduce stopping power. If a hydraulic leak is not repaired, the system will eventually lose enough fluid that the brakes will fail altogether, possibly resulting in an accident.

Brake pedal assembly and master cylinder service are common brake repair jobs. This chapter contains service procedures for working on these components. Pedal service is usually limited to adjusting the freeplay. However, master cylinder service is much more involved and includes procedures for inspection, testing, replacement, and overhaul.

BRAKE PEDAL ASSEMBLY SERVICE

Brake pedal assembly service includes pedal and linkage inspection, pedal freeplay adjustment, and pedal or bushing replacement. The inspection verifies that the pedal assembly is in good condition and works freely. The pedal and linkage must be working properly or pedal freeplay cannot be adjusted accurately.

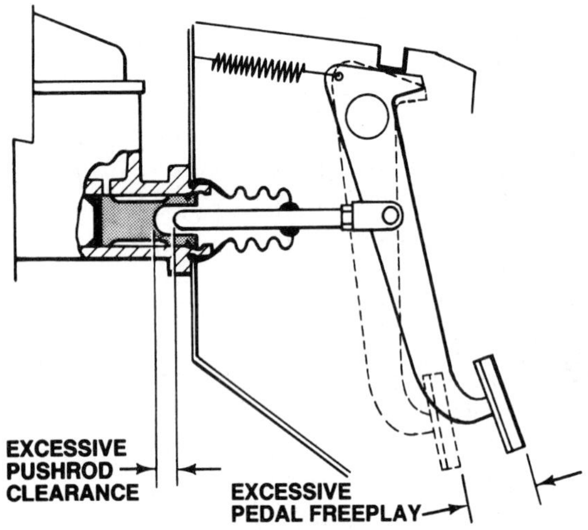

Figure 5-1. Excessive brake pedal freeplay reduces pedal reserve.

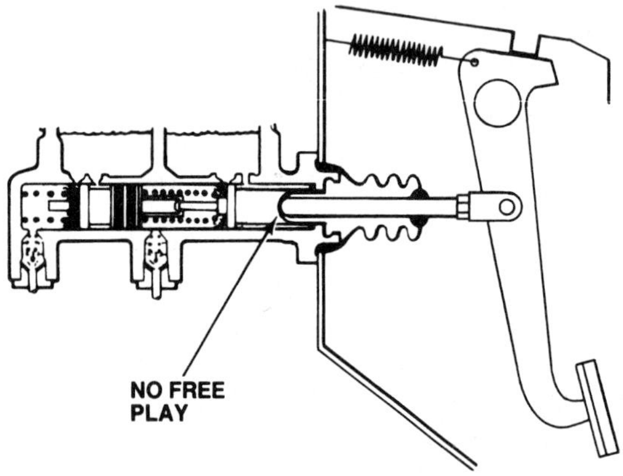

Figure 5-2. If the brake pedal has no freeplay, the brakes may be slightly applied at all times.

Figure 5-3. Change the brake pedal pad for a new one, if needed.

Brake pedal freeplay is determined by the clearance between the pedal pushrod and the master cylinder primary piston. Proper freeplay is important because too much freeplay causes excessive brake pedal travel, figure 5-1. This reduces the pedal height and gives the driver less effective travel, or pedal reserve, with which to compensate for vapor lock or brake fade.

If there is no brake pedal freeplay, figure 5-2, the master cylinder pistons cannot return all the way. When this happens, the primary cup seals come to rest slightly in front of, rather than behind, the compensating ports. With the seals in this position, the brakes are held in a partially applied position that causes brake drag, premature wear of the shoes and pads, and possibly heat fade. In addition, fluid cannot pass between the reservoir and the cylinder bore to compensate for temperature changes; as fluid trapped in the lines expands from the extra heat, it eventually causes the brakes to lock.

With the seals held in front of the compensating ports, there is yet another way the brakes can lock. Every time the brake pedal is released, the one-way pumping action of the master cylinder cup seals allows additional fluid into the hydraulic system. After a certain number of stops (the exact number varies with the brake system) the volume of fluid trapped in the system will become so great that the shoes and pads will be held in solid contact with the drums and rotors.

Pedal Linkage Inspection

The first step when inspecting the brake pedal linkage is to check the rubber pedal pad. If it is worn, replace it with a new part, figure 5-3. Next grasp the pedal pad and move the pedal arm from side to side to check for wear. A small amount of side play is acceptable; larger amounts indicate that the linkage has loose attaching hardware, or missing or worn bushings. Tighten the hardware and replace worn parts as needed. Finally, depress the pedal by hand and release it. If it does not move in and out smoothly without binding, locate the source of the friction and repair as necessary.

Pedal Freeplay Adjustment

Many cars have no provision for brake pedal freeplay adjustment; tolerances in the design allow an acceptable amount of freeplay with any combination of master cylinder and brake pedal assembly. Brake pedal assemblies that do have provisions for freeplay adjustment are set at the factory, and do not normally need adjustment in the field unless the master cylinder is rebuilt or replaced. To check the pedal freeplay:

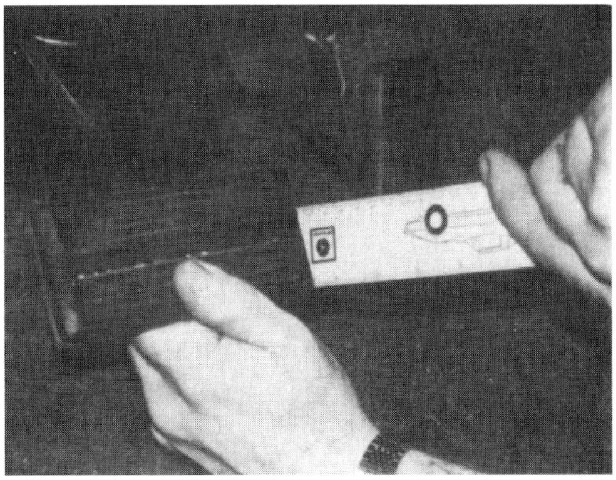

Pedal Assembly and Master Cylinder Service

Figure 5-4. Measuring brake pedal freeplay.

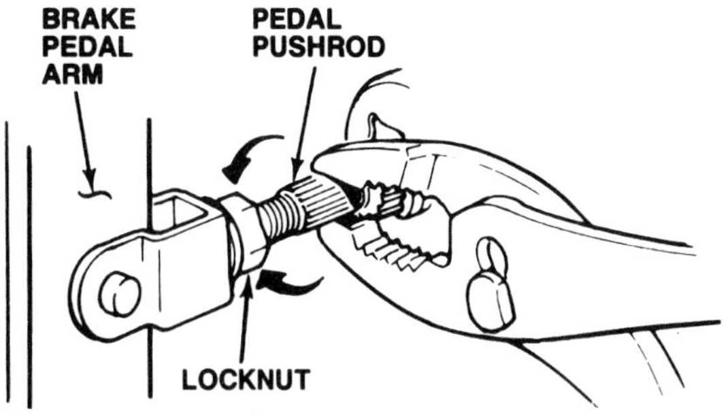

Figure 5-5. Adjusting pedal freeplay at the pedal pushrod.

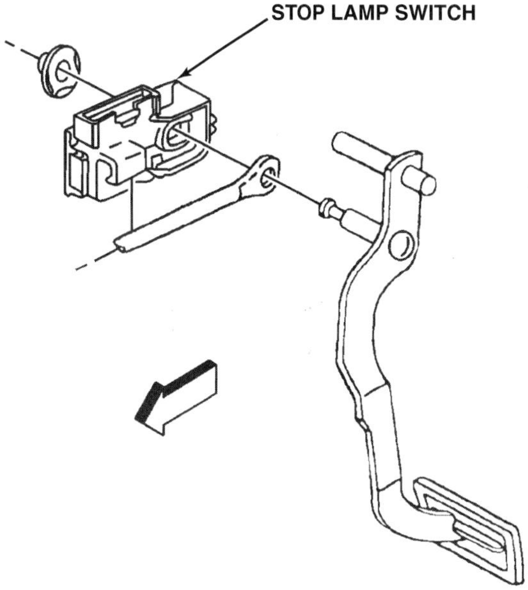

Figure 5-6. This brake lamp switch is attached to the brake pedal linkage and the booster pushrod. (Courtesy of General Motors Corporation, Service and Parts Operations)

1. If the vehicle is equipped with a power booster, pump the brake pedal until the reserve is depleted and the pedal becomes hard.
2. Place a ruler along the axis of brake pedal travel, figure 5-4, and slowly apply the pedal by hand until all of the slack in the linkage is eliminated and a slight resistance is felt.
3. Observe the distance the pedal moved from the relaxed position to the position where resistance is first met; this is the freeplay. Most automakers require that pedal freeplay be between ⅛ and ½ inch (3 and 13 mm). The exact amount varies from one vehicle to another, however, so always check the manufacturer's specification for the car you are servicing.

Freeplay is adjusted by shortening or lengthening the brake pedal pushrod. To adjust the pedal freeplay on most vehicles, loosen the locknut on the pushrod, rotate the pushrod in one direction or the other, figure 5-5, until you obtain the correct freeplay, then tighten the locknut. Some imported vehicles have an eccentric hinge bolt at the end of the pushrod that connects to the brake pedal. To adjust this type of linkage: loosen the hinge bolt locknut, turn the hinge bolt to obtain the proper freeplay, then tighten the locknut.

Many vehicles have a mechanical stoplight switch on the brake pedal linkage, figure 5-6. If adjusting the pedal freeplay affects the relationship between the switch and the linkage, adjust the stoplight switch as described in Chapter 6.

Replacement of the brake pedal or pedal bushings requires the removal of the pedal pivot pin or bolt, figure 5-7. This can be a simple or complex job, depending on the vehicle. It may be necessary to first remove the steering column before the pivot bolt can be removed, figure 5-8. Some vehicles require that the pedal assembly be replaced as a unit, figure 5-9. The brake technician should refer to the available service information for a specific vehicle before tackling a brake pedal replacement.

MASTER CYLINDER INSPECTION AND TESTING

If a problem is suspected in the master cylinder, a detailed external inspection should be made to determine if the cylinder requires additional service. If you determine that additional service is required, an internal inspection should be done to determine whether the cylinder can be rebuilt, or if it must be replaced with a

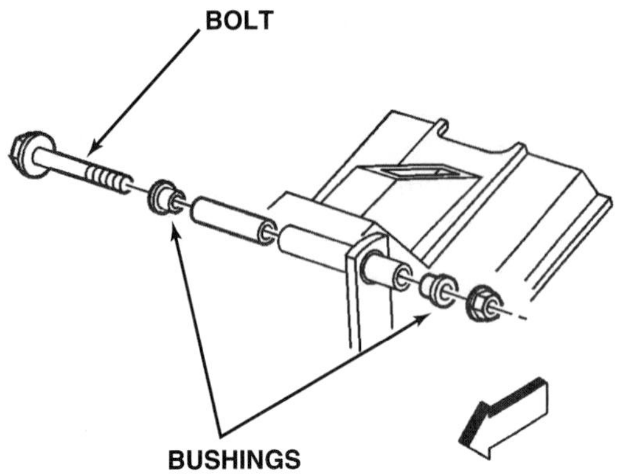

Figure 5-7. After removing the pivot bolt, the nylon bushings can be replaced. (Courtesy of General Motors Corporation, Service and Parts Operations)

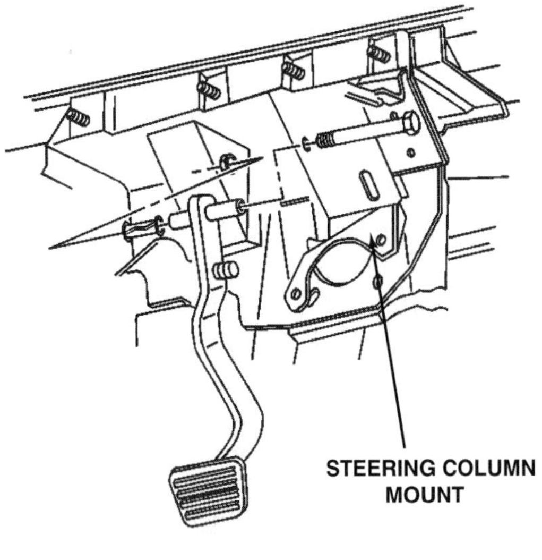

Figure 5-8. The steering column has been removed to gain access to the pivot bolt. (Courtesy of General Motors Corporation, Service and Parts Operations)

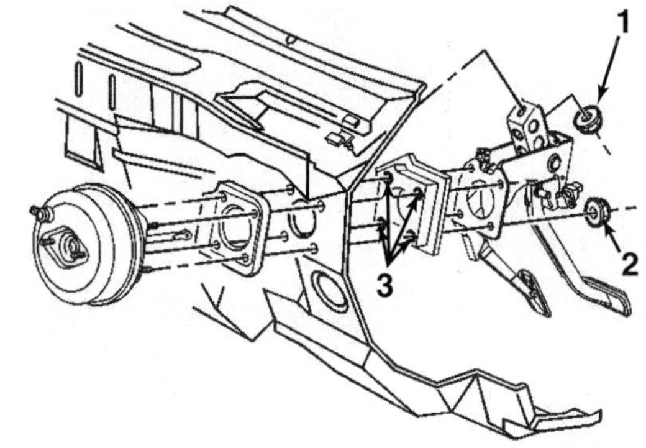

Figure 5-9. On some vehicles, the brake pedal and mounting are replaced as an assembly. (Courtesy of General Motors Corporation, Service and Parts Operations)

new part. External inspections and tests are described below. Internal inspections are covered in the overhaul section later in the chapter.

The two most common reasons master cylinders have to be rebuilt or replaced is that they are leaking fluid externally or fluid is internally bypassing the piston seals. Both of these problems occur as a result of wear and fluid contamination. Rubber seals naturally wear as they slide against the cylinder bore, and the normal buildup of rubber dust and other contaminants in the brake fluid accelerates this process. The metal cylinder bore walls also wear, although at a much slower rate than the seals. Another problem with piston seals is that the rubber they are made from ages with time and becomes inflexible, which reduces its sealing ability.

Fluid contamination occurs when a foreign liquid enters the hydraulic system. If the contaminant is a petroleum-based product, it quickly attacks the rubber seals and causes them to soften and swell to the point where they lose their sealing ability. Cylinders that suffer this type of damage can usually be rebuilt if the sealing surfaces of the bore are in good condition. If the contaminant is moisture, rust and corrosion form on the cylinder bore and destroy the sealing surface. Although this process takes longer than the damage caused by improper fluids, it is much more likely to require cylinder replacement.

Master Cylinder Inspection

To inspect a master cylinder, wipe the fluid reservoir cover clean, and remove it from the master cylinder. Hold the reservoir cover up to the light and make sure the vent holes are open. The holes must be open to maintain atmospheric pressure above the fluid in the reservoir.

Check the condition of the reservoir cover diaphragm seal, figure 5-10, a seal in good condition has no cuts or tears, and the rubber is firm and not distorted in any way. A cut or torn diaphragm allows the brake fluid to absorb moisture from out of the atmosphere and must be replaced. A swollen or misshapen diaphragm is a sign that the brake fluid is contaminated, probably with some type of petroleum-base liquid. In this case, you will have to disassemble the entire brake system,

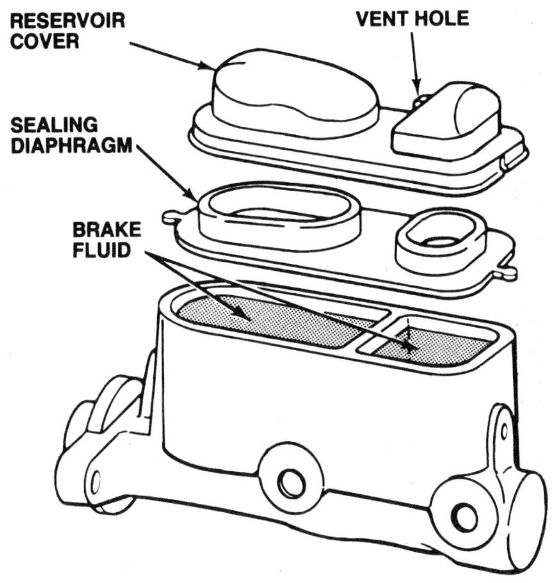

Pedal Assembly and Master Cylinder Service

Figure 5-10. The vent holes, diaphragm seal, and fluid level can all be inspected when the reservoir cover is removed.

flush it clean of contaminated fluid, and rebuild the hydraulic components using all-new rubber parts.

Next, check the brake fluid level as covered in Chapter 2 a low fluid level may be caused simply by brake lining wear, but it can also be a sign of leaks in the hydraulic system. Inspect the outside of the master cylinder for leaks, paying particular attention to the fluid outlet fittings. If the cylinder has a plastic fluid reservoir, check the seals where the reservoir joins to the cylinder body.

On vehicles without a power booster, reach under the dashboard and squeeze the rubber boot at the back of the master cylinder to check for fluid leakage from the rear seal. If the car is equipped with a vacuum-assisted power booster, look for fluid stains on the front of the booster below the master cylinder. If you suspect a leak but there are no external signs of one, you will have to loosen the master cylinder mounting bolts and pull the cylinder away from the booster to check for leaks. If a fluid leak is fairly large, or the vacuum supply hose attaches near the bottom of the booster power chamber, you can sometimes remove the hose and inspect inside it for signs of brake fluid that has leaked from the rear master cylinder seal.

Master Cylinder Testing

A visual inspection checks the external aspects of the master cylinder; however, there are also special tests than can pinpoint whether a particular problem is within the master cylinder, or elsewhere in brake system. The tests below apply to most of the master cylinders now on the market. However, certain cylinders have special features that require unique test procedures, or special caution when performing otherwise routine tests. If you are unfamiliar with a particular master cylinder, consult the factory shop manual for any special instructions that may apply to that design.

Quick-take-up Valve Test

The quick-take-up (QTU) valve is a special fluid control valve installed in the rear chamber of the fluid reservoir on some General Motors and Ford master cylinders. The QTU valve regulates the flow of fluid between the reservoir and master cylinder bore, and enables the cylinder to move the large initial volume of fluid needed to take up the clearances in the low-drag brake calipers used with this type of master cylinder.

There is no direct method of testing the QTU valve, however, a problem with the valve may be indicated by a couple of common brake system problems. For example, excessive pedal travel will result if fluid is bypassing the valve when the brakes are first applied; check for a damaged, missing, or unseated QTU valve. If the brake pedal returns slowly when the brakes are released, the QTU valve may be clogged so that fluid flow out of the cylinder bore is restricted. If no other cause for these problems can be found, remove the valve, and clean or replace it as needed.

Compensating Port Test

The compensating port test is directly related to brake pedal freeplay as discussed earlier in the chapter. If there is no pedal freeplay, the compensating ports in the master cylinder may be closed. When this happens, fluid cannot flow from the cylinder bore back into the reservoir, and the brakes are always partially applied. The results are brake drag, premature wear of the shoes and pads, brake fade, and possibly brake lockup.

The compensating port test can be used to determine if the ports are open; however, you must use special caution when performing this test. If the brake pedal is not applied *slowly*, fluid can be pumped from the ports with enough velocity to spray onto the underside of the hood. This can damage the vehicle finish, or cause personal injury. Wear proper eye protection while performing this test, and never put your face directly over the master cylinder reservoir.

To check if the compensating ports are open, remove the reservoir cover and have an assistant *slowly* apply the brake pedal while you observe the fluid in the reservoir. As the pedal is applied, a small amount of fluid should be forced out of the cylinder bore through the compensating port in each chamber of the reservoir; this causes a small jet or spurt of fluid to appear on the surface of the brake fluid, figure 5-11.

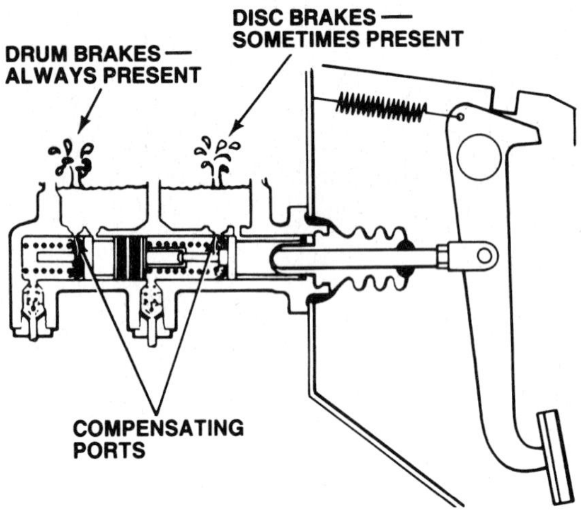

Figure 5-11. Spurts of fluid in the reservoir as the brakes are applied indicate that the compensating ports are open.

The fluid spurt in a reservoir that serves only disc brakes will generally be somewhat smaller than the spurt in a reservoir that serves only drum brakes. In some cases, a spurt may not be present at all. This occurs because the caliper pistons, which are held in place by the relatively light tension of their O-ring seals, will start to move under much less pressure than the wheel cylinder pistons, which must work against the much higher tension of the brake shoe return springs.

When performing the compensating port test on a QTU master cylinder, there are some special points and precautions to keep in mind. In these cylinders, the QTU valve initially restricts fluid flow through the rear compensating port, so a jet of fluid will not appear in the reservoir. However, once the clearance in the brake system is taken up and pressure reaches 70 to 100 psi, the QTU valve check ball unseats and a large quantity of fluid is pumped into the reservoir very rapidly. This can create a safety hazard, so have your assistant apply the brake pedal very lightly (perhaps by hand) so the opening pressure of the QTU valve is not exceeded.

If fluid spurts do not appear when the brakes are applied, the compensating ports are clogged or the pedal freeplay is too tight. Check and adjust the pedal freeplay as described earlier. If spurts still do not appear, and the car has manual brakes, the master cylinder will have to be removed and disassembled to determine why the compensating ports are obstructed. If spurts still do not appear, and the car has a vacuum power booster, back off the master cylinder mounting bolts approximately ⅛ inch (3 mm) and repeat the compensating port test. If the spurts now appear, the power booster output pushrod must be adjusted because it is holding the master cylinder in the applied position. To make this adjustment, you must remove the master cylinder and use a special gauge. See Chapter 11 for details.

External Leak Test

A master cylinder reservoir that is low on fluid, or has run dry and allowed air to enter the hydraulic system, can be an indication of two things: normal brake lining wear, or a fluid leak in the brake hydraulic system. Major external leaks in the hydraulic system are usually obvious. If the leak is at the back of the master cylinder and the car has manual brakes, there will be fluid on the floor inside the car, and an odor of brake fluid in the passenger compartment. If the leak is from a brake line, wheel cylinder, or caliper, there will usually be fluid stains on the backing plate, inside the wheel, or elsewhere under the car.

Minor fluid leaks are not always easy to spot, however. Most cars today have power boosters that can conceal an external leak from the back of the master cylinder. And, because brake fluid is water soluble, small amounts of brake fluid from minor leaks under the car can easily be washed away by car washes or travel on wet roads. Minor wheel cylinder leaks often do not pass enough fluid for the fluid to become visible outside the drum. Finally, a few cars route portions of the brake lines through concealed areas of the car interior, such as under the rear seat, where a leak may not be immediately apparent.

The external leak test is used to check for fluid leakage out of the hydraulic system. To perform the external leak test:

1. Fill the master cylinder reservoir at least half full of brake fluid, and note the exact level.
2. If the reservoir has run dry and air has entered the hydraulic system, bleed the brakes before continuing with the test.
3. Apply the brake pedal several times. If there is a leak in the system, the pedal will go at least half way to the floor under firm pressure.
4. Check the fluid level in the master cylinder reservoir. If the level has dropped, there is an external leak from the system.

Internal Leak Test

In addition to external leaks, the brake system can also suffer internal leakage in the master cylinder. In normal operation, brake fluid in front of the master cylinder piston primary cup seals is forced into the hydraulic system. However, if the seals cannot contain the pressure created, fluid bypasses around the outside of the seals, figure 5-12, creating an internal leak. Because the volume of the brake hydraulic system is reduced as the master cylinder pistons move forward,

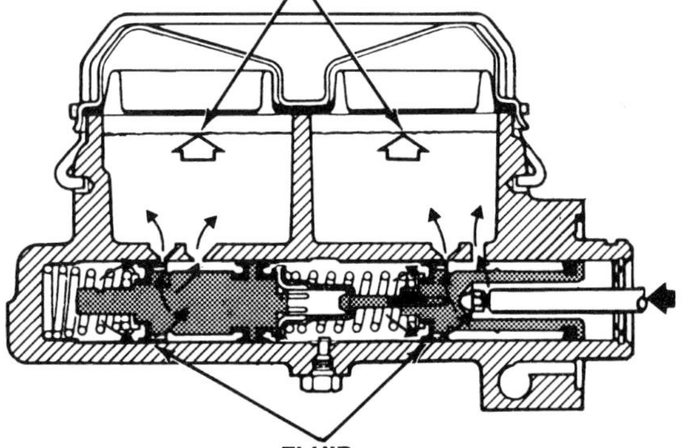

Pedal Assembly and Master Cylinder Service

Figure 5-12. Internal leakage past the piston seals causes the fluid level in the reservoir to rise as the brakes are applied.

Figure 5-13. The first step to removing a master cylinder is to disconnect the fluid lines.

fluid displaced past the seals escapes through the compensating and replenishing ports, causing the fluid level in the master cylinder reservoir to rise.

The internal-leak, or bypass, test checks the sealing ability of the master cylinder piston primary seals. This test is usually performed if there is no indication of an external leak in the brake hydraulic system but the brake warning light is illuminated. To perform the internal leak test:

1. Fill the master cylinder reservoir at least half full of brake fluid.
2. Have an assistant slowly apply and release the brake pedal as you observe the fluid level in the reservoir.
3. If the fluid level rises as the pedal is applied and falls when the pedal is released, fluid is bypassing the seals in the master cylinder.

Another way to test for an internal leak is to hold a constant, firm pressure on the brake pedal for approximately one minute. If the pedal sinks slowly toward the floor and there are no signs of external leaks, fluid is bypassing the master cylinder seals. This test is effective for diagnosing minor internal leakage because the extended time that pressure is held on the brake pedal allows enough fluid to bypass the seals so that the leak can be detected at the brake pedal.

MASTER CYLINDER REPLACEMENT

When an external inspection reveals a problem with the master cylinder, the cylinder will have to be removed from the car for further service. To remove a master cylinder:

1. Disconnect the brake lines from the master cylinder fluid outlets with a flare-nut wrench, figure 5-13. To prevent fluid spillage, plug the outlets with plastic or rubber plugs available from the aftermarket.
2. If the cylinder is so equipped, detach the wiring harness connector from the fluid level warning switch on the reservoir, or the pressure differential switch on the master cylinder body.
3. If the car has manual brakes, determine if the brake pedal pushrod is mechanically connected to the master cylinder. If so, disconnect the pushrod from the brake pedal linkage.
4. Unbolt the master cylinder from the firewall or the power booster, figure 5-14, and remove it from the car. Keep the cylinder upright to prevent fluid spillage, figure 5-15.

With the cylinder off the car, make an internal inspection immediately to determine whether the cylinder can be rebuilt. This procedure is covered in the overhaul section later in the chapter. When the rebuilt, or new replacement, master cylinder is ready, install it on the car as follows:

1. Bench bleed the master cylinder as described in Chapter 3.
2. If the vehicle has a vacuum power booster, and the master cylinder was not returning all the way, check the adjustment of the booster output pushrod as described in Chapter 11.
3. Install the master cylinder on the firewall or power booster, and tighten the mounting bolts to the proper torque.

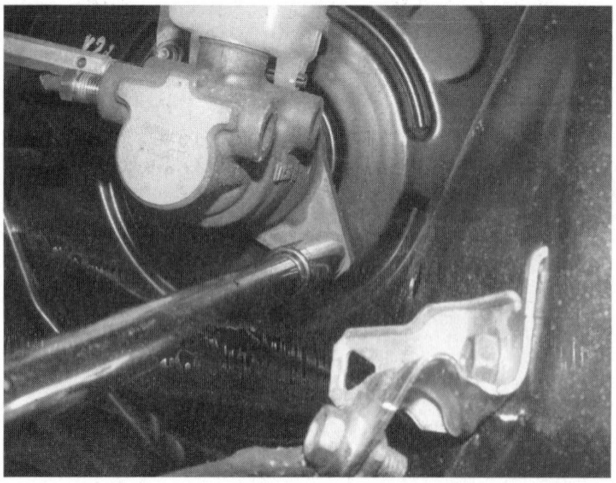

Figure 5-14. Remove the nuts and washers from the master cylinder mounting flange.

Figure 5-15. Carefully remove the master cylinder from the brake booster.

4. Connect the brake lines to the master cylinder fluid outlets and tighten them with a flare-nut wrench.
5. If the cylinder is so equipped, attach the wiring harness connector to the fluid level warning switch on the reservoir, or the pressure differential switch on the master cylinder body.
6. On cars with manual brakes, connect the brake pedal pushrod to the pedal linkage if it was detached when the cylinder was removed. Check and adjust the pedal freeplay and mechanical stoplight switch as described above and in Chapter 6.
7. Check the factory shop manual for the vehicle manufacturer's recommendations on brake bleeding. If the brake pedal feels high and firm, the brake system may not require additional bleeding. If the brake pedal feels spongy, bleed the master cylinder on the car. If the pedal remains spongy, or the master cylinder was replaced as part of a complete brake system overhaul, bleed the entire system using one of the methods discussed in Chapter 3.

MASTER CYLINDER OVERHAUL

Once an external inspection has revealed that the master cylinder will require further service, the next step is to disassemble the cylinder and determine whether it can be rebuilt or if it must be replaced. In the past, most cylinders were rebuilt and returned to service. Today, the trend is to replace defective cylinders.

There are several reasons hydraulic cylinders are rebuilt less often today. First, most master cylinders have aluminum bodies whose bore *cannot* be honed; this makes overhaul impossible in many cases. Second, hydraulic cylinder overhaul, particularly on dual master cylinders, requires a fair amount of time and skill on the part of the technician. At today's shop labor rates, it is often less expensive for the customer in the long run if the cylinder is replaced. Finally, considering the brake system's critical part in vehicle safety and the large number of lawsuits filed in recent years, cylinder replacement can be more appealing because it places a portion of the liability for the repair job on the manufacturer of the replacement part.

Overhaul Kits

The job of overhauling a master cylinder involves replacing all of the cylinder components that are subject to wear. These parts are purchased in an overhaul or rebuild kit, figure 5-16. A rebuild kit will usually not include every part in the cylinder; the exact contents vary based on the supplier and the cost of the kit.

All kits contain the rubber parts most likely to wear, but better kits contain added items such as a wiper boot with special grease to seal and lubricate it, tubing seats for the fluid outlets, assembly lubricant, and primary and secondary pistons with return springs. The best kits come with the seals already installed on the pistons; this is especially helpful because installing these seals can be difficult, and the seals are easily damaged. Certain special parts, such as QTU valves and reservoir cover diaphragms, are never included in a rebuild kit and must be obtained separately.

When rebuilding a master cylinder, it is helpful to know beforehand exactly what parts you need and what parts are included in the rebuild kit. This ensures that you will have everything available you need to complete the job. It also saves you having to clean old parts that will be replaced anyway.

Pedal Assembly and Master Cylinder Service

Figure 5-16. A typical master cylinder rebuild kit.

Cylinder Internal Inspection

Overhauling a master cylinder involves replacing the parts most likely to wear. Essentially, this means replacing everything but the cylinder body and, in some cases, the metal pistons. This means that to determine whether a master cylinder can be rebuilt, you must inspect the condition of the cylinder body, and the cylinder bore in particular.

If the master cylinder is equipped with bleeder screws, the first inspection step is always to attempt to loosen the screws with a bleeder wrench. It is not unusual for bleeder screws to become rusted or corroded in place so they cannot be removed. These "frozen" bleeder screws are particularly common in aluminum cylinders where the dissimilar metal of the steel bleeder screw causes electrolysis. In most cases, cylinders with frozen bleeder screws should be replaced. The exceptions are when a replacement cylinder is unavailable, or its cost is so high that the time and effort spent on bleeder screw removal can be justified.

Once you are sure the bleeder screws are free, disassemble the cylinder and wipe the bore clean. Shine a light into the cylinder and inspect the bore. If the cylinder is made of cast iron and the bore is in good condition, or only lightly scratched, pitted, scored, or rusted, the cylinder can probably be honed and rebuilt. If the bore is deeply scored, the cylinder must be replaced. If deep scores are honed out, so much metal is removed that the cylinder bore becomes oversize and the piston cup seals will not seal properly because they lose tension against the cylinder wall. Also, if a cast-iron cylinder shows any sign of having been rebuilt before, such as honing marks in the bore or nonstock rubber parts, it is best to replace the cylinder rather than risk another rebuild.

If an aluminum master cylinder is scratched, pitted, scored, or corroded in any way, the cylinder must be replaced. Aluminum cylinders cannot be honed because they have a wear-resistant, anodized finish. Honing would cut through the anodizing and the resulting bare aluminum finish would corrode very rapidly and be too rough for good sealing.

Cylinder Honing

Honing is a procedure in which abrasive stones are rotated inside the cylinder bore to remove a small amount of metal, along with any scratches, pitting, scuff marks, and rust. Honing restores the sealing surface for the piston seals; however, the new finish is never as smooth as the "bearingized" surface of a new cylinder. As a result, the cup seals in a rebuilt cylinder that has been honed wear faster than those in a replacement cylinder. Many shops today will only rebuild a master cylinder if the bore does not need to be honed. In addition, some manufacturers recommend against honing the cylinders on their cars. Check the factory shop manual for the exact recommendations on the car you are servicing.

If the bore of a cast-iron master cylinder can be honed, follow this procedure:

1. Clamp the cylinder in a vise by its mounting flange. Do not clamp on the cylinder body or the bore may be distorted.
2. Select a suitably sized cylinder hone and chuck it in a drill motor.
3. Lubricate the cylinder bore with brake fluid, and insert the hone into the bore, figure 5-17.
4. Operate the drill motor at approximately 500 rpm, and move the hone back and forth with smooth, even strokes.
5. Keep the bore lubricated with brake fluid, and hone for approximately 10 seconds. Let the hone come to a full stop, then remove it from the cylinder bore.
6. Wipe the bore clean with a rag, and check the surface finish; it should be clean and free of rust, corrosion, and scratches. The hone should also have created an even crosshatch pattern as shown in figure 5-18.
7. If necessary, repeat the honing process for another 10 seconds. If the bore does not clean up after several repetitions of this procedure, replace the cylinder.

After the bore is honed, thoroughly clean the cylinder with a non-petroleum-base brake cleaning solvent or soap and water to remove all residue and grit.

Cylinder Bore Measurement

After the cylinder has been honed, you must measure the size of the cylinder bore to make sure that too much metal has not been removed.

Figure 5-17. Lightly hone the cylinder using fine grit stones lubricated with brake fluid.

Figure 5-19. Using a feeler gauge to check cylinder bore to piston clearance.

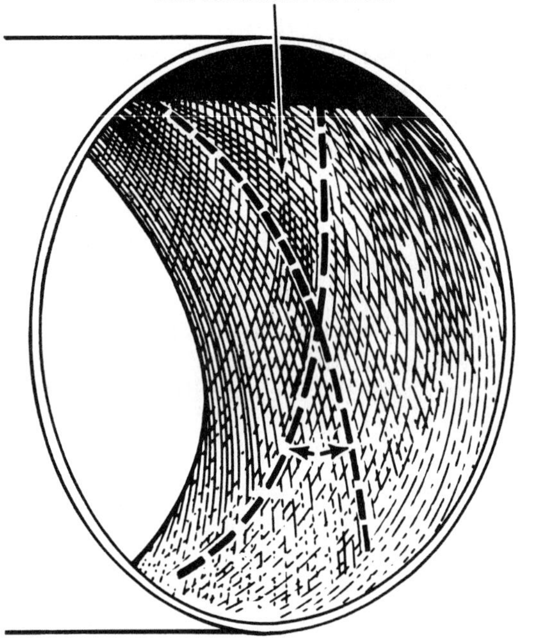

Figure 5-18. Proper honing will leave an even crosshatch pattern in the cylinder bore.

To check the bore using a feeler gauge, place a narrow (¼ inch or 6 mm wide) strip of .006 inch (.15 mm) feeler gauge inside the bore. Attempt to insert one of the cylinder pistons into the bore with the feeler gauge in place, figure 5-19; if the piston will fit, the bore is oversize and the cylinder must be replaced. Traditionally, most manufacturers have allowed up to .006 inch (.15 mm) of piston clearance; however, many newer cylinders with smaller diameters require tighter clearances. If you are unsure of the proper specification, consult the shop manual for the vehicle you are servicing.

MASTER CYLINDER OVERHAUL PROCEDURES

The following pages provide step-by-step overhaul procedures for a General Motors quick-take-up master cylinder and a typical dual-piston master cylinder. While these are not the only cylinders in use today, they are representative of those found on many vehicles. Before beginning any overhaul, read completely through the procedure to obtain a better idea of the entire job.

The first procedure covers the General Motors aluminum QTU master cylinder. This master cylinder is typical of the step-bore-type master cylinder used by many manufacturers. The master cylinder has a built-in pressure differential switch and dual proportioning valves that thread directly into the fluid outlets to the rear brakes.

The second procedure covers a standard-bore, dual-piston master cylinder and is of a type used by many vehicle manufacturers. It has a removable reservoir, a fluid level switch, and proportioning valves that are part of the master cylinder body.

Pedal Assembly and Master Cylinder Service

GENERAL MOTORS ALUMINUM QTU MASTER CYLINDER OVERHAUL

1. Remove the master cylinder reservoir cover and pour the brake fluid into a drain pan.

2. Clamp the cylinder in a vise by its mounting flange, and position a drain pan under it to catch any fluid released during disassembly.

3. Remove the fluid reservoir with a pry bar. Do not remove the quick-take-up valve from the cylinder body unless it is being replaced.

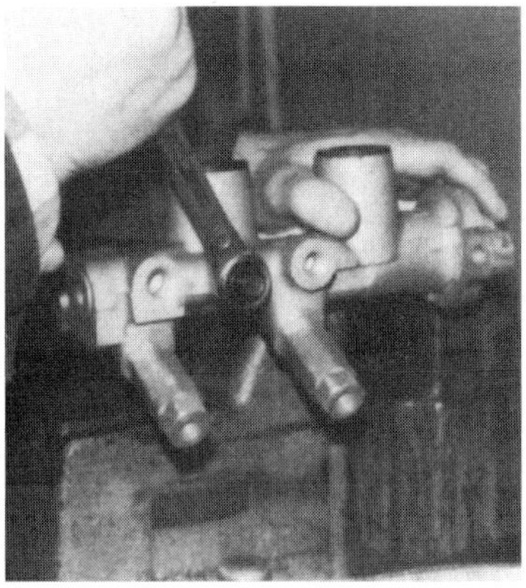

4. Unscrew and remove the pressure differential switch.

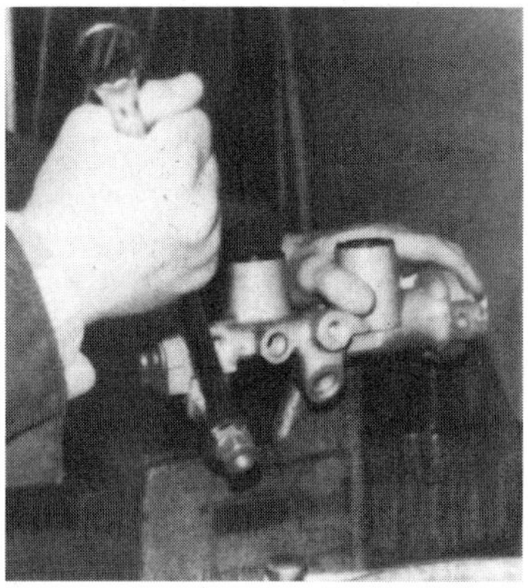

5. Unscrew and remove the two proportioning valves.

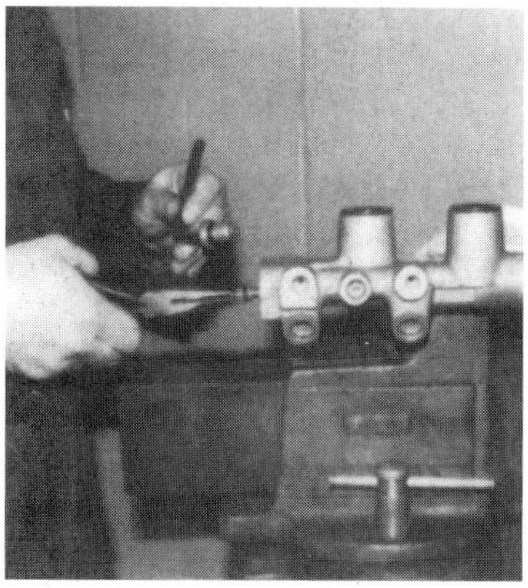

6. Unscrew the Allen-head plug and remove the pressure differential switch piston.

7. Depress the primary piston and remove the retaining lock ring from its groove at the open end of the cylinder.

8. Release the primary piston and allow return spring pressure to force it from the bore.

9. Remove the cylinder from the vise and strike its open end against a wood block to remove the secondary piston, spring retainer, and spring.

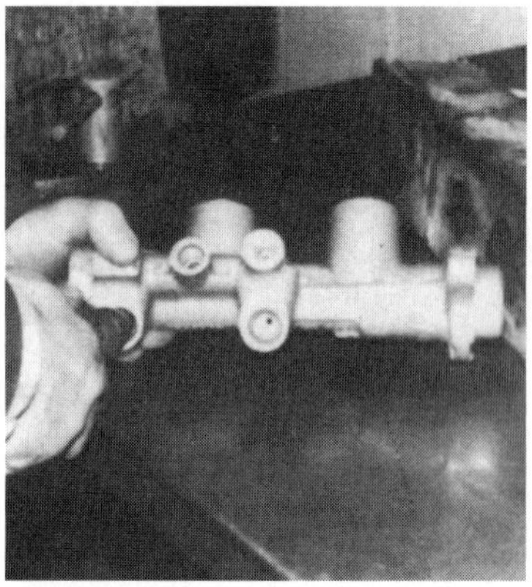

10. To remove frozen pistons, place the open end of the cylinder against a wood block, then apply compressed air to one forward fluid outlet while blocking the other.

11. Inspect the cylinder bore, and replace the cylinder if any damage is visible.

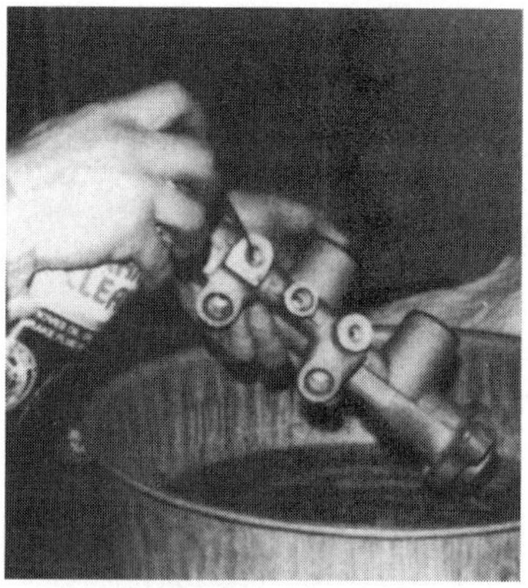

12. Thoroughly clean the master cylinder body, bore, and passages with a non-petroleum-base brake cleaner.

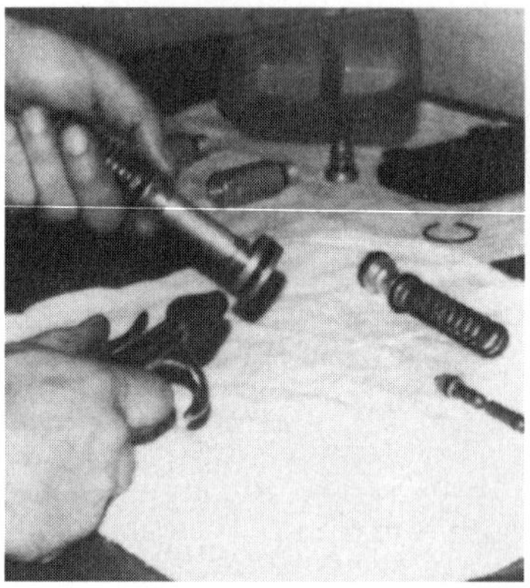

13. Thoroughly clean and dry the cylinder internal parts, including those from the rebuild kit, and lay them out on a clean shop towel.

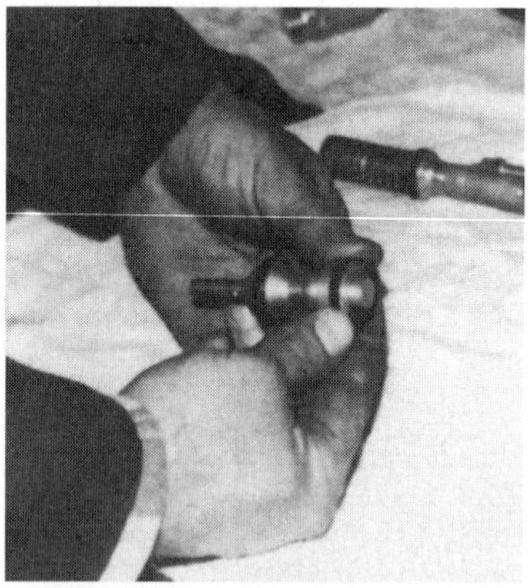

14. Lubricate the new seals with brake fluid or assembly lube and install them on the secondary piston.

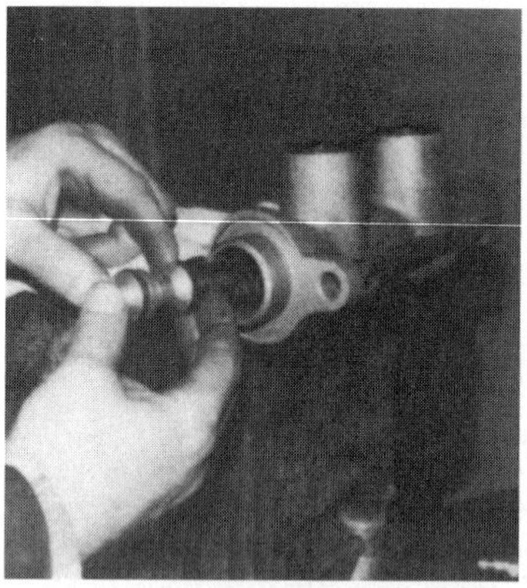

15. Lubricate the secondary piston assembly with brake fluid or assembly lube and install the spring, spring retainer, and piston into the cylinder bore.

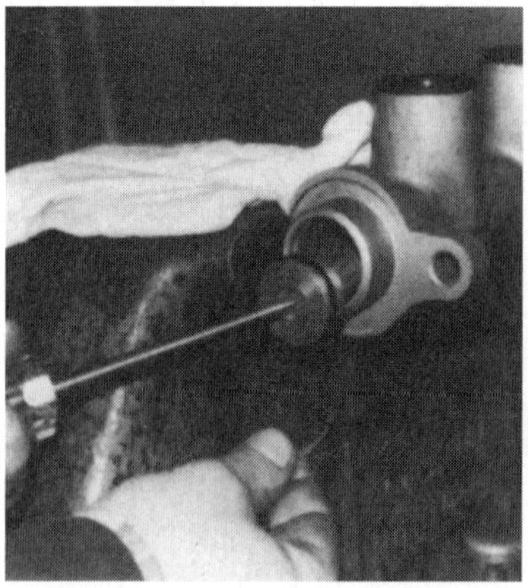

16. Lubricate the primary piston assembly with brake fluid or assembly lube and install the piston into the cylinder bore.

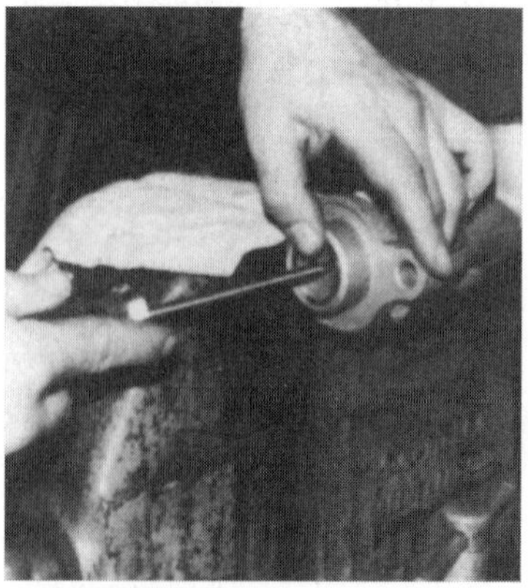

17. Depress the primary piston and install the retaining lock ring into its groove at the open end of the cylinder.

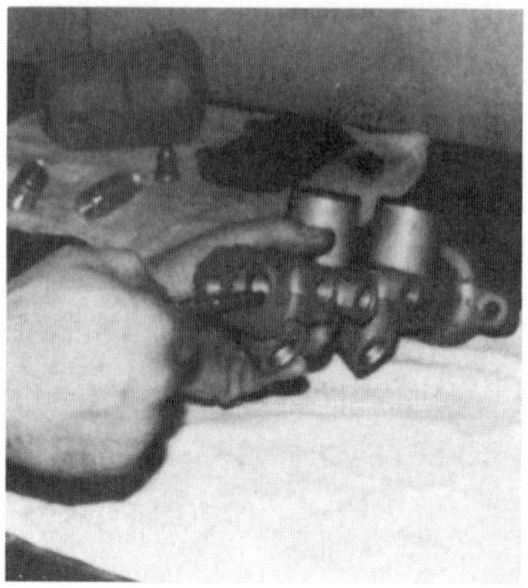

18. Lubricate the pressure differential switch piston with brake fluid or assembly lube and install it into the master cylinder body.

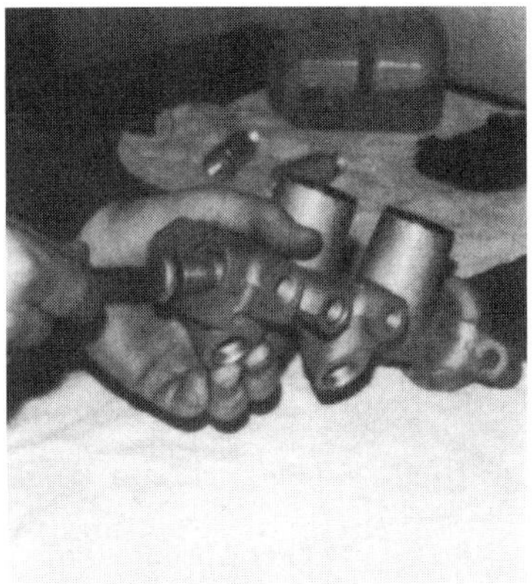

Pedal Assembly and Master Cylinder Service

97

19. Install a new O-ring on the Allen-head plug, and screw the plug into the cylinder body. Torque the plug to 40–140 inch-pounds (4.5–16 Nm).

20. Install a new O-ring on the pressure differential switch, and screw the switch into the cylinder body. Torque the switch to 15–50 inch-pounds (1.7–5.6 Nm).

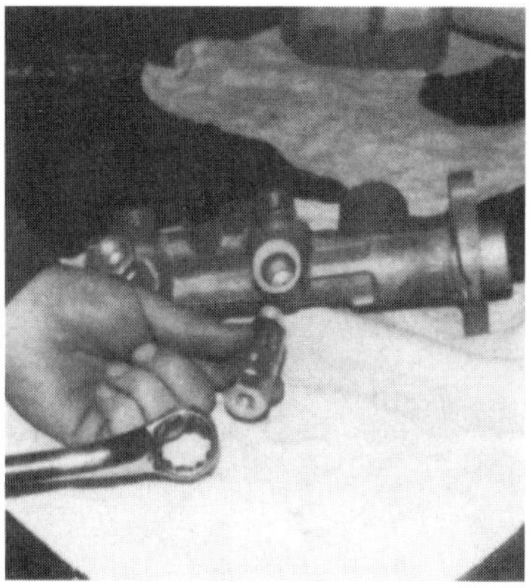

21. Install the proportioning valves onto the master cylinder body. The valves may be aluminum or steel. Never mix the two types; use either two aluminum or two steel valves.

22. Lubricate the new fluid reservoir grommets, and install them into the master cylinder body.

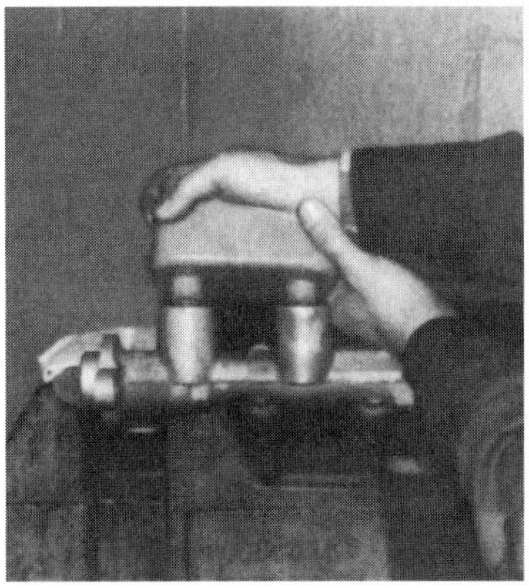

23. Install the fluid reservoir into grommets at an angle, then rock it back and forth under pressure until it is seated.

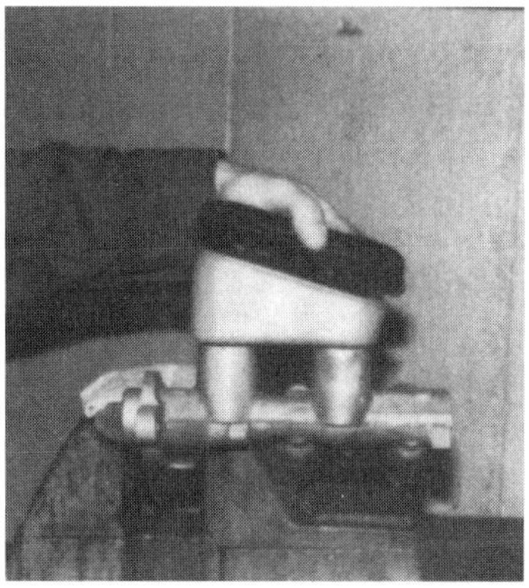

24. Install the reservoir cover and diaphragm on the master cylinder.

DUAL-PISTON MASTER CYLINDER OVERHAUL

1. Drive out the roll pins that secure the reservoir to the master cylinder.

2. Remove the reservoir.

3. Use a small pick or screwdriver to remove the piston retaining ring.

4. Tap the cylinder on a block of wood to get the pistons to slide out.

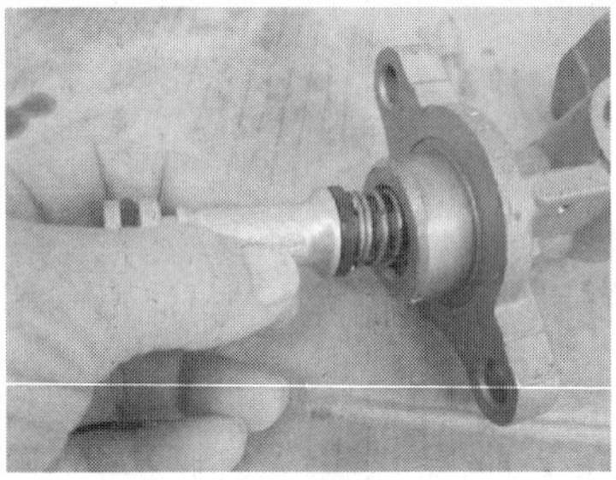

5. Remove the primary piston and spring.

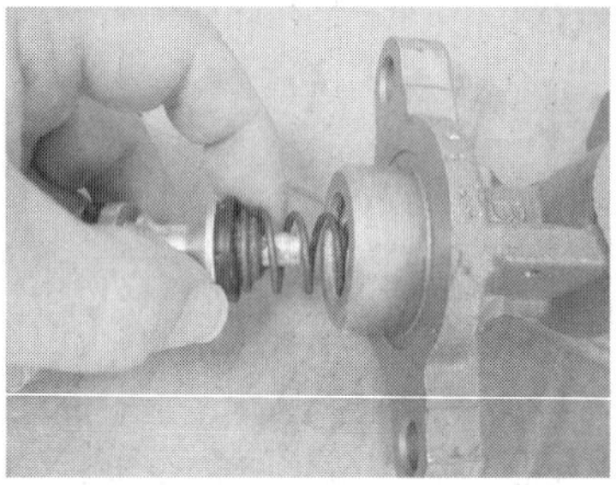

6. Remove the secondary piston and spring.

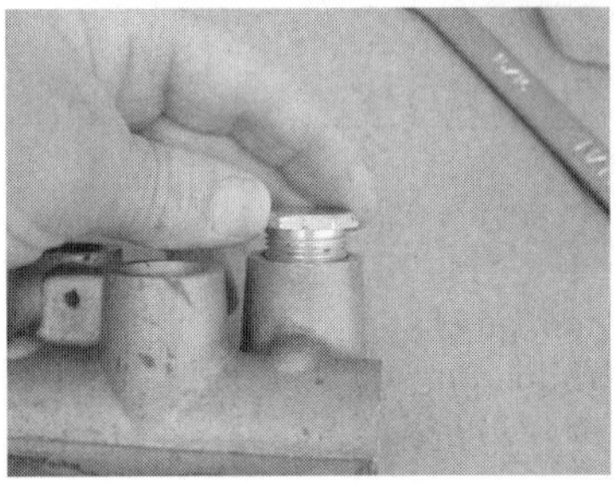

7. Remove the proportioning valve cap, and . . .

8. . . . remove the proportioning valve.

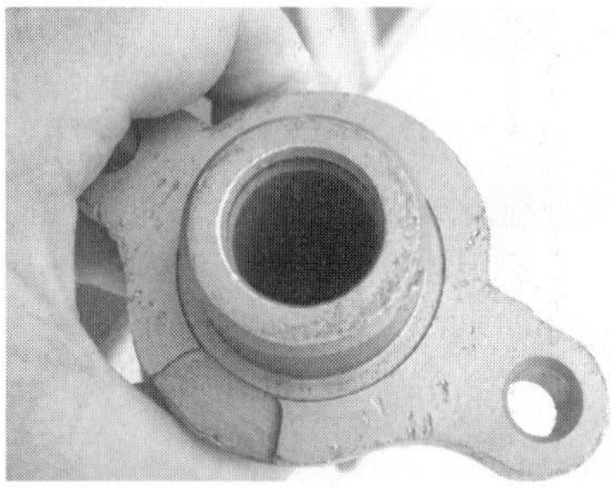

9. Throughly clean the master cylinder, and inspect it for any damage. This cylinder cannot be honed, so any badly worn or corroded cylinder will have to be replaced.

10. The disassembled master cylinder.

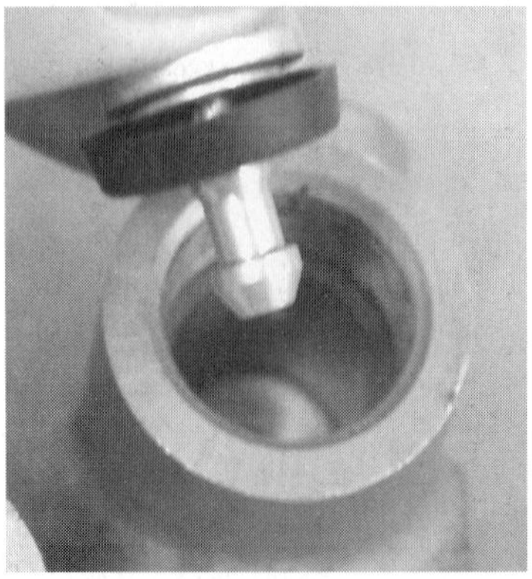

11. Install new seals on the proportioning valve and install it.

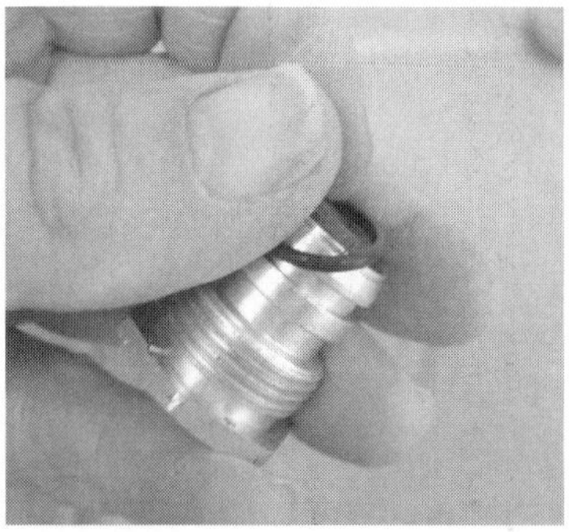

12. Install new O-rings on the proportioning valve cap.

Pedal Assembly and Master Cylinder Service

13. Install and torque the proportioning valve caps.

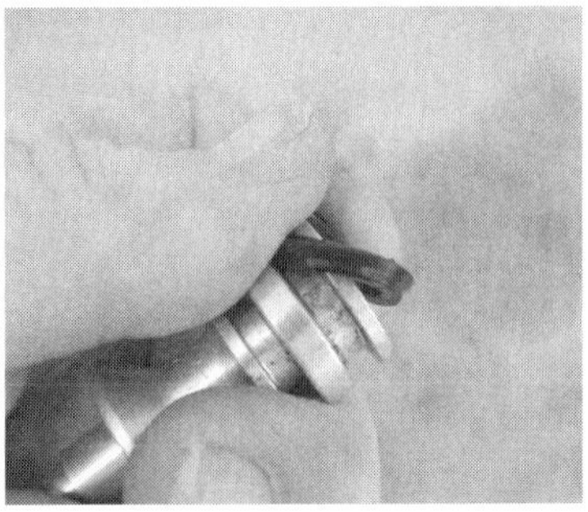

14. Install new sealing cups on the primary and secondary pistons.

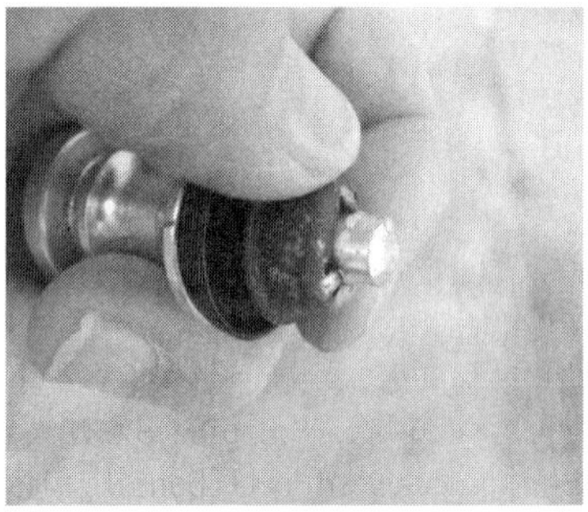

15. Install the spring seat, if used.

16. Lubricate the cylinder and new seals with clean brake fluid, and install the pistons and springs.

17. While holding the primary piston down, install the retaining ring.

18. Install the reservoir and tap in the roll pins to hold it in place.

6
Hydraulic Valves and Electrical Component Service

OBJECTIVES

Upon completion and review of this chapter, you will be able to:

- Locate and identify metering valves, proportioning valves, and combination valves.
- Test the operation of the metering valve.
- Test the operation of the proportioning valve using pressure gauges.
- Replace a metering or proportioning valve.
- Check and adjust a height-sensing proportioning valve.
- Use basic electrical troubleshooting tools.
- Test a stoplight (brake light) switch.
- Replace and adjust a stoplight switch.
- Test the proper operation of the red brake warning lamp.
- Check the parking brake warning light operation.
- Test the proper operation of the fluid level warning system.
- Test the proper operation of the pressure differential warning switch, if equipped.

INTRODUCTION

Hydraulic valves in the brake system ensure that brake fluid reaches the wheel friction assemblies at the correct time and/or pressure. A faulty valve can cause premature or excessively hard brake application that can lock the wheels and lead to an accident. The first portion of this chapter describes the testing and replacement of hydraulic valves.

Brake system electrical components consist primarily of the stoplights and system warning lights, along with the switches that control them. The second part of this chapter details the testing, adjustment, and replacement of these parts. Brake electrical diagnosis and repair related to antilock brake systems (ABS) are covered in Chapter 12 and Chapter 13.

HYDRAULIC CONTROL VALVE SERVICE

The hydraulic control valves used in the brake system are the metering valve and the proportioning valve. These are used to regulate the timing and amount of hydraulic pressure supplied to the wheel friction assemblies. The control valves are usually located on or near the master cylinder, and can be separate valves or joined together into a combination valve. Height-sensing proportioning valves are located under the car near the rear axle.

Hydraulic control valve service includes procedures for testing and replacement. With the exception of certain height-sensing proportioning valves, neither metering valves nor proportioning valves can be repaired or adjusted; leaking or faulty valves must be replaced. If the defective valve is part of a combination valve, the entire valve assembly must be replaced.

Metering Valve Tests

The metering valve withholds hydraulic pressure from the front disc brakes until the shoes of the rear drum brakes have contacted the drums. A faulty metering valve will usually allow the front brakes to apply early and lock prematurely, especially on slick pavement. A metering valve can also seize shut and prevent any pressure from reaching the front brakes, although this is an uncommon type of failure.

If front brake locking causes you to suspect a faulty metering valve, give the valve a visual inspection. Check around the rubber boot at the valve stem for leakage, figure 6-1; a trace of moisture is normal, but an excessive amount indicates a defective valve. Have an assistant apply the brake pedal while you watch the valve stem. As pressure to the front brakes builds, the valve stem should move. If it does not, replace the valve. More accurate metering valve tests can be performed in two ways, with a pressure bleeder or with pressure guages, as explained below.

Pressure Bleeder Metering Valve Test

A brake system pressure bleeder can be used to test a metering valve because the pressure provided by the bleeder is sufficient to close the valve, but not high enough to reopen it. To test a metering valve with a pressure bleeder:

1. Connect the pressure bleeder to the master cylinder as described in Chapter 3, and charge the bleeder to 40 psi (275 kPa).
2. *Do not* disarm the metering valve with an override tool.
3. Pressurize the brake system with the power bleeder, and open a front brake bleeder screw. If fluid flows from the bleeder, the metering valve is not closing properly and must be replaced.

Pressure Gauge Metering Valve Test

The most precise method of testing metering valve operation is to use a pair of pressure gauges to measure the actual closing and opening points of the valve. This test requires an assistant to apply the brake pedal, two gauges that read from 0 to a minimum of 500 psi (0 to 3450 kPa), and the appropriate fittings to attach the gauges to the hydraulic system. To test a metering valve using gauges:

1. Tee Gauge 1 into the brake line from the master cylinder to the metering valve, figure 6-2, so the gauge does not block the flow of fluid to the metering valve.
2. Connect Gauge 2 to one of the metering valve outlets leading to the front brakes.
3. Have an assistant slowly apply the brake pedal while you observe both gauges.
4. If the metering valve is working properly, the gauge readings will rise at the same rate, figure

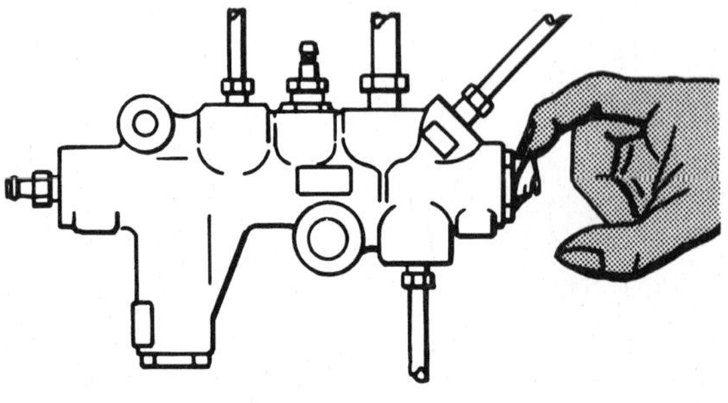

Figure 6-1. Visual inspection of a metering valve for leakage.

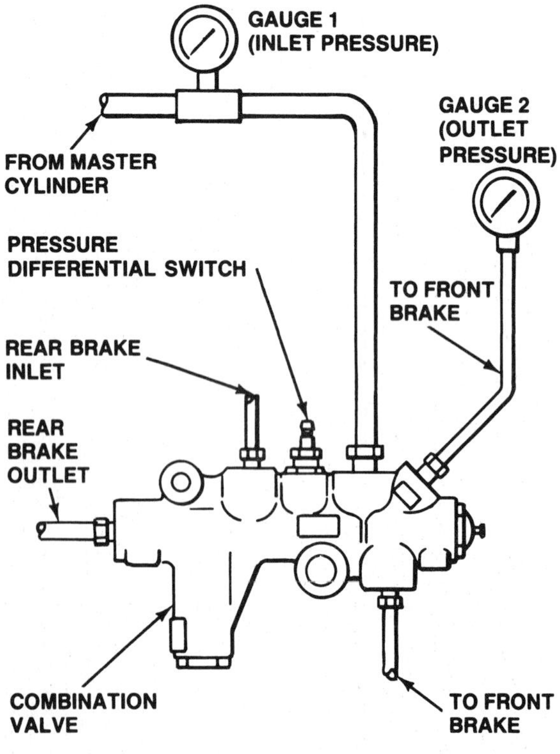

Figure 6-2. Proper gauge connections for testing a metering valve.

Hydraulic Valves and Electrical Component Service

6-3A, until they reach the valve closing point. Depending on the vehicle this will be somewhere between 3 and 30 psi (20 and 210 kPa).

5. When the metering valve closes, the reading on Gauge 2 will remain constant; however, the pressure reading on Gauge 1 will continue to increase, figure 6-3B.
6. At a reading of approximately 75 to 300 psi (520 to 2070 kPa) on Gauge 1, the metering valve will open. The reading on Gauge 2 will then increase to match that on Gauge 1, and from that point on, both gauges will have identical readings, figure 6-3C.

If the pressures indicated on the gauges do not follow the patterns described above, the metering valve is defective and must be replaced.

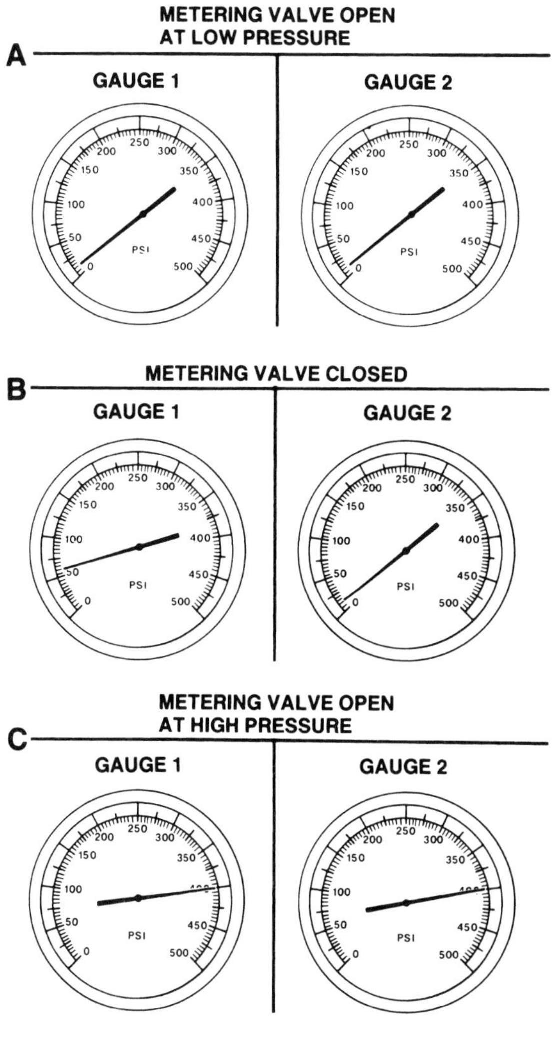

Figure 6-3. Typical gauge readings during a metering valve test.

Proportioning Valve Tests

The proportioning valve slows the rate of pressure increase to the rear brakes once a certain pressure, called the split point, has been reached. A faulty proportioning valve usually allows rear brake pressure to increase too rapidly, causing the rear wheels to lock prematurely during hard stops or on slippery pavement. The proportioning valve can also fail in such a way that no pressure is allowed to the rear brakes, although this is an uncommon type of failure.

Proportioning valve operation can only be tested with pressure gauges. You will need an assistant to apply the brake pedal, two gauges that read from 0 to 1000 psi (0 to 6900 kPa), and the appropriate fittings to attach the gauges to the hydraulic system. You also need to know the split point of the proportioning valve on the particular make and model of vehicle being tested. Most split points are between 300 and 500 psi (2070 and 3450 kPa), but check the factory shop manual to be sure.

On cars where the dual braking system is split front to rear, only a single gauge hookup and test are required, figure 6-4. On cars with diagonal-split braking systems and dual proportioning valves, the tests will have to be performed twice, once for each half of the hydraulic system, figure 6-5. To test the proportioning valve:

1. Attach Gauge 1 to one of the front wheels at the brake caliper. Bleed the air out of the gauge hose using the gauge bleeder valve.
2. Attach Gauge 2 to the same side rear caliper (front/rear split system) or to the opposite rear

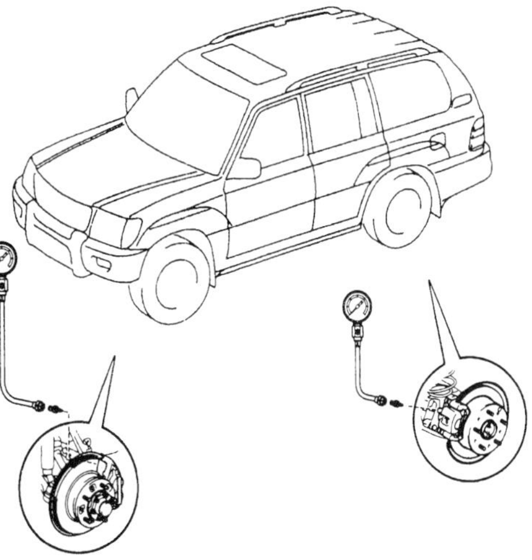

Figure 6-4. Proper gauge connections for testing the proportioning valve on a front/rear-split brake system. (Courtesy of Toyota Motor Sales U.S.A., Inc.)

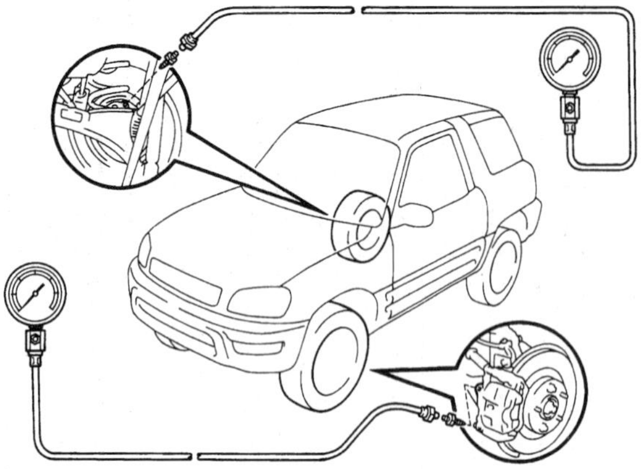

Figure 6-5. Proper gauge connections for testing the proportioning valve to the right rear brake on a diagonal-split brake system. (Courtesy of Toyota Motor Sales U.S.A., Inc.)

wheel (diagonal-split system). Bleed the air out of the hose.
3. Have an assistant slowly apply the brake pedal and observe both gauges.
4. The readings on both gauges should rise at an identical rate until the split point pressure is reached, figure 6-6A.
5. After the split point is reached, the pressure reading on Gauge 2 will increase at a slower rate than the reading on Gauge 1, figure 6-6B. In other words, less pressure will be allowed to the rear brakes than is being produced by the master cylinder.

If the pressures indicated on the gauges do not follow the patterns described above, the proportioning valve is defective and must be replaced.

Metering and Proportioning Valve Replacement

Metering and proportioning valve replacement can involve changing a separate valve or a combination valve. The special brake tools required for valve replacement are flare-nut wrenches and brake bleeding equipment. To replace a valve:

1. Disconnect the brake lines from the valve with flare-nut wrenches.
2. If the valve contains a pressure differential switch, disconnect the vehicle wiring harness from the switch.
3. Unbolt the valve from its mounting, and remove it taking care not to spill brake fluid on the vehicle finish.
4. Bolt the new valve to the mounting bracket.

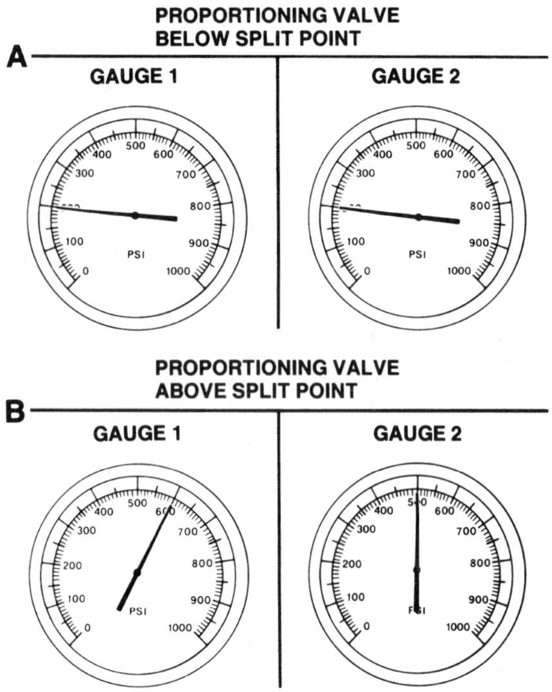

Figure 6-6. Typical gauge readings during a proportioning valve test.

5. Connect the brake lines to the valve and tighten them to the manufacturer's specifications.
6. If the valve contains a pressure differential switch, connect the vehicle wiring harness to the switch.
7. If the valve being replaced is a height-sensing proportioning valve, adjust it as described below.
8. Bleed the brake hydraulic system using one of the methods detailed in Chapter 3.
9. If the valve is equipped with a pressure differential switch that must be manually recentered, do so as described in Chapter 3.

Proportioning Valve Adjustment

On vehicles not equipped with antilock brake systems (ABS), there may be a height-sensing proportioning valve that must be adjusted when it is replaced. The adjustment ensures that the proportioning action takes effect at the correct hydraulic pressure in relation to vehicle loading. There are nearly as many adjustment procedures as there are variable proportioning valves. The adjustment procedures are given below for three types of valves. Consult the factory shop manual for the exact procedure on other types of valves.

The height-sensing proportioning valve on Chevrolet/GMC trucks and vans requires a special plastic ad-

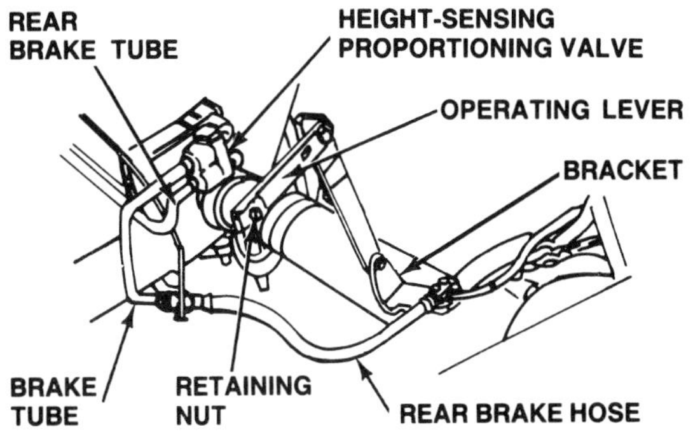

Hydraulic Valves and Electrical Component Service

Figure 6-7. The Chevrolet/GMC height-sensing proportioning valve.

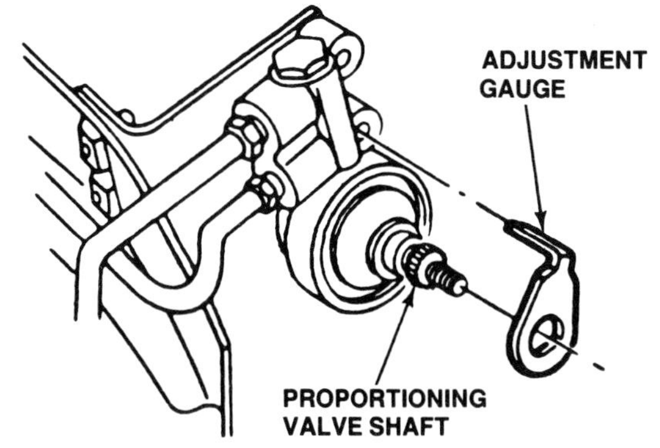

Figure 6-8. Install the plastic adjustment gauge to properly position the proportioning valve shaft.

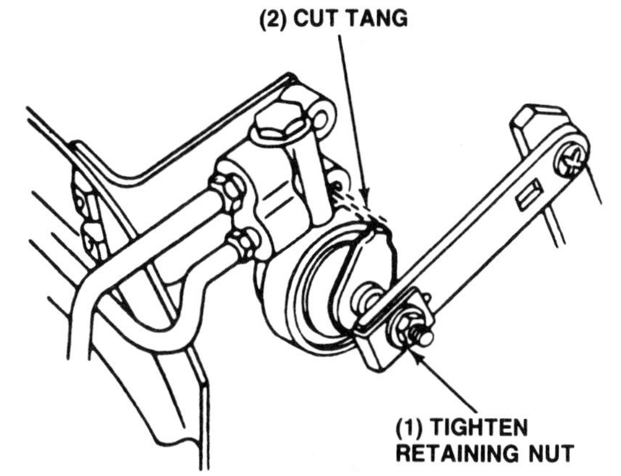

Figure 6-9. Cut the tang from the adjustment gauge after the operating lever is installed.

justment gauge available from the dealer. This gauge is a one-time use item that is installed on the valve to hold it in position during installation. Once the valve operating lever is tightened in place, a tang on the gauge is cut away to allow unrestricted valve operation. To adjust the Chevrolet/GMC height-sensing proportioning valve:

1. Raise the vehicle and support it so that the axle hangs free.
2. Remove the retaining nut and operating lever from the valve shaft, figure 6-7.
3. Rotate the valve shaft as needed to install the adjustment gauge, figure 6-8. The D-shaped hole in the center of the gauge fits over a matching shape on the valve shaft, and the tang of the gauge fits into the lower hole on the valve body.
4. Position the operating lever on the shaft and use a C-clamp or Channel-Lock pliers to press the lever and its plastic bushing over the serrations on the shaft until it is fully seated. Do not use the retaining nut to seat the lever; this can rotate the valve shaft and disturb the adjustment.
5. Install the retaining nut and torque it to 70 to 98 in-lb (8 to 11 Nm).
6. Sever the tang on the adjustment gauge to allow the valve shaft to rotate freely, figure 6-9.

The height-sensing proportioning valve on some Dodge trucks adjusts differently:

1. Park the unloaded vehicle on a level surface. Do not raise or support the vehicle.
2. Push the operating lever inward toward the proportioning valve and away from the stopper bolt, figure 6-10.
3. Measure the distance "A" from the lever hole to the spring support hole. The distance should be 163 to 167 mm (6.42 to 6.57 inches).
4. To adjust the distance, loosen the spring support bolt and slide the spring support until the distance is correct.

The adjustment of the height-sensing proportioning valve on some Toyota trucks, vans, and station wagons involves the use of pressure gauges and weight scales, figure 6-11. To adjust the valve on Toyota models:

1. Raise the vehicle on a lift and install the pressure gauges, one at the front caliper and one at the rear wheel cylinder or caliper. Bleed the air from the gauges.
2. Lower the vehicles onto the weight scales. The valve must be adjusted with a specified weight on the rear wheels. This will require weight to be added to the rear of the vehicle. Refer to the shop manual to get the specified weight. Read the actual vehicle weight on the rear scales and add weight until the specified weight is reached.

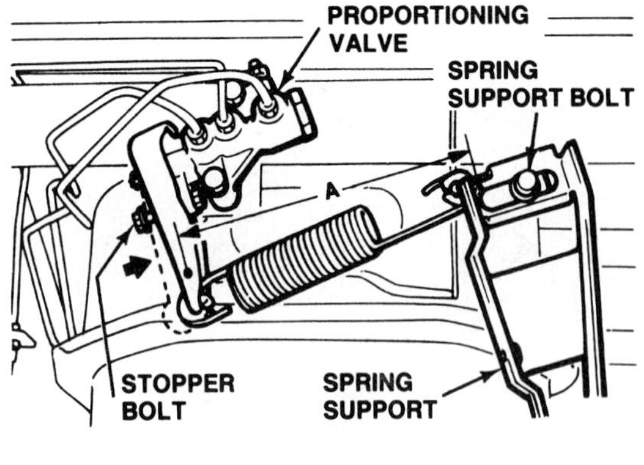

Figure 6-10. This height-sensing proportioning valve is adjusted by setting the spring length, dimension "A."

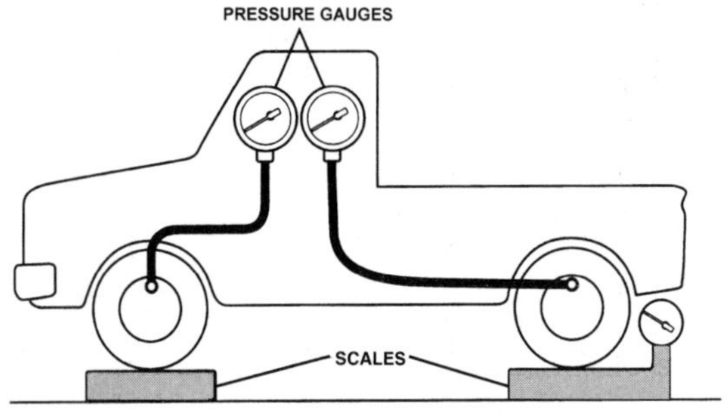

Figure 6-11. Adjustment of the load-sensing height proportioning valve may require the use of scales and pressure gauges. (Courtesy of Toyota Motor Sales U.S.A., Inc.)

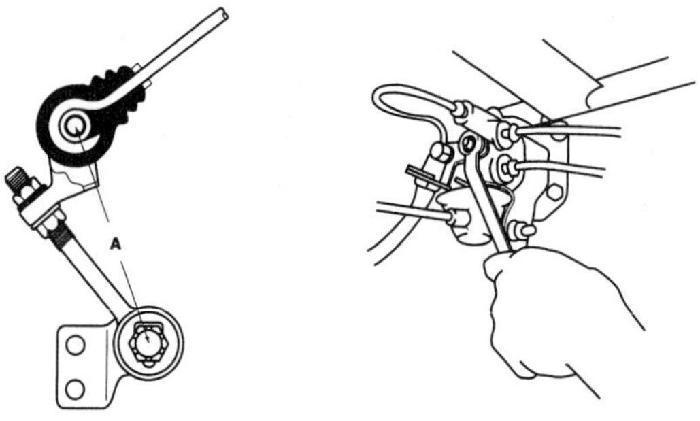

Figure 6-12. Adjust the load-sensing proportioning valve at the linkage or at the valve mounting bolts. (Courtesy of Toyota Motor Sales U.S.A., Inc.)

3. Compare the pressure of the front brakes to the pressure of the rear brakes in two or three stages as specified in the shop manual. Pressure readings should be taken within two seconds of reaching the specified front pressure.
   a. First, the front pressure is brought to a specified pressure (example: 1138 psi) and the rear pressure should be within a specified pressure range (example: 583 to 768 psi).
   b. Second, without releasing the brake pedal, increase the front pressure (example: 1422 psi) and the rear pressure should increase (example: 688 to 873 psi).
4. If the rear pressures are not within the specified range, adjust distance A, figure 6-12.
   a. If the pressure is too low, lengthen distance A.
   b. If the pressure is too high, shorten distance A.
5. If the pressure cannot be brought into the specified range, adjust the position of the proportioning valve body.
   a. If pressure is low, lower the valve body.
   b. If pressure is high, raise the valve body.

BRAKE ELECTRICAL COMPONENT TESTS

The electrical components in the brake system can be broken down into two main circuits. The first is the stoplight circuit, which is made up of the stoplights and the stoplight switch. The second is the brake system warning light circuit, which consists of the warning light, the parking brake switch, and either a pressure differential switch or a brake fluid level switch. Defective parts in either of these circuits must be replaced; they cannot be repaired.

The first step in diagnosing *any* brake system electrical problem is to check the fuses, light bulbs, bulb sockets, wiring, and connectors for obvious problems. Burned out fuses and bulbs, corroded sockets and connections, and broken or grounded wiring are all common problems that cause electrical circuit failure.

The procedures described below are for common types of switches and lights in the brake system; they do not deal with problems involving the vehicle wiring harness or electronic brake system controls. As a general rule, unless you are familiar with the design of a particular system, it is best to consult a factory shop manual for detailed electrical troubleshooting instructions.

On many late-model vehicles, the brake system warning lights and/or stoplights may be integrated into the vehicle body control computer system, vehicle alarm system, or the ABS warning system. ABS warning systems will be covered in Chapter 12 and Chapter 13. For more information on the electronic and integrated systems, see the Chek-Chart Automotive Series text *Automotive Electrical and Electronic Systems*.

Electrical Troubleshooting Tools

The basic tools required for most brake system electrical troubleshooting are a jumper wire, a test light, and

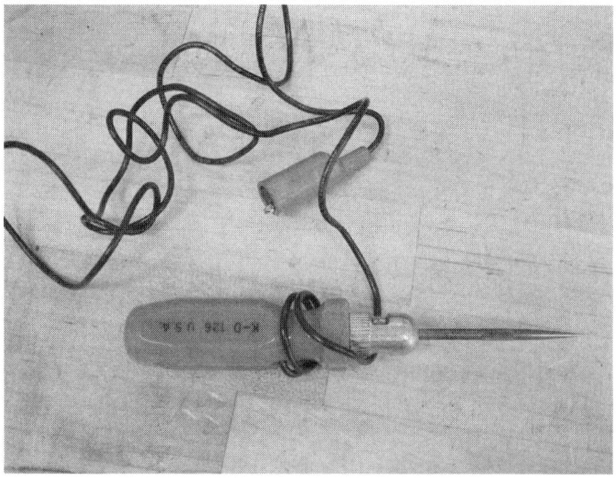

Hydraulic Valves and Electrical Component Service

Figure 6-13. A test light is useful for making quick checks of some electrical circuits.

a digital multimeter (DMM). A jumper wire is simply a length of insulated wire with an alligator clip or probe on each end. A jumper wire is commonly used to bypass a switch in a circuit to help determine whether the switch or another part of the circuit is faulty. A test light, figure 6-13, is used to make quick checks of power and ground circuits.

A digital multimeter (DMM), figure 6-14, can measure resistance, voltage, and amperage, among its many functions. In brake system electrical troubleshooting, the DMM is commonly used to check the brake switch for proper operation. When the switch is closed, it has full continuity, or 0 ohms of resistance. When the switch is open, it has no continuity, or an infinite amount of resistance. DMMs are battery powered and can be damaged if there is any current flow in the circuit while testing resistance. For this reason, the ignition switch should always be OFF and the switch disconnected from the vehicle's wiring when testing for resistance.

The DMM DC volts setting is used to check for the presence of voltage in the circuits, figure 6-14. When the switch is in this position, the system fuses and switch power supply can be checked.

STOPLIGHT CIRCUIT TESTS AND ADJUSTMENTS

There are two potential problems in the stoplight circuit; either the stoplights are always on, or they fail to come on when the brakes are applied. Most of these problems result from burned out fuses or bulbs, a faulty stoplight switch, or a switch that is out of adjustment.

Some early cars have hydraulic stoplight switches mounted on the brake master cylinder or in a nearby junction block. However, virtually all late-model cars have mechanical switches on the brake pedal linkage.

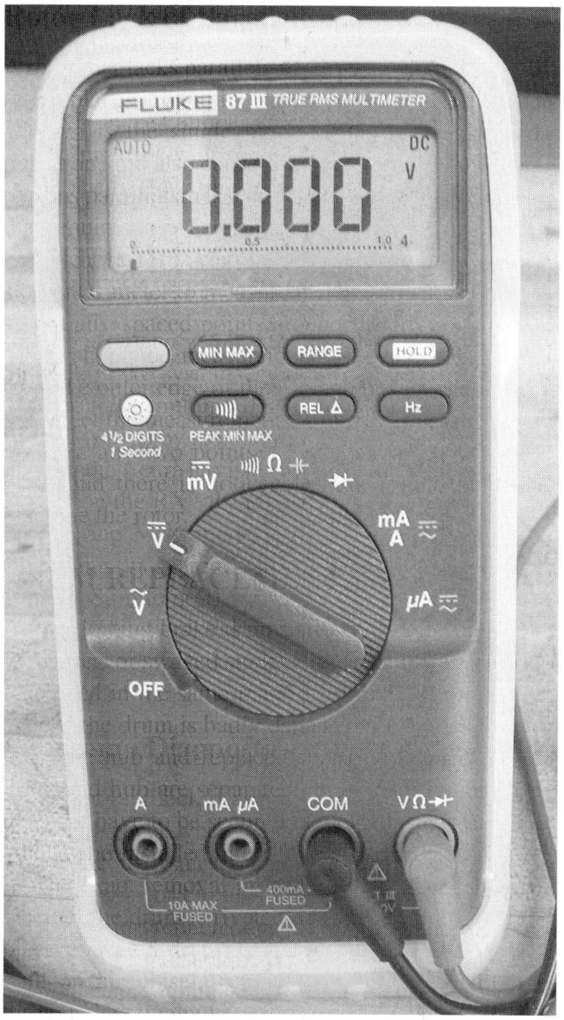

Figure 6-14. The digital multimeter (DMM) can be set to test for voltage in electrical circuits.

Hydraulic switches close once a preset level of pressure is reached in the brake system; hydraulic switches do not require adjustment. Mechanical switches close when the plunger is depressed, or when the plunger extends under internal spring pressure. Most mechanical switches require adjustment when they are installed.

Stoplight Switch Test—Stoplights Always On

1. Confirm that the stoplights are always on by observation. On some vehicles, the ignition switch must be ON for the stoplights to operate.
2. Locate the stoplight switch on the pedal linkage or under the hood and detach the wiring harness connector.
   a. If the stoplights stay on with the harness disconnected, the stoplight circuits are being

powered by a fault in the wiring. Locate and repair the short circuit in the wiring harness.

b. If the stoplights go out when the harness is disconnected and the car has a hydraulic stoplight switch, go to step 3.

c. If the stoplights go out with the harness disconnected and the car has a mechanical stoplight switch, proceed to step 4.

3. Check the brake pedal for proper freeplay to make sure the master cylinder is not being held in the applied position.

a. If there is freeplay, replace the stoplight switch.

b. If there is no freeplay, adjust the pedal linkage to establish the proper freeplay. Reconnect the stoplight switch and repeat the test starting at step 1.

4. Loosen the stoplight switch retaining bolts so that the switch plunger no longer contacts the brake pedal linkage.

5. Set the DMM on Ohms and connect the test leads to the stoplight switch. Move the switch plunger in and out through its full range of travel.

a. If the meter reads very low or zero resistance at one end of the switch travel, figure 6-15, and infinite resistance at the other, figure 6-16, the switch is OK. Adjust the switch as described below.

b. If the meter reads zero resistance at all times, replace the switch and adjust the new switch as described below.

Stoplight Switch Test—Stoplights Never On

1. Turn the ignition switch ON, if necessary, and have an assistant push on the brake pedal. Confirm that the stoplights do not illuminate.
2. Turn the ignition switch OFF, if it was ON.
3. Locate the stoplight switch on the pedal linkage or under the hood and disconnect the wiring harness connector.
4. Connect a jumper wire between the two wires of the harness connector.
5. Turn the ignition switch ON, if necessary, and check if the stoplights are illuminated.

a. If the stoplights are on, go to step 6 to check the switch.

b. If the stoplights are not on, locate and repair the open circuit in the wiring harness.

6. Turn the ignition switch OFF, if it was ON.

a. If the car has a hydraulic stoplight switch, go to step 7.

b. If the car has a mechanical stoplight switch, go to step 8.

7. Connect the leads of an ohmmeter to the terminals of the switch. Have an assistant apply and release the brake pedal while you observe the ohmmeter. If the reading is not zero resistance when the brakes are applied and infinite resistance when the brakes are released, replace the switch.

8. Loosen the stoplight switch retaining bolts so that the switch plunger is no longer in contact with the brake pedal linkage.

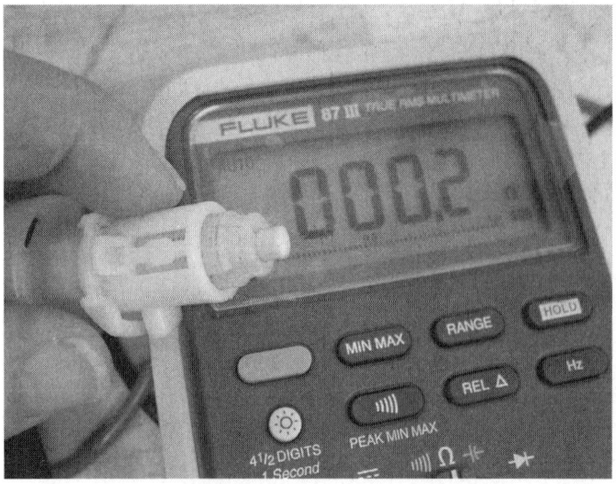

Figure 6-15. With the brake switch released, the meter reads low resistance. This means the switch is closed and the brake lights will go on.

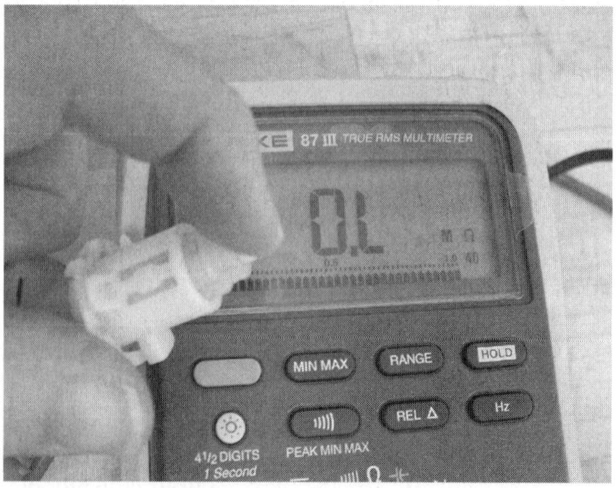

Figure 6-16. With the switch closed, the meter reads OL (over limit), meaning the resistance is very high. This means the switch is open and the brake lights will be off.

Hydraulic Valves and Electrical Component Service

9. Connect the test leads of an ohmmeter to the stoplight switch (see figure 6-14), then move the switch plunger in and out through its full range of travel.
   a. If the meter reads zero resistance at one end of the switch travel and infinite resistance at the other, adjust the switch as described below.
   b. If the meter reads infinite resistance at all times, replace the switch and adjust the new switch as described below.
10. Set the DMM to measure DC volts. Connect the DMM black lead to a good ground. With the switch connected and the ignition ON (if needed), back probe the switch connector with the red lead. There should be a reading of 12 volts or more on one wire and no voltage on the other of the two wires.
    a. If there is no voltage on either wire, repair the vehicle wiring or fuses that supply power to the switch.
    b. If there is voltage present on one wire, go to step 11.
11. Push the brake pedal down and check for voltage at both wires.
    a. If there is voltage at both wires, the switch is working. If the stoplights do not come on, repair the wiring between the stoplight switch and the stoplights.
    b. If there is still only voltage on one wire, as measured above, the switch is faulty. Replace and adjust as described below.

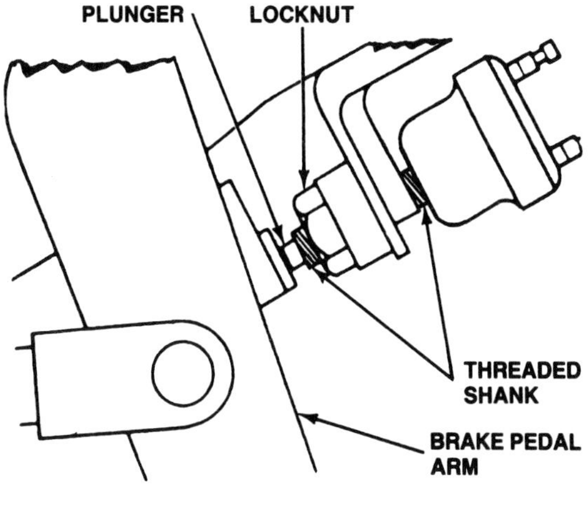

Mechanical Stoplight Switch Adjustment

Whenever a mechanical stoplight switch is replaced the new switch must be adjusted. There are many different ways to adjust these switches. Most imported cars have a stoplight switch with a threaded body that is secured in position by a locknut. Some Chrysler vehicles have a stoplight switch that is adjusted using a spacer gauge. And finally, many cars from Chrysler and General Motors have a semiautomatic adjustment mechanism.

To adjust a stoplight switch with a threaded shank, figure 6-17:

1. Disconnect the wiring harness connector from the switch, and connect an ohmmeter to the switch terminals.
2. Loosen the locknut on the threaded shank of the stoplight switch body.
3. Screw the switch in or out to adjust the clearance between the brake pedal arm and the switch plunger so that the ohmmeter reads zero resistance (the switch is closed) when the brake pedal is depressed approximately ½ inch (13 mm).
4. Tighten the locknut and disconnect the ohmmeter.
5. Attach the wiring harness connector to the switch and check the stoplights for proper operation.

To adjust a stoplight switch using a spacer gauge, figure 6-18:

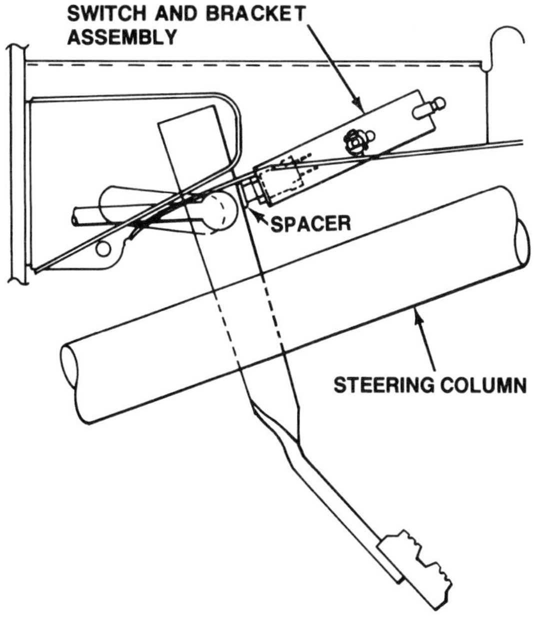

Figure 6-17. To adjust a stoplight switch with a threaded shank, loosen the locknut and thread the switch in or out of its bracket.

Figure 6-18. Some stoplight switches are adjusted with a spacer between the switch plunger and brake pedal arm.

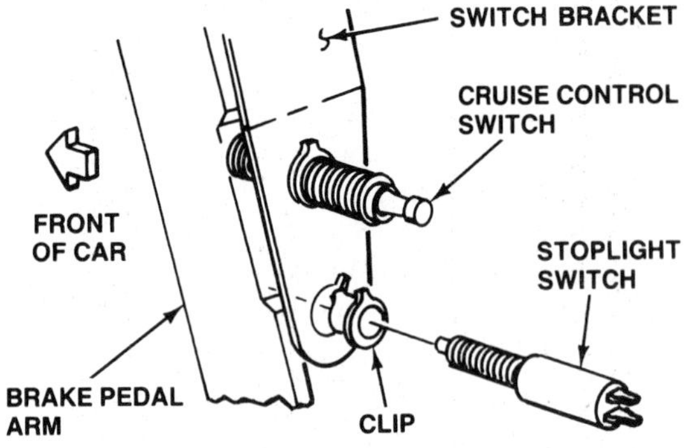

Figure 6-19. This stoplight switch ratchets in the tubular clip to adjust semiautomatically.

1. Loosen the screw securing the switch bracket assembly, and slide the assembly away from the brake pedal.
2. Press brake pedal firmly and allow it to return freely. *Do not* pull back on the pedal.
3. Place the spacer gauge between the switch plunger and the brake pedal arm.
4. Slide the switch bracket assembly toward the brake pedal until the switch plunger is bottomed against the spacer gauge.
5. Tighten the screw securing the switch bracket assembly and remove the spacer gauge.
6. Check the stoplights for proper operation.

To adjust a stoplight switch with a semiautomatic adjusting mechanism, figure 6-19:

1. Depress the brake pedal and insert the switch into the tubular clip on the brake pedal mounting bracket; the switch will click when it is fully seated.
2. Pull back on the brake pedal to adjust the switch position. The switch will ratchet in the tubular clip and emit a series of clicks as it does so.
3. Release the pedal and repeat step 2 until clicks stop.
4. Attach the wiring harness connector to the switch and check the stoplights for proper operation.

To adjust the stoplight switch on late-model General Motors vehicles, use the following procedure, figure 6-20.

NOTE: Proper stoplight switch adjustment is essential. Improper stoplight switch adjustment may cause brake drag, heat buildup, and excessive brake lining wear. Adjust the stoplight switch and the cruise control at the same time.

1. Insert the stoplight switch (3) into the retainer (2) until the switch body is seated on the retainer.

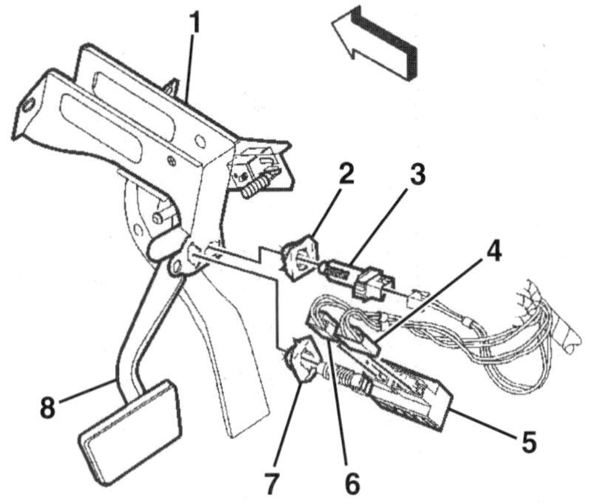

Figure 6-20. Adjust the stoplight switch (3) by pushing it into the retainer (2), lifting the brake pedal (8), and twisting the switch 90 degrees clockwise to lock it in place. The cruise control switch (5) is adjusted in the same manner. (Courtesy of General Motors Corporation, Service and Parts Operations)

2. Pull the brake pedal (8) upward against the internal pedal stop.
3. Turn the switch (3) 90 degrees clockwise. The switch will lock into position.
4. Adjust the cruise control switch (5) in the same manner.
5. If either switch does not "snap" or lock into position, the retainer or switch body may be damaged. Replace as necessary.

Stoplight Switch Replacement

Stoplight switch replacement is a fairly basic procedure. Hydraulic switches require only removal and installation. Mechanical switches must be adjusted as described above after they are installed.

To replace a hydraulic stoplight switch:

1. Disconnect the wiring harness connector from the switch.
2. Unscrew the switch from the master cylinder or junction block.
3. Screw the new switch into the master cylinder or junction block.
4. With the switch slightly loose, have an assistant *slowly* apply the brake pedal and hold it to the floor. Brake fluid will be forced out around the threads of the switch along with any air that may have entered the system. Wear safety glasses to prevent eye injuries from fluid spray, and use a rag or drain pan to catch the fluid and prevent damage to the vehicle finish.

Hydraulic Valves and Electrical Component Service

5. Tighten the switch and have your assistant slowly release the brake pedal. Repeat steps 5 and 6 until no air comes from the system.
6. Attach the wiring harness connector to the switch and check the stoplights for proper operation.

To replace a mechanical stoplight switch:

1. Disconnect the wiring harness connector from the switch.
2. Remove any nuts, bolts, or screws securing the switch in place, then remove the switch from its bracket.
3. Place the new switch in the bracket, and install the mounting nuts, bolts, or screws loosely.
4. Adjust switch as described above, then tighten it securely in position.
5. Attach the wiring harness connector to the switch and check the stoplights for proper operation.

To replace the stoplight switch on late-model General Motors vehicles:

1. Gain access to the switch by removing the under dash sound insulator.
2. Disconnect the electrical connector.
3. Turn the switch 90 degrees counterclockwise while pulling on the switch. The switch will unsnap and pull out of the retainer.
4. Inspect the switch retainer for damage. Replace, if necessary.
5. Insert the new switch into the retainer until the switch body contacts the retainer.
6. Pull the pedal upward until it contacts the pedal stop.
7. Turn the switch 90 degrees clockwise until it locks in place.
8. Reinstall the wiring harness connector and sound insulator.
9. Check for proper operation of the stoplights.

WARNING LIGHT CIRCUIT TESTS

All cars are equipped with one or more red brake warning lights (RBWL) on the instrument panel, figure 6-21. On vehicles with a single RBWL, the light serves two purposes and is activated in two ways. The minor function of the light is to serve as a parking brake warning indicator. A switch on the parking brake linkage turns the light on when the parking brake is applied. The major function of the light is as an indicator of trouble within the brake hydraulic system. For this purpose, the light is activated by either a pressure differential switch or a brake fluid level switch. All cars manufactured since 1967 are equipped with one or the other of these switches.

Figure 6-21. Typical brake system warning lights.

Vehicles may have more than one brake warning light. For example, there may be a warning light for the fluid level and another for the parking brake. Also, vehicles with ABS will have a separate amber-colored ABS warning light. An ABS fault will turn on the ABS light and may also turn on the RBWL.

The brake fluid level switch turns on the brake system warning light when the fluid level in the master cylinder reservoir falls below a predetermined level; this can be caused by wear of the brake linings or a leak in the hydraulic system. A pressure differential switch turns on the brake system warning light when there is a significant difference in pressure between the two hydraulic circuits of the dual braking system.

Problem diagnosis in the brake system warning light circuit begins by testing the warning light bulb or bulbs. After the bulbs have been tested, the parking brake switch and either the pressure differential switch or the brake fluid level switch are tested, depending on which is fitted to the vehicle being serviced. A scan tool may be required to properly diagnose and repair the warning light system.

Warning Light Bulb Tests

Most vehicles rely on one or two bulbs for the brake system warning light. The brake system warning lights are tested each time the vehicle is started and should be checked whenever the brake system is serviced. The exact procedure for testing the warning light bulb varies from car to car, but most tests are performed by turning the ignition switch to a certain position without starting the engine.

To perform the warning light test on some vehicles, turn the ignition switch to either the ON or START position. The warning light will illuminate as long as the engine is not running. On other vehicles, turn the ignition switch to a point *between* the ON and START positions. Once again, the warning light will illuminate when the engine is not running.

Once the engine is running, the warning light bulb on most cars can be tested simply by applying the parking barke, assuming of course that the parking brake warning light switch and wiring are operating properly. Consult the shop or owner's manual if you are in doubt about the proper test for a given car.

Bulb Check Failures

If the bulb fails to light during the above bulb tests, it must be repaired before continuing. Some things to check are:

- *Bulb burned out*—Remove the bulb and replace it with a new one.
- *No power to the bulb*—There may also be a general failure of other bulbs or the instruments. Check for burned or corroded fuses.
- *No ground at the bulb*—Refer to a wiring schematic to determine how the bulb is grounded. This may involve the ignition switch, body control module, or ABS control module.
- *Instrument cluster fault*—There may be a problem with the instrument cluster printed circuits or computer. Follow the manufacturer's instructions to use a scan tool to test the instrument cluster.
- *Vehicle communication fault*—Most late-model vehicles use a communications network to operate the various warning lights. Use the scan tool to check for communication faults.

Parking Brake Switch Test

If the bulb test above indicates that the warning light is operating properly, yet the light does not illuminate when the ignition is ON and the parking brake is applied, there is a problem in the parking brake switch circuit. This is usually caused by a parking brake switch that fails to close and complete the circuit. To test the parking brake switch:

1. Turn the ignition switch OFF.
2. Locate the parking brake switch on the pedal, lever, or handle linkage and disconnect the wiring harness connector from the switch.
3. If the harness connector contains a single wire, connect the wire to ground. If the connector has two wires, connect a jumper wire between them.
4. Turn the ignition switch ON, and check if the warning light is illuminated.

   a. If the light is on, replace the parking brake switch.
   b. If the light is not on, locate and repair the open circuit in the wiring harness.

Although it rarely happens, the parking brake switch can also jam in the ON position, or short internally, causing the warning light to stay lit all the time. If you suspect this problem, simply detach the wiring harness connector from the parking brake switch while the ignition is on and the light is illuminated. If the light goes out when the connector is detached, repair or replace the parking brake switch.

FAILURE WARNING SYSTEM SWITCH TESTS

If the brake system warning light flashes when the brakes are applied, or is on constantly when the parking brake is not applied (and the parking brake switch has been ruled out as the problem), the warning system is probably doing its job and indicating that a problem exists in the brake hydraulic system. However, it is also possible that there may be a failure within the warning system itself.

Before you test the failure warning system, perform these preliminary checks to determine if the problem is in the brake hydraulic system. If the car is equipped with a fluid level switch, check the fluid level in the master cylinder reservoir; if it is low, adjust it as necessary. If the car is equipped with a pressure differential switch, detach the wiring harness connector from the switch terminal. If the light no longer comes on when you perform either of the above operations, do a complete brake system inspection. A low fluid level signals a leak in the hydraulic system, or worn brake linings that need to be replaced. A pressure differential switch that is activated indicates there is a leak in the system.

If the brake fluid level is okay and there are no signs of leaks anywhere in the hydraulic system, it is possible that the pressure differential or fluid level switch is defective and keeping the light on. The procedures for testing these switches are given below.

Pressure Differential Switch Test

If the brake system warning light on a car equipped with a pressure differential switch flashes when the brakes are applied, or remains on when there are no external signs of leakage from the hydraulic system, the switch may need to be manually recentered; this is usually required only on domestic models built before 1971, and certain later imports. However, pressure differential switches with centering springs, as used on all late-model cars, can also require manual centering if

Hydraulic Valves and Electrical Component Service

the switch piston sticks in its bore. See Chapter 3 for switch centering procedures.

If the warning light comes on again after the switch has been manually centered, the master cylinder is bypassing internally and creating a pressure difference between the two hydraulic circuits. Rebuild or replace the master cylinder to solve the warning light "problem."

It is also possible that a defective pressure differential switch will not turn the warning light on, even though a leak exists in the hydraulic system. If a leak is present and bulb test indicates that the warning light is operating properly, test the pressure differential switch as follows:

1. Turn the ignition switch ON.
2. Detach the wiring harness connector from the pressure differential switch, and use a jumper wire to connect the harness wire to ground, figure 6-22. Observe the warning light:
   a. If the light illuminates, go to step 3.
   b. If the light does not illuminate, locate and repair the open circuit in the wiring harness.
3. Attach the wiring harness connector to the pressure differential switch, and have an assistant apply the brake pedal with light to moderate pressure.
4. Open the left front bleeder screw and have your assistant observe the warning light:
   a. If the warning light illuminates, the switch is good. Close the bleeder screw and recenter the pressure differential switch as described in Chapter 3.
   b. If the warning light does not illuminate, go to step 5.
5. Close the bleeder screw and have your assistant release the brake pedal, then reapply it with light to moderate pressure.
6. If the car has a front/rear-split braking system, open a rear bleeder screw. If the car has a diagonal-split braking system, open the right front bleeder screw. Have your assistant observe the warning light:
   a. If the warning light illuminates, the switch is good. Close the bleeder screw and recenter the pressure differential switch as described in Chapter 3.
   b. If the warning light does not illuminate, replace the switch.

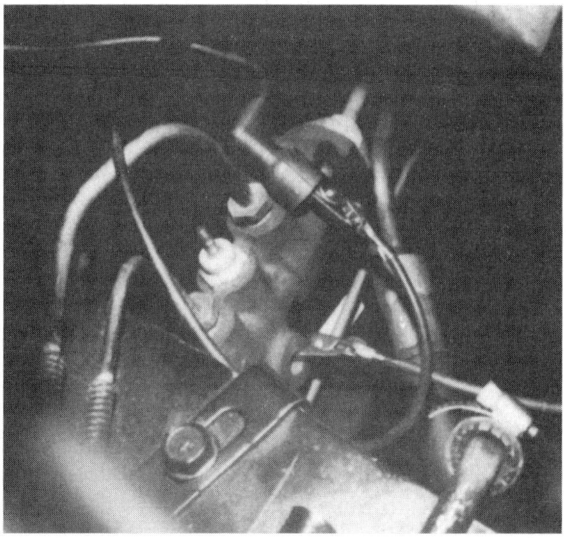

Fluid Level Switch Tests

Fluid level switches come in two varieties, those where the float remains in the reservoir, and those where the float is attached to the reservoir cap. Both are basic on/off switches, and fail by sticking in either the open or closed position.

Float in Reservoir—Switch Test

To test a fluid level warning switch with a float that remains in the reservoir:

1. Perform a bulb test to confirm that the warning light is operating properly.
2. Adjust the fluid level in the master cylinder reservoir to the full mark.
3. Turn the ignition switch ON and observe the warning light.
   a. If the warning light illuminates, go to step 4.
   b. If the warning light does not illuminate, go to step 5.
4. Detach the wiring harness connector from the fluid level switch.
   a. If the warning light goes out, replace the reservoir and switch assembly.
   b. If the warning light remains lit, locate and repair the short in the wiring harness.
5. Remove the master cylinder fluid reservoir cap, and use a clean screwdriver or other probe to gently push the float to the bottom of its travel, figure 6-23, simulating a low fluid level. Observe the warning light:
   a. If the warning light illuminates, the switch is good.

Figure 6-22. Ground the pressure differential switch wire to test the wiring harness portion of the circuit.

Figure 6-23. Push the float down to test the fluid level switch.

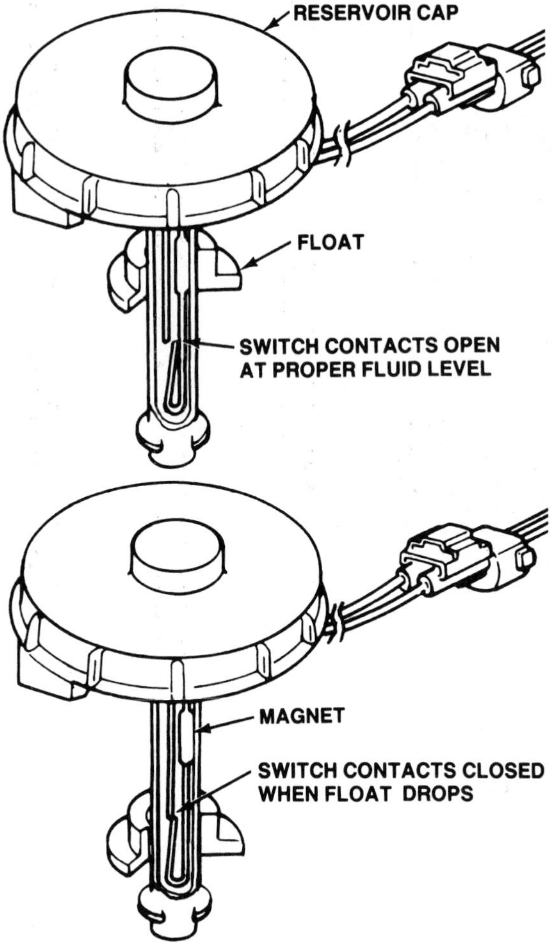

  b. If the warning light does not illuminate, go to step 6.
6. Detach the wiring harness connector from the switch, and use a jumper wire to bridge the two wires in the connector. Observe the warning light:
   a. If the warning light illuminates, replace the fluid reservoir and switch assembly.
   b. If the warning light does not illuminate, locate and repair the open circuit in the wiring harness.

Float on Reservoir Cap—Switch Test
Many imported cars use a fluid level warning switch in which the float is attached to the master cylinder fluid reservoir cap. To test this type of switch:

1. Perform a bulb test to confirm that the warning light is operating properly.
2. Adjust the fluid level in the master cylinder reservoir to the full mark.
3. Turn the ignition switch ON, and with the reservoir cap in place, observe the warning light.
   a. If the warning light illuminates, go to step 4.
   b. If the warning light does not illuminate, go to step 5.
4. Detach the wiring harness connector from the fluid level switch.
   a. If the warning light goes out, replace the cap and switch assembly.
   b. If the warning light remains lit, locate and repair the short in the wiring harness.
5. Remove the master cylinder fluid reservoir cap, and allow float to drop to the bottom of its travel,

Figure 6-24. Allow the float to drop to the bottom of its travel to manually close this type of fluid level switch.

  figure 6-24, simulating a low fluid level. Observe the warning light:
   a. If the warning light illuminates, the switch is good.
   b. If the warning light does not illuminate, go to step 6.
6. Detach the wiring harness connector from the cap and switch assembly, and use a jumper wire to bridge the two wires in the connector. Observe the warning light:
   a. If the warning light illuminates, replace the cap and switch assembly.
   b. If the warning light does not illuminate, locate and repair the open circuit in the wiring harness.

7 Drum Brake Service

OBJECTIVES

Upon completion and review of this chapter, you will be able to:

- Remove a fixed or floating brake drum.
- Inspect drum brake linings.
- Inspect drum brake hardware.
- Perform a brake pedal travel test.
- Adjust manually adjusting drum brakes.
- Perform an anchor adjustment.
- Replace brake shoes.
- Perform the initial adjustment to starwheel automatic adjusting brakes.
- Burnish-in brake shoes.
- Inspect and replace a wheel cylinder.
- Overhaul a wheel cylinder.
- Replace brake shoes on the Chrysler leading-trailing brake.
- Replace brake shoes on the Chrysler dual-servo brake.
- Replace brake shoes on the GM dual-servo brake.
- Replace brake shoes on the Ford leading-trailing brake.

INTRODUCTION

Drum brake service consists of five main operations: drum removal, brake inspection, brake adjustment, shoe replacement, and wheel cylinder service. The operations are listed in this order because you must remove the brake drum before you can inspect the friction assembly or replace the brake shoes. And, while it is possible to adjust the brakes without first inspecting them, this is not recommended. Wheel cylinder service is also a part of drum brake repair.

Manually adjusted drum brakes were once used on all four wheels of every car, and brake adjustment and shoe replacement were common service procedures. Today, all brakes are self-adjusting, and drum brakes are used exclusively on the lightly loaded rear wheels. This means that except for routine inspection, rear drum brake service is usually not required until the car has high mileage, a hydraulic problem with the wheel cylinder, or a mechanical failure of some part in the friction assembly. When this occurs, it is best to do a complete brake overhaul rather than a single repair.

This chapter explains the procedures used to remove brake drums, inspect drum brake friction assemblies, manually adjust drum brakes, replace brake shoes and repair wheel cylinders. It also describes detailed shoe replacement procedures for several specific drum brakes. Although this chapter focuses primarily

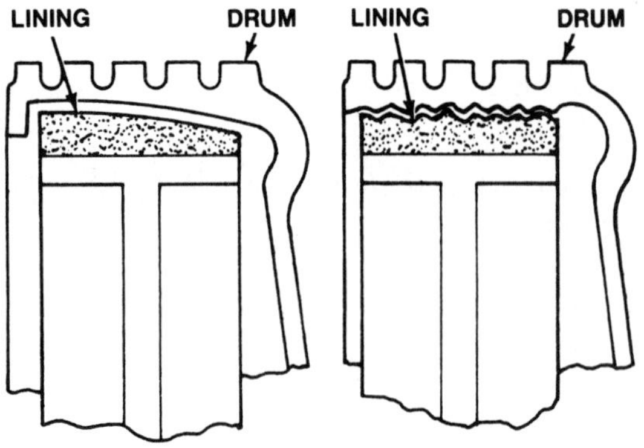

Figure 7-1. Brake lining and friction surface wear can make a drum difficult to remove.

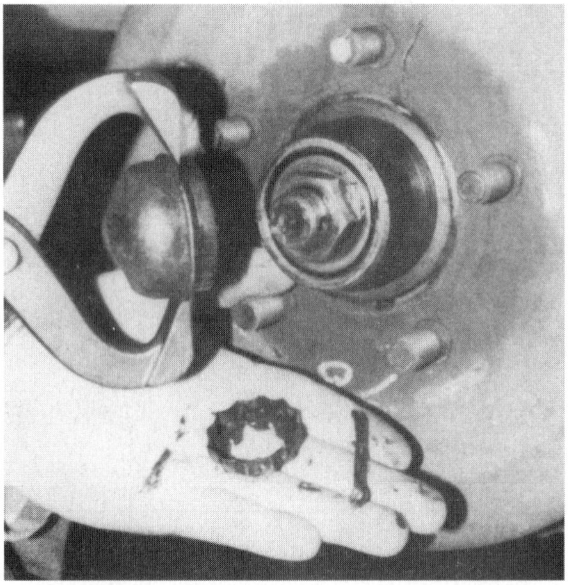

Figure 7-2. This nut adjusts the wheel bearings and retains the drum on the spindle.

on rear drum brakes, most of the information applies to front drum brakes as well.

BRAKE DRUM REMOVAL

Before you can inspect a drum brake or replace its shoes, you must first remove the drum to gain access to the friction assembly. To do this, it may be necessary to: loosen the parking brake cable and service brake adjustment, remove a drum retaining device, and break the drum loose from accumulated rust and corrosion. Whenever you remove a drum, mark it with an L (left) or an R (right) so you can replace it in the same position.

The removal procedures differ for fixed and floating drums, however, either type can be difficult or impossible to remove unless the parking and service brake adjustments are loosened first. This occurs because wear at the open edge of the drum, or scoring of the brake linings and drum friction surface, creates a ridge or a series of interlocking grooves that hold the drum in place, figure 7-1. If you cannot remove a drum once the retaining devices are removed and the drum is loose on the hub or axle, loosen the parking and service brake adjustments as described later in the chapter so the high points on the linings and drum clear one another. Refer to figure 7-22 and figure 7-23.

Fixed Drum Removal

Fixed brake drums that are cast as a unit with the hub assembly are common on the rear axles of FWD cars, and the front axles of older RWD cars with front drum brakes. There are two kinds of fixed drums: those whose hubs contain wheel bearings, and those whose hubs have a tapered opening that fits directly onto the axle. Both types are held in place by a single large retaining nut.

In most applications, the nut that retains a fixed brake drum also secures the wheel bearings in the hub. When tapered-roller bearings are fitted, the retaining nut is used to adjust bearing end play, and is typically finger tight or torqued to only a few inch-pounds. If ball bearings are used, a spacer and shim pack between the inner and outer bearings sets the bearing clearance, and the retaining nut is tightened to a moderately high torque.

To remove a fixed drum that contains wheel bearings:

1. Use a pair of dust cap pliers to remove the cap from the center of the hub and expose the retaining nut, figure 7-2.
2. Remove the retaining nut. Most cars have a nut secured by a castellated nut lock and a cotter pin; remove the pin along with any other locking devices, then unscrew the nut. Some imported cars have a split nut with a pinch bolt; loosen the bolt, then unscrew the nut.
3. Pull outward on the drum and slide it off the spindle. Take care not to let the thrust washer and outer wheel bearing fall on the ground as they clear the end of the spindle. Also, do not drag the inner wheel bearing across the retaining nut threads on the spindle.

Sometimes, the inner races of the inner wheel bearing will stick or have a light press fit on the spindle. In these cases, the drum will be difficult to remove unless you use a puller, figure 7-3. When doing this, the inner bearing may remain on the spindle, forcing the grease seal out of the hub. Once the drum is off the car, use a

Drum Brake Service

Figure 7-3. A puller may be required to remove a fixed drum if the inner wheel bearing sticks on the spindle.

Figure 7-4. Nuts that retain drums with tapered hubs are tightened to high torques.

Figure 7-5. Taper-hub drum pullers are tightened against the axle with a hammer and lever.

puller or a pair of pry bars to carefully remove the inner bearing and grease seal.

Once the drum is off the car, inspect the grease in the hub and on the wheel bearings. If the grease appears in good condition, set the drum on the bench, open side down, and cover the outer bearing and hub opening so the bearings will not become contaminated. If the grease appears old and dirty, repack the wheel bearings before you reinstall the drum. As a general rule, always repack the wheel bearings when performing a complete brake job. See Chapter 14 for information on wheel bearing service.

Taper-hub Fixed Drum Removal

Some cars and light trucks have fixed drums that install directly on the rear driven axles. The hubs of these drums have a tapered opening that fits over a matching taper on the axle; a groove in the hub fits over a locating key in the axle to prevent drum slippage. Once the drum retaining nut is removed, a special puller is required to remove the drum because it becomes tightly wedged onto the axle.

The retaining nuts of fixed drums with tapered hubs are tightened to a high torque and require a great deal of force to remove or install. Unless you take certain precautions, this force may damage the axle and drivetrain, or cause personal injury. Always loosen the retaining nuts, or do final tightening, with the car on the ground and the weight of the vehicle on the wheels. Firmly apply the parking brake, or have an assistant apply the service brakes, to reduce shock loading on the axle and drivetrain as you remove or install the retaining nut.

To remove a fixed drum that is a taper fit on the axle:

1. Remove the cotter pin from the drum retaining nut.
2. Use an impact wrench or large breaker bar to loosen the retaining nut, figure 7-4.
3. Raise and properly support the vehicle, then remove the wheels from the brake drums.
4. Unscrew the retaining nut from the axle, then loosen the parking and service brake adjustments to ensure that the drum will clear the brake shoes.
5. Attach the drum puller as shown in figure 7-5, then use a hammer and the special lever to tighten the shaft against the axle until the puller is under heavy pressure.
6. Strike the end of the shaft two or three heavy blows with a three- to five-pound hammer, figure 7-6.
7. Check the pressure on the puller shaft; if it is reduced, the drum is moving. Retighten the shaft and strike it several more blows with the hammer. Continue to tighten and strike the shaft until the drum pops free.

Figure 7-6. Strike the puller shaft to dislodge the drum from the axle.

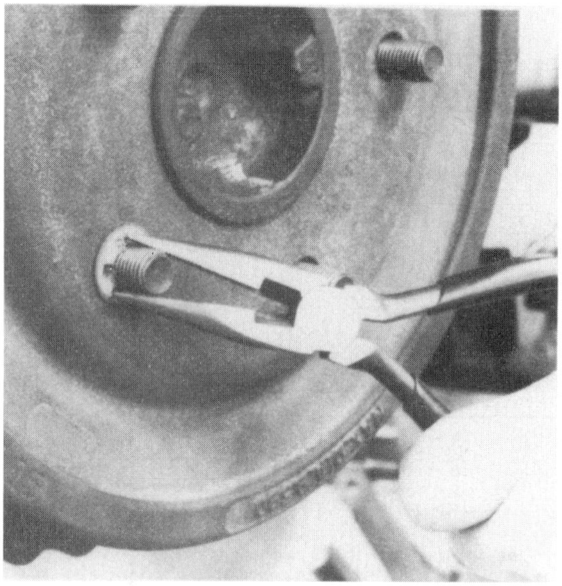

Figure 7-7. Remove speed nuts with pliers.

If pressure on the puller does not decrease when the shaft is struck with the hammer, and you are trained in the proper use of an oxyacetylene torch, heat the hub where the drum fits on the axle. Do not apply excessive heat or drum and axle damage may occur. Again strike the shaft and check for drum movement. Continue to heat the hub, and tighten and strike the puller shaft, until the drum pops free.

Floating Drum Removal

Floating brake drums are held in place by the wheel and lug nuts during normal operation. However, they may also be retained by speed nuts over the wheel studs, or bolts or screws threaded through the drum into the hub or axle flange. To remove speed nuts, grasp them with a pair of pliers and unscrew them from the studs, figure 7-7. On most cars, you can discard the speed nuts because they are unnecessary once the car has left the factory. However, certain Ford cars have high shoulders on the wheel studs that can catch the drum and hold it in a cocked position when the wheel is installed. To prevent the possibility of drum damage in these applications, replace the speed nut after the brake work is completed. To remove bolts or screws that retain a drum, use the appropriate tool, figure 7-8. Set aside the bolts or screws so you can reinstall them when the drum is replaced.

Once the retaining devices are removed, the drum should move freely on the hub or axle, and slip off over the brake shoes. If necessary, loosen the parking and service brake adjustments until the drum will clear the

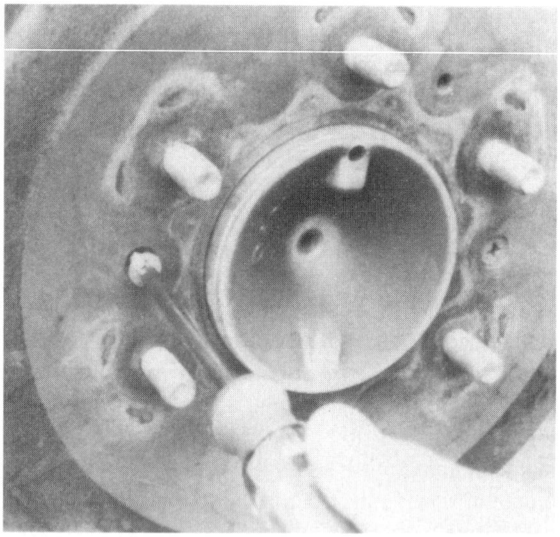

Figure 7-8. Use the appropriate tool to remove screws or bolts that retain drums.

shoes. If the drum does not move on the hub or axle once the brake adjustments are loosened, the drum is rusted or corroded in place. Where the frozen drum mounts on the hub assembly of a nondriven axle, it is often faster and easier to remove the drum and hub as a unit, like a fixed drum, rather than attempt to separate the drum from the hub. However, when the drum is on a driven axle, or must be removed from the hub for replacement, use this procedure:

1. Use a pointed probe to scribe the joint where the drum mounts on the hub or axle. This breaks the

Drum Brake Service

Figure 7-9. A few well-placed blows can free a frozen drum from the hub or axle.

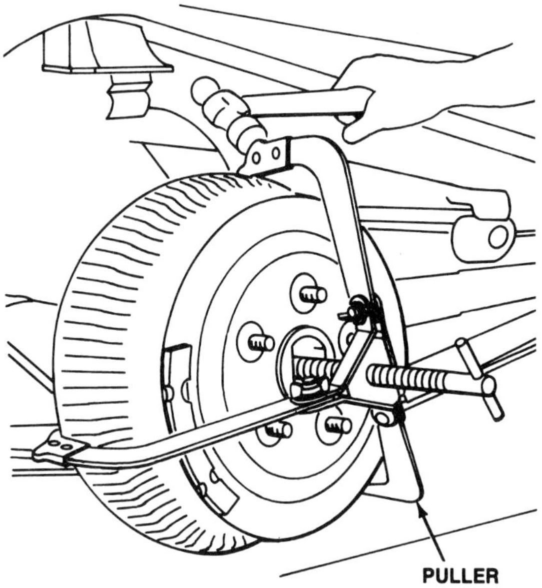

Figure 7-10. A puller is a last resort when removing floating drums.

surface tension, and like a glass cutter, helps crack the joint free.

2. Strike the outer edge of the drum several solid blows with a three- to five-pound hammer at approximately a 45-degree angle, figure 7-9. A "dead-blow" urethane hammer loaded with lead shot works very well for this purpose.
3. If the drum does not come free, spray penetrating oil around the stud holes and the joint where the drum mounts on the hub or axle. Allow the oil to soak in for a few minutes, then strike the drum several more blows with the hammer.
4. Some drum brakes have two threaded holes in the drum web that allow bolts to be threaded into the drum to push it off of the hub. When using threaded holes to push the drum off of the hub, first clean out the threads with the proper size bottoming tap. These threads are almost always metric threaded. Be sure to use the correct tap.
5. If the drum still does not come free, install a three-jaw puller on the drum, figure 7-10. Tighten the puller shaft against the end of the spindle or axle, and strike the puller several solid blows with a metal hammer. The special puller shown in the illustration is designed with hammer pads on the puller arms that allow force to be applied at the edges of the drum. On a standard three-jaw puller, strike the puller shaft to free the drum.
6. If the drum still does not come free, and you are trained in the proper use of an oxyacetylene torch, heat the drum in the area where it mounts on the hub or axle. Continue to heat the drum, and tighten and strike the puller, until the drum comes free.
7. Once the drum is off the car, clean all traces of penetrating oil from the drum and hub or axle flange to prevent contamination of the brake linings.

The methods of drum removal described above should be exercised with caution. Excessive hammer blows, puller force, or heat can warp a drum in the process of removing it. Whenever a drum is removed using one of these methods, it should be checked for damage and distortion as described in Chapter 9 before it is returned to service. In addition, high heat on a hub that contains wheel bearings can melt the grease and lead to seal and bearing failure. If a hub that has been heated contains wheel bearings, repack the bearings and replace the grease seal before you return the car to service.

BRAKE INSPECTION

Rear drum brake shoes wear more slowly and require less frequent service than either drum brake shoes or disc brake pads on the front-wheel brakes. This occurs because rear drum brakes provide as little as 20 percent of the total vehicle braking. Also, when compared to disc brake pads, drum brake shoes have greater friction material surface area to absorb heat and distribute wear. Because the rear brake linings wear so slowly, rear brake inspection is an often overlooked part of vehicle maintenance.

Most vehicle manufacturers recommend that drum brake friction assemblies be inspected every 7500 miles (12,000 km). You should also inspect the drum brakes

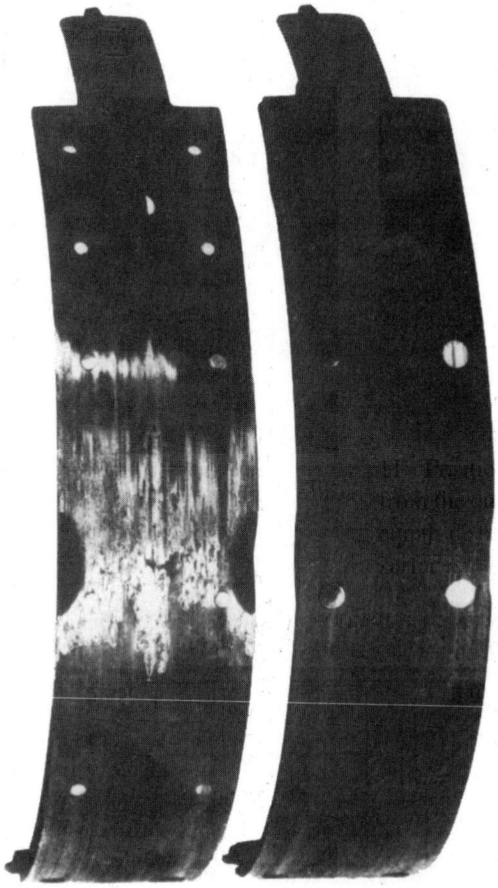

Figure 7-11. Metal-to-metal contact is the destructive result of brake neglect.

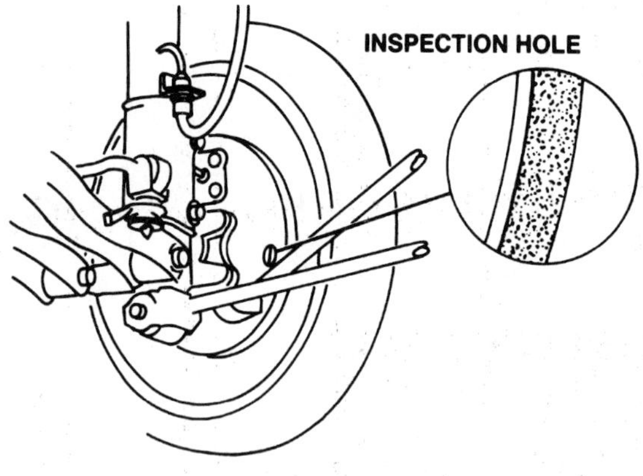

Figure 7-12. A lining inspection hole in the brake backing plate.

before you perform a manual adjustment, or whenever you do any work on the front disc brakes. Unfortunately, many car owners wait to have the brakes inspected until they hear the grinding noise that means a lining is worn completely away, and a shoe lining table is making metal-to-metal contact with a brake drum, figure 7-11. Once this happens, the drum must be machined or replaced as described in Chapter 9. It is much better to replace a set of brake shoes sooner than absolutely necessary, rather than risk drum damage by trying to get the maximum possible life from the linings.

Although some backing plates and brake drums contain inspection holes that allow you to check lining thickness, figure 7-12, you cannot do a complete brake inspection unless you remove the drum. Once the drum is off the car, inspect it as described in Chapter 9. Next, thoroughly clean the friction assembly with a brake washer, or a brake vacuum fitted with a high efficiency particulate air (HEPA) filter. Brake dust and other grit increase lining wear and cause brake noise, and a clean friction assembly is easier to inspect.

When the friction assembly is clean and dry, make a simple three-step inspection. First, check the condition of the brake shoes and linings. Second, make sure there are no fluid leaks from the wheel cylinder or axle, and check the wheel cylinder operation. And finally, confirm that all the brake hardware is mounted properly, in good condition, and operating as designed. These operations are detailed below. Additional checks, made with the friction assembly disassembled, are covered in the brake shoe replacement section later in the chapter.

Lining Inspection

The thickness of the brake linings is the primary factor that determines the need for replacement, so check them first. The linings must be thick enough that the vehicle can be operated safely until the next inspection. As a general rule, replace the brake shoes if the linings are worn to within $\frac{1}{32}$ inch (.030" or .75 mm) of the lining table on bonded linings, or the same distance above the rivet heads on riveted linings, figure 7-13. Also inspect the linings for physical damage such as cracks, loose or missing rivets, or separation of a bonded lining from the lining table. If any of these problems are present, replace the shoes.

The linings on both shoes should be worn approximately the same amount. If one lining of a dual-servo brake is worn much more than the other, make sure the primary and secondary shoes are installed in their proper positions; the shoe with the smaller lining should be toward the front of the vehicle. If the brake shoes are applied to serve as the parking brake, and are worn excessively at the ends acted on by the parking brake strut, the parking brake may be adjusted too tight. If the linings are worn only in the center or at one end, the shoes are not properly arced to the curvature of the drum, or standard shoes have been installed in an oversize drum. This is not a major problem on to-

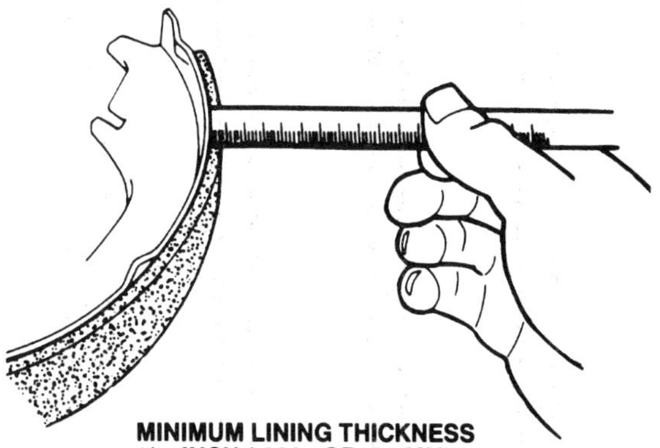

Drum Brake Service

Figure 7-13. Replace the shoes when the linings wear below the minimum safe thickness.

Figure 7-14. A glazed brake shoe lining.

Figure 7-15. A shoe lining suffering from fluid contamination.

Figure 7-16. Inspecting a wheel cylinder for fluid leaks.

day's lightly loaded rear drum brakes; however, it is a concern on front drum brakes. At least two-thirds of the linings on both shoes of a front drum brake should contact the drum. If not, replace the shoes and drums.

Next, inspect the faces of the brake shoe linings. They should be relatively smooth with a dull finish. A hard lining with a shiny or polished surface, figure 7-14, is glazed and must be replaced. If the lining has been contaminated by brake fluid from a leak at the wheel cylinder, or a differential lubricant that has leaked past the axle seals, figure 7-15, the friction surface will be darkened. If the leak is severe, the lining will appear "smeared" and paint will often be stripped from the brake shoe and friction assembly hardware. Where the contamination is limited to less than 10 percent of the lining surface, you can usually clean and reuse the brake shoes. In most cases, however, you will have to replace the shoes because contamination soaks deep into the lining material and cannot be washed away with brake cleaner.

Wheel Cylinder and Axle Inspection

Detailed inspection of the wheel cylinder is covered later in this chapter; however, there are some basic checks you should make during a routine brake inspection. First, inspect the outside of the wheel cylinder for signs of leakage; minor stains caused by fluid seepage are considered normal. Next, fold back the cylinder dust boots and look for signs of liquid, figure 7-16; if you find more than a slight amount of dampness, the cylinder must be rebuilt or replaced.

If there are no fluid leaks, check for free movement of the wheel cylinder pistons. With the brake drum from only a single wheel removed, have an assistant gently apply and release the brake pedal while you verify that both brake shoes move outward and return smoothly to their stops. If a shoe does not apply, or returns slowly to its anchor, a piston is frozen or sticking, and the wheel cylinder should be rebuilt or replaced. On brakes without piston stops, use two large screwdrivers to make sure the pistons are not pushed out of the cylinder bore. Insert the tips of the screwdrivers under the lip at the edge of the backing plate, then lever the screwdriver shafts against the brake shoes to prevent them from moving outward too far.

On cars with a live rear axle, inspect the backing plate where the axle exits its housing. If there is any sign of lubricant leakage, replace the axle seal to prevent contamination of the brake linings.

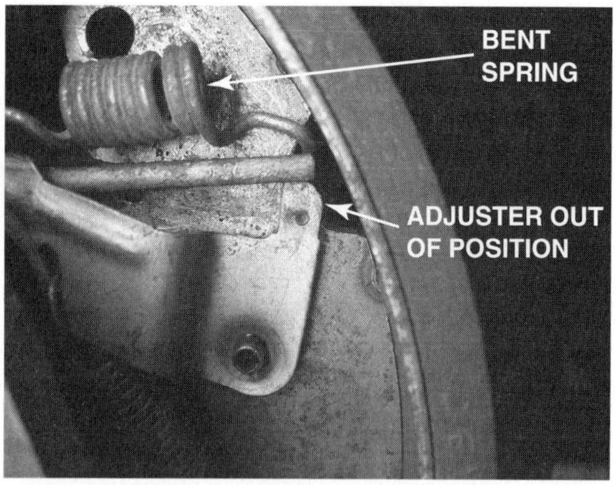

Hardware Inspection

Drum brake hardware consists of the shoe holddown devices, the shoe return springs, the automatic adjuster linkage, and the parking brake linkage. Replace any hardware that is not in perfect condition, and always replace the same hardware on both friction assemblies of an axle to maintain even braking from side to side.

Make sure the holddown springs, clips, pins, and washers are all present and securely fastened in place. If you pry the shoes slightly away from the backing plate and release them, the holddowns should pull the shoes back into place. While you have the shoes up off the backing plate, inspect the support pads for grooves, notches and any other wear, and make sure the pads are properly lubricated with brake grease.

Inspect for bent, broken, or distorted shoe return springs, and look for nicks in the springs that can weaken them. Also check the springs for discoloration and burnt paint that indicate the springs have been overheated. Excessive heat removes the temper from the springs and causes them to loose tension.

Check the condition of the automatic adjuster hardware, figure 7-17. The parts of a link-type adjuster should fit snugly together without excessive play. Adjusting cables should not have any loose or frayed strands, and the cable guide should not be worn. To test the operation of the adjuster, pry the appropriate brake shoe away from its anchor several times, figure 7-18, and check that the adjuster pawl rotates the starwheel to move the brake shoes apart. Be sure to adjust the starwheel back to its original position before you reinstall the brake drum.

Finally, make sure that when the parking brake pedal, lever, or handle is operated, the linkage in the

Figure 7-17. Close inspection of this brake assembly reveals a bent return spring and an incorrectly installed automatic adjusting lever.

Figure 7-18. Levering a brake shoe outward should actuate the automatic adjuster.

friction assembly moves the shoes apart, figure 7-19. The linkage cable should not have any loose or frayed strands, and it should return smoothly when the parking brake is released. If there is an anti-rattle spring on the parking brake strut, it should hold the strut under a con-

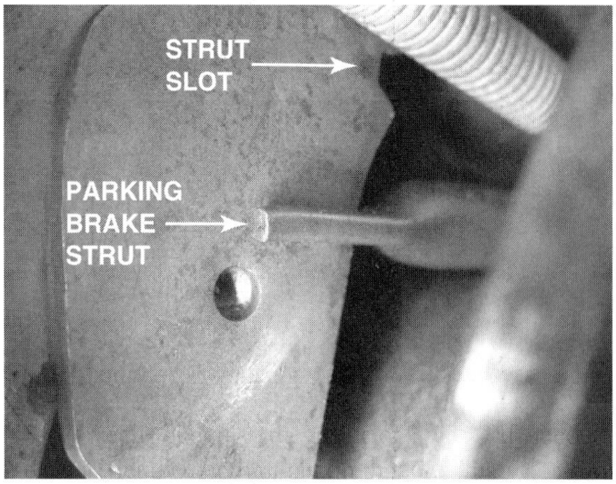

Drum Brake Service

Figure 7-19. The parking brake strut on this brake assembly has slipped out of the strut slot.

stant tension to prevent noise. See Chapter 10 for detailed parking brake inspection and repair information.

BRAKE ADJUSTING

When a drum brake is properly adjusted, the shoes retract only a short distance from the drum when the brakes are released. The exact lining-to-drum clearance varies with the brake design, but it is usually between .006″ and .015″ (.15 and .40 mm). Ideally, you want the smallest clearance possible without brake drag, plus a little extra clearance to allow for heat expansion of the shoes as the brakes are used.

Today, most drum brakes have automatic adjusters that eliminate the need for periodic manual adjustment. As the linings wear, the adjusters automatically reposition the shoes farther outward on the backing plates to maintain the proper lining-to-drum clearance. Manual adjustment of the brakes on cars with automatic adjusters is unnecessary unless scoring makes the brake drum difficult to remove, the brake shoes are replaced, or the automatic adjusters fail.

Drum brakes without automatic adjusters were once used on all cars, and can still be found on some older models. These brakes require periodic manual adjustment of the lining-to-drum clearance. The frequency of these adjustments varies with the type of friction material, the size of the brakes in relation to the weight of the car, the type of roads on which the car is driven, and the driving habits of the vehicle operator.

When a drum brake is adjusted properly, a minimum amount of pedal travel is required to apply the brakes, and there is plenty of pedal reserve to compensate for any brake fade that may occur. As the brake linings wear and the lining-to-drum clearance increases, brake pedal travel also increases, and pedal reserve is reduced. As a general rule, you should check and adjust drum brakes with manual adjusters every six months or 7500 miles (12,000 km), or whenever there is excessive brake pedal travel.

Brake Pedal Travel Test

Although excessive brake pedal travel is the main symptom of brakes that need adjustment, a low pedal can also be caused by other problems such as air in the hydraulic system. A low brake pedal caused by brake lining wear has a firm feel once the brakes are applied. If the pedal has ecessive travel but a spongy feel once the brakes are applied, there are other problems in the brake system.

When a car with front disc brakes has a parking brake that applies the shoes of the rear drum service brakes, a simple test can help you isolate the cause of the low pedal, and determine if the rear brakes need adjustment. The test uses the parking brake linkage to apply the brake shoes against the drum; because this eliminates all lining-to-drum clearance, it will also eliminate excessive pedal travel if brake adjustment is the cause. To perform the test:

1. With the parking brake released, apply the service brakes and note the amount of brake pedal travel.
2. Release the service brakes and apply the parking brake.
3. With the parking brake engaged, apply the service brakes several times; this moves the wheel cylinder pistons outward in their bores to take up the slack created when the parking brake was applied.
4. Once the brake pedal travel has stablized, compare it to the travel you observed in step 1.

If the pedal travel remains the same, the drum brakes are adjusted properly and the excessive travel is caused by air in the hydraulic system, or a problem with the front disc brakes. If pedal travel returns to normal when the parking brake is applied, adjust the rear brakes.

Parking Brake Caution

On cars where the parking brake applies the rear drum service brake shoes, another symptom of lining wear will be increased travel of the parking brake pedal, lever, or handle. However, unless you check and adjust the rear service brakes *before* you adjust the parking brake linkage, problems will result. Like a brake shoe adjuster, the parking brake linkage moves the shoes outward toward the drum. If you adjust the parking brake without first adjusting the wheel brakes, the parking brake linkage may hold the brake shoes off their anchors. Although this reduces the lining-to-drum clearance and returns the travel of the parking brake control and service brake pedal to normal, it places the parking brake cables under a constant strain that will cause them to stretch and eventually break. As the cables stretch, the brake adjustment will be lost and pedal travel will again increase. Also, because the shoes cannot return to their anchors when the brakes are released, they may not center properly in the drum, resulting in brake drag and increased lining wear.

Whenever you adjust the service brakes, always fully release the parking brake pedal, lever, or handle. If you suspect the parking brake linkage may be improperly adjusted and is partially applying the brake shoes, loosen the parking brake adjustment until there is slack in the cables. Once you complete the service brake adjustment, adjust the parking brake as described in Chapter 10.

BRAKE ADJUSTING PROCEDURE

The exact procedure for adjusting brakes varies with the type of adjuster. However, there are common steps that apply to all brake adjustment. First, raise and properly support the vehicle so the wheels to be adjusted hang free. Unless the brake adjusters or parking brake linkage have been overtightened, the wheels should rotate with no apparent drag. If loosening the adjustments does not free up the wheels, locate and repair the problem before you adjust the brakes.

Next, reduce the lining-to-drum clearance by tightening the adjuster as described in one of the sections below. As you do this, rotate the wheel in the direction that energizes the shoe or shoes being adjusted. This keeps the shoes centered in the drum and properly seated against their anchors. When you adjust a dual-servo or double-leading brake, rotate the wheel in the direction of forward travel. On a leading-trailing brake with a single adjuster, rotate the wheel back and forth as you tighten the adjuster. If a leading-trailing brake has a separate adjuster for each shoe, rotate the wheel in the direction of forward travel to adjust the leading shoe and in the direction of reverse travel to adjust the trailing shoe.

Continue to tighten the adjuster until there is a consistent heavy drag on the wheel, or the brake locks. Then, back off the adjustment the amount specified by the vehicle manufacturer, or until the wheel just turns free. Repeat the adjustment procedure at the other wheels as needed.

Problem Adjustments

On some cars, you may be able to tighten the adjuster a great deal after the linings make contact with the drum. Then, to get free wheel rotation, you will have to back off the adjustment so far that excessive brake pedal travel remains a problem. The pedal may also have a "springy" feel when this occurs. These are all signs that the brake linings are not properly arced to the curvature of the drum (a common problem when standard linings are installed in an oversize drum), or that the shoes are bent or warped. In either case, the lining makes only partial contact when it first touches the drum; further tightening of the adjuster flexes the shoe and brings the lining into greater contact with the drum.

The best repair in these situations is to replace or arc the brake shoes; however, this is not always a realistic option. When the problem is relatively minor, back off the brake adjuster the amount recommended by the manufacturer, and then an additional amount until there is a *very light* drag at the wheel and the brake pedal is reasonably high. A light drag is also acceptable with new brake shoes because it represents only a small area of lining contact with the drum. This portion of the lining will quickly wear away in the first few miles of driving.

SPECIFIC BRAKE ADJUSTERS

Manually adjusted brakes use four different adjuster designs: starwheel, cam, wedge, and anchor. The first three types are used to set the proper clearance between the brake linings and the drum. Anchor adjusters are used on some early brakes to center the brake shoes in the drum, and are always used with another type of adjuster, usually a starwheel, that adjusts the actual lining-to-drum clearance.

Starwheel Brake Adjustment

Starwheel brake adjusters are the most common type, and they are manufactured in both manual and automatic adjusting versions. Starwheel brake adjusters are usually adjusted through an access hole in the brake backing plate. However, some cars with automatic starwheel adjusters have the access hole in the brake drum web, and the tire and wheel must be removed to manually adjust the brakes.

Most brakes that use this adjuster design have a single starwheel adjuster between the shoes that adjusts both shoes at the same time. Some leading-trailing and double-leading brakes use two starwheel adjusters, one at each shoe, to adjust the shoes independently. When you service a brake with dual starwheels, complete the adjustment on one shoe, then proceed to the other.

Drum Brake Service

Manual Starwheel Adjustment

All starwheel adjusters are first turned in one direction to reduce the lining-to-drum clearance and tighten the adjustment, and then turned in the opposite direction to increase the lining-to-drum clearance and loosen the adjustment. With manual starwheel adjusters, lining-to-drum clearance is usually reduced by levering the starwheel upward as viewed through the access hole in the backing plate. This is not a hard and fast rule, however, and the direction of rotation that tightens or loosens the adjustment will vary from car to car, and sometimes from one side of the vehicle to the other!

To adjust the brakes on a car with manual starwheel adjusters:

1. Remove the plug covering the access hole in the backing plate or brake drum.
2. Insert a brake spoon of the appropriate size and shape through the access hole, figure 7-20, and engage the teeth on the starwheel.
3. Use a lever action to rotate the starwheel and reduce the lining-to-drum clearance. As you rotate the starwheel, the spring holding it in position should snap from one tooth to the next and cause a clicking sound.
4. When there is heavy drag at the wheel, or the brake locks, lever the starwheel in the opposite direction to increase the lining-to-drum clearance. Loosen the adjustment until the wheel just turns free, or you have rotated the starwheel the number of clicks specified by the vehicle manufacturer. As many as 20 to 30 clicks are required in some cases, so check the factory shop manual for the proper number.
5. Reinstall the plug in the adjuster access hole to prevent water and dirt from entering the friction assembly.

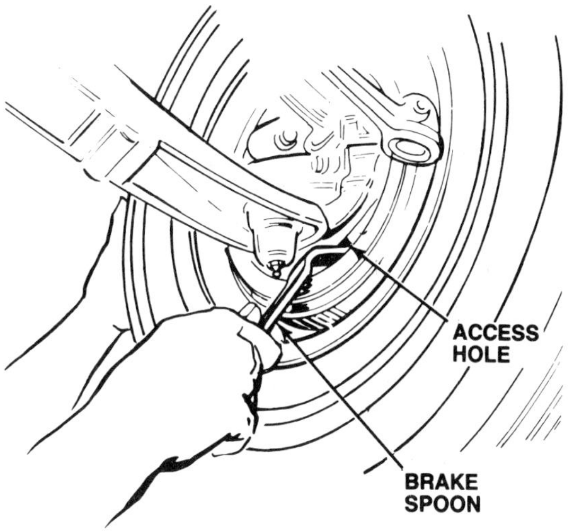

Automatic Starwheel Adjustment

Automatic starwheel adjusters require manual adjustment when scoring makes it difficult to remove the brake drum, when the brake shoes are replaced, or if the automatic adjusters fail. On some cars with automatic starwheel adjusters, the backing plate or drum is lanced for an access hole, figure 7-21, but the metal insert is still in place. To manually adjust the brakes on these cars, remove the insert from the lanced area with a hammer and punch. Take care so that the insert does not fall through the hole into the drum. Once the adjustment is complete, install a metal or rubber plug in the hole to prevent dirt and moisture from affecting braking. The plugs are available from auto dealers and aftermarket brake parts suppliers.

Figure 7-20. Use a brake spoon to turn a starwheel adjuster.

Figure 7-21. A lanced area must be removed to reach the brake adjuster on some cars.

The adjustment procedure is basically the same as for manual starwheel adjusters, with one exception: automatic starwheel adjusters cannot be loosened unless the adjuster ratchet pawl is held away from the starwheel. If you attempt to rotate the starwheel backwards against the pawl, you will round off the edge of the pawl and burr the teeth on the starwheel. If the damage is bad enough, the automatic adjusting mechanism will not operate properly.

To manually reduce the lining-to-drum clearance in a drum brake with automatic starwheel adjusters, use a

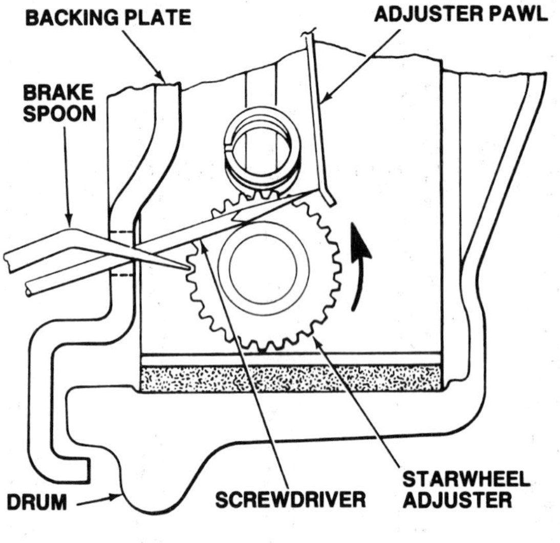

Figure 7-22. Using a screwdriver to push the automatic adjuster pawl out of the way.

brake spoon to rotate the starwheel as described above. The adjuster design will allow the starwheel to rotate only in the tightening direction, and the starwheel teeth will ratchet past the pawl at this time. If the brake adjustment loosens as you rotate the starwheel in the only direction it will turn, the starwheel adjuster assembly is installed backwards, or the assemblies have been swapped from side to side on the axle.

To loosen the adjustment, use a standard screwdriver or wire hook to hold the adjuster pawl out of the way. When the access hole is in the backing plate, use the screwdriver to push the lever away from the starwheel, figure 7-22. When the access hole is in the drum, use a wire hook to pull the self-adjuster lever away from the starwheel, figure 7-23. In either case, push or pull the pawl just hard enough to disengage it from the starwheel. If you use too much force you may bend parts of the automatic adjuster mechanism.

Cam Brake Adjustment

Cam-type manual adjusters are relatively rare, and are found primarily on older brakes. One adjuster is used on each brake shoe, and the shoes are adjusted independently. To adjust a cam-type adjuster, rotate the hex head of the adjuster stud that extends through the backing plate, figure 7-24. In most cases, lining-to-drum clearance is reduced as the wrench on the adjuster is moved downward. Some adjuster studs have arrows on them to indicate the tightening direction.

To adjust a brake equipped with cam-type adjusters, rotate the adjuster stud of the leading shoe to reduce the lining-to-drum clearance. When there is heavy drag at the wheel, or the brake locks, loosen the adjustment so

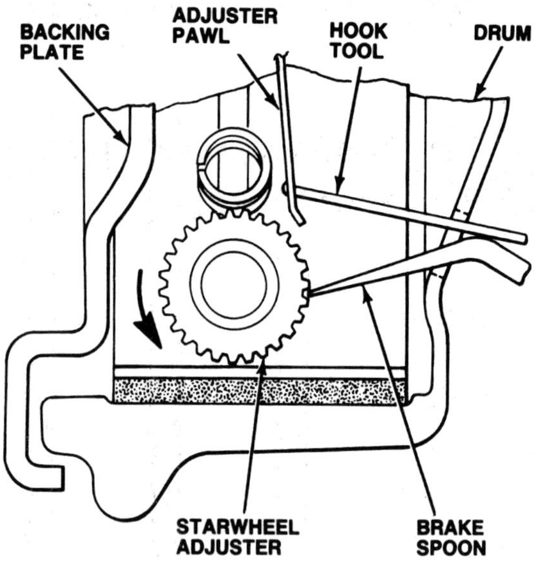

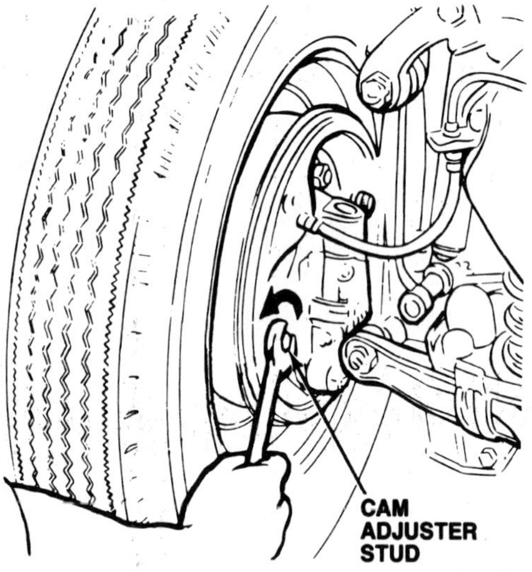

Figure 7-23. Using a wire hook to pull the automatic adjuster pawl out of the way.

Figure 7-24. Cam adjusters are rotated with conventional wrenches.

the wheel just turns free. Repeat this process on the trailing shoe.

Wedge Brake Adjustment

Wedge-type manual adjusters are found on older imported cars. With this design, you adjust both brake shoes at the same time by rotating a single adjusting bolt that extends through the backing plate, figure 7-25. Some bolts have a common hex head, but many have a metric-sized square head. Special tools are available to

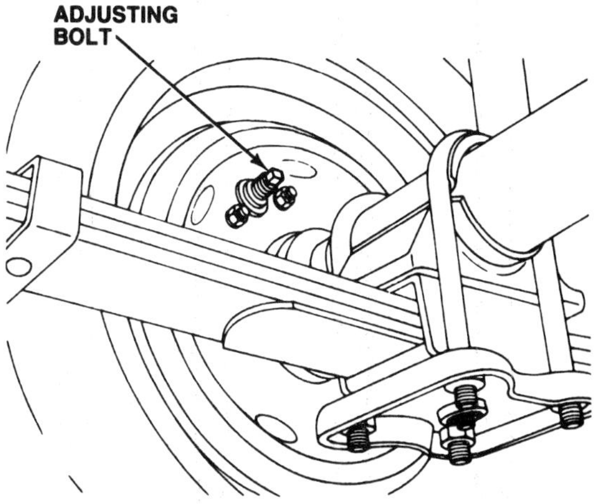

Drum Brake Service

Figure 7-25. The adjusting bolt of a wedge adjuster.

fit these square-head bolts; however, a tight-fitting wrench or an 8-point socket of the proper size can also be used to make the adjustment. In all cases, turning the bolt in a clockwise direction so it threads into the backing plate (travels outward on the vehicle) reduces the brake lining-to-drum clearance.

To adjust a brake with a wedge-type adjuster, rotate the adjusting bolt in a clockwise direction to reduce the lining-to-drum clearance. As the shoes move closer to the brake drum, the flats on the tapered end of the bolt inside the brake will cause the bolt to alternately tighten and loosen, and the brake will grab and release at the same time. When you can tighten the adjusting bolt no farther, loosen the bolt the number of flats recommended by the vehicle manufacturer, or until the wheel just turns free.

Anchor Brake Adjustment

Anchor adjusters are used on some older brakes to center the shoes in the drum for better lining contact and more effective braking. If the shoes are not properly centered, it is impossible to accurately adjust the lining-to-drum clearance. Anchor adjusters were dropped from domestic car brakes in the late 1950s when undersize- and cam-ground brake shoes made them unnecessary. Imported cars continued to use anchor adjusters into the 1960s, and some large truck brakes still have adjustable brake shoe anchors.

As mentioned earlier, anchor adjusters are always used with another type of adjuster that sets the lining-to-drum clearance. In normal driving conditions, only the clearance between the brake linings and drum requires periodic attention. This operation is called a minor brake adjustment, and depending on the type of shoe adjuster used, the procedure is identical to one of those described earlier.

Anchor adjustment is normally needed only when the brake shoes are replaced, or at high-mileage intervals when significant lining wear has taken place. This operation is called a major brake adjustment. During a major brake adjustment, you adjust the shoes and the anchor at the same time. The method used to do this varies depending on whether the brake is fitted with an eccentric anchor or a slotted anchor.

Eccentric Anchor Adjustment

To adjust an eccentric anchor, tighten the shoe adjuster until a medium drag is felt when turning the wheel with one hand. Loosen the anchor pin locknut one-half turn, figure 7-26A, and slowly rotate the pin in the direction of forward wheel rotation until you feel the least amount of drag as you rotate the wheel. Hold the anchor pin in position and tighten the locknut, then finish adjusting the lining-to-drum clearance as described earlier.

Slotted Anchor Adjustment

To adjust a slotted anchor, tighten the shoe adjuster until a heavy drag is felt while turning the wheel with both hands. Loosen the anchor pin locknut one full turn, figure 7-26B, then tap the anchor pin and backing plate with a plastic hammer to allow the shoes to center in the drum. If the amount of drag on the wheel changes, retighten the shoe adjuster and again tap the anchor pin and backing plate. Repeat this procedure until the drag on the wheel remains constant, then tighten the anchor pin locknut to the manufacturer's specification. Finish adjusting the lining-to-drum clearance as described earlier.

BRAKE SHOE REPLACEMENT

Brake shoes are sold and serviced as axle sets. An axle set consists of four shoes, one pair for the friction assembly at each wheel. Shoes from different manufacturers should never be mixed. Although they will fit and may appear the same, the friction coefficients of the linings may be quite different. Even if only one shoe of an axle set is badly worn, the entire set should be replaced after the problem causing uneven wear has been repaired.

The most efficient way to replace the brake shoes on an axle is to disassemble and service both friction assemblies at the same time. However, if you are unfamiliar with a particular brake design, a good practice is to work on only one wheel at a time so the other brake can serve as a model for assembly. This is important because even a small error in assembly can have a big effect on brake operation. If you do disassemble both

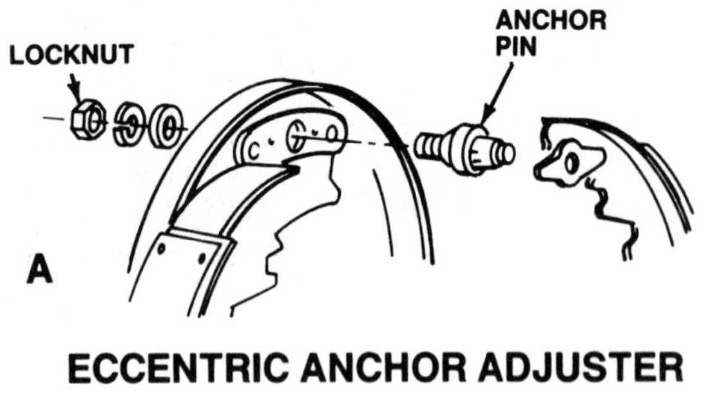

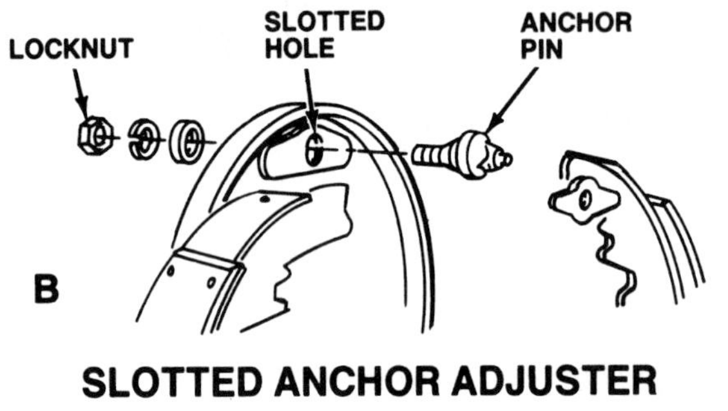

Figure 7-26. The locknuts for adjustable anchors are on the backside of the backing plate.

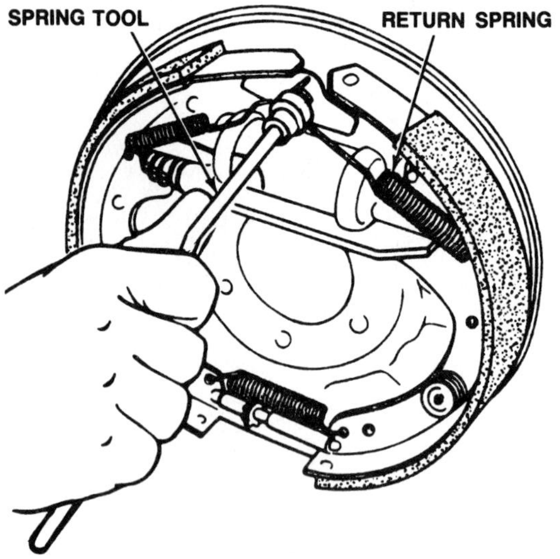

Figure 7-27. Removing a brake return spring.

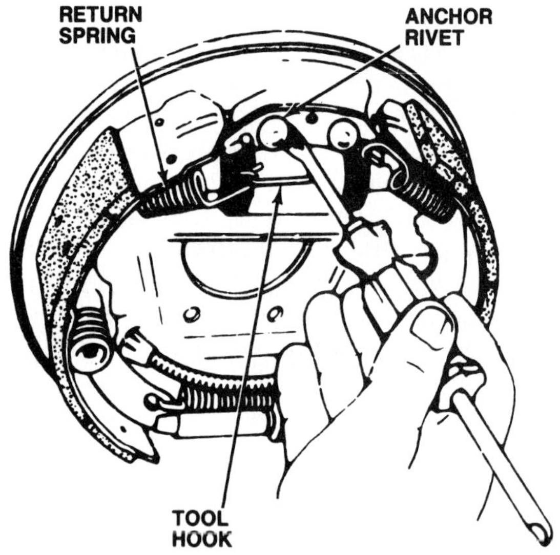

Figure 7-28. Removing a brake return spring on a GM brake.

brakes at the same time, keep the parts for each wheel separated. Many parts that appear the same on both friction assemblies, starwheel adjusters for example, are actually different from side to side.

The exact procedure used to replace a set of brake shoes varies with the design of the friction assembly. Step-by-step shoe replacement procedures for several typical drum brake friction assemblies are provided at the end of the chapter. The sections below describe a general procedure that includes the common operations required to disassemble, inspect, and reassemble drum brakes.

Brake Disassembly

The first step in any shoe replacement job is to remove the brake drum as described earlier in the chapter. After that point, however, the order in which the many parts of the friction assembly are disassmbled varies from one brake to another. The shoe return springs are often the first parts removed. Before you remove the springs, note how they are installed, which holes they fit into in the shoe webs, and how the springs overlap on the anchor post (where applicable).

Springs that hook over an anchor post are removed with a special tool as shown in figure 7-27. Place the tool over the post and hook the flange under the end of the spring; rotate the tool to lever the spring up and off the anchor. Once the springs are free, remove the anchor plate and adjuster cable or linkage (if fitted) from the anchor post.

The special tool used to remove the return springs from the rear drum brakes on FWD General Motors cars, figure 7-28, works somewhat differently. Attach the hook of the tool to the end of the return spring, then lever the shaft of the tool against the anchor rivet to remove the spring. Return springs that install between two brake shoes can be removed with a pair of brake spring pliers; however, this is often unnecessary because once the shoes are removed from the anchor,

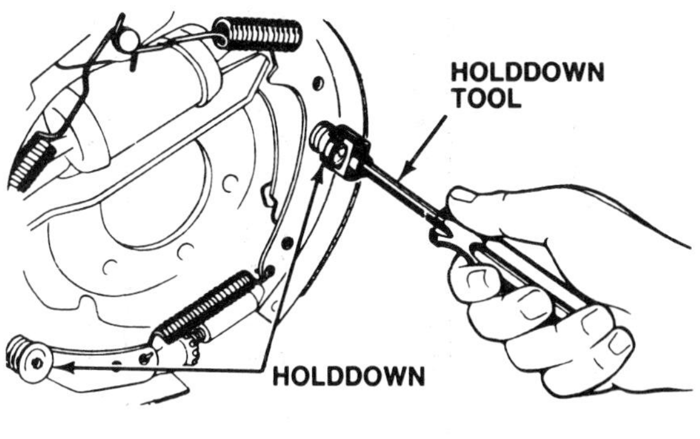

Drum Brake Service

Figure 7-29. Removing a brake shoe holddown.

they can be collapsed together to release the tension on the shoe-to-shoe spring.

The next step in disassembly is often to remove the brake shoe holddowns. Most holddown devices can be removed by hand or with common hand tools, although there are special tools available to make the job easier. The most common of these is used with spring-and-pin holddowns, figure 7-29. To remove the hold down, place the tool over the spring retaining washer; while holding the pin in place from the backside of the backing plate, push the tool inward and rotate it to release the washer from the flattened end of the pin. When a spring clip is used with a holddown pin, depress the clip by hand and slide it out from under the pin. To remove a coiled spring "beehive" holddown, insert a Phillips screwdriver into the coil, and while holding the retaining clip in place from the backside of the backing plate, push the screwdriver inward and disengage the hook on the spring from the retaining clip.

Once the return springs and shoe holddowns are removed, disassembly of the friction assembly can be completed. In most cases, simply reposition the brake shoes as needed so the shoe-to-shoe return springs, automatic adjusting mechanism, and parking brake linkage can be disconnected. To prevent problems on assembly, note the location of each part you remove, and how the part is installed.

Brake Detailed Inspection

Once the friction assembly is disassembled, inspect the brake drum as described in Chapter 9 and determine whether it needs to be turned or replaced. Even though a drum removed from a car may appear in perfect condition, it often has minor wear and distortion that cannot be spotted visually, but will affect braking performance. Because of this, it is common practice to always turn the drums when replacing brake shoes in order to guarantee a good job. If the drum hub contains the wheel bearings, you should also repack the bearings when you replace the brake shoes. Information on bearing service is located in Chapter 14.

Next, inspect the brake backing plate and its mounting bolts. If the plate is bent or cracked, replace it. If the mounting bolts are loose, torque them to the car manufacturer's specifications. Also, check the shoe support pads for grooves, notches, or any other signs of wear. Minor wear is considered normal; grind or file the pads smooth to repair the problem. If the pads are deeply grooved, replace the backing plate. If a replacement backing plate is unavailable, and you are trained in the proper use of an oxyacetylene torch, it is acceptable to build up the worn support pads with brazing rod then grind or file them smooth.

Once you are sure the backing plate is in good condition inspect the wheel cylinder as described later in this chapter. Just as drums are turned whenever the brake shoes are replaced, it is common practice to always rebuild or replace the wheel cylinders as well. Unless this is done, the thicker linings on the new shoes will force the wheel cylinder pistons back over portions of the bore that may have become rusted or corroded. This will quickly cause a fluid leak that will contaminate the linings, cause an expensive comeback, and result in an unhappy customer. Rebuilding or replacing the wheel cylinders is inexpensive insurance.

When you replace a set of brake shoes, most vehicle manufacturers recommend that you automatically replace the shoe return springs as well. They do this because faulty springs are sometimes hard to spot. Even if a spring appears in perfect condition, it may have lost part of its tension from the hundreds of thousands of times it has been stretched in normal brake operation.

If you are unsure about whether the springs need to be replaced, here are some guidelines and simple tests to follow. Always replace springs that are bent, broken, distorted or have nicks in them. Burnt paint or obvious discoloration on a spring are sure signs that it has been overheated and lost tension, and should be replaced. Most brake shoe return springs have closed-coil construction, and can be visibly tested by holding them up to a light. If you can see light shining between the individual coils of the spring, it has stretched and should be replaced. Closed-coil springs can also be checked using the drop test. Drop the spring from waist height onto a concrete floor; if there is a dull thud as it hits the ground, the spring is probably in good condition; however, if there is a ringing noise as it hits the floor, the spring has open space between its coils and should be replaced.

In addition to the shoe return springs, manufacturers also recommend you always replace shoe holddown hardware and automatic adjuster cables. Like return springs, these parts are difficult to inspect. For example, you cannot tell if a holddown spring or pin is weakened unless it has obvious physical damage; in the same manner, a stretched adjuster cable looks perfectly normal until you compare its length to that of a new one. These parts play a major role in smooth and quiet brake operation; if any of them brake loose in operation, severe lining damage and drum scoring will result. The cost of these components is small compared to repairing the problems they will cause if they fail.

The final parts to inspect are those in the automatic adjusting mechanism and parking brake linkage. These differ depending on the design of the brake; however, look for bent components and wear at the points where the parts contact one another. If the car has starwheel adjusters, disassemble the adjuster assembly and clean it thoroughly, figure 7-30. Replace the adjuster if the starwheel teeth are rounded. Use a wire brush to clean any rust and grime from the adjuster threads, then lubricate the threads with brake grease and screw the adjuster together through its full range of travel. If the threads bind at any point, repair the problem or replace the adjuster.

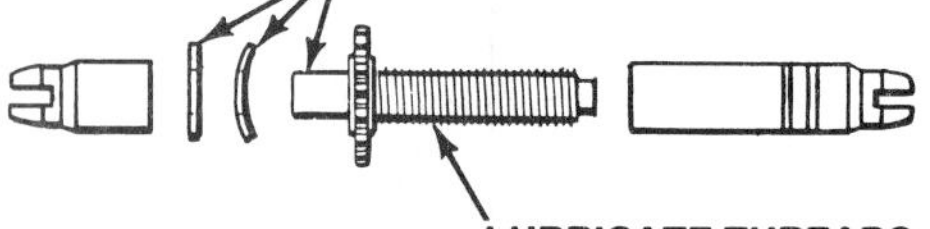

Brake Assembly

Drum brake assembly is essentially the reverse of disassembly, although there are some things to be aware of. Most of these points concern making sure that all parts are reinstalled in their proper locations. There are also a few special techniques used to install specific brake components.

If the brake inspection revealed problems with the brake wheel cylinders, refer to the section later in this chapter, Wheel Cylinder Service. The wheel cylinders must be overhauled or replaced before continuing with the brake assembly procedure. After servicing the wheel cylinder, return here.

The first step in assembly is to compare the replacement brake shoes to the original equipment parts. The replacement shoes do not have to be absolutely identical to the original parts; however, they should have the appropriate holes in the shoe webs, and the linings should be the same basic size and shape as those on the originals. If there are major differences in the construction of the shoes or the sizes of the linings, contact your parts supplier and make sure you have the proper shoes for the application.

Next, determine where the shoes belong on the car. Although they may physically fit in more than one position, most brake shoes are designed to be installed in a particular spot. On a dual-servo brake, for example, the primary shoe generally has a smaller lining than the secondary shoe, and the friction materials used for the two linings may be differ as well. Always install the primary shoe so it is pulled away from the anchor when

Figure 7-30. Starwheel adjusters must be clean and properly lubricated to work correctly.

the brakes are applied with the wheel turning in the direction of forward rotation. Some leading-trailing brakes are also designed to use shoes that have different friction characteristics. In these applications, install the replacement shoes in the same relative locations as the original equipment parts. If you have any question about the proper shoe positions, consult the component manufacturer or the shop manual of the vehicle being serviced.

Once you have determined the proper locations for the replacement shoes, remove any parking brake linkage pieces or similar parts from the old shoes. Transfer these parts to the appropriate replacement shoes, and install them using new fasteners. Lubricate the shoe support pads on the backing plate with brake grease, figure 7-31, then assemble the shoes on the backing plate. The procedure required to do this varies with the design of the friction assembly; basically, however, you reposition the shoes as needed until the parking brake linkage, brake adjuster, and the shoes themselves are all fitted together in their proper positions.

While assembling a friction assembly, be sure to use only the parts intended for that side of the car. For example, all starwheel adjusters look alike, but right-side adjusters usually have left-hand threads, while left-side adjusters have right-hand threads. If an adjuster is installed on the wrong side, the automatic adjusting mechanism will increase the lining-to-drum clearance rather than reduce it. Some starwheel adjusters are marked L or R to indicate the side of the car on which they belong.

Once the shoes are assembled in position, install the holddowns to secure the shoes in place. On pin and spring holddowns, insert the pin through the holes in the backing plate and brake shoe web. Then, while holding the pin in place from the backside of the backing plate, use the special tool to compress the spring and retaining washer over the end of the pin. Rotate the washer as needed to lock it onto the flattened end of the pin. Where a spring clip is used with a holddown pin, compress the clip by hand and slip it into position under the flattened end of the pin. To install a coil-spring "beehive" holddown, hold the retaining clip in place

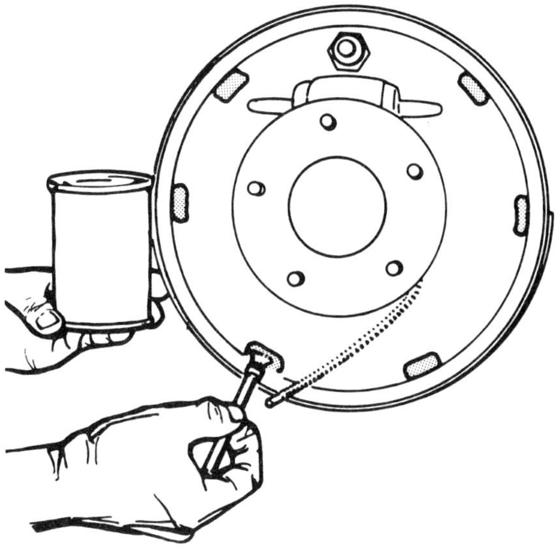

Drum Brake Service

Figure 7-31. Lubricate the shoe contact pads with high-temperature brake grease or silicone grease. Do not use wheel bearing grease.

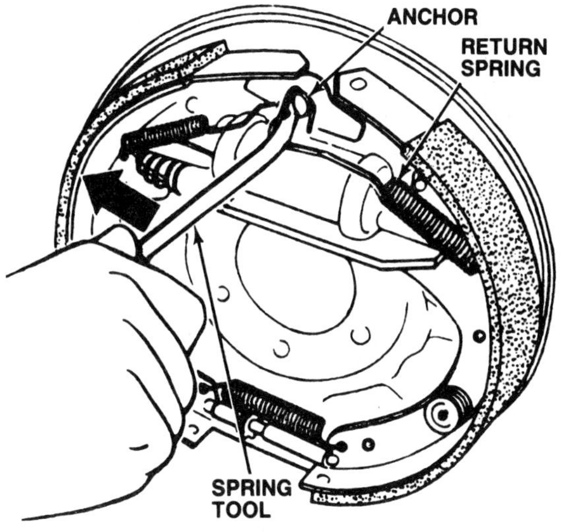

Figure 7-32. Installing a shoe return spring on an anchor post.

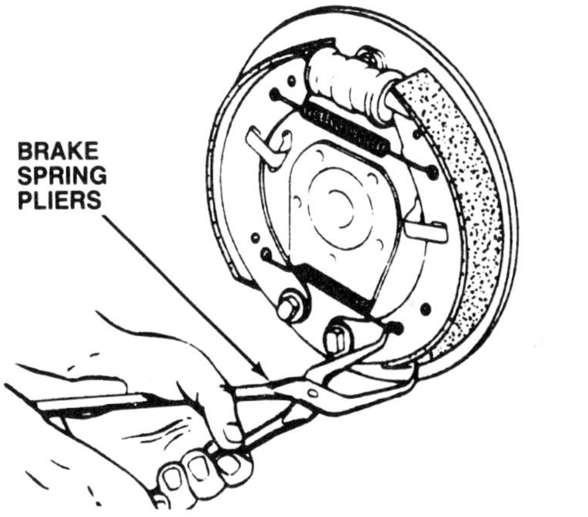

Figure 7-33. Installing a shoe-to-shoe return spring.

from the backside of the backing plate, then use a Phillips screwdriver to push the spring inward and engage its hook into the retaining clip.

The final step in drum brake assembly is to install the shoe return springs. It is very important to install the proper spring in the proper direction, in the proper location. Some springs can be installed only one way, and their proper position is easy to identify. Different paint colors are often used to distinguish similar springs that have different tensions. Certain springs have a longer straight section and attachment hook at one end than at the other. These springs must be installed facing a specific direction, or the coiled section of the spring will interfere with another part of the friction assembly. Sometimes, there are several holes in the shoe web where a spring can be attached. If you install a spring in the wrong hole, it will affect the rate at which the brake shoes apply and release. If you failed to note how the springs were installed when you disassembled the friction assembly, consult a shop manual for the proper locations.

Return springs are installed in two basic ways, and both methods require a special tool. To install a spring that fits over an anchor post, attach the appropriate end of the spring into the hole in the shoe web. Then, place the notched end of the spring tool on the anchor post, and drape the hook end of the spring over the tool shaft, figure 7-32. Finally, taking care not to overstretch the spring, lever the tool back so the spring slides down the shaft and into place on the anchor.

Shoe-to-shoe return springs are installed using brake spring pliers, figure 7-33. Install one end of the spring into its hole in the brake shoe web, and place the other end over the hooked arm of the brake spring pliers. Position the pliers over the shoe the spring is to be attached to; the pointed arm of the plier should contact the lining at the same level as the hole the spring is to engage. If possible, position the pointed arm on a lining rivet; otherwise, position it directly on the lining and use extra caution to prevent damage. Squeeze the handle of the pliers to stretch the spring to the appropriate length, then insert the end of the spring into the hole in the web. Remove the plier, and make sure both ends of the spring are fully engaged in the web holes.

INITIAL BRAKE ADJUSTMENT

When you replace a set of brake shoes, you generally bottom the adjuster mechanism so the shoes are at their smallest diameter. This makes it easier to install the return springs, and ensures that the brake drum will easily slip over the shoes. However, once the brake is assembled, and you are sure the drum fits, you must adjust the initial lining-to-drum clearance so the brake pedal travel will be satisfactory. On cars with starwheel brake adjusters, the initial adjustment is usually done before the drum is installed. On cars without starwheel brake adjusters, the initial adjustment is performed after the brake drum is installed.

Initial Adjustment—Starwheel Adjusters

Both manual and automatic starwheel brake adjusters make their adjustments in very small increments. If you attempt to adjust the brakes manually after the drum is installed, more than a hundred clicks of the adjuster may be required to get the proper clearance. This is both tiring and time-consuming. When you make the initial adjustment before you install the drum, final manual adjustment will be quick and easy, or you can use the automatic adjusters to make the final adjustment during the test drive.

To perform the initial adjustment, place a shoe-setting caliper in the brake drum as shown in figure 7-34. Slide the caliper back and forth and spread the jaws until they span the drum at its widest point. Tighten the lock screw to fix the caliper at this setting. Depending on the brand of tool being used, the opening on the opposite side of the caliper is now set to equal the drum diameter, or be approximately .020″ (.50 mm) smaller than the drum diameter to provide a clearance of .010″ (.25 mm) between the drum and each brake shoe.

Remove the caliper from the drum, and place the open side over the brake shoes as shown in figure 7-35. If the caliper opening matches the drum diameter, rotate the starwheel adjuster as needed until there is approximately .020″ (.50 mm) clearance between the caliper opening and the shoes at their widest point. If the caliper setting includes the desired lining-to-drum clearance, rotate the starwheel adjuster as needed until the caliper just slides over the shoes at their widest point. Hold the automatic adjuster pawl out of the way while turning the starwheel so neither becomes burred. On brakes with dual starwheel adjusters, rotate each starwheel an equal amount.

Once the initial adjustment is completed, install the brake drum and check to make sure the brake pedal is fairly high and firm. On cars with manual starwheel adjusters, perform a final brake adjustment as described earlier in the chapter. On cars with automatic

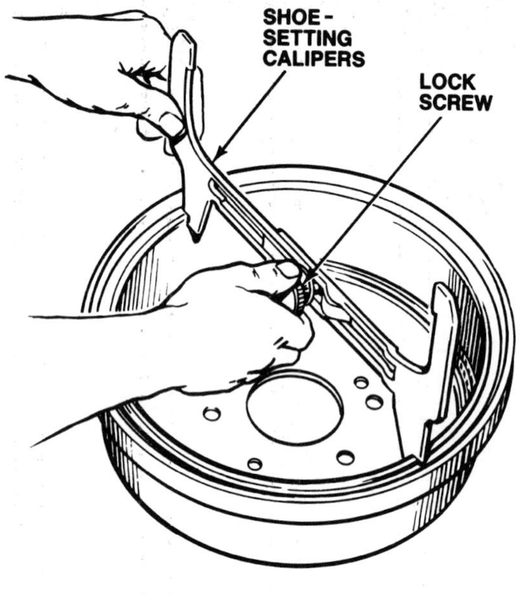

Figure 7-34. Measure the brake drum diameter with a shoe-setting caliper. (Courtesy of General Motors Corporation, Service and Parts Operations)

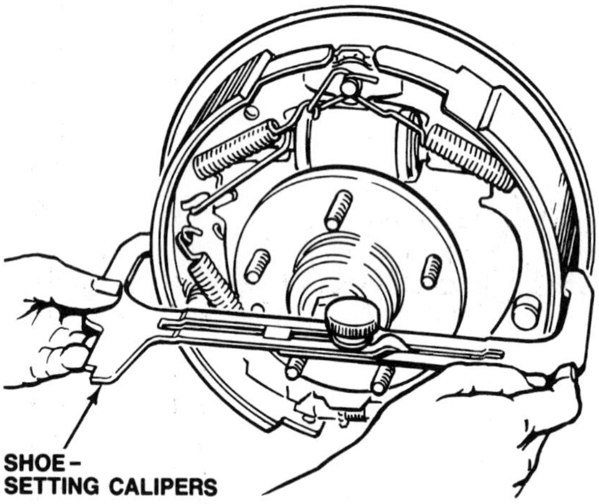

Figure 7-35. Transfer the drum measurement to the shoes with the shoe-setting caliper. (Courtesy of General Motors Corporation, Service and Parts Operations)

starwheel adjusters, take the car for a test drive and apply the brakes several times while traveling forward or in reverse (depending on the design of the adjuster) to complete the adjustment.

Initial Adjustment—Drum Installed

On cars without starwheel brake adjusters, the initial adjustment is generally made with the drum installed because other adjuster designs make it quick and easy

Drum Brake Service

to set the lining-to-drum clearance. To perform the initial adjustment on brakes with cam- or wedge-type manual adjusters, follow the procedures for manual adjustment described earlier in the chapter.

A few brakes have automatic adjusters that can take up large amounts of lining-to-drum clearance very rapidly. On these brakes, the initial adjustment is made after the brake drum is installed by simply applying the brake pedal or parking brake lever a few times.

BRAKE SHOE BURNISH-IN

Whenever new brake shoes are installed, they require a short time of relatively light use called a burnishing-in or bedding-in period. There are two reasons for this. First, new shoes do not make full contact with the drum friction surface. A short period of light braking allows the shoes and drums to become "familiar" with one another and wear into better contact.

The second reason a burnish-in period is needed is because new brake linings are not fully cured when they come from the factory; there are still binding resins and other chemicals that have not completely evaporated from the friction material. Final curing takes place over the first few hundred miles of driving as the shoes are repeatedly heated and cooled.

If new brakes are used hard immediately and become too hot, residual resins boil out of the shoes as gases and liquids. If these gases and liquids come out in great enough quantities, they will lubricate the friction material and cause a type of brake fade called green fade. When green fade occurs, the shoes will be glazed when they return to normal operating temperature. Glazed shoes do not have the proper friction coefficient for smooth operation, are usually very noisy, and must be replaced.

Brake Burnishing Procedure

Whenever you replace any of the friction materials in a brake system, take the car for a test drive afterward to make sure the brakes are operating properly. During the test drive, perform the simple procedure below to burnish-in the new shoes and/or pads:

1. Drive the car at approximately 30 mph (50 kph). Check your rear-view mirror to make sure it is safe to do so, then apply the brakes with *moderate to firm* pressure to slow the car to about 5 mph (8 kph).
2. Accelerate back to speed, and drive for approximately 15 seconds to allow the brakes to cool. Make another stop as described in step 1. Continue to alternate stops with cooldown periods until you have made about a half dozen stops in this manner.
3. Accelerate to approximately 55 mph (88 kph). Check your rear-view mirror to make sure it is safe to do so, then apply the brakes with *moderate to firm* pressure to slow the car to about 20 mph (30 kph).
4. Accelerate back to speed, and drive for approximately 30 seconds to allow the brakes to cool. Make another stop as described in step 3. Continue to alternate stops with cooldown periods until you have made about a half dozen stops in this manner.
5. When you deliver the car to its owner, caution them that the brakes should not be used hard for approximately 100 miles of in-town driving, or 300 miles of highway driving. This will ensure that the brakes will become properly burnished in.

WHEEL CYLINDER SERVICE

A leaking wheel cylinder presents two main problems. First, it eventually drains half the brake hydraulic system and allows air to enter; this results in a major loss of braking power. Second, as it leaks, the wheel cylinder contaminates the brake linings with fluid; this reduces stopping power, causes the brakes to slip or grab, and makes the car pull to one side during braking. A leaking wheel cylinder must be rebuilt or replaced. If the brake linings have been contaminated with fluid, the entire wheel friction assembly will require an overhaul.

Wheel Cylinder Inspection

To inspect a wheel cylinder, remove the brake drum, then grasp the wheel cylinder and attempt to move it. If any movement is detected, make sure all of the mounting hardware is in place and properly tightened. Some imported cars have wheel cylinders that slide in a slot on the backing plate. These cylinders are designed to move, so simply make sure the mounting clips are present and properly installed, and the dust boot that seals the slot is in good condition.

Inspect the outside of the wheel cylinder for signs of leakage; minor stains caused by fluid seepage are considered normal. Fold back the cylinder dust boots and look for signs of liquid; if you find more than a slight amount of dampness, the cylinder must be rebuilt or replaced.

Next, check for free movement of the wheel cylinder pistons. With the brake drum from only a single wheel removed, have an assistant gently apply and release the brake pedal while you verify that both brake shoes move outward and return smoothly to their stops. On brakes without piston stops, use two large screwdrivers to make sure the pistons are not pushed out of the cylinder bore. Insert the tips of the screwdrivers under the lip at the edge of the backing plate, then lever the screwdriver shafts against the brake shoes to prevent them from moving outward too far.

Depending on the brake design, a frozen wheel cylinder piston can prevent one or both of the brake shoes from applying. This increases the amount of force that must be applied to the brake pedal for a given stop, and causes a pull toward the side of the car that does not have the frozen piston. A sticking piston that slows or prevents full return of the brake shoes will cause the brakes to drag, resulting in rapid lining wear, and possibly heat fade.

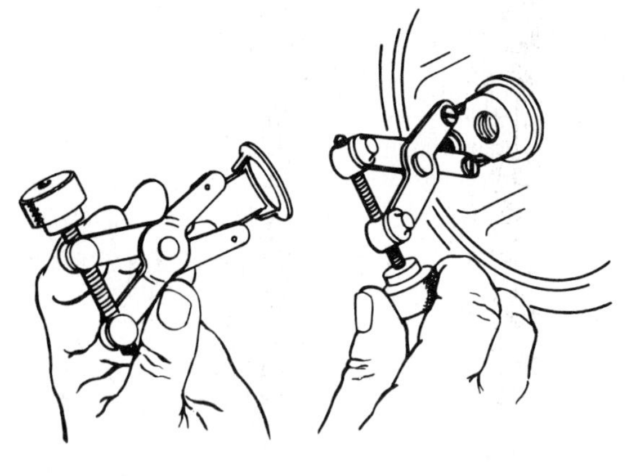

Wheel Cylinder Replacement

When an external inspection reveals that a wheel cylinder needs further service, it does not necessarily mean the cylinder must be removed from the car. Many wheel cylinders can be taken apart, internally inspected, and rebuilt while they are still mounted on the backing plate. Wherever possible, leave the cylinder in place while you perform an internal inspection (described in the overhaul section later in the chapter) to determine whether the cylinder can be rebuilt or if it must be replaced. However, if the wheel cylinder is recessed into the backing plate, or the backing plate incorporates piston stops, the cylinder will have to be removed from the backing plate for any further work.

To remove a wheel cylinder:

1. Remove brake drum and disassemble the friction assembly as described earlier in this chapter.
2. Disconnect the steel brake line or rubber hose from the wheel cylinder as described in Chapter 4.
3. Remove the retaining hardware that holds the cylinder to the backing plate. Most cars use a pair of bolts for this purpose, but some GM cars have a retaining clip that requires a special tool, figure 7-36, to bend back the retainer tabs and release the wheel cylinder. A pair of awls can also be used if the special tool is unavailable. On imported cars that use a sliding wheel cylinder, release the retaining clips taking care to note the relative positions of the various parts.

If the cylinder had to be removed from the car to perform an internal inspection, do so at this time. Once the cylinder is rebuilt, or a new replacement part is obtained, install the wheel cylinder as follows:

1. Position the wheel cylinder on the backing plate, and loosely thread the brake hose or tubing fitting into the cylinder.
2. Install the wheel cylinder mounting hardware. If applicable, torque the mounting bolts to the

Figure 7-36. A GM wheel cylinder retaining clip being removed with a special tool.

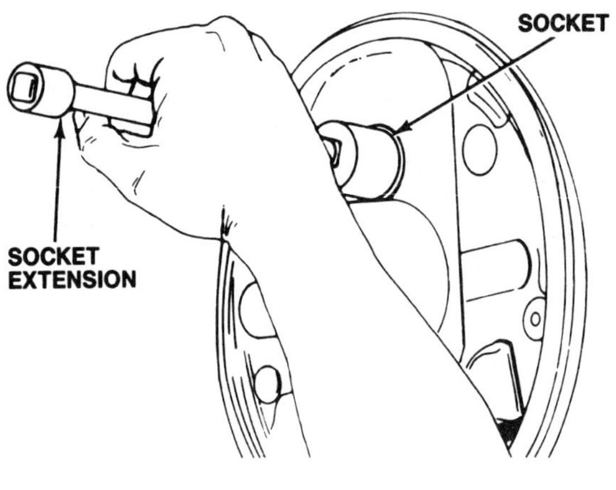

Figure 7-37. Installing the GM wheel cylinder retaining clip. (Courtesy of General Motors Corporation, Service and Parts Operations)

proper tightness. On GM cars with a retaining clip, hold the wheel cylinder in place with a block of wood between the cylinder and axle flange, then tap the retainer into place with one of the special tools available for this purpose, figure 7-37, or a 1⅛-inch 12-point socket; make sure the retainer tabs fully engage the slot on the cylinder. If the car was equipped with a bracket to keep the wheel cylinder from rotating, the bracket *must* be reinstalled. On imported cars with sliding cylinders, install the retaining clips in the correct order and make sure they are properly locked together. Install the dust boot to prevent dirt from entering the friction assembly through the slot.
3. Tighten the brake hose or tubing fitting where it enters the wheel cylinder, and finish installing the brake line.

Drum Brake Service

4. Assemble the friction assembly and install the brake drum.
5. Bleed the brakes as described in Chapter 3.

Wheel Cylinder Overhaul

Once an external inspection has revealed that the wheel cylinder will require further service, the next step is to disassemble the cylinder and determine whether it can be rebuilt or if it must be replaced. In the past, most cylinders were rebuilt and returned to service. Today, the trend is to replace defective cylinders.

There are many reasons wheel cylinders are rebuilt less often today. Hydraulic cylinder overhaul requires a fair amount of time and skill on the part of the technician. At modern shop labor rates, it is often less expensive for the customer in the long run if the cylinder is replaced. Considering the brake system's critical part in vehicle safety, and the large number of lawsuits filed in recent years, cylinder replacement can be more appealing because it places a portion of the liability for the repair job on the manufacturer of the replacement part.

Overhaul Kits

The job of overhauling a wheel cylinder involves replacing all of the cylinder components that are subject to wear. These parts are purchased in an overhaul or rebuild kit. A rebuild kit will usually not include every part in the cylinder; the exact contents vary based on the supplier and the cost of the kit. For example, all wheel cylinder rebuild kits contain new rubber cup seals and dust boots, but better quality kits may also include new pistons, cup expanders, and the cup expander spring. Some kits for imported cars even include a rubber dust cover for the bleeder screw.

When rebuilding a hydraulic cylinder, it is helpful to know beforehand exactly what parts you need, and what parts are included in the rebuild kit. This ensures that you will have everything available you need to complete the job. It also saves you having to clean old parts that will be replaced anyway.

Cylinder Internal Inspection

As stated in the previous section, overhauling a hydraulic cylinder involves replacing the parts most likely to wear. Essentially, this means replacing everything but the cylinder body and, in some cases, the metal pistons. This means that to determine whether a wheel cylinder can be rebuilt, you must inspect the condition of the cylinder body, and the cylinder bore in particular.

If a wheel cylinder is equipped with bleeder screws, the first inspection step is always to attempt to loosen the screws with a bleeder wrench. It is not unusual for bleeder screws to become rusted or corroded in place

Figure 7-38. The condition of the bore is a primary factor in determining whether a hydraulic cylinder can be rebuilt.

so they cannot be removed. In most cases, cylinders with frozen bleeder screws should be replaced. The exceptions are when a replacement cylinder is unavailable, or its cost is so high that the time and effort spent on bleeder screw removal can be justified.

Once you are sure the bleeder screws are free, disassemble the cylinder and wipe the bore clean. Shine a light into the cylinder and inspect the bore, figure 7-38. If the cylinder is made of cast iron and the bore is in good condition, or only lightly scratched, pitted, scored, or rusted, the cylinder can probably be honed and rebuilt. If the bore is deeply scored, the cylinder must be replaced. If deep scores are honed out, so much metal is removed that the cylinder bore becomes oversize and the piston cup seals will not seal properly because they lose tension against the cylinder wall. Also, if a cast-iron cylinder shows any sign of having been rebuilt before, such as honing marks in the bore or nonstock rubber parts, it is best to replace the cylinder rather than risk another rebuild.

If an aluminum wheel cylinder is scratched, pitted, scored, or corroded in any way, the cylinder must be replaced. Aluminum cylinders cannot be honed because they have a wear-resistant, anodized finish. Honing would cut through the anodizing and the resulting bare aluminum finish would corrode very rapidly and be too rough for good sealing.

Bleeder Screw Removal

If it is necessary to remove a frozen bleeder screw, spray the screw threads with penetrating oil and allow it to soak in for at least 10 minutes. Then, place a deep socket over the bleeder screw so it contacts the body of the cylinder around the base of the screw. Wearing safety glasses to prevent injuries, strike the socket several medium-firm blows; this should slightly deform the metal of the cylinder and break the surface tension between the bleeder screw threads and those in the cylinder opening. Attempt to remove the bleeder screw with the appropriate wrench, but do not apply too much turning force or you will twist the end of the screw off. Once this happens, it is virtually impossible to remove the portion of the screw that remains in the cylinder.

Repeat the procedures with the penetrating oil, socket and hammer, and bleeder wrench as needed until the screw is free. To make this process easier, special hammer sockets are available from the aftermarket that allow you to apply both hammer blows and turning force at the same time, figure 7-39. Once you remove a bleeder screw, buff its threads clean on a wire wheel, and run a drill bit through its passageways to make sure they are clear.

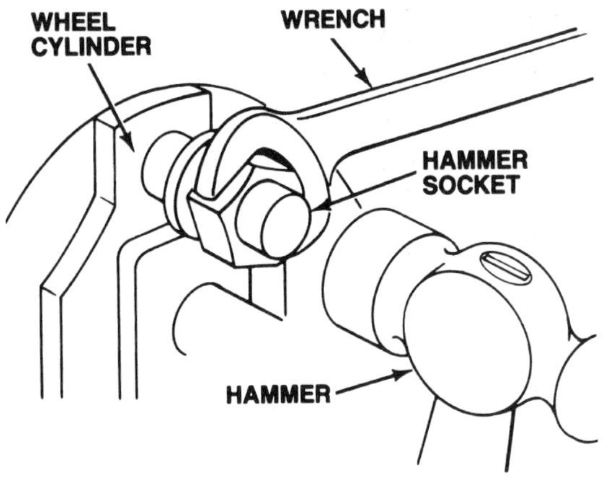

Cylinder Honing

Honing is a procedure in which abrasive stones are rotated inside the cylinder bore to remove a small amount of metal, along with any scratches, pitting, scuff marks, and rust. Honing restores the sealing surface for the piston seals; however, the new finish is never as smooth as the "bearingized" surface of a new cylinder. As a result, the cup seals in a rebuilt cylinder that has been honed wear faster than those in a replacement cylinder. Many shops today will only rebuild a wheel cylinder if the bore does not need to be honed. In addition, some manufacturers recommend against honing the cylinders on their cars. Check the factory shop manual for the exact recommendations on the car you are servicing.

If the bore of a cast-iron wheel cylinder can be honed, follow this procedure:

1. If a wheel cylinder is to be honed on the car, make sure it is tightly attached to the backing plate. Otherwise clamp the cylinder in a vise by its mounting flange. Do not clamp on the cylinder body or the bore may be distorted.
2. Select a suitably sized cylinder hone and chuck it in a drill motor.
3. Lubricate the cylinder bore with brake fluid, and insert the hone into the bore, figure 7-40.
4. Operate the drill motor at approximately 500 rpm, and move the hone back and forth with smooth, even strokes. Allow the hone to extend just beyond the open ends of the cylinder to ensure that the entire length of the bore is honed. Use extra caution when honing with a stone hone; if the stones come out of the bore, they can strike the vise or backing plate and be broken. Stones may also be torn loose and thrown free, possibly causing injury. Always wear safety glasses when honing hydraulic cylinders.
5. Keep the bore lubricated with brake fluid, and hone for approximately 10 seconds. Let the hone come to a full stop, then remove it from the cylinder bore.
6. Wipe the bore clean with a rag, and check the surface finish; it should be clean and free of rust, corrosion, and scratches. The hone should also have created an even crosshatch pattern.
7. If necessary, repeat the honing process for another 10 seconds. If the bore does not clean up after several repetitions of this procedure, replace the cylinder.

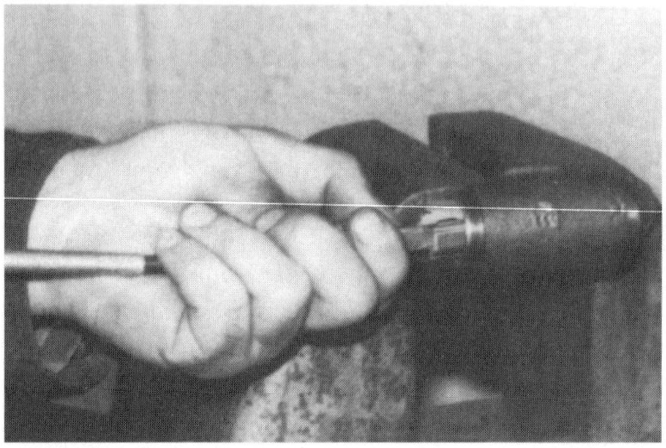

Figure 7-39. A hammer socket is a special tool used to remove frozen bleeder screws.

Figure 7-40. Insert the hone all the way into the cylinder before starting the drill motor.

After the bore is honed, thoroughly clean the cylinder with a non-petroleum-base brake cleaning solvent to remove all residue and grit.

Cylinder Bore Measurement

After the cylinder has been honed, you must measure the size of the cylinder bore to make sure that too much metal has not been removed. There are two methods that can be used to do this; one uses a feeler gauge strip, and the other uses a go/no-go gauge.

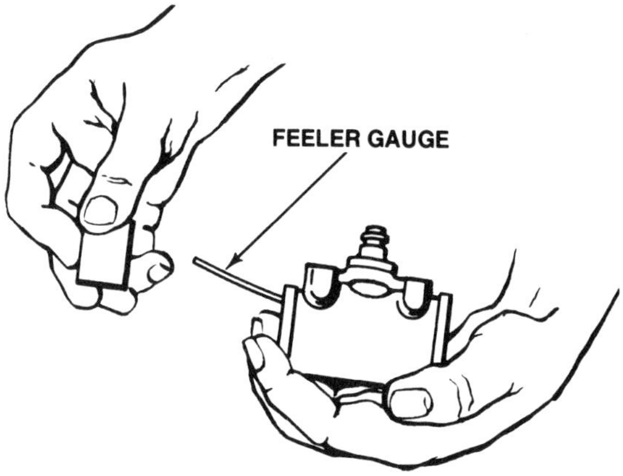

Drum Brake Service

Figure 7-41. Using a feeler gauge to check cylinder bore size.

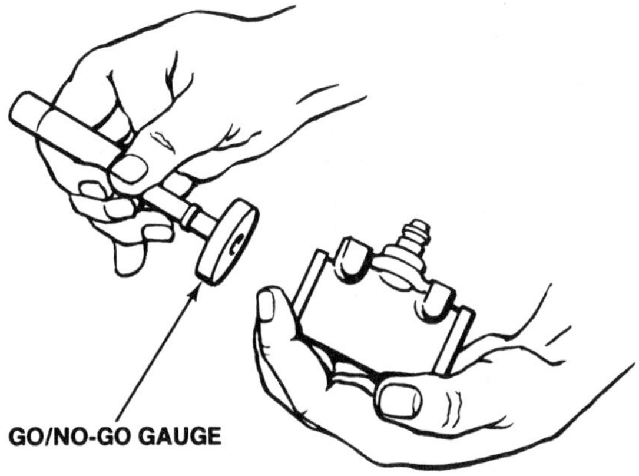

Figure 7-42. Using a go/no-go gauge to check cylinder bore size.

To check the bore using a feeler gauge, place a narrow (¼ inch or 6 mm wide) strip of .006 inch (.15 mm) feeler gauge inside the bore. Attempt to insert one of the cylinder pistons into the bore with the feeler gauge in place, figure 7-41; if the piston will fit, the bore is oversize and the cylinder must be replaced. Traditionally, most manufacturers have allowed up to .006″ (.15 mm) of piston clearance; however, many newer cylinders with smaller diameters require tighter clearances. If you are unsure of the proper specification, consult the shop manual for the vehicle you are servicing.

To check the bore with a go/no-go gauge, select the proper size of plug from the gauge kit and attach it to the handle. The correct plug is the same size as the nominal cylinder bore plus .006″ (.15 mm). Attempt to insert the plug into the bore, figure 7-42; if it will fit, the bore is too far oversize and the cylinder must be replaced. Although go/no-go gauges were once quite common, they are seldom used today because of the wider variations in clearance specifications mentioned above.

Wheel Cylinder Overhaul Procedures

The following pages provide step-by-step overhaul procedures for a typical two-piston wheel cylinder. Before you begin any overhaul, read completely through the procedure to obtain a better idea of the entire job.

It is common practice to overhaul wheel cylinders while they are mounted on the backing plate, if possible. This holds the cylinder solidly in position, and reduced the time required for the job. However, as discussed earlier, some wheel cylinders must be removed for rebuilding because they are recessed into the backing plate, or the backing plate is fitted with piston stops. When a wheel cylinder is rebuilt off the car, it is mounted in a vise.

TWO-PISTON WHEEL CYLINDER OVERHAUL

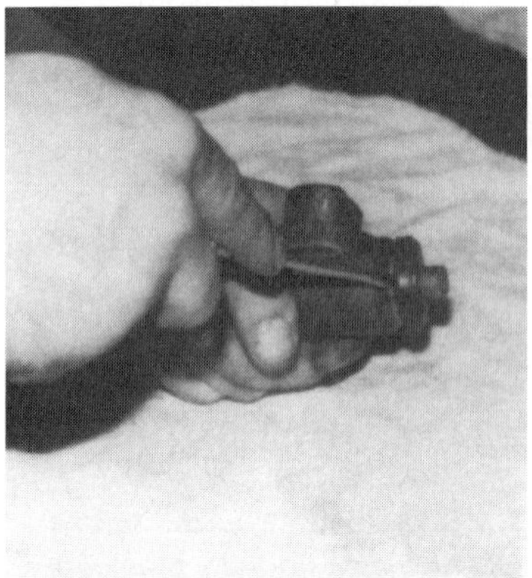

1. Remove the shoe links and rubber boots from the ends of the cylinder.

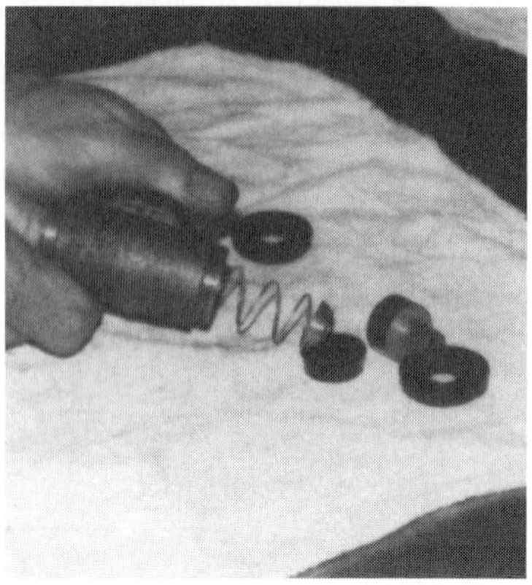

2. Press out the pistons, cups, and cup expander assembly by hand or with a wooden punch.

3. Inspect the cylinder bore. If there is any damage, replace an aluminum cylinder, or hone a cast-iron part.

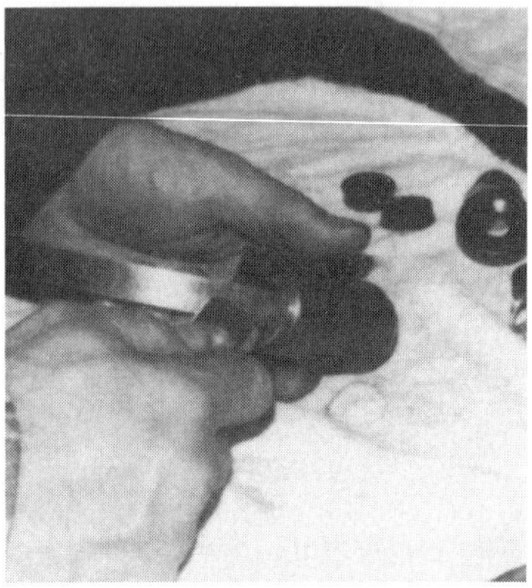

4. Measure the bore and replace the wheel cylinder if the bore is too far oversize.

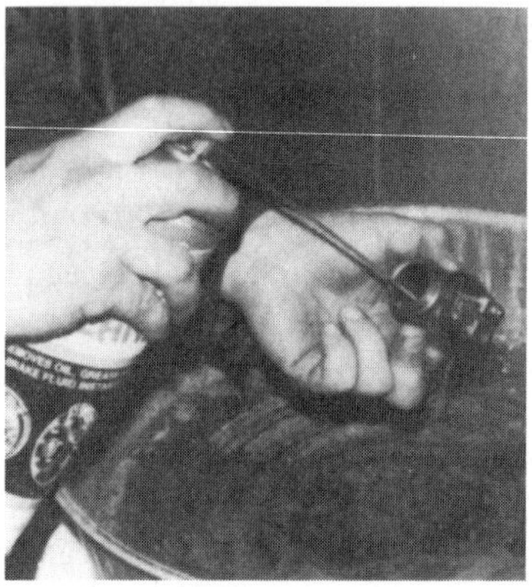

5. Thoroughly clean the wheel cylinder body with a non-petroleum-base brake cleaner.

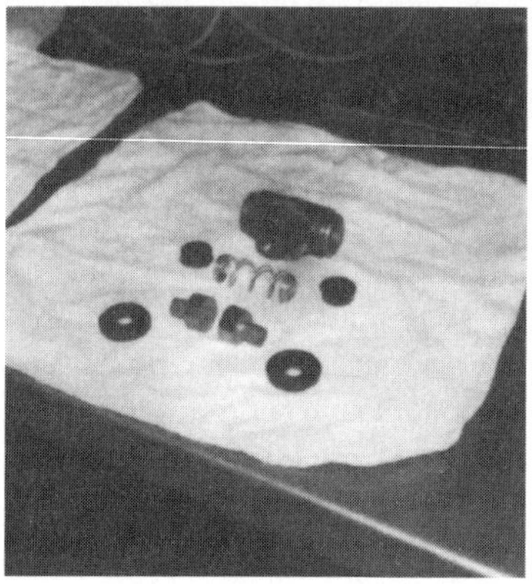

6. Thoroughly clean and dry the cylinder internal parts, including those from the rebuild kit, and lay them out on a clean shop towel.

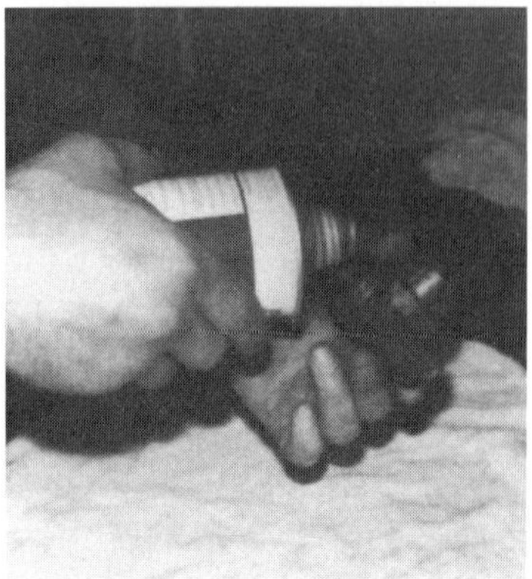

7. Lubricate the cylinder bore with brake fluid or assembly lube.

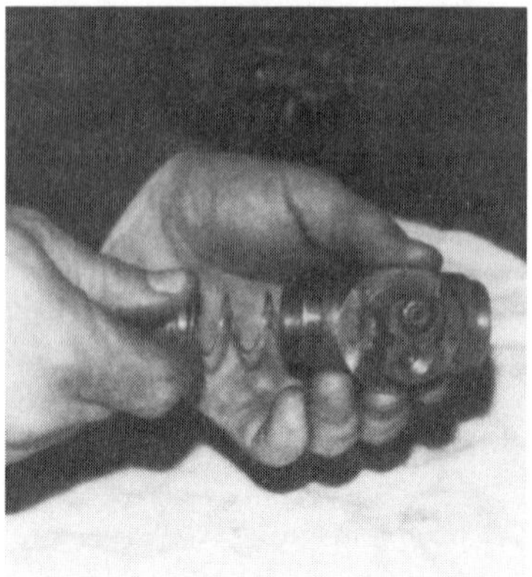

8. Check that the cup expanders are secure on the spring ends, and install the assembly into the cylinder bore.

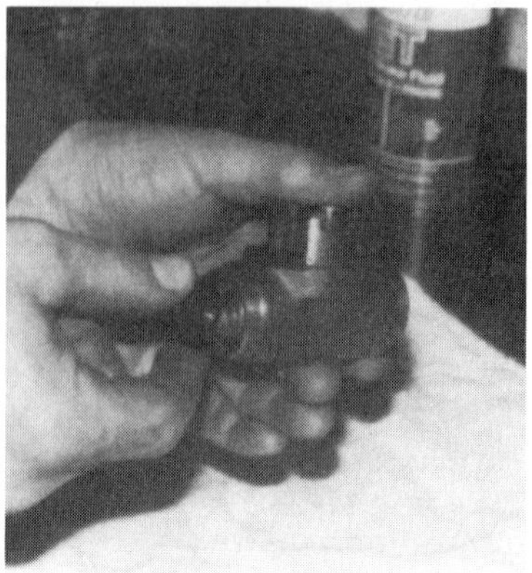

9. Lubricate the cup seals and install them into the cylinder bore, one at each end, with the lip facing inward. Make sure the seals do not cock in the bore.

Drum Brake Service

TWO-PISTON WHEEL CYLINDER OVERHAUL

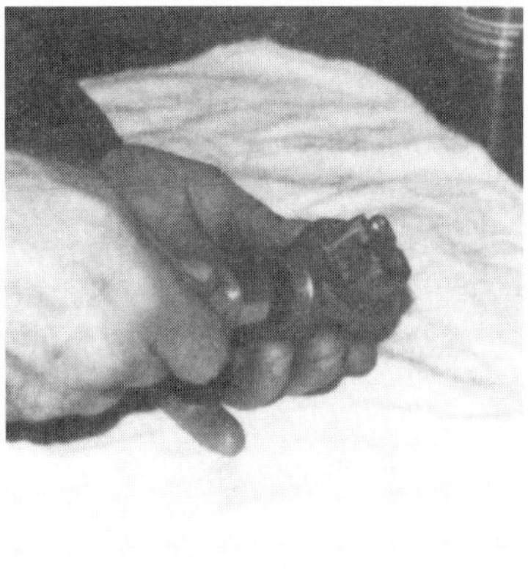

10. Lubricate the pistons and install them into the cylinder body, one at each end, with the flat side contacting the backs of the cup seals.

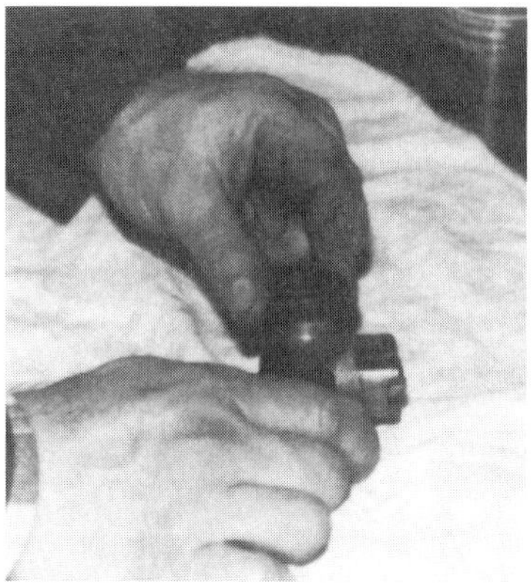

11. While holding the pistons in position, install the dust boots on each end of the cylinder.

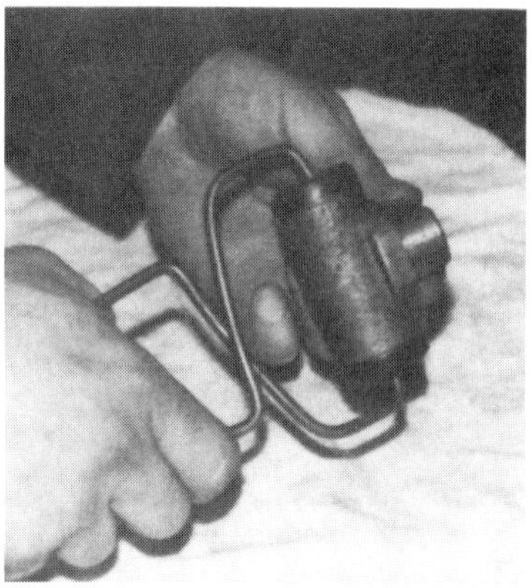

12. If the cup expander spring has very strong tension, use a wheel cylinder clamp to hold the assembly together.

SHOE REPLACEMENT PROCEDURES

The following pages contain shoe replacement procedures for four different drum brake friction assemblies:

- Chrysler leading-trailing brake with manual adjuster
- Chrysler dual-servo brake with cable-type starwheel automatic adjuster
- General Motors dual-servo brake with lever-type starwheel automatic adjuster
- Ford leading-trailing brake with strut-quadrant automatic adjuster.

While there are many other drum brakes that are not covered, these are popular designs that include many common variations in drum brake construction and overhaul procedures. With the knowledge gained from reading this chapter, and the experience of going through the shoe replacement procedure for each of these brakes, you should be able to understand the various other friction assemblies you will encounter.

Chrysler Leading-Trailing Brake with Manual Adjuster

The Chrysler leading-trailing brake has been used on the rear wheels of man. FWD Chrysler Corporation vehicles. The early version, covered in the shoe replacement procedures, has a manual starwheel adjuster; later models have automatic adjusters. Chrysler uses a fixed drum with this friction assembly, so the wheel bearings should be repacked and adjusted when the brake shoes are replaced. See Chapter 14 for information on wheel bearing service.

Chrysler Dual-Servo Brake with Cable-Type Starwheel Automatic Adjuster

The Chrysler dual-servo brake with cable-type starwheel automatic adjuster has been used in both front- and rear-wheel applications on all RWD Chrysler Corporation cars since 1969. This brake comes in 9-, 10-, and 11-inch diameters, but the service procedures for all three are the same. The only difference between the front and rear designs is that the front brake does not have a parking brake mechanism. Fixed drums are used on front brakes so the wheel bearings should be repacked and adjusted when the shoes are replaced. See Chapter 14 for information on wheel bearing service.

GM Dual-Servo Brake with Lever-Type Starwheel Automatic Adjuster

The General Motors dual-servo brake with lever-type starwheel automatic adjuster is used as the rear brake on most FWD General Motors cars. This brake has been built in two versions, but both operate the same. On early brakes, the adjuster lever actuating link installs through a hole in the shoe anchor. On later models, the link hooks over a post on the anchor. In all other respects, the operation and servicing of these brakes is identical.

Ford Leading-Trailing Brake with Strut-Quadrant Automatic Adjuster

The Ford 7-inch (180-mm) leading-trailing brake with strut-quadrant automatic adjuster is used on all Escort/Lynx three-door models except those with styled steel wheels. This is a somewhat unusual design that is similar to the brakes on the Merkur XR4Ti. Ford uses a fixed drum with this friction assembly, so the wheel bearings should be repacked and adjusted when the brake shoes are replaced. See Chapter 14 for information on wheel bearing service.

Although the shoe replacement procedure for this brake includes instructions for disassembling the adjuster, this is only necessary if the teeth on the adjuster quadrant or pin are damaged, and a part must be replaced. In most cases, simply pull the quadrant back against spring tension, and reposition it so the pin fits into the third or fourth notch at the narrow end of the quadrant. This shortens the adjuster strut to its minimum length, and makes it easy to install the brake drum.

Drum Brake Service

CHRYSLER LEADING-TRAILING BRAKE WITH MANUAL ADJUSTER

1. Pull back the spring on the parking brake cable and unhook the cable from the parking brake lever.

2. Remove both shoe-to-anchor springs.

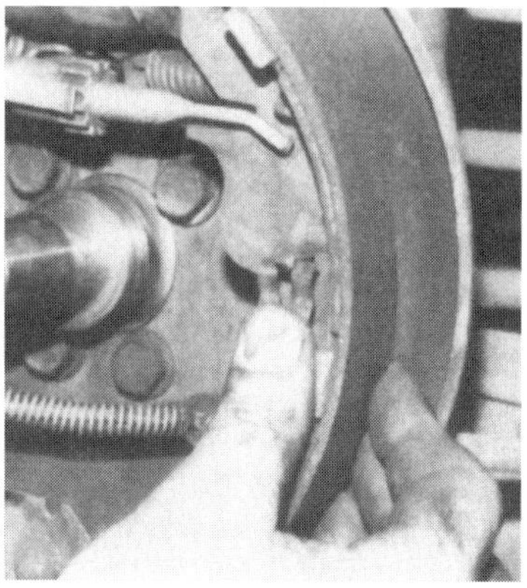

3. Remove the shoe holddown springs, and withdraw the pins from the backing plate.

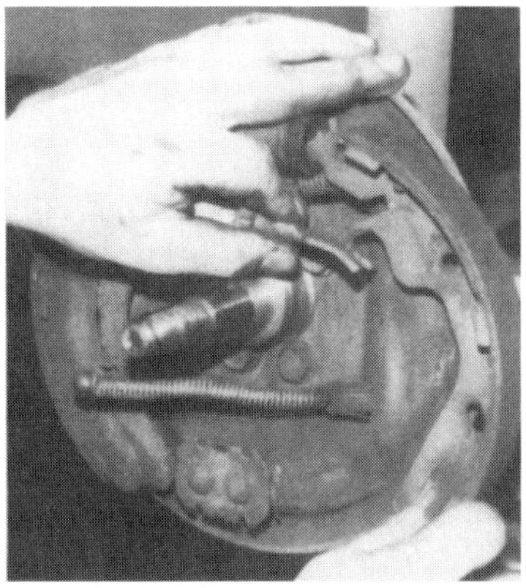

4. Fully back off the shoe adjustment, then spread the shoes and remove the adjuster screw assembly.

5. Raise the parking brake lever, and remove the trailing shoe from under the anchor plate to release tension on the return spring.

6 Unhook the return spring from the backing plate, and remove the trailing shoe assembly.

7. Remove the leading shoe from under the anchor plate to release tension on the return spring.

8. Unhook the return spring from the backing plate, and remove the leading shoe.

9. Lubricate the shoe support pads on the backing plate.

CHRYSLER LEADING-TRAILING BRAKE WITH MANUAL ADJUSTER

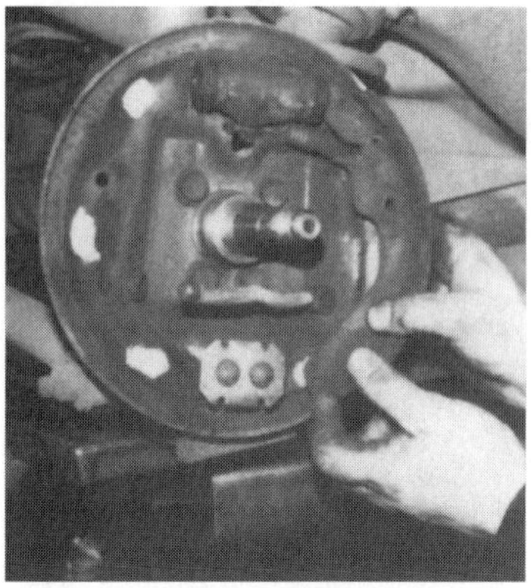

10. Hook the return spring of the leading shoe into the backing plate, then move the shoe into position with its end under the anchor plate.

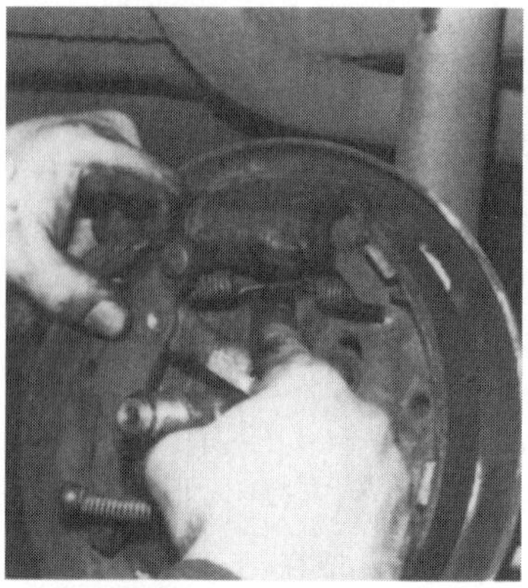

11. Hook the return spring of the trailing shoe into the backing plate, then move the shoe into position with its end under the anchor plate.

12. Spread the shoes as needed to install the adjuster screw assembly. The forked end of the screw must curve downward.

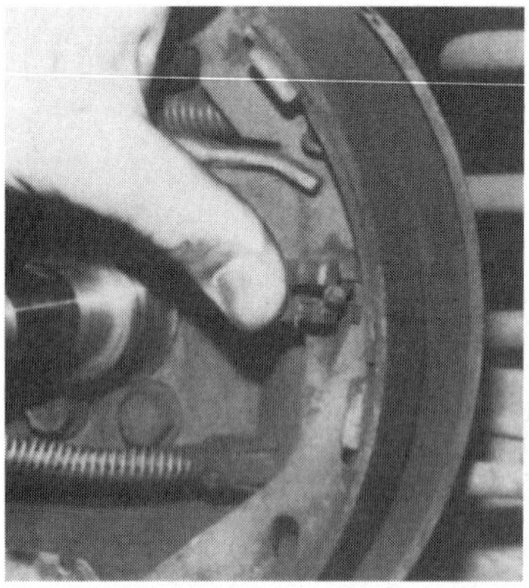

13. Insert the holddown pins through the backing plate and shoes, then install the holddown springs on the pins.

14. Install both shoe-to-anchor springs.

15. Pull back the spring on the parking brake cable, and attach the cable to the parking brake lever. Position the cable washer (if fitted) between the spring and lever.

Drum Brake Service

CHRYSLER DUAL-SERVO BRAKE WITH CABLE-TYPE STARWHEEL AUTOMATIC ADJUSTER

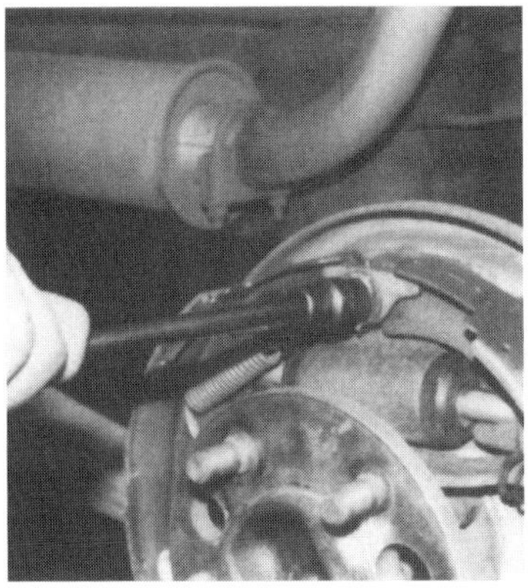

1. Remove the shoe return springs from the anchor post.

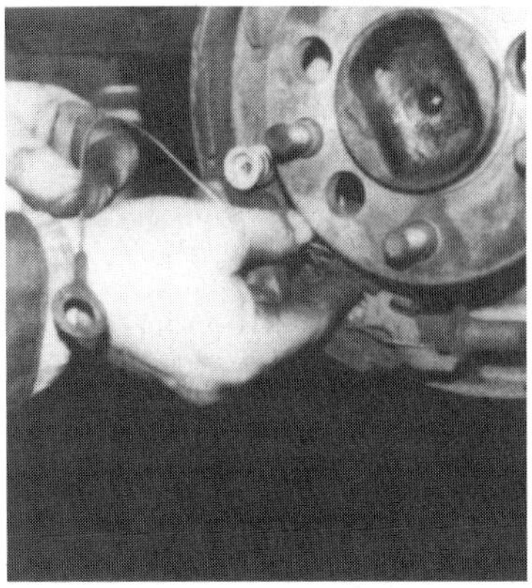

2. Lift the eye of the automatic adjuster cable off the anchor, unhook the cable from the adjusting pawl, and remove the cable.

3. Remove the anchor plate from the anchor post.

4. Remove the adjuster cable guide from the secondary shoe.

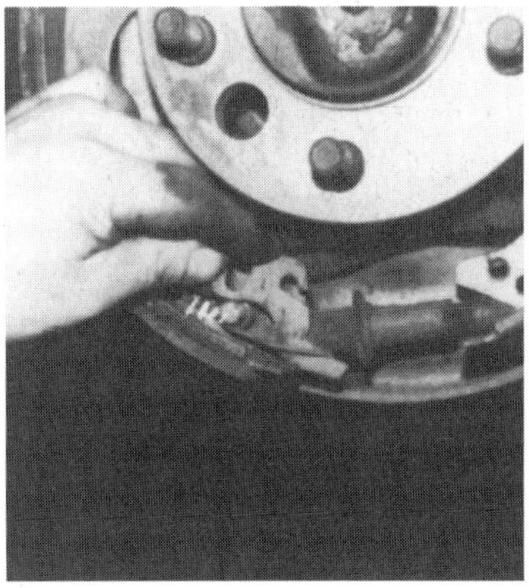

5. Slide the adjuster pawl forward to clear the pivot, and pull it out from under the pawl spring.

6. Remove the pawl spring from the pivot.

7. Remove the shoe-to-shoe return spring.

8. Spread the shoes and remove the starwheel adjuster assembly.

9. Remove the shoe holddown springs, and withdraw the pins from the backing plate.

CHRYSLER DUAL-SERVO BRAKE WITH CABLE-TYPE STARWHEEL AUTOMATIC ADJUSTER

10. Spread the shoes and remove the parking brake strut and anti-rattle spring.

11. Disconnect the parking brake cable, and lift out the shoes.

12. Remove the parking brake lever from the old secondary shoe, and install it on the new shoe.

13. Connect the parking brake cable to the lever, then position the secondary shoe on the backing plate and install its holddown.

14. Slide the anti-rattle spring over the end of the parking brake strut, and fit the strut into the slot in the parking brake lever.

15. Position the primary shoe on the backing plate so it engages the parking brake strut, then install the shoe holddown.

16. Install the anchor plate and the eye of the adjuster cable over the anchor post.

17. Install the primary shoe return spring through the shoe web and over the anchor post.

18. Install the cable guide onto the secondary shoe so the hole in the guide aligns with the hole in the shoe web.

Drum Brake Service

CHRYSLER DUAL-SERVO BRAKE WITH CABLE-TYPE STARWHEEL AUTOMATIC ADJUSTER

19. Install the secondary shoe return spring through both the cable guide and shoe web, and over the anchor post.

20. Use a pair of pliers to squeeze the end of each spring around the anchor post until it is parallel with the incoming spring wire.

21. Install the starwheel adjuster assembly. The left assembly is cadmium plated and stamped with an L. The right assembly is black and stamped with an R.

22. Install the shoe-to-shoe return spring.

23. Install the adjuster pawl spring over the pivot on the secondary shoe web.

24. Install the adjuster pawl under the spring, route the adjuster cable through the cable guide, and attach the end of the over-travel spring to the pawl.

GM DUAL-SERVO BRAKE WITH LEVER-TYPE AUTOMATIC STARWHEEL ADJUSTER

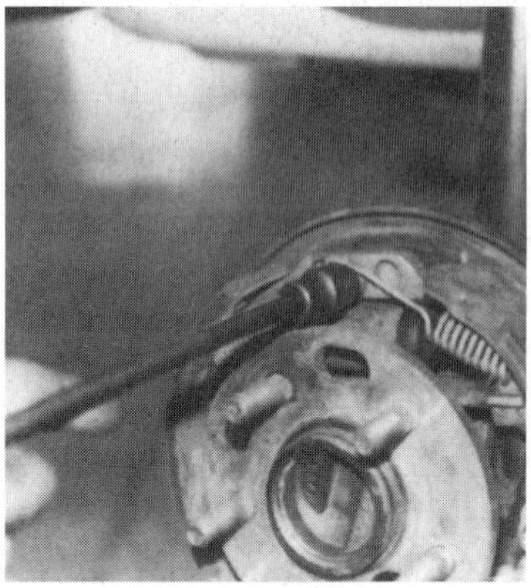

1. Remove both shoe return springs from the anchor.

2. Remove the shoe holddown springs, and withdraw the pins from the backing plate.

3. Lift upward on the adjuster lever, and remove the actuating link from the anchor.

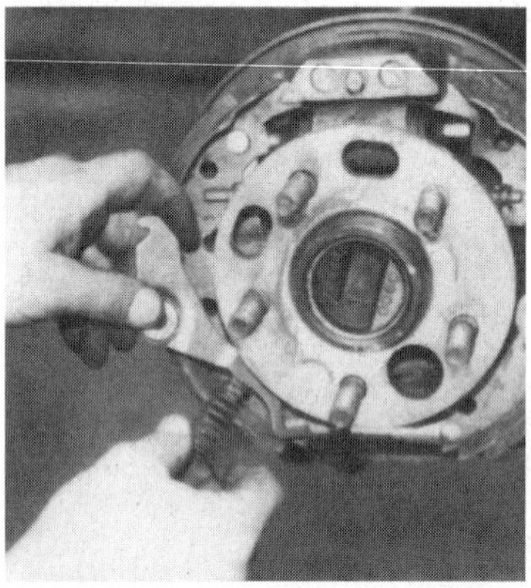

4. Remove the adjuster lever, pivot, and lever return spring from the secondary shoe.

5. Spread the shoes and remove the parking brake strut and anti-rattle spring.

6. Disconnect the parking brake cable, and remove the shoes, starwheel adjuster assembly, and shoe-to-shoe return spring.

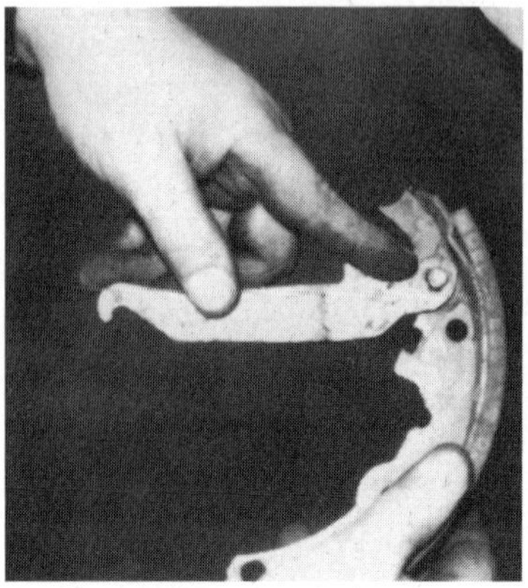

7. Remove the parking brake lever, pin, and retaining clip from the old secondary shoe, and install them on the new shoe.

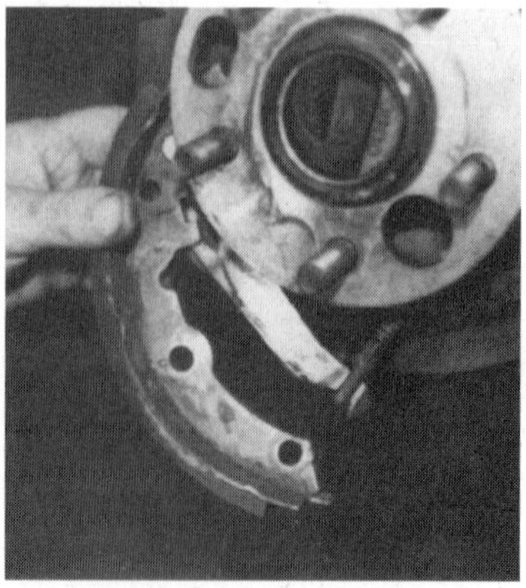

8. Connect the parking brake cable to the lever on the secondary shoe.

9. Install the starwheel adjuster and shoe-to-shoe return spring between the shoes, then position the shoes on the backing plate.

Drum Brake Service

GM DUAL-SERVO BRAKE WITH LEVER-TYPE AUTOMATIC STARWHEEL ADJUSTER

10. Spread the shoes and install the parking brake strut so the end with the anti-rattle spring engages the primary shoe.

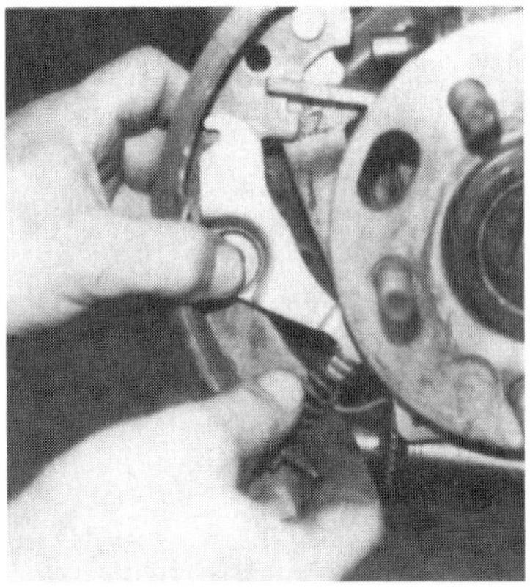

11. Install the adjuster lever, pivot, and lever return spring pivot, and lever return spring on the secondary shoe.

12. Install the actuating link into the hole or over the post in the anchor.

13. Lift upward on the adjuster lever, and connect the link to the lever.

14. Insert the holddown pins through the backing plate and shoes, then install the holddown springs on the pins.

15. Hook the shoe return springs into their holes in the shoe webs, then install the springs onto the anchor.

FORD LEADING-TRAILING BRAKE WITH STRUT-QUADRANT AUTOMATIC ADJUSTER

1. Remove the shoe holddown springs, and withdraw the pins from the backing plate.

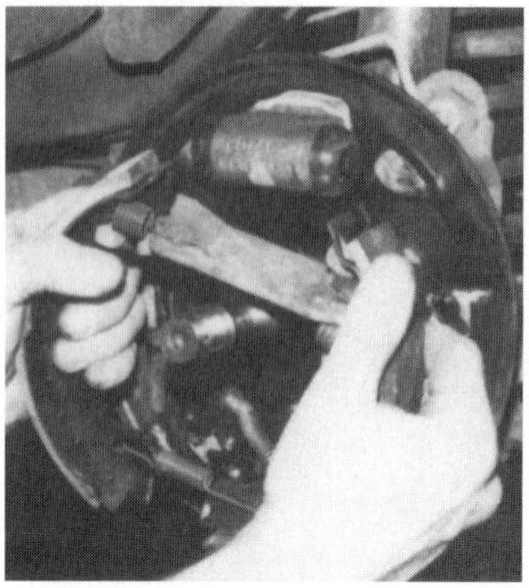

2. Lift the assembly of the brake shoes, adjuster strut, parking brake lever, and shoe-to-shoe return spring off of the backing plate.

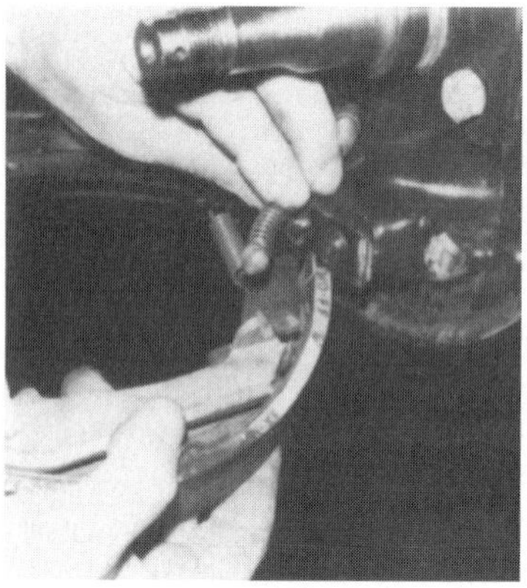

3. Disconnect the parking brake cable from the lever.

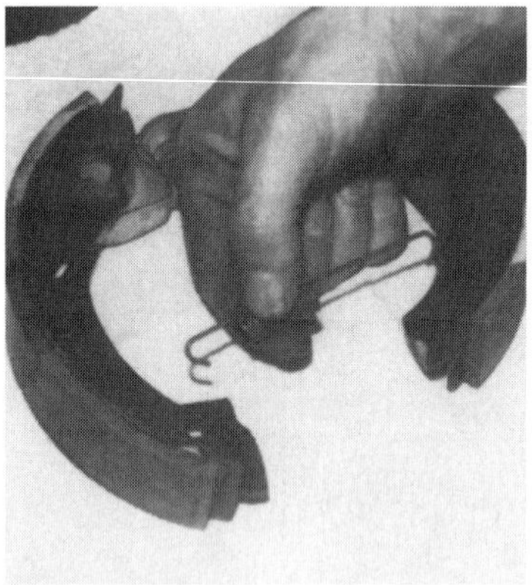

4. Remove the shoe-to-shoe return spring.

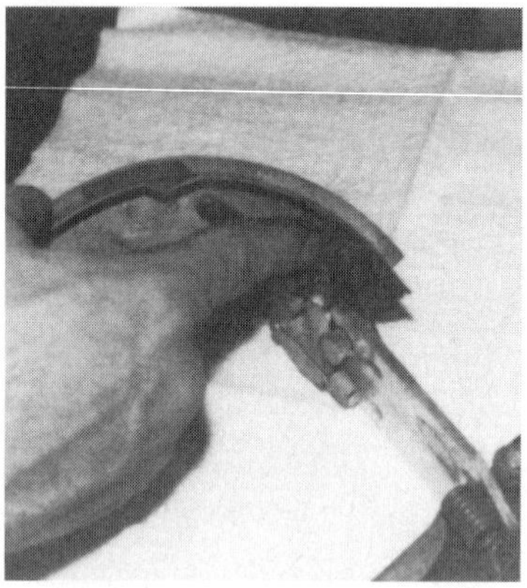

5. Rotate the leading shoe outward to release tension on the return spring, then remove the spring.

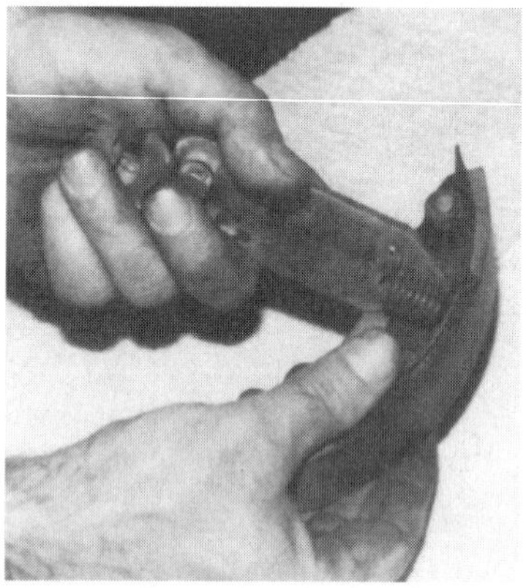

6. Pull the adjuster strut away from the secondary shoe and pivot it downward to release tension on the return spring, then remove the spring.

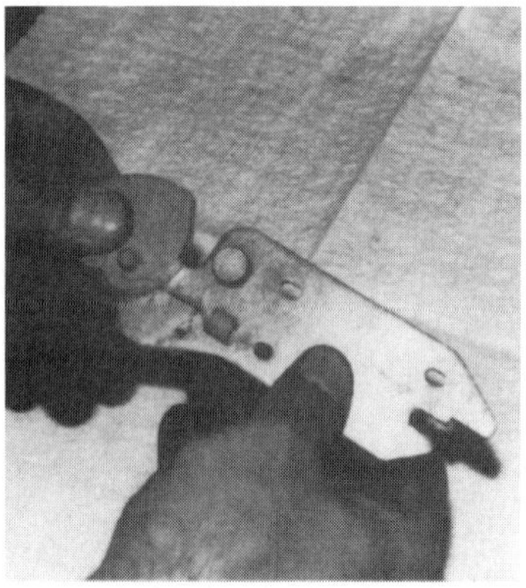

7. Pull the adjuster quadrant away from the knurled pin, and rotate the quadrant until its teeth no longer mesh with the pin.

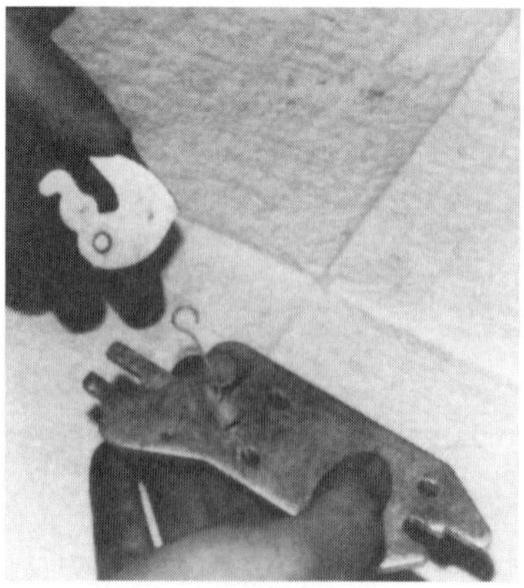

8. Carefully unhook the quadrant spring, taking care not to overstretch it, and remove the quadrant from the slot in the strut.

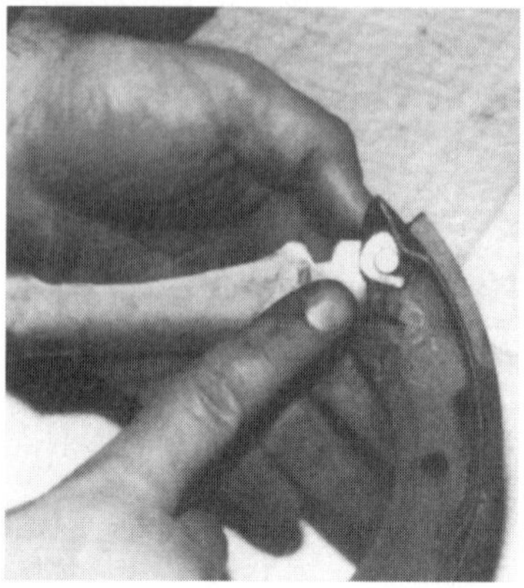

9. Remove the parking brake lever, pin, and retaining clip from the old trailing shoe, and install them on the new shoe.

Drum Brake Service

FORD LEADING-TRAILING BRAKE WITH STRUT-QUADRANT AUTOMATIC ADJUSTER

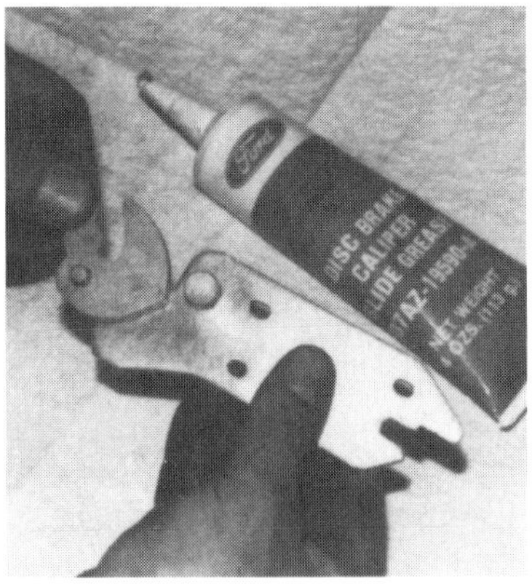

10. Lubricate the contact surface between the adjuster quadrant and strut with brake grease, then install the quadrant into the slot in the strut.

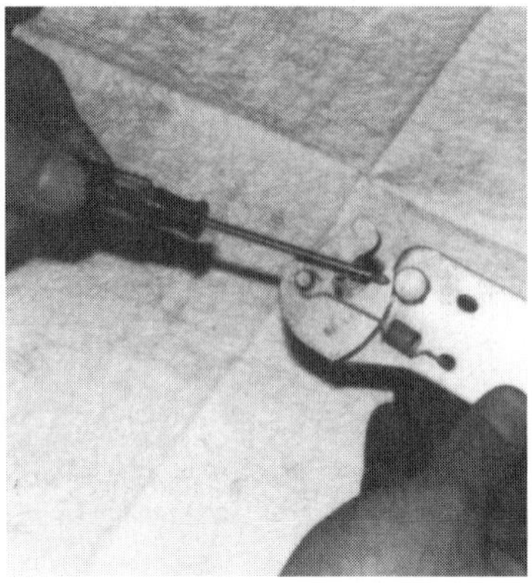

11. Install the quadrant spring, and rotate the quadrant until the third and fourth notch on its narrow end meshes with the pin.

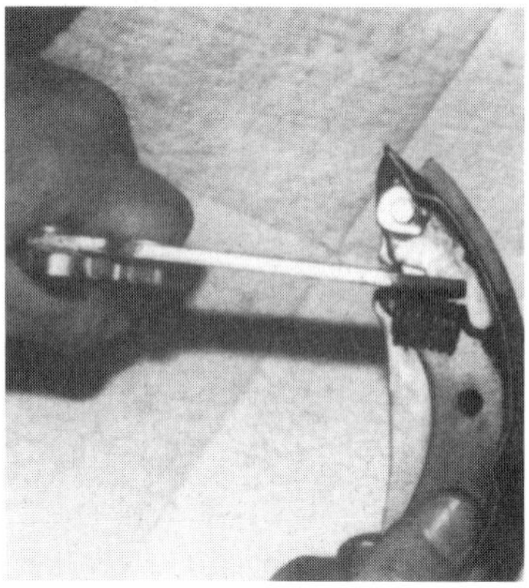

12. Hook the shoe return spring into its holes in the trailing shoe and strut, then pivot the strut upward into position.

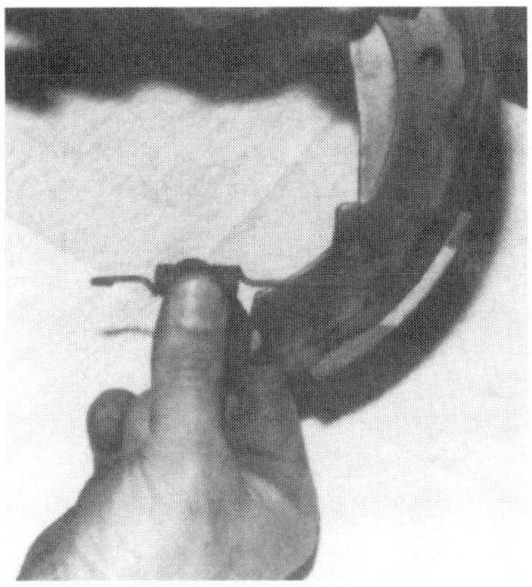

13. Install the shoe-to-shoe return spring so the long, straight section of the spring is attached to the trailing shoe.

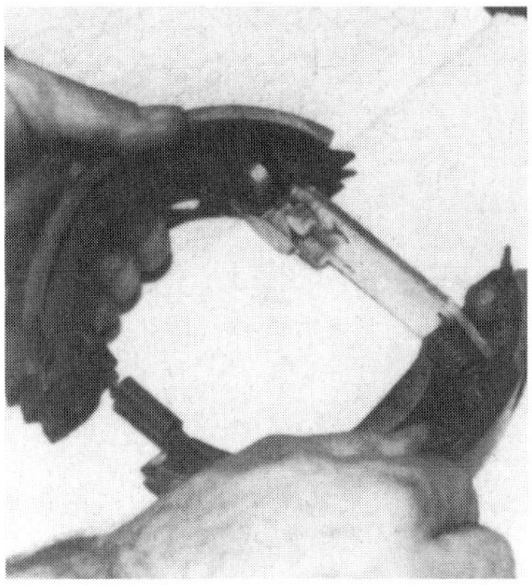

14. Hook the shoe return spring into its holes in the leading shoe and strut, then pivot the shoe rearward into position.

15. Lubricate the shoe support pads on the backing plate.

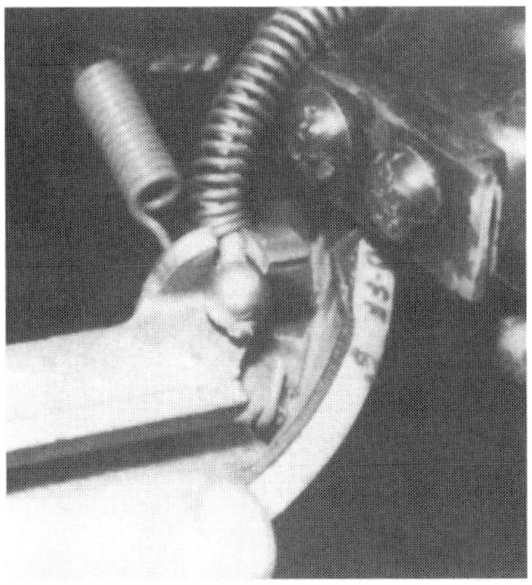

16. Connect the parking brake cable to the lever.

17. Install the assembly of the brake shoes, adjuster strut, parking brake lever, and shoe-to-shoe return spring onto the backing plate.

18. Insert the holddown pins through the backing plate and shoes, then install the holddown springs on the pins.

8 Disc Brake Service

OBJECTIVES

Upon completion and review of this chapter, you will be able to:

- Inspect brake pads on or off the car.
- Replace brake pads.
- Burnish-in brake pads.
- Perform a caliper external inspection.
- Remove a caliper piston by mechanical, compressed air, or hydraulic means.
- Remove and install dust boots and piston seals.
- Inspect caliper pistons.
- Inspect, hone, and measure a caliper bore.
- Overhaul a fixed caliper.
- Overhaul a single-piston floating caliper.
- Overhaul a two-piston floating caliper.
- Overhaul a rear brake caliper.

INTRODUCTION

Disc brake service consists of two main operations, pad replacement and caliper overhaul. With the exception of brake fluid level checking, pad replacement is probably the most common form of brake system service. This is because the brake pads are designed to wear as they generate the friction that stops the car.

When replacing brake pads, the caliper is usually removed from the brake rotor, or at least partially disassembled. The caliper is inspected at this time, and then rebuilt or replaced as needed. Caliper overhaul or replacement can also be required because of fluid leaks, or because a caliper piston is frozen in its bore.

This chapter explains the procedures used to inspect and replace brake pads and calipers. It also describes detailed pad replacement and caliper overhaul procedures for several specific brake assemblies.

BRAKE PAD INSPECTION

Front disc brake pads wear more quickly and require more frequent service than either drum brake shoes or disc brake pads on the rear-wheel brakes. This occurs because front disc brakes provide as much as 80 percent of the total vehicle braking. And, compared to drum brake shoes, disc brake pads have less surface area to absorb heat and distribute wear.

Because front brake pads wear at a rapid rate, most vehicle manufacturers recommend that they be inspected approximately every 7500 miles (12,000 km), or anytime the wheels are removed. Some brake pads are fitted with mechanical wear indicators that contact the rotor and make a high-pitched squeal or scraping noise when the pads are worn to the point where they

Figure 8-1. Rotor damage occurs if brake pads are not replaced before the linings are worn away.

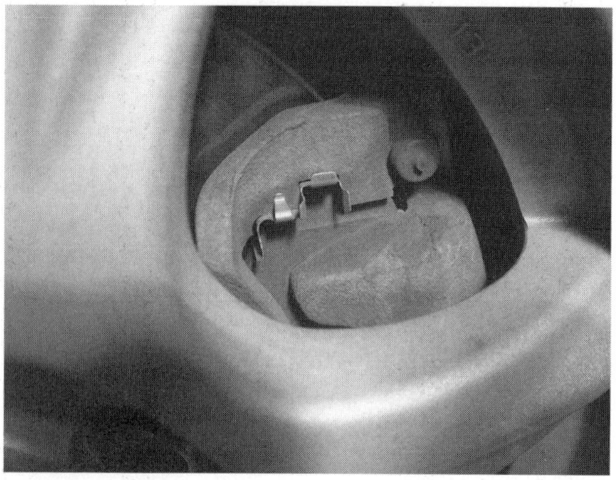

Figure 8-2. On many vehicles, it is possible to inspect the brake pads without removing the wheels.

Figure 8-3. The wheels must be removed on some vehicles before the pads can be inspected.

need to be replaced. Other cars have electrical wear indicators that illuminate a warning light on the instrument panel. The brake pads should be inspected at regular intervals, or whenever any of the above indications of wear are present.

Unfortunately, many car owners wait until they hear a grinding noise from their brakes before having the pads checked. By then it is too late because the noise indicates that the lining material is worn completely away, and a pad backing plate is making metal-to-metal contact with a brake rotor, figure 8-1. Once this happens, the rotor must be machined or replaced as described in Chapter 9. Brake pads are inexpensive compared to rotor service, and it is much better to change a set of brake pads sooner than absolutely necessary, rather than risk rotor damage by trying to get the maximum possible life from the pads.

There are two types of brake pad inspections. The first is a routine check of lining thickness while the pads are still installed on the car. This inspection is a part of regular vehicle maintenance, and helps determine when the pads should be replaced. Sometimes, a routine pad inspection can also indicate a problem with a caliper. The second type of inspection is made when pads with plenty of lining material are removed from the car in the course of other brake service. This inspection helps determine if the pads can be reused.

On-Car Pad Inspection

The exact method of pad inspection on the car varies with the design of the brake caliper. Some pads can be inspected with the wheels on the car either directly or by using a small mirror, figure 8-2. Other brakes require that the wheels be removed before the pads can be viewed clearly, figure 8-3. There are three things to look for when inspecting brake pads: thickness, taper wear, and uneven wear.

The thickness of the lining material is the main factor that determines whether the pads should be replaced. Check the thickness of the lining material, and compare your measurement to the manufacturers specifications. As a general rule, the lining should be at least $\frac{1}{32}$ inch (.030″ or .75 mm) above the rivet heads on riveted pads, or the same distance above the backing plate on bonded pads, figure 8-4. If the pads are thinner than this, replace them.

Next, inspect the pads for taper wear in which the pads are thinner at one end than at the other. Some pad taper wear is normal in floating calipers because the

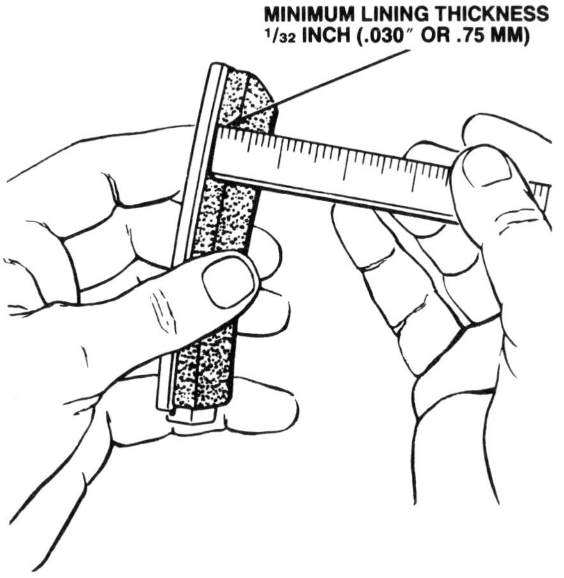

Disc Brake Service

Figure 8-4. Lining thickness determines when a brake pad needs to be replaced.

Figure 8-5. A glazed brake pad lining.

caliper body tends to flex slightly on its mountings. The leading edges of brake pads may also wear faster than the trailing edges because they operate at higher temperatures. However, if there is more than 1/8 inch (3 mm) of taper wear, you should replace the pads and inspect the caliper for possible problems that may be contributing to the taper wear. This test does not apply on certain vehicles from the early 1970s that use tapered brake pads in a unique pivoting brake caliper.

Next, compare the amount of wear on the two pads in each caliper, then compare the amount of pad wear between the two calipers on the same axle; all of the pads should be worn about the same amount. Uneven wear between pads in the same caliper can be caused if the rotor is rough on one side, causing that pad to wear more rapidly. In a fixed caliper, a frozen piston will cause uneven wear between the two pads. Uneven pad wear occurs in floating and sliding calipers when the mounting hardware rusts or corrodes, causing the caliper to bind where it moves on the anchor plate. A rough rotor can also cause unequal pad wear from one side of the car to the other, but the most common cause is a frozen caliper piston on the side with the least wear.

Whenever you find a caliper with unevenly worn pads, or a car with unequal side-to-side pad wear, locate and repair the cause of the wear problem before you install new pads. Never swap brake pads to the opposite side of the rotor or car in an attempt to balance out wear and extend the life of the brakes. This is not cost effective, and will leave you open to liability problems if there is an accident.

Off-Car Pad Inspection

Brake pads that have plenty of lining material remaining are often removed in the course of other brake system service, such as rebuilding a leaking or frozen caliper, or turning a brake rotor. These pads can often be reused; however, you should first inspect them for damage and contamination that is difficult to see while the pads are on the car. The major difference in inspecting the brake pads off the car as opposed to checking them on the car is that you can examine the friction surface that contacts the brake rotor. Normally, this surface is relatively smooth with a dull finish. A shiny or polished lining is glazed, figure 8-5, and should be replaced.

Also check the lining surface for signs of contamination from brake fluid that has leaked past the piston seal and dust boot. Fluid contamination will cause the lining to darken, and where the leak is severe, the lining will appear "smeared" and the paint will often be stripped from the pad backing plate, figure 8-6. Brake pads that have been soaked with brake fluid must be replaced. However, where the contamination is limited to less than 10 percent of the lining surface, you may be able to clean and reuse the brake pads.

In addition to glazing and contamination, inspect the pads for physical damage. Look for large cracks in the lining, loose or missing rivets, a bent backing plate, or a bonded lining that is separating from the backing plate, figure 8-7. If any of these problems are present, replace the pads.

BRAKE PAD REPLACEMENT

Brake pads are sold and serviced as axle sets. An axle set consists of four pads, the inner and outer pad for the caliper at each wheel. Pads from different manufacturers should never be mixed. Although they will fit and may appear the same, the friction coefficients of the linings may be quite different. Even if only one pad of

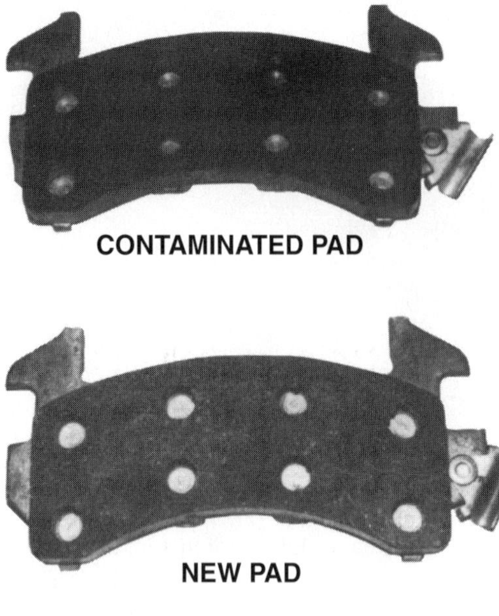

CONTAMINATED PAD

NEW PAD

Figure 8-6. A brake pad suffering from fluid contamination.

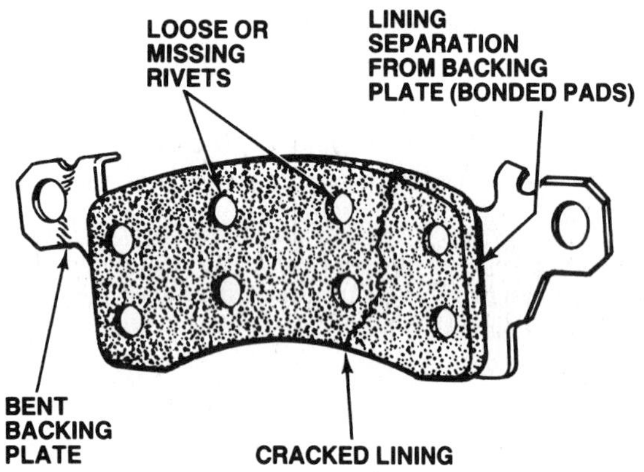

LOOSE OR MISSING RIVETS
LINING SEPARATION FROM BACKING PLATE (BONDED PADS)
BENT BACKING PLATE
CRACKED LINING

Figure 8-7. Replace any pad that has physical damage.

an axle set is badly worn, the entire set should be replaced after the problem causing the uneven wear has been repaired.

When you replace a set of brake pads, most vehicle manufacturers recommend that you also replace the bushings, O-rings, retaining bolts, retaining clips, and any other caliper mounting hardware unless it is in perfect condition. These parts play a major role in smooth and quiet brake operation, and they are relatively inexpensive compared to the cost of a comeback. The necessary parts for all common calipers are sold as a "small parts kit," which is available from the dealer or the aftermarket.

Pad Removal

The exact procedure used to replace a set of brake pads varies with the design of the caliper. However, there are a number of basic steps common to any pad replacement job; these are described below. Detailed procedures for replacing the pads in typical brake calipers are included in the photo sequences at the end of this section.

Brake Fluid Considerations

As discussed in Chapter 3, it is normal for the fluid level in the master cylinder reservoir to slowly drop as the brake pads wear down. The caliper pistons move out of their bores as the pads wear, and fluid from the master cylinder fills the space behind the pistons, thus lowering the fluid level. Just the opposite will occur if the pistons are pushed back into their bores, as is done when replacing brake pads; the fluid level will rise as the pistons are bottomed. This must be accounted for when replacing brake pads.

Two methods can be used to make space for the fluid that will be displaced when the caliper pistons are bottomed in their bores to install the new and thicker pads. The first method removes fluid from the reservoir, and the second method allows the fluid to be bled from the caliper.

In the first method, the technician removes some of the brake fluid from the master cylinder reservoir with a brake fluid syringe, figure 8-8. When removing brake fluid from the reservoir, wear safety glasses to prevent eye injury from accidental fluid spray. Also, take suitable precautions to keep brake fluid from coming in contact with the vehicle finish.

If the hydraulic system of a car has a front/rear split, remove about two-thirds of the fluid from the larger reservoir chamber that supplies the front disc brakes. If the hydraulic system has a diagonal or triagonal split, remove about one-half of the fluid from each of the equally sized reservoir chambers. Be sure to replace the reservoir caps or cover after lowering the fluid level; this prevents any damage from brake fluid that may spray out through the compensating ports as the caliper pistons are bottomed in their bores.

The second method allows the fluid to be bled from the caliper bleed screw as the piston is bottomed in the caliper bore. This method is recommended by many manufacturers, especially on vehicles equipped with antilock brake systems (ABS). Releasing the fluid at the caliper bleed screw keeps any possibly contaminated fluid from being pushed into and through the ABS hydraulic controller, where it may cause problems.

Attach a clear plastic tube to the brake bleeder screw and place the other end in a catch bottle, figure 8-9. Open the bleeder screw and allow the fluid to bleed off

Disc Brake Service

Figure 8-8. Lower the fluid level in the master cylinder reservoir before replacing brake pads.

Figure 8-9. Open the bleeder screw when bottoming the piston to keep any dirty fluid from being pushed back up into the ABS modulator.

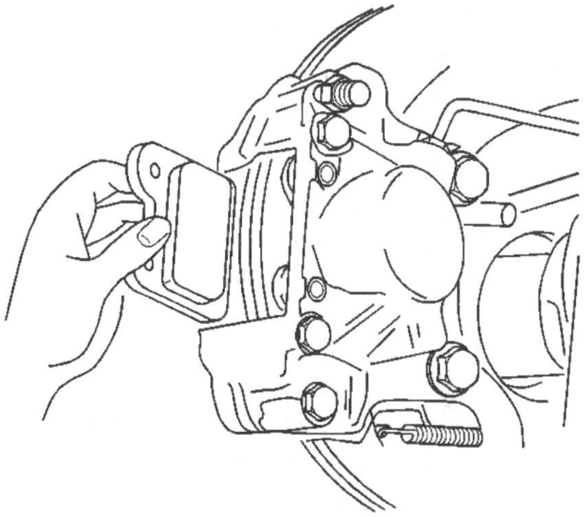

into the catch bottle as the piston is bottomed, then close the bleeder screw. When using this method, some technicians will first slightly depress the brake pedal with a brake pedal depressor. This moves the master cylinder piston seals past the compensating ports so that no fluid can move upward to the master cylinder.

Removing the Caliper Pads
Raise the car until the wheels hang free, then support it securely in position. It will be easier to replace the pads if the car is at a convenient working level, so take into account the position you will be in when servicing the brakes. If you will be standing, raise the car so that the brakes are at waist or shoulder level; if you will be seated on a stool, the brakes should be around knee height. Once the car is in position, remove the wheels to gain access to the calipers.

On fixed brake calipers, remove the pad retaining pins, and use a pair of pliers to pull the pads straight out of the caliper, figure 8-10. If there is a ridge at the edge of the rotor that prevents a pad from being easily removed, insert a screwdriver between the rotor and pad, and pry the caliper piston back into its bore until there is sufficient clearance to remove the pad. If the pads are rusted or seized in the caliper body, use a screwdriver or a pair of pliers to work the pads back and forth until they can be removed. In severe cases, a hook attached to a slide hammer can be inserted through one of the retaining pin holes in the pad backing plate, figure 8-11; a few blows with the slide hammer should pull the pad out of the caliper.

Figure 8-10. On a fixed caliper, remove the retaining pins and slide the pads out from the caliper. Do *not* disassemble the caliper to remove the pads. (Courtesy of General Motors Corporation, Service and Parts Operations)

Removing the pads from a sliding or floating caliper generally requires that the movable portion of the caliper be separated or pivoted away from the anchor plate. Use the appropriate wrench to remove the attaching hardware, and lift or swing the caliper body away from the anchor plate. Take special care when removing rusted or frozen caliper attaching hardware; a broken fastener could result in the need for costly caliper replacement. Whenever you remove a caliper during brake pad replacement, hang it from the suspension by a wire, figure 8-12, so there is no strain on the brake hose that might cause internal or external damage.

Figure 8-11. A slide hammer will remove frozen brake pads from a fixed caliper.

Figure 8-12. Hang calipers from the suspension to prevent brake hose damage.

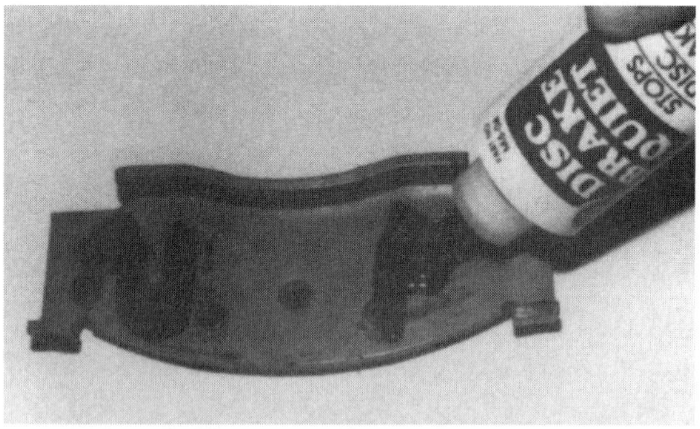

Figure 8-13. Anti-squeal coatings applied to pad backing plates can help reduce brake noise.

Once the caliper is secured, remove the brake pads from the caliper and/or anchor plate. Be sure to note the presence and position of any springs, shims, wear sensors, or other parts; detach these items and transfer them to the new pads as necessary. Compare the new pads to the old parts to be sure you have the proper replacements.

Pad Installation

Before you install the new pads, inspect the brake rotor as described in Chapter 9, and inspect the brake caliper as described later in this chapter. These inspections will help you determine if additional service is necessary to these components. The caliper external inspection procedure also describes how to bottom the caliper pistons in their bores so that the new brake pads can be installed.

Because disc brakes are so prone to noise, many shops make it standard practice to apply an anti-squeal coating to the backing plates of new brake pads, figure 8-13. Many new pad sets come with a small tube of this coating, and several brands are available from the aftermarket. Follow the manufacturer's instructions for the product you choose, and allow the coating to set up properly before you install the pads.

The new brake pads may come with anti-squeal shims and hardware, figure 8-14. This is especially true if the new pads are purchased from the dealer or manufacturer. Often, aftermarket replacement pads do not include new shims; use the old shims when installing the new pads, if possible. The shims are required to reduce noise, so be careful to not throw the shims away along with the old pads.

Installing new brake pads is essentially the reverse of removing them, with a few important differences. First, install the pads into the caliper or anchor plate as dictated by the brake design. The pads in fixed calipers slip into place, and spring clips on the retaining pins and/or shims between the caliper pistons and pad backing plates prevent the pads from vibrating and causing brake noise. The pads in floating and sliding calipers usually have spring clips or bent tabs on the backing plate that lock them securely into the caliper or anchor plate to prevent vibration and brake noise. Bend the springs or tabs as necessary so the pad fits firmly in position.

Once the pads are in position, secure them in the appropriate manner. Once again, the exact method for doing this is determined by the brake design. With a fixed caliper, install the retaining pins. With a sliding caliper, lubricate the ways with high-temperature brake grease, position the caliper body onto the ways over the rotor, and install the retaining hardware. With a floating caliper, lubricate the caliper bushings and retaining bolts with high-temperature brake grease, and position the caliper body over the rotor. Install the retaining bolts and torque them to the manufacturer's specifications.

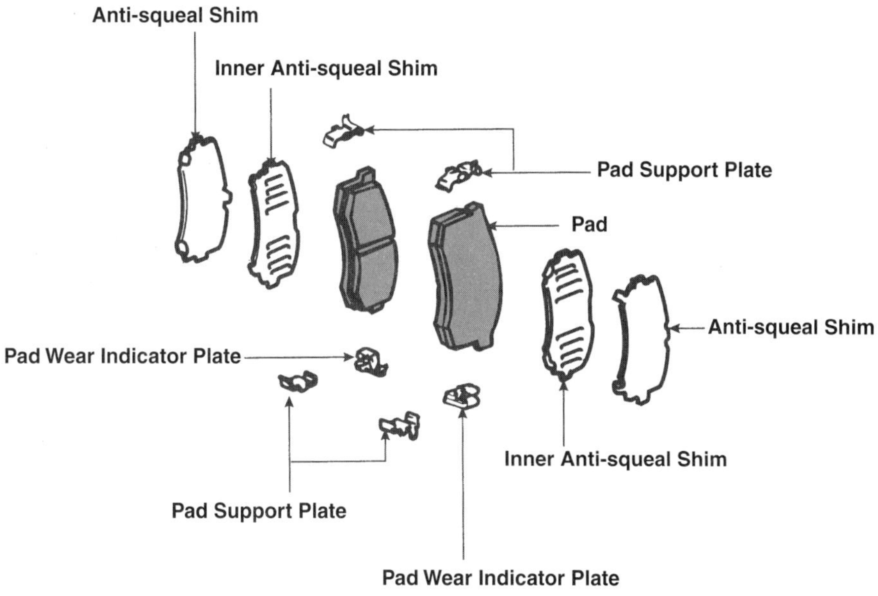

Disc Brake Service

Figure 8-14. Various shims and clips may be required to reduce noise. (Courtesy of Toyota Motor Sales U.S.A., Inc.)

New Pad Seating

Before driving the vehicle, the new pads must be seated against the brake rotor. If you fail to make this initial brake application, an accident may occur when you drive the vehicle out of the service bay and discover that it has no brakes the first time you apply the pedal. This is because the caliper pistons are bottomed in their bores and the space between the pad surface and the rotor is excessive. The master cylinder moves to the end of its travel before the pads contact the rotor, resulting in no braking.

Top up the brake fluid in the master cylinder reservoir. Slowly and carefully pump the brake pedal, in short strokes, until the pads contact the rotor. At this time the pedal will become firm and the vehicle is safe to drive.

NOTE: It is not uncommon for the master cylinder to fail shortly after having the pads changed on older vehicles. Be careful to *not* stroke the master cylinder all the way to the bottom if its bore. Doing this may damage the cylinder seals as they are forced over possibly corroded sections of the master cylinder bore, resulting in a leak or damage to the master cylinder.

If you cannot get a high, firm pedal, bleed the brakes as described in Chapter 3. If bleeding fails to restore a good brake pedal, and no other cause can be found for the problem, it is possible that rust and corrosion in the caliper bore have disturbed the piston's seal. When this happens, air continually enters the hydraulic system, and the caliper soon starts to leak fluid. This problem should have been noticed when bottoming the piston, but if not, the calipers should be removed and rebuilt at this time.

Once good pedal height and feel are achieved, adjust the fluid level in the master cylinder to the full mark, and securely install the reservoir cover or caps. Turn the ignition ON, release the parking brake, and make sure the brake system warning light is not illuminated. If the light is on constantly, center the pressure differential switch as described in Chapter 3. Install the wheels, lower the vehicle to the ground, and test drive the car to make sure the brakes operate properly.

BRAKE PAD REPLACEMENT PROCEDURES

The following pages contain brake pad replacement procedures for two typical vehicles:

- Passenger car front brakes (General Motors)
- Typical Asian import (Mazda) front and rear brakes

While there are many different types of calipers and pads, these examples show some of the procedures that are common to all brake pad replacement jobs. Also shown are some special steps required when changing some rear disc brake pads.

GENERAL MOTORS FRONT PAD REPLACEMENT

1. Use a hex wrench to remove the caliper mounting bolts.

2. Remove the caliper and pads from the brake rotor.

3. Remove the pads from the caliper.

4. Hang the caliper with wire or a hook. Do not let the caliper hang from the brake hose.

5. Measure the rotor thickness and machine the rotor if necessary.

6. Install the machined rotor.

7. Bottom the caliper piston and install the new pads.

8. Slide the caliper and new pads into position on the rotor and steering knuckle.

9. Install and tighten the caliper mounting bolts.

Disc Brake Service

MAZDA FRONT PAD REPLACEMENT

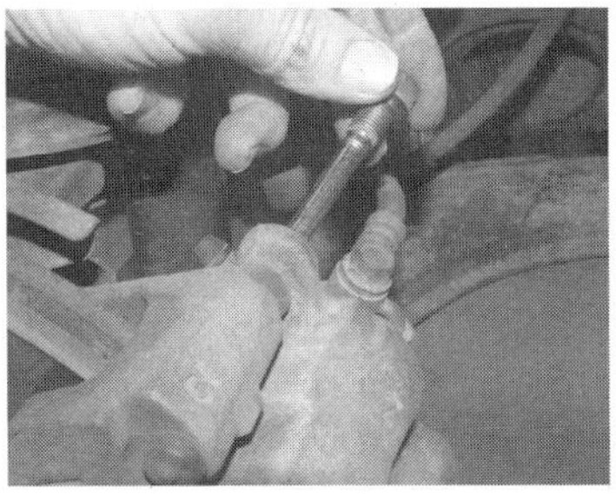

1. Remove the top caliper mounting bolt.

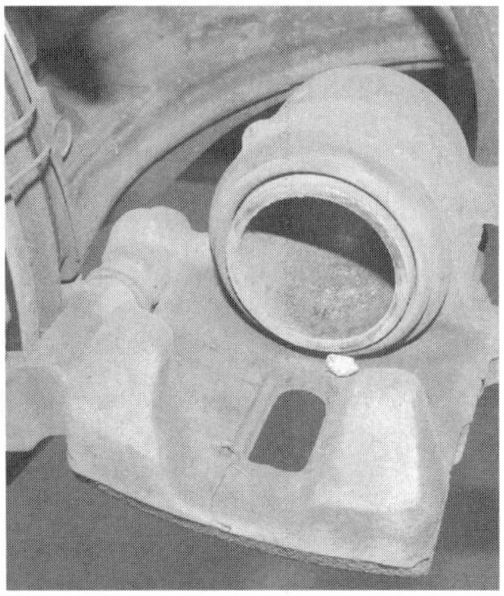

2. Pivot the caliper down, leaving it attached to the lower caliper pin. Note the position of the "V-springs."

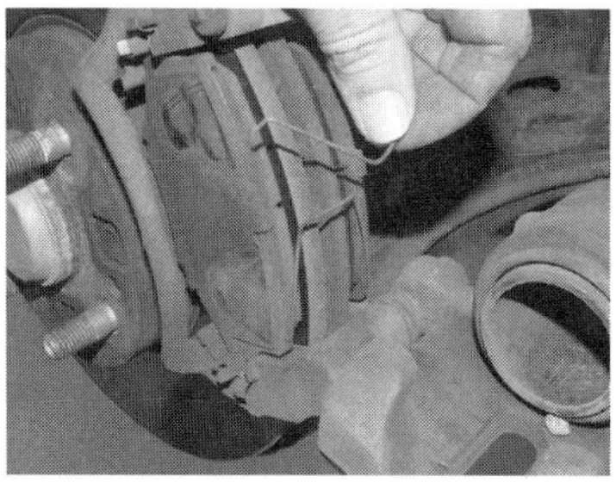

3. Remove the V-springs.

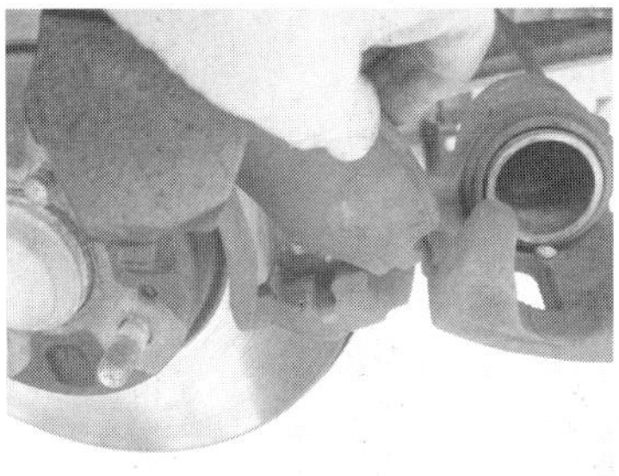

4. Remove the brake pads.

5. Check the rotor thickness.

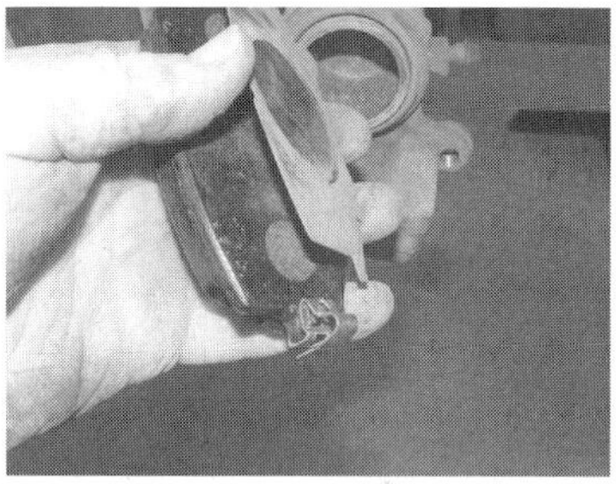

6. Prepare the new pads by installing the wear indicator and the shim.

7. Install the new brake pads.

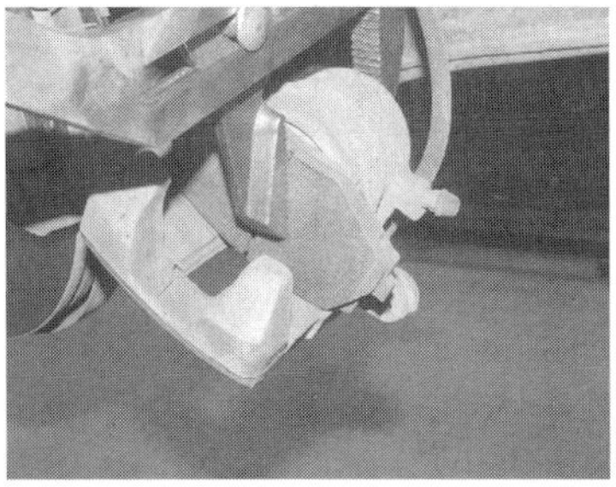

8. Using an old pad and large pliers, bottom the piston in the caliper bore.

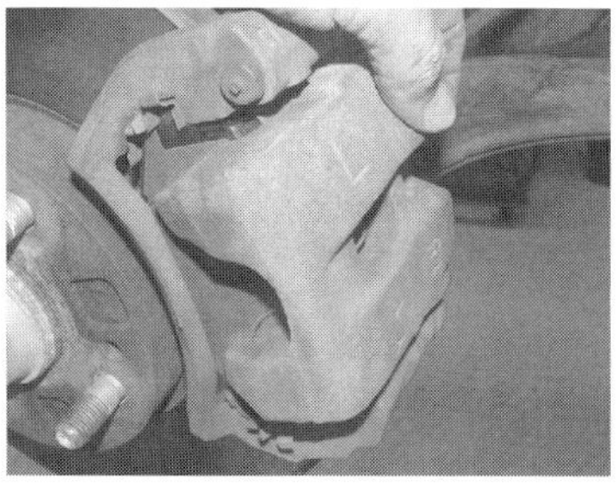

9. Install the V-springs and caliper.

MAZDA FRONT PAD REPLACEMENT

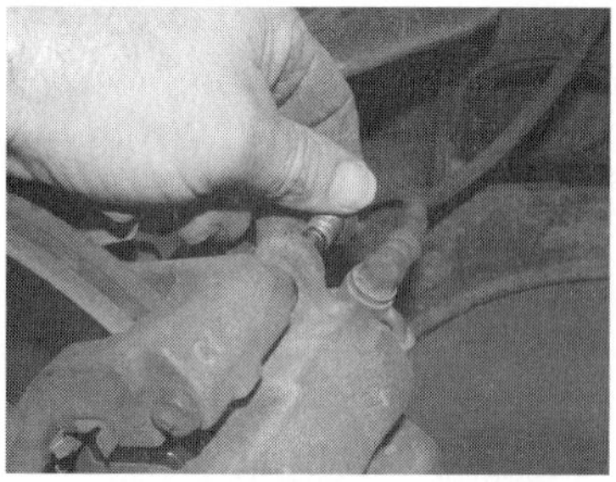

10. Install the upper caliper bolt.

11. Torque the bolt to 60 ft-lb (72 Nm).

MAZDA REAR PAD REPLACEMENT

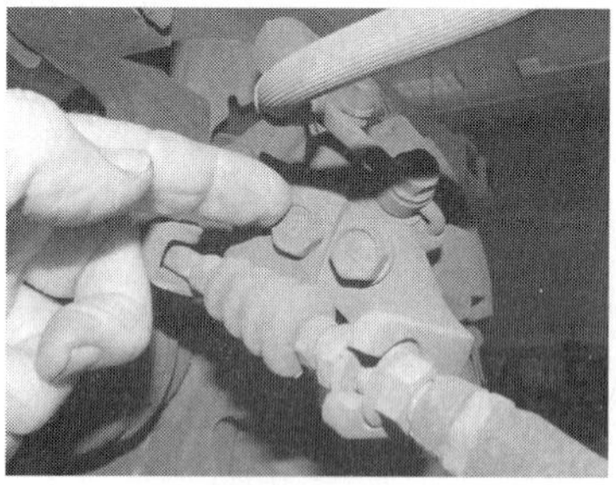

1. The rear caliper has an adjuster screw under this plug that needs to be loosened before removing the caliper.

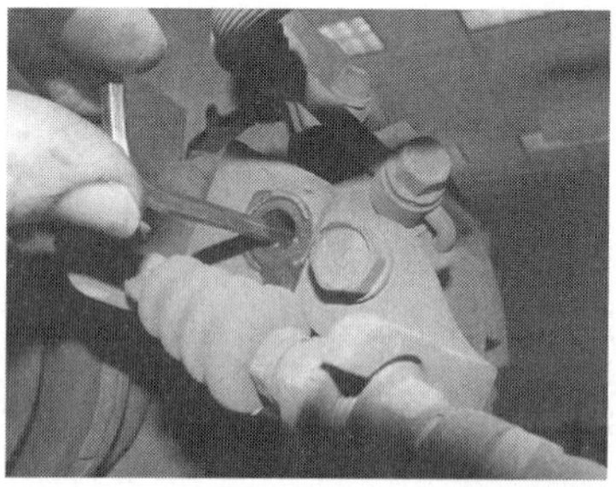

2. Remove the access plug and use a hex wrench to turn the adjuster counterclockwise. This will retract the caliper piston.

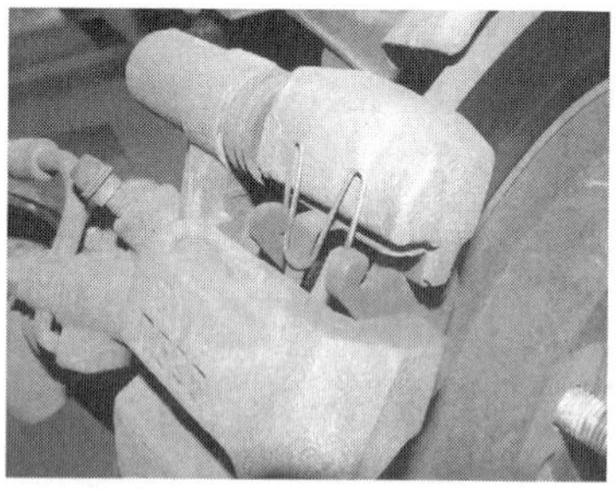

3. Note the position of the "M-springs" before removing the caliper.

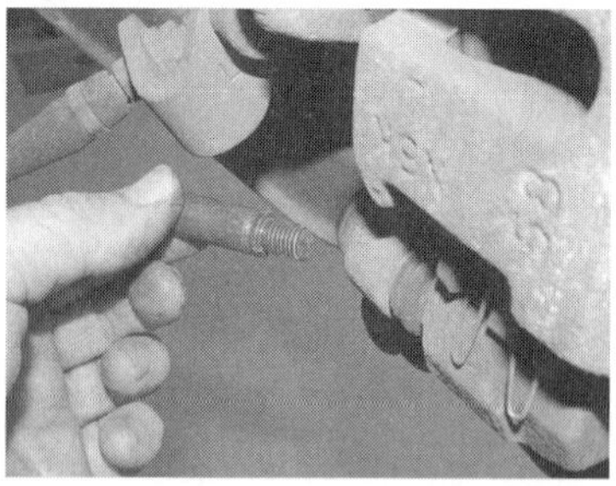

4. Remove the lower caliper mounting bolt.

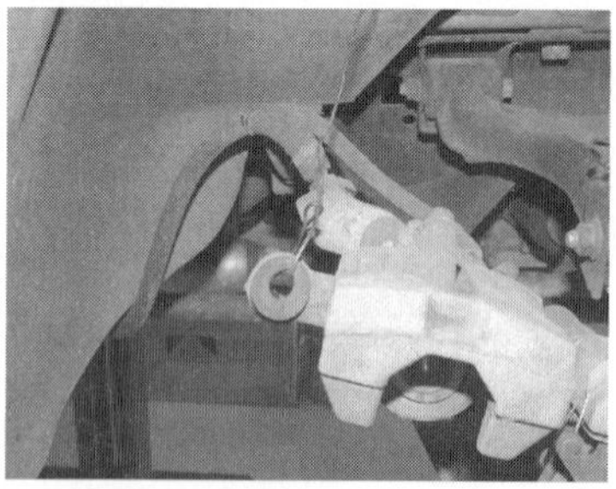

5. Pivot the caliper up and secure it with wire.

6. Remove the M-springs and...

Disc Brake Service

MAZDA REAR PAD REPLACEMENT

7. . . . remove the worn pads.

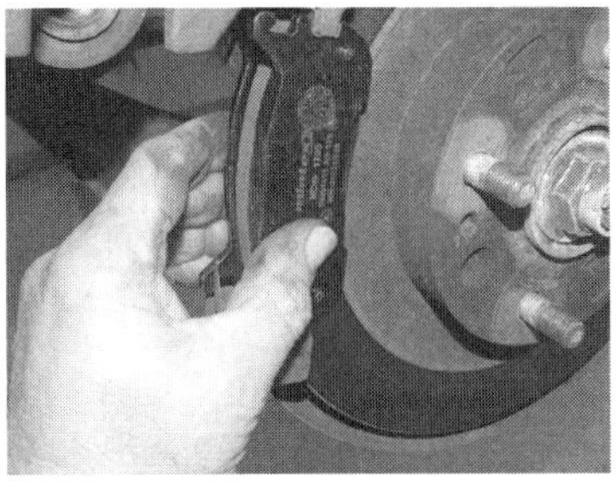

8. Install the new brake pads.

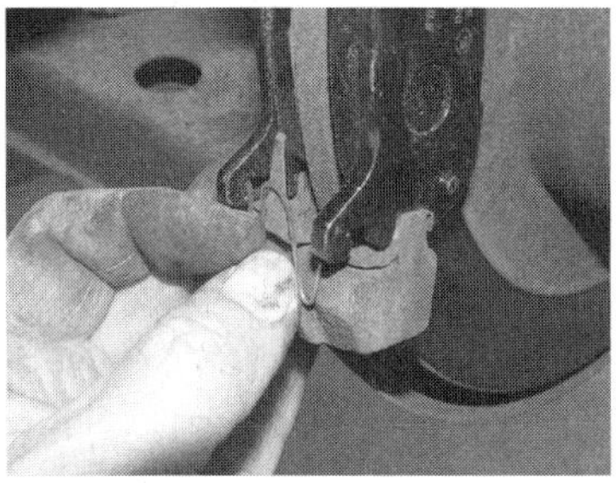

9. Install the upper and lower M-springs.

10. Install the caliper and tighten the mounting bolt.

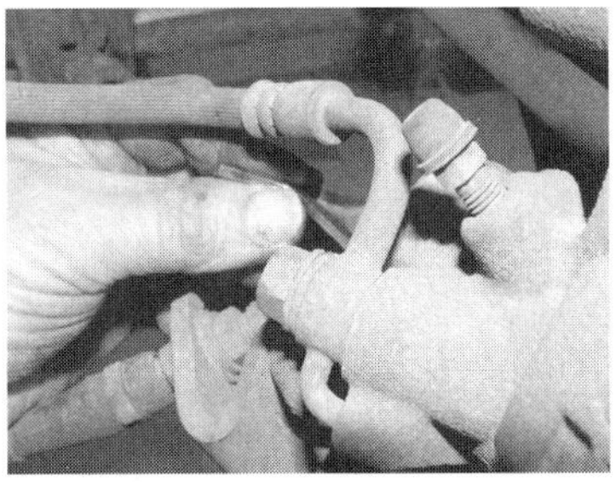

11. Turn the parking brake adjuster clockwise until the pads contact the rotor.

12. Tighten the adjuster until the rotor cannot be turned by hand.

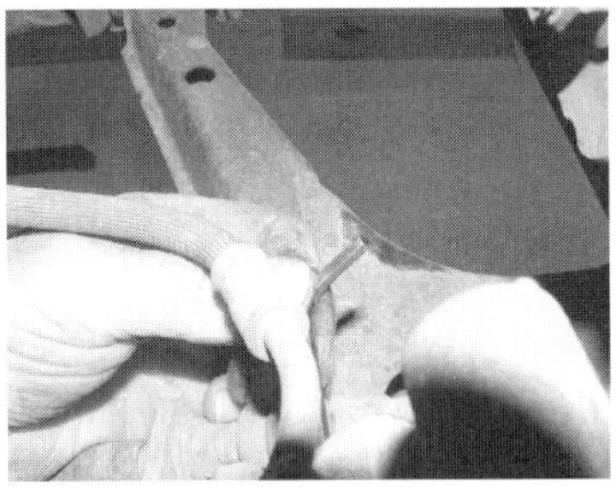

13. Back off the adjuster ⅓ of a turn. This sets the proper parking brake clearance. Install the adjuster plug.

14. Finish by installing the wheels and torquing the lug nuts.

BRAKE PAD BURNISH-IN

Whenever new brake pads are installed, they require a short time of relatively light use called a burnishing-in or bedding-in period. There are two reasons for this. First, regardless of whether the rotors have been refinished or not, new pads do not make full contact with the friction surface. A short period of light braking allows the pads and rotors to become "familiar" with one another and wear into better contact.

The second reason a burnish-in period is needed is because new brake pads are not fully cured when they come from the factory; there are still binding resins and other chemicals that have not completely evaporated from the friction material. Final curing takes place over the first few hundred miles of driving as the pads are repeatedly heated and cooled.

If new brakes are used hard immediately and become too hot, residual resins boil out of the pads as gases and liquids. When these gases and liquids come out in great enough quantities, they lubricate the friction material and cause a type of brake fade called green fade. Once green fade occurs, the pads will be glazed when they return to normal operating temperature. Glazed pads do not have the proper friction coefficient for smooth operation, and must be replaced.

Pad Burnishing Procedure

Whenever you replace any of the friction materials in a brake system, take the car for a test drive afterward to make sure the brakes are operating properly. During the test drive, perform the simple procedure below to burnish-in the new shoes and/or pads:

1. Drive the car at approximately 30 mph (50 kph). Check your rear-view mirror to make sure it is safe to do so, then apply the brakes with *moderate to firm* pressure to slow the car to about 5 mph (8 kph).
2. Accelerate back to speed, and drive for approximately 15 seconds to allow the brakes to cool. Make another stop as described in step 1. Continue to alternate stops with cooldown periods until you have made about a half dozen stops in this manner.
3. Accelerate to approximately 55 mph (88 kph). Check your rear-view mirror to make sure it is safe to do so, then apply the brakes with *moderate to firm* pressure to slow the car to about 20 mph (30 kph).
4. Accelerate back to speed, and drive for approximately 30 seconds to allow the brakes to cool. Make another stop as described in step 3. Continue to alternate stops with cooldown periods until you have made about a half dozen stops in this manner.
5. When you deliver the car to its owners caution them that the brakes should not be used hard for approximately 100 miles of in-town driving, or 300 miles of highway driving. This will ensure that the brakes become properly burnished in.

BRAKE CALIPER EXTERNAL INSPECTION

Whenever you replace a set of brake pads, or have the calipers off the car for any reason, you should inspect the calipers to determine if they need an overhaul. Some manufacturers and technicians maintain that the calipers should be rebuilt every time the pads are replaced; others believe that new pads can be installed without overhauling the calipers if the calipers pass a simple inspection. Keep in mind that a set of brake pads usually lasts a minimum of 30,000 miles (48,000 km). If you decide to replace a set of brake pads without rebuilding the calipers, you should be confident the calipers will not leak, seize, or otherwise fail before the new pads are worn out.

If the brake calipers are not rebuilt when the pads are changed, the replacement pads generally do not last as long as the original parts. This happens for two reasons: first, because the rotor friction surface is not as smooth as it was originally; and second, because the rubber used to make fixed piston seals loses flexibility with age, and will not retract the piston and pads as far from the rotor. Both of these conditions increase brake drag, which accelerates the rate of lining wear.

The next section describes an external caliper inspection procedure, but in addition to the items described, there are a number of other factors that affect the need to rebuild brake calipers. It is impossible to give precise recommendations for every situation, but consider the following items when you make your decision.

A caliper overhaul is more likely to be needed on a car that:

- Has over 50,000 miles (80,000 km) on it and the brake system has never been serviced
- Is more than five years old and the brake system has never been serviced
- Is driven in snowbelt areas where salt is used on the roads
- Is driven in areas with high humidity and rainfall
- Is driven in mountainous regions or in heavy-duty service.

On the other hand, unless there are obvious signs of a problem, a caliper overhaul is less likely to be needed on a car that:

- Has fewer than 50,000 miles (80,000 km) and has had regular brake system service

Disc Brake Service

Figure 8-15. Rebuild the brake caliper if the dust boot is damaged in any way.

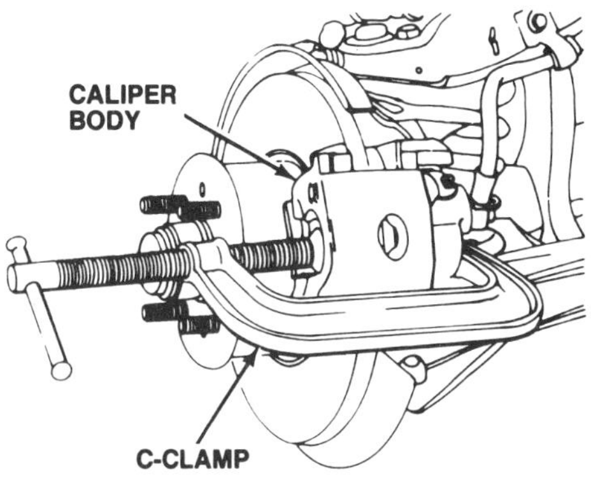

- Is less than five years old and has had regular brake system service
- Is driven in sunbelt areas where humidity, rainfall, and snowfall are minimal.

Caliper External Inspection Procedure

Once the brake pads are removed, inspect the entire outside of the caliper body; if there are cracks or any other major damage, replace the caliper. Next, visually inspect the dust boot around the piston, figure 8-15; make sure it is fully seated in the caliper body and does not have any holes or tears in it. A leaking dust boot allows moisture and dirt into the caliper bore that will quickly destroy the piston, seal, and bore finish. Also inspect the caliper for brake fluid leakage around the boot, or fluid deposits on the brake pads that can indicate a leaking caliper seal. A leaking seal could result in a total loss of braking in at least half of the split braking system. If the dust boot is unseated or damaged in any way, or there are any signs of fluid leakage, rebuild or replace the caliper.

If the dust boot is in good condition and there are no signs of leaks, bottom the caliper pistons in their bores. On single-piston calipers, use a C-clamp, figure 8-16, or a large pair of slip-joint pliers, figure 8-17; take care not to tear or dislodge the dust boot. On multi-piston fixed calipers, insert a screwdriver or pry bar between the rotor and an old brake pad, and lever the pistons back into their bores, figure 8-18. Rear disc brake calipers that are applied to serve as the parking brake require a special turning tool to thread the piston back into the bore on the automatic adjuster screw, figure 8-19.

Figure 8-16. Bottoming a caliper piston with a C-clamp.

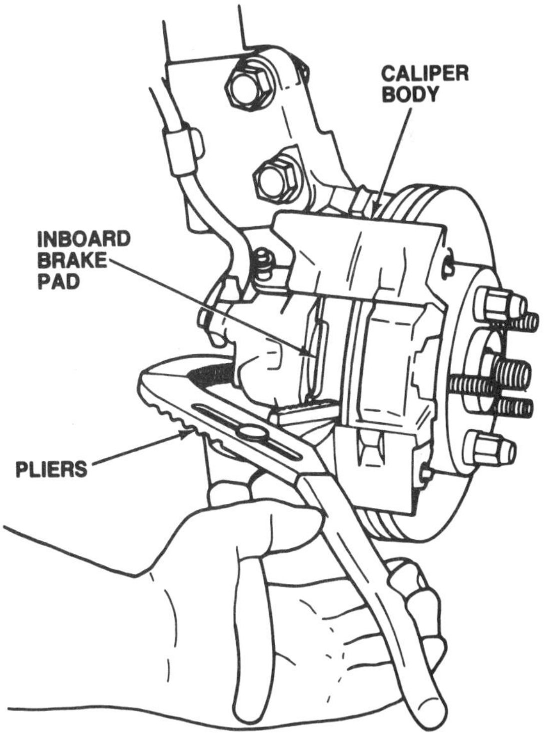

Figure 8-17. Bottoming a caliper piston with slip-joint pliers.

Remember that as you bottom a piston, the fluid inside the caliper is displaced into the hydraulic system under pressure. If other pistons in the hydraulic system, such as those in the wheel cylinders or the caliper on the other side of the car, are not restrained, this pressure may be sufficient to push them out of their bores. Unless these parts are to be rebuilt anyway, take precautions to prevent this from happening. Service one axle or wheel at a time, or insert a block of wood into the opposing caliper to prevent its piston from coming out of the bore.

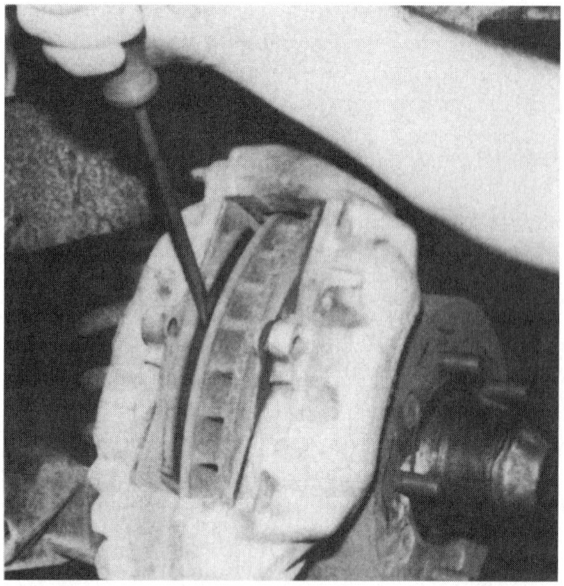

Figure 8-18. Bottoming the caliper pistons in a fixed brake caliper.

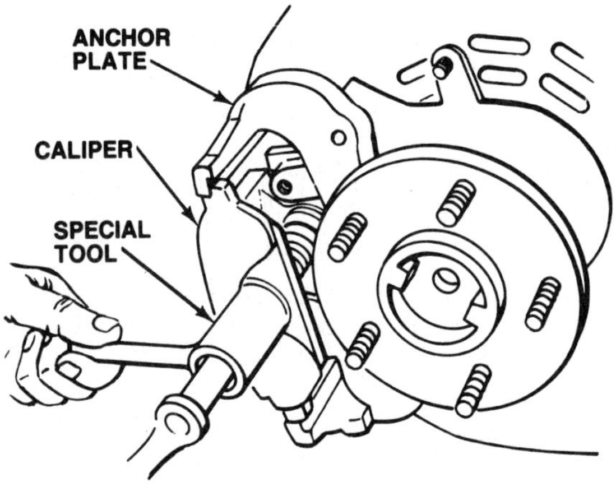

Figure 8-19. A special tool is required to bottom some rear disc brake caliper pistons.

As you bottom the pistons, note the "feel" of the piston movement. A moderate amount of force should be sufficient to move the pistons, and they should slide smoothly into the caliper bores. Furthermore, all of the pistons in a multi-piston caliper, and those in the calipers on both sides of the car, should require about the same amount of force to bottom. If these conditions are met, and the car does not fall into any of the "likely to need an overhaul" catagories discussed above, you can be reasonably safe in assuming that the calipers are in good condition and do not need to be overhauled.

If a piston is frozen or difficult to bottom, the piston and/or bore is rusted or corroded, and the caliper must be overhauled or replaced. Do not return a caliper in marginal condition to service. Even though you may be able to bottom a rusted, corroded, or dirty piston in its bore, the piston will not seal properly and the caliper will begin to leak fluid, which will contaminate the new pads and cause a comeback.

Just as brake pads are always replaced in axle sets, *both* calipers on an axle should be overhauled if it is determined that one needs to be rebuilt. This ensures that even braking action is maintained, and that the brakes at both wheels have a similar service life.

Loaded Calipers

If it is determined that the calipers must be rebuilt or replaced, it may be faster and more cost-effective to install a loaded caliper, figure 8-20. This is a rebuilt caliper that comes with new brake pads already installed on the caliper. Loaded calipers are available for most popular vehicle applications and are usually less expensive than buying the pads and rebuilt caliper separately.

BRAKE CALIPER OVERHAUL

Every brake caliper requires certain special overhaul procedures, but just as with brake pad replacement, *all* overhaul procedures have some things in common. Step-by-step overhaul procedures for several calipers are provided at the end of the chapter. The sections below describe a general procedure that includes the common operations of bleeder screw removal, piston removal, dust boot and piston seal removal, internal inspection, honing, and caliper assembly.

Before you begin an overhaul on any caliper, attempt to loosen the bleeder screw with a bleeder screw wrench. It is not unusual for bleeder screws to become rusted or corroded in place so they cannot be removed. These "frozen" bleeder screws are particularly common in aluminum calipers where the dissimilar metal of the steel screw causes electrolysis. In most cases, calipers with frozen bleeder screws should be replaced. The exceptions are when a replacement caliper is unavailable, or its cost is so high that the time and effort spent on bleeder screw removal can be justified.

Bleeder Screw Removal

If it is necessary to remove a frozen bleeder screw, spray the screw threads with penetrating oil and allow it to soak in for at least 10 minutes. Then, place a deep socket over the bleeder screw so it contacts the body of the caliper around the base of the screw. Wearing safety glasses to prevent injuries, strike the socket several medium-firm blows; this should slightly deform the metal of the caliper and break the surface tension

Disc Brake Service

Figure 8-20. A loaded caliper comes with a new or rebuilt caliper and new brake pads.

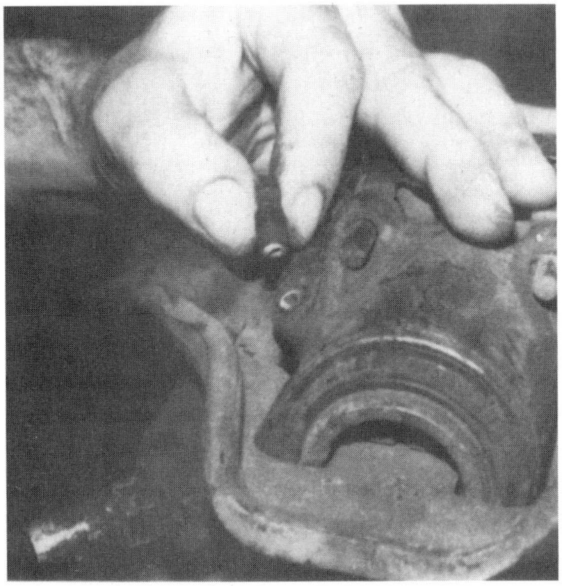

Figure 8-21. Caliper bleeder screws are almost impossible to remove once they become frozen in place.

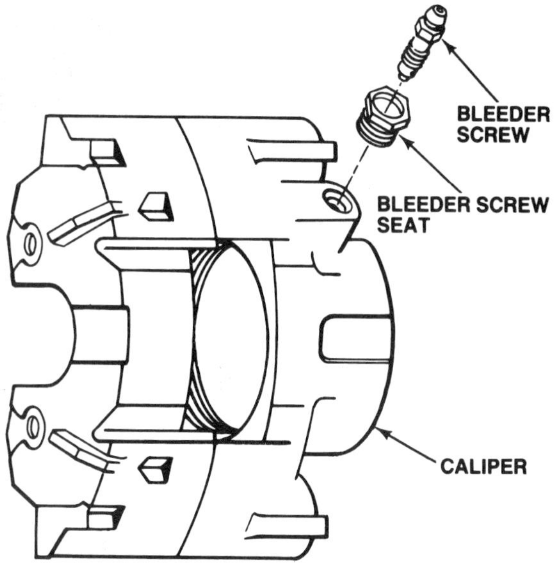

Figure 8-22. A universal replacement bleeder screw assembly.

between the bleeder screw threads and those in the caliper opening. Attempt to remove the bleeder screw with the appropriate wrench, but do not apply too much turning force or you will twist the end of the screw off, figure 8-21. Once this happens, it is virtually impossible to remove the portion of the screw that remains in the caliper.

Repeat the procedures with the penetrating oil, socket and hammer, and bleeder wrench as needed until the screw is free. As discussed in chapter 7, special hammer sockets are available from the aftermarket that allow you to apply both hammer blows and turning force at the same time. Once you remove a bleeder screw, buff its threads clean on a wire wheel, and run a drill bit through its passageways to make sure they are clear. In some cases this is not necessary because a new bleeder screw is included in the caliper overhaul kit. Do not reinstall the bleeder screw until after the caliper and screw threads have both been thoroughly cleaned and are ready to be assembled.

When a bleeder screw breaks off, or cannot be removed using any of the techniques above, the caliper should be replaced. If a replacement caliper is unavailable, there are replacement bleeder screw assemblies available from the aftermarket, figure 8-22. These require that you drill out the old bleeder screw, and thread the caliper body to accept the new bleeder screw seat. Because bleeder screws are usually made of very hard steel, this operation can be quite difficult, and is often best done by a machine shop equipped with the proper tooling.

BRAKE CALIPER PISTON REMOVAL

Other than bleeder screw removal, the only potentially difficult part of a brake caliper overhaul is removing the piston or pistons from the caliper. Pistons fit in their bores with only a few thousandth of an inch clearance, so even a small amount of rust or corrosion can make a piston extremely hard to remove. Unless a piston is free in its bore, or only slightly stuck, a great deal of force will be required to remove it. This force is usually generated in one of three ways: with a mechanical removal tool, or by applying air pressure or hydraulic pressure to the fluid inlet fitting of the caliper.

The problems involved in caliper piston removal are worse with multi-piston calipers. With a single-piston caliper, air or hydraulic pressure only has to act on one piston; when that piston is forced from its bore, you can proceed with the overhaul. However, with a multi-piston caliper, the pressure acts with equal force on all of the pistons, which means that the piston that is least stuck will be forced out of its bore first. Once this happens, pressure is no longer contained within the caliper, and another method must be used to remove the remaining, more securely frozen, caliper pistons.

In some cases, you can work around this difficulty by removing the bridge bolts and splitting the caliper into its component halves. For example, if a two-piston caliper is split, pressure can be applied to each half to remove the pistons individually. This is not always an option, however, because some manufacturers state that their calipers should not be split. And, with four-piston calipers, there will always be two pistons in each caliper half.

One way of dealing with this problem is to use a C-clamp or other means of holding the free pistons in their bores while the frozen pistons are forced out with air or hydraulic pressure. Sometimes, if the caliper is installed on the car, the brake rotor will prevent the pistons from coming entirely out of the bores. In this case, pressure can be applied until all of the pistons contact the rotor, then the caliper is removed from the car. If the rotor does not have sufficient thickness to keep the pistons in their bores, a thin wooden block or a worn-out brake pad can be inserted between the pistons and the rotor. Generally, even a badly frozen piston can be removed manually once it is at least 75 percent of the way out of its bore.

One final caution is necessary before describing the various caliper piston removal procedures. There will always be at least a little brake fluid in the caliper when removing the pistons. Depending on the method used, this fluid will be sprayed or spilled from the caliper when the piston comes out of its bore. When you remove caliper pistons, wear safety glasses to protect your eyes, and take precautions to ensure that brake fluid does not come in contact with the vehicle finish or other painted surfaces.

Mechanical Piston Removal

Special tools are available to mechanically remove brake caliper pistons that are free, or only mildly stuck, in their bores. These tools are not widely used because it is generally faster and easier to use air pressure when removing these types of pistons (see figure 8-23). However, mechanical removal tools can work well on multi-piston calipers to remove the second piston from a caliper half once another method has been used to remove the first one.

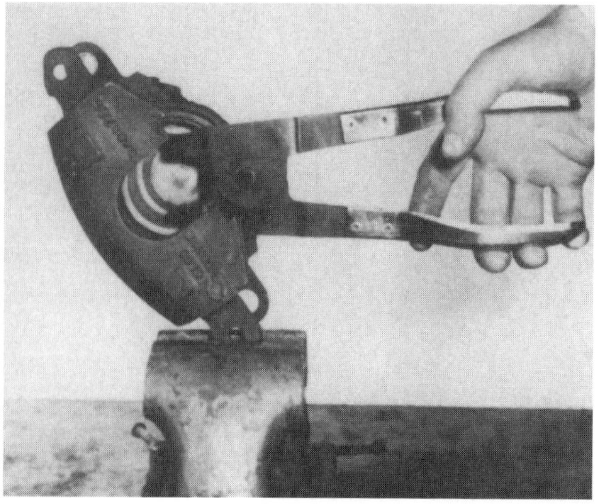

Figure 8-23. Removing a caliper piston with a mechanical tool.

The advantages to removing caliper pistons mechanically are that the tools are simple and relatively inexpensive, and a source of compressed air is not required. The main disadvantage is that mechanical removal tools are human powered, and usually do not provide enough leverage to remove even moderately rusted or corroded pistons.

To remove a caliper piston with a mechanical tool:

1. Remove the caliper from the vehicle and clamp it in a vise.
2. Grip the inner bore of the piston with the removal tool. With a plier-type tool, simply squeeze the handles together tightly. With a mechanically tightened tool, rotate the Allen bolt until the jaws of the tool are tightly clamped against the inner bore of the piston.
3. Rotate the piston back and forth until it is free, and pull outward with a twisting motion to remove the piston from its bore, figure 8-23.

If a piston cannot be removed with a manual tool, you will have to use either air pressure or hydraulic pressure, as described below, to remove the piston.

Compressed-Air Piston Removal

Using compressed air to remove caliper pistons is a common procedure. This method works well when the piston is free, or somewhat firmly stuck, in the caliper bore. The advantages of removing pistons in this way are that it can be done by a single technician, and sufficient force is available from the compressed air supply in most shops to remove all but severely frozen pistons. For example, 100 psi (690 kPa) of air pressure applied to a 1½-inch (38-mm) diameter caliper piston

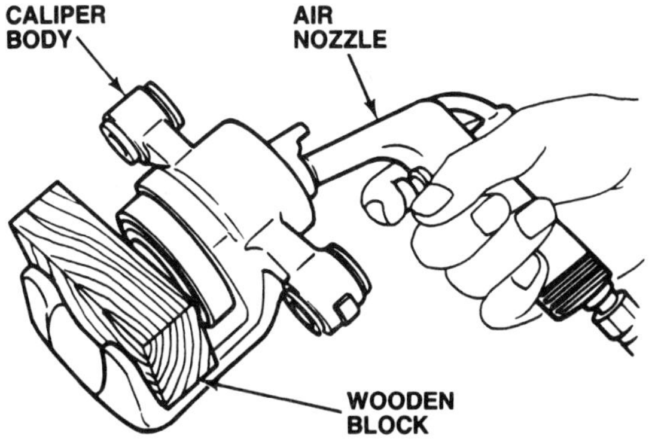

Disc Brake Service

Figure 8-24. Wooden blocks help prevent damage when caliper pistons are removed from their bores.

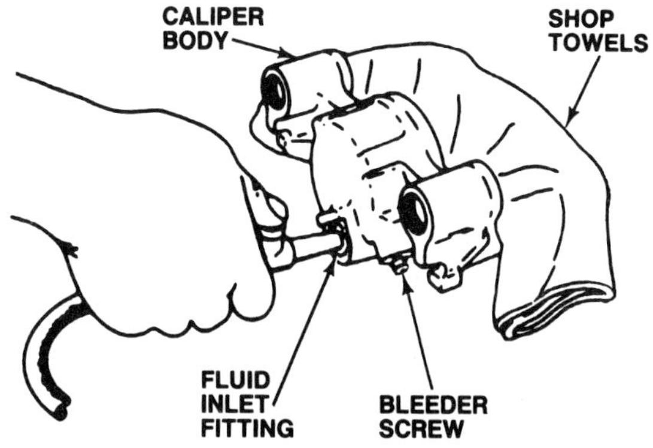

Figure 8-25. Apply air pressure to the caliper fluid inlet to force the piston out of its bore.

creates more than 550 pounds (250 kg) of force to drive the piston out of the bore.

The primary disadvantage of using compressed air to remove caliper pistons is that it is very difficult to regulate the amount of pressure applied to the piston. Compressed air contains a great deal of energy that is released very suddenly when the piston pops free. When too much pressure is used, the piston can be damaged as it is driven from the bore with great force, and brake fluid in the caliper may spray out, causing further damage or injury. Use *extreme* caution when you remove caliper pistons in this manner.

To remove a caliper piston with compressed air:

1. Remove the caliper from the vehicle and clamp it in a vise by its mounting flange.
2. Insert a wooden block or bundle of shop towels between the piston and caliper body to prevent damage to the piston when it comes out of the caliper bore, figure 8-24.
3. Cover the caliper body in shop towels to trap any brake fluid spray that may occur when the piston comes out of its bore.
4. Place a rubber-tipped air nozzle into the caliper fluid inlet, and carefully apply air pressure to force the piston out of the bore, figure 8-25. Use the minimum amount of pressure necessary, and *keep fingers and hands away from the piston.*

If full shop air pressure is insufficient to remove the piston from its bore, you will have to use hydraulic pressure to remove the piston.

Hydraulic Piston Removal

Using hydraulic pressure to remove caliper pistons is both the most effective and the safest method. The most common method of hydraulic piston removal is to use the vehicle brake hydraulic system to force the pistons from their bores while the calipers are still mounted on the car. In this manner, both front calipers can be serviced at the same time.

The advantages of this method are that it is relatively fast, does not require special tools, and provides plenty of pressure to do the job. While compressed air can provide several hundred pounds of force to remove a piston, hydraulic pressure can supply well over a thousand pounds! If hydraulic pressure cannot remove a piston from its bore, there is probably so much damage to the piston and bore that the caliper should be replaced anyway. Hydraulic pressure can also be applied with much greater control than air pressure, which reduces the chances of damage caused by flying pistons or brake fluid.

The disadvantages of using hydraulic pressure to remove pistons are that it requires an assistant, and cannot be used if there is air in the hydraulic system or the master cylinder is bypassing internally. In addition, extra fluid may have to be added to the master cylinder reservoir in order to move the pistons all the way out of their bores.

To remove a caliper piston from its bore using the brake hydraulic system:

1. With fixed brake calipers, remove the brake pads from the calipers. If the brake rotor is not thick enough to prevent the pistons from coming out of their bores, insert a set of worn-out brake pads or thin wooden shims between the caliper pistons and the rotor.
2. With floating or sliding calipers, remove the calipers from over the brake rotors and hang them from the suspension to prevent damage to the brake hose. Insert thick wooden blocks into the calipers between the pistons and caliper bodies to prevent the pistons from coming out of their bores, figure 8-26.

Figure 8-26. Wooden blocks can also prevent caliper pistons from coming entirely out of their bores.

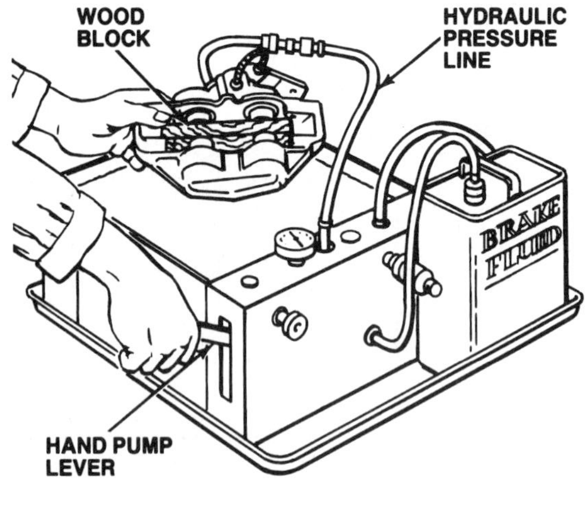

Figure 8-27. Removing a caliper piston with a special hydraulic service bench.

3. Place drain pans under the calipers to catch brake fluid in the event that a piston does come out of its bore.
4. Have an assistant *slowly* apply the brake pedal to force the pistons from their bores; several pedal strokes may be needed to move all of the pistons out against the rotors or wooden blocks.
5. Determine which piston was the last to be fully extended; this is the most frozen piston. If the piston is in a fixed caliper, remove worn out pad or wooden shim from between the rotor and the most frozen piston; if no pad or shim was used, remove the caliper from over the rotor, and secure the less frozen pistons in their bores with C-clamps or other suitable tools. If the most frozen piston is in a sliding or floating caliper, remove the wooden block from that caliper.
6. Have your assistant *slowly* apply the brake pedal until the most frozen piston comes entirely out of its bore.
7. Remove both from the vehicle and finish removing the other pistons with a mechanical tool or compressed air.

Caliper Hydraulic Service Bench

Pistons can also be removed hydraulically with a special caliper service bench. The principle is the same as described above, but rather than using the vehicle brake hydraulic system to do the job, you remove the calipers from the car and attached them to the hydraulic hose of the service bench, figure 8-27. You then pump the hand lever, which is connected to a small master cylinder that provides pressurized fluid to force the piston out of the caliper.

The advantages to this method are that an assistant is not needed, and the condition of the vehicle brake hydraulic system is not a factor in obtaining sufficient pressure to free a frozen piston. The disadvantages are the cost of the specialized caliper service bench, and the fact that only one caliper can be serviced at a time.

Dust Boot and Piston Seal Removal

Once the piston is out of the caliper, remove the dust boot. If the boot is a press fit in the caliper and remains attached to it, use a screwdriver to pry the boot out, figure 8-28. Take care not to scratch the caliper bore as you remove the boot. If the boot is a stretch fit over the piston and remains attached to that part, simply pull it free and set it aside.

Next, remove the piston seals. If the caliper has stroking seals, insert a probe under the seals and lever them off of the pistons. If the caliper has fixed seals, insert a probe under the seals and pry them out of the grooves in the caliper bores, figure 8-29. To avoid scratching or otherwise damaging the pistons, caliper bore, or seal groove, always use a wooden or plastic probe to remove seals. Damage in these areas can cause fluid leaks when the caliper is reassembled. If a fixed seal is any shape other than square cut, note how it fits into the groove so that you can install the new seal in the same manner.

Once the caliper is disassembled, clean the body and pistons with brake cleaning solvent. If the parts are particularly dirty, use a soft bristle brush to help remove any contamination. Do not use a wire brush or you may damage the piston sealing surface, the seal groove, or the caliper bore. Rubber parts such as boots and seals do not need to be cleaned because they will be replaced with new parts from the rebuild kit. When

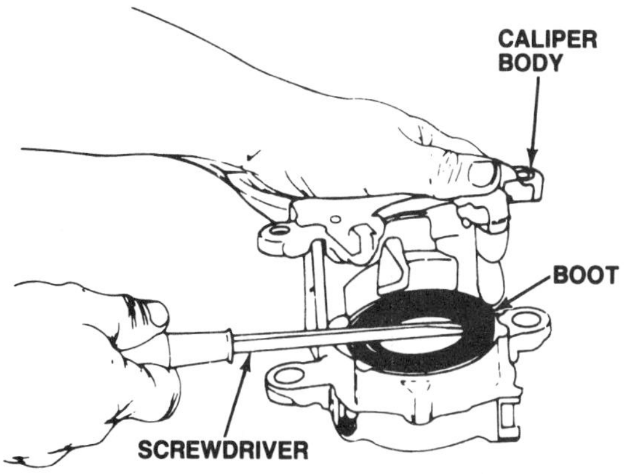

Disc Brake Service

Figure 8-28. Removing a dust boot that is a press fit in the caliper body. (Courtesy of General Motors Corporation, Service and Parts Operations)

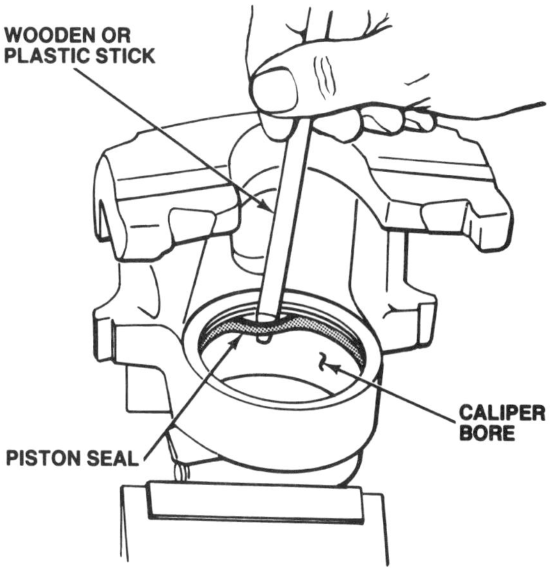

Figure 8-29. The final step in caliper disassembly is to remove the piston seal.

the caliper and pistons are clean, allow them to dry and make sure no liquid solvent remains in the fluid passages of the caliper body.

BRAKE CALIPER INTERNAL INSPECTION

Once the caliper body and piston are cleaned, inspect the caliper bore for scoring, rust, corrosion, and wear. This is particularly important on calipers that have stroking seals because the bore provides the sealing surface; even a small imperfection in the bore can create a fluid leak. Minor rust and corrosion can be removed from the bore with crocus cloth or by honing as described later in the chapter. However, if the bore of a caliper with stroking seals is significantly damaged, the caliper must be replaced.

The bore condition of calipers with fixed seals is less critical because the piston provides the sealing surface. Inspect the bores of these calipers for major defects that might prevent the piston from moving freely, and make sure the edges of the seal groove are not rusted or corroded, and do not have any nicks or burrs that can cut the seal or affect its sealing ability. As long as the seal groove is in good condition, and the bore diameter remains within specifications, calipers with fixed seals can be honed clean of even major rust and corrosion. However, if the seal groove is damaged in any way, or honing makes the bore oversize, the caliper must be replaced.

Caliper Piston Inspection

Caliper pistons are made of cast-iron, steel, aluminum, or phenolic resin. As mentioned above, pay particular attention when you inspect pistons used in calipers with fixed seals because the outside diameter of the piston provides the sealing surface for the caliper seal. On pistons used with stroking seals, the important area is the groove in which the seal fits. In both cases, the piston will have to be replaced if the critical surface is not smooth, clean and entirely free of defects.

Inspect cast-iron, steel, and aluminum pistons for rust, corrosion, nicks, and scoring in their sealing areas, figure 8-30. If a cast-iron or steel piston is chrome plated to provide a better sealing surface, make sure the plating is not flaking away anywhere. All aluminum pistons are anodized to provide a durable finish, and this surface should not be damaged in any way. If cast-iron, steel, or aluminum pistons have any of these problems, you should replace them.

Inspect pistons made of phenolic resin for cracks or chips, figure 8-30 and figure 8-31. Minor cracks or chips that extend partially across the piston face are acceptable, as are minor nicks and gouges at the outer edge of the piston, providing they do not extend into the dust boot groove. Replace any piston if cracks extend across the face of the piston, or nicks and gouges enter the dust boot groove. Finally, inspect the outer diameter of the piston, it should be smooth and even. If the surface is scuffed or scored in any way, replace the piston.

BRAKE CALIPER HONING

In the early years of disc brakes, calipers had stroking seals that would seal against the caliper bore even with a relatively large amount of clearance between the piston and bore. As a result, honing the caliper

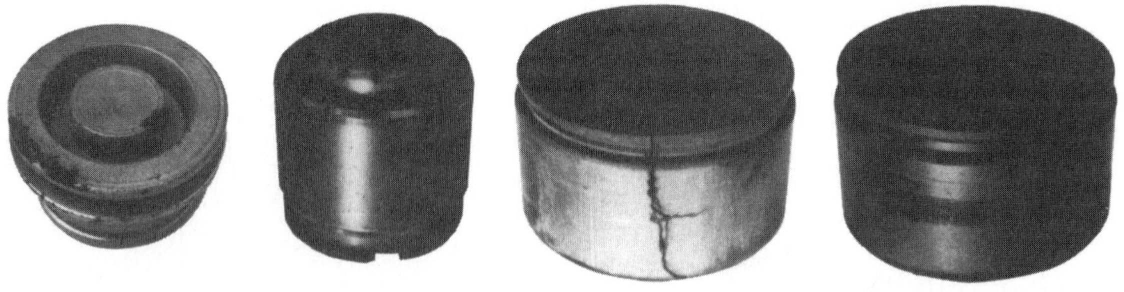

Figure 8-30. Typical caliper piston damage.

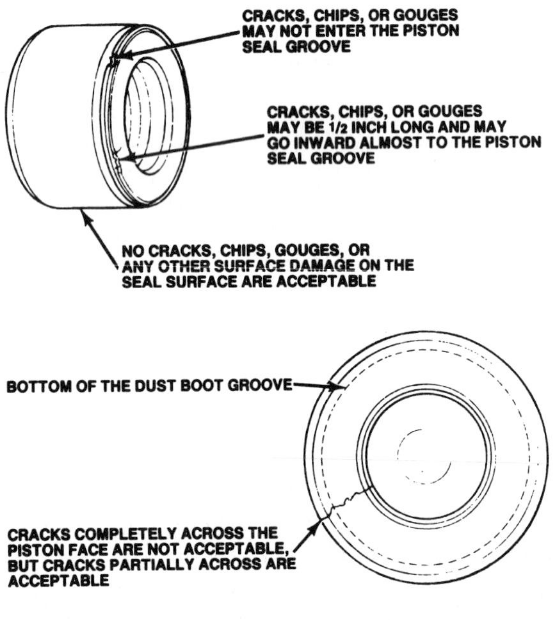

Figure 8-31. Phenolic caliper pistons commonly suffer minor cracking.

bore to restore the sealing surface was a routine part of a caliper overhaul. The fixed seals used in virtually all brake calipers today require smaller piston-to-bore clearances in order to seal properly. For this reason, modern calipers are honed rarely, if at all, and only to remove rust, corrosion, or minor scoring that might interfere with the free movement of the piston.

On calipers with stroking seals, honing remains an acceptable rebuilding procedure that can provide a less expensive alternative to caliper replacement. However, just as with master cylinders and wheel cylinders that have been honed, the resulting sealing surface is not nearly as smooth as the finish on the original part. As a result, a honed caliper will not provide the same service life as a new part.

Whether it is used to restore the sealing surface of a caliper with stroking seals, or simply to clean up the bore of a caliper with fixed seals, the honing procedure is the same. Remember to always compress the arms of the hone manually when you move the stones into or out of the caliper bore. Never drag the stones straight out of the bore or you will cause scratches that may result in a leak. To hone a brake caliper:

1. Mount the caliper in a vise so you have clear access to the bore. Do not clamp on the cylinder body or the bore may be distorted.
2. Select the proper size caliper hone and chuck it in a drill motor. Use a hone with fine stones.
3. Lubricate the bore and hone with clean brake fluid, then place the hone into the bore. Start the drill motor, and rotate the hone at approximately 500 rpm, figure 8-32. If the caliper uses stroking seals, stroke the hone gently in and out of the bore to obtain a crosshatch pattern for good sealing. If the caliper uses fixed seals, you can simply hold the hone steady in the bore because the honing pattern does not matter.
4. After about 10 seconds, remove the hone, wipe the bore clean, and check the finish. It should be clean, smooth, and free of damage. Repeat the honing sequence as needed. If the bore does not clean up after several attempts, replace the caliper.
5. After you are finished honing, thoroughly clean the caliper bore, seal groove, and fluid inlet passage with brake cleaner. Allow the caliper to dry, and make sure all traces of grit and residue are cleaned away.
6. Measure the caliper bore as described in the next section.

Caliper Bore Measurement

If the dust boots remain intact and the brake fluid in the system is changed regularly, there is usually little or no

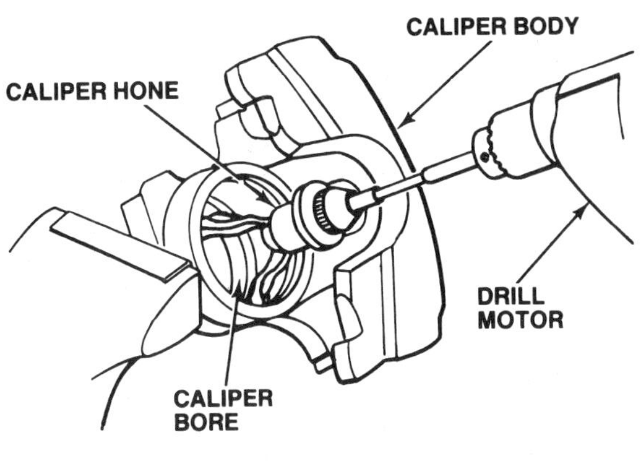

Disc Brake Service

Figure 8-32. Honing a brake caliper bore.

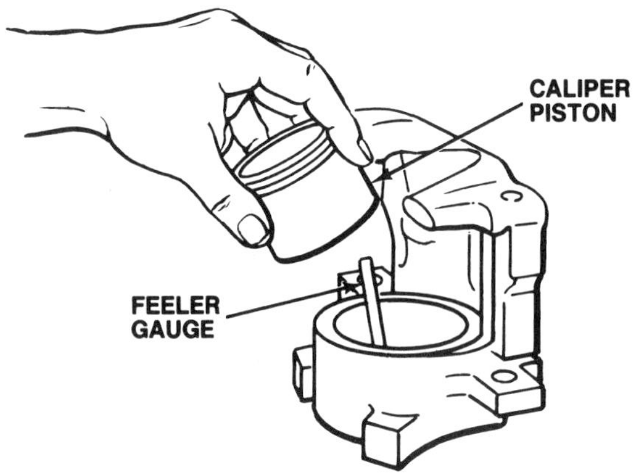

Figure 8-33. Checking the caliper piston-to-bore clearance.

caliper piston and bore wear during normal operation. However, whenever you hone a caliper, you must measure the bore to make sure it has not been honed too far oversize. This is particularly true when a great deal of honing is required to clean up the bore, or when honing calipers with fixed seals.

If the clearance is too great in a caliper with stroking seals, the lip of the seal will seat against the caliper bore with less pressure. This reduces the ability of the seal to contain fluid within the caliper, and shortens the service life of the caliper. Most manufacturers specify between .004″ and .010″ (.10 and .25 mm) piston-to-bore clearance for calipers with stroking seals. Consult the factory shop manual for the car you are servicing to get an exact figure.

If the clearance is too great in a caliper with fixed seals, seal damage can result, and the self-adjusting action of the caliper may be affected. As a general rule, the maximum piston to bore clearance for fixed seal calipers is .002″ to .005″ (.06 to .13 mm) when using metal pistons, and .005″ to .010″ (.13 to .25 mm) when using phenolic pistons. Once again, consult the factory shop manual for the car you are servicing to get an exact figure.

To measure the caliper piston-to-bore clearance, insert a feeler gauge strip whose thickness is equal to the maximum allowed clearance into the caliper bore, figure 8-33. Attempt to insert the piston into the bore alongside the feeler gauge strip. If the piston will enter the bore, repeat the check with a new piston. If a new piston will also enter the bore, replace the caliper.

Sleeved Brake Calipers

Although honing is an acceptable procedure, it is not always the best form of repair. Many calipers with stroking seals are found on older collectible or special-interest cars that get little use. And many of these same

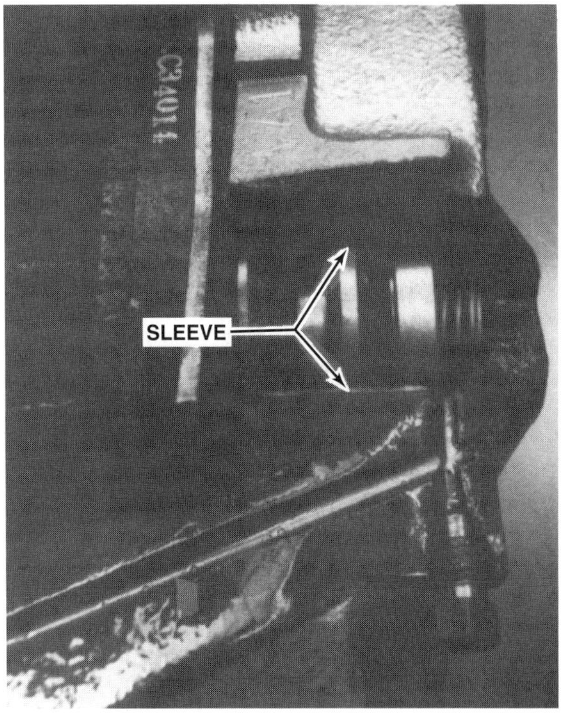

Figure 8-34. Stainless steel sleeves extend the service life of older calipers with stroking seals.

calipers have relatively poor dust and water sealing that makes them prone to rust, corrosion, and fluid leaks. To provide a more permanent repair for these cars (the Chevrolet Corvette in particular), several aftermarket firms sell sleeved brake calipers.

To improve both the sealing and the service life of these calipers, the bores are machined oversize, and stainless steel sleeves are installed, figure 8-34. The sleeve is a press fit into the bore, and provides a very smooth sealing surface. At the same time, stainless steel is far more durable and rust resistant than the original cast-iron caliper bore, which ensures a long service life. If the car you are working on fits into one of the categories described above, you may want to recommend sleeved calipers to the customer rather than a rebuild of the old parts.

BRAKE CALIPER ASSEMBLY

Once you have disassembled, inspected, cleaned, honed, and measured the caliper and caliper piston, obtain any replacement parts you may need, along with the proper overhaul and small parts kits. Before you begin to reassemble a caliper, make sure your hands are completely clean. Dirty hands will contaminate the caliper with grit or oil, and cause early failure. To help ease assembly, have a container of fresh brake fluid or assembly lube handy.

Piston Seal Installation

The first step in assembling a caliper is to install the piston seals. On calipers with fixed seals, thoroughly lubricate the O-ring seal and the seal groove in the caliper bore. Using your fingers, position one edge of seal in the groove, then work the seal around the bore diameter gently until it is fully seated, figure 8-35. Do not twist or roll the seal. Square-cut O-ring seals can be installed facing either way; however, if the seal is any shape other that square-cut, install it in the same manner as the original part.

On calipers with stroking seals, thoroughly lubricate the lip seal and the seal groove in the caliper piston. Using your fingers only, stretch the seal over the end of the piston and into place in the seal groove, figure 8-36. Take special care not to cut or damage the seal, particularly the edge of the sealing lip, in any way. The sealing lip of a stroking seal must face the bottom of the caliper bore when the piston is installed.

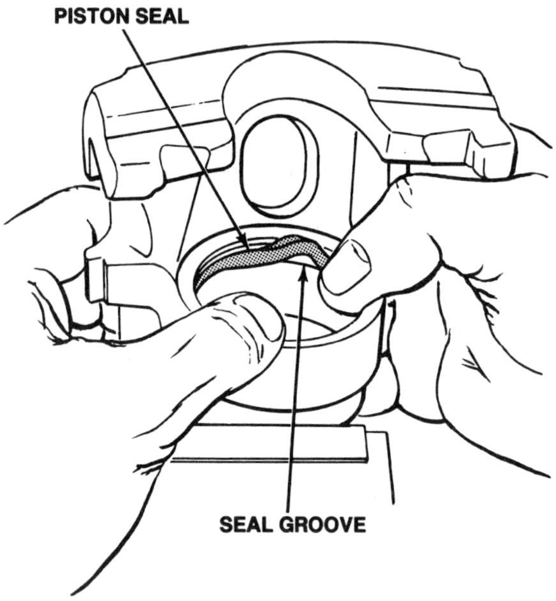

Piston and Dust Boot Installation

Once the seals are installed, the next, and essentially final, step in caliper assembly is to install the piston and dust boot. If piston removal is the most potentially difficult part of caliper disassembly, then piston and dust boot installation can be considered the most difficult part of reassembly. The procedure used to do this varies with the design of the dust boot, and all three common methods are described below.

Press-fit Dust Boot Installation

The brake calipers on General Motors cars, late-model Chrysler products (primarily FWD), and some imports use a dust boot with a metal reinforcing ring around the outer edge that is press fit into the caliper body. These

Figure 8-35. Installing a fixed caliper piston seal.

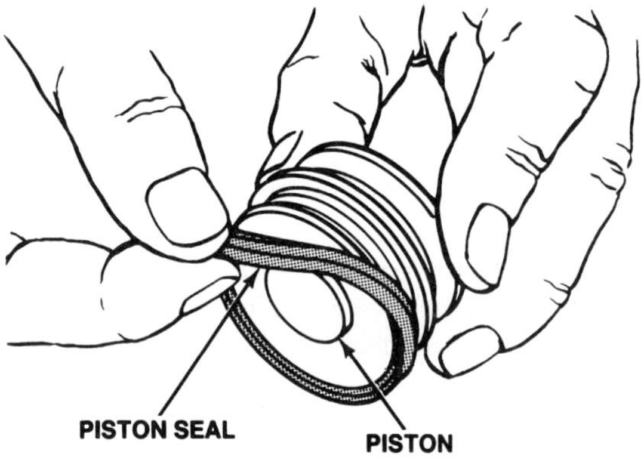

Figure 8-36. Installing a stroking caliper piston seal.

boots require a special driver to install properly. To install the pistons and dust boots on these calipers:

1. Lubricate the piston and slip it into the dust boot until the boot snaps into the groove in the piston.
2. Using only hand pressure, work the piston into the caliper bore past the O-ring seal. Bottom the piston in the bore.
3. Use a hammer and a dust boot driver of the proper size to seat the metal reinforcing ring at the outer edge of the boot into the groove in the caliper body, figure 8-37.

Retaining Ring Dust Boot Installation

The brake calipers on Volkswagens and many Japanese imports may use a dust boot with a separate metal ring that secures the outer edge of the boot into the

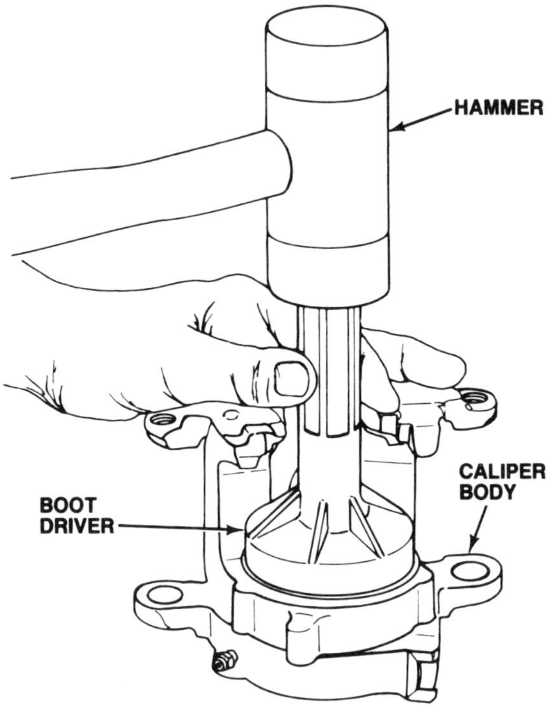

Disc Brake Service

Figure 8-37. Use a hammer and special driver to seat dust boots that are a press fit in the caliper body. (Courtesy of General Motors Corporation, Service and Parts Operations)

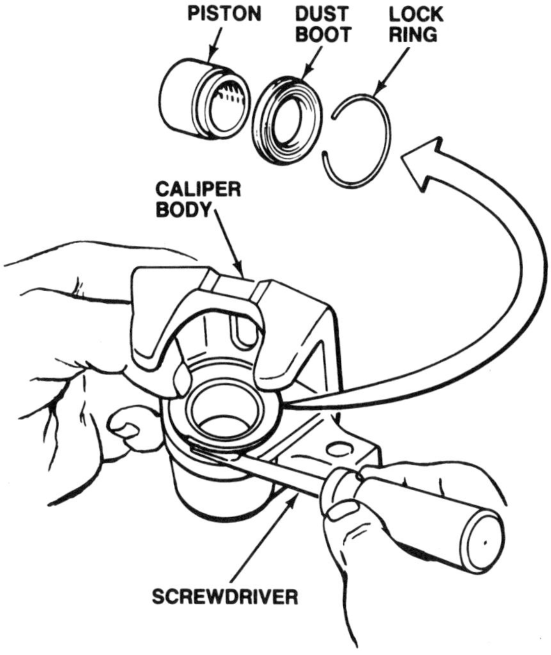

Figure 8-38. Some calipers use a separate retaining ring to lock the dust boot into the caliper body.

caliper body. No special tools are required to assemble this type of caliper. To install the pistons and dust boots into these calipers:

1. Lubricate the piston and slip it into the dust boot until the boot snaps into the groove in the piston.
2. Using only hand pressure, work the piston into the caliper bore past the O-ring seal. Bottom the piston in the bore.
3. Using your fingers, position the outer edge of the boot into the groove in the caliper body; the boot *must* seat properly.
4. Install the metal ring to lock the boot into the groove, figure 8-38.

Lip/Groove Dust Boot Installation

The brake calipers on some Ford Motor Company cars and older Chrysler products (as well as a few newer ones) use a dust boot with a lip around the outer edge that fits into a groove in the caliper bore. Although special tools are not essential to assemble these calipers, a set of metal or plastic rings about one-half inch high will make the job easier. These rings are available from several aftermarket sources. To install the pistons and dust boots on these calipers:

1. Select the ring that just barely fits over the caliper piston.
2. Lubricate the inner edge of the dust boot, and install it over the ring chosen in step 1.
3. Install the lip at the outer edge of the dust boot into the groove in the caliper bore. Reach through the ring with your fingers and make sure the lip is fully seated in the groove.
4. Lubricate the piston and slip it through the ring into the caliper bore, figure 8-39. Using only hand pressure, work the piston past the O-ring seal until it is bottomed in the bore.
5. Carefully remove the ring from the dust boot so that the boot snaps into place on the piston.

There are two common ways to install the pistons and dust boots into these calipers without using the special rings; however, both require a certain "touch," and may require several attempts before the caliper can be assembled properly. The cost of the rings is so low as to make these methods impractical except where the rings are unavailable.

The first method is to install the piston and dust boot entirely by hand:

1. Lubricate the caliper bore, and position the dust boot over the opening.
2. Use your fingers to "pucker" the boot, and carefully work the lip at its outer edge into the groove in the caliper bore, figure 8-40.

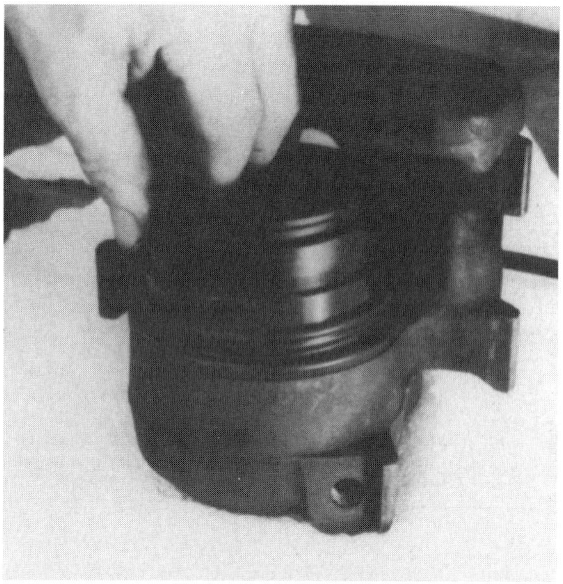

Figure 8-39. Special rings make it easier to install dust boots that fit into grooves in the caliper bore.

Figure 8-41. Using compressed air to install the piston through a lip/groove dust boot.

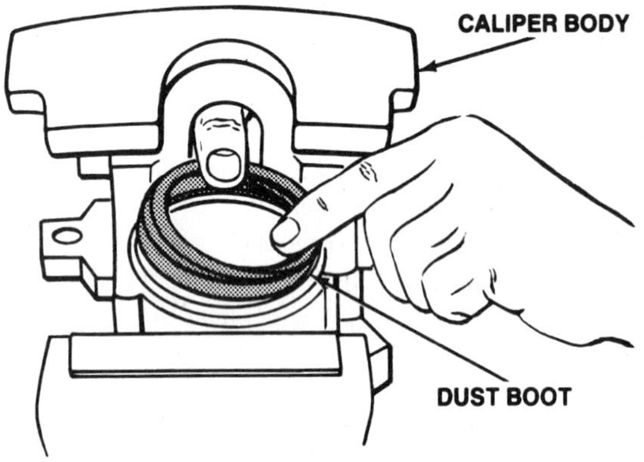

Figure 8-40. Manually installing a lip/groove dust boot.

3. Center the piston over the caliper bore and lightly rest it against the inner edge of the dust boot to "seal" the bore.
4. Apply a small amount of compressed air at the caliper fluid inlet fitting. As the dust boot begins to inflate, increase the amount of air until you can work the piston through the boot, figure 8-41.
5. Once the boot is over the end of the piston, release the air pressure, and slide the piston into the caliper bore past the O-ring seal. Take care not to dislodge the boot from its groove in the process.

BRAKE CALIPER OVERHAUL PROCEDURES

The following pages contain brake caliper overhaul procedures and information on some popular caliper types. These include:

- General Motors single-piston floating caliper
- General Motors four-piston fixed caliper
- Toyota four-piston fixed caliper
- Ford single-piston rear caliper
- General Motors single-piston rear caliper
- General Motors two-piston floating caliper

While there are many other calipers that are not covered, these are popular designs that include most of the common variations in caliper construction and overhaul procedure that you are likely to encounter. With the knowledge gained from reading this chapter, and the experience of going through the overhaul procedure

3. Once the lip is fully seated, carefully stretch the dust boot and slide the piston through it into the caliper bore and past the O-ring seal. Take care not to dislodge the boot from its groove in the process.

The second method of installing the pistons and boots without the special rings uses compressed air. Because water or oil in the compressor storage tank can contaminate the caliper, you should only use this procedure if you know that your compressed air supply is clean and dry.

1. Manually install the lip at the outer edge of the dust boot into the groove in the caliper bore.
2. Lubricate the piston and the inner edge of the dust boot.

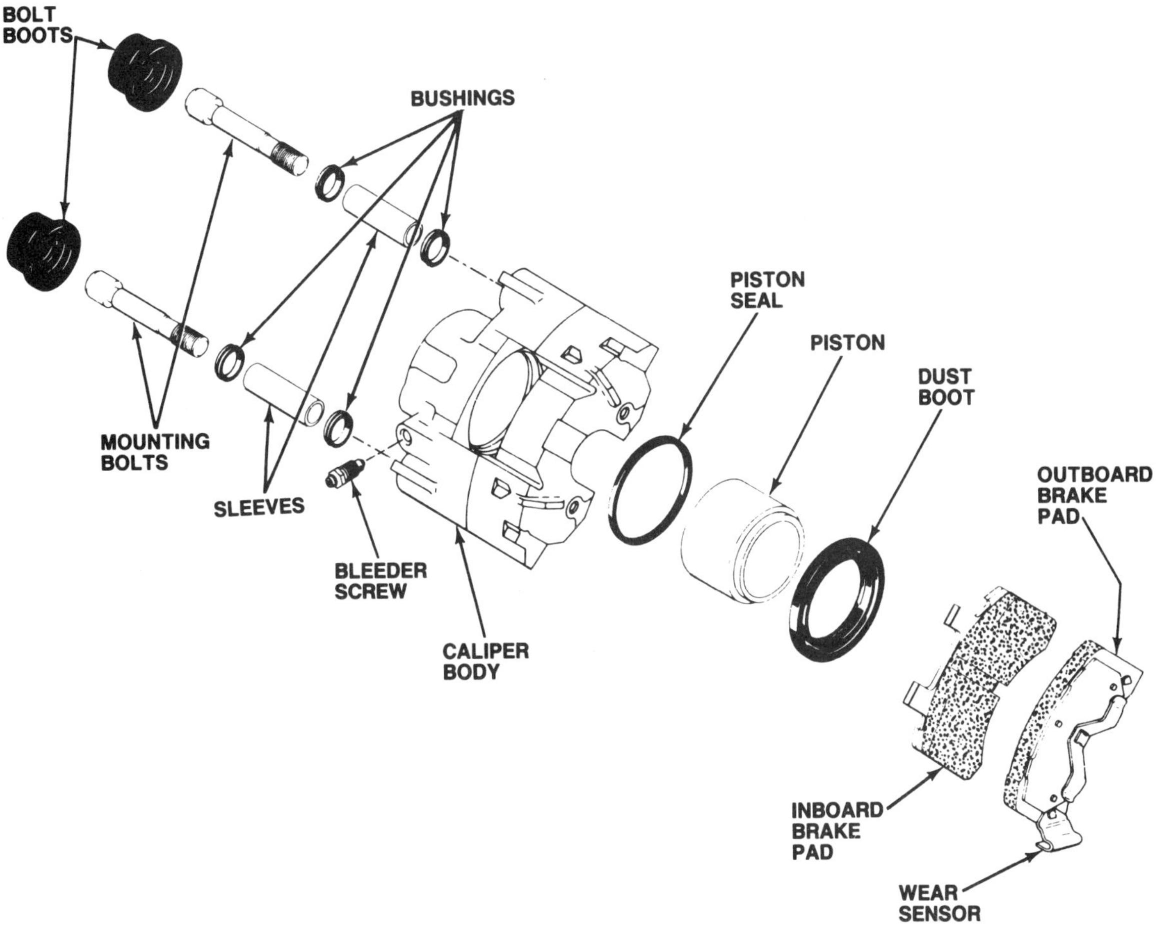

Disc Brake Service

Figure 8-42. The General Motors Series 3200/3300 single-piston, floating caliper.

for each of these calipers, you should be able to overhaul the various other calipers you will encounter.

The procedures for removing the caliper from the vehicle are the same as described earlier in this chapter under Brake Pad Replacement. This is the first step in the removal of the caliper for overhaul. Additional details are covered in the following section.

GM Single-Piston Floating Caliper Service

The General Motors Series 3200/3300 single-piston, floating caliper, figure 8-42, has been used on a variety of General Motors cars in basically the same form since 1980. This caliper is similar to other front calipers used throughout the General Motors line, and the overhaul procedures for all of them are essentially the same. There are three things to watch for when overhauling these calipers: proper lubrication of the mounting hardware, the tightness of the outboard brake pad in the caliper, and the position of the brake lining wear sensor.

All of these calipers float on rubber bushings that slide along steel sleeves held in place by the caliper mounting bolts. In some cases, the mounting bolt also provides part of the sliding surface. While the exact configuration of the bushings, sleeves, and bolts varies, these parts must be in perfect condition and properly lubricated with high-temperature brake grease, figure 8-43, to ensure smooth caliper operation. To prevent comebacks, replace these parts every time the brake pads are changed or the caliper is rebuilt.

To prevent brake noise, the inboard brake pads on most General Motors calipers are retained by a spring clip that snaps into the caliper piston. Spring clips are used on some outboard pads as well. However, most outboard brake pads are retained by tabs on the backing plate that are bent in some manner to secure the pad tightly in the caliper body. Depending on the caliper design, there are two ways in which this is done. Where the

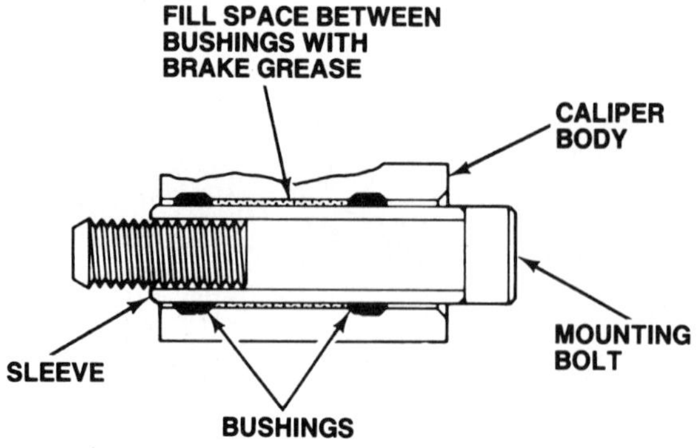

Figure 8-43. Proper lubrication is the key to smooth operation of floating calipers.

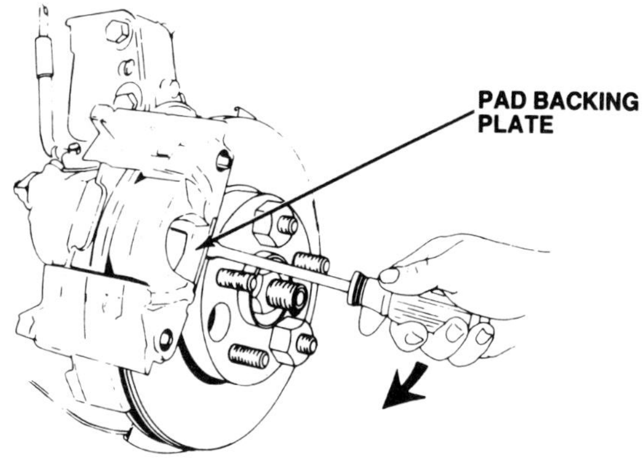

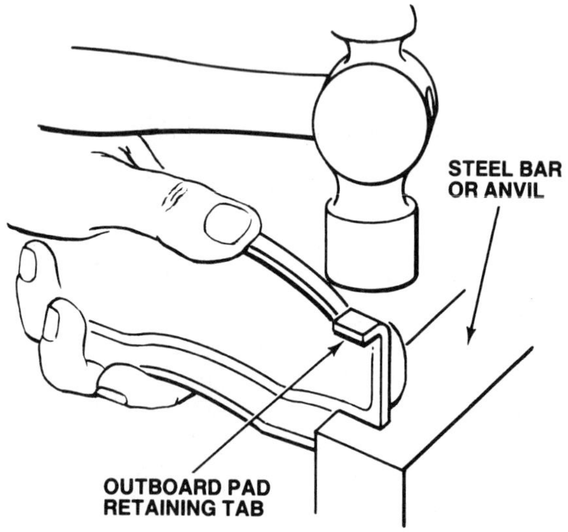

Figure 8-44. Some brake pad retaining tabs can be bent off the car.

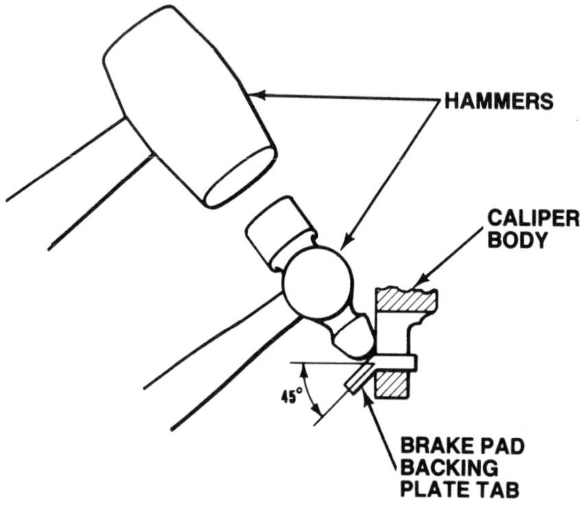

Figure 8-45. Levering a pad into position to clinch the retaining tabs.

Figure 8-46. Use two hammers to clinch the tab where it extends through the hole in the caliper body.

tabs extend over the top of the caliper body, bend them with a hammer off the car, figure 8-44, until the pad snaps into place in the caliper with a slight preload.

Where the tabs extend through holes in the caliper body, a more complex procedure is called for:

1. Once the new pads are installed, insert a large screwdriver or pry bar between the flange on the bottom of the pad and the rotor hat, figure 8-45.
2. Lever the pad upward so that the flange is firmly seated against the caliper body.
3. Have an assistant apply and hold the brake pedal with firm pressure to lock the pad in position.
4. Use a ball-peen hammer and a larger brass hammer to clinch the tabs against the caliper body as shown in figure 8-46.

The outboard pads on General Motors calipers are usually interchangeable side to side except for the position of the wear sensor. When the caliper is installed on the car, the wear sensor *must* be at the leading edge of the caliper during forward rotor rotation. That is, the rotor should sweep across the sensor before it reaches the brake lining. Make sure you use the proper pad on each side of the car.

Disc Brake Service

GENERAL MOTORS SINGLE-PISTON FLOATING CALIPER SERVICE

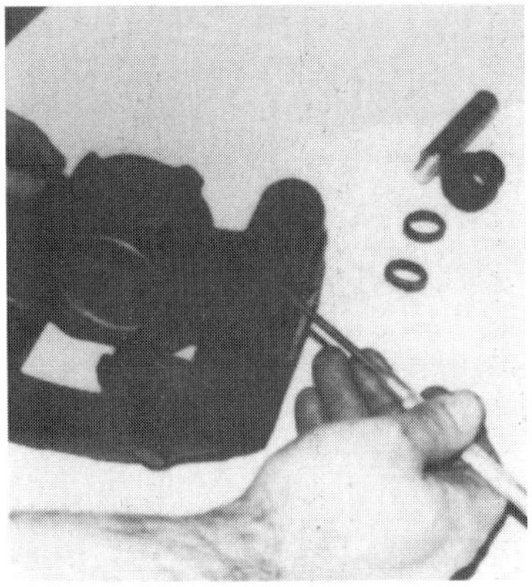

1. Remove the sleeves and bushings from the caliper mounting bolt holes.

2. Remove the caliper piston using one of the methods described earlier, then remove the bleeder screw.

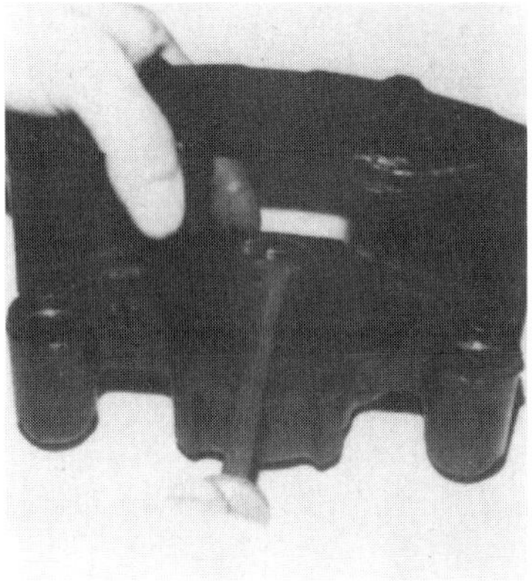

3. Pry the dust boot out of the caliper body with a screwdriver.

4. Remove the piston seal from its groove in the caliper bore.

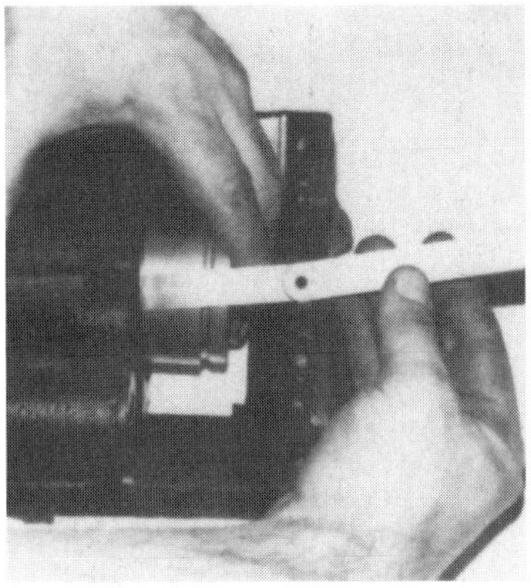

5. Clean and inspect the caliper body and piston. Hone the caliper bore if necessary, and measure the piston-to-bore clearance.

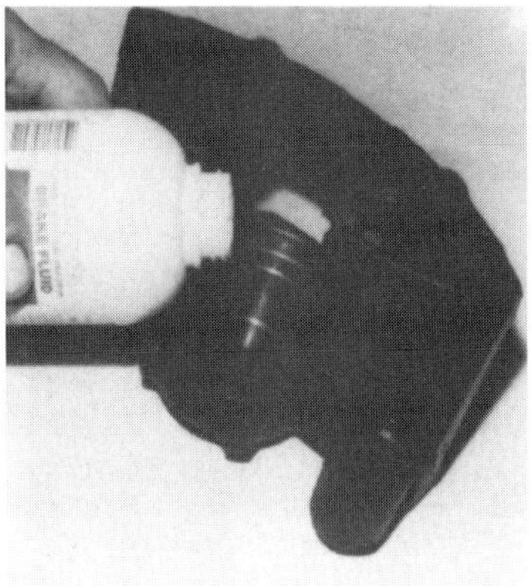

6. Lubricate the caliper bore and the new piston seal. Install the seal into its groove in the caliper bore.

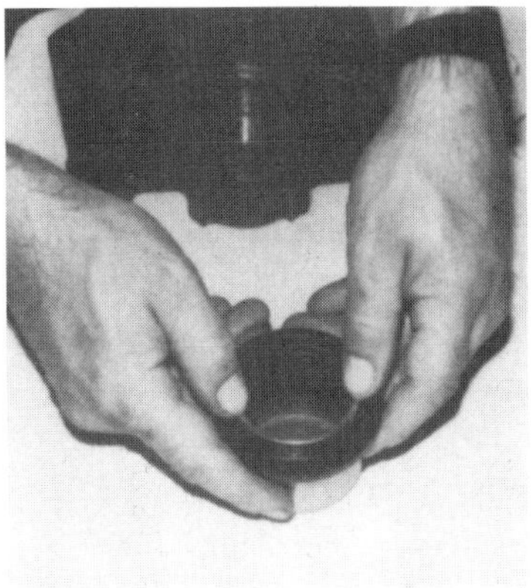

7. Install the new dust boot into its groove on the piston.

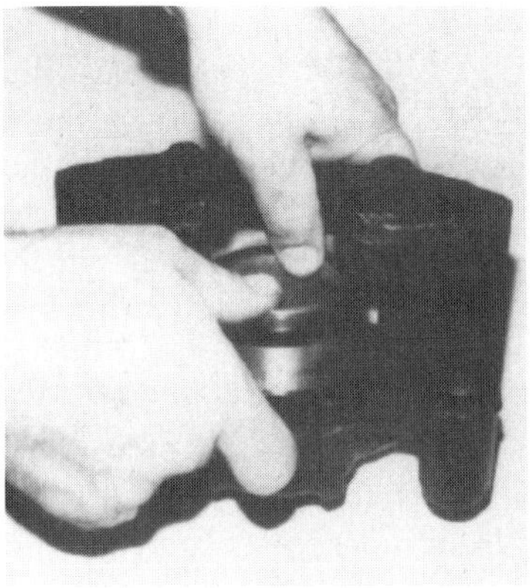

8. Lubricate the piston and install it into the caliper bore until it is bottomed.

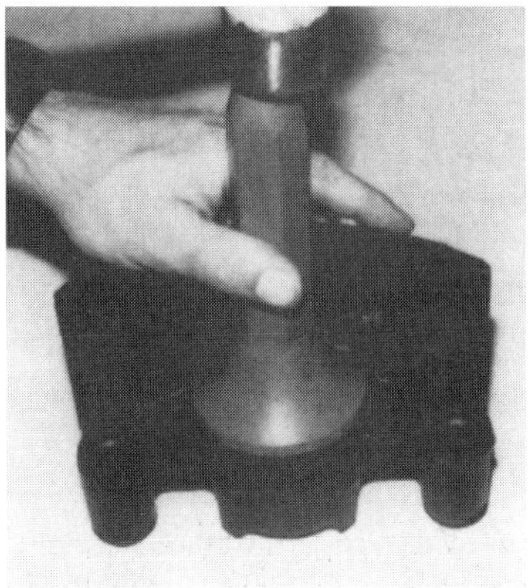

9. Seat the reinforcing ring at the outer edge of the dust boot into the caliper body with a hammer and boot driver.

GENERAL MOTORS SINGLE-PISTON FLOATING CALIPER SERVICE

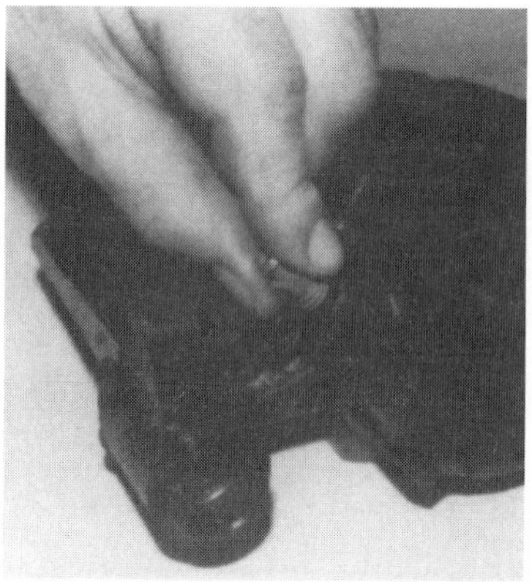

10. Install the bleeder screw in the caliper.

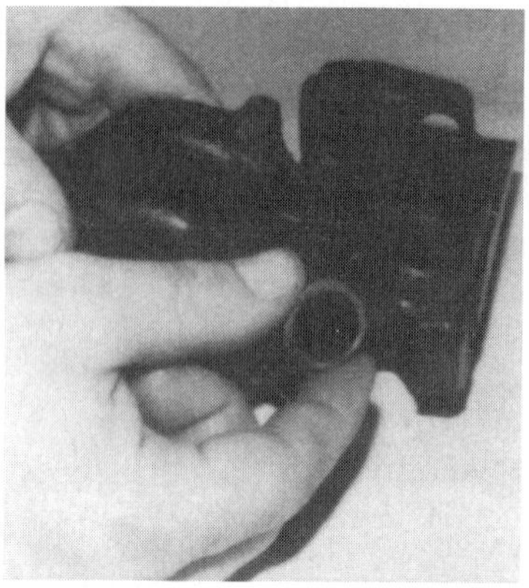

11. Lubricate the new bushings with brake grease and install them into the mounting bolt holes.

12. Lubricate the outside of the new sleeves with brake grease and install them into the mounting bolt holes.

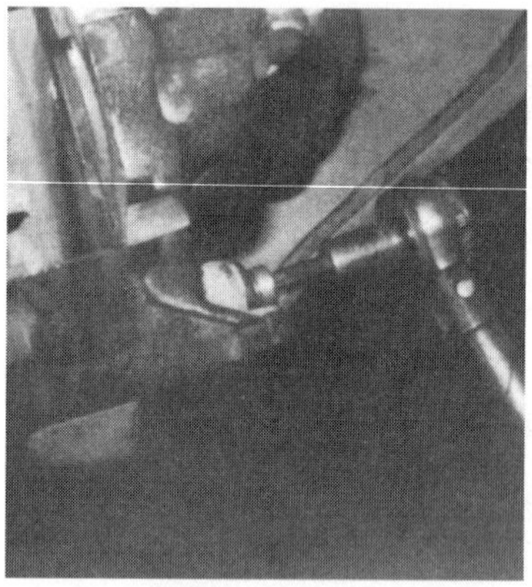

13. Install the caliper mounting bolts and torque them to 38 ft-lb (51 Nm). Install the protective rubber boots over the bolt heads.

14. If the caliper was rebuilt, connect the brake hose to the fluid inlet of the caliper. Torque the bolt to 33 ft-lb (45 Nm). Bleed the brakes as described in Chapter 3.

Four-Piston Fixed Caliper Service

Used on many high-performance and other heavier vehicles, four- and six-piston fixed calipers are manufactured in two styles. Early types used stroking piston seals, and current types use square-cut seals as used on single-piston calipers. The procedure for overhauling each is slightly different.

General Motors Four-piston Fixed Caliper Service

The General Motors four-piston caliper with stroking seals, shown in figure 8-47, is typical of older fixed caliper designs. Introduced in 1965, this caliper was used on all four wheels of the Corvette through 1982 and some other General Motors products in the 1967 to 1969 model years. The caliper shown is the version used from 1965 to 1966. The 1967 and later calipers use the same service procedures but have a one-piece piston design without the plastic insulator.

There are several special procedures involved in working on these calipers. First, because of the piston shape, the outer edges of the dust boots should be removed from the caliper body before the pistons are removed from their bores. To do this, insert a flat-blade screwdriver under the edge of the dust boot reinforcing ring, and using the piston as a fulcrum, lever the ring out of its groove in the caliper body, figure 8-48.

When you install the pistons into their bores, use extra care to avoid damaging the sealing lip of the stroking seal. Special tools are available to ease seal installation; however, a little caution and a thin feeler gauge strip are usually all that is required to work the lip past the edge of the caliper bore, figure 8-49.

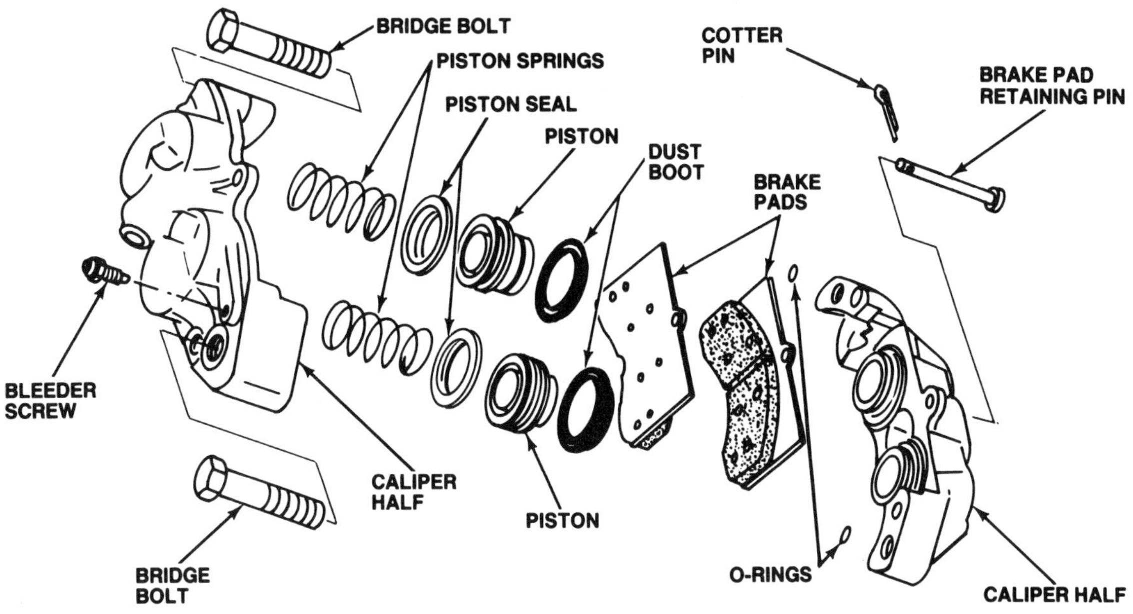

Disc Brake Service

Figure 8-47. The General Motors 4-piston fixed brake caliper.

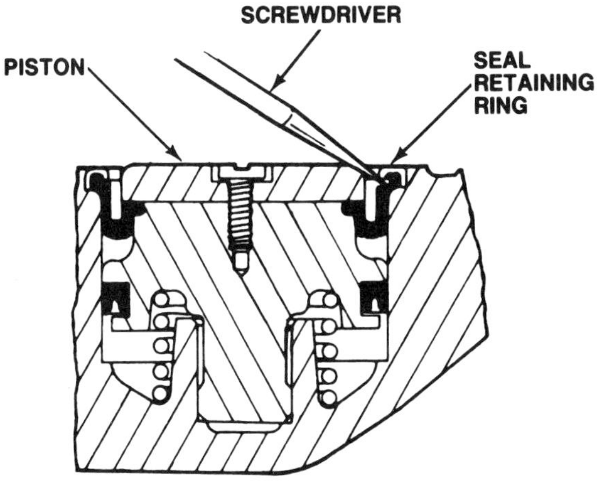

Figure 8-48. Removing a dust boot from the GM fixed brake caliper.

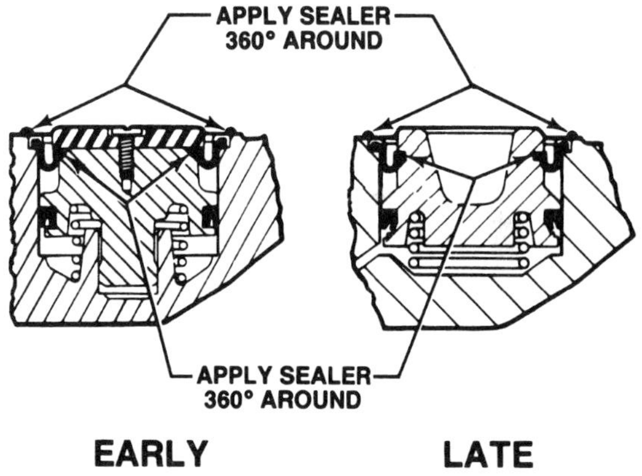

Figure 8-50. Silicone sealer is required to improve dust boot sealing on the GM fixed brake caliper.

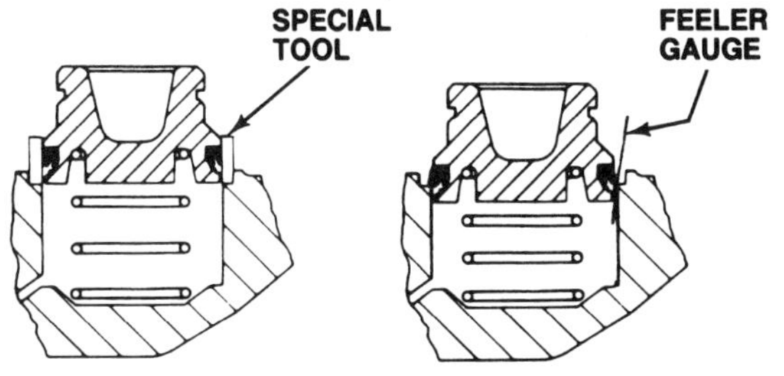

Figure 8-49. Stroking seals require special care during installation.

Finally, this caliper design is known for its poor sealing, which makes it prone to rust, corrosion, and fluid leaks. This often causes severe damage to the caliper bore, and rebuilt calipers with stainless steel sleeves are common in this application. To ensure a long service life, special sealing procedures are required. Before you install the dust boot, apply a bead of silicone sealer to the dust boot groove in the piston. Once the piston is installed in the bore and the boot is driven into its groove in the caliper body, apply a second bead of sealer around the outer edge of the boot, figure 8-50.

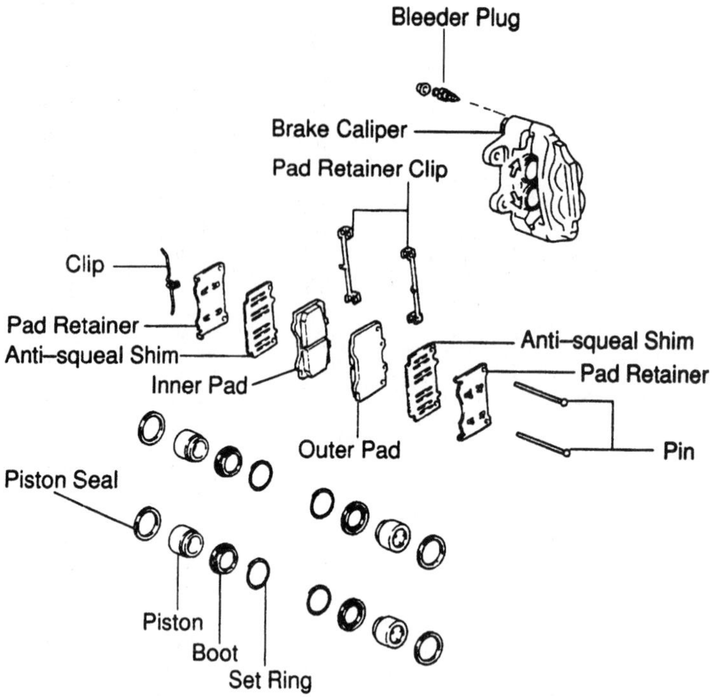

Figure 8-51. This Toyota four-piston caliper assembly is similar to many other import types. (Courtesy of Toyota Motor Sales U.S.A., Inc.)

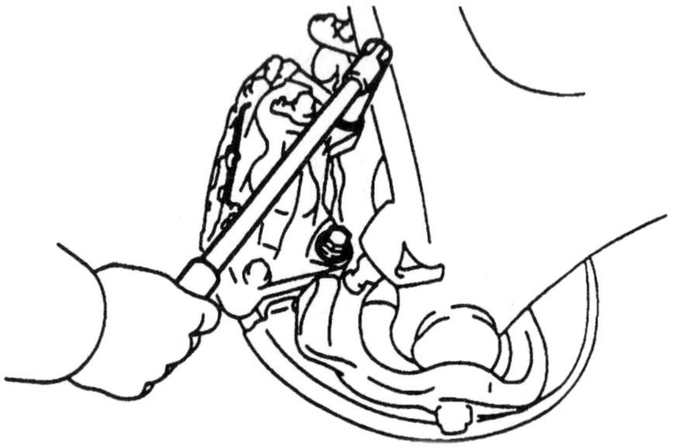

Figure 8-52. Remove the caliper mounting bolts and remove the caliper from the vehicle. (Courtesy of Toyota Motor Sales U.S.A., Inc.)

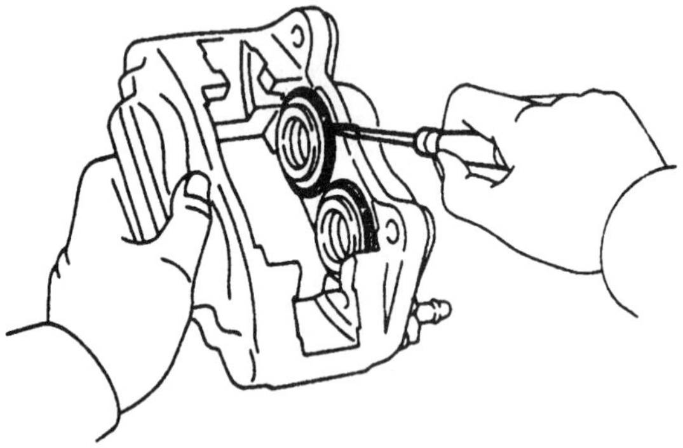

Figure 8-53. Remove the boot retainers and then the dust boots. Do *not* remove the bridge bolts to separate the caliper halves. (Courtesy of Toyota Motor Sales U.S.A., Inc.)

Because this is a fixed caliper, it is not necessary to remove the caliper body from the car when you replace the brake pads. On the other hand, if the caliper is going to be rebuilt, it can be removed from the car with the brake pads still in place.

Late-model, Four-piston Fixed Caliper Service

Service of late-model, four- and six-piston fixed calipers differs from the earlier stroking type in two ways. First, since the piston provides the sealing surface for the seal, honing of the bore is not needed in

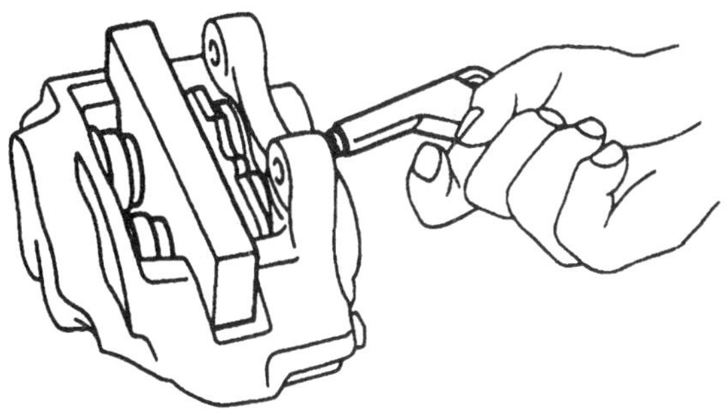

Disc Brake Service

Figure 8-54. Using a wooden block, carefully remove the pistons with compressed air. (Courtesy of Toyota Motor Sales U.S.A., Inc.)

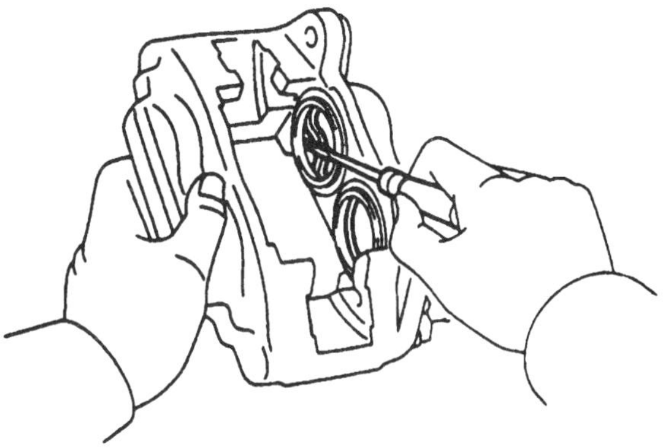

Figure 8-55. Remove the piston seals and inspect the caliper bore. (Courtesy of Toyota Motor Sales U.S.A., Inc.)

order to provide a proper seal. Secondly, the manufacturers do *not* recommend the removal of the bridge bolts during overhaul. The bridge bolts are to remain in place, and the caliper seals can be replaced without splitting the caliper halves.

A typical four-piston caliper assembly is shown in figure 8-51. Follow these steps.

- The overhaul begins with the removal of the caliper from the vehicle, figure 8-52.
- Remove the pads and then remove the four-piston dust boot retainers and the dust boots, figure 8-53.
- Using a wooden block, remove the pistons with compressed air, figure 8-54. It may be necessary to remove, clean, and reinstall each piston in turn during the overhaul.
- Use a small tool to remove the square-cut piston seals, figure 8-55.
- Cleaning and reassembly are similar to that of the single-piston caliper, previously described.

Ford Single-Piston Rear Caliper Service

Ford has used two types of single-piston, sliding rear brake calipers with integral parking brake mechanisms. The type shown in figure 8-56 was used beginning in 1975 until 1989 on some models. The later type of rear caliper is a cam and plunger type, used in 1989 and later models. The later type caliper service procedure is similar to that used with the General Motors rear caliper, described later (see that section for details). Due to their relative complexity, the earlier type caliper service is explained here.

There are several special considerations you should be aware of when overhauling these calipers. First, they are specific left- and right-side parts with unique parking brake levers, pistons, and internal thrust screws. Do not mix calipers or their components from side to side; and make sure any replacement parts are for the proper caliper. Many of the caliper parts are marked to indicate the side of the car on which they belong.

Second, the design of the self-adjuster mechanism in this caliper prevents the piston from being forced back into the bore in the usual manner. A special piston turning tool, figure 8-19, is required to thread the piston back into its bore once the brake pads are removed.

Because of the adjuster design, it may be difficult to remove one of these calipers if there is a ridge at the outer edge of the rotor, or the brake pads are badly worn and interlock with scoring on the rotor. If you encounter this problem, remove the parking brake cable and lever, and loosen the parking brake end retainer up to one-half turn; this allows the piston to move slightly back into the bore, and makes it possible to remove the caliper from the rotor. Take care when removing the caliper in this manner; if the end retainer is loosened more than one-half turn, the seal between the caliper body and thrust screw may be broken. Brake fluid will then leak into the parking brake mechanism, and the caliper will have to be disassembled to clean and relubricate the mechanism. If the caliper is being overhauled, this is not a concern, and the retainer can be unscrewed as necessary to remove the caliper.

Once the caliper is disassembled, clean and inspect the caliper body and all of the other parts except the piston. Hone the caliper bore if necessary, and measure the piston-to-bore clearance. Inspect the thrust screw bore; it must be smooth and free of pits. The thrust screw threads, seal groove, ball pockets, and bearing surface must show no signs of wear or pitting. Inspect the thrust bearing for wear or corrosion, and also the bearing surface inside the end retainer. Replace any of these parts that are not in perfect condition.

Next, wipe the caliper piston/adjuster assembly clean; do not use liquid cleaners because they may

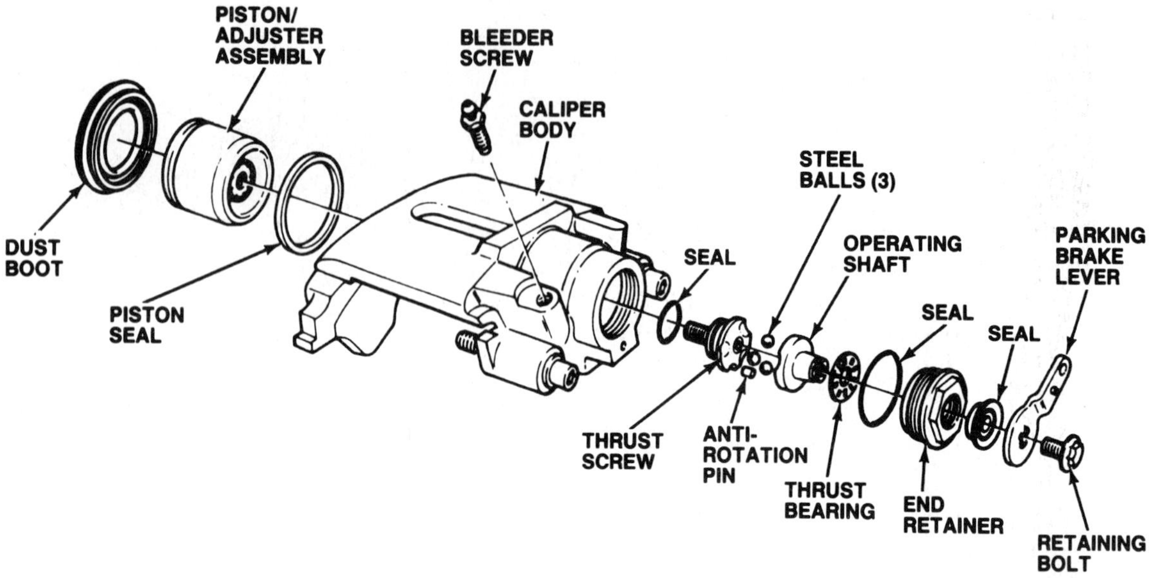

Figure 8-56. The Ford single-piston, sliding rear brake caliper with integral parking brake mechanism.

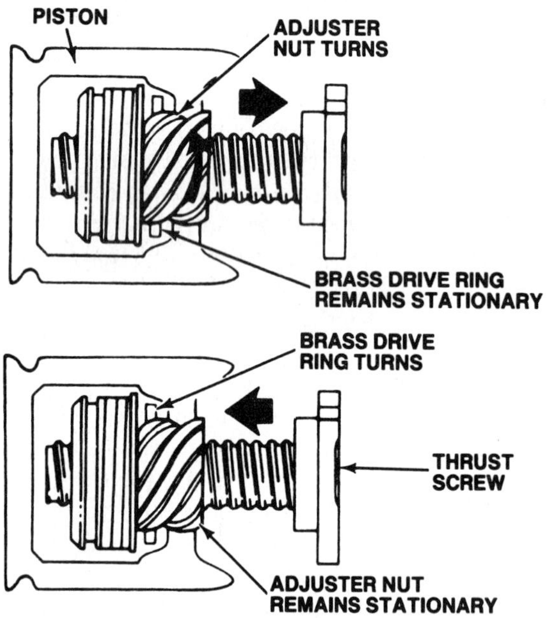

Figure 8-57. Testing the Ford rear brake caliper piston/adjuster mechanism.

remain inside the piston and contaminate the hydraulic system. Inspect the piston sealing surface for damage, and flush any old brake fluid from the piston with new fluid. Inspect the adjuster assembly for a loose fit in the piston, and check the adjuster operation. As shown in figure 8-57, thread the thrust screw into the piston/adjuster assembly. Pull the two pieces apart about ¼ inch (6 mm), the brass drive ring should remain stationary and the adjuster nut should turn. When the two pieces are released, the nut should remain stationary and the drive ring should rotate. The piston/adjuster assembly cannot be taken apart for service. Replace the entire assembly if the adjuster is loose in the piston, or does not function as described above.

Finally, when you have completed the overhaul of one of these calipers, adjust the parking brake mechanism. With the engine running, apply the brake pedal lightly 40 times, allowing a one second pause between applications. With the engine not running, apply the pedal with moderate pressure 30 times. Once you have finished this procedure, adjust the parking brake linkage as described in Chapter 10.

Disc Brake Service

FORD SINGLE-PISTON REAR CALIPER SERVICE

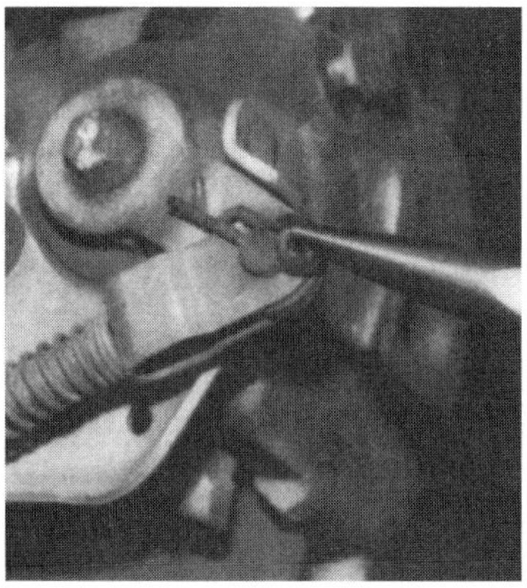

1. Remove the clip and pin, and disconnect the parking brake cable from the caliper lever.

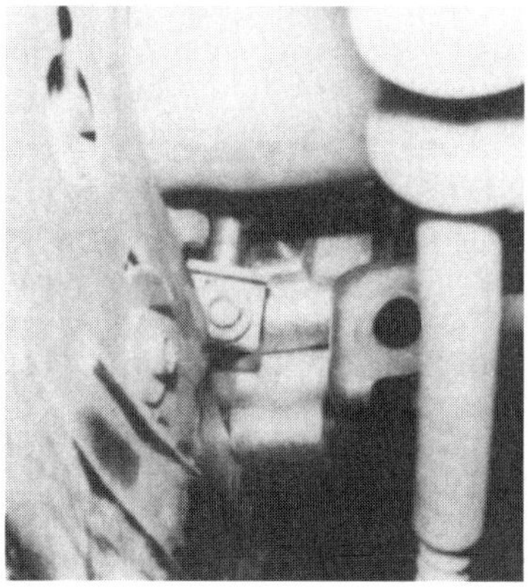

2. Make sure the bleeder screw is free, then disconnect the brake hose from the fluid inlet.

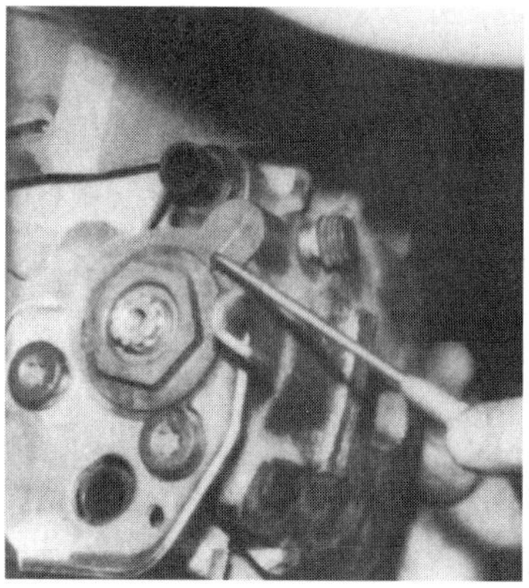

3. Remove the parking brake lever. Scribe the end retainer for reference, and loosen it one-half turn.

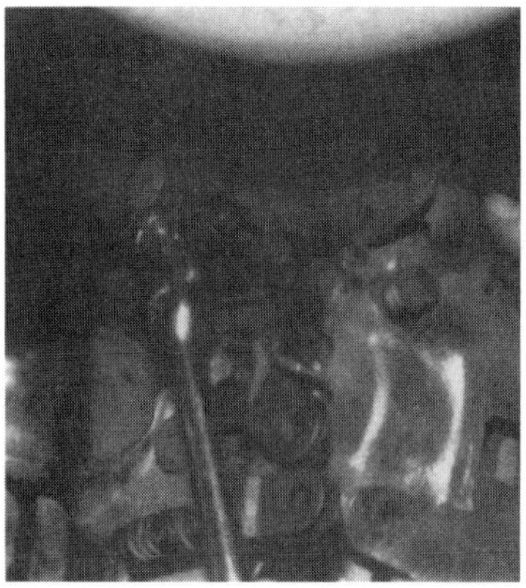

4. Remove the caliper mounting pins and pin bushings.

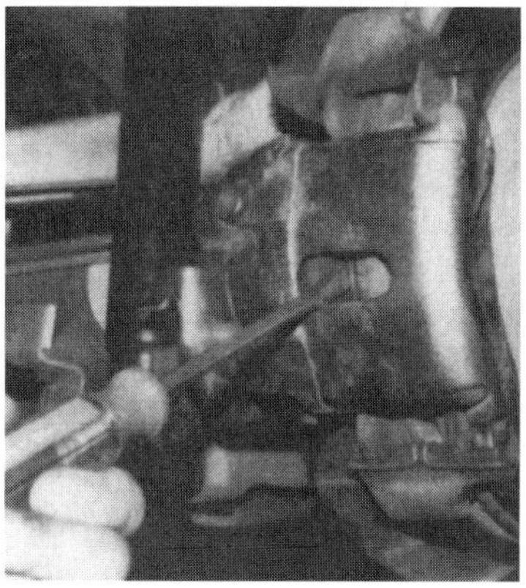

5. Pry the piston into its bore, and lift the caliper off of the rotor.

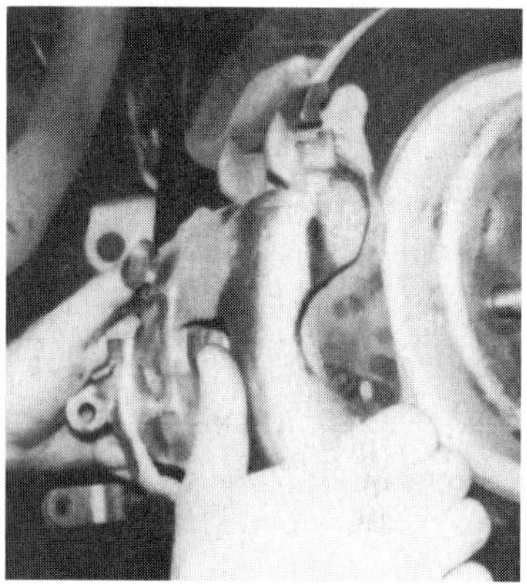

6. Lift the caliper off the rotor and clamp it in a vise.

7. Remove the bleeder screw and parking brake lever, then unscrew the caliper end retainer.

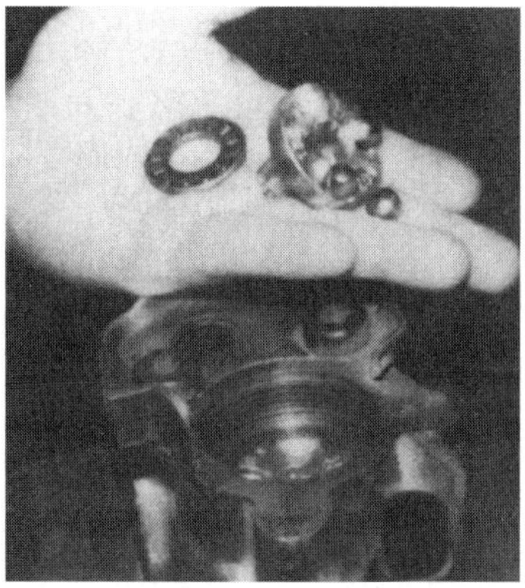

8. Lift the thrust bearing, operating shaft, and three steel balls out of the caliper.

9. Remove the anti-rotation pin with a magnet or tweezers. If the pin is free, go to step 12; otherwise, go to step 10.

FORD SINGLE-PISTON REAR CALIPER SERVICE

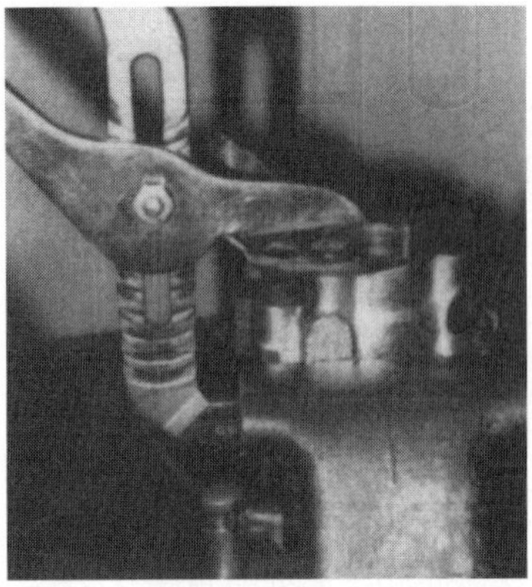

10. Bottom the caliper piston in the caliper bore with a pair of slip-joint pliers (this is possible with the end retainer removed).

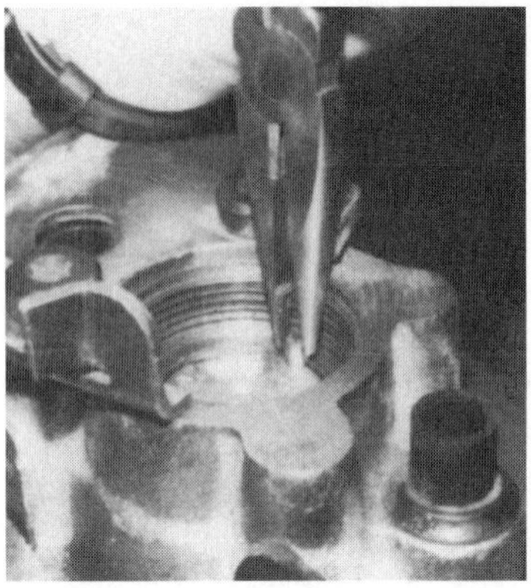

11. Tap the thrust screw into the caliper until the anti-rotation pin stands proud, then remove the pin with a pair of pliers.

12. Remove the thrust screw by rotating it counterclockwise with a ¼-inch Allen wrench.

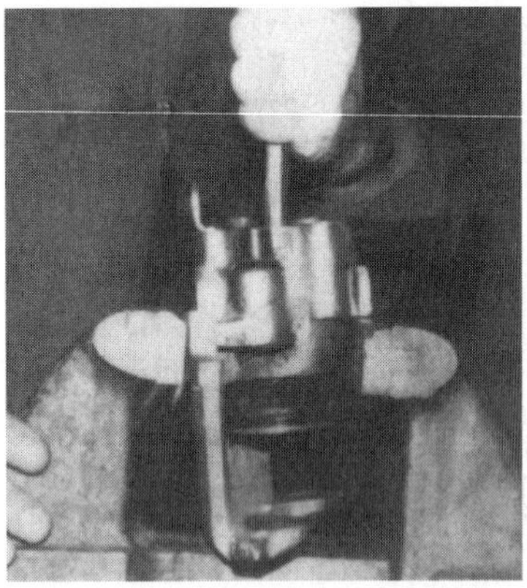

13. Push the caliper piston out of its bore using a punch inserted into the opening in the backside of the piston.

14. Remove and discard the dust boot, piston seal, thrust screw O-ring seal, end retainer O-ring seal, and end retainer lip seal.

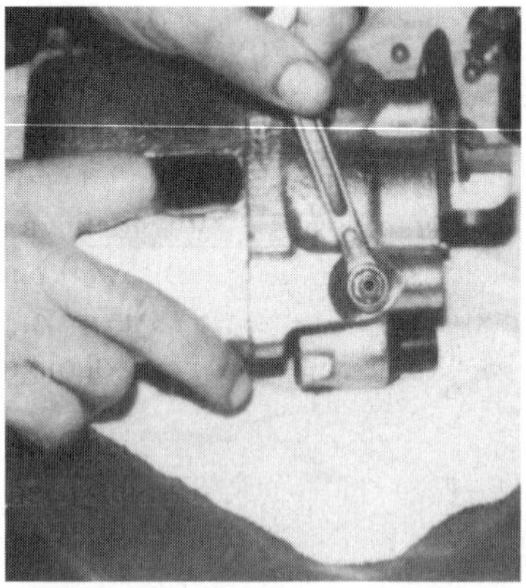

15. Install and tighten the bleeder screw.

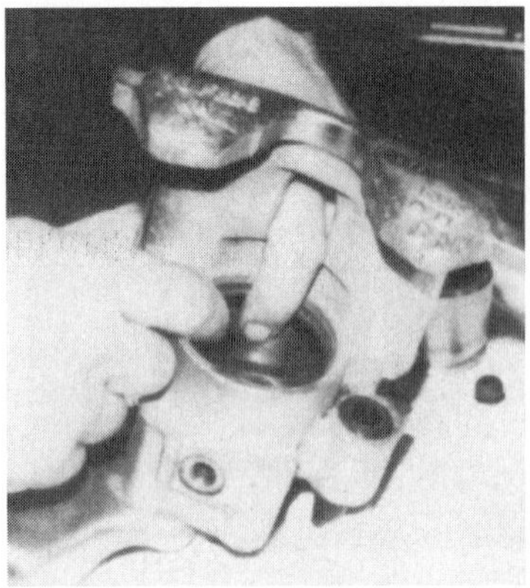

16. Lubricate the caliper bore and the new piston seal. Install the seal into its groove in the caliper bore.

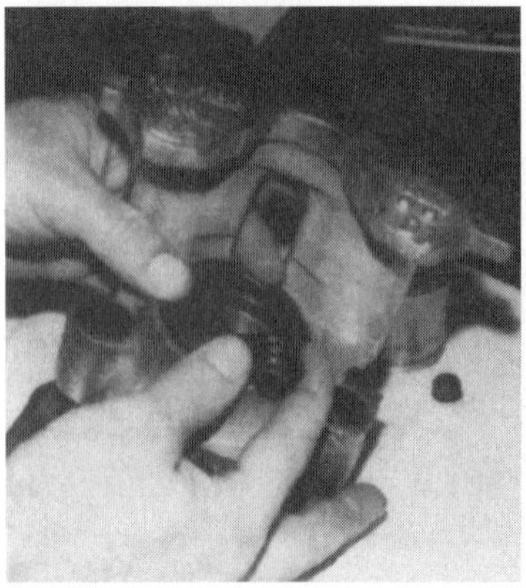

17. Install the outer edge of the new dust boot into its groove in the caliper bore.

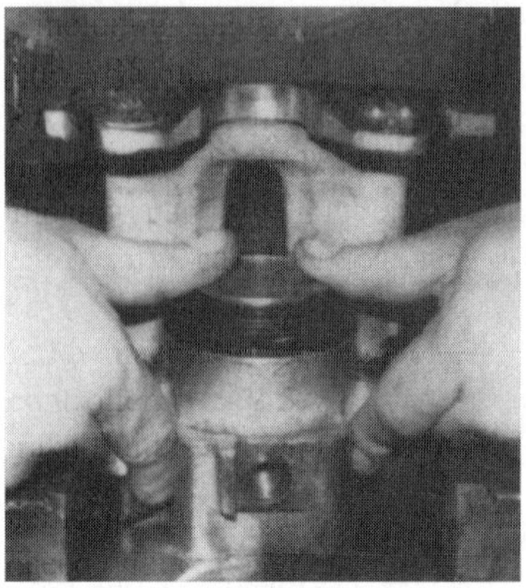

18. Coat the piston with brake fluid and install it through the dust boot into the caliper bore.

Disc Brake Service

FORD SINGLE-PISTON REAR CALIPER SERVICE

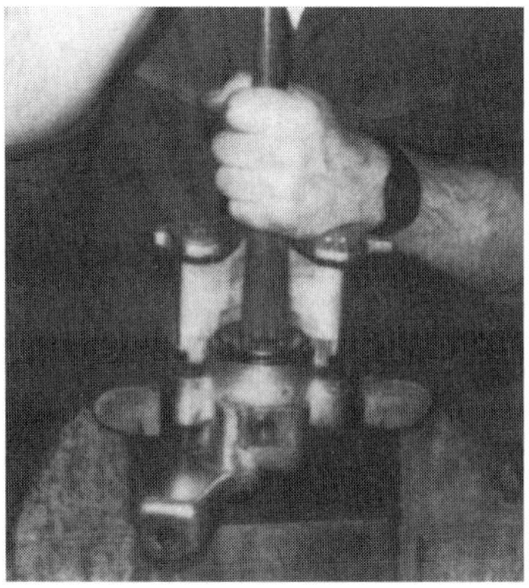

19. Seat the inner edge of the dust boot into its groove on the piston, and bottom the piston in the caliper bore.

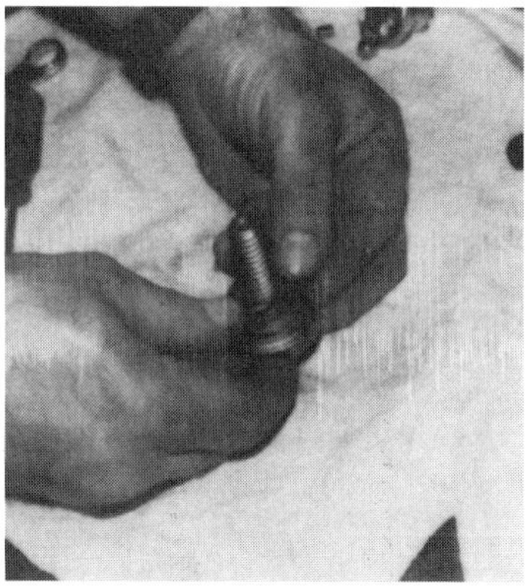

20. Lubricate the new O-ring seal and install it on the thrust screw.

21. Thread the thrust screw into the piston with a ¼-inch Allen wrench. The top of the thrust screw should be flush with the bottom of the threaded bore.

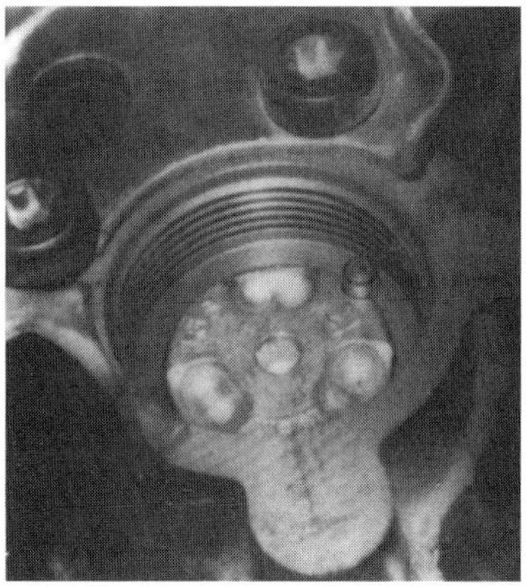

22. Align the notch in the thrust screw with the notch in the caliper housing, then install the anti-rotation pin.

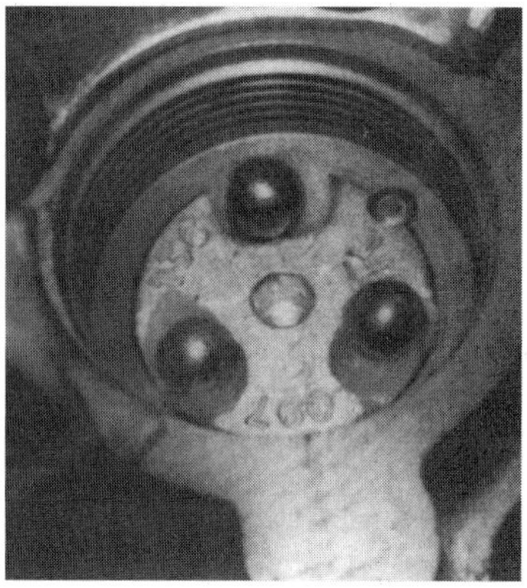

23. Coat the end of the thrust screw with high-temperature brake grease, and install a greased ball in each of the three pockets.

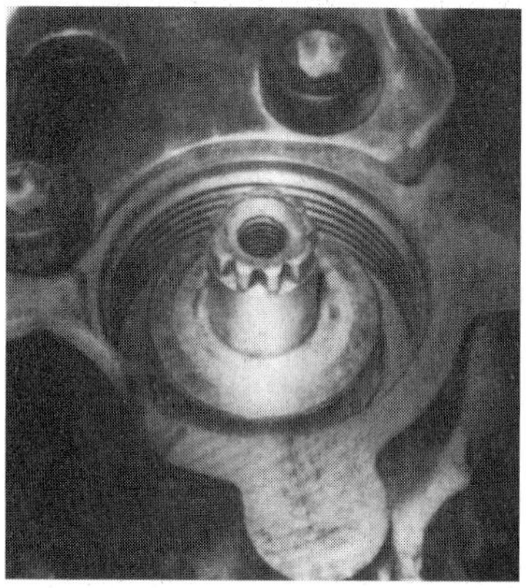

24. Grease the face of the operating shaft, and install it over the balls.

25. Grease the thrust bearing and install it on the operating shaft.

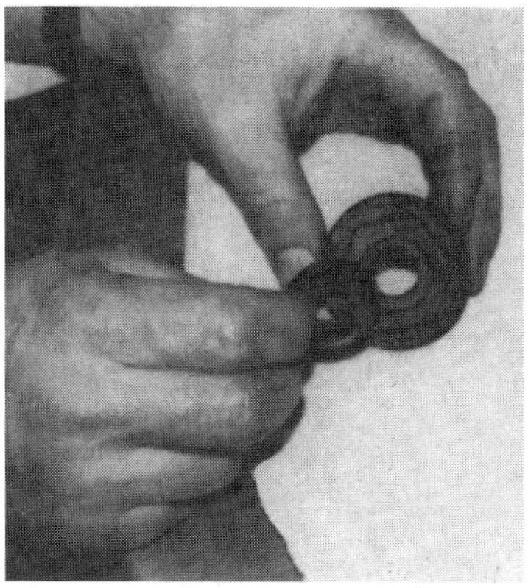

26. Grease the bearing surface inside the end retainer, then grease and install a new O-ring and lip seal on the end retainer.

27. Thread the end retainer into the caliper body while holding a downward pressure on the operating shaft to prevent dislocating the balls.

FORD SINGLE-PISTON REAR CALIPER SERVICE

28. Tighten the end retainer to 75 to 95 ft-lb (102 to 128 Nm).

29. Install the parking brake lever and tighten the retaining screw to 16 to 22 ft-lb (22 to 29 Nm). The lever should rotate freely.

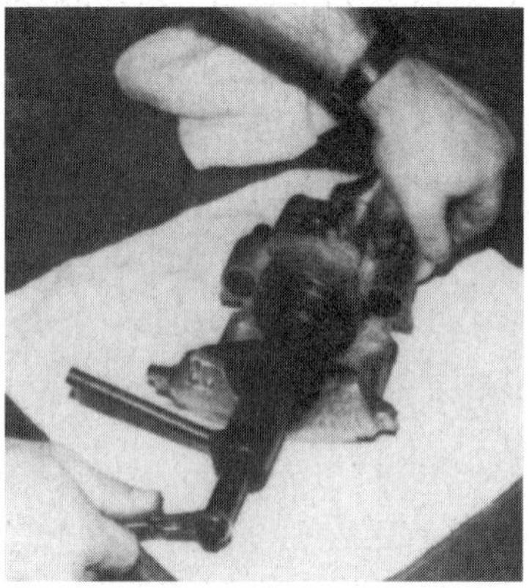

30. Rotate the piston in a clockwise direction with the turning tool. Though it will continue to turn, the piston is bottomed when there is no more inward movement.

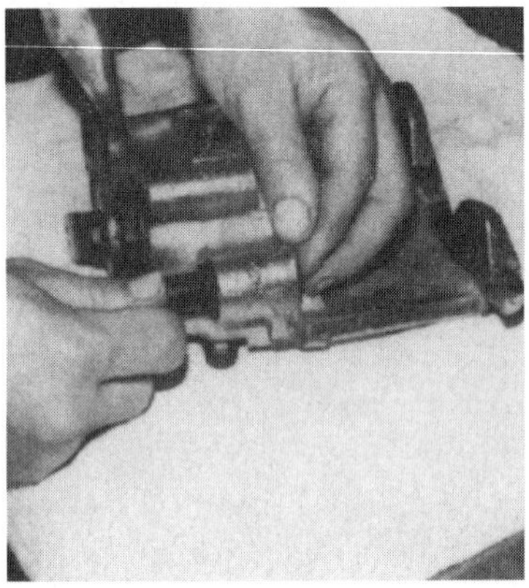

31. Sand or wire brush any rust out of the bushing bores of the caliper, then install new mounting pin bushings.

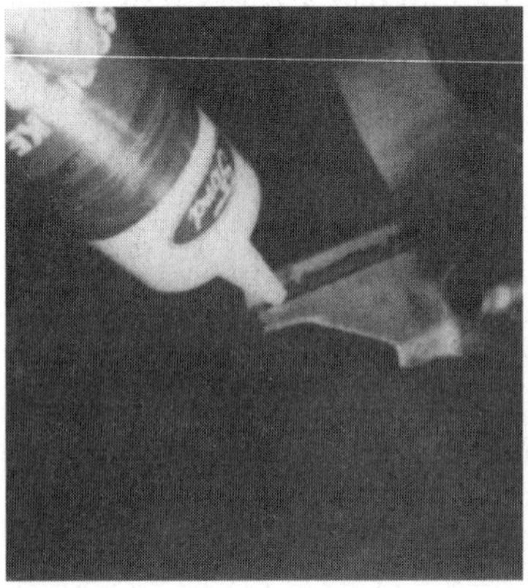

32. Grease the anchor plate sliding ways and install the inner brake pad.

33. Position the caliper on the car and pull it outward until the inner pad is in firm contact with the rotor.

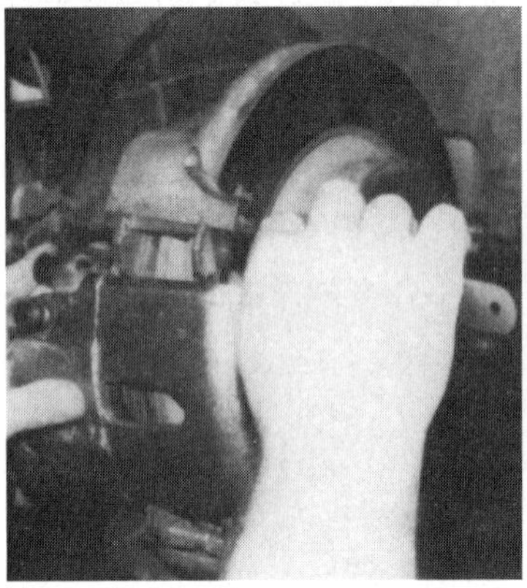

34. The clearance between the outer pad and caliper must be less than 3/32 inch (2.4 mm) or the piston/adjuster assembly will be damaged when the service brakes are applied.

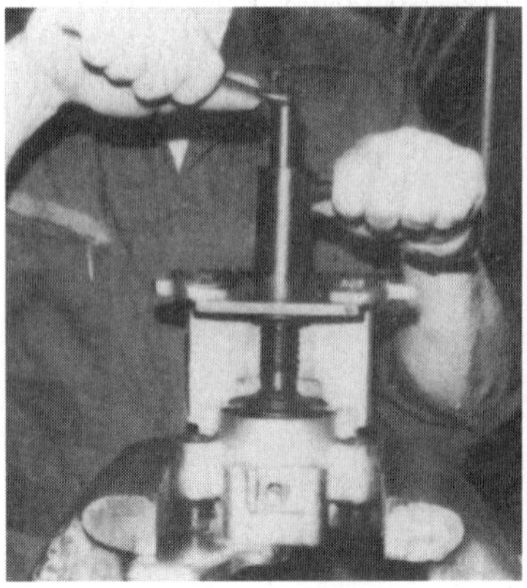

35. Using the turning tool, unscrew the piston as needed to obtain the proper clearance; 1/4 turn equals approximately 1/16 inch (1.6 mm).

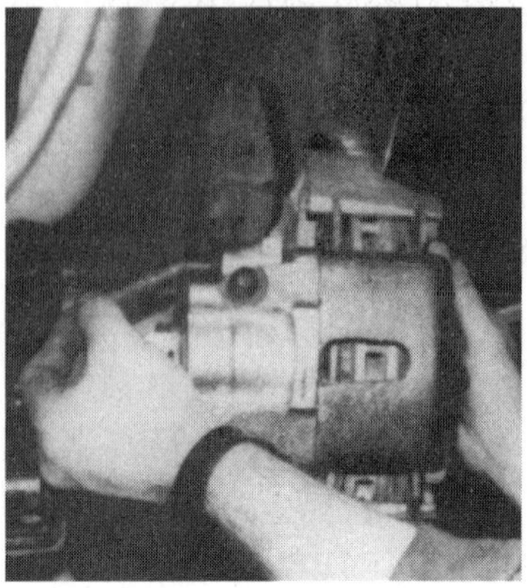

36. Grease the mounting pins and install them in the caliper. Tighten them to 29 to 37 ft-lb (39 to 50 Nm).

Disc Brake Service

FORD SINGLE-PISTON REAR CALIPER SERVICE

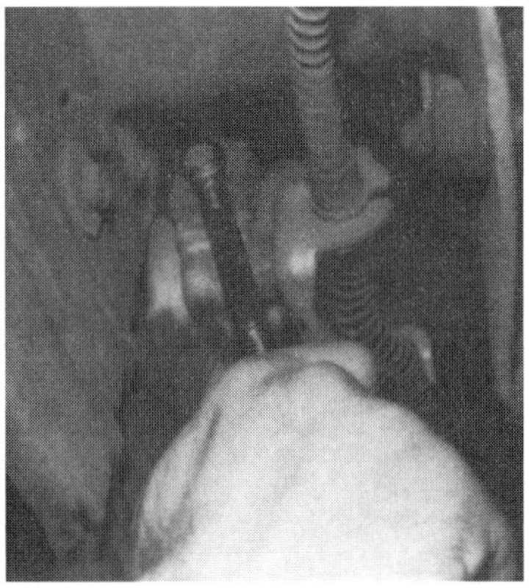

37. Connect the brake hose to the fluid inlet of the caliper. Bleed the brakes as described in Chapter 3.

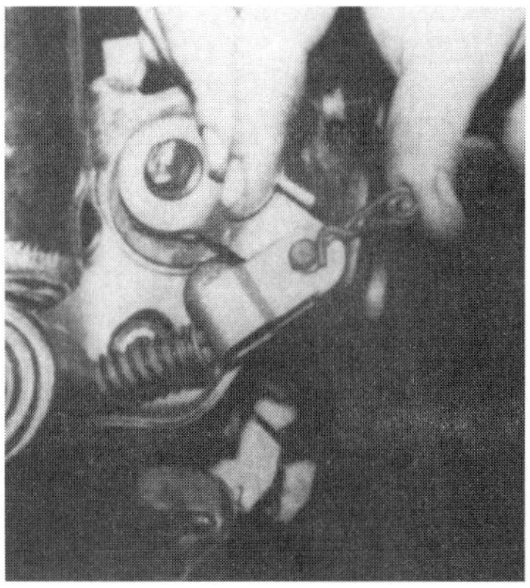

38. Connect the parking brake cable and adjust the caliper mechanism and linkage as described earlier.

General Motors Single-Piston Rear Caliper Service

The General Motors 3500 Series single-piston, floating rear brake caliper with integral parking brake mechanism, figure 8-58, is used on many GM rear disc brake applications. The construction and operation of this caliper are similar to that of the 3200/3300 front brake caliper described earlier. The major external difference is the parking brake actuating lever, bracket, and associated hardware. Several different lever designs are used, but all consist of essentially the same parts; a typical installation is shown in figure 8-59.

Because this caliper is similar to other General Motors designs, all of the service tips, precautions, and special instructions described earlier for the 3200/3300 calipers apply to this unit as well. In addition, there are several other things to be aware of when you overhaul one of these calipers.

First, General Motors rear calipers, like Ford designs, are specific left- and right-side units that cannot be swapped from side to side. Also like the Ford rear caliper, the piston in the General Motors caliper contains the self-adjusting mechanism. Never clean the piston/adjuster assembly with liquid cleaners that can be trapped inside and contaminate the brake hydraulic system.

The self-adjusting mechanism of the General Motors caliper cannot be tested when the caliper is disassembled, so before you remove the caliper from the car, check the range of movement of the parking brake lever. If the lever is frozen, or rotates more than approximately 45 degrees, the self-adjusting mechanism is damaged and the piston/adjuster assembly must be replaced.

Second, and unlike the Ford design, the piston in the General Motors rear caliper can be bottomed in its bore using conventional methods once the parking brake lever has been removed. General Motors recommends a C-clamp for this purpose, figure 8-60. With the parking brake lever removed, place the C-clamp across the inboard side of the caliper body and the backing plate of the outboard brake pad. Do not allow the C-clamp to contact the actuator screw or the self-adjusting mechanism in the piston may be damaged.

Third, when you install the inboard brake pad, the D-shaped tabs on the pad backing plate must engage

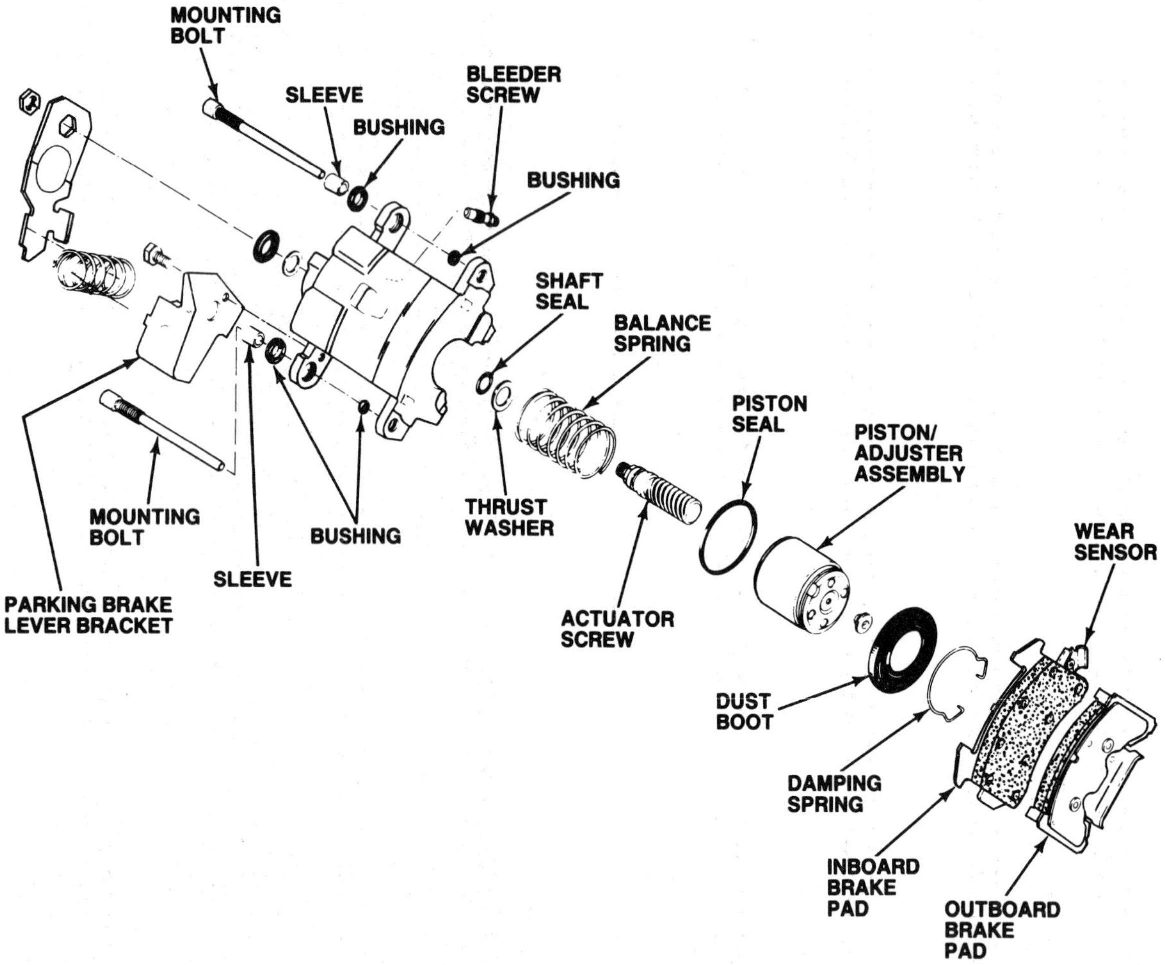

Figure 8-58. The GM single-piston, floating rear brake caliper with integral parking brake mechanism. (Courtesy of General Motors Corporation, Service and Parts Operations)

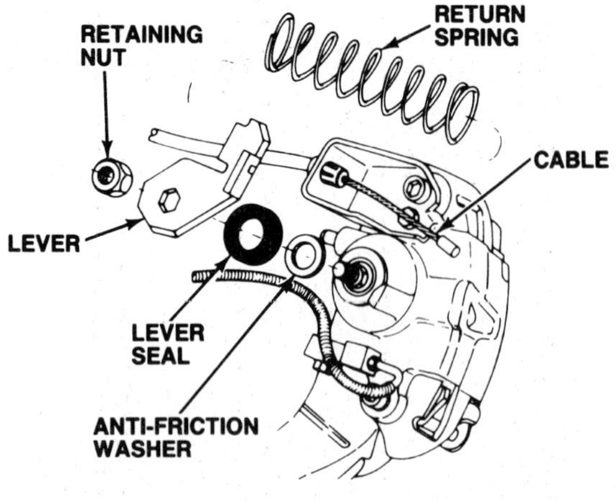

Figure 8-59. The parking brake lever components of a General Motors rear brake caliper. (Courtesy of General Motors Corporation, Service and Parts Operations)

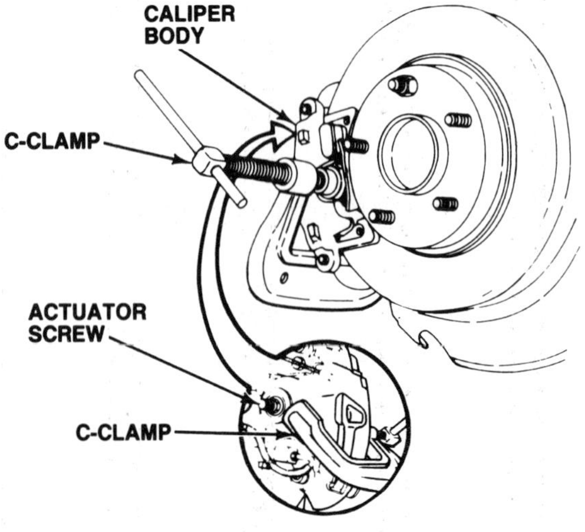

Figure 8-60. Bottoming the piston in a GM rear disc brake caliper. (Courtesy of General Motors Corporation, Service and Parts Operations)

Disc Brake Service

the notches in the caliper piston, figure 8-61; rotate the piston as needed to obtain the proper alignment. To install the pad, hold it at an angle in the caliper, and slide the edge of the backing plate under the ends of the damping spring. Then, lift the pad up against spring tension, and engage the D-shaped tables into the piston notches. When installed properly, the pad will seat flat against the piston.

Finally, whenever new pads are installed in this caliper, or an overhaul is completed, adjust the parking brake cables as described in Chapter 10. Then, set the clearance between the brake pads and the rotor by applying the brake pedal at least three times with about 175 lb (778 N) of force. This allows the self-adjusting mechanism in the piston to take up the slack. When the clearance is correct, the parking brake pedal will have a high, firm feel.

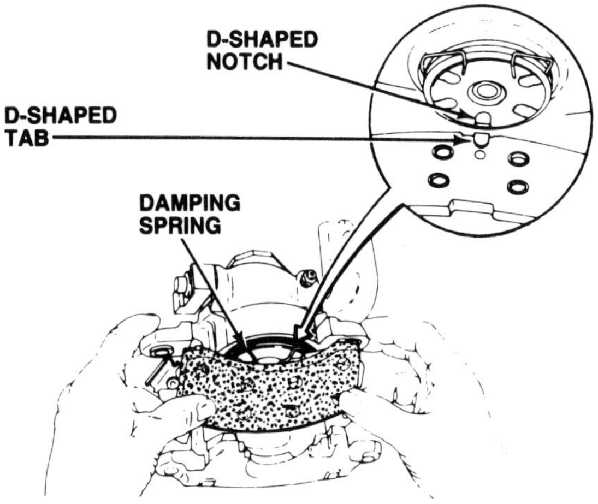

Figure 8-61. Proper inboard brake pad mounting on the GM rear brake caliper.

GENERAL MOTORS SINGLE-PISTON REAR CALIPER SERVICE

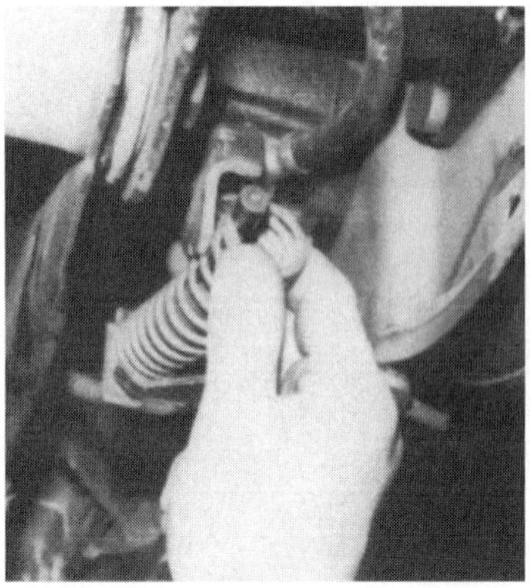

1. Loosen tension on the parking brake cable at the equalizer, then disconnect the cable from the lever on the caliper.

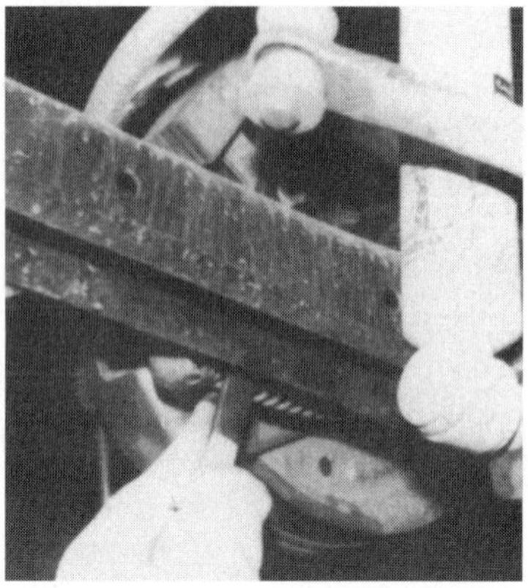

2. Unscrew the retaining nut, and remove the parking brake lever, return spring, lever seal, and anti-friction washer.

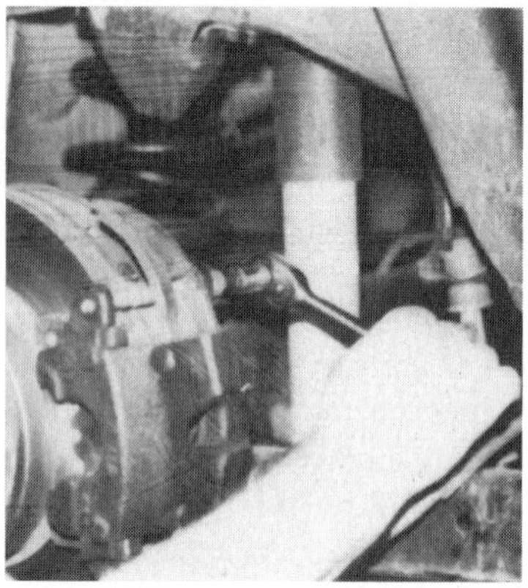

3. Unscrew and remove the caliper mounting bolts.

4. Use a small screwdriver to pry the two-way check valve out of the piston.

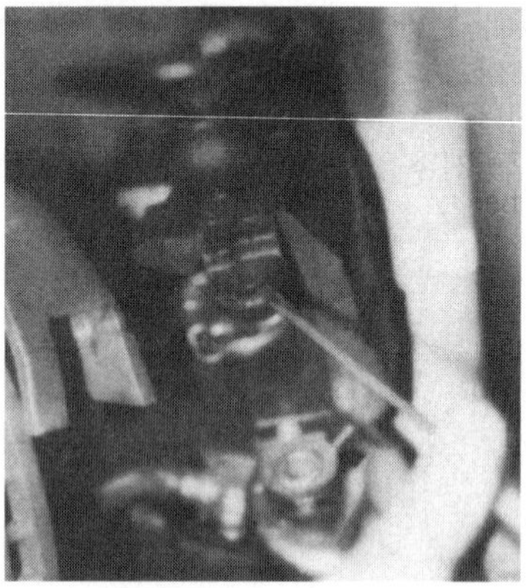

5. Remove the sleeves and bushings from the caliper mounting bolt holes. If the caliper is not being rebuilt, go to step 24.

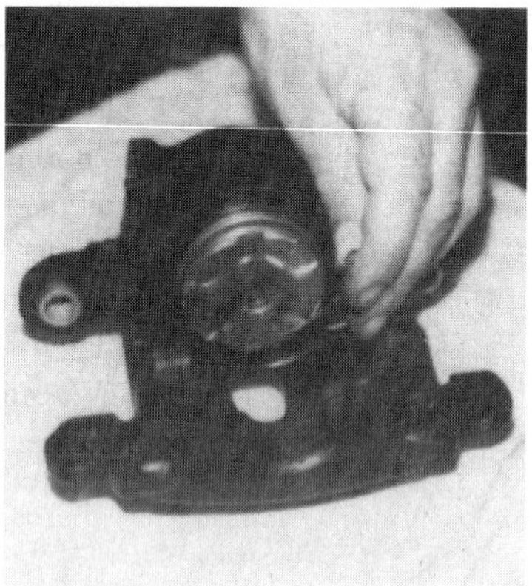

6. Remove the brake pad damping spring from the end of the piston.

7. Mount the caliper in a vise, then use a wrench to rotate the actuator screw and force the piston out of its bore.

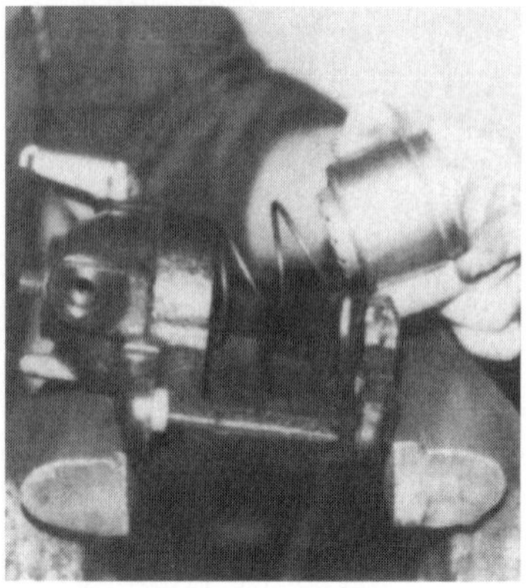

8. Remove the balance spring from the caliper bore.

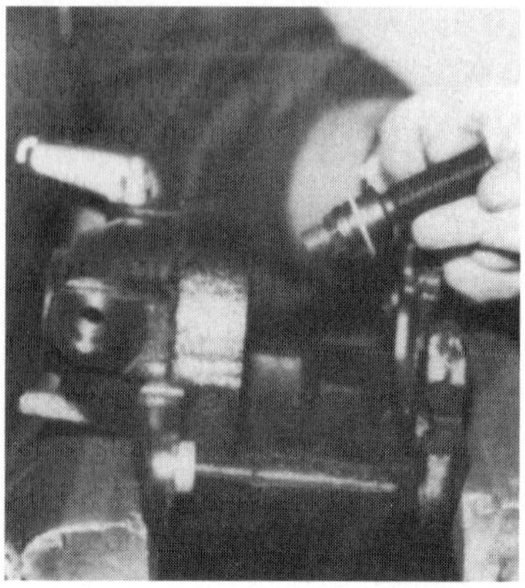

9. Remove the actuator screw and thrust washer from the caliper bore. Remove the shaft seal from its groove in the actuator screw.

Disc Brake Service

GENERAL MOTORS SINGLE-PISTON REAR CALIPER SERVICE

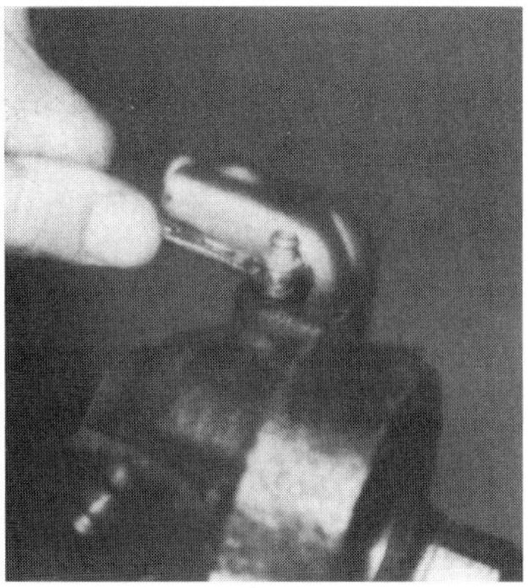

10. Remove the bleeder screw.

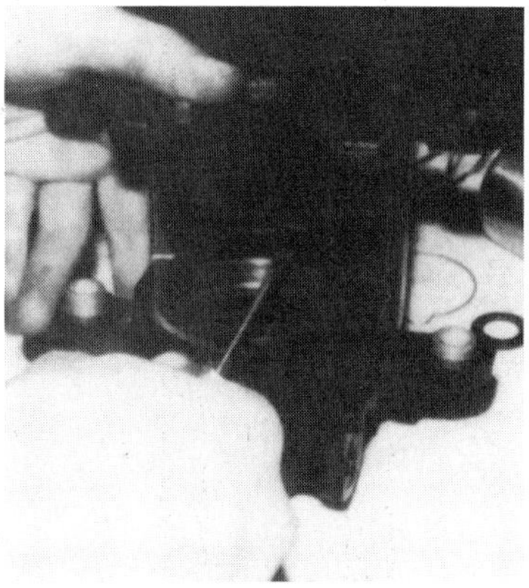

11. Pry the dust boot out of the caliper body with a screwdriver.

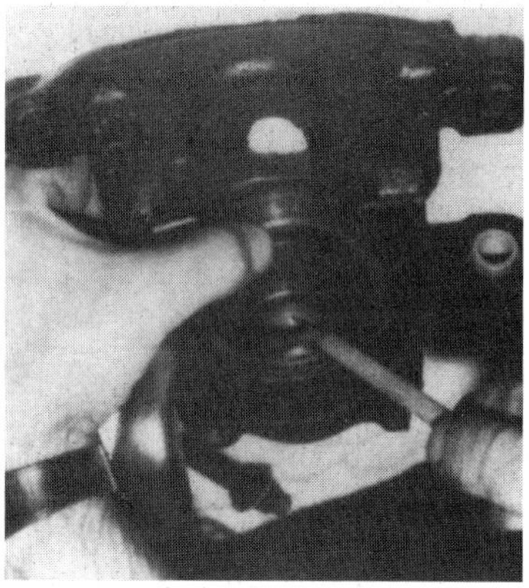

12. Remove the piston seal from its groove in the caliper bore.

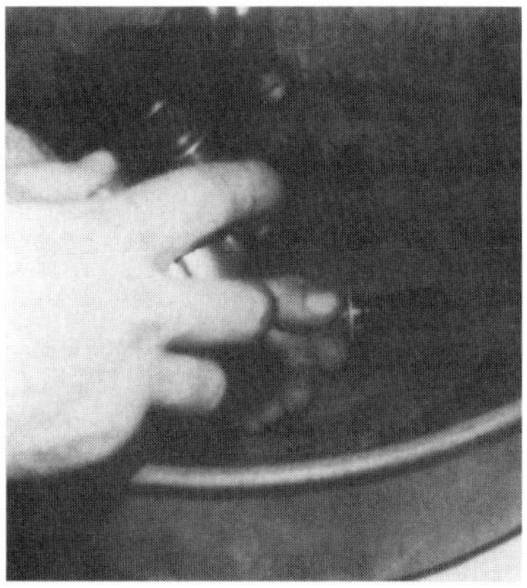

13. Clean and inspect the caliper body and other components. Hone the caliper bore if necessary, and measure the piston-to-bore clearance.

14. Install the bleeder screw in the caliper body and tighten it to 80 to 140 in-lb (9 to 16 Nm).

15. Lubricate the caliper bore and the new piston seal. Install the seal into its groove in the caliper bore.

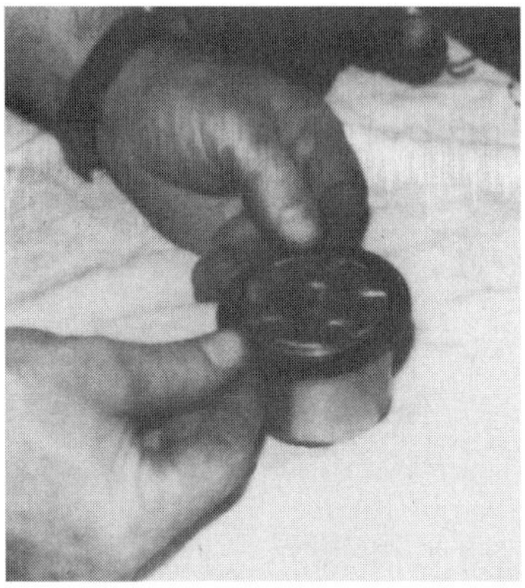

16. Install the new dust boot into its groove on the piston.

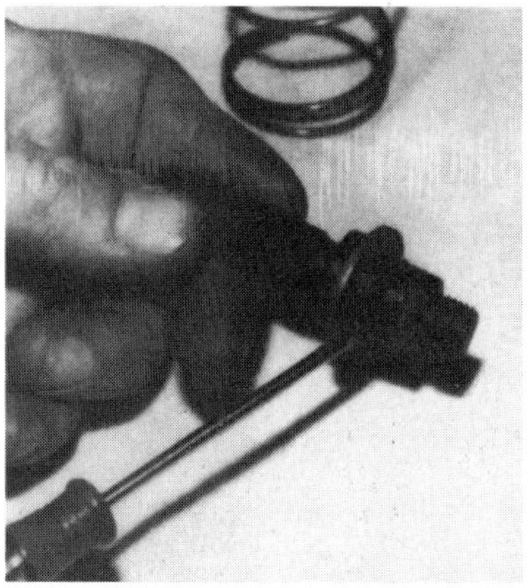

17. Lubricate the new shaft seal and install it into its groove on the actuator screw.

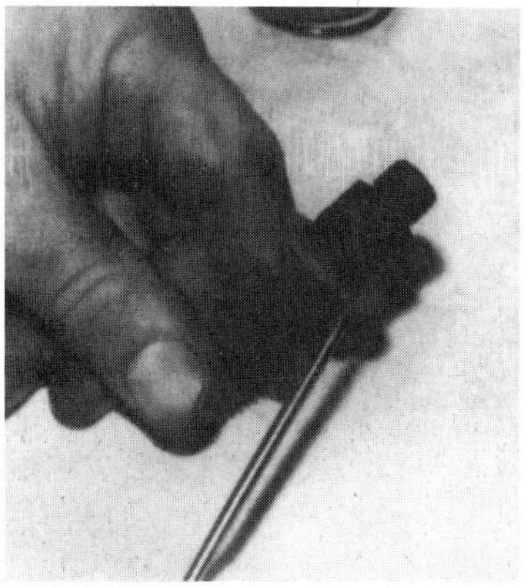

18. Position the thrust washer on the actuator screw so the rounded edge will contact the caliper body when the screw is installed.

GENERAL MOTORS SINGLE-PISTON REAR CALIPER SERVICE

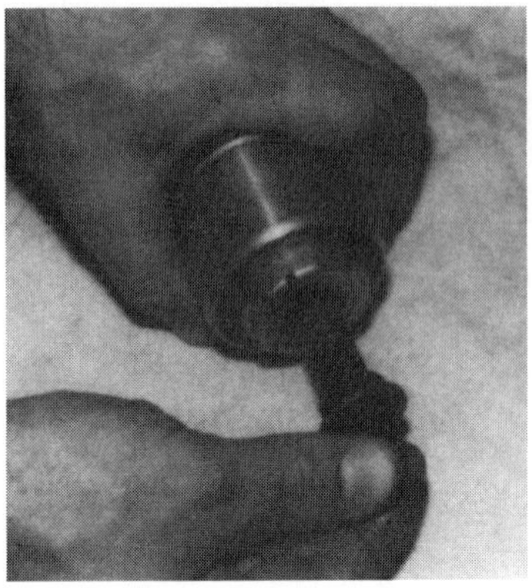

19. Lubricate the actuator screw threads, and install the screw into the piston.

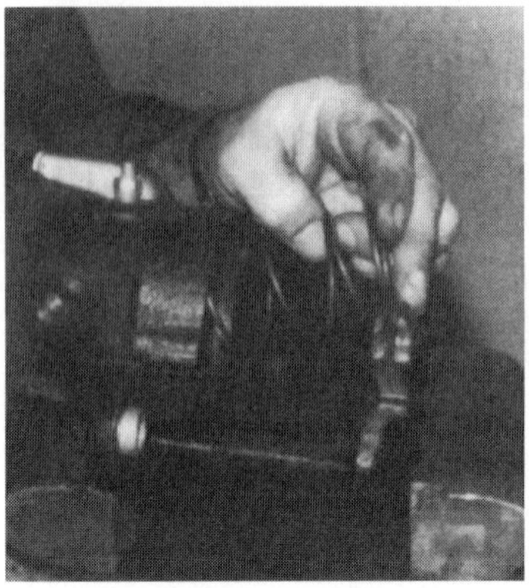

20. Install the balance spring in the caliper bore.

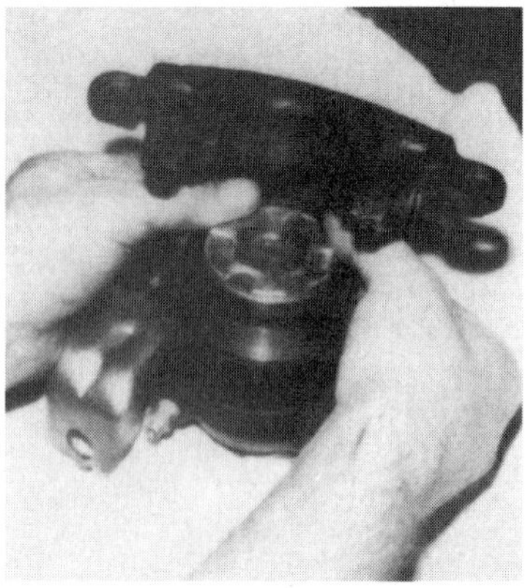

21. Lubricate the piston and install it into the caliper bore until it is bottomed.

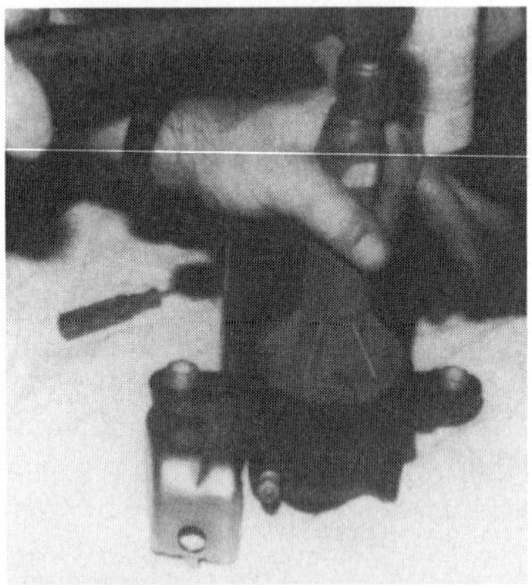

22. Seat the reinforcing ring at the outer edge of the dust boot into the caliper body with a hammer and boot driver.

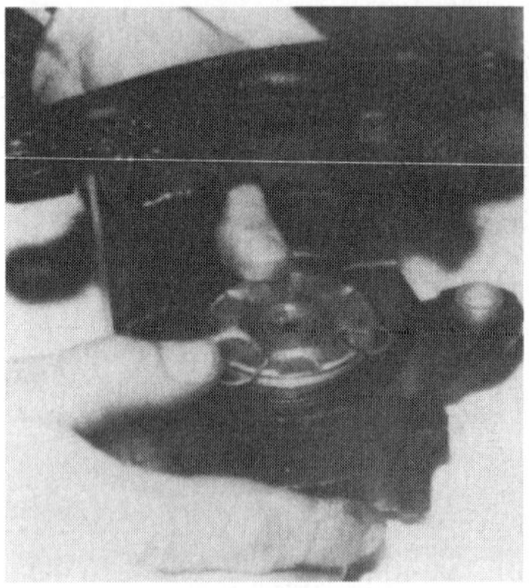

23. Install the brake pad damping spring in the groove at the end of the piston.

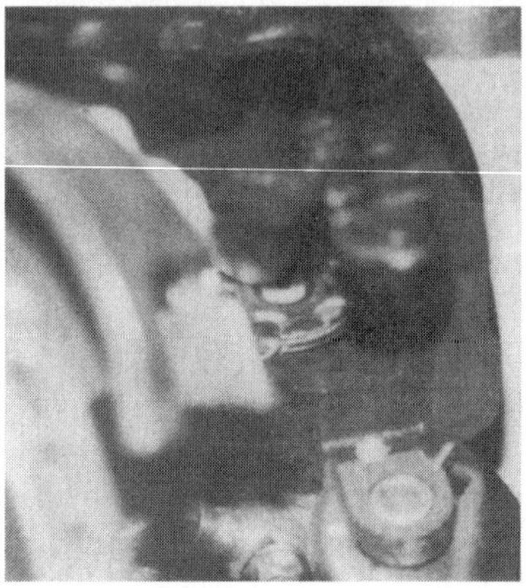

24. Lubricate the new two-way check valve with brake fluid and install it into the piston.

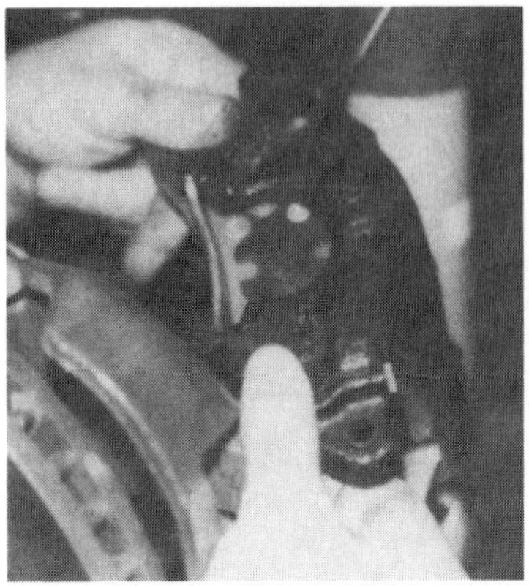

25. Install the outboard pad in the caliper as described earlier.

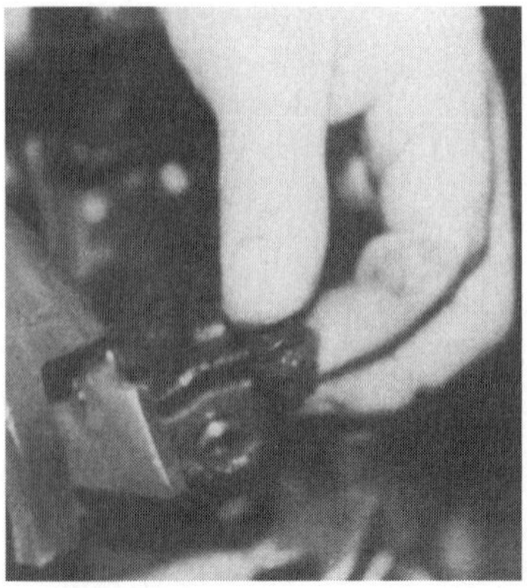

26. Lubricate the new bushings with brake grease and install them into the mounting bolt holes in the caliper body.

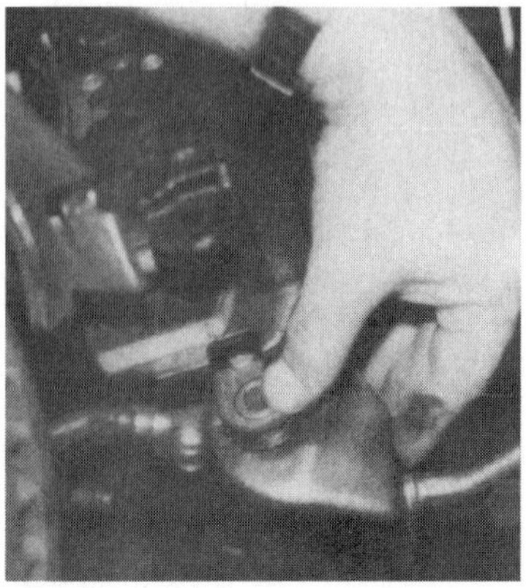

27. Lubricate the outside of the new sleeves with brake grease and install them into the mounting bolt holes.

Disc Brake Service

GENERAL MOTORS SINGLE-PISTON REAR CALIPER SERVICE

28. Position the caliper over the rotor, then lubricate and install the caliper mounting bolts. Torque them to 30 to 45 ft-lb (41 to 61 Nm).

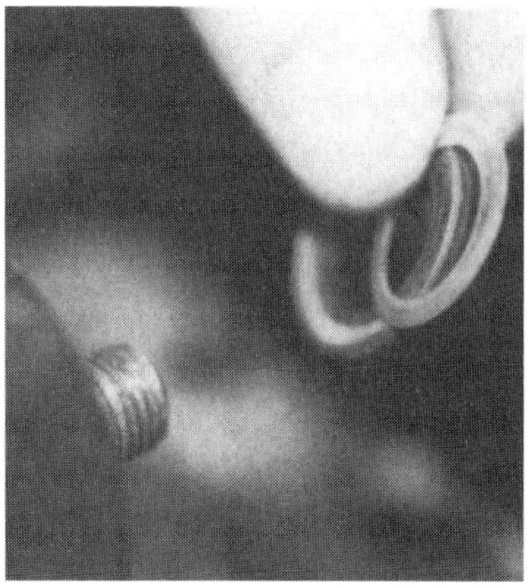

29. Grease the new anti-friction washer and lever seal, and install them on the end of the actuator screw.

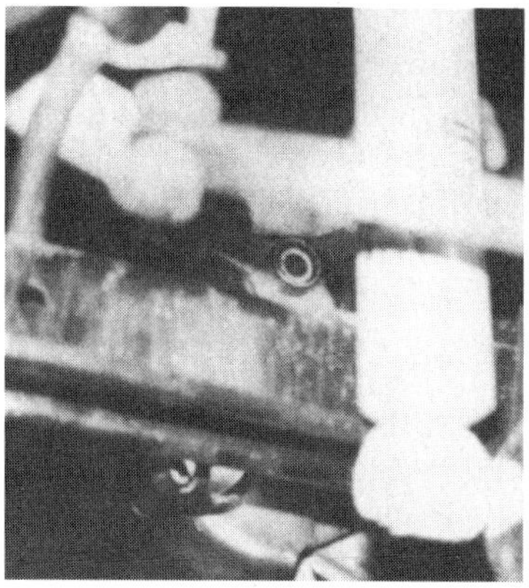

30. Install the parking brake lever, and while holding it away from the stop, tighten the retaining nut to 30 to 40 ft-lb (41 to 54 Nm).

31. Connect the parking brake cable to the lever, and install the return spring. Adjust the cables as described in Chapter 10.

32. If the caliper was rebuilt, connect the brake hose to the caliper fluid inlet. Torque the bolt to 22 to 33 ft-lb (30 to 45 Nm). Bleed the brakes as described in Chapter 3.

General Motors Two-Piston Floating Caliper

General Motors began using a two-piston floating caliper in 2001 on many models, including Chevrolet light- and medium-duty trucks and SUVs, figure 8-62. This type of caliper is used by many other manufacturers, including Ford, Nissan, Toyota, and Cadillac.

Service for the two-piston floating caliper is similar to a single-piston caliper, with the exception of the extra steps needed to remove the second piston. Using a caliper from a Cadillac CTS as an example, the final photo sequence in this chapter shows how to rebuild the General Motors two-piston floating caliper.

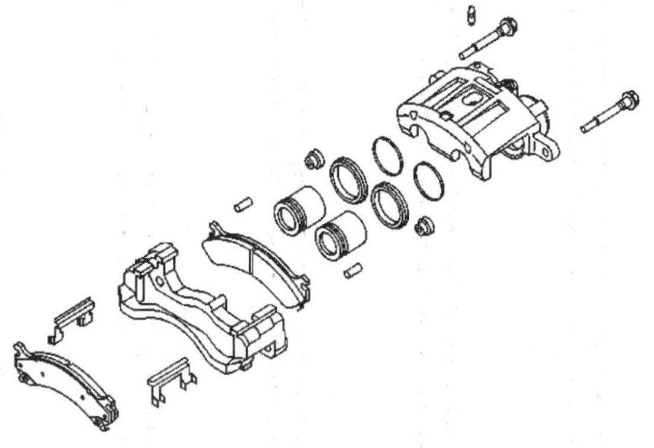

Figure 8-62. The GM double-piston floating caliper.
(Courtesy of General Motors Corporation, Service and Parts Operations)

GENERAL MOTORS TWO-PISTON FLOATING CALIPER SERVICE

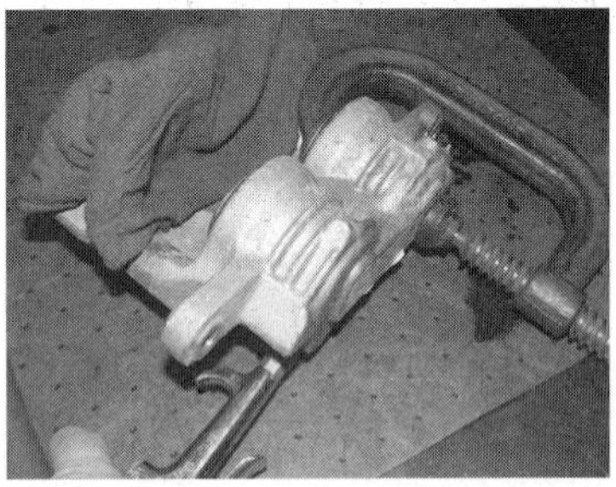

1. Use a C-clamp to clamp one piston in place. Cushion the caliper with a shop towel and blow the other piston out with air.

2. Remove the first piston.

3. Use the C-clamp and a round tool or wood block to seal off the open piston bore and blow out the second piston.

4. Pry out the dust seals.

5. Carefully remove the old piston seals. Do not scratch the caliper bore.

6. Inspect the piston and replace it if necessary.

Disc Brake Service

GENERAL MOTORS TWO-PISTON FLOATING CALIPER SERVICE

7. Install the new piston seals into the caliper. Install the new dust boot on the piston before installing the piston.

8. Install the piston.

9. Make sure the piston is properly aligned. Use the C-clamp and carefully seat the piston.

10. Use a seal driver to seat the dust boot.

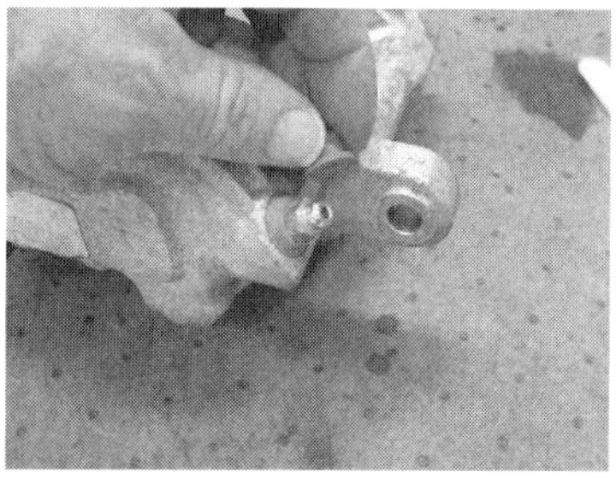

11. Clean and install the bleeder screw. Be sure to install the new bleeder cap.

9
Brake Drum and Rotor Machining

OBJECTIVES

Upon completion and review of this chapter, you will be able to:

- Visually inspect a drum or rotor for scoring, cracking, heat checking, and hard spots.
- Measure a brake drum for oversize, tapered, or barrel-shaped wear.
- Measure a brake drum for bellmouth, out-of-round, or eccentric distortion.
- Measure a rotor for thickness, taper variation, parallelism, and runout.
- Recognize drum and rotor problems and explain the complications they can cause.
- Replace a riveted or swaged floating drum.
- Explain drum and rotor metal removal limits.
- Explain special considerations involved in machining new drums and rotors.
- Describe lathe care.
- Explain lathe settings.
- Mount and center both a drum and rotor on a lathe.
- Turn both a drum and rotor off the car.
- Turn a rotor on the car.
- Grind a drum.
- Resurface a rotor.

INTRODUCTION

Brake drums and rotors provide the surfaces that the shoes and pads rub against to create the friction that stops the vehicle. Although drums and rotors are not considered disposable parts like the brake linings that help them do their job, they are subjected to great deal of heat and friction. As a result, drums and rotors suffer several types of wear, damage, and distortion. If these problems are minor, a drum or rotor can be machined to restore the friction surface; if the problems are severe, the drum or rotor must be replaced.

This chapter describes the procedures used to inspect and machine brake drums and rotors. Instructions are also provided on how to replace brake drums that are riveted or swaged onto their hub.

DRUM AND ROTOR SERVICE

As discussed in the *Classroom Manual,* the size, shape, and finish of drum and rotor friction surfaces are critical to safe and efficient braking. If these factors are not maintained within specific tolerances, brake shoe or pad wear increases, braking force becomes erratic, the brake pedal pulsates, and brake noise and vibration occur. In extreme cases, a drum or rotor can fail entirely.

To identify problems and determine if additional service is required, you should inspect the drums and rotors: whenever you service the brakes, if there is noise and vibration from the brakes, or if a road test reveals a pulsating brake pedal. A brake drum must be removed from the vehicle (see Chapter 7) before it can be inspected, but you can inspect the outboard friction surface of a brake rotor simply by removing the wheel. To thoroughly inspect a rotor, however, you may have to remove the brake caliper (see Chapter 8) to get a clear view of the inboard friction surface.

Some shops bypass the inspection and automatically turn drums and rotors any time they replace the shoes or pads. This is generally a good policy on drum brakes because the drums are already off the car, and drums are subject to a number of problems that can be difficult to spot until a drum is machined in a lathe. In addition, today's lightly loaded rear drum brakes are serviced at infrequent intervals, which makes a complete brake job, including turning the drums, a good way to go.

On disc brakes, however, automatically turning the rotors is not a good policy. All of the problems that require rotors to be machined can be identified by an inspection. In addition, the extra work required to remove and reinstall the rotors increases the cost of the job, while any metal removed from a rotor that is in serviceable condition needlessly shortens its service life.

Brake drum and rotor inspections consist of two parts, a visual inspection followed by one or more careful measurements. Once you have completed a thorough inspection, you will know if the drum or rotor is in serviceable condition, must be machined to restore the friction surface, or is beyond saving and must be replaced.

VISUAL DRUM AND ROTOR INSPECTION

The visual inspection checks a drum or rotor for obvious defects such as scoring, cracking, heat checking, and hard spots. Before you start the inspection, wipe the drum or rotor friction surface clean with a shop towel soaked in brake cleaner; this will make it easier to spot any problems. If you are inspecting a rotor that has rust buildup on its friction surfaces as a result of disuse, sand away the rust with medium-grit sandpaper or abrasive cloth. If the rust buildup cannot be easily removed by hand, resurface the rotor as described later in the chapter.

During the visual inspection, if you find any problem that requires the drum or rotor to be machined, immediately measure the drum or rotor as described later in the chapter. If the visual inspection reveals no problems, but there are other symptoms of brake trouble such as noise, vibration, or brake pedal pulsation, measure the drum or rotor anyway. If a visual inspection reveals no problems, and there are no other symptoms of brake trouble, the drum or rotor is most likely in serviceable condition. However, you should *always* measure the drum inside diameter, or rotor thickness, to make sure it is within legal limits.

Visual Inspection Procedure

First, inspect the drum or rotor friction surface for scoring and grooves, figure 9-1. If a badly scored or grooved friction surface is not refinished, lining wear will increase, and the brakes may be noisy. To determine the depth of any scores or grooves, use a micrometer with a pointed anvil or a depth micrometer. The maximum amount of allowable scoring or grooves will vary, according to the vehicle. Generally, the smaller the vehicle, the smaller the depth of allowable scoring. For example, a subcompact may allow grooves up to .015″ (.38 mm) while a full-size pickup or sports utility vehicle may allow as much as .060″ (1.5 mm). Scores or grooves this deep are not usually harmful to brake performance and need not be turned if they also pass the measurement inspection, described in the next section.

Second, inspect the drum or rotor for cracks, figure 9-2. A cracked drum or rotor is unsafe and may fail completely if left in service. Cracks can occur anywhere, but drums usually crack near the bolt circle or web, or at the open edge of the friction surface. Rotors usually crack at the outer edge of their friction surface. Do not confuse small surface cracks with cracks that reach deeply into the structure of the drum or rotor. If any cracks are visible, replace the drum or rotor.

Third, inspect the drum or rotor for heat checking, figure 9-3. Heat checking creates a rough friction surface that increases lining wear and may cause a slight pedal pulsation or brake noise. Heat checking appears as many small, interlaced cracks on the friction surface. If the heat checking is minor and the drum or rotor checks good in other respects, machine the drum or rotor. If heat checking is widespread, and there are other problems, it may be better to replace the drum or rotor.

Finally, inspect the drum or rotor for hard spots, figure 9-4. These are round, bluish/gold, glassy appearing areas on the friction surface that can increase lining wear, or cause brake chatter and a pulsating pedal. It is possible to machine hard spots flush with the friction surface; however, most hard spots cannot be removed entirely because they penetrate too far into the metal. Machining down hard spots requires special equipment and is time-consuming, so most manufacturers today recommend that drums and rotors with hard spots be replaced.

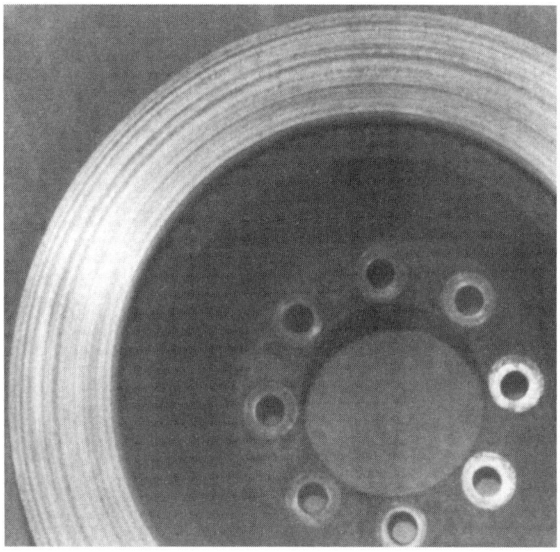

Brake Drum and Rotor Machining

Figure 9-1. Inspect for scores and grooves in the friction surface.

Figure 9-2. Inspect the entire surface of a drum or rotor for cracks.

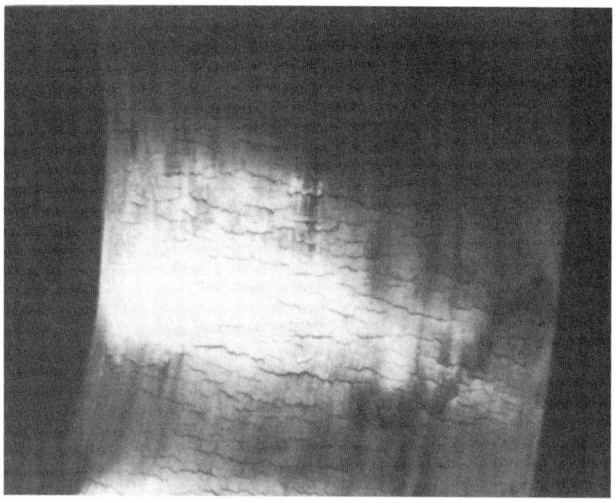

Figure 9-3. Inspect the friction surface for heat checking.

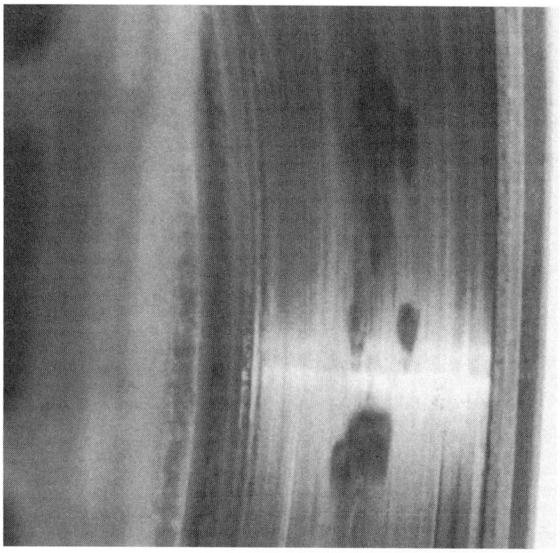

Figure 9-4. Inspect the friction surface for hard spots.

BRAKE DRUM MEASUREMENT

Brake drums are measured to identify wear and distortion that are not visually apparent. When drums wear, they become oversize, tapered, or barrel-shaped. Distorted drums become bellmouthed, out-of-round, or eccentric. You can measure most of these problems using a drum micrometer or an inside micrometer. However, some forms of drum wear and distortion cannot be identified until the drum is turned in a brake lathe.

Drum Inside Diameter

Anytime a brake drum is removed from the car, you should measure its inside diameter to check for wear. To do this, note the discard diameter stamped or cast into the drum, then position the drum so the open side is facing up. On early brake drums that do not have a discard diameter marked on them, consult a shop manual for the proper dimension. Next, adjust a drum micrometer to the nominal drum diameter as described in Chapter 1, and insert the micrometer into the brake drum, figure 9-5. Hold the anvil steady against the friction surface, and slide the dial end of the micrometer back and forth until the highest reading is obtained on the dial scale. Repeat this process at two or three locations around the drum, then compare the largest reading to the discard diameter.

On most vehicles, if the inside diameter is not at least .030″ (.75 mm) smaller than the drum discard diameter, replace the drum. The amount of additional metal required to allow for wear in service varies depending on the manufacturer; check the shop manual

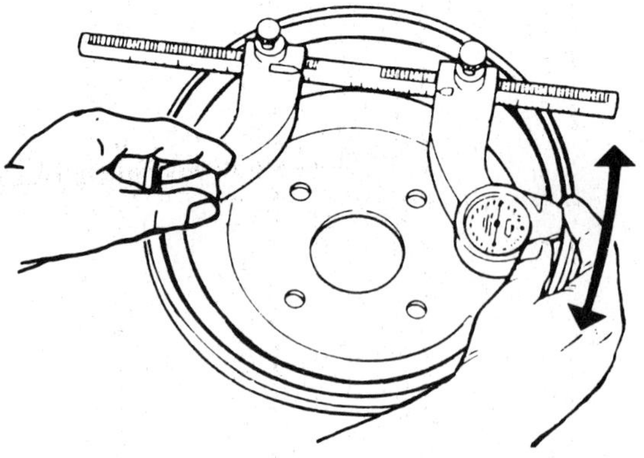

Figure 9-5. Use a drum micrometer to check the inside diameter of the brake drum.

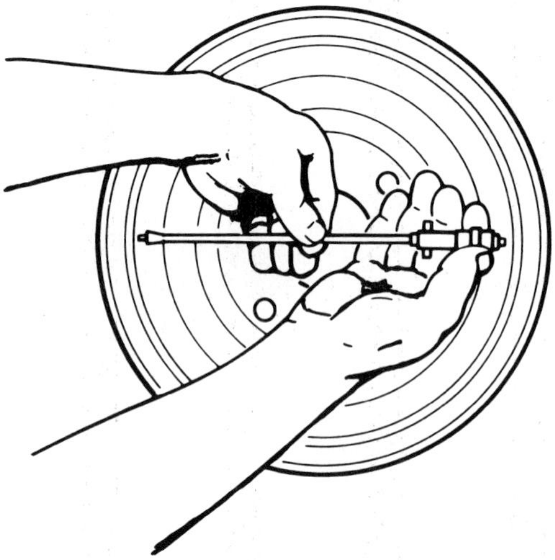

Figure 9-6. Use an inside micrometer to check a drum for taper wear, barrel wear, or bellmouth distortion.

of the car you are servicing for the exact value. If the drum needs to be turned, there must be sufficient metal remaining so the inside diameter will be at least .030″ (.75 mm) smaller than the discard diameter *after* the drum is turned. Ford Motor Company drums, and those on some other vehicles, are marked differently. Replace one of these drums whenever its inside diameter exceeds the "maximum diameter" stamped or cast into the drum. If you are unsure of what the measurements on a drum mean, consult a shop manual to be sure.

Drum Taper Wear, Barrel Wear, and Bellmouth Distortion

Taper wear, barrel wear, and bellmouth distortion are problems that cause variations in brake drum diameter between the open and closed edges of the friction surface. A drum with taper wear has a larger diameter at the closed edge than at the open edge. A drum with barrel wear has a larger diameter at the center than at either edge. A drum with bellmouth distortion has a larger diameter at the open edge than at the closed edge. If new brake shoes are installed into a drum with any of these problems, a spongy brake pedal, brake fade caused by poor lining-to-drum contact, and uneven lining wear will result.

Taper wear can sometimes cause a spongy brake pedal, but barrel wear and bellmouth distortion have no symptoms that are obvious to the driver. These problems can sometimes be spotted by ridges or lips worn into the drum friction surface; other times, unusual wear patterns on the brake linings will reveal the problem. Generally, however, these types of wear and distortion are discovered when the drum is turned on a lathe and the tool bit contacts the drum only at one, the other, or both edges.

You can also identify these problems by measuring the drum inside diameter at several points across the friction surface. A drum micrometer cannot reach deeply enough into the drum to make these measurements, so you must use an inside micrometer instead. Position the micrometer as shown in figure 9-6 and take three measurements, one at the open edge of the drum, one at the center of the friction surface, and one at the closed edge of the drum. If the highest and lowest of these measurements vary by more than .006″ (.15 mm), machine the drum.

Out-of-Round Drum Distortion

The diameter of an out-of-round drum varies when measured at several points around its circumference. This causes a pulsating brake pedal; brake vibration; and, sometimes, grabby, erratic braking. To check for an out-of-round drum, use a brake drum micrometer to measure the drum inside diameter at four locations 45 degrees apart from one another, figure 9-7. If the highest and lowest measurements vary by more than .006″ (.15 mm), machine the drum.

Eccentric Drum Distortion

Eccentric brake drum distortion exists when the geometric center of the friction surface is different from that of the hub. This makes the drum rotate with a cam-like motion that causes the shoe contact pads on the backing plate to wear, and creates noise whenever the brakes are applied. Eccentric drum distortion cannot be detected visually or with common measuring tools. This condition is usually identified when a drum is turned on a lathe and the tool bit contacts the friction surface on only one side of the drum.

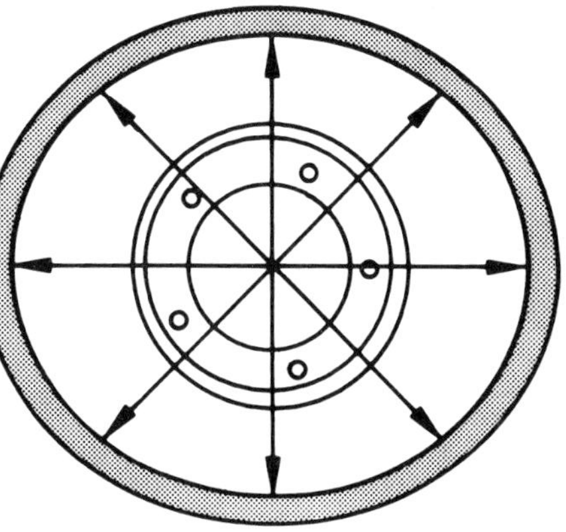

Brake Drum and Rotor Machining

Figure 9-7. Measure the drum inside diameter at four places around the drum to check for out-of-roundness.

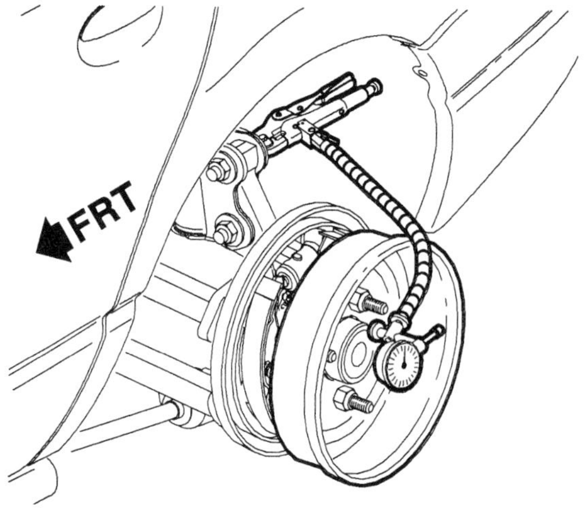

Figure 9-8. Use this setup to check the brake drum for runout. (Courtesy of General Motors Corporation, Service and Parts Operations)

Brake Drum and Hub Radial Runout Check

To check for radial runout of the brake drum, remove the brake drum and clean the surfaces of the drum and hub. Install the drum on the hub backward and secure it with the wheel nuts, also installed backward, with the flat side toward the drum, figure 9-8. Using a dial indicator as shown, measure the total combined runout of the hub and drum. The runout should be less than 0.011″ (0.28 mm), or as listed in the manufacturer's service information. If the runout exceeds this amount, mount the drum on a lathe and recheck the runout:

1. If the drum still has excessive runout, machine or replace the drum.
2. If the drum, mounted on the lathe, now has reduced or no excessive runout, check the hub and wheel bearing for damage. Hub runout should be 0.005″ (0.13 mm) or less.

BRAKE ROTOR MEASUREMENT

Like brake drums, brake rotors are measured to identify wear and distortion that are not visually apparent. When rotors wear, they become too thin or have taper variation. Distorted rotors have lateral runout, or the two friction surfaces are not longer parallel. You can measure all types of rotor wear and distortion using an outside micrometer and a dial indicator.

Brake rotor dimensions are held to much tighter tolerances than drum dimensions. This makes the proper use of accurate measuring tools a critical part of rotor inspection. If you have any questions on how to use and read a micrometer, see Chapter 1 for instructions.

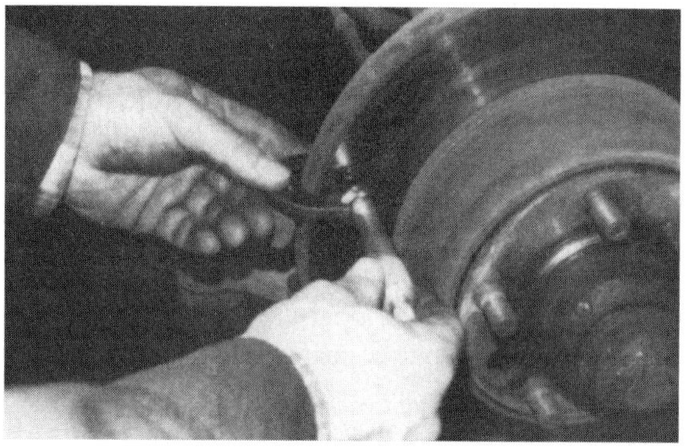

Figure 9-9. Measure the thickness, parallelism, and taper variation of a rotor with an outside micrometer.

Rotor Thickness

Anytime you inspect a brake rotor, measure its thickness to check for wear. On some vehicles, it may be necessary to remove the caliper in order to do this. To check a rotor for wear, note the discard dimension stamped or cast into the rotor. On early brake rotors that do not have a discard dimension marked on them, consult a shop manual for the proper measurement. Next, position an outside micrometer 1 inch (25 mm) in from the outer edge of the friction surface, and measure the rotor thickness, figure 9-9. Compare the measured thickness to the discard dimension.

If the rotor thickness is not at least .015″ to .030″ (.40 to .75 mm) larger than the rotor discard dimension, replace the rotor. The amount of additional metal required to allow for wear in service varies depending on the manufacturer; check the shop manual of the car you are servicing for the exact value. If the rotor needs to be turned, there must be sufficient metal remaining so the thickness will be at least .015″ to .030″ (.40 to .75 mm) larger than the discard dimension *after* the rotor is turned. Ford Motor Company rotors, and those on some other cars, are marked differently. Replace one of these rotors whenever its thickness is less than the "minimum thickness" stamped or cast into the outside of the rotor. If you are unsure of what the measurements on a rotor mean, consult a shop manual to be sure.

Rotor Taper Variation

A rotor with taper variation has a different thickness at the outer edge of its friction surface than at the inner edge. If the variation is too great, new brake pads will not contact the rotor squarely, and the caliper pistons may bind in their bores.

To check for taper variation, use an outside micrometer with a deep frame to measure the rotor thickness at the outer edge just below the ridge, then at the inner edge of the area swept by the brake pads. If a micrometer with a deep frame is unavailable, use a conventional outside micrometer to make the outer measurement as described above, then measure inward as far as the micrometer can reach. In either case, subtract the smaller measurement from the larger one to obtain the taper variation. Repeat these measurements at four points around the rotor. If the variation is greater than .003″ (.08 mm) at any point, machine the rotor.

Rotor Lateral Runout

Lateral runout is a side-to-side movement of the rotor as it turns. Excessive runout can cause brake pedal pulsations, vibration during braking, and increased brake pedal travel from too much pad knockback. For the best braking performance, the lateral runout should be less than .003″ (.08 mm). However, depending on the vehicle manufacturer, anywhere between .002 ″ and .008″ (.05 and .20 mm) runout is allowed. It is only necessary to check lateral runout on one side of the rotor; runout never varies significantly between the two sides.

You check for lateral runout while the rotor is mounted on the vehicle and rotating on the wheel bearings. When making this check, it is very important not to mistake bearing play for lateral runout. Adjustable wheel bearings can be tightened to eliminate play as a factor; nonadjustable wheel bearings cannot. As a result, a different procedure is required to check rotor runout with each type of wheel bearing.

To check the lateral runout of a rotor mounted on adjustable wheel bearings:

1. Raise and properly support the vehicle so the wheel with the rotor to be checked hangs free, then remove the wheel.
2. If the car has floating rotors, install and torque the lug nuts to hold the rotor tightly on the hub.
3. Pry the brake pads back so they do not drag against the rotor. Use one of the methods described in Chapter 8.
4. Tighten the wheel bearing adjusting nut with a wrench to a snug fit. There should be no play, but the rotor should still turn without binding. See Chapter 14 for information on adjusting wheel bearings.
5. Mount a dial indicator on the suspension, and position the plunger so it contacts the rotor at a 90-degree angle about 1 inch (25 mm) from the outer edge, figure 9-10.
6. Rotate the rotor until the lowest reading shows on the indicator dial, then zero the dial, figure 9-11.
7. Rotate the rotor until the highest reading shows on the dial; this is the lateral runout, figure 9-12.

Because the play cannot be adjusted out of nonadjustable wheel bearings, it must be subtracted from the final reading on the dial indicator to determine the true runout. To check the lateral runout of a rotor mounted on nonadjustable wheel bearings:

1. Raise and properly support the vehicle so the wheel with the rotor to be checked hangs free, then remove the wheel.
2. If the vehicle has floating rotors, install two lug nuts to hold the rotor tightly on the hub.
3. Pry the brake pads back so they do not drag against the rotor. Use one of the methods described in Chapter 8.
4. Mount a dial indicator on the suspension, and position the plunger so it contacts the rotor at a 90-degree angle about 1 inch (25 mm) from the outer edge, figure 9-10.
5. Push inward on the hub with moderate pressure, and rotate the rotor until the lowest reading shows on the indicator dial; set the dial to zero, figure 9-11.
6. Pull outward on the hub with moderate pressure, and record the measurement shown on the indicator dial; this is the bearing end play.
7. Rotate the rotor until the highest reading shows on the indicator dial, then pull outward on the hub with moderate pressure; record the reading shown on the indicator dial.
8. Subtract the bearing end play reading in step 6 from the total reading in step 7; the result is the rotor lateral runout.

Brake Drum and Rotor Machining

Figure 9-10. Check the lateral runout of a rotor with a dial indicator.

Figure 9-11. Turn the outside of the dial to zero the dial indicator.

Figure 9-12. When the rotor is rotated, the dial needle shows the lateral runout.

Rotor Lack of Parallelism

A rotor that lacks parallelism varies in thickness at different places around its friction surfaces. Lack of parallelism is the single biggest cause of brake pedal pulsation, and also causes braking vibration. For these reasons parallelism is a critical form of rotor distortion that requires very careful measurement.

To check for variations in parallelism, use an outside micrometer to measure the rotor thickness at 6 to 12 equally spaced points around the friction surface. Make all of the measurements the same distance in from the outer edge of the rotor so taper variation will not affect the measurements. If the thickness variation between any two points is greater than .0005" (.013 mm), and there is noticeable brake pedal pulsation, machine the rotor.

DRUM REPLACEMENT

A few floating brake drums are attached to their hubs with rivets or swaged studs. This assembly is generally machined in the same manner as a fixed drum. However, if the drum is badly damaged, it can be removed from the hub and replaced separately. Once the old drum and hub are separated, the new drum generally does not have to be secured in place. Instead, it is machined and installed like a floating drum.

The exact removal procedure varies depending on whether the drum is riveted or swaged in place. To replace a riveted drum, cut off the heads of the rivets with an air chisel, figure 9-13. Drill a small hole through the remaining portion of each rivet, then drive the rivets out with a hammer and punch to separate the drum and hub.

To replace a drum that is held in place by swaged studs, you will need a special cutter designed to machine away the swaged portion of the stud shoulders. Chuck the cutter in a drill motor, position it over the stud, start the drill motor, and press the cutter down firmly for about 10 seconds, figure 9-14. Remove the

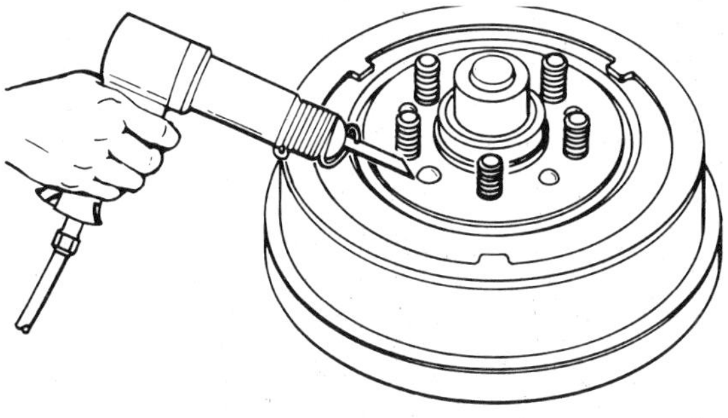

Figure 9-13. Using an air chisel helps remove rivets that hold a drum and hub together.

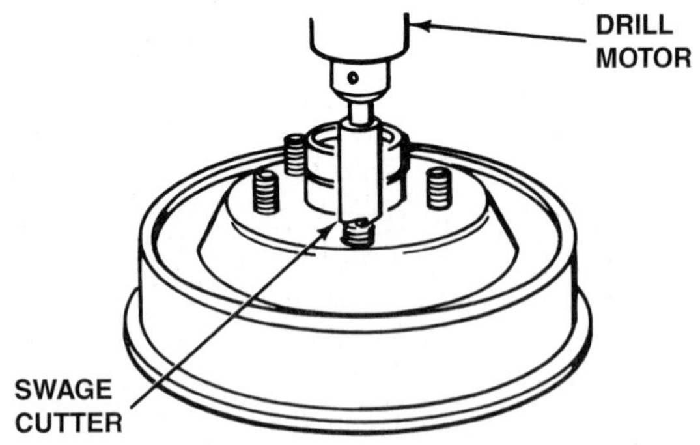

Figure 9-14. Using a cutter to remove the swaged portion of a wheel stud.

cutter and determine if all of the swaged metal has been removed. Repeat this process as needed until the swaged portion on all of the studs has been cut away, then separate the drum and hub.

DRUM AND ROTOR REFINISHING

As discussed in the *Classroom Manual,* there are three methods used to machine or refinish brake drums and rotors. *Turning* removes metal from drum and rotor friction surfaces with a steel tool bit to repair most forms of wear, damage, and distortion. *Grinding* removes metal from drum friction surfaces with an abrasive stone wheel to machine hard spots level with the rest of the friction surface. *Resurfacing* removes very small amounts of metal from rotor friction surfaces with a spinning abrasive disc, and is commonly done to create a nondirectional finish that speeds the bedding-in of new brake pads. Resurfacing can also be done to remove rust, brake lining deposits, and minor rotor damage. Except when a rotor is turned on the car, all of these operations are performed with the drum or rotor off the car and mounted in a brake lathe.

Metal Removal Considerations

Regardless of the procedure you use to machine a drum or rotor, you should only remove the minimum amount of metal necessary to restore the friction surface. This helps ensure the longest possible service life for the drum or rotor. On rotors used with sliding or floating calipers, you can machine different amounts of metal from each friction surface; however, you must machine rotors used with fixed calipers equally on both sides.

Never machine a drum or rotor unless you also machine the drum or rotor on the other end of the same axle. This keeps braking force and fade resistance equal from side to side, and prevents brake pull. This is especially important with drum brakes where the inside diameters of drums on the same axle should be kept within .010″ to .020″ (.25 to .51 mm) of each other. To help keep the drum diameters equal, machine the more badly worn drum first, then machine the other drum to match. In the same manner, machine a new drum to match the diameter of an old drum on the same axle.

BRAKE LATHE OPERATION

Once you inspect a brake drum or rotor and determine it needs to be machined, the next step is to mount and center the drum or rotor in a brake lathe. If you are servicing drum brakes, you removed the drums from the car for inspection. If you are servicing disc brakes, remove the rotors at this time unless you are using an on-car lathe to machine them.

To remove a brake rotor, first remove the brake caliper as described in Chapter 8. Then, you can remove a floating rotor by removing any attaching hardware, and sliding it off the hub. Remove a fixed rotor in the same manner as a fixed drum, and remember that whenever you machine a fixed drum or rotor you must also service the wheel bearings. Details on wheel bearing service are contained in Chapter 14.

Lathe Care

Before you mount a drum or rotor on a brake lathe, make sure the arbor shaft and adapters are wiped clean, figure 9-15. Any dirt, metal chips, or other contaminants, figure 9-16, will affect the alignment of the drum or rotor on the lathe, and the quality of the final cut. Always handle lathe parts carefully — scratches, nicks, and dents on these parts will also adversely affect the accuracy of the machining operation.

To ensure a good friction surface finish, always use sharp tool bits when turning a drum or rotor. Also, make sure the bits are rounded and not pointed. This is especially important on drum brakes where a pointed bit can cut a "thread" into the friction surface. This can cause the linings to "thread" outward when the brakes are applied. The result will be shoe misalignment with the drum, less effective braking, increased lining wear, and a clicking noise as the shoes snap back into place when the brakes are released.

Mounting Drums and Rotors

Fixed drums and rotors are mounted on the brake lathe arbor shaft differently than floating drums and rotors. Fixed drums and rotors mount using tapered or radiused cone adapters, figure 9-17, that fit into the wheel bearing races in the drum or rotor hub. Floating drums and rotors mount using two basket adapters,

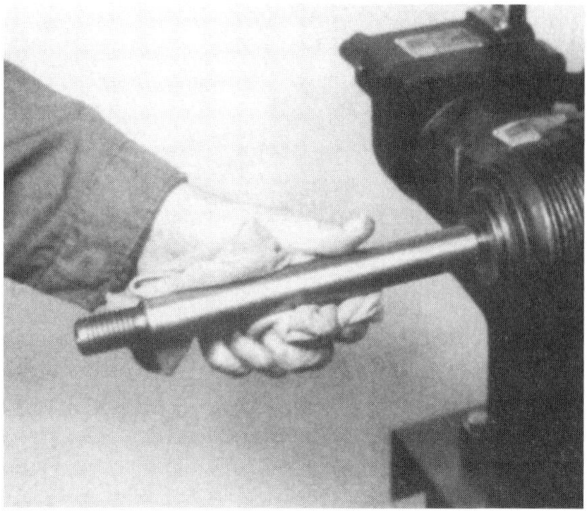

Brake Drum and Rotor Machining

Figure 9-15. Wipe the arbor shaft clean before mounting a drum or rotor on a brake lathe.

Figure 9-16. Dirt and metal chips on the arbor shaft and adapters can greatly affect the accuracy of a lathe.

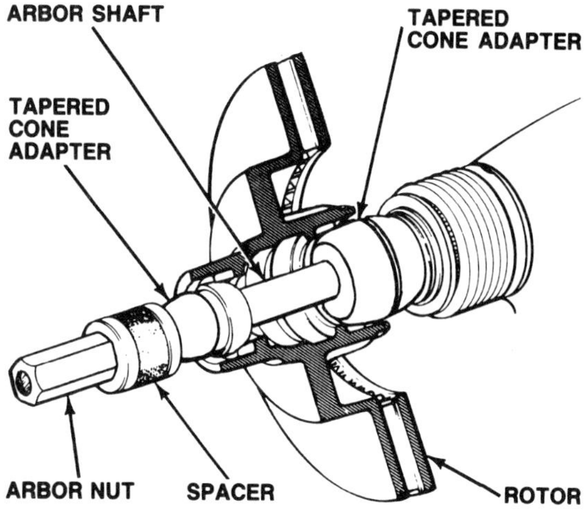

Figure 9-17. A typical mounting for a fixed drum or rotor.

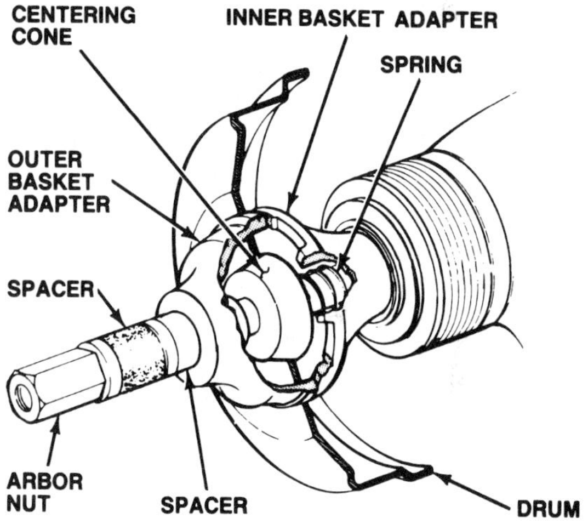

Figure 9-18. A typical mounting for a floating drum or rotor.

figure 9-18, or hubless adapters, figure 9-19, that press against the inner and outer sides of the drum web or rotor hat; the drum or rotor is centered by a spring-loaded cone that fits into the center hole.

To mount a fixed drum or rotor on a brake lathe:

1. Remove the inner bearing grease seal. Remove both the inner and outer wheel bearing roller assemblies.
2. Use a shop towel to wipe the bearing races clean of all dirt and grease.
3. Inspect the races for fit and damage:
   a. If you can turn any race with your fingers, figure 9-20, replace the drum or rotor along with the bearings.
   b. Replace any damaged or worn races as described in Chapter 14.
4. Select the cone adapters that fit into the bearing races, figure 9-21. Generally, a small cone fits the outer race and a large cone fits the inner race.
5. Slide the cone adapter for the inner bearing race onto the arbor shaft so the tapered side faces out.
6. Slide the drum or rotor onto the arbor shaft so that the inner bearing race fits over the adapter.

Figure 9-19. Hubless or composite rotors may need to use these hubless adapters when being mounted on the lathe.

Figure 9-20. Check the bearing races before mounting the drum or rotor on the lathe.

Figure 9-21. Cone adapters used to mount fixed drums and rotors on a brake lathe.

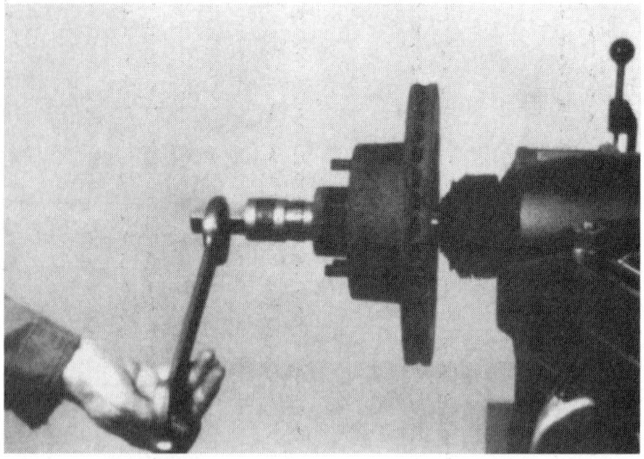

Figure 9-22. Tighten the arbor nut to hold the drum or rotor onto the arbor shaft.

Figure 9-23. Basket adapters and centering cones used to mount floating drums and rotors on a brake lathe.

7. Slide the cone adapter for the outer bearing race onto the arbor shaft, tapered side in, and install it into the outer bearing race.
8. Place spacers between the outer cone adapter and the arbor nut as needed, figure 9-22, then securely tighten the nut so the drum or rotor is held solidly in position.

To mount a floating drum or rotor on a brake lathe:

1. Clean the inside, outside, and center hole of the drum web or rotor hat with a wire brush so it is free of rust and dirt.
2. Scrape the inside, and lightly file the outside, of the drum web or rotor hat so both surfaces are clean and free of high spots.
3. Select the centering cone that fits the center hole in the drum or rotor, figure 9-23.
4. Slide one of the basket adapters onto the arbor shaft with the open side facing out.
5. Slide the spring onto the arbor shaft.
6. Slide the centering cone onto the arbor shaft with the tapered side facing out.
7. Install the drum or rotor onto the arbor shaft with the outside of the drum web or rotor hat facing out.
8. Install the other basket adapter onto the arbor shaft with the open side pressing against the drum or rotor.

Brake Drum and Rotor Machining

9. Place spacers between the outer basket adapter and the arbor nut as needed, figure 9-22, then securely tighten the nut so the drum or rotor is held solidly in position.

Silencing Bands and Straps

After the brake drum or rotor is mounted on the lathe, install a silencing band or strap around the outer edge. The band or strap prevents vibrations during machining; without it, the cutting tool will chatter on the friction surface, making it impossible to produce a smooth finish. Brake rotors usually use a rubber silencing band, figure 9-24A, while brake drums use a wider, rubber strap, Figure 9-24B. To install the band or strap, stretch it around the rotor or drum, and secure it so it remains tightly in place.

Solid brake rotors, or vented rotors less than 1/2 inch (13 mm) thick, may be too thin for a silencing band to remain in place. In these cases, a special damper like that shown in figure 9-25 can be used. To install the damper, bolt it to the lathe and position the adjustable arms so the pads contact the rotor on opposite sides, about 180 degrees apart.

Centering Drums and Rotors

Once the silencing band or strap is in position, the next step is to make sure the drum or rotor is properly centered. If a drum or rotor is not centered accurately, you can easily cut more runout into it than it had to begin with! Use the procedure below to check the centering of a drum or rotor. When you check a rotor, it is only necessary to make scratch cuts on one of the friction surfaces. Always wear safety glasses when operating a brake lathe to prevent eye injury from flying metal chips.

To check that the drum or rotor is centered:

1. Back the tool bit or bits away from the drum or rotor, and rotate the drum or rotor by hand through at least one full turn to make sure everything clears.
2. Start the lathe, and advance the tool bit until it just touches the friction surface at about its midpoint. This scratch cut should be not more than .001″ (.025 mm) deep.
3. Back the tool bit away from the friction surface and stop the lathe.
   a. If the scratch cut appears all around the friction surface, the drum or rotor is properly mounted and centered, and you can proceed with machining.
   b. If the scratch cut appears only part of the way around the friction surface, figure 9-26, go to step 4.

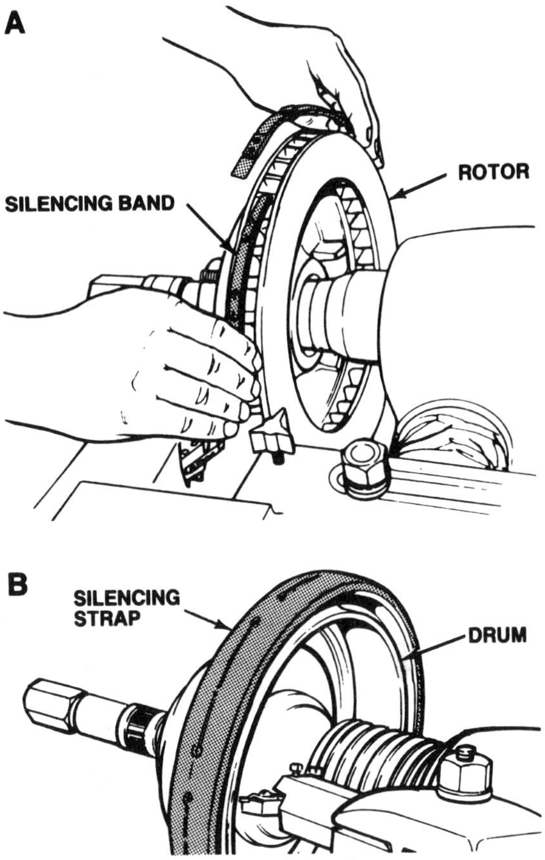

Figure 9-24. A silencing band or strap improves the quality of the machined surface.

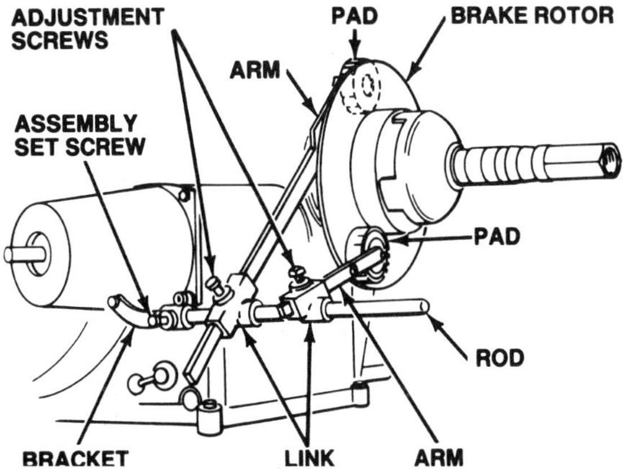

Figure 9-25. Use a damper to quell vibrations on solid rotors.

4. Loosen the arbor nut, rotate the drum or rotor 180 degrees on the arbor shaft, and retighten the arbor nut.
5. Start the lathe and advance the tool bit so it again just touches the friction surface, this time at a

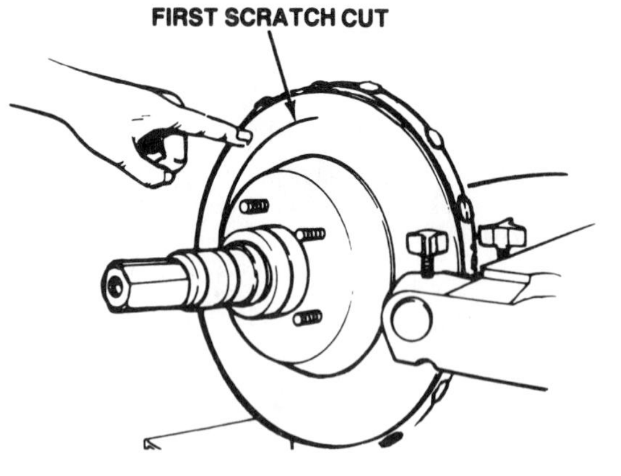

Figure 9-26. A scratch cut in only part of the friction surface may indicate a mounting problem or lathe damage.

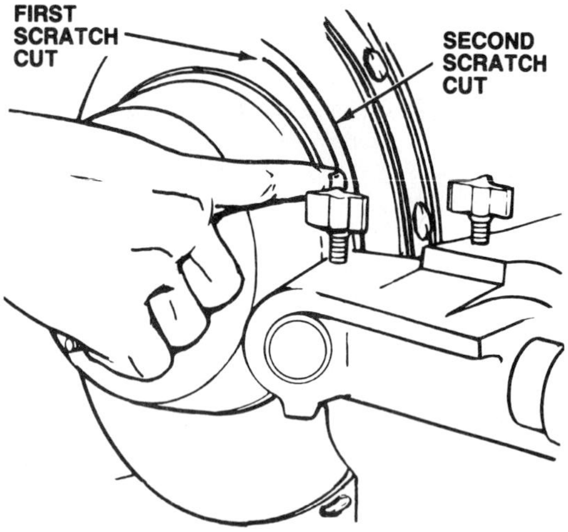

Figure 9-27. If the second scratch cut is next to the first, the drum or rotor is mounted properly and the lathe is okay.

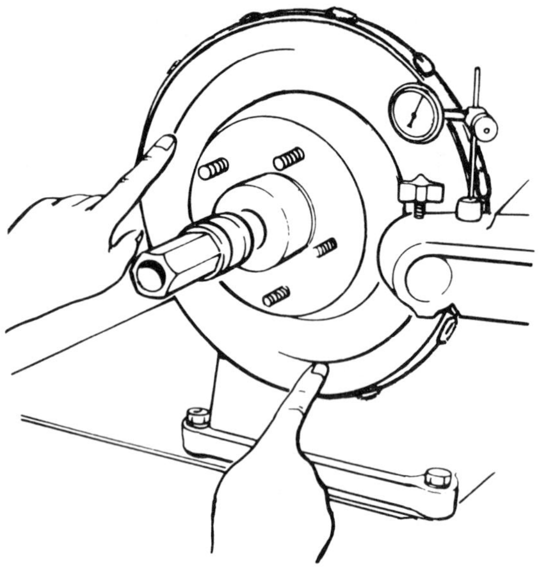

Figure 9-28. If the second scratch cut is opposite the first, check the mounting of the drum or rotor.

point next to the first scratch cut. As with the first cut, the second scratch cut should be not more than .001″ (.025 mm) deep.

6. Back the tool bit away from the friction surface and stop the lathe.
   a. If the second scratch cut appears on the friction surface at the same location as the first cut, figure 9-27, the drum is out of round or the rotor has runout. The drum or rotor is properly centered, and you can proceed with machining.
   b. If the second scratch cut appears in the friction surface opposite the first cut, figure 9-28, go to step 7.
7. Remove the drum or rotor from the lathe, and make sure the mounting adapters fit properly.

Clean the adapters and arbor shaft, and inspect them for dirt, metal chips, rust, nicks, dents, and burrs.

8. Remount the drum or rotor, and repeat steps 2 through 6. If the two scratch cuts are still on opposite sides of the friction surface, have your tool representative check the lathe and arbor shaft for runout or damage.

Lathe Settings

Once you have mounted and centered the brake drum or rotor on the lathe, it is ready to be machined. However, in order to obtain the proper friction surface finish, you must adjust three settings: rpm, crossfeed, and depth of cut. The rpm is the speed at which the drum or rotor rotates on the lathe. The crossfeed is the distance the tool bit moves across the friction surface for each revolution of the drum or rotor. The depth of cut is the amount of metal the tool bit removes from the overall brake drum diameter, or one friction surface of the rotor. There are many brands of brake lathes on the market, but they all have some means of adjusting these three settings.

The drum or rotor rpm is usually constant throughout the machining operation; however, the crossfeed and depth of cut vary depending on whether you are making a rough cut or a finish cut. One or more rough cuts are used to remove major damage, and quickly get the drum or rotor close to finished size. The final cut is a finish cut that produces a smooth finish on the friction surface. Rough cuts are made with a faster cross-

Brake Drum and Rotor Machining

feed and a deeper depth of cut than those used for finish cuts. As a general rule, faster rpm, slower crossfeed, and shallower depth of cut, all contribute to a smoother friction surface finish.

Lathe Setting Recommendations

To recap, the rpm is the speed at which the drum or rotor rotates on the lathe. If you do not want to constantly readjust the lathe speed, you can turn both drums and rotors at 150 rpm; however, rotors end up with a better friction surface finish if they are turned at 200 rpm. The rpm should be the same for both the rough cuts and the finish cut.

The crossfeed is the distance the tool bit moves across the friction surface for each revolution of the drum or rotor. When you turn brake drums, use a crossfeed of .020″ (.50 mm) per revolution for the rough cut, and a much slower .005″ (.15 mm) per revolution for the finish cut. When you turn brake rotors, use a crossfeed of .006″ to .010″ (.15 to .25 mm) per revolution for the rough cut, and a much slower .002″ (.05 mm) per revolution for the finish cut.

The depth of cut is the amount of metal the tool bit removes from the overall brake drum diameter, or one friction surface of the rotor. When you turn drums, use up to a .015″ (.40 mm) depth of cut for the rough cut, and a much shallower .005″ (.15 mm) depth of cut for the finish cut. When you turn rotors that will run against organic or synthetic brake pads, use a .006″ (.15 mm) depth of cut for both the rough cut and the finish cut. When you turn rotors that will run against semimetallic brake pads, use a .006″ (.15 mm) depth of cut for the rough cut, and a much shallower .002″ (.05 mm) depth of cut for the finish cut. Some technicians prefer to take *only* .002″ (.05 mm) cuts on a rotor that will be used with semimetallic pads.

TURNING A BRAKE DRUM

Once you have mounted and centered the drum on the lathe, it is ready to be turned. Because every brake lathe operates differently, read the instructions for the particular lathe you are using, and familiarize yourself with the controls. The following procedure is a general guide for machining a drum. The photo sequence shows the steps required to turn a drum on one specific type of brake lathe. Always wear safety glasses when operating a brake lathe to prevent eye injury from flying metal chips.

First, adjust the lathe rpm to the proper setting. Advance the tool bit to the open edge of the drum and machine away the ridge of rust and metal that forms there. Next, move the tool bit to the closed edge of the drum and remove the ridge of rust and metal there as well. As you remove these ridges, note the point on the friction surface where the drum diameter is smallest. Position the tool bit in this location and zero the micrometer scale on the handwheel controlling depth of cut. This is your reference point for setting the depth of cut.

Move the tool bit to the closed edge of the drum (if it is not already there) and adjust the depth of cut for a rough cut as described earlier in the chapter. To a large extent, the depth of cut is determined by the condition of the drum; the greater the damage, the deeper the cut you can take, up to a maximum of .015″ (.40 mm). All drum lathe handwheels that control depth of cut are calibrated to show the amount of metal removed from the overall drum diameter. For example, if you set the handwheel on .010″ (.25 mm), the lathe really cuts .005″ (.13 mm) deep into the friction surface.

Adjust the crossfeed for a rough cut as described earlier in the chapter, and engage the mechanism. The tool bit will automatically move from the closed edge of the drum out to the open edge of the drum. Turn the drum with rough cuts as needed until all defects are removed or nearly removed. Complete the drum turning operation with a finish cut that removes the last traces of defects from the drum and provides a smooth friction surface. After the finish cut, some sources recommend you lightly sand across the friction surface with sandpaper or abrasive cloth. This removes any trace of "thread" left by the tool bit that could increase lining wear and cause a brake noise.

Once you are completely finished machining the drum, wipe the friction surface with a shop towel soaked in brake cleaner. This removes loose metal shavings and other particles that can become embedded in the brake linings and score the drum friction surface. Finally, remeasure the drum inside diameter as described earlier to make sure it is within legal limits.

Chapter Nine

TURNING A BRAKE DRUM

1. Loosen the boring bar locknut.

2. Pull the boring bar back to prevent damage to the bar or tool bit when mounting the drum.

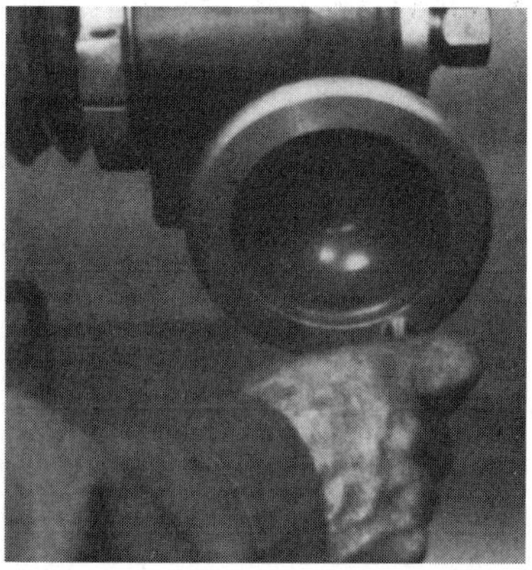

3. Crank the spindle handwheel back fully, then forward approximately five turns.

4. Crank the depth-of-cut handwheel in fully, then back out approximately two turns.

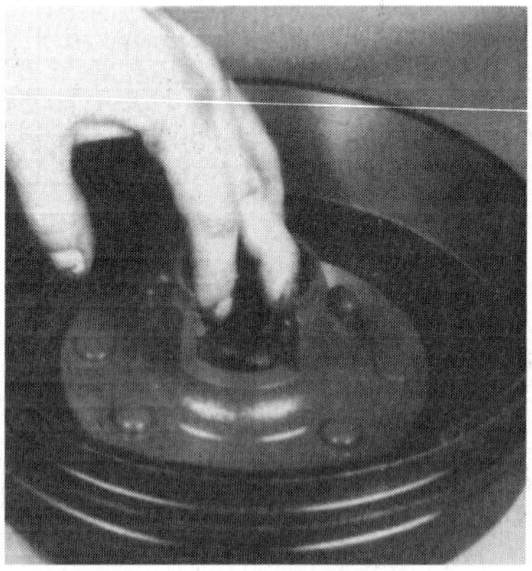

5. On fixed drums, check the bearing races for looseness in the hub. Replace the drum if a race is loose.

6. Install a fixed drum on the arbor shaft using the appropriate adapters as described earlier.

7. Install a floating drum on the arbor shaft using the appropriate adapters as described earlier.

8. Tighten the arbor shaft nut, but do not overtighten it.

9. Install the rubber silencer strap on the drum.

Brake Drum and Rotor Machining

TURNING A BRAKE DRUM

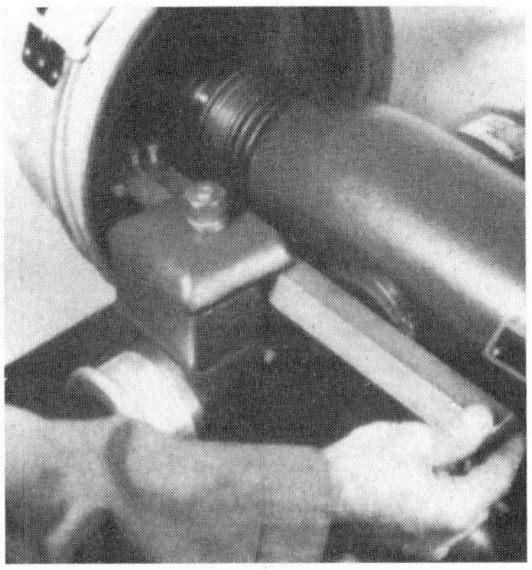

10. Slide the boring bar and pivot the bar holder until the tool bit contacts the friction surface just beyond the rust ridge.

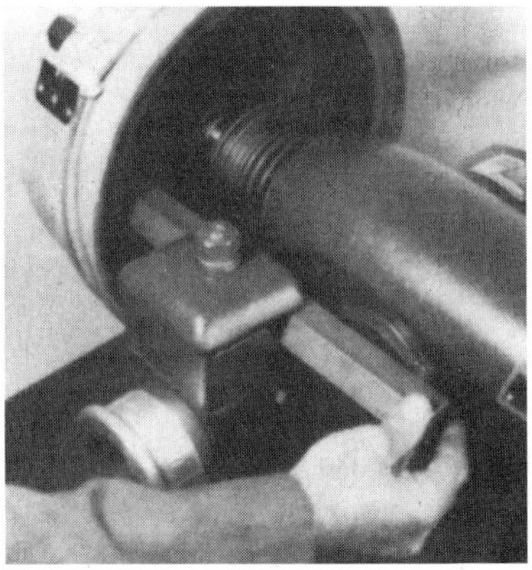

11. Keeping the tool bit in contact with the friction surface, bottom the boring bar in the drum.

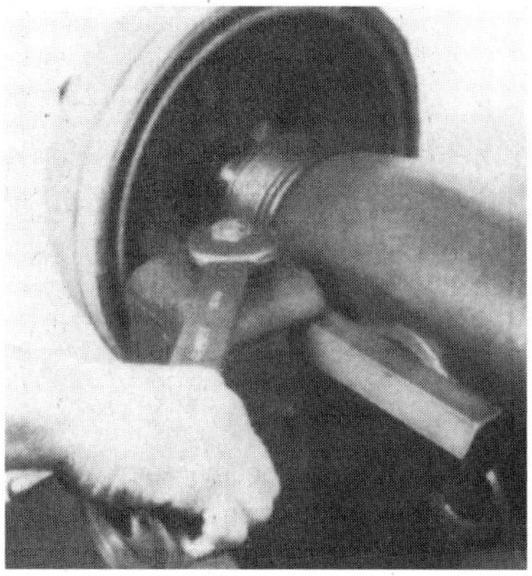

12. Tighten the boring bar locknut.

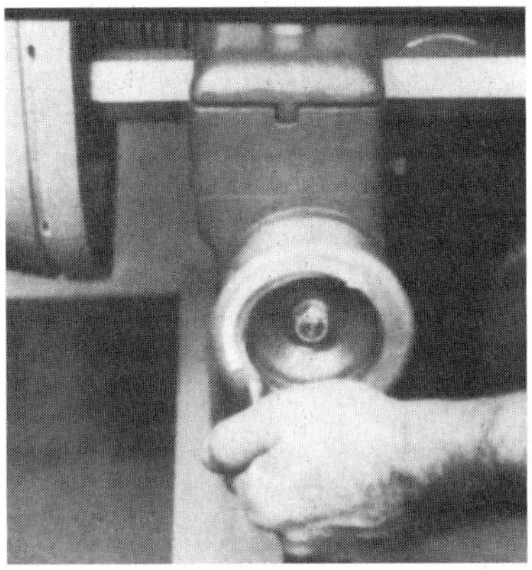

13. Crank the depth-of-cut handwheel one turn inward to move the tool bit away from the friction surface.

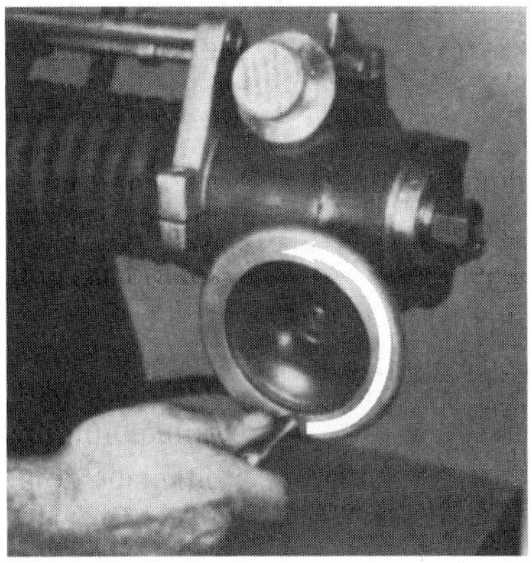

14. Crank the spindle (drum) outward . . .

15. . . . until the tool bit is ⅛ inch (3 mm) away from the open edge of the drum.

16. Set the crossfeed shutoff bushing against its left stop and tighten the knurled lock knob.

17. Make sure the drive belt is in the proper pulley for the correct turning rpm.

18. Start the lathe, and make a pair of scratch cuts to check for drum runout and centering as described earlier.

Chapter Nine

TURNING A BRAKE DRUM

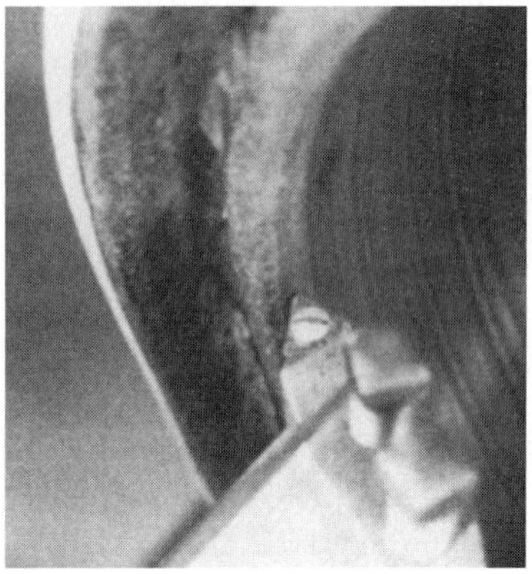

19. Position the spindle so the tool bit is centered over the rust ridge.

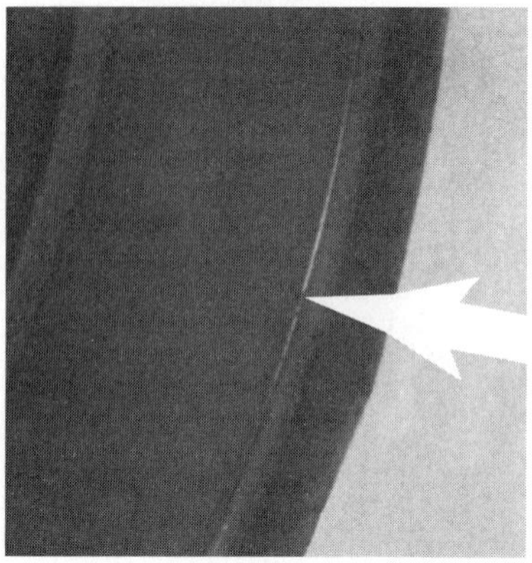

20. Advance the tool bit toward the rust ridge until very light contact is made.

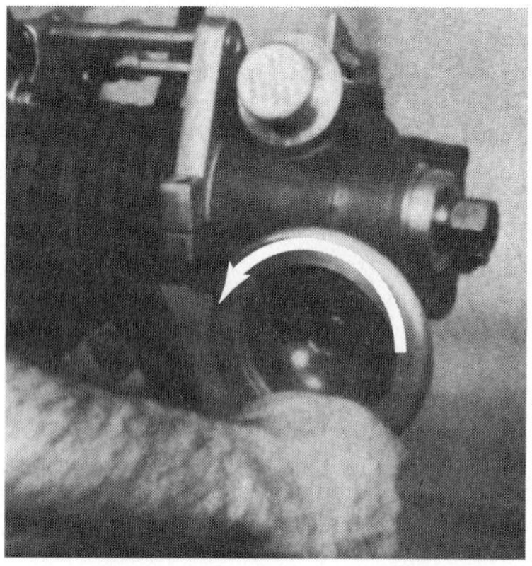

21. Crank the spindle handwheel until the edge of the drum clears the tool bit.

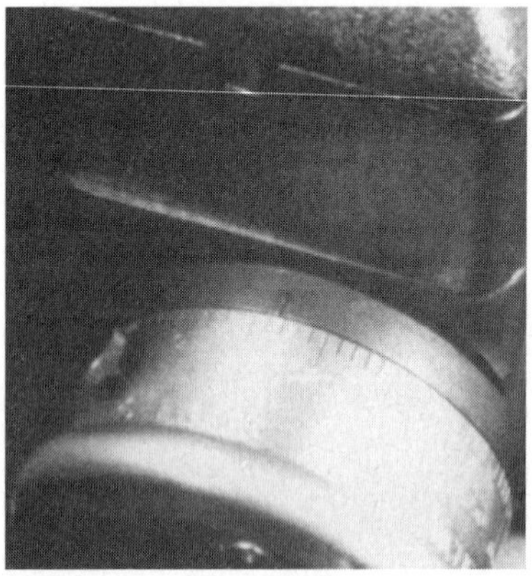

22. Turn the depth-of-cut handwheel counterclockwise about .005″ (2 ½ graduations).

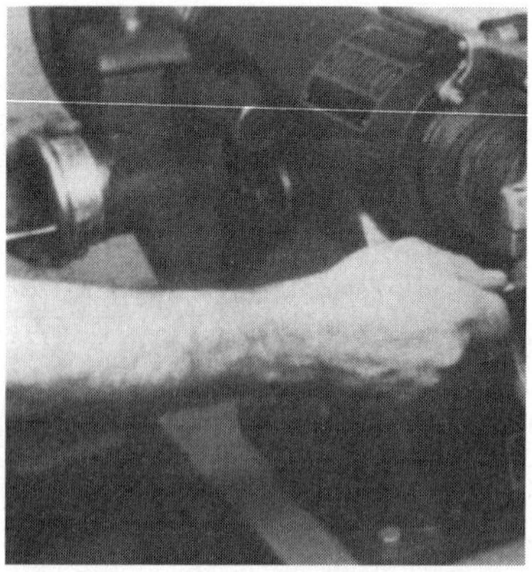

23. Hold the depth-of-cut handwheel stationary, and crank the spindle handwheel to advance the drum . . .

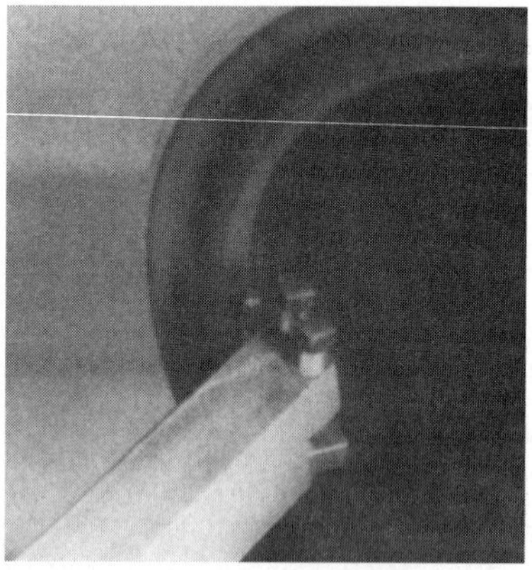

24. . . . and machine away a portion of the rust ridge.

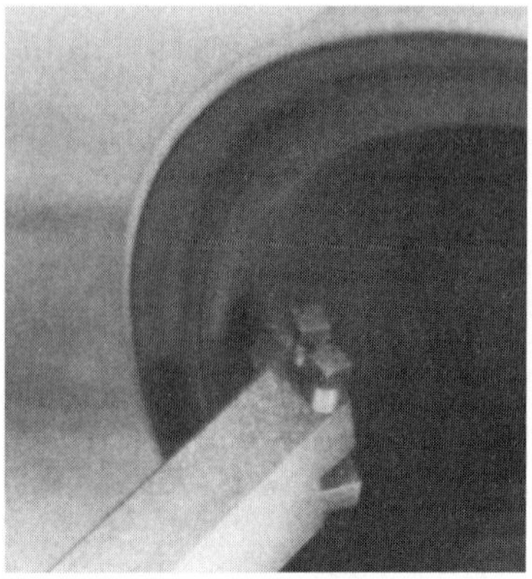

25. Repeat steps 20 through 23 until the ridge is removed and the tool bit contacts the worn portion of the friction surface.

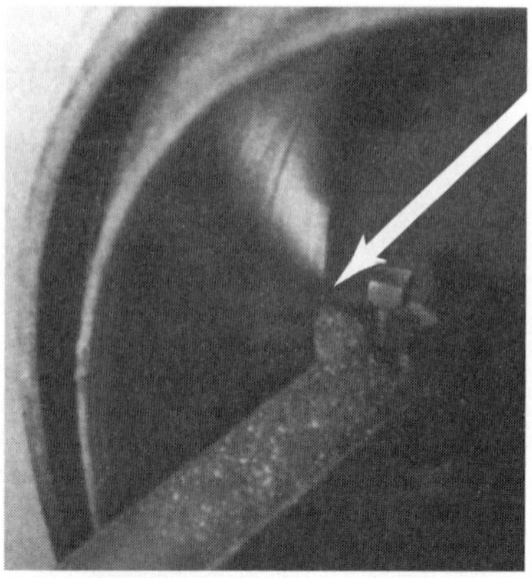

26. Advance the tool bit to the unworn shoulder at the closed edge of the drum . . .

27. . . . adjusting the depth-of-cut handwheel as needed to maintain light contact with the friction surface.

Brake Drum and Rotor Machining

TURNING A BRAKE DRUM

28. Advance the tool bit slowly by hand to machine away the shoulder of unworn metal at the closed edge of the drum.

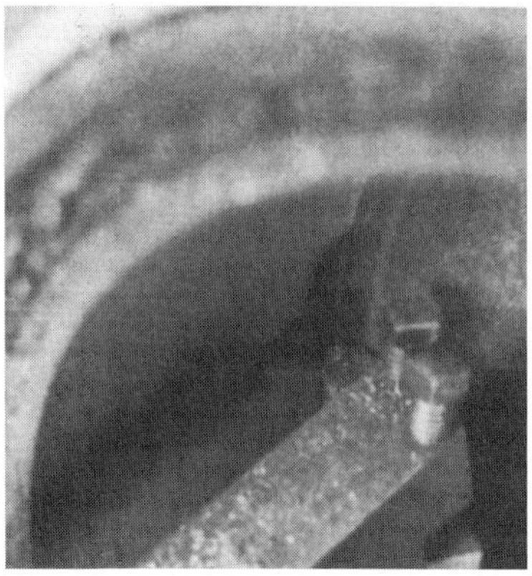

29. The bit will make a scraping noise when it contacts the bottom of the drum.

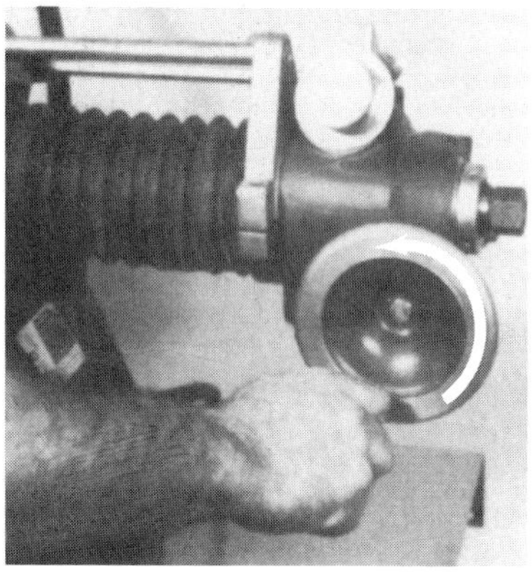

30. Crank the spindle handwheel counterclockwise until the scraping sound stops.

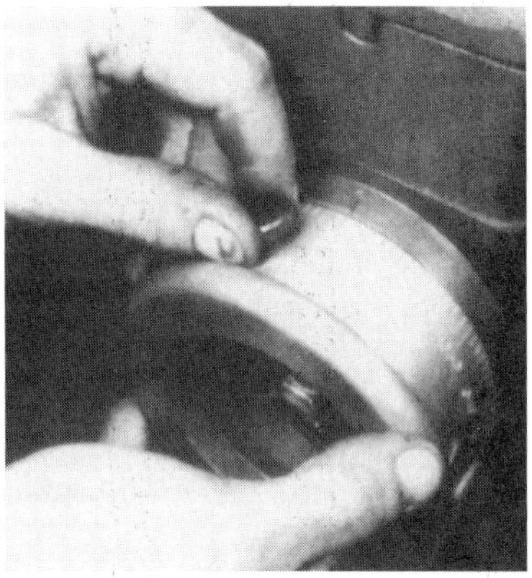

31. Zero the micrometer dial of the depth-of-cut handwheel, then tighten the dial lockscrew.

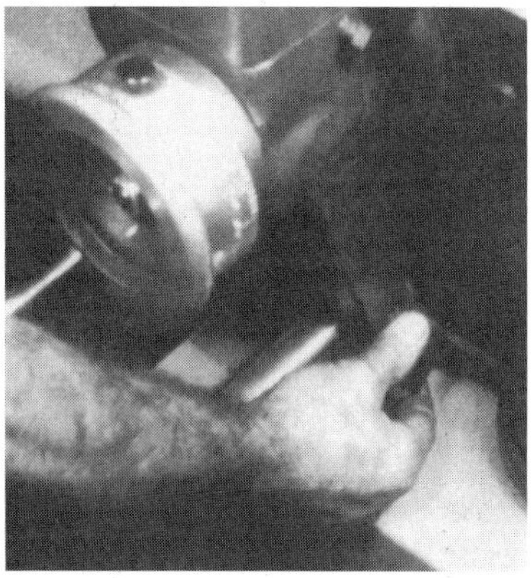

32. Rotate the depth-of-cut handwheel to advance the tool bit into the drum the desired amount; tighten the handwheel lock.

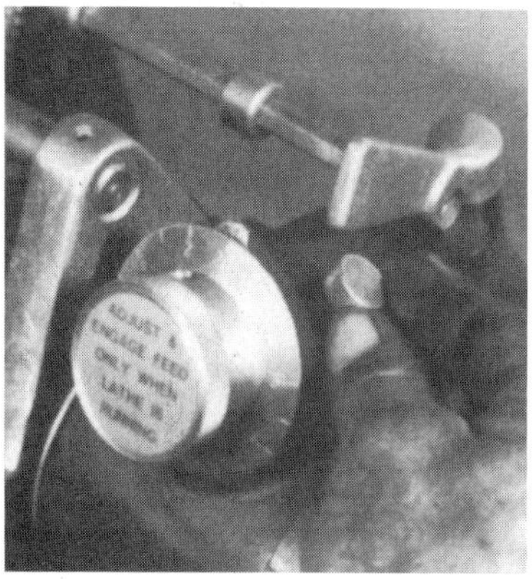

33. Loosen the crossfeed lockscrew.

34. Set the crossfeed control to the desired speed, and tighten the lockscrew.

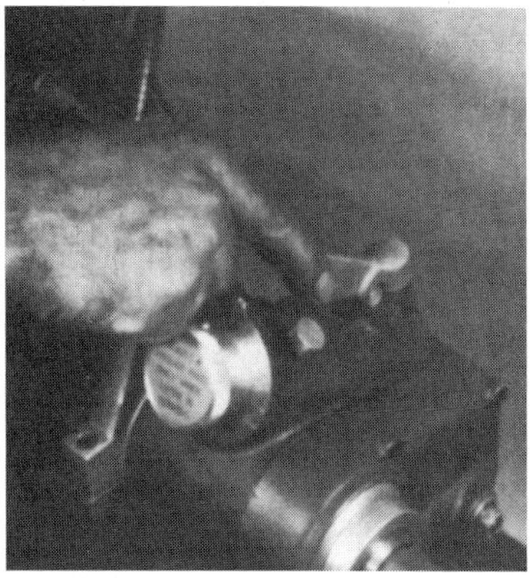

35. Engage the crossfeed mechanism. The shutoff bushing will turn off the lathe when the tool bit clears the drum.

36. Inspect the drum; repeat steps 29 through 31, making rough and finish cuts, until the friction surface is smooth.

ROTOR TURNING PROCEDURES

Two types of lathes are available for turning rotors, off-vehicle freestanding lathes that require the rotors be removed from the vehicle, and on-vehicle lathes that turn the rotors while they are still mounted on the vehicle. The following sections provide step-by-step procedures for using both types.

Virtually all modern brake lathes have two tool bits that straddle the rotor and refinish both friction surfaces at the same time. This makes the job go faster, and produces a better friction surface finish because distortion is reduced when pressure is applied equally to both sides of the rotor. Because two-bit lathes (no pun intended) are the most common type, they are the only kind dealt with below.

TURNING A BRAKE ROTOR OFF THE VEHICLE

Once you have mounted and centered the rotor on the brake lathe as described earlier, the rotor is ready to be turned. Because every lathe operates differently, read the instructions for the particular unit you are using, and familiarize yourself with the controls. The following procedure is a general guide for turning a rotor. The photo sequence shows the steps required to turn a rotor using one specific type of brake lathe. Always wear safety glasses when operating a brake lathe to prevent eye injury from flying metal chips.

First, adjust the lathe rpm to the proper setting. Advance the tool bit to the outer edge of the rotor and machine away the ridge of rust and metal that forms there, then move the tool bit to the inner edge of the friction surface and remove the ridge of rust and metal there as well.

Position the tool bits at approximately the center of the rotor, and advance each bit until it lightly contacts the rotor surface. Zero the micrometer scales on the handwheels controlling depth of cut. These are your reference points for setting the depth of cut. Move the tool bits to the inner edge of the rotor, and turn the handwheels to set the depth of cut on both bits for a rough cut as described earlier in the chapter. To a large extent, the depth of cut is determined by the condition of the rotor; the greater the damage, the deeper the cuts you can take, up to a maximum of .006" (.015 mm) on each side. All rotor lathe handwheels that control depth of cut are calibrated to show the amount of metal removed from the friction surface. If you set each handwheel at .005" (.13 mm), the lathe will cut a total of .010" (.25 mm) from the thickness of the rotor.

Adjust the crossfeed for a rough cut as described earlier in the chapter, and engage the mechanism. The tool bit will automatically move from the inner edge of the rotor to the outer edge. Turn the rotor with rough cuts as needed until all defects are removed or nearly removed. Finish turning the rotor with a finish cut that removes the last traces of defects from the rotor, and provides a friction surface finish compatible with the type of brake lining material used. Many manufacturers recommend that after the finish cut you should apply a nondirectional finish to the friction surfaces with a resurfacing attachment as described later in the chapter.

Once you are completely finished machining a rotor, wipe the friction surfaces clean with a shop towel soaked in brake cleaner. This removes loose metal shavings that could become embedded in the brake linings and score the rotor friction surface. Remeasure the rotor thickness as described earlier in the chapter to make sure it is within legal limits.

Brake Drum and Rotor Machining

TURNING A BRAKE ROTOR OFF THE VEHICLE

1. If the lathe is designed to machine both drums and rotors, install the saddle mount cutting tool assembly.

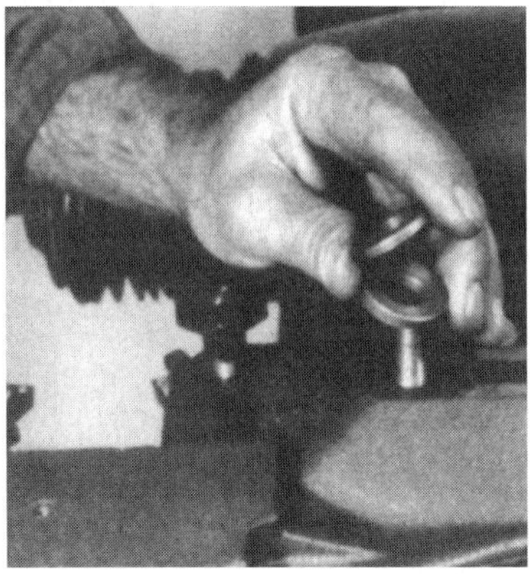

2. Install the washers over the boring bar clamp stud with the convex and concave sides facing one another.

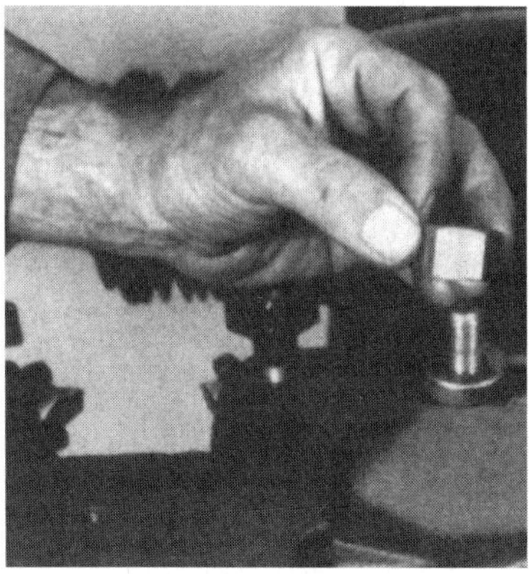

3. Install the locknut on the boring bar clamp stud, but do not tighten it completely at this time.

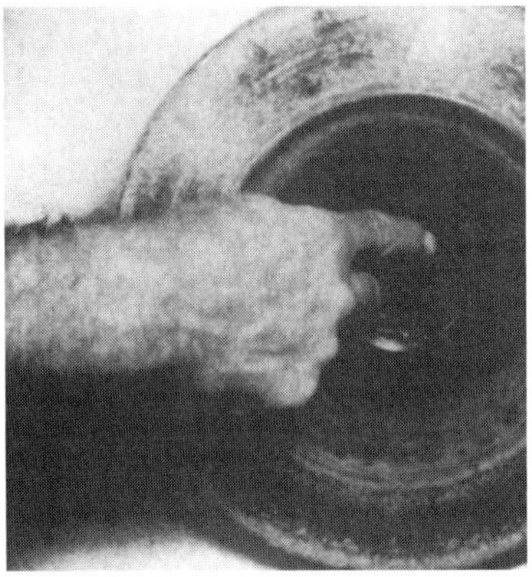

4. On fixed rotors, check the bearing races for looseness in the hub. Replace the rotor if a race is loose.

5. Install a fixed drum on the arbor shaft using the appropriate adapters as described earlier.

6. Install a floating drum on the arbor shaft using the appropriate adapters as described earlier.

7. Tighten the arbor shaft nut, but do not overtighten it.

8. Install a rubber silencing band on vented rotors.

9. Install a damper assembly on rotors where a rubber silencing band will not work.

TURNING A BRAKE ROTOR OFF THE VEHICLE

10. Swing the cutting tool assembly into position.

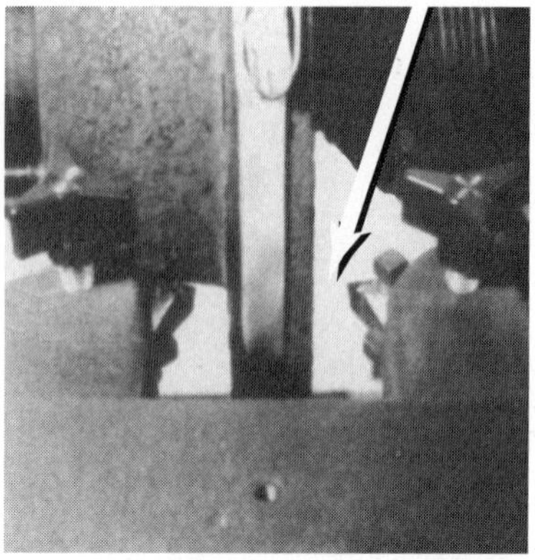

11. Position the tool bits ½ inch in from the outer edge of the rotor, and equal distances from the friction surfaces.

12. Tighten the locknut on the boring bar clamp stud.

13. Make sure the drive belt is in the proper pulley for the correct turning rpm.

14. Install the safety shield to stop flying metal chips.

15. Start the lathe, and make a pair of scratch cuts to check for rotor runout and centering as described earlier.

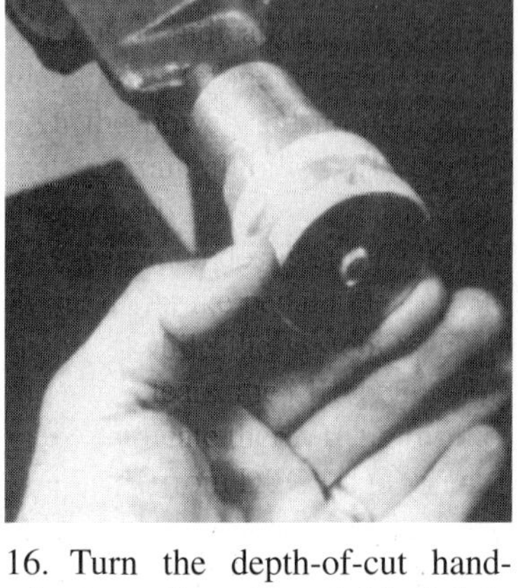

16. Turn the depth-of-cut handwheels until each tool bit lightly contacts the rotor friction surface.

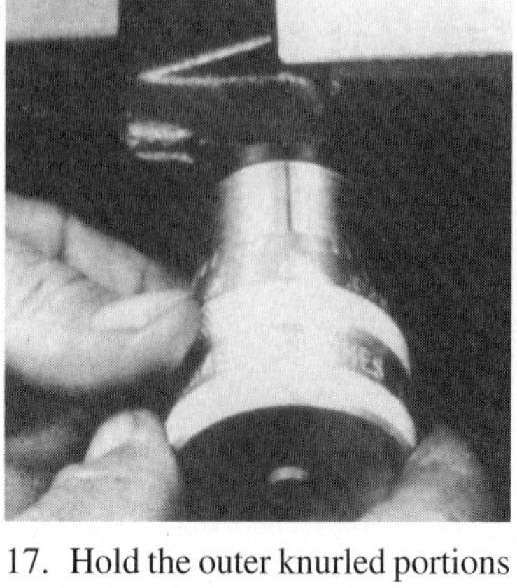

17. Hold the outer knurled portions of the handwheels stationary, and zero the depth-of-cut collars.

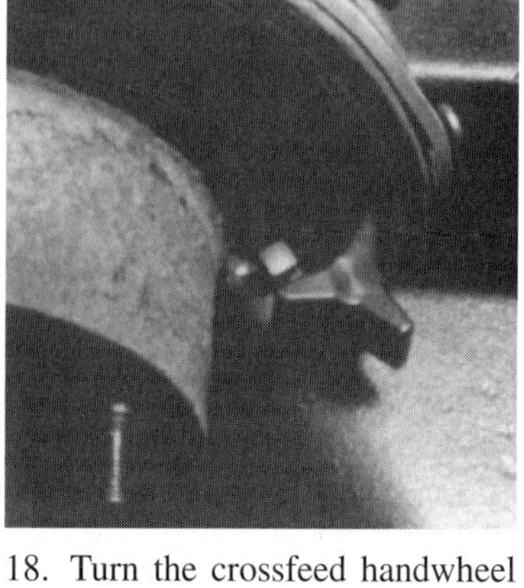

18. Turn the crossfeed handwheel until the tool bit on the outer face of the rotor is at the inside edge of the friction surface.

Brake Drum and Rotor Machining

TURNING A BRAKE ROTOR OFF THE VEHICLE

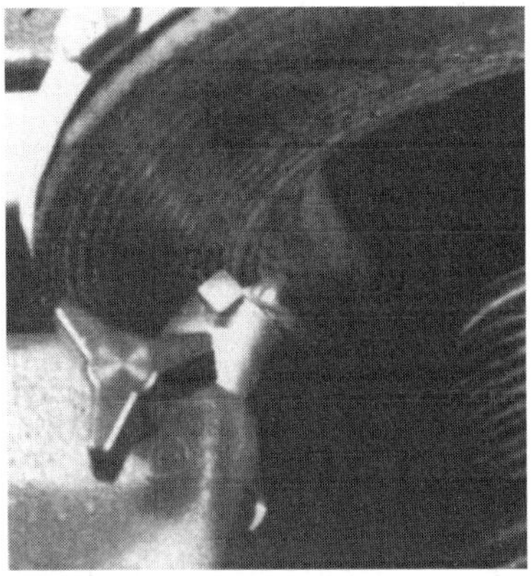

19. The tool bit on the inner friction surface will be off the friction surface entirely.

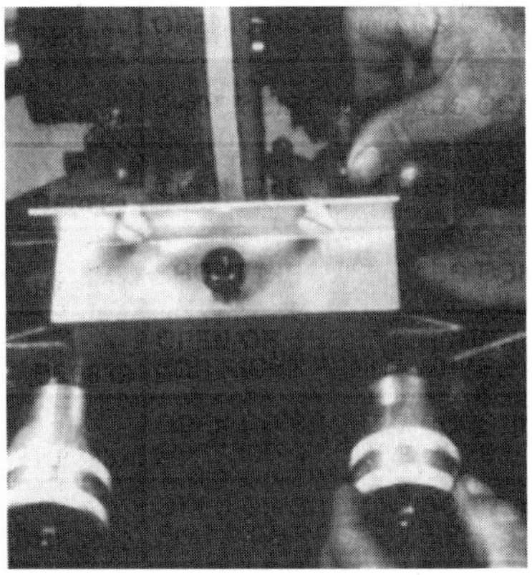

20. Rotate the depth-of-cut handwheels to advance the tool bits into the rotor the desired amount; tighten the handwheel locks.

21. Engage the crossfeed mechanism by moving the gearbox control to the "slow" position.

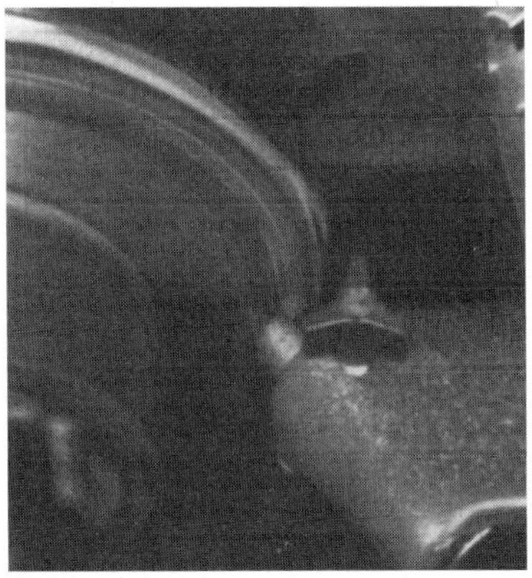

22. Once the crossfeed is engaged, the tool bits will advance to the outer edge of the rotor.

23. When the tool bits clear the rotor, disengage the crossfeed by moving the gearbox lever to the "off" position.

24. Stop the lathe and inspect both the outer...

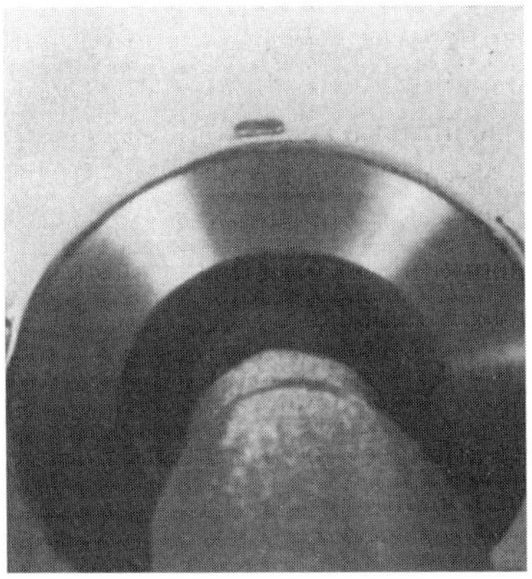

25. ...and the inner friction surfaces of the rotor.

26. Repeat steps 18 through 25, making rough and finish cuts, until both friction surfaces are smooth.

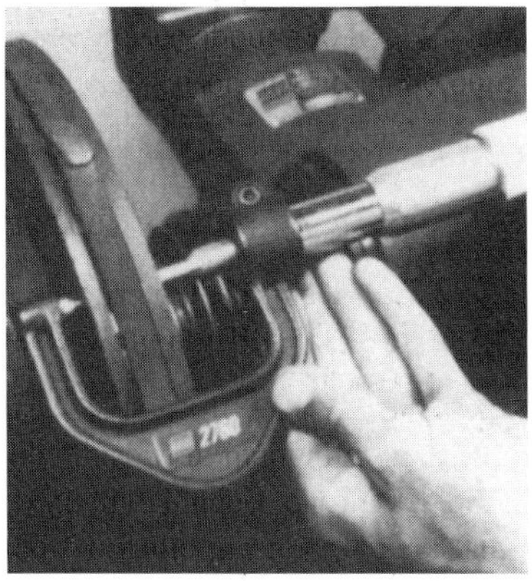

27. Measure the rotor thickness to make sure it is within legal limits.

TURNING A BRAKE ROTOR ON THE VEHICLE

The on-vehicle lathe machines rotors while they are still on the vehicle. One type of on-vehicle lathe bolts in place of the brake caliper and uses the vehicle powertrain to turn the rotor. Because the spindle and wheel bearings serve as the arbor shaft for the lathe, it is very important that the wheel bearings be in good condition and properly adjusted (where possible).

The latest style of on-vehicle lathe attaches to the hub of the vehicle and uses an electric motor and gear reduction to turn the rotor. The photo sequence details the procedure for turning a rotor using this type of on-vehicle lathe. Every lathe operates differently, however, so read the instructions for the unit you are using, and familiarize yourself with its controls.

TURNING A BRAKE ROTOR ON THE VEHICLE

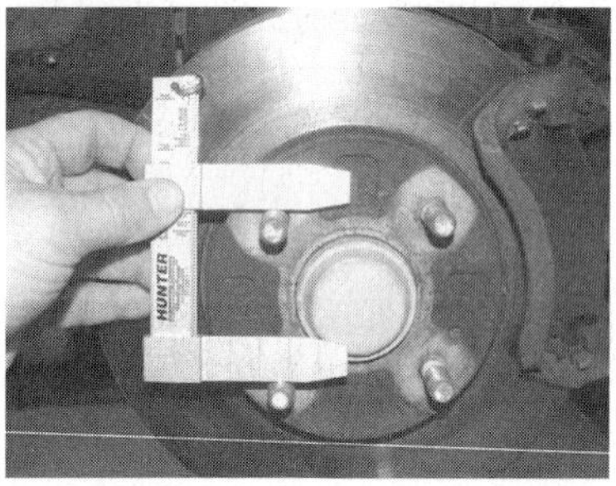

1. After removing the wheel and caliper, use the gauge to measure the wheel studs spacing. This reads which adapter ring to use.

2. Select the proper adapter and install it using about 30 ft-lb torque. Do *not* use an impact gun.

3. Install the universal adapter to the adapter ring.

4. Turn the handwheel to back the twin cutters away from the rotor before attaching the lathe.

5. Align the lathe flange with the universal adapter and thread the flange in place.

6. Tighten the lathe flange and compensator to the adapter.

7. Follow the lathe manufacturer's instructions to compensate the lathe runout. This usually involves a special mount and a dial indicator.

8. Adjust the compensator until the lathe runout is less than .002".

9. Set the cutting bits in the same way as on a bench lathe. Cut off the inner and outer lip.

Brake Drum and Rotor Machining

TURNING A BRAKE ROTOR ON THE VEHICLE

10. Move the cutters to the inside of the rotor. Set the depth of cut, in this case .1 mm, and make the first cut.

11. If needed, make a second cut. This rotor shows a thickness variation (low spot) on the outer edge and will need a second cut.

12. After machining the left rotor, remove the lathe and set it up on the right side of the vehicle.

13. The lathe setup on the right side is the same as the left except that the lathe is mounted upside down. Compensation is performed on the bottom rather than the top.

RESURFACING A BRAKE ROTOR

If the brake lathe tool bits are sharp, and you follow the recommended rpm, crossfeed, and depth-of-cut settings when turning a rotor, you will generally get an acceptable surface finish. However, many manufacturers recommend that the rotor friction surface also be resurfaced after turning to give it a nondirectional finish. This is especially important when semimetallic brake pads are fitted. Brake rotors are resurfaced with a lathe attachment that applies a spinning abrasive disc against the friction surfaces. You should resurface a brake rotor immediately after it has been turned, while it is still mounted and centered on the brake lathe.

To resurface a rotor, use the special attachment, figure 9-29, and install an abrasive disc of the proper grit on the disc holder. For organic or synthetic brake pads, use 50- to 80-grit abrasive paper. For semimetallic brake pads, 120-grit paper will provide the smoother surface needed for proper break-in.

Start the lathe, and hold the abrasive disc against the rotor for 15 seconds, then stop the lathe and inspect the rotor friction surface for a good crosshatch pattern. Repeat this process as necessary.

Figure 9-29. A brake rotor resurfacing attachment.

10
Parking Brake Service

OBJECTIVES

Upon completion and review of this chapter, you will be able to:

- Perform the brake pedal travel test for disc and drum brakes.
- Perform the parking brake control test.
- Perform the parking brake release test.
- Perform the parking brake performance test.
- Adjust parking brake shoes.
- Adjust the parking brake cables of disc and drum parking brakes.
- Replace parking brake cables.
- Service parking brake shoes and pads.
- Diagnose and repair parking brake release systems.

INTRODUCTION

The parking brakes keep the vehicle from rolling when it is parked, and provide a limited amount of stopping power if there is a failure in the service brake hydraulic system. Three main types of parking brakes are currently used on automobiles and light trucks: integral drum parking brakes that apply the shoes of the rear drum service brakes, auxiliary drum parking brakes that apply a set of small brake shoes against drums inside the rear brake rotors, and caliper-actuated disc parking brakes that use a mechanical linkage to apply the service brake pads of the brake calipers.

Parking brake service consists of three basic operations: testing the parking brake system, adjusting the parking brake linkage, and replacing the parking brake cables. In addition to these basic jobs, auxiliary drum parking brakes require periodic replacement of the parking brake shoes, and the vacuum parking brake release mechanism on some cars may require diagnosis and repair.

PARKING BRAKE TESTING

Parking brake problems, like almost all automotive problems, are easiest to diagnose if you approach them in an organized way. You can isolate a problem in the parking brake system using a four-step test procedure. First, perform a brake pedal travel test to confirm that the parking brake is the source of the problem. Second, perform a parking brake control test to determine if the parking brake adjustment is correct. Third, perform a release test to make sure the parking brake is not causing brake drag. And finally, do a performance test to find out if the parking brake has sufficient holding power.

Brake Pedal Travel Test—Drum Brakes

The integral drum parking brakes used on most cars apply the shoes of the rear drum service brakes. As a result, the adjustment of the service brakes affects the performance of the parking brake as well. If there is excessive lining-to-drum clearance, the parking brake linkage may not have sufficient travel to take up the slack and still apply the brake with enough force to hold the car in place.

To test the adjustment of the service brakes, apply the brake pedal, figure 10-1, and note the amount of travel. If the travel is excessive, you must adjust or repair the service brakes before you adjust the parking brakes. Refer to Chapter 7 for complete drum brake diagnosis and service procedures.

On many Asian imports, the rear brake shoe self-adjusters may be actuated by the parking brake strut or lever assembly, figure 10-2. These vehicles depend on the regular use of the parking brake to maintain proper shoe-to-drum clearance in the rear brakes. If the vehicle is equipped with an automatic transmission, the chances are that the parking brake is never used, resulting in excessive rear shoe clearance, a low brake pedal, and no parking brake operation. Follow this procedure to correct the situation:

1. Park the vehicle in a quiet area so that the clicking of the rear adjusters can be heard during this procedure.
2. With the engine off and the brake pedal not depressed, hold the parking brake lever release button down and pump the lever up and down.
3. One or two "clicks" will be heard each time the lever is pulled. This is the result of the adjuster arm ratcheting on the adjuster starwheel.
4. Repeat steps 2 and 3 until the clicking stops. The brake shoe clearance is now correct.
5. If there is no "clicking" sound and the brake clearance does not improve, the adjusters are frozen and must be repaired.

Figure 10-1. The brake pedal must be high and firm before the parking brakes can be adjusted.

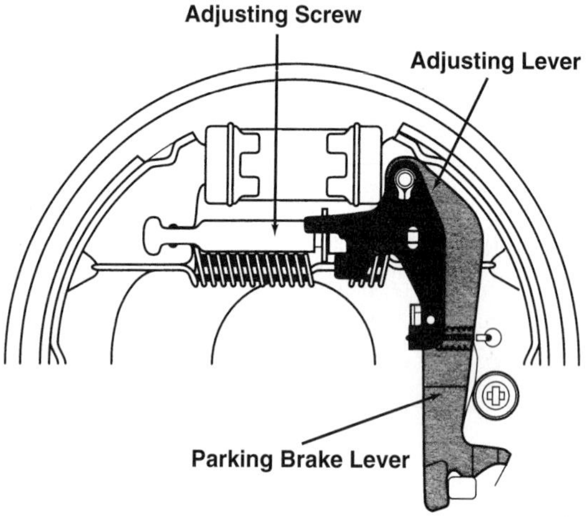

Figure 10-2. This Toyota drum brake adjuster is actuated by the parking brake lever. (Courtesy of Toyota Motor Sales U.S.A., Inc.)

Brake Pedal Travel Test—Disc Brakes

A low brake pedal on a vehicle with a caliper-actuated disc parking brake also indicates a problem in the service brake system. However, if the low pedal is accompanied by excessive travel of the parking brake control, the problem is most likely caused by a defective adjuster in one or both of the brake calipers that function as the parking brake.

In order to apply the caliper for parking brake service, rear disc brakes have mechanical adjusters built into their caliper pistons. If these adjusters fail to operate properly as the brake pads wear, the piston will not adjust outward, causing the symptoms described above. To determine if this is the problem, follow the procedures described in the next two sections. In some cases, you may be able to free the adjuster and reestablish the proper lining-to-rotor clearance; however, most of the time you will have to rebuild the caliper and repair or replace the piston/adjuster assembly.

Screw-actuated Rear Disc Parking Brake

The screw-type actuators used on some rear calipers (General Motors and others) with disc parking brakes are known for problems with frozen adjusters. On these vehicles, it is extremely important that the car

Parking Brake Service

owner apply the parking brake regularly. This keeps the actuator screw threads clean so the automatic adjusting mechanism in the piston will work properly. If both the service brake pedal and parking brake control have excessive travel on one of these cars, attempt to adjust the caliper pistons.

1. Pull and hold the parking brake pedal release handle to prevent the pedal mechanism from locking.
2. Repeatedly apply the parking brake pedal.
3. If the travel of both the service brake pedal and the parking brake control does not decrease, the adjuster is frozen and you must rebuild the caliper and replace the piston/adjuster assembly as described in Chapter 8.

NOTE: If the brake pads are worn out, replace the pads before working on the parking brake.

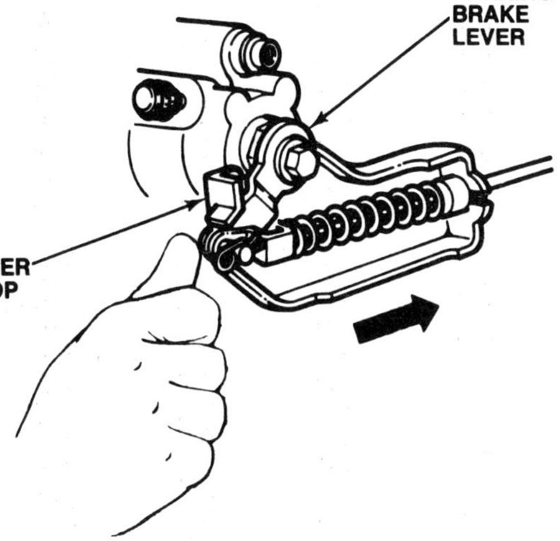

Ball-and-ramp-actuated Rear Disc Parking Brake

The ball-and-ramp- or cam-and-pin-actuated rear calipers (Ford Motor Company and others) with disc parking brakes are less subject to adjuster problems than the screw-type design, but they do have occasional failures. To determine if the piston in this type of rear caliper is properly adjusted, push the parking brake lever in the apply direction under firm hand pressure, figure 10-3. If the lever moves more than 20 degrees, attempt to adjust the caliper pistons.

1. With the engine idling, apply the brake pedal 40 times with approximately 15 lb (67 N) of force; allow one second between each pedal application.
2. With the engine not running, apply the pedal 30 times with approximately 90 lb (400 N) of force; allow one second between each pedal application.
3. If the travel of both the service brake pedal and the parking brake control does not decrease, the adjuster is frozen and you must rebuild the caliper and replace the piston/adjuster assembly as described in Chapter 8.

NOTE: If the brake pads are worn or there is excessive clearance between the pad and rotor with the pedal released, correct this first. Replace the pads and set the initial clearance as described in Chapter 8. The adjusters will not work correctly if the initial clearance is too wide.

Figure 10-3. Push the parking brake lever forward to check the piston adjustment in a rear brake caliper.

Other Rear Disc Parking Brake Adjusters

Many import vehicles use a screw-type adjuster to set the initial pad-to-disc clearance on caliper-actuated parking brakes. As noted above, the proper operation of the adjuster depends on having the proper clearance. If the pads do not firmly contact the rotor surface, the adjusters will not function. To set the initial adjustment of this type of caliper:

1. After installing the new pads, locate the adjuster screw or bolt. It may be located under a plug or cover, figure 10-4.
2. Turn the adjuster bolt until the pads lightly touch the rotor.
3. Back off the adjuster one-third to one-half of a turn, figure 10-5.
4. Replace the adjuster concealment plug.

Parking Brake Control Test

If the service brake pedal is high and firm, the next step is to apply the parking brake control, figure 10-6, and check its travel. The parking brake should be fully applied when the control has moved through one- to two-thirds of its available travel. Some manufacturers specify that the brake should be fully applied when the parking brake control ratchet has made a certain number of clicks, usually five to seven.

If the control travels more than the specified amount, the parking brake adjustment is too loose. A loose adjustment can leave the parking brake linkage with insufficient travel to take up the slack in the linkage and still apply the brake with enough force to hold the vehicle in place. If the control travels less than the

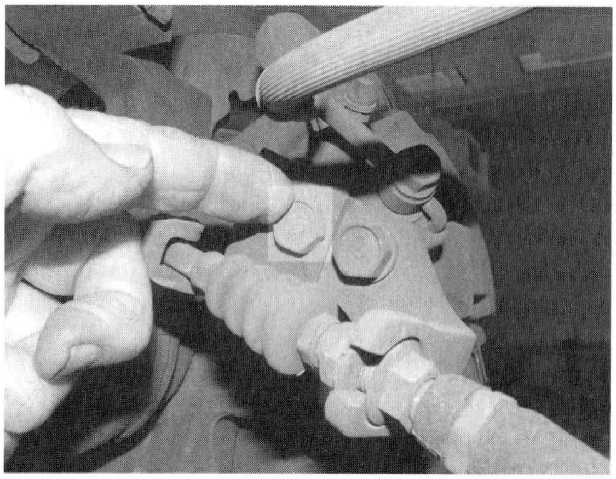

Figure 10-4. On this rear caliper with integral parking brake, the adjuster is under this plug.

Figure 10-5. The adjusting screw is turned with a hex wrench. After the initial adjustment, the parking brake is self-adjusting.

Figure 10-6. Apply the parking brake control to check the linkage adjustment.

specified amount, the parking brake adjustment is too tight. A tight adjustment may cause the brake shoes or pads to drag against the drum or rotor. This creates heat that can lead to brake fade, rapid wear of the brake linings, and distortion of the drum or rotor. Adjust the parking brakes if the control requires more or less movement than specified to apply the brakes.

Release Test

If both the service brake pedal and parking brake control have acceptable travel, raise and support the vehicle so the wheels with the parking brakes hang free. With the parking brake control fully released, rotate the wheels by hand and check for drag, figure 10-7. If either brake drags, check for sticking or frozen parking brake cables, or a problem in the service brake friction assembly.

Inspect parking brake cables for broken strands along the sections of cable that are visible. Then, have an assistant operate the parking brake control while you observe that the cables move freely in and out of their housings. If any cable has broken strands or does not move freely, replace it as described later in the chapter.

On vehicles with dual-servo brakes, a slightly overtightened parking brake will sometimes cause the brakes to drag in one direction but not the other. This occurs because the overtightened adjustment prevents the shoe with the weaker return spring from fully returning against the anchor when the service brakes are released.

As with any disc brake, a small amount of drag is considered normal in a rear brake caliper. However, if there is excessive drag on vehicles with rear disc parking brakes, make sure the parking brake levers on both rear calipers are fully returned. If the calipers are fitted with external lever stops, the levers should contact the stops when the parking brake control is released. If the levers are not fully returned or against their stops, adjust the parking brake. If adjusting the parking brake does not eliminate the drag, the caliper has a sticking piston, or the caliper floating or sliding surfaces are in need of lubrication. If there is excessive drag in a rear brake caliper, locate and repair the problem as described in Chapter 8.

Performance Test

If both the service brake pedal and parking brake control have acceptable travel, and the wheels with the parking brakes turn freely, the final test is to check the parking brake performance. Stop the vehicle facing uphill on a grade of approximately 20 percent, then firmly apply the parking brake and release the service brakes. The vehicle should hold its position and not

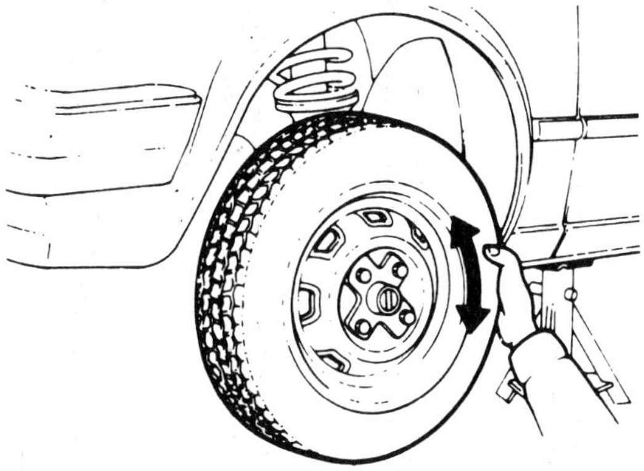

Parking Brake Service

Figure 10-7. There should be no drag at the wheels with the parking brake control released.

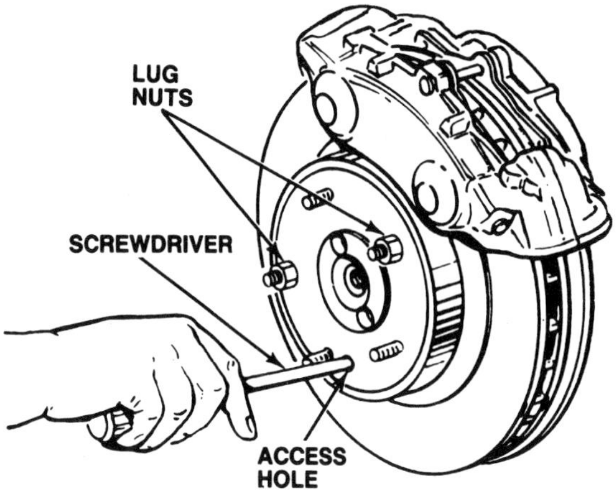

Figure 10-8. Auxiliary drum parking brake shoes are adjusted through an access hole in the rotor/drum.

creep or roll. Repeat the test with the vehicle facing downhill.

If the vehicle fails the performance test, it usually indicates a problem in the service brake friction assembly. A worn out service brake, or one with contaminated linings, cannot generate enough friction for the parking brake to work properly. However, some parking brakes, particularly caliper-actuated disc designs, have marginal holding power unless a great deal of force is applied to the parking brake control. Some drivers who complain of parking brake problems may simply be unable to apply the parking brake control hard enough. To a certain extent, you must depend on experience to help identify when a parking brake has sufficient braking power, and when it does not.

PARKING BRAKE ADJUSTMENT

Most vehicle manufacturers recommend that the parking brake be tested and adjusted (if necessary) at regular intervals, generally twice a year or every 7500 miles (12,000 km). More frequent adjustment may be required if the vehicle is used in severe service that involves extensive use of the parking brake. Naturally, the parking brake must also be adjusted whenever a cable is replaced, or the wheel brakes that contain the parking brakes are serviced.

Parking brake adjustment involves two basic procedures. The first, parking brake shoe adjustment, is required only on cars that have auxiliary drum parking brakes. The second procedure, cable adjustment, is required on all parking brake systems, both disc and drum.

PARKING BRAKE SHOE ADJUSTMENT

As with any drum brake, the shoes in auxiliary drum parking brakes must be adjusted periodically to maintain the proper lining-to-drum clearance. On a few imported cars, this adjustment is made by adjusting the parking brake cables. However, most of these brakes use manual starwheel adjusters to set the lining-to-drum clearance independent of the cable adjustment.

On some vehicles, you reach the adjuster through an access hole in the outer face of the rotor/drum, figure 10-8. However, on some imported cars, one of the wheel lug bolt holes serves as the access hole; this allows adjustment with the wheel installed. Because access to the adjusters on auxiliary drum parking brakes is relatively easy, a standard screwdriver is often used in place of a brake spoon to rotate the starwheel.

All auxiliary drum parking brake shoes are adjusted the same way, and the procedure is essentially the same as for a drum service brake with a manual starwheel adjuster. To adjust an auxiliary drum parking brake:

1. Shift the transmission into neutral, and release the parking brake control.
2. Raise and properly support the vehicle so the wheels to be adjusted hang free.
3. If the brake is adjusted through an access hole in the outer face of the rotor/drum, remove the wheel and reinstall two of the lug nuts to retain the rotor/drum securely in place. If the brake is adjusted through a lug bolt hole, remove one of the lug bolts.
4. Loosen the parking brake cable adjustment until there is slack in the cables.
5. Turn the rotor/drum or wheel until the access hole aligns with the starwheel inside the friction assembly.
6. Insert a standard screwdriver through the access hole and use a lever action to rotate the starwheel

and reduce the lining-to-drum clearance. The direction of rotation used to tighten or loosen the adjustment varies from car to car, and usually from one side of the vehicle to the other. As you rotate the starwheel, the spring holding it in position should snap from one tooth to the next and cause a clicking sound.

7. Tighten the adjuster until there is heavy drag at the wheel or the brake locks (it will be necessary to remove the screwdriver to check this), then lever the starwheel in the opposite direction to increase the lining-to-drum clearance. Loosen the adjustment the number of clicks specified by the vehicle manufacturer, typically five to seven, or until the wheel just turns free.

PARKING BRAKE CABLE ADJUSTMENT

Whenever the parking brake is applied, there is constant tension on the cables that connect the parking brake control to the friction assemblies. Regular use of the parking brake stretches the cables, and increases the amount of parking brake control travel required to apply the parking brake. When the amount of travel becomes too great, the cable adjustment is tightened to shorten the working length of the cables and reduce parking brake control travel to the proper amount.

The service brakes must be in good operating condition before you can adjust the parking brake cables. If the brake pedal travel tests described earlier revealed a low brake pedal, adjust or repair the drum service brakes as described in Chapter 7, or the disc service brakes as described in Chapter 8, before you adjust the parking brake cables.

In addition to the reasons already given, you must adjust the service brakes before the parking brakes because certain cars have a parking brake linkage with a separate cable for each friction assembly, figure 10-9. No equalizer is used in this system, and the parking brake control moves each cable the same amount. If the wheel brakes do not have similar lining-to-drum clearance, the more loosely adjusted brake will not grab as hard when the parking brake is applied, and the tighter brake may drag when the parking brake is released.

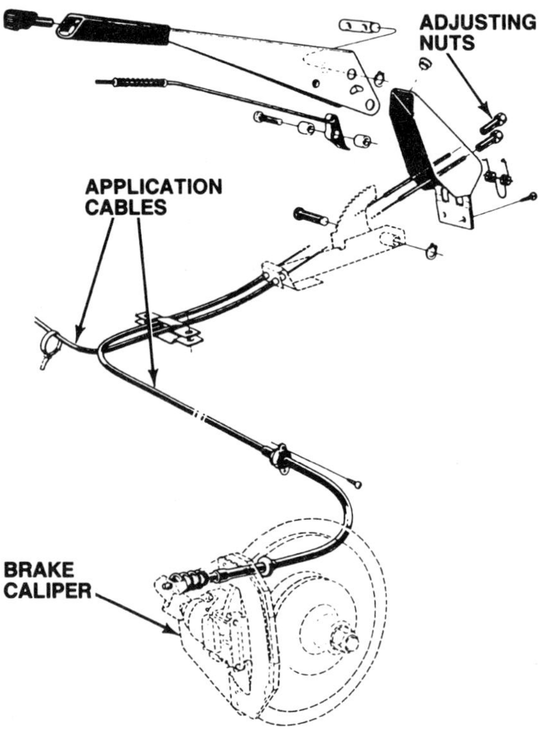

Cable Adjusters

When the parking brake is controlled by a foot pedal or underdash handle, the cable adjuster is generally located under the vehicle at an intermediate lever or equalizer, figure 10-10. If the parking brake is controlled by a

Figure 10-9. Parking brakes with a separate cable for each wheel require that the service brakes be properly adjusted.

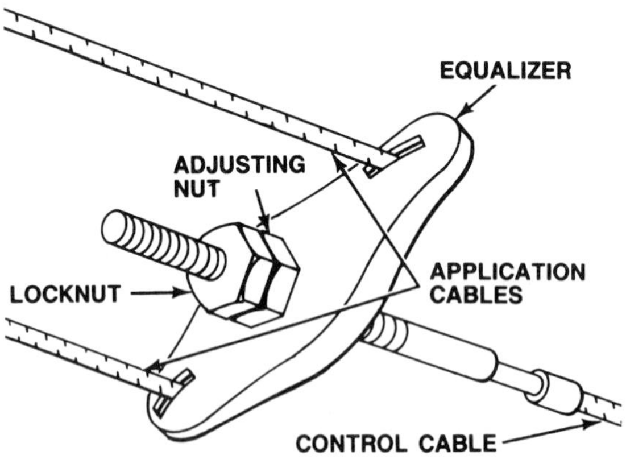

Figure 10-10. Many parking brake cables are adjusted under the car at an equalizer.

floor-mounted lever, the cable adjuster is usually inside the car on the lever assembly, figure 10-11. When the adjuster is mounted inside the car, you often have to remove a rubber boot or plastic cover to reach it.

Many cable adjusters use two jam nuts—an adjusting nut and a locknut—to set the cable length. A few cables have a single self-locking adjusting nut. If the nuts are rusted, corroded, or seized to the threaded ad-

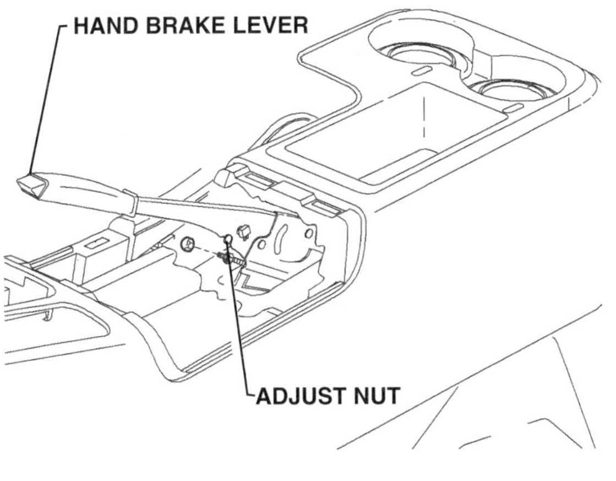

Parking Brake Service

Figure 10-11. Some parking brake cables are adjusted inside the car at the parking brake lever. (Courtesy of General Motors Corporation, Service and Parts Operations)

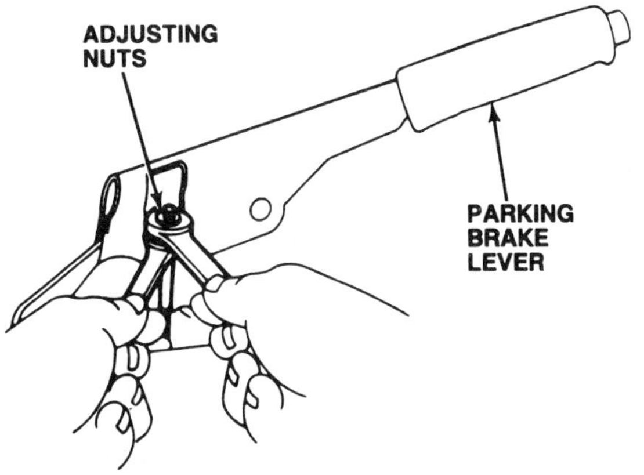

Figure 10-12. Two open-end wrenches are normally used to adjust parking brake cables.

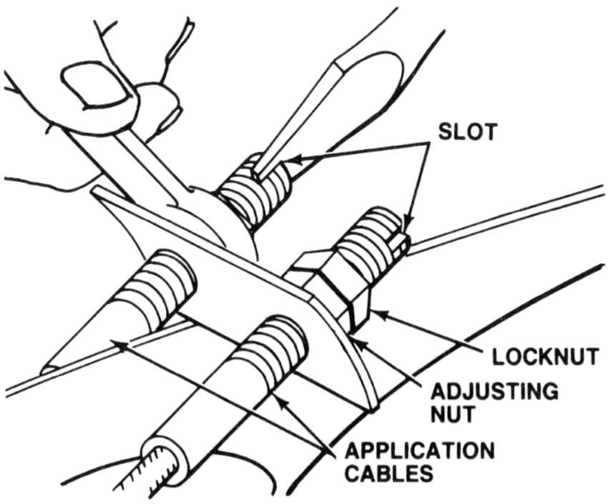

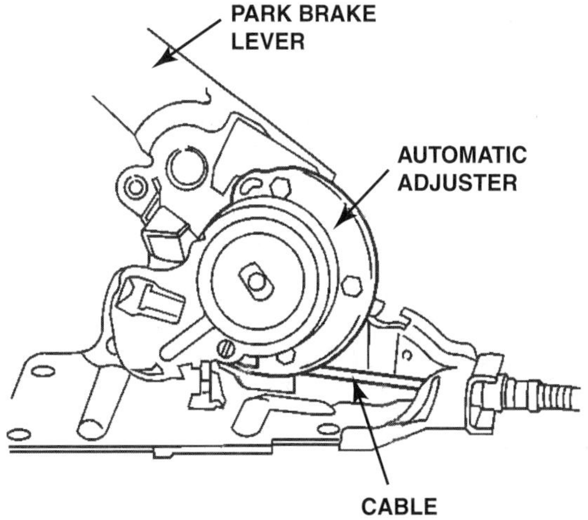

Figure 10-13. Always hold the parking brake cable stationary when you turn the adjusting nut.

Figure 10-14. Some vehicles use an adjuster assembly that automatically adjusts the parking brake cable with five to six pulls of the brake lever. (Courtesy of General Motors Corporation, Service and Parts Operations)

juster rod, soak the assembly with penetrating oil before you attempt to make the adjustment; this will help prevent the nuts and rod from being stripped.

To adjust the cable, hold the adjusting nut in place with an open-end wrench, then loosen the locknut with a second wrench, figure 10-12. Rotate the adjusting nut to draw the end of the cable through the lever or equalizer to shorten the working length of the cable. Once the adjustment is complete, hold the adjusting nut in place with an open-end wrench, and tighten the locknut against it with a second wrench. On systems with a separate adjustment for each cable, tighten the cables equally.

It is very important not to twist the cables when making an adjustment. This places the cables under additional stress, and leads to premature failure. If necessary, use a pair of locking pliers on an unthreaded section of the threaded rod to hold the rod stationary while you tighten the adjusting nut. Some adjusters have a slot in the end of the rod, figure 10-13, so you can insert a screwdriver to stop the cable from twisting.

Some vehicles may use an automatic cable adjuster, figure 10-14. The adjuster automatically adjusts the cable tension. To adjust this type of adjuster:

1. Using the appropriate tool, rewind the adjuster about 270 degrees.
2. After installing the new cable, firmly apply the parking brakes four to six times. This will activate the self-adjusting system.

Cable Adjustment—Drum Brakes

The cable adjustment for any kind of drum parking brake is similar whether it is an integral drum parking brake or a rear-disc auxiliary drum parking brake. To adjust the parking brake cable:

1. Shift the transmission into neutral, and fully release the parking brake control.
2. Raise and properly support the vehicle so the wheels with the parking brakes hang free.
3. Tighten the cable adjustment until the brakes begin to drag as you rotate them by hand.
4. Loosen the cable adjustment until the brakes just turn free.
5. Apply the parking brake and make sure it is fully engaged when the parking brake control has moved through one- to two-thirds of its available travel.
6. Apply and release the parking brake several times, then check that the wheels still turn free when the parking brake control is fully released. Loosen the adjustment slightly if necessary.

Some vehicle manufacturers recommend an alternative parking brake adjusting procedure similar to the one above, except that the parking brake control is partially applied during the adjustment. This helps prevent overadjustment by ensuring that there will be sufficient slack in the cables when the parking brake is released. To adjust the parking brake in this manner:

1. Shift the transmission into neutral, and apply the parking brake control as specified by the vehicle manufacturer. Most recommend that the control be engaged from one to seven clicks.
2. Raise and properly support the vehicle so the wheels with parking brakes hang free.
3. Tighten the cable adjustment until the brakes begin to drag as you rotate them by hand.
4. Fully release the parking brake control, and check that the wheels spin freely. Loosen the adjustment slightly if necessary.

Cable Adjustment—Disc Brakes

The cables that operate both General Motors and Ford caliper-actuated rear disc parking brakes can be adjusted using the following common procedure:

1. Shift the transmission into neutral, and fully release the parking brake control.
2. Raise and properly support the vehicle so the wheels with the parking brakes hang free.
3. Loosen the cable adjustment until there is slack in the cables, then make sure the parking brake

Figure 10-15. The parking brake levers on disc brake calipers must be fully returned when the brake is released.

levers on both calipers are fully returned. If the calipers are fitted with external lever stops, the levers should contact the stops when the parking brake control is released.
4. Tighten the cable adjustment until all of the slack is removed and either parking brake lever just starts to move.
5. Loosen the cable adjustment until both levers are again fully returned, figure 10-15.
6. Apply and release the parking brake several times, then make sure the parking brake levers still return all the way when the parking brake control is fully released. Loosen the adjustment slightly if necessary.

If the parking brake control travel is still excessive after you have adjusted the cables, the automatic adjuster in one or both caliper pistons is not operating properly. You can attempt to adjust the piston as described earlier in the chapter, but you will probably have to overhaul the caliper and replace the piston/adjuster assembly as described in Chapter 8.

PARKING BRAKE CABLE REPLACEMENT

In dry climates, parking brake cables often last the life of the car. However, in areas with lots of wet and cold weather, cables are subjected to rain, snow, and road salt that greatly increase rust and corrosion. This damage results in two distinct problems. First, the inner cable may stick or seize in its housing. And second,

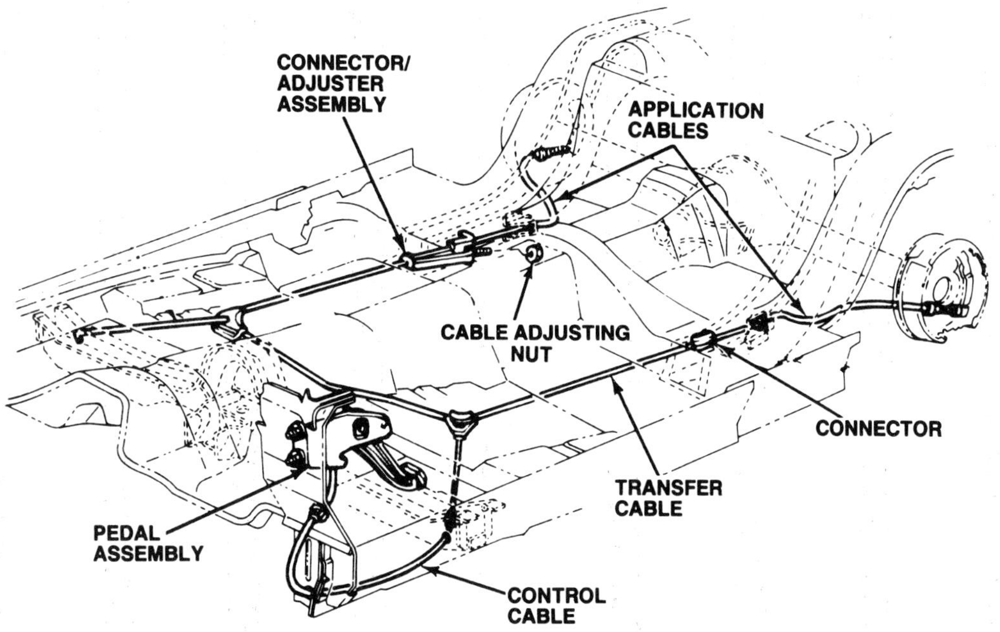

Parking Brake Service

Figure 10-16. A typical four-cable parking brake linkage.

damage to exposed sections of cable can cause individual strands to snap until the cable is frayed to the point where it breaks entirely.

Various attempts have been made to help prevent parking brake cable damage. A few older cables have a grease fitting for lubrication, and some automakers recommend that exposed sections of inner cable be lightly greased. However, for the most part, modern parking brake cables are sealed and do not require regular maintenance. If a parking brake cable is frayed or broken, you must replace it. Generally, sticking and seized cables should also be replaced because the time and effort required to free them can seldom be justified.

Freeing Sticking and Seized Cables

If a replacement cable is unavailable and you must free up a sticking or seized parking brake cable, use penetrating oil to soak the inner cable where it enters the housing. Most cable damage is confined to within a few inches of where the cable enters the housing. Allow the oil to soak in for several minutes, then work the inner cable back and forth until it loosens up. If used with extreme care, heat applied near the ends of the housing can sometimes help free a sticking or seized cable.

Once the inner cable begins to move, pull it out of the housing as far as possible and clean the contamination from its surface with solvents and abrasive cloth. Continue to apply penetrating oil, move the cable in and out of the housing, and clean the cable as needed. When the cable is completely free, grease the exposed sections with brake grease to help prevent future problems.

Cable Replacement Procedures

Parking brake linkages have from one to four cables that can be arranged in a wide variety of configurations. A typical domestic linkage, figure 10-16, has a control cable that runs from the parking brake control to the equalizer or adjuster, a transfer cable that runs from the equalizer or adjuster to near the rear wheels, and two application cables that run from connectors at the ends of the transfer cable to the parking brake levers at the wheels. The sections below describe typical procedures used to remove and install these three types of cables. Most other cables are replaced in a manner similar to one of these cables, or using some combination of the procedures described.

Whenever you replace a parking brake cable, check to see if you will need any additional parts before you order the new cable. Cable mounting hardware is often badly corroded, and will break apart when you remove the old cable. If the mounting hardware is in good condition, transfer it to the new cable. After you have installed the new cable, adjust it as described earlier, then apply the parking brake hard three or four times to pre-stretch the cable; readjust the cable if necessary.

Control Cable Replacement

The control cable is often attached to the parking brake pedal assembly under the dash. Typically, the cable will be concealed in the underdash wiring where it will be difficult to reach the cable end and disconnect it from the pedal linkage. In these situations, you may want to disconnect the battery ground cable to eliminate any chance of creating an electrical short circuit while working around the wiring. However, keep in mind that doing this on a modern car with computer controls will erase the computer memories for such convenience items as the radio, climate control, and power seats.

Installing a new parking brake control cable can also be difficult if you have to thread the cable through a hard-to-reach opening in the firewall or floor pan. To make the job easier, connect a wire about 50 inches (130 cm) long to the end of the cable that is removed last. Pull the old cable through the firewall or floor pan, then disconnect the wire from the cable, leaving the wire in the place normally occupied by the cable. Connect the wire to the end of the new cable that is installed first, then use the wire to guide and pull the new cable into position through the firewall or floor pan.

To replace a parking brake control cable:

1. Fully release the parking brake control.
2. Raise and properly support the vehicle.
3. Disconnect the lower end of the cable from the equalizer or adjuster.
4. Disconnect the brackets, clips, and screws that hold the cable to the frame or body.
5. Disconnect the upper end of the cable from the parking brake control.
6. Remove the cable by pulling the upper end down through the hole in the firewall or floor pan. On some cars, the lower end of the cable is pulled up through the inside of the vehicle.
7. Insert the new cable through the firewall or floor pan as described above.
8. Connect the upper end of the cable to the parking brake control.
9. Attach the mounting hardware to the new cable and screw or clip the cable to the frame or body.
10. Connect the lower end of the cable to the equalizer or adjuster.

Transfer Cable Replacement

Parking brake transfer cables are the easiest to replace because the job is done entirely from under the car; there is no need to work inside the vehicle, or disassemble a friction assembly as is required when you replace an application cable.

To replace a parking brake transfer cable:

1. Fully release the parking brake control.
2. Raise and properly support the vehicle.
3. Loosen the parking brake adjustment, then disconnect the transfer cable from the adjuster or equalizer, and the application cable connectors.
4. Disconnect the brackets, clips, and screws that hold the cable to the frame or body.
5. Connect the new transfer cable to the adjuster or equalizer.
6. Attach the mounting hardware to the new cable and screw or clip the cable to the frame or body.
7. Connect the cable to the application cable connectors.

Application Cable Replacement

Parking brake application cables are easy to install on cars that have caliper-actuated disc parking brakes, however, they are somewhat more difficult to install when they actuate an integral drum parking brake. In these cases, you must disassemble the drum brake friction assembly in order to disconnect the cable end from the parking brake lever on the brake shoe, and release the cable housing from the brake backing plate. Details on drum brake disassembly and assembly can be found in Chapter 7.

To replace a parking brake application cable on a car with either an integral drum or caliper-actuated disc parking brake:

1. Fully release the parking brake control.
2. Raise and properly support the vehicle.
3. Loosen the parking brake adjustment, and disconnect the application cable from the equalizer or adjuster, or the transfer cable connector.
4. Disconnect the brackets, clips, and screws that hold the cable to the frame or body:
   a. With caliper-actuated disc parking brakes, go to step 5.
   b. With integral drum parking brakes, go to step 7.
5. Disconnect the cable from the parking brake lever on the caliper.
6. Connect the new cable to the parking brake lever on the caliper. Go to step 11.
7. Disassemble the service brake as necessary, then disconnect the end of the cable from the parking brake lever on the brake shoe.
8. Use a pair of pliers or a hose clamp to compress the fingers of the cable retaining clip, figure 10-17, then remove the cable from the backing plate.
9. Install the new cable through the backing plate, and make sure the retaining clip locks into place.
10. Connect the end of the cable to the parking brake lever on the brake shoe, then reassemble the service brake.
11. Attach mounting hardware to the new cable, and screw or clip the cable to the frame or body.
12. Connect the end of the cable to the equalizer or adjuster, or the transfer cable connector.

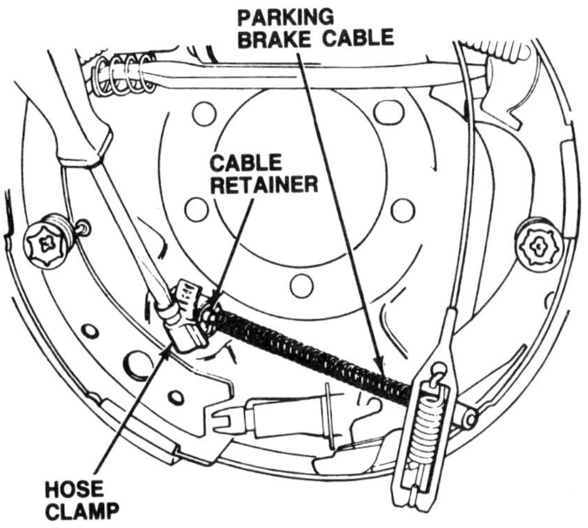

Parking Brake Service

Figure 10-17. Compress the parking brake cable retainer with pliers or a hose clamp.

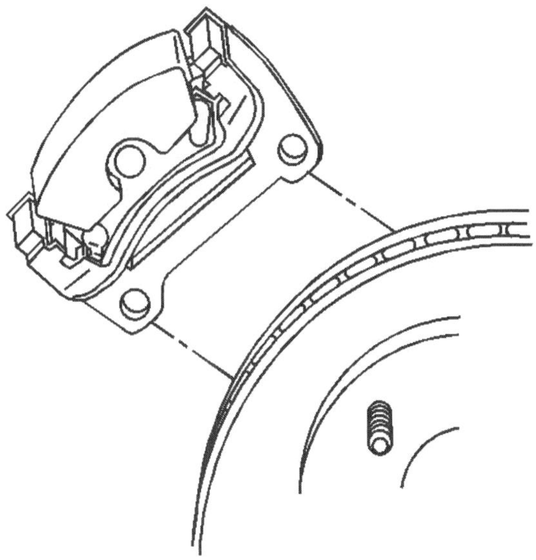

Figure 10-18. Remove the brake caliper and mounting bracket as an assembly. (Courtesy of General Motors Corporation, Service and Parts Operations)

PARKING BRAKE SHOE AND PAD SERVICE

Integral drum and caliper-actuated disc parking brakes use the service brake shoes and pads as the parking brake friction material. In these applications, you simply change the brake shoes or pads as needed in the course of normal service. The inspection and replacement procedures for shoes and pads are covered in Chapter 7 for drum brakes, and Chapter 8 for disc brakes.

The linings of the small shoes used in auxiliary drum parking brakes are made of soft friction materials that provide a high coefficient of friction for better holding power. These shoes usually last the life of the car, or require replacement only at high-mileage intervals, because the parking brake only holds the vehicle in place and is not normally called upon to slow or stop the car. However, because the linings are softer than those in service brake systems, they will wear very quickly if the parking brake is overadjusted and drags, or if the driver forgets and drives even a short distance with the parking brake engaged.

For the same reasons described above, the friction surface of the small parking brake drum inside the rotor is not normally subject to significant wear. This is important because, unlike a service-brake drum, the parking brake drum cannot be turned to refinish the friction surface. To do so would excessively weaken the rotor structure, which could lead to a brake failure.

Shoe replacement on auxiliary drum parking brakes is very similar to the same job on service drum brakes. If anything, the job is easier because the parking brake friction assemblies do not have wheel cylinders or automatic adjusters to deal with. To replace the auxiliary drum parking brake shoes, remove the caliper and rotor as described in Chapter 8. Then, refer to the drum brake inspection and service procedures in Chapter 7.

Parking Brake Shoe Replacement

One popular style of parking brake uses a combination brake shoe and spring assembly, sometimes called a uni-shoe. To change this type of brake shoe follow these steps:

1. Jack up and support the vehicle. Remove the wheel.
2. Remove the brake caliper and mount bracket as an assembly, figure 10-18.
3. Remove the brake rotor, figure 10-19.
4. Disconnect the parking brake cable, figure 10-20. This will release any tension on the shoe actuator, making it easier to remove the shoe.
5. The shoe will have a wire-type retainer or a spring clip holding the shoe to the backing plate, figure 10-21. Remove the wire-type clip or slide the shoe until it clears the retaining clip.
6. Spread the shoe slightly and remove it from the actuator/adjuster, figure 10-22.
7. To reinstall the shoe, reverse these instructions.

AUTOMATIC RELEASE SYSTEMS

Many full-size and luxury vehicles have automatic release mechanisms on their parking brake pedal. Using either vacuum or electric solenoids, these systems are designed to release the parking brake when

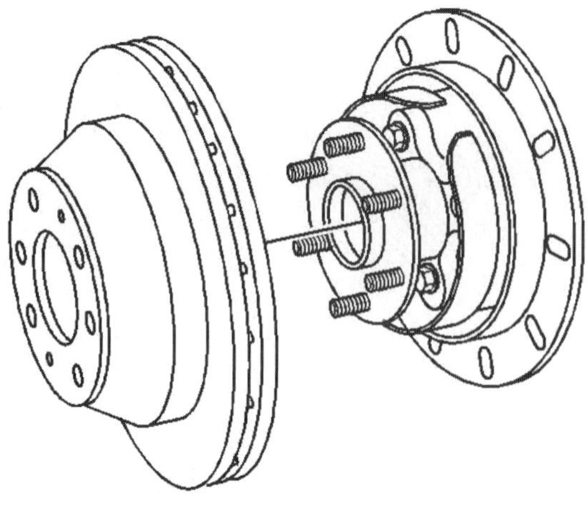

Figure 10-19. Remove the brake rotor. (Courtesy of General Motors Corporation, Service and Parts Operations)

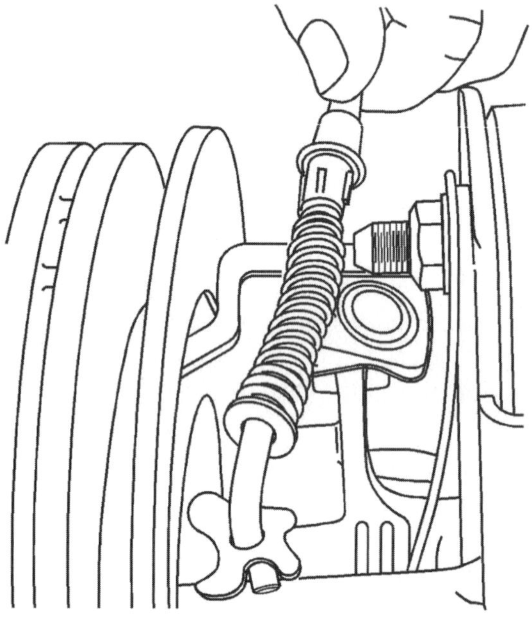

Figure 10-20. Disconnect and remove the parking brake cable. (Courtesy of General Motors Corporation, Service and Parts Operations)

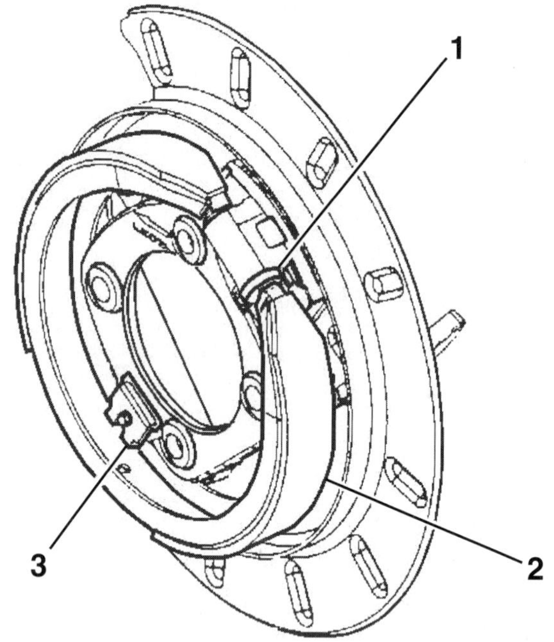

Figure 10-21. Slide the brake shoe (2) until it clears the retainer clip (3) and the actuator (1). (Courtesy of General Motors Corporation, Service and Parts Operations)

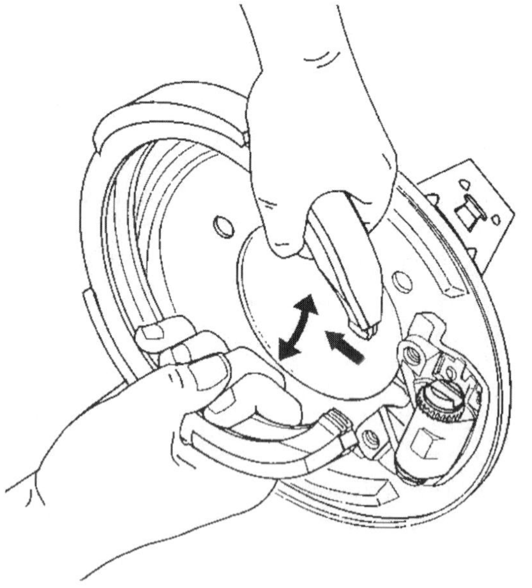

Figure 10-22. Spread the shoe slightly and remove it. (Courtesy of General Motors Corporation, Service and Parts Operations)

the transmission is placed in Drive or Reverse. All of these systems include a manual override lever to release the brake should the automatic release system fail.

Vacuum Release Parking Brake

On the vacuum-operated system, when the transmission is placed in Drive or Reverse, a switch closes and completes an electrical circuit that activates a vacuum solenoid. The solenoid then applies vacuum to a servo on the parking brake assembly, and the servo pulls a lever to release the parking brake, figure 10-23.

The automatic parking brake release system requires a minimum of 10 in. Hg (35 kPa) of vacuum for proper operation. Before you proceed to more involved diagnosis, make sure the engine has good man-

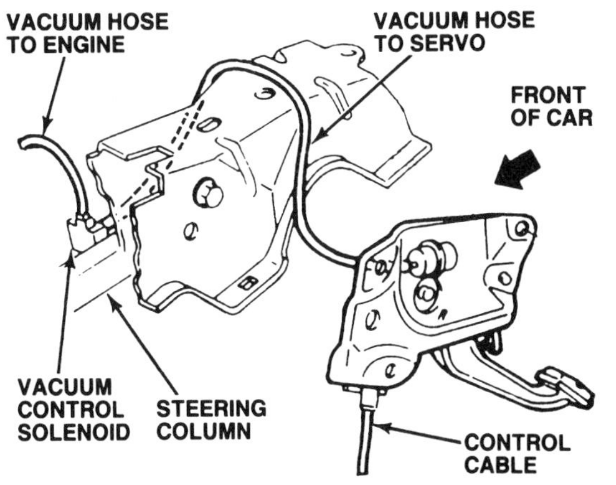

Parking Brake Service

Figure 10-23. A vacuum parking brake release mechanism.

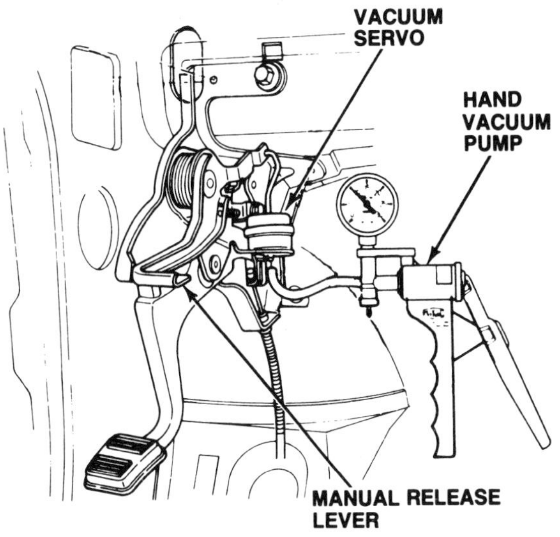

Figure 10-24. Using a vacuum pump to test the parking brake vacuum servo.

ifold vacuum at idle, and that all the vacuum hoses in the system are in good condition and tightly attached. To check the operation of the automatic parking brake release system:

1. Apply the parking brake, then pull the manual release lever, figure 10-24:
   a. If the parking brake releases, go to step 2.
   b. If the parking brake does not release, locate and repair the problem in the pedal assembly.
2. With the service brakes applied, start the engine and allow it to idle.
3. Place the transmission shift lever in Neutral, then apply the parking brake.
4. Move the shift lever to Drive or Reverse:
   a. If the parking brake pedal releases, the system is operating properly and no further service is required.
   b. If the parking brake does not release, go to step 5.
5. Remove the vacuum hose from the servo unit and connect a vacuum gauge to the hose.
6. Have an assistant apply the service brakes and move the shift lever to Drive or Reverse:
   a. If intake manifold vacuum is shown on the gauge, go to step 7.
   b. If low or no vacuum is shown on the gauge, go to step 8.
7. Use a hand pump to apply a minimum of 10 in. Hg (35 kPa) of vacuum to the servo, figure 10-24:
   a. If the servo does not hold a vacuum, replace the servo.
   b. If the servo holds a vacuum, check the servo link connection to the release lever, or locate and repair the problem with the pedal assembly.
8. Remove the vacuum supply hose from the vacuum control solenoid, and connect a vacuum gauge to the hose:
   a. If manifold vacuum is shown on the gauge, locate and repair the electrical problem with the solenoid, switch, or wiring of the system.
   b. If no or low vacuum is shown on the gauge, replace the obstructed vacuum supply hose.

Computer-Controlled Parking Brake Release

Many luxury vehicles have changed from a vacuum-operated parking brake release system to a computer-controlled system that uses the vehicle body control system and release solenoids. The solenoids are located on the parking brake apply assembly, figure 10-25. These systems require the use of a computer scan tool during diagnosis.

To check the operation of the release system:

1. Apply the parking brake.
2. Start the engine and allow it to idle. Check that the red parking brake warning light is on.
3. Step on the brake pedal and shift the transmission into reverse or any drive gear.
   a. If the parking brake pedal releases and the red warning light goes out, the system is working as it should and no further service is needed.
   b. If the pedal does not release, go to step 4.

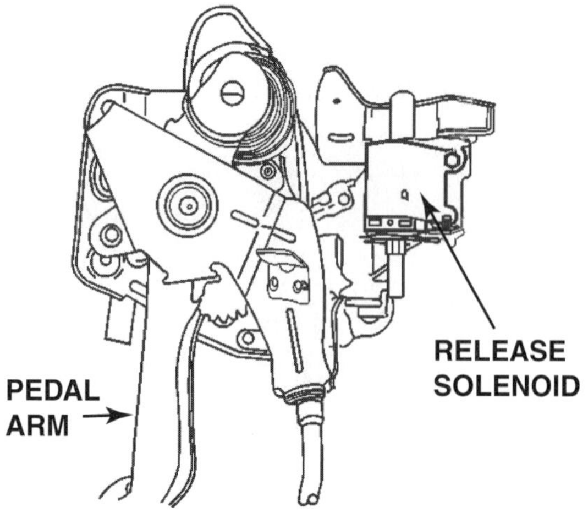

Figure 10-25. This automatic parking brake release system uses release solenoids that are controlled by the vehicle body control system. (Courtesy of General Motors Corporation, Service and Parts Operations)

4. Install and power up the scan tool. Check the appropriate control module for any diagnostic trouble codes (DTCs) that relate to the parking brake.
   a. If there are DTCs, go to the related chart in the service information.
   b. If there are no DTCs, go to step 5.
5. Using the scan tool, command the parking brake release solenoids on and off. Listen for them to click as they are switched off and on.
   a. If the solenoids click but the pedal does not release, look for a mechanical problem with the pedal assembly.
   b. If the solenoids do not click when commanded by the scan tool, check the solenoids, fuses, and related relays. Also check the control module and the vehicle communications system for proper operation. Use the vehicle's specific service information or shop manual to do this.

11
Power Brake Service

OBJECTIVES

Upon completion and review of this chapter, you will be able to:

- Perform the vacuum booster function test.
- Perform the vacuum booster leak test.
- Perform the vacuum supply test.
- Adjust vacuum booster output pushrods.
- Replace a vacuum booster.
- Inspect a Hydro-Boost system.
- Perform the Hydro-Boost function test.
- Perform the Hydro-Boost accumulator test.
- Replace a Hydro-Boost.
- Bleed a Hydro-Boost system.
- Perform the Powermaster function test.
- Perform the Powermaster external leak test.
- Perform Powermaster electrical tests.
- Perform the Powermaster pressure tests.
- Perform the Powermaster internal leak test.
- Replace a Powermaster.
- Fill and bleed a Powermaster.

INTRODUCTION

Passenger vehicle power brake systems use a vacuum or hydraulic power booster to increase brake application force and reduce the amount of foot pressure required on the brake pedal. Some integral-type antilock brake systems (ABS) combine the power assist function and the ABS controller/actuator into one unit. A failure in either a power brake or antilock system will not prevent the brake system from stopping the car; however, braking does require greater effort without power brakes, and greater skill without antilock brakes.

As discussed in the *Classroom Manual,* three types of power boosters are used on cars today. The most common is the vacuum booster, which is used by all automakers and comes in both single- and dual-diaphragm forms. Another common design is the hydraulic booster, which is powered by the power steering pump. An example is the Bendix Hydro-Boost, used primarily by General Motors and the Ford Motor Company. A third design is the electrohydraulic booster, which combines the master cylinder, an electrohydraulic pump, and a hydraulic booster into one compact unit; ABS functions may also be part of the unit. Examples of this type, used by General Motors, are the Powermaster I and II (non-ABS) and the Powermaster III (with ABS).

A variety of antilock brake systems are used on import and domestic vehicles. Some antilock systems combine the antilock and power assist functions in one integrated unit. Systems that operate in this way are the

Bendix 9 and 10 ABS, Bosch 3 ABS, Delco Powermaster III ABS, and Teves Mk II ABS. Service for these systems is covered in Chapter 12 and Chapter 13.

Power brake service consists primarily of testing and replacing the three types of power boosters. Although it is possible to rebuild Hydro-Boost units and some vacuum boosters, most shops today simply install a factory-rebuilt assembly. When a vacuum booster is rebuilt or replaced, its output pushrod may need adjustment. And, when a hydraulic or electrohydraulic booster is replaced, the power brake system must be bled of air in order to function properly.

VACUUM BOOSTER TESTING

Vacuum boosters are generally trouble free, and do not require regular service other than a function test during routine brake system inspection. A problem with the vacuum power booster is unusual in a vehicle less than five years old and many vacuum boosters last the life of the vehicle. When a vacuum booster does fail, the service brake pedal height remains normal, but pedal feel becomes much harder, and significantly greater pedal force is required to slow and stop the car. Usually, it is impossible to apply enough force at the pedal to lock the brakes.

Because other problems in the brake system can also increase the force required to apply the brakes, the first step in vacuum booster diagnosis is to perform a function test to determine if the booster is the source of the problem. Depending on the function test results, you may also perform vacuum supply and booster leak tests described in this section to further identify the problem.

Vacuum Booster Function Test

The booster function test determines if the booster is receiving adequate vacuum and creating brake application force. With the ignition OFF, apply the brake pedal repeatedly with medium pressure until the booster reserve is depleted. There should be a power-assisted feel for at least two brake applications before the pedal becomes hard. If the pedal feels hard immediately, or after only one brake application, there may be a problem with the booster vacuum supply, or the booster may have a vacuum leak.

Once the reserve is depleted, hold medium pressure on the brake pedal and start the engine. If the booster is working properly, the pedal will drop slightly toward the floor as the engine begins to run, and less force will be required to hold the pedal in place. If the booster passes the function test, proceed to the booster leak test. If there is no noticeable change in the pedal position or feel, the booster is not operating properly, and you should perform the vacuum supply test.

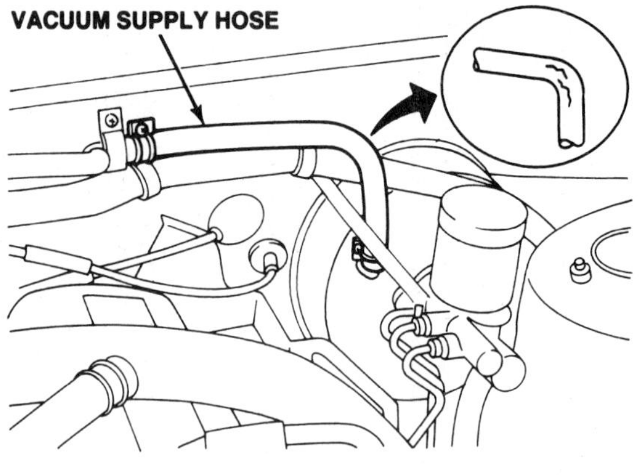

Figure 11-1. Vacuum supply hoses often crack where they bend.

Vacuum Supply Test

The vacuum supply test consists of several checks and inspections that make sure the power booster is receiving enough vacuum to function properly. There are two reasons the booster may not receive sufficient vacuum: either there is an obstruction or leak in the vacuum supply hose, or the amount of vacuum generated by the engine and/or vacuum pump is below specifications.

First, visually inspect the vacuum supply hose to the booster. Look for kinks or other indications that the hose may be blocked. If the car has a vacuum hose filter, remove the filter and blow through it to make sure it is clear. Next, inspect the hose for holes or cracks, figure 11-1. Make sure the fittings are tight where the hose connects to the booster check valve and vacuum source. Start the engine and allow it to idle, then listen along the hose for hissing noises that indicate a vacuum leak.

If the vacuum supply hose is clear and free from leaks, check the level of vacuum supplied by the engine or vacuum pump. With the ignition OFF, pump the brake pedal to deplete the booster reserve. Disconnect the vacuum supply hose from the booster, and connect a vacuum gauge to the hose using a cone-shaped adapter, figure 11-2. On all cars except those with electric vacuum pumps, start the engine and allow it to idle, then observe the vacuum reading on the gauge. The proper amount of vacuum will vary with the application, but the reading at idle should typically be between 15 and 20 in. Hg (50 and 70 kPa).

Sometimes, a vacuum supply hose that is restricted but not completely plugged, will allow a satisfactory reading on a vacuum gauge, but prevent a sufficient "volume" of vacuum from reaching the booster. To quickly check for this problem, disconnect the vacuum supply hose from the booster while the engine is idling. If the engine does not stall almost immediately from the extra air drawn in through the

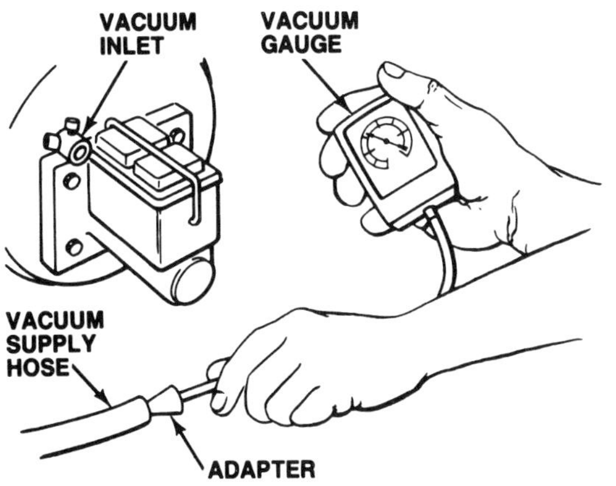

Power Brake Service

Figure 11-2. Use a vacuum gauge to check the vacuum supply to the booster.

supply hose, check for a restricted hose or filter. If the vacuum reading is within specifications, and the vacuum supply hose is not restricted, perform the booster leak test.

If the vacuum reading is less than 15 in. Hg (50 kPa), repair the problem at the vacuum source. If the vacuum source is a mechanically driven vacuum pump, rebuild or replace the pump as necessary. If the vacuum source is the engine, you will have to locate and repair the cause of the low manifold vacuum. This may be something as simple as improperly adjusted ignition timing, or as major as valvetrain and piston ring wear. After the vacuum source is repaired, repeat the booster function test. If the booster still fails the test, perform the booster leak test.

Electric Vacuum Pump

On vehicles with an electric vacuum pump, connect a vacuum gauge to the booster vacuum supply hose as described above, then turn the ignition ON, but do not start the engine. The vacuum pump should begin to run, and the reading on the vacuum gauge should increase. When vacuum level reaches the point specified in the factory shop manual, the vacuum pump should stop running. If the pump does not run at all, or continues to run after the proper vacuum level is reached, consult the shop manual for instructions on the diagnosis and repair of the pump electrical circuit. After the vacuum source is repaired, repeat the booster function test. If the booster still fails the test, perform the booster leak test.

Supplemental Brake Assist (SBA)

Some vehicles use a supplemental brake assist (SBA) unit to create vacuum for the brake booster in case of a low or no vacuum condition to the booster. The SBA unit is controlled by a microprocessor and contains a pressure sensor and various circuits. It communicates with the instrument panel cluster whenever a problem occurs, causing a SERVICE BRAKE BOOSTER or REDUCED BRAKE POWER message to appear on the instrument cluster.

The SBA uses self-diagnostics to test system operation. The diagnostics test circuit operation and pump motor operation each time the vehicle is driven. If a fault occurs the warning messages will appear on the instrument cluster. This will also cause a diagnostic trouble code (DTC) to set in the instrument cluster.

The self-diagnostic system of the SBA can be used to test the operation of the system.

1. Disconnect and plug the engine vacuum supply hose from the SBA pump.
2. Start the engine and let it idle.
3. Pump the brake several times. This will exhaust the vacuum from the brake booster.
4. The drop in vacuum will be sensed by the SBA pressure sensor, causing the pump to run. This will also set a DTC and cause a warning message to appear in the instrument cluster.
5. If the warning message appears and the pump runs the system is OK.
6. Refer to the manufacturer's service information if more testing is needed.
7. Shut off the engine and reconnect the vacuum hose.
8. Use a scan tool to clear the DTC.

Vacuum Booster Leak Test

The vacuum booster leak test consists of two parts that determine if the booster can maintain a vacuum reserve when the brakes are released, and contain vacuum within the booster when the brakes are applied. To check the ability of the booster to hold a vacuum when the brakes are released, run the engine at a fast idle for 30 seconds, then release the throttle and turn the ignition OFF. Wait two minutes, then apply the brake pedal repeatedly with medium force. There should be a power-assisted feel for at least two brake applications before the pedal feel becomes hard. If the booster passes this test, perform the brakes applied leak test below.

If you feel no power assist, either the booster vacuum check valve is leaking, or the booster has an unapplied vacuum leak. To test the vacuum check valve, disconnect the vacuum supply hose from the intake manifold or vacuum pump, and blow into the hose, figure 11-3. If air passes through the valve into the booster, replace the check valve. If air does not pass through the check valve, rebuild or replace the booster.

To check the ability of the booster to hold a vacuum while the brakes are applied, start the engine and allow it to idle. Close the car doors and windows, then listen carefully as you apply the brakes. If the engine begins

Figure 11-3. Testing a vacuum booster inlet check valve.

to run rough, or there is a continuous hissing noise from the area where the brake pedal pushrod enters the booster, the booster has an internal vacuum leak and must be rebuilt or replaced.

VACUUM BOOSTER OUTPUT PUSHROD ADJUSTMENT

Like the input pushrod from the brake pedal, the vacuum booster output pushrod must be adjusted to the proper length. A pushrod that is too long holds the master cylinder in a partially applied position that prevents the brakes from releasing completely. This causes brake drag, premature wear of the pad and shoe linings, and possibly brake fade. A pushrod that is too short does not usually cause significant brake problems, although it does increase brake pedal travel slightly, and can cause a clunk or groaning noise from the booster in some applications.

Pushrod Adjustment Test

To determine if the booster output pushrod is too long, remove the cover or caps from the master cylinder fluid reservoir(s), and have an assistant *gently* apply the brakes. If fluid spurts from the compensating ports as the brakes are applied, the pushrod adjustment is satisfactory. Because brake fluid can spray when performing this test, wear safety glasses to prevent eye injuries, and use a fender cover to protect the vehicle finish.

If there are no spurts of fluid, check and adjust the brake pedal freeplay as described in Chapter 5, then repeat the test. If there are still no spurts, loosen the master cylinder retaining nuts and pull the cylinder away from the booster approximately ⅛ inch (3 mm). Repeat the test. If fluid spurts now appear, adjust the booster output pushrod. If spurts do not appear, the master cylinder should be disassembled to determine why the compensating ports are obstructed.

Pushrod Adjusting Methods

On most cars, you should adjust the booster output pushrod whenever you install a new or rebuilt vacuum power booster, or if the system fails the pushrod adjustment test above. However, some manufacturers do not recommend, or provide specifications for, booster pushrod adjustment. In these applications, you simply install the new booster and hope that the pushrod was properly adjusted at the factory.

To adjust the pushrod on a power booster that is already installed on the car, you must separate the cylinder from the booster. To do this, remove the master cylinder retaining nuts, and pull the cylinder forward and away from the booster. If you do this carefully, you generally do not have to disconnect the brake lines from the cylinder. Once the master cylinder is free from the booster, support it so there is no stress on the brake lines.

Where pushrod adjustment *is* recommended, a go/no-go gauge is commonly used to check the pushrod position. Most gauges are flat pieces of metal or plastic with calibrated notches cut in them, figure 11-4, although some import cars use a variable gauge. The procedure used to adjust the output pushrod is basically the same for all vacuum boosters; the most common variations are described below.

Ford Booster Pushrod Adjustment

Ford power boosters are adjusted when they are installed on the car and the engine is idling. To adjust the output pushrod, place the "minimum" side of the go/no-go gauge over the pushrod. In this position, a 5-lb (22-N) force against the pushrod should seat the legs of the gauge flat against the booster housing, figure 11-5. If necessary, hold the pushrod with a pair of pliers and turn the self-locking adjusting nut with a wrench, figure 11-6, until there is the proper preload when the gauge contacts the pushrod. To double check the adjustment, place the "maximum" side of the go/no-go gauge over the pushrod so the legs of the gauge seat flat against the booster housing. In this position, the end of the pushrod should not contact the gauge.

General Motors Pushrod Adjustment

General Motors power boosters are adjusted off the car, or on the car with the engine not running. To adjust the output pushrod, place the go/no-go gauge

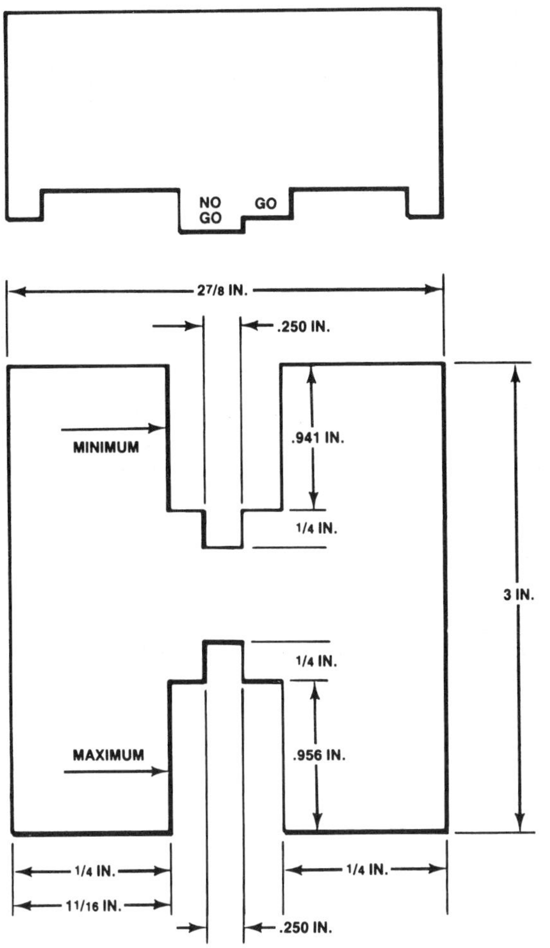

Power Brake Service

Figure 11-4. Typical vacuum booster output pushrod adjusting gauges.

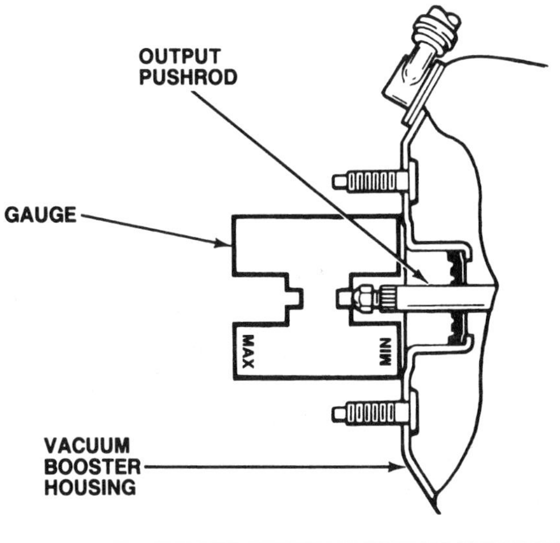

Figure 11-5. Adjusting the output pushrod on a vacuum booster.

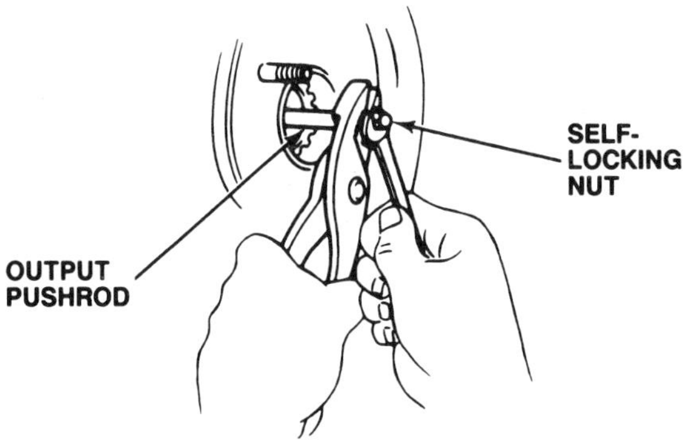

Figure 11-6. Use a wrench and a pair of pliers to adjust the booster output pushrod length.

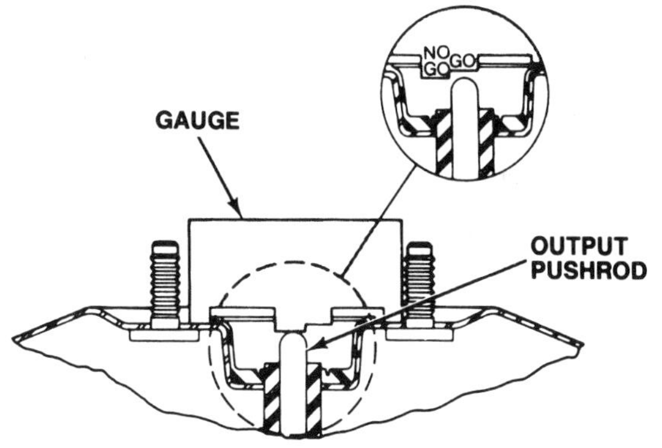

Figure 11-7. A properly adjusted output pushrod on a GM vacuum booster.

over the pushrod so the legs of the gauge seat flat against the booster housing, figure 11-7. Slide the gauge from side to side to check the pushrod length. The pushrod tip should *always* contact the lower "no-go" section of the gauge, but *never* contact the upper "go" section of the gauge. If the pushrod length is not within these limits, obtain an adjustable pushrod from a General Motors dealer. To set the proper length, hold the pushrod with a pair of pliers and turn the adjusting nut with a wrench.

Variable Gauge Pushrod Adjustment

Some imported cars use a variable gauge to transfer an adjustment measurement from the master cylinder to the booster output pushrod. To adjust an output pushrod using a variable gauge, figure 11-8, place the gauge on the master cylinder and screw the threaded pin downward until it lightly contacts the master cylinder primary piston. Then, turn the gauge over and place it on the power booster as shown in figure 11-9. Adjust the booster output pushrod until it lightly contacts the head of the threaded pin on the gauge.

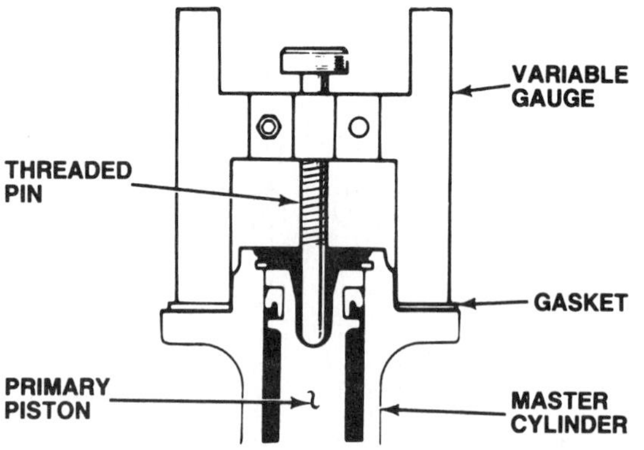

Figure 11-8. Initial setting of a variable gauge used to adjust the booster output pushrod.

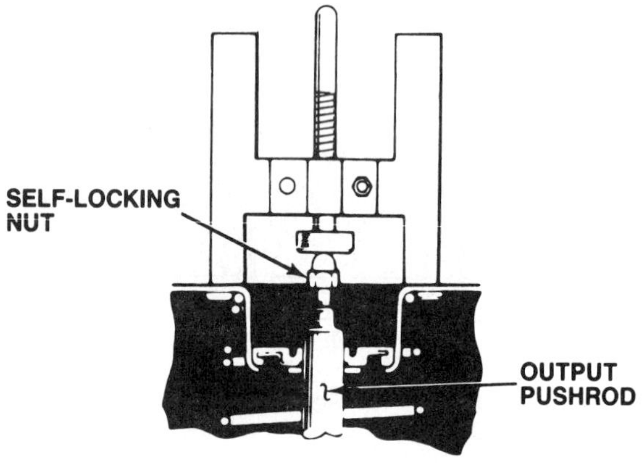

Figure 11-9. Using a variable gauge to check the vacuum booster output pushrod length.

VACUUM BOOSTER REPLACEMENT

All vacuum boosters are replaced in basically the same way. The generic procedure below can be used to replace the vacuum power brake booster on most cars.

1. Remove or reposition any wires, brackets, hoses, or other components that obstruct access to the booster.
2. Disconnect the vacuum supply hose from the booster.
3. Remove the master cylinder retaining nuts, and pull the cylinder away from the booster. In most cases, you do not have to disconnect the brake lines if you do this carefully. Be sure to support the cylinder so there is no stress on the brake lines.
4. Disconnect the brake pedal pushrod from the pedal arm on figure 11-10. To do this, it may be necessary to remove the stoplight switch.
5. Remove the retaining nuts that hold the booster to the firewall, figure 11-11, then withdraw the booster from the vehicle.

Figure 11-10. The pedal pushrod must be disconnected before the booster can be removed.

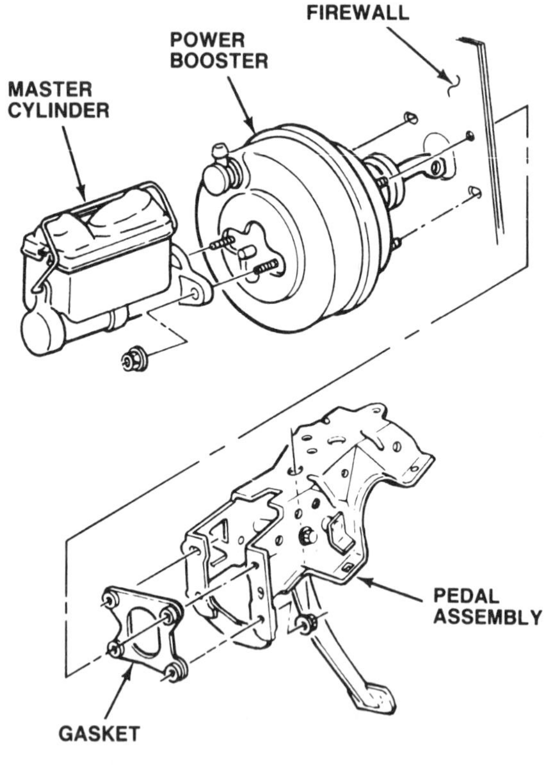

Figure 11-11. A typical vacuum booster installation.

NOTE: Some late-model General Motors vehicles use a twist-and-lock type of mount for the vacuum booster. A special tool bolts in place of the master cylinder, figure 11-12. Using a large open-end wrench, turn the booster counterclockwise until it releases from the bulkhead, figure 11-13.

6. Check and adjust the output pushrod of the replacement booster as described above.

Power Brake Service

Figure 11-12. Use this special tool to turn the booster counterclockwise.

Figure 11-13. The booster on this vehicle uses a twist-lock mount.

7. Position the new booster on the firewall, then install and tighten the retaining nuts.
8. Connect the brake pedal pushrod to the pedal arm.
9. Install and adjust the stoplight switch if you removed it in step 4. See Chapter 6 for information on switch adjustment.
10. Position the master cylinder on the booster, then install and tighten the retaining nuts.
11. If you removed the brake lines from the master cylinder in step 3, reconnect them at this time and bleed the brakes as described in Chapter 3.
12. Connect the vacuum supply hose to the booster.
13. Install any wires, brackets, hoses, or other components removed in step 1.
14. Start the engine to build vacuum in the booster, then perform a booster function test.

HYDRO-BOOST TESTING

Just as with a vacuum power booster, a failure in a Bendix Hydro-Boost system causes a high, hard brake pedal that makes it difficult for the driver to slow and stop the car. Because the Hydro-Boost system depends on the power steering pump for its boost pressure, a power brake problem may be accompanied by erratic steering feel. And, if air enters the power steering system and causes cavitation, there may be pulsations in the brake pedal as well.

To diagnose a Hydro-Boost malfunction, perform a pre-test inspection to eliminate any outside problems, then perform a function test to determine if the Hydro-Boost unit is the source of the problem. Depending on the function test results, you may also perform one or more of the other tests in this section to help further identify the problem. All of the tests apply to both Hydro-Boost I and Hydro-Boost II systems unless otherwise noted.

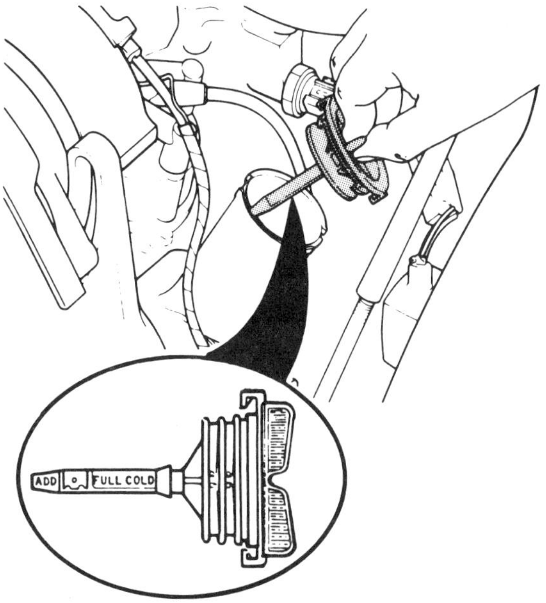

Figure 11-14. The power steering fluid level must be correct for the Hydro-Boost unit to operate properly.

Hydro-Boost Pre-Test Inspection

Because the Hydro-Boost system is powered by the power steering system, the first step in any diagnosis is to check for power-steering-related problems. Start by checking the fluid level in the power steering pump reservoir. During parking and other low speed maneuvers, a low fluid level can cause a moan or low-frequency hum, accompanied by a vibration in the brake pedal or steering column.

To check the fluid level, remove the cap/dipstick from the power steering reservoir and check the fluid level on the dipstick, figure 11-14. Some manufacturers recommend you check the level with the fluid at operating temperature, others say to check the level

Figure 11-15. Belt problems usually occur on the underside of the belt that runs against the pulleys.

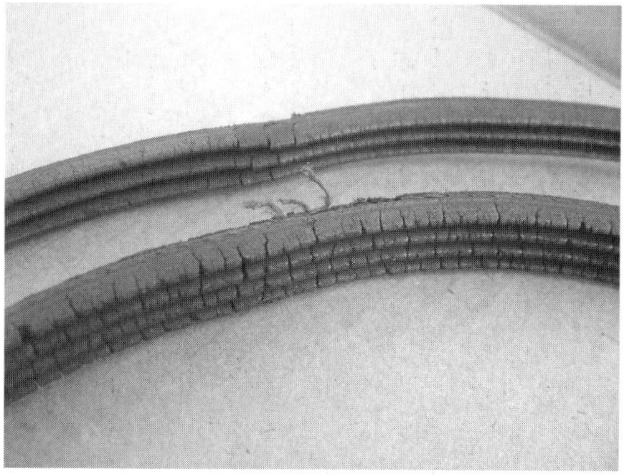

Figure 11-16. These cracked and frayed belts should be replaced.

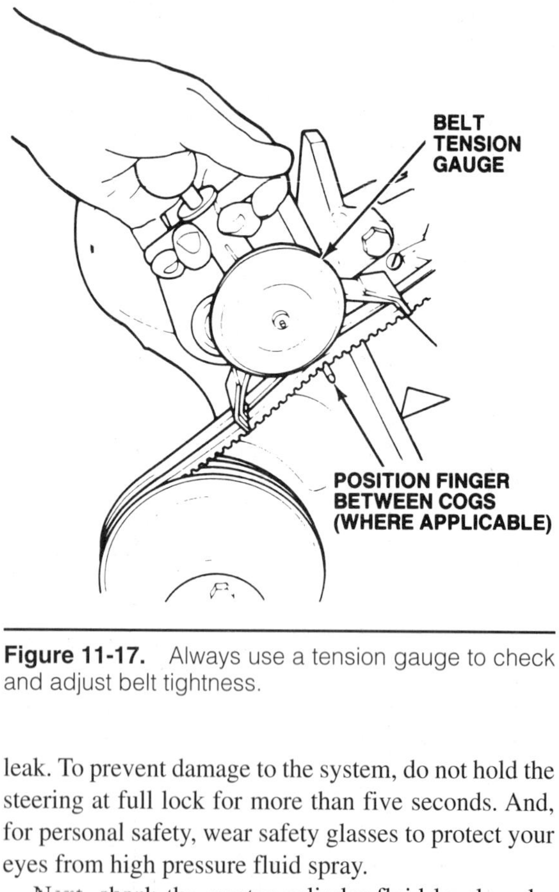

Figure 11-17. Always use a tension gauge to check and adjust belt tightness.

when the fluid is cold. Some dipsticks have markings for both hot and cold fluid levels. If the level is low, top up the reservoir with the type of fluid recommended by the vehicle manufacturer. Using the wrong fluid can damage rubber seals and hoses in the power steering and Hydro-Boost systems.

Next, inspect the power steering pump drive belt, figure 11-15. Check the portions of the belt that run against the pulleys for cracks, fraying, separation, brittleness, grease and oil contamination, glazing, and excessive wear, figure 11-16. Replace the belt if any of these conditions are present.

Once you have made sure the pump drive belt is in good condition, or installed a new belt, check and adjust the belt using a strand tension gauge, figure 11-17. If the pump is driven by a flat serpentine belt, use a gauge designed for that type of belt construction. A belt that is too tight quickly wears out. A loose belt slips under load and allows the power steering pump to slow. This reduces the output of the pump and leads to erratic power assist to the brake and steering systems. Belt tensions differ for new and used belts, and the correct specifications for both can be found in the vehicle owner's and shop manuals. A used belt is any belt that has been tensioned and run for more than 10 or 15 minutes.

Next, inspect all of the power steering and Hydro-Boost lines, hoses, and connections, figure 11-18, for leaks, kinks, and wear. Tighten or replace parts as necessary. To confirm a leak, observe the suspected leak location while an assistant runs the engine at a fast idle and turns the steering wheel to full lock in either direction. This greatly increases pressure in the hydraulic system, and will force fluid out of even a small leak. To prevent damage to the system, do not hold the steering at full lock for more than five seconds. And, for personal safety, wear safety glasses to protect your eyes from high pressure fluid spray.

Next, check the master cylinder fluid level as described in Chapter 3. If the fluid level has dropped low enough for air to enter the system and give the pedal a spongy feel, it will be hard to judge the condition of the Hydro-Boost unit in the tests below. Top up the master cylinder and bleed the brake system as required before proceeding.

Finally, make sure the engine idle speed is set to the proper rpm. If the idle speed is too low, the power steer-

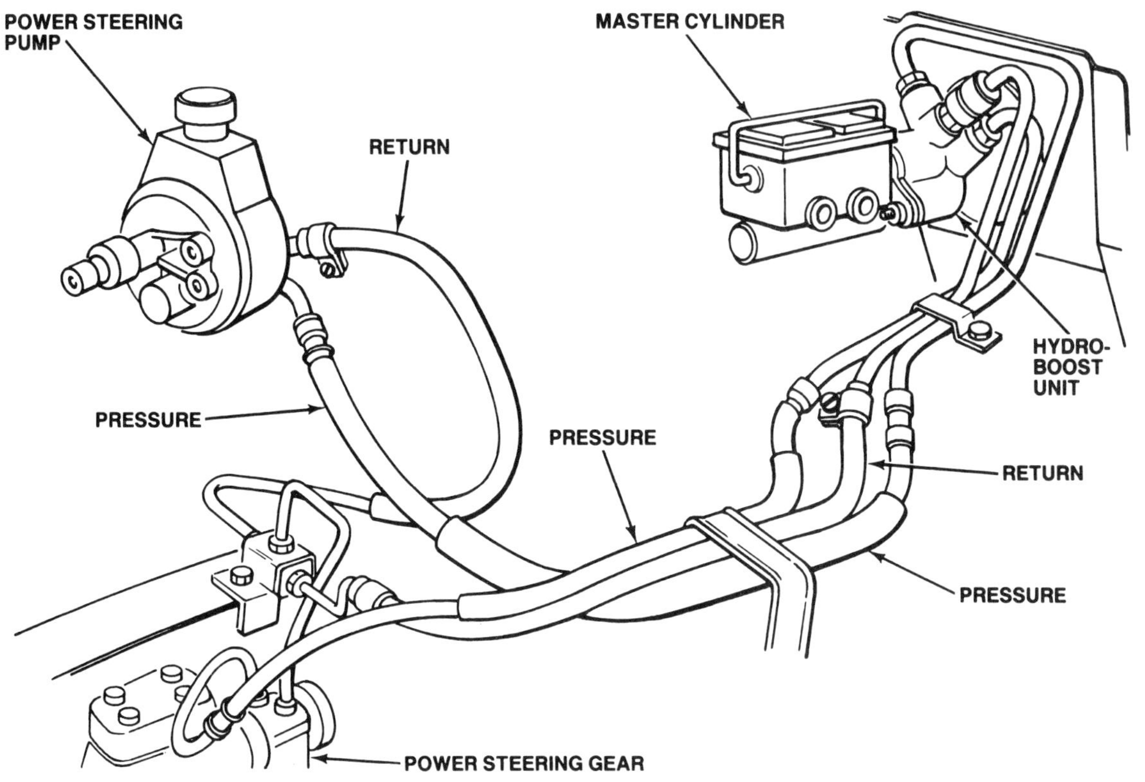

Power Brake Service

Figure 11-18. The extensive plumbing of the Hydro-Boost system can lead to fluid leaks.

ing pump will not turn fast enough to produce the pressure required for the Hydro-Boost unit to operate properly. If this happens, the results of the tests below may not be valid.

Hydro-Boost Function Test

The function test checks the ability of the Hydro-Boost unit to provide power assist. With the engine not running, apply the brake pedal five or more times with medium force to discharge the accumulator. The pedal feel will harden noticeably when the accumulator is discharged. Next, apply the brake pedal with medium force, and start the engine. If the booster is working properly, the pedal will drop toward the floor, then push back upward slightly. If the booster passes this test, perform the accumulator test below. If there is no change in the pedal position or feel, the booster is not working, and you should perform the power steering pump test to determine whether the problem is in the pump or the booster.

Power Steering Pump Test

The power steering pump test checks whether the pump produces enough fluid pressure and flow to enable the Hydro-Boost unit to provide full power brake

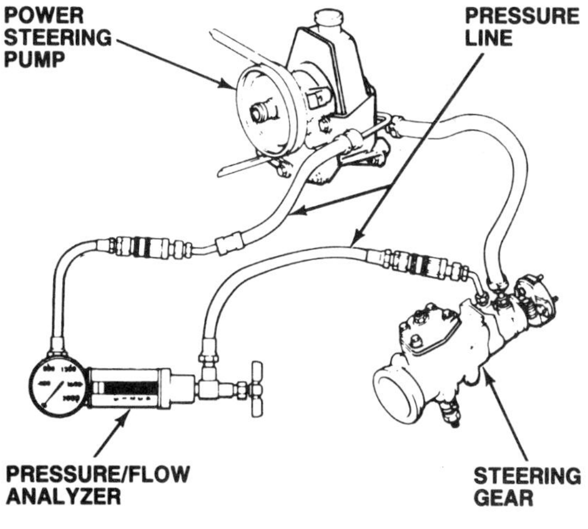

Figure 11-19. Pressure/flow analyzer installation to check the power steering pump output.

assist. To perform the power steering system test, drive the vehicle until the power steering fluid is at operating temperature, then shut off the engine. Disconnect the pressure line to the Hydro-Boost unit at the power steering pump end, and install a special pressure/flow analyzer (Kent-Moore No. J 25323 or equivalent) in series between the pump and hose, figure 11-19.

Start the engine, and follow the instructions that come with the analyzer to check the fluid pressure and flow provided by the power steering pump. Typical readings at idle are between 80 and 150 psi (550 and 1035 kPa) of pressure, with a flow rate between 1.25 and 1.75 gallons per minute. The exact specifications vary with the application, so check the factory shop manual for the car you are servicing. If the pump pressure and flow are within specifications, but the booster still fails a function test, rebuild or replace the Hydro-Boost unit. If the readings are below the normal ranges, rebuild or replace the power steering pump, then repeat the function test.

Hydro-Boost Accumulator Test

The accumulator test checks the operation of the booster reserve system by making sure the accumulator can hold a charge of hydraulic pressure. The accumulator test consists of two parts that check the ability of the reserve system to hold a short-term charge and a long-term charge.

To test the ability of the system to store a short-term charge, start the engine and allow it to idle. Charge the accumulator by turning the steering wheel slowly one time from lock to lock; do not hold the steering at full lock for more than five seconds. Shut off the engine and release the steering wheel, then repeatedly apply the brake pedal with medium force. If the accumulator can hold a charge, a Hydro-Boost I unit will provide two or three power assisted applications; a Hydro-Boost II unit will provide one or two.

To test the ability of the system to store a long-term charge, start the engine and recharge the accumulator as described above. As the accumulator charges on a Hydro-Boost I system, you should hear a slight hissing sound as fluid rushes through the accumulator charging orifice. Once the accumulator is charged, shut off the engine and do not apply the brake pedal for one hour. At the end of the hour, repeatedly apply the brake pedal with medium force. Once again, a Hydro-Boost I unit should provide two or three power assisted applications; a Hydro-Boost II unit should provide one or two.

If the Hydro-Boost unit fails these tests, it usually means the accumulator of a Hydro-Boost I unit, or the accumulator/power-piston assembly of a Hydro-Boost II unit, is leaking and the booster must be rebuilt or replaced. However, if a Hydro-Boost I system fails the test but does not make the hissing sound that indicates the accumulator is charging, the fluid in the system is probably contaminated, and you may be able to solve the problem by flushing the Hydro-Boost system.

Flushing the Hydro-Boost System

If you suspect fluid contamination in a Hydro-Boost system, flush the power booster, power steering pump, and fluid lines as follows:

1. Raise and properly support the front of the car so the wheels can be steered freely.
2. Disconnect the fluid pressure line at the steering gear, and place the end of the line in a drain pan.
3. Disable the vehicle ignition system to prevent the engine from starting. On diesel engines, disconnect the power supply wire to the fuel injection pump.
4. Have an assistant crank the engine, and at the same time, pump the brake pedal and slowly turn the steering wheel from lock to lock. To prevent starter damage, do not crank the engine for longer than 30 seconds at a time; allow the starter to cool for two minutes between cranking periods.
5. As the engine is cranking, fluid will be pumped from the system into the drain pan. As this occurs, continuously add new fluid to the power steering reservoir to maintain a minimum fluid level.
6. Once you have added approximately three quarts of fluid, have your assistant stop cranking the engine, then reconnect the pressure line to the power steering gear.
7. Lower the car, check and adjust the power steering fluid level, then start the engine and turn the steering wheel slowly from lock to lock several times.
8. Shut the engine off, then check and adjust the power steering fluid level.
9. Repeat the accumulator test. If the accumulator still will not hold a charge, rebuild or replace the Hydro-Boost unit.

HYDRO-BOOST REPLACEMENT

The accumulator of a Hydro-Boost unit holds over 1000 psi (6900 kPa) of pressure. As a result, it is *extremely important* to discharge the accumulator before you disconnect any of the lines or hoses attached to the booster. To discharge the accumulator, apply the brake pedal five or more times with medium force while the engine is not running. The pedal feel will harden noticeably when the accumulator is discharged.

To replace a Hydro-Boost power booster:

1. Remove or reposition any wires, brackets, hoses, or other components that obstruct access to the booster.
2. Remove the master cylinder retaining nuts, and pull the cylinder away from the booster. In most cases, you do not have to disconnect the brake

Power Brake Service

lines if you do this carefully. Be sure to support the cylinder so there is no stress on the brake lines.

3. Remove the three hydraulic lines from the power booster. Cap the lines to avoid fluid loss and prevent contaminants from entering the system.
4. Disconnect the brake pedal pushrod from the pedal arm. To do this, it may be necessary to remove the stoplight switch.
5. Remove the retaining nuts that hold the booster to the firewall, then withdraw the booster from the vehicle.
6. Position the new booster on the firewall, then install and tighten the retaining nuts.
7. Connect the brake pedal pushrod to the pedal arm.
8. Install and adjust the stoplight switch if you removed it in step 4. See Chapter 6 for information on switch adjustment.
9. Connect the three hydraulic lines to the power booster.
10. Position the master cylinder on the booster, then install and tighten the retaining nuts.
11. If you removed the brake lines from the master cylinder in step 2, reconnect them at this time and bleed the brakes as described in Chapter 3.
12. Install any wires, brackets, hoses, or other components removed in step 1.
13. Bleed the Hydro-Boost system as described in the next section, then perform a function test.

HYDRO-BOOST BLEEDING

Hydro-Boost power brake boosters are basically self-bleeding unless large quantities of air get into the power steering system, such as when it is opened for service. Air in the booster hydraulic circuits can cause noises and vibrations in the brake pedal and steering column during parking and other low speed maneuvers. To bleed the Hydro-Boost system, follow the procedure below. Once most of the air has been bled from the system in this manner, normal braking and steering will purge any small air pockets that remain in the system.

After you have finished bleeding a Hydro-Boost I system, there may be a gulping noise when the brake pedal is applied. The noise is caused by small amounts of air trapped in the system, and will go away after running the engine for a few minutes and lightly pumping the brake pedal. Once the noise disappears, check the fluid level in the power steering pump and add fluid if necessary.

To bleed a Hydro-Boost power brake system:

1. Check and adjust the power steering fluid level.
2. Disable the vehicle ignition system to prevent the engine from starting. On diesel engines, disconnect the power supply wire to the fuel injection pump.
3. Crank the engine with the starter for several seconds.
4. Recheck the power steering fluid level, and top it up as necessary. Repeat steps 3 and 4 until the fluid level remains constant.
5. Reconnect any wires removed in step 2, and start the engine.
6. Turn the steering wheel slowly from lock to lock two times.
7. Shut off the engine, and discharge the accumulator.
8. Restart the engine and turn the steering wheel slowly from lock to lock two times.
9. Shut off the engine, then check and adjust the power steering fluid level.
10. If fluid foaming occurs when bleeding the Hydro-Boost system, shut off the engine and allow the car to sit for one hour. Then, check and adjust the power steering fluid level, and repeat the bleeding procedure.

POWERMASTER TESTING

The General Motors Powermaster brake system does not rely on hydraulic pressure from an outside source such as the power steering pump. Instead, the unit has a self-contained electrohydraulic pump, and requires only a 12-volt power source to provide braking assist. As with other power boosters, a failure of the Powermaster system causes a high, hard brake pedal that makes it difficult for the driver to slow and stop the car. A Powermaster failure may also be indicated by illumination of the brake warning light on the instrument panel, or by unusual operation of the electrohydraulic pump motor.

Before you suspect a faulty Powermaster unit, be sure the problem you are dealing with is booster related. For example, a faulty Powermaster cannot cause a low brake pedal; only about 1/8 inch (3 mm) of pedal pushrod travel is required to activate the booster valves. The Powermaster also cannot cause such common problems as brake pull, a pulsating or spongy pedal, brake squeal, or a failure in one half of the dual-circuit braking system.

If you suspect a problem with the Powermaster unit, check and adjust the fluid level in the reservoir as detailed in Chapter 3, then perform a function test. Depending on the results, perform the additional tests detailed below for external leaks, electrical problems, improper system pressures, and internal leaks. If the results of any test indicate that the Powermaster booster needs repair, the unit must be replaced. There are no rebuild kits available at this time.

Several Powermaster tests require that the electrohydraulic pump be allowed to run in order to pressurize the system. When doing these tests, do not allow the pump to run for more than 20 seconds at a time, or it may overheat. To prevent pump damage, turn off the ignition and allow the pump to cool for two minutes between each operating cycle.

Powermaster Function Test

The Powermaster function test is a preliminary diagnostic procedure with several steps that check different aspects of the Powermaster system. To perform the test:

1. Inspect the outside of the Powermaster for signs of brake fluid leaks:
   a. If there are no signs of leakage, go to step 2.
   b. If there is leakage, perform the external leak test below.
2. Apply the brake pedal with firm pressure and hold:
   a. If the pedal remains at a fixed height, go to step 3.
   b. If the pedal drops toward the floor, the master cylinder section of the Powermaster is bypassing internally. Replace the Powermaster.
3. Pump the brake pedal at least 10 times with the ignition OFF to discharge the accumulator. The pedal feel will harden noticeably when the accumulator is discharged.
4. Release the parking brake.
5. Turn the ignition switch to RUN. The brake warning light should come on and the electric pump motor should begin to operate. After approximately 20 seconds, the pump motor should stop and the light should go out.
   a. If the pump motor and warning light operate as described, go to step 6.
   b. If the pump motor does not run, perform the electrical checks below.
   c. If the pump motor runs for longer than 20 seconds, perform the pressure tests below.
6. Leave the ignition switch in the RUN position, and do not apply the brake pedal for five minutes. If the pump motor begins to operate during that time, perform the internal leak test.

External Leak Test

External leakage from a Powermaster unit is usually easy to spot because the accumulator is pressurized to over 500 psi (3,450 kPa). As a result, even a small leak will cause fluid to seep or spray from the unit. Even when the leak is quite small, the Powermaster reservoir quickly runs dry of fluid.

To locate the source of a leak, wipe the Powermaster assembly and hoses clean with a rag soaked in brake cleaner or alcohol, and install a fender cover to protect the vehicle finish from possible brake fluid spray. Top up the reservoir with fresh brake fluid, and turn the ignition switch ON. As the pump motor runs to charge the accumulator, check for leaks at the reservoir cover, reservoir mounting grommets, pressure switch, accumulator, hose and pipe connections, and under the dash at the end of the pedal pushrod. Once you locate the leak, replace defective parts or tighten connections as needed. If fluid is leaking from around the brake pedal pushrod, replace the Powermaster unit.

If there is a great deal of fluid on the outside of the Powermaster reservoir, but the fluid level inside is normal, the fluid spill was probably caused by an overfilled reservoir and not by a leak. If the reservoir is filled when the accumulator is charged, excess fluid will be forced past the reservoir cover as fluid is returned to the reservoir from the accumulator during normal brake operation.

Electrical Checks

The electrohydraulic pump of the Powermaster unit draws a great deal of current. In order for the booster to operate properly, it must have a constant 12-volt power supply, and the battery must be in good condition and fully charged. If the pump motor does not run during a function test, check the 30-amp Powermaster fuse, and make sure all electrical connections at the Powermaster unit are tight. If the fuse and connections are both okay, consult the factory shop manual of the vehicle being serviced for diagnosis information on the Powermaster electrical circuit.

Pressure Tests

The Powermaster pressure tests are used to determine why the electrohydraulic pump motor runs too long or too often. There are three separate tests to check the upper limit pressure, the lower limit pressure, and the accumulator precharge pressure. Perform all three tests if the Powermaster function test or internal leak test instructs you to do so.

To perform the pressure tests requires a special pressure testing gauge (Kent-Moore No. J 35126 or equivalent). The tool consists of a high-pressure gauge, a bleeder valve, and a bleeder hose. To install the gauge, discharge the accumulator by applying the brake pedal at least ten times with medium pressure while the ignition is OFF. The pedal feel will become noticeably harder when the accumulator is discharged. Remove the pressure switch from the Powermaster unit, install the gauge in its place, figure 11-20, then install the pressure switch into the opening in the gauge

Power Brake Service

Figure 11-20. The special pressure test gauge installed on the Powermaster.

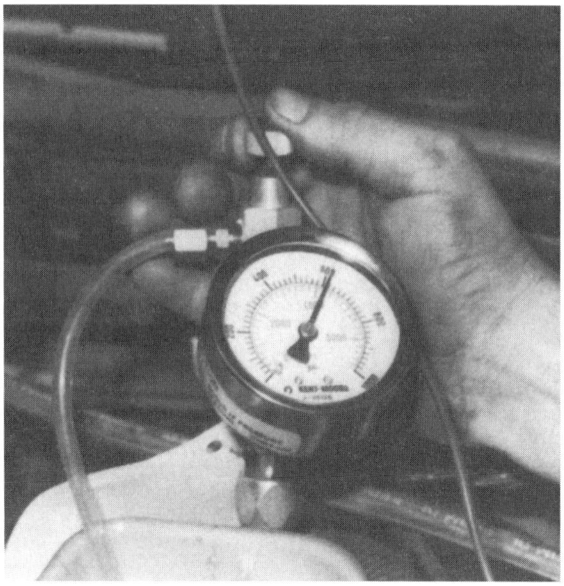

Figure 11-21. The Powermaster test gauge showing the correct reading for the upper limit pressure check.

Figure 11-22. Open the bleeder valve on the test gauge to perform the Powermaster lower limit pressure check.

mounting boss. Route the bleeder hose from the gauge into the booster side of the fluid reservoir.

Upper Limit Pressure Test

The upper limit test checks the pressure at which the electrohydraulic pump shuts off. To perform the upper limit pressure test, close the bleeder valve on the special tool, then turn the ignition ON and allow the pump motor to run. The pump should shut off when the pressure reading on the gauge reaches 635 to 735 psi (4,380 to 5,070 kPa), figure 11-21. If the pressure exceeds the upper limit, replace the pressure switch. If the pressure never reaches the upper limit and the pump motor runs longer than 20 seconds, replace the pump.

Lower Limit Pressure Test

The lower limit test checks the pressure at which the electrohydraulic pump turns on. To perform the lower limit pressure test, turn the ignition ON and wait until the pump motor shuts off, indicating that the accumulator is fully charged. Make sure the bleeder hose from the gauge is routed into the booster side of the fluid reservoir, then slowly open the bleeder valve, figure 11-22. Watch the reading on the gauge, and note the pressure at which the pump motor begins to run; this should be between 490 and 530 psi (3380 to 3655 kPa). If the pump starts to run at a higher pressure, or does not start to run at the lower limit, replace the pressure switch.

Accumulator Precharge Pressure Test

The accumulator precharge pressure test checks the ability of the accumulator to hold a charge of hydraulic pressure. To perform the test, turn the ignition OFF, and have an assistant discharge the accumulator by repeatedly applying the brake pedal with medium force. As he does so, observe the gauge and note the pressure reading just before the brake pedal becomes hard. This is the accumulator precharge pressure, which should be between 200 and 300 psi (1,380 and 2,070 kPa).

Another way to test the accumulator precharge pressure is to discharge the accumulator as described above, then turn the ignition ON. The pressure reading on the

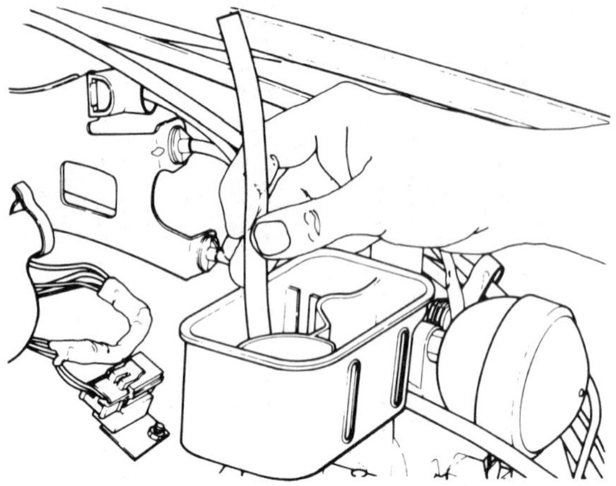

Figure 11-23. Use a clear plastic hose to check for internal leaks in the Powermaster.

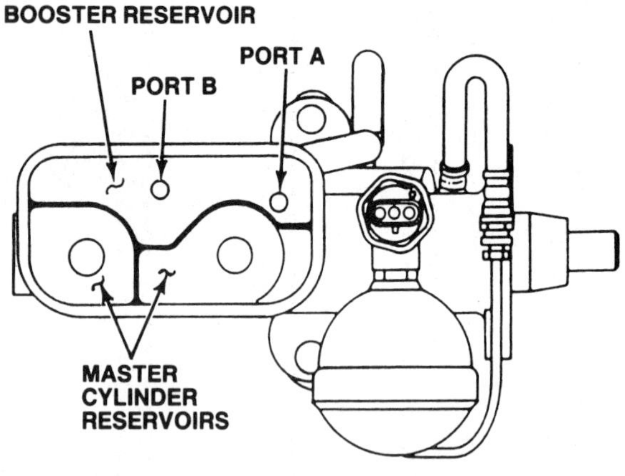

Figure 11-24. The Powermaster fluid return port (A) and supply port (B).

gauge should immediately jump to the precharge pressure. If the Powermaster fails either of the precharge tests, replace the accumulator.

Internal Leak Test

If there is no evidence of an external leak, but the pump motor runs within a 5-minute period when the brake pedal is not applied and the ignition is ON, suspect an internal leak. To test for this problem:

1. Turn the ignition ON and pump the brake pedal until the electrohydraulic pump motor begins to run.
2. Stop pumping the brake pedal, wait until the pump motor stops running, then turn the ignition OFF.
3. Hold a clear plastic hose, figure 11-23, over the fluid return port in the booster section of the Powermaster fluid reservoir, port B in figure 11-24:
   a. If brake fluid rises up the tube, fluid is leaking past the check valve. Replace the Powermaster.
   b. If fluid does not rise in the tube, go to step 4.
4. Hold a clear plastic hose over the pump supply port in the booster section of the Powermaster fluid reservoir, port A in figure 11-24:
   a. If fluid rises up the tube, there is a leak past the internal valves. Replace the Powermaster.
   b. If fluid does not rise in the tube, perform the pressure tests above.

POWERMASTER REPLACEMENT

The accumulator of a Powermaster unit holds over 500 psi (3,450 kPa) of pressure. As a result, it is *extremely important* to discharge the accumulator before you disconnect any of the lines or hoses attached to the booster. To discharge the accumulator, apply the brake pedal 10 or more times with medium force while the ignition is OFF. The pedal feel will harden noticeably when the accumulator is discharged.

To replace a Powermaster brake booster:

1. Remove or reposition any wires, brackets, hoses, or other components that obstruct access to the booster.
2. Detach the electrical connectors from the pressure switch and electrohydraulic pump.
3. Disconnect the brake lines from the master cylinder portion of the Powermaster.
4. Disconnect the brake pedal pushrod from the pedal arm. To do this, it may be necessary to remove the stoplight switch.
5. Remove the retaining nuts that hold the booster to the firewall, then withdraw the booster from the vehicle.
6. Bench bleed the master cylinder portion of the Powermaster as described in Chapter 3.
7. Position the new booster on the firewall, then install and tighten the retaining nuts.
8. Connect the brake pedal pushrod to the pedal arm.
9. Install and adjust the stoplight switch if you removed it in step 4. See Chapter 6 for information on switch adjustment.
10. Connect the brake lines to the master cylinder portion of the Powermaster.
11. Attach the electrical connectors to the pressure switch and electrohydraulic pump.
12. Install any wires, brackets, hoses, or other components removed in step 1.
13. Fill and bleed the Powermaster unit as described below.

Power Brake Service

POWERMASTER FILL AND BLEED

The master cylinder section of the Powermaster unit should be bench bled in a conventional manner before the booster is installed on the car. However, once the Powermaster unit is in place, you must use the procedure below to fill and bleed the booster section of the unit. During this process, do not allow the pump to run for longer than 20 seconds at a time.

To fill and bleed a Powermaster booster:

1. Remove the fluid reservoir cover and fill the booster side of the reservoir with fresh DOT 3 brake fluid.
2. Turn the ignition switch ON. As the pump motor runs, the fluid level in the booster side of the reservoir will drop as the accumulator is charged. Add fluid as needed to prevent the reservoir from running dry.
3. When the pump motor stops, adjust the fluid level so the ports in the bottom of the reservoir are just covered, then install the reservoir cover.
4. Turn the ignition OFF, and discharge the accumulator. Pump the brake pedal 10 or more times with medium force. The pedal feel will harden noticeably when the accumulator is discharged.
5. Remove the reservoir cover, and top up the fluid level to the "maximum" mark on the reservoir.
6. Reinstall the reservoir cover and turn the ignition ON to charge the accumulator. Add fluid as needed to prevent the reservoir from running dry.
7. Repeat steps 4 through 6 a total of 10 to 15 times to purge all of the air from the booster. When you are completed, the fluid level in the booster side of the reservoir should always return to the "maximum" mark when the accumulator is discharged.

12
Antilock Brake Basics

OBJECTIVES

Upon completion and review of this chapter, you will be able to:

- Properly relieve accumulator pressure on integral ABS.
- Monitor the ABS warning lamp to determine if a problem exists.
- Diagnose ABS problems by symptom.
- Perform antilock system basic diagnostic checks.
- Perform preliminary inspections.
- Verify ABS operation.
- Perform voltage checks on the ABS pump circuit.
- Pressure test an integral antilock system.
- Isolate the source of a pressure loss.
- Test a wheel speed sensor using a DVOM.
- Test a wheel speed sensor using an oscilloscope.
- Adjust wheel speed sensor air gap.
- Replace a wheel speed sensor.

INTRODUCTION

This chapter describes basic troubleshooting techniques and service precautions that are common to all antilock brake systems (ABS). Chapter 13 covers diagnostic and service procedures for specific systems.

Troubleshooting antilock brake problems can sometimes be done without referring to service literature. More often, it requires detailed diagnostic charts found in shop manuals. These charts define the various ABS fault codes. They also provide a step-by-step diagnostic procedure to pinpoint the faulty circuit or component in the least amount of time. These charts decrease the time and money otherwise spent repairing working systems.

Many ABS applications require a scan tool to access the ABS control module for diagnostic purposes, as well as for performing some service procedures such as system bleeding. Refer to Chapter 13 for accessing the ABS electronics on specific systems.

SERVICE BASICS

Before discussing the basics of troubleshooting ABS, keep the following basic brake system service points in mind. Most ABS and non-ABS-equipped vehicles use essentially the same brake service procedures. This includes techniques for replacing brake pads and shoes, and refinishing rotors and drums. Some antilock systems may require special brake bleeding procedures.

On vehicles with nonintegral ABS, the basic brake components are usually identical to those used on the same model without the antilock brake option. For

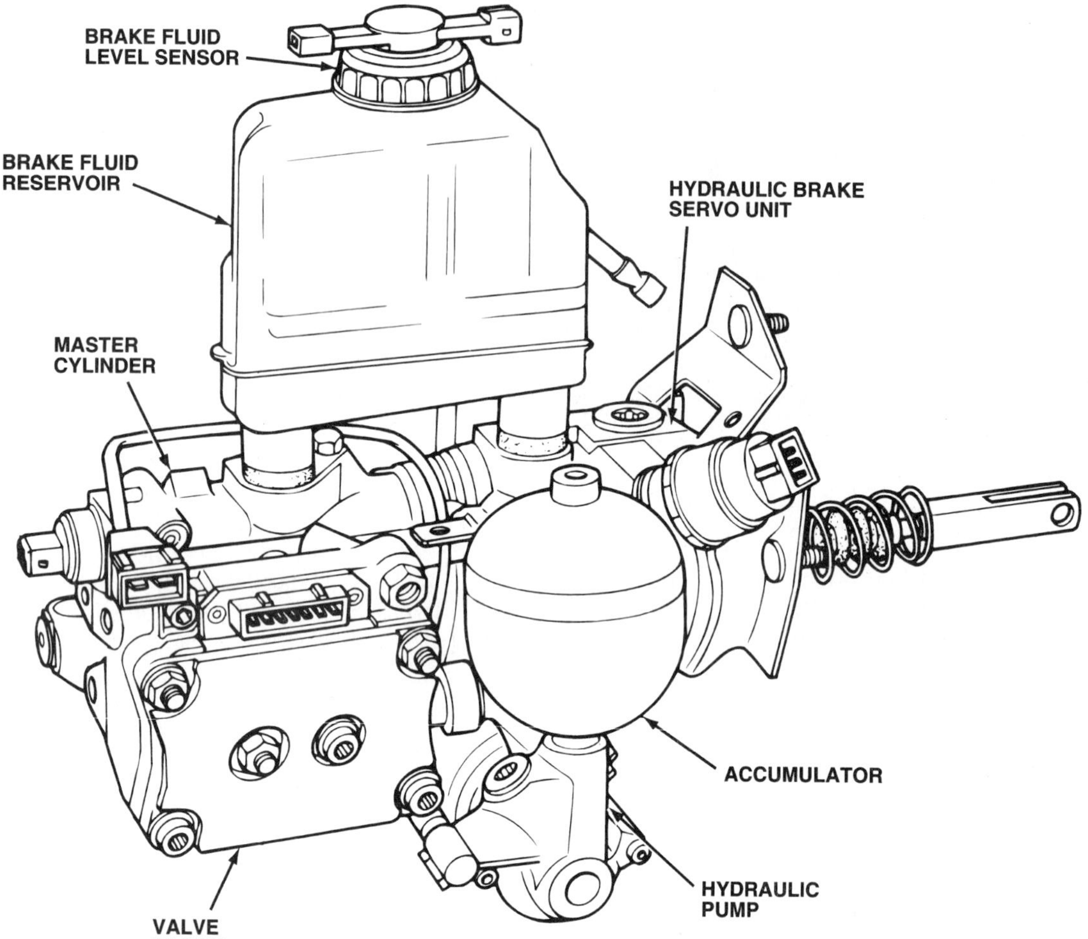

Figure 12-1. On integral ABS with a hydraulic pump and accumulator, you must pump the brake pedal to relieve accumulator pressure before you begin working on the system.

example, between the two vehicles, the brake linings, calipers, wheel cylinders, and brake hoses may share the same replacement part numbers. However, the master cylinder may be different on some, but not on all applications. The brake rotors and drums may also be different, depending on if the wheel speed sensor tone ring is a part of the assembly, or a separate part.

Modern brake systems, whether ABS or not, require either DOT 3 or 4 brake fluid. Always use the type of fluid specified by the vehicle manufacturer. DOT 5 silicone brake fluid is generally not recommended for ABS applications.

When working on integral ABS that use a pump and accumulator rather than a conventional vacuum booster, be sure to vent all pressure from the accumulator before opening any lines or beginning any brake work, figure 12-1. Pump the brake pedal 25 to 40 times while the ignition is off to relieve pressure. Some ABS applications create hydraulic pressures as high as 2700 psi (18,660 kPa). Generally, you can monitor the gradual decrease in pressure remaining in the system by sensing the increasing effort required to depress the brake pedal. Again, do not open any brake line or attempt to service or remove any component on an integral master cylinder assembly without first fully discharging the accumulator!

An ABS Problem or a Base Brake Problem?

During normal braking, ABS does not affect the operation of the brakes. Pressurized fluid from the master cylinder pushes the caliper and wheel cylinder pistons out so the linings contact the rotors and drums. The pressure of the fluid normally does not change as it passes through the ABS modulator. In most cases, an ABS malfunction will not affect normal braking. However, there are exceptions, which will be explained later. Typically, an ABS problem only affects the ABS portion of the braking system.

Antilock Brake Basics

SEQUENCE NUMBER	LAMP SEQUENCE	SYMPTOM DESCRIPTION	PERFORM TEST
1	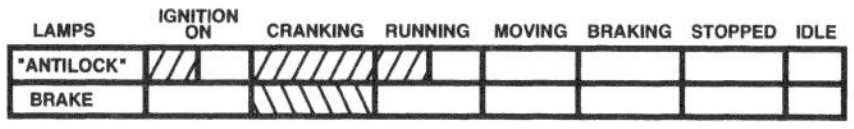	NORMAL LAMP SEQUENCE WITH -EXCESSIVE PEDAL TRAVEL OR SPONGY PEDAL -ANTILOCK BRAKING OPERATION OR VALVE CYCLING DURING NORMAL STOPS ON DRY PAVEMENT -POOR VEHICLE TRACKING DURING ANTILOCK BRAKING	H C D
2	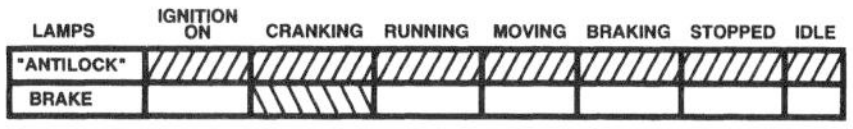	CONTINUOUS "ANTILOCK" LAMP NORMAL "BRAKE" LAMP	A
3	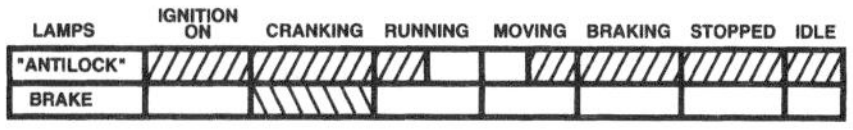	"ANTILOCK" LAMP COMES ON AFTER VEHICLE STARTS MOVING NORMAL BRAKE LAMP	C
4	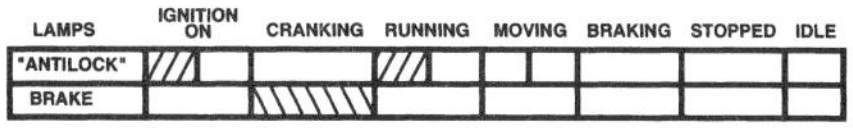	NO "ANTILOCK" LAMP WHILE CRANKING NORMAL "BRAKE" LAMP	E
5	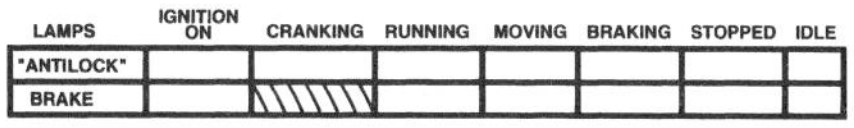	NO "ANTILOCK" LAMP NORMAL "BRAKE" LAMP	F
6	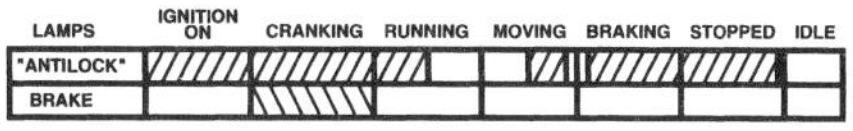	INTERMITTENT "ANTILOCK" LAMP WHILE DRIVING NORMAL "BRAKE" LAMP	G
7	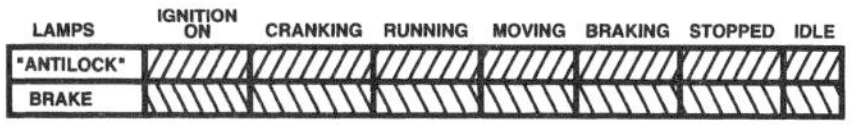	CONTINUOUS "ANTILOCK" LAMP CONTINUOUS "BRAKE" LAMP	B
8	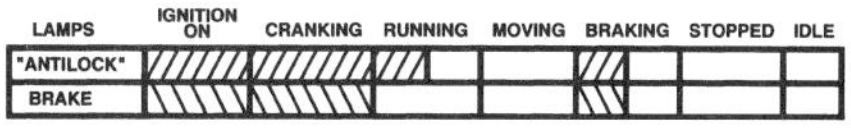	"ANTILOCK" AND "BRAKE" LAMPS COME ON WHILE BRAKING	B
9	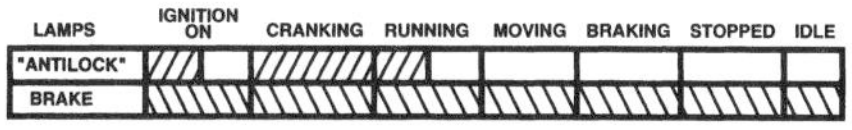	NORMAL "ANTILOCK" LAMP CONTINUOUS "BRAKE" LAMP	B
10	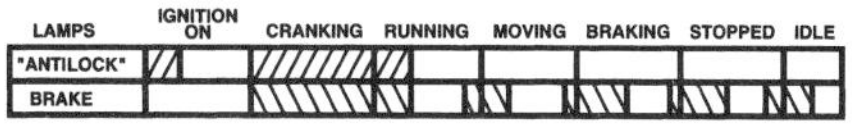	NORMAL OR CONTINUOUS "ANTILOCK" LAMP FLASHING "BRAKE" LAMP	B

Figure 12-2. This lamp sequence chart refers you to a specific troubleshooting procedure. To use it properly, you must note during what driving conditions the warning lamps light up, and how long they stay lit.

You can detect most ABS problems by monitoring when the ABS warning lamp, BRAKE warning lamp, or both, illuminate. One or both lamps may fail to go out, come on intermittently, or remain on continuously while driving, figure 12-2. Simultaneously, the driver may have noticed a change in the braking characteristics of the vehicle, or a complete loss of ABS function.

Guard against hasty diagnoses that blame the ABS system for conventional brake problems. In general, service grabbing, pulling, dragging, or noisy brakes by following the procedures in the brake system diagnosis chapter. Make sure the service brakes are in good working order before searching for an ABS problem. Remember, most ABS only activates when the wheel speed sensors detect a wheel decelerating too quickly, causing an interruption of traction. Integral ABS systems with power assist serve as the exception. Servicing procedures for these systems will be addressed later in the chapter.

Brake Symptoms

We covered all the common symptoms of the conventional brake system in Chapter 2 of this manual. This section describes how the diagnosis of some common brake symptoms may be different with ABS.

- *Noise*—Most ABS systems make noise when operating. Typically, the ABS solenoids in the modulator assembly will buzz and click. Diagnoses for other brake noises are the same as for conventional brake systems.

- *Pulling*—Faults with the ABS system usually do not cause brake pull; pulling is most often the result of a conventional brake system failure. Although unlikely, certain ABS failures can cause the brakes to pull. An ABS isolation valve for a front wheel circuit that remains energized or stuck closed will block pressure to the affected wheel. This will cause a pull toward the unaffected side when the brakes are applied. Similarly, an ABS dump valve for a front wheel circuit that remains energized or stuck open will prevent the affected brake from being applied and results in a pull to the opposite side. ABS valves that fail to close are often caused by contamination that interferes with the movement of the valve. Look for debris or corrosion within the hydraulic system when you suspect a sticking ABS valve.
- *Pedal vibration*—The rapid cycling of brake pressure in the hydraulic circuits during an ABS stop pulsates the brake pedal. The amount of pulsation varies with the type of ABS and vehicle application. Pulsation should only occur during a hard, ABS-assisted stop or when braking on a slick surface. It should not occur during normal braking. If it does, especially when accompanied by a shuddering or jerky stop, examine the brake rotors for warpage. An out-of-round drum, loose wheel bearings, or loose brake parts can also cause pedal pulsation during normal braking.
- *Grabbing*—If the brakes feel jerky or lockup easily during normal braking, check for contaminated linings, as shown in Chapters 7 and 8. Also examine the drums and rotors for severe scoring, as shown in Chapter 9. These problems affect ABS operation as well as normal braking. On most antilock systems, low-speed wheel lockup does not indicate a problem. The vehicle must exceed 4 to 6 mph (6 to 10 kph) before the wheel speed sensors provide reliable speed signals and ABS becomes operational.
- *Dragging*—Although unlikely, ABS with traction control may apply the brake on a drive wheel continuously if there is current constantly flowing through the traction control solenoids and pump.
- *Gradually sinking brake pedal*—For this problem, check for a worn master cylinder. For systems that have a brake fluid level indicator, check for an illuminated ABS or BRAKE warning lamp. On trucks with Kelsey-Hayes rear-wheel antilock brakes (RWAL or RABS), dirt in the ABS control valve can prevent the dump valve from fully seating. This allows brake fluid to leak past the valve, causing the pedal to sink. Refer to Chapter 13 of this manual for diagnostic techniques.
- *Hard pedal*—Increased pedal effort may indicate an ABS problem, but only on integral ABS. The electric pump and accumulator on these systems provide normal power assist. Problems such as a faulty pump, pump relay, or a pressure loss in the accumulator reduces boost and increased pedal effort is needed to stop the vehicle. Usually, the ABS warning lamp will light, and the ABS control module will deactivate itself. With a hard pedal on vehicles with hydroboost power brakes, look for a loose power steering pump belt, low fluid level, leaky hoses, or faulty valves in the hydroboost unit.

Preliminary Checks

In addition to the preliminary checks for conventional brake components recommended in Chapter 2 and throughout the book, examine the following items before inspecting ABS components:

- *Charging system and battery*—Antilock systems require proper system voltage to operate; make sure the generator and battery are functioning properly. Most ABS will be disabled at less than 11 volts.
- *Fuses*—Check the ABS control module fuse, main relay fuse, and pump motor fuse. Also check instrument cluster fuses that could affect the warning lamps.
- *Connectors*—Check for corroded or loosely installed connections on the following parts: the main relay, pump motor, pump motor relay, pressure switch, main valve, valve block, fluid level sensor, control module, and wheel speed sensors.
- *Grounds*—Check for excessive voltage drop across system ground connections, especially those for the control module, pump motor, relay, and hydraulic modulator assembly.

Verifying ABS Operation

In most vehicles, when the antilock system is working normally, the ABS warning lamp should illuminate as a bulb check for a few seconds when the ignition is first switched on. It is possible for the accumulator to discharge if the vehicle has been sitting for several days. In this case, the warning lamp may remain on for up to 30 seconds as pressure builds in the accumulator.

During engine cranking expect the ABS warning lamp, and possibly the BRAKE warning lamp, to remain on, figure 12-3. When the engine starts, the BRAKE lamp should go out, and then, after a short de-

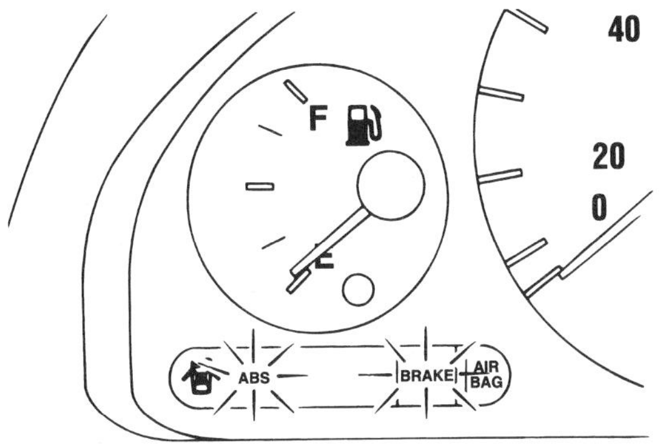

Antilock Brake Basics

Figure 12-3. On most systems, both the ABS and BRAKE warning lamps should come on as a bulb check when the ignition is first switched on.

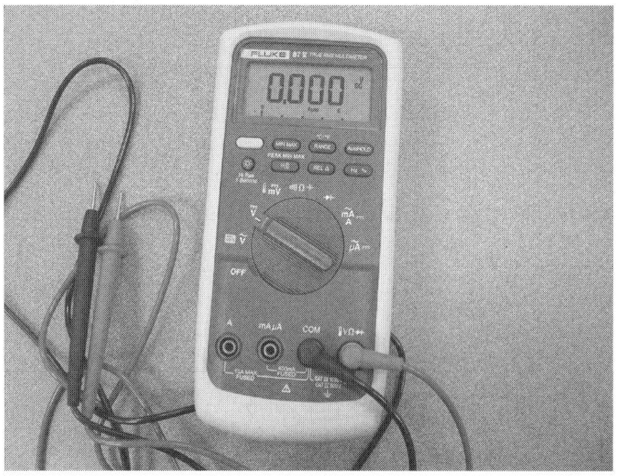

Figure 12-4. A good quality digital volt-ohmmeter (DVOM) is essential for troubleshooting ABS electronic circuits.

lay, the ABS lamp should switch off. On vehicles with traction control, the traction control warning lamp will generally function similar to the ABS lamp. All of the warning lamps should remain off at all other times.

Test the ABS system by driving on a wet or slick surface at 20 to 25 mph (32 to 48 kph) and stopping suddenly. If the ABS works, expect to feel feedback in the brake pedal and hear the buzzing and clicking noises mentioned previously. The vehicle should stop in a straight line without skidding or locking up the wheels.

If the ABS does not engage during the test, check the operation of the ABS warning lamp. Explore the conventional brake system, or look for an intermittent ABS fault, if a functioning lamp does not light.

ABS Monitoring Equipment

Verifying ABS operation usually requires the use of electronic test equipment. A high-impedance digital volt-ohmmeter (DVOM) is essential, figure 12-4. You must have accurate wiring diagrams and service specifications as well. Standard electronic test equipment, such as a breakout box and scan tool, will also prove beneficial. The scan tool is required for servicing some systems, and other test equipment is also available. Here we will briefly discuss ABS test equipment.

Dedicated System Testers

For certain systems, dedicated test equipment is available. These tools check ABS operation by passing current through various electrical circuits and cycling the solenoids. Due to high cost and limited applications, only technicians working at new car dealerships are likely to use these tools, figure 12-5. On most systems, similar tests can be performed using a DVOM and a breakout box, or a scan tool. For additional information on dedicated service equipment, see the section on Bosch ABS in Chapter 13 of this manual.

Scan Tools

A scan tool can check for diagnostic trouble codes (DTC), as well as display data stream parameters and perform functional tests on some systems, figure 12-6. Functional testing allows you to quickly check the operation of the pump and the modulator solenoids and motors. However, some test functions require bidirectional communication between the scan tool and ABS control module. This allows the scan tool to receive and give commands to the ABS control module. Some manufacturers limit bidirectional communications information, and these features are only available with their factory scan tool, figure 12-7.

When scan tool testing reveals ABS codes in memory, refer to the appropriate diagnostic chart for troubleshooting. Often, it will be necessary to perform pinpoint tests using a DVOM and breakout box to isolate the source of the problem.

Diagnosis with the ABS Warning Lamp

If the ABS warning lamp is off, do not assume the system is operating as it should. The bulb may be burned out, or the fuse that supplies it may be blown. Check bulb operation during the timed bulb check period when the ignition switch is initially turned on. If the bulb illuminates and extinguishes after several seconds, and there are no other brake system complaints, then the ABS is probably operational. We say "probably" because the only way to know for sure is to test the system.

If the ABS warning lamp comes on and remains on, the system has detected a fault that requires further diagnosis. A BRAKE warning lamp that remains on or comes on while driving usually indicates a problem with the hydraulic system, not an ABS failure. There

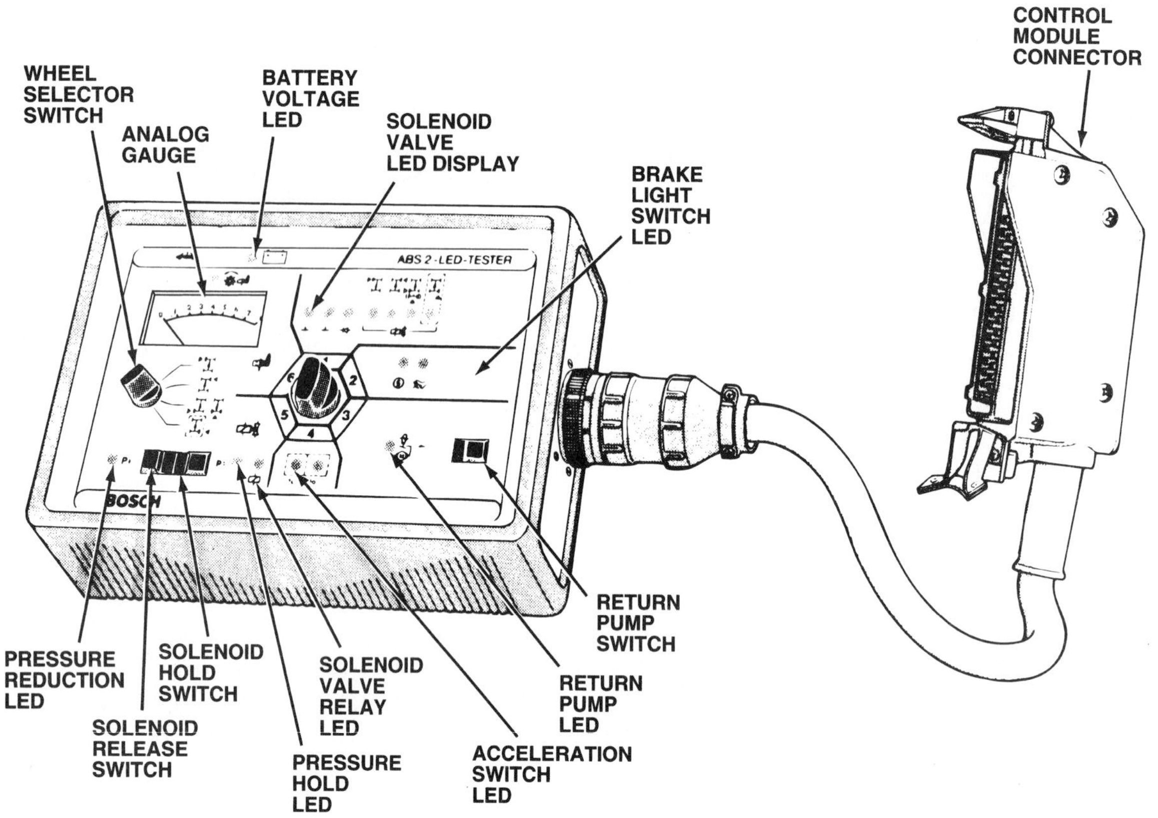

Figure 12-5. Some equipment, such as this Bosch ABS 2 LED tester, is designed to perform functional tests on specific ABS applications.

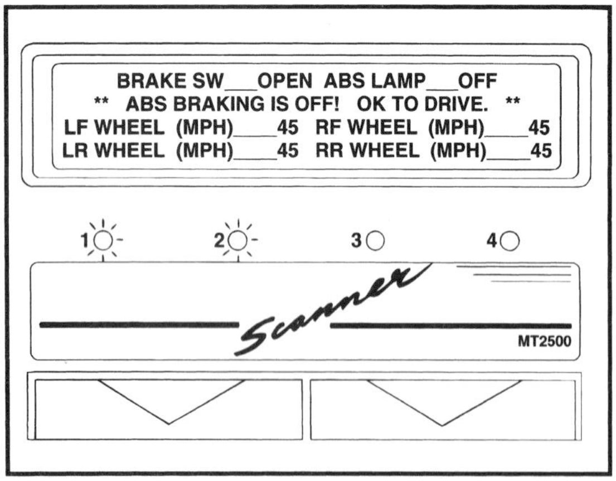

Figure 12-6. You can monitor the ABS data stream with a scan tool, as well as perform functional tests on some systems.

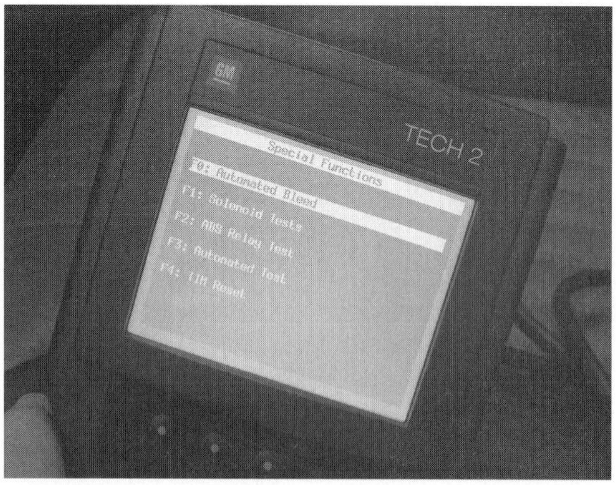

Figure 12-7. This scan tool has bidirectional functions that allow the technician to operate and test the ABS.

may be a fluid leak or loss of pressure, both threats to safe braking. Investigate the cause immediately. Be aware: Some systems use the BRAKE warning lamp to alert the driver of an ABS problem when the ABS lamp or circuit is malfunctioning.

If the ABS lamp comes on and remains on or flashes, the self-diagnostic program of the ABS control module has detected a system failure. How the warning lamp reacts can provide clues to the nature of the problem.

Antilock Brake Basics

An ABS warning lamp that comes on when the car first starts to move generally indicates a problem with one wheel speed sensor. Speed sensor failures can also cause ABS to engage during normal stops on dry pavement.

Most systems perform a self-test to check the integrity of the circuits when the ignition is turned on. Once the vehicle gets underway, a second self-test momentarily energizes solenoids, valves, and motors to check for a dynamic response. Should the system detect a fault during either self-test, the warning lamp illuminates and the control module suspends ABS operation.

On vehicles with integral ABS, if both the BRAKE and ABS warning lamps illuminate and power assist is low, suspect an inoperative pump or an accumulator pressure leak. If power assist is normal and both warning lamps are on, check the fluid level and fluid level sensor. If level is normal and the sensor is working, take a brake pressure reading.

When the ABS is combined with a traction control system, both systems automatically deactivate when the warning lamp comes on as a failsafe procedure. This should not affect normal braking, and does not pose any danger to the safe operation of the vehicle under normal driving conditions. Vehicles with integral ABS will also deactivate power-assisted braking. If the ABS warning light is on and remains on, first check for obvious problems such as low fluid level. Next, use the procedures in Chapter 13 of this manual to retrieve diagnostic trouble codes. Refer to a diagnostic chart for the specific vehicle being serviced to conduct circuit voltage, resistance, and continuity tests.

ONBOARD DIAGNOSTICS

Most antilock brake systems have comprehensive self-diagnostic capability; early Bosch systems are exceptions. See the following chapter of this manual for specific ABS diagnostic procedures.

The ABS control module generates diagnostic trouble codes. Each diagnostic trouble code (DTC) represents a specific failure, such as a signal loss from a wheel speed sensor, erroneous voltage feedback from a modulator solenoid, or an intermittent signal from a pump motor relay circuit. On some applications, a low-pressure switch is used to detect pressure loss in the accumulator, and a switch circuit failure will also set a DTC. Be aware: The ABS self-diagnostic routine monitors ABS functions only, and will not recognize problems or set codes, for the conventional brake system.

On some vehicles, retrieve codes by grounding the ABS control module diagnostic connector, and counting the number of times the ABS warning lamp flashes, figure 12-8. On some others, you access codes by pushing buttons on the control panel of the climate control system in a specified sequence to display results on the vehicle information center or digital speedometer. For some applications, a scan tool must be used to retrieve codes from the ABS control module, figure 12-9.

Even when not required, the scan tool offers several advantages. Rather than flash codes, the scan tool displays codes numerically, making them easier to read and eliminating the possibility of miscounting lamp flashes. On some systems, the scan tool can also clear codes at the press of a button. As previously mentioned, the scan tool can also perform functional tests of system components on some applications.

Fault Code Diagnosis

Although a DTC will pinpoint the specific faulty circuit, it will not tell you the exact nature of the fault, or the exact location of the problem. The DTC is simply a guide to point you in the right direction. Additional testing is needed to locate the defective component, connection, or wiring. To identify the problem from your list of possibilities, first refer to the diagnostic procedure found in the shop manual, figure 12-10. As you follow the sequence, each step eliminates working components and subsystems to lead you to the source of the failure. Often, these charts are quite lengthy and involve a number of continuity, resistance, and voltage checks. Carry out each test in the exact order prescribed. Skipping steps, or taking other shortcuts, can lead to false conclusions and compound the problem. Using the factory procedure, you can efficiently identify the problem.

Multiple Diagnostic Trouble Codes

When there are multiple ABS codes in memory, they will display either in numerical sequence or the sequence in which you must repair them. Troubleshooting codes in correct order is important, as one code may be responsible for setting other codes. Follow the steps included in the diagnostic chart in sequence, until you eliminate all possibilities.

When diagnosing a system using codes, always attempt to make the codes reappear to be sure the problem still exists. First, record and then clear all the codes present. Inspect the wiring for obvious problems, such as loose or corroded connectors. Then test drive the vehicle, perform a wiggle test, or do both. Note if the ABS warning lamp comes back on, or if the same codes reappear on your scan tool.

When more than three codes appear, the real problem may be a loose or corroded connection shared by multiple circuits. It is extremely rare to have more than one component fail at the same time. Consult a wiring

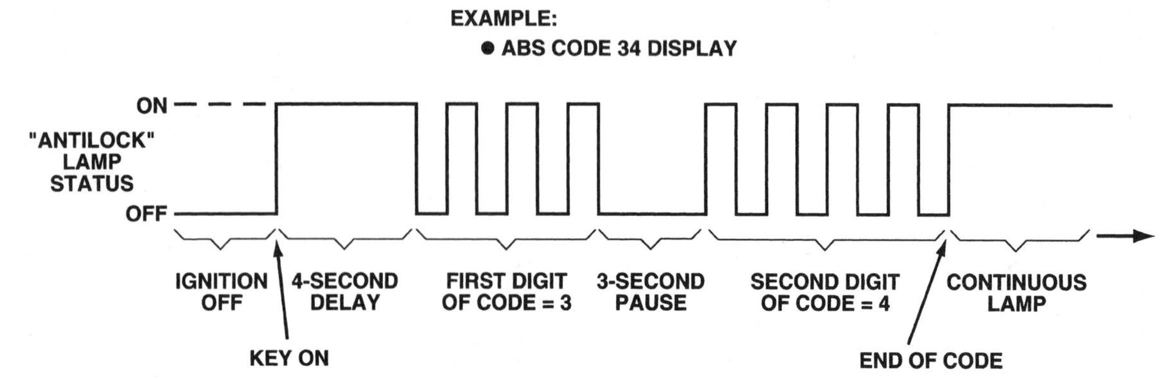

Figure 12-8. Some systems display codes by flashing the warning lamp. The example shows how a code 34 would be displayed on a General Motors vehicle with Teves Mark II ABS.

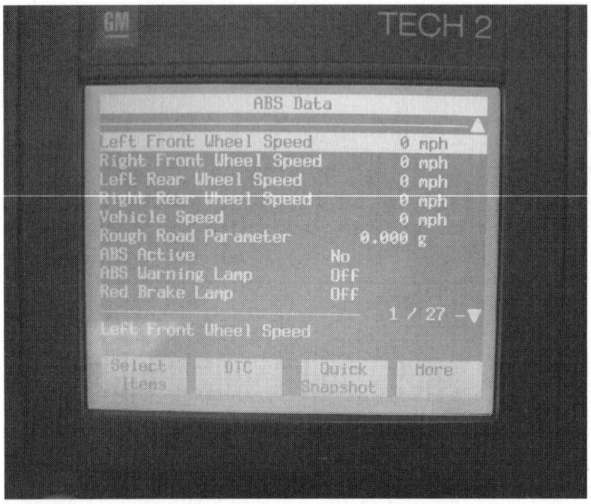

Figure 12-9. The scan tool can be used to monitor ABS functions and read trouble codes.

diagram to determine which parts share common circuits on both the powerside and groundside.

False Codes

ABS control modules sometimes generate "false" codes. You can waste time replacing operating parts in an attempt to cure a false code. System software design sometimes is at fault. For example, on a Jeep Cherokee, Wagoneer, or Grand Cherokee, a wheel speed sensor code may be set if the rear wheels break traction while accelerating on ice or mud in the two-wheeldrive mode. False wheel speed sensor codes can also be triggered on some vehicles if a wheel rotates or spins while the ignition switch is in the on position. In these cases, the ABS control module sets a code because the speed signal from one wheel disagrees with the signals from the other sensors. Turn the switch off when changing a tire or working on the brakes.

Changing tire size can trigger wheel speed sensor codes and cause ABS performance problems as well. If replacement tires or wheels have a larger or smaller diameter than the original equipment, rotational speed, and thus wheel speed sensor voltage, will vary. This can be especially critical if there is a difference in tire diameter between the front and rear axles. Keep in mind: The ABS is calibrated for a specific size of tire for a specific size wheel, and most manufacturers recommend not changing tire sizes.

ABS PERFORMANCE CHECKS, PRECAUTIONS, AND PROCEDURES

Following are some general service precautions that apply to all vehicles with ABS:

- Never connect or disconnect ABS electrical connectors while the ignition is on. Doing so creates momentary high-voltage spikes that can damage delicate electronic components.
- Disconnect the wiring harness from the ABS control module before any type of arc, MIG or TIG welding is done on the vehicle.
- Do not charge the battery in the vehicle with a high-amp fast charger unless the battery cables have been disconnected.
- Heat can also damage the ABS control module, so it should be removed before a repainted vehicle is put into a bake oven.
- After replacing an ABS component, check the system thoroughly to make sure it functions correctly.
- Use only top quality replacement parts in the brake system to ensure proper ABS operation.
- With integral ABS, always relieve accumulator pressure before servicing the system. Do this by depressing the brake pedal with a steady force 25 to 40 times while the ignition switch is off.

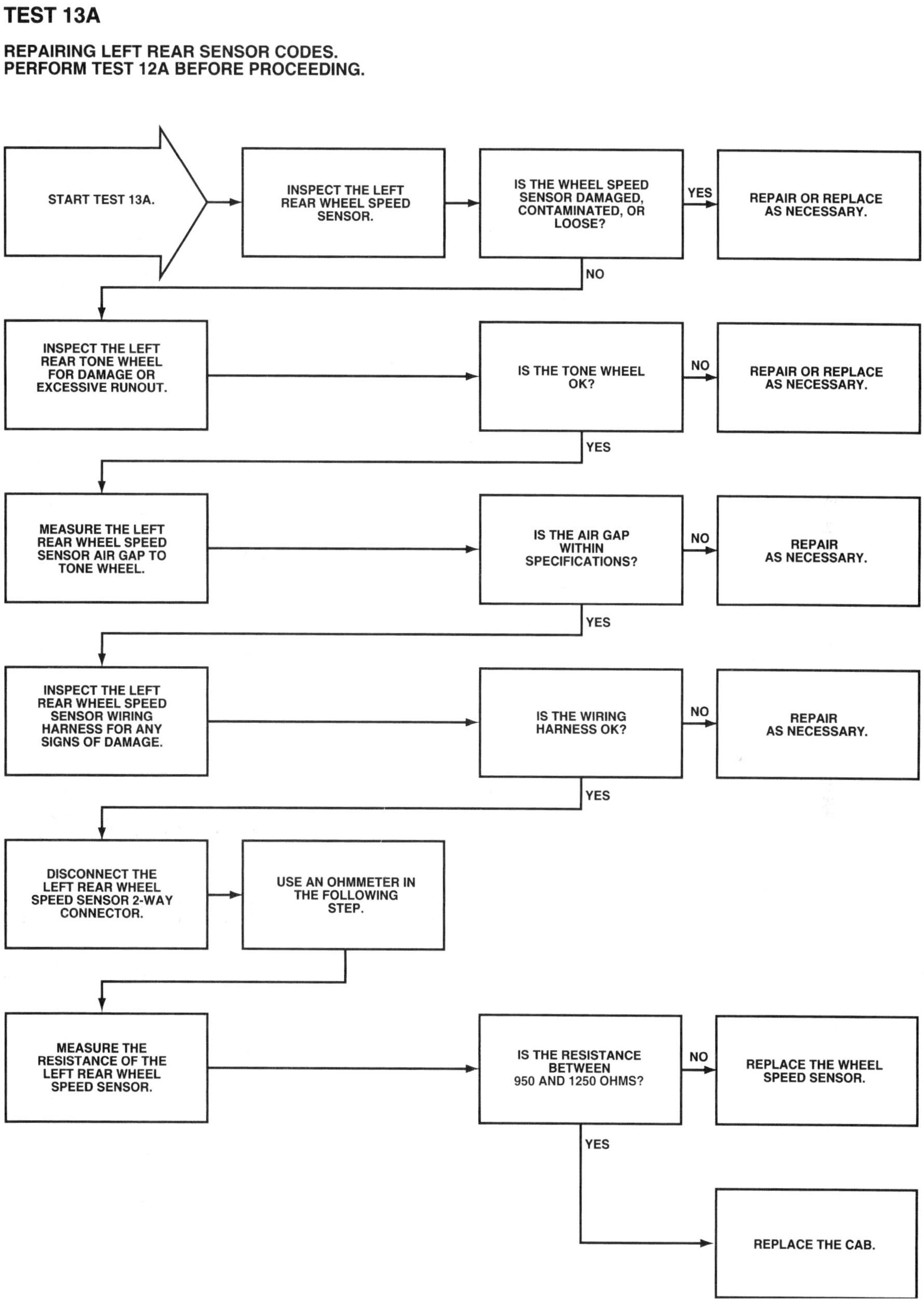

TEST 13A

REPAIRING LEFT REAR SENSOR CODES.
PERFORM TEST 12A BEFORE PROCEEDING.

```
START TEST 13A. → INSPECT THE LEFT REAR WHEEL SPEED SENSOR. → IS THE WHEEL SPEED SENSOR DAMAGED, CONTAMINATED, OR LOOSE? —YES→ REPAIR OR REPLACE AS NECESSARY.
                                                              │NO
                                                              ↓
INSPECT THE LEFT REAR TONE WHEEL FOR DAMAGE OR EXCESSIVE RUNOUT. → IS THE TONE WHEEL OK? —NO→ REPAIR OR REPLACE AS NECESSARY.
                                                                   │YES
                                                                   ↓
MEASURE THE LEFT REAR WHEEL SPEED SENSOR AIR GAP TO TONE WHEEL. → IS THE AIR GAP WITHIN SPECIFICATIONS? —NO→ REPAIR AS NECESSARY.
                                                                  │YES
                                                                  ↓
INSPECT THE LEFT REAR WHEEL SPEED SENSOR WIRING HARNESS FOR ANY SIGNS OF DAMAGE. → IS THE WIRING HARNESS OK? —NO→ REPAIR AS NECESSARY.
                                                                                    │YES
                                                                                    ↓
DISCONNECT THE LEFT REAR WHEEL SPEED SENSOR 2-WAY CONNECTOR. → USE AN OHMMETER IN THE FOLLOWING STEP.
                                                               ↓
MEASURE THE RESISTANCE OF THE LEFT REAR WHEEL SPEED SENSOR. → IS THE RESISTANCE BETWEEN 950 AND 1250 OHMS? —NO→ REPLACE THE WHEEL SPEED SENSOR.
                                                              │YES
                                                              ↓
                                                              REPLACE THE CAB.
```

Figure 12-10. A flowchart, like this one for the left rear wheel speed sensor on a Chrysler, leads you to the source of a failure through a process of elimination.

The following are typical checks that apply to systems with integral ABS. On these designs, the master cylinder, pump, accumulator, and modulator are combined in an assembly.

Pump and Accumulator Checks

After relieving accumulator pressure, switch the ignition on to check pump operation. If you do not hear the pump engage, check for voltage available at the pump, and take a voltage-drop reading across the ground connection at the pump. Normal voltage available at the pump along with a low voltage drop across the ground connection indicates a defective pump assembly. Replace the pump. A low- or zero-voltage reading at the pump indicates a problem in the power supply; check the relay and wiring harness. A high voltage drop indicates a problem on the ground side of the circuit.

Check accumulator pressure by connecting a high-pressure gauge between the accumulator and modulator assembly using the appropriate adapter, figure 12-11. Remember to relieve accumulator pressure before loosening any connections to install the gauge. When you switch the ignition on, the accumulator should quickly pressurize the brake fluid to about 600 to 1200 psi (4137 to 8274 kPa). Then, pressure should slowly climb to peak-specified pressure, which is sometimes as high as 2700 psi (18,616 kPa). Always refer to the appropriate shop manual for exact specifications.

Next, leave the ignition on and pump the brake pedal until the pump motor restarts. When the pump stops, switch the ignition off, wait three minutes, then note the pressure. Wait five more minutes, and note the pressure again. Accumulator pressure leakdown should not exceed 20 psi (138 kPa) in 5 minutes. If the leakdown is greater, look for leaks in the pump, the master cylinder, or booster assembly.

To locate the pressure leak, switch the ignition on and allow the pump to run for one minute. Then, switch the ignition off and disconnect the return hose from the fluid reservoir. Plug the reservoir outlet and hold the free end of the return hose in a suitable container. Watch the open end of the hose and note what happens during the next five minutes. If no fluid flows through the hose, the problem lies in the master cylinder and booster assembly. If fluid flows from the hose, the pump is leaking and the assembly should be replaced.

Wheel Speed Sensor Service

Wheel speed sensor circuits are often the cause of many ABS problems. These components may suffer from physical damage, buildup of metallic debris on the sensor tip, corrosion, poor electrical connections, and damaged wiring.

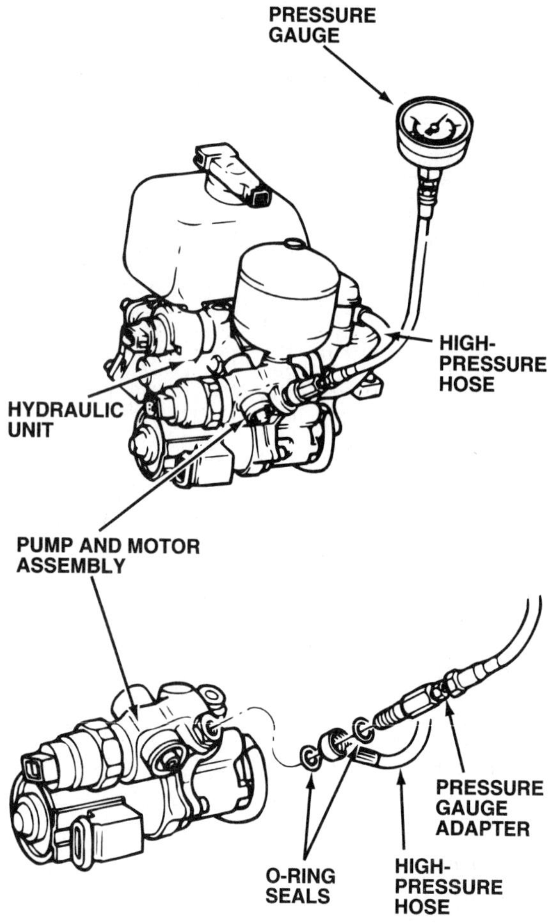

Figure 12-11. Install a high-pressure gauge to check hydraulic pressures on integral ABS with a pump and accumulator.

DVOM Testing

Test a wheel speed sensor by measuring its output voltage and circuit continuity. To save time, use a breakout box and a DVOM. With a DVOM alone, you must connect the test leads to each of the four wheel speed sensors. With a breakout box and a DVOM, you have the convenience of probing all four wheel sensor signal wires at one location, figure 12-12. In addition, since the breakout box cable connects to the ABS harness near the ABS module, your wheel speed sensor resistance checks include the wiring to the sensors as well. Follow the equipment manufacturer's instructions for connecting the breakout box to the vehicle, and for probing the appropriate pins on the breakout box with your DVOM.

Rotate the wheel you are testing by hand at a rate of about one revolution per second. Note the voltage reading from the sensor. A functioning wheel speed sensor generally produces an alternating current (AC) voltage that ranges from about 50 to 700 mV. Refer to the shop manual for exact specifications.

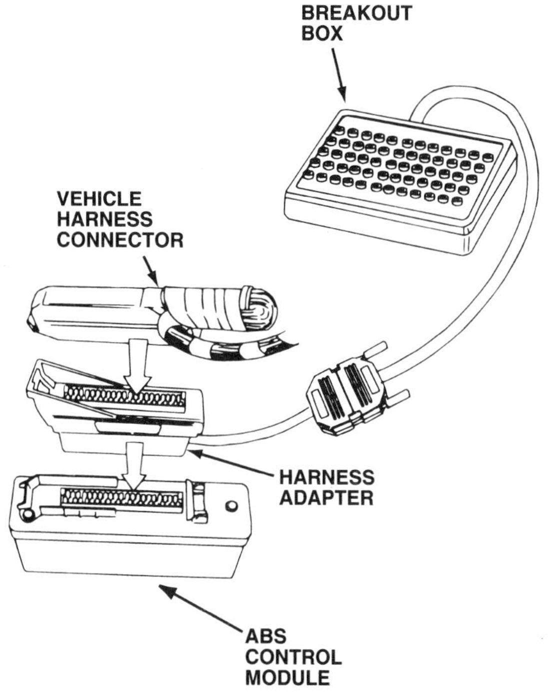

Antilock Brake Basics

Figure 12-12. A breakout box allows you to monitor all controlled circuits directly at the ABS control module with a DVOM.

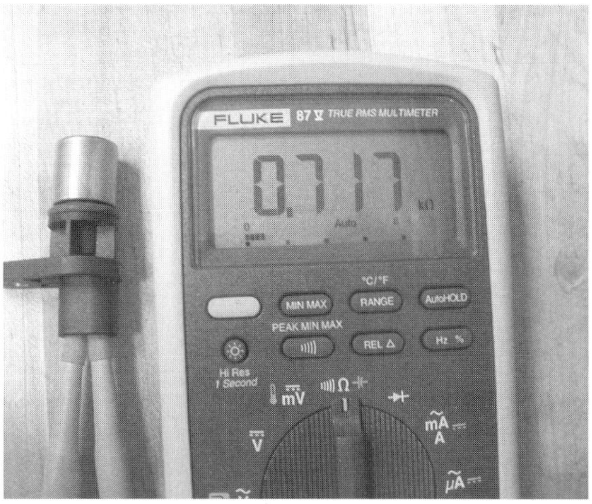

Figure 12-13. Measure the resistance across the coil of a wheel speed sensor with a DVOM.

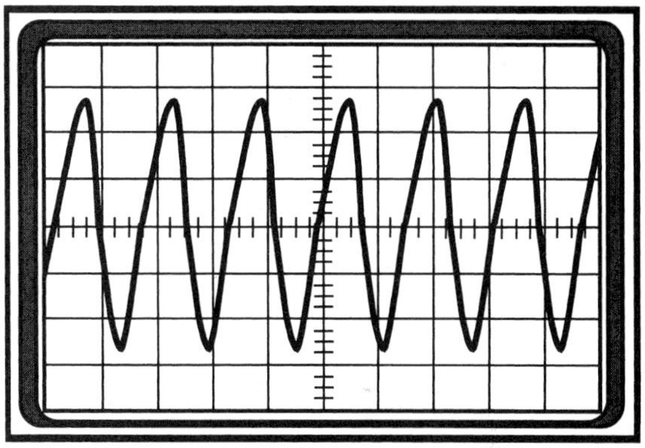

Figure 12-14. You can use a laboratory oscilloscope to monitor the sine wave voltage trace an operating wheel speed sensor generates.

If voltage readings are low, switch the ignition off and check the resistance across the sensor. You can do this with the DVOM using the breakout box. Readings from a breakout box represent the combined resistance of the wiring harness between the breakout box and the sensor, as well as the resistance of the sensor itself. Expect the value to be between 800 and 1400 ohms; check the shop manual for exact specifications. If the resistance is out of range, disconnect the sensor from the wiring harness and check resistance across the sensor coil, figure 12-13. If the sensor is shorted or open, replace it. If resistance meets specifications, test the wiring harness for loose or corroded connections, frayed insulation, or other damage.

Locate grounds or shorts in the wheel speed sensor cables by testing for continuity between the wiring connectors. It is best to simply replace defective wiring, rather than to repair it by splicing, soldering, or taping. Road debris and suspension travel can wear wheel sensor wiring faster than the wiring for other system components.

Oscilloscope Testing

The ability of a laboratory oscilloscope to display voltage as a function of time provides the best means of evaluating the condition of a wheel speed sensor. For example, a missing or damaged tooth on a sensor tone ring may affect ABS operation, yet produce no change in voltage according to a DVOM. However, on the oscilloscope, every time the missing tooth passes under the tip of the sensor, a visible fluctuation in voltage will appear.

You can connect the scope either to the breakout box or directly to the wheel speed sensor. A good sensor will produce an alternating current sine wave that changes both in frequency and amplitude in proportion to wheel speed, figure 12-14. As the wheel turns faster, signal frequency and amplitude should also increase.

Damaged or missing teeth on the sensor tone ring will cause flat spots, or gaps, in the sine wave pattern, figure 12-15. A bent axle or hub will produce a wavelike pattern that fluctuates as the strength of the sensor signal changes with every revolution.

An excessively wide air gap between the tip of the sensor and the tone ring, or a buildup of metallic debris

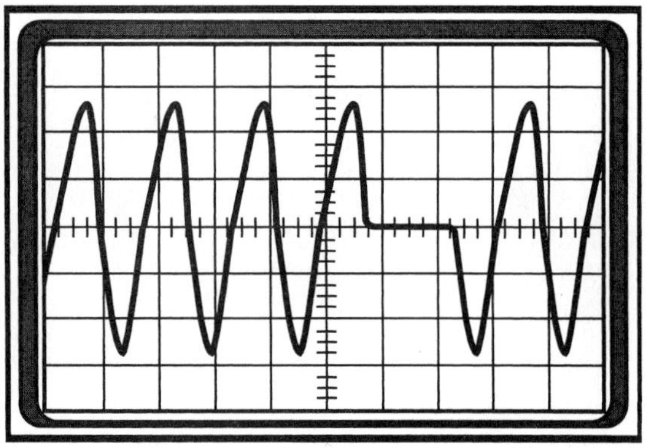

Figure 12-15. A broken tooth on a wheel speed sensor tone ring shows up on the scope trace as a missing wave.

on the end of the sensor will cause a weak signal. Visually, the peaks and valleys of the voltage trace will appear diminished, or erratic. High internal resistance may cause a weak signal as well.

Digital Wheel Sensor Testing
Beginning in 2003, some manufacturers are using wheel speed sensors that output a DC digital square wave, rather than the AC sine wave of a magnetic sensor. See the *Classroom Manual* for more information on their operation.

While the internal circuits are different, the active digital wheel speed sensor (General Motors) and the magneto-resistive wheel speed sensor (Daimler-Chrysler) produce their output signal in a similar manner. The sensor receives a 12-volt reference voltage to power the sensor circuits. The wheel speed sensor (WSS) returns a small current to the ABS controller. The return current toggles between low (about 7 mA) to high (about 14 mA) in response to the position of the tone wheel.

To test this type of sensor:

1. Begin by testing for the proper reference voltage from the ABS controller.
   a. Using the schematic, identify the sensor voltage supply wire, figure 12-16.
   b. Disconnect the sensor or back probe the sensor and, with the key ON, check for about 12 volts at the supply wire, figure 12-17.
   c. If there is no voltage, repair the open circuit or check the ABS controller.
   d. If there is voltage, continue with step 2.
2. To check the sensor output, the sensor must be powered up and the signal wire measured with an ammeter. To do this:
   a. Turn the ignition OFF. Install a jumper wire from the vehicle harness to the sensor on the 12-volt circuit (just tested in step 1). The sensor is grounded through the vehicle hub.
   b. Set the DVOM to measure milliamps. Install the meter in series in the sensor signal wire, figure 12-18.
3. Turn the ignition ON. Very slowly rotate the wheel and watch for the amperage reading to switch from high (11–16 mA) to low (4–8 mA).
4. Rotate the wheel as fast as possible and watch for the amperage to be steady between 7.5 and 12 mA.
5. Turn OFF the ignition before disconnecting the test equipment. If the signal wire is opened while the ignition is ON, a DTC will set.

NOTE: If a DTC is set while doing this test, the electronic brake control module (EBCM) will disable the sensor circuit and set a DTC. This may falsely appear as a bad sensor. Make sure the amperage fuse in the DVOM is functional before performing this test.

Wheel Speed Sensor Adjustment
On ABS applications with adjustable wheel speed sensors, always refer to a shop manual for the proper air gap setting. Most sensors adjust by first loosening a set screw, then inserting a nonmagnetic brass or plastic feeler gauge between the tip of the sensor and a high point on the tone ring, figure 12-19. Adjust the position of the sensor so there is a slight drag on the feeler gauge, then tighten the setscrew to lock the sensor in place.

When installing new sensors, look for a piece of paper or plastic on the tip end of the unit. This is more than a protective covering, and must be left in place during installation. The paper or plastic is the precise thickness to guarantee a correct air gap between the tip of the sensor and the tone ring. Adjust the sensor so the tip just touches the tone ring and you can slip the paper or plastic out without ripping it. Tighten the setscrew, and the air gap is properly set.

Some manufacturers recommend leaving a paper covering in place; the motion of the tone ring removes it after the vehicle is driven for several miles. This is the way sensors are generally installed at the factory, and it is not unusual to find traces of the covering still on the sensor when the vehicle is in for service.

When reinstalling a used sensor, be sure that there is no trace of the original paper or plastic covering remaining on the tip. If there is, it will be impossible to properly set the air gap with a feeler gauge. Carefully clean the tip of the sensor to avoid damaging the unit.

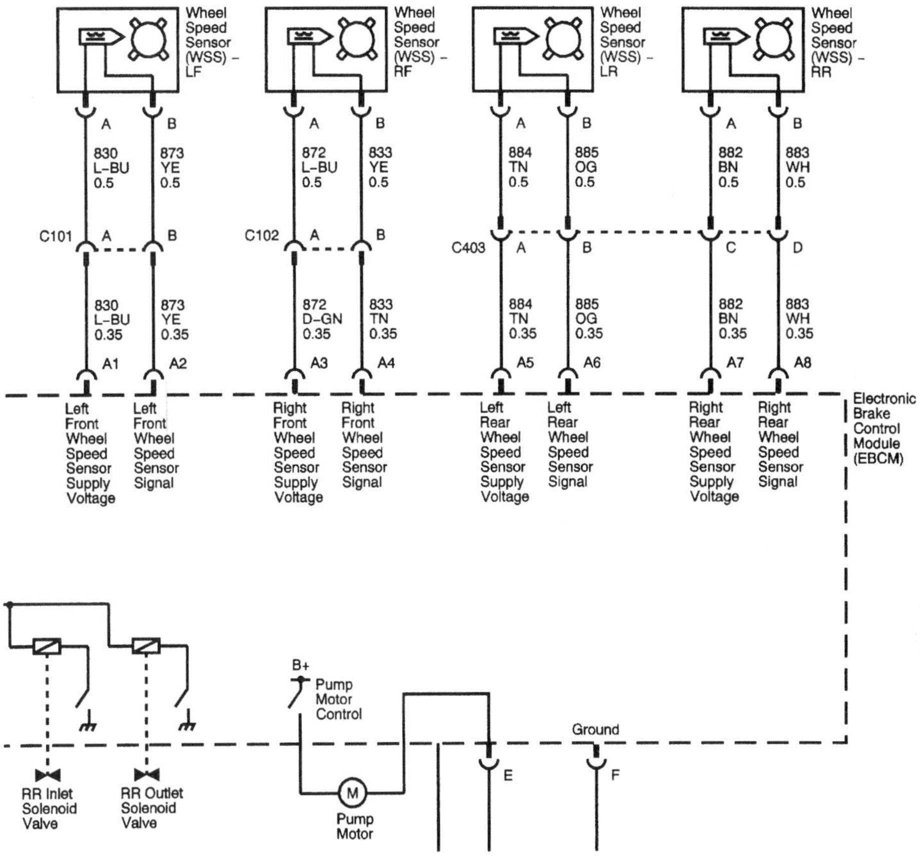

Antilock Brake Basics

Figure 12-16. This ABS schematic shows the wire color for the wheel speed sensors. (Courtesy of General Motors Corporation, Service and Parts Operations)

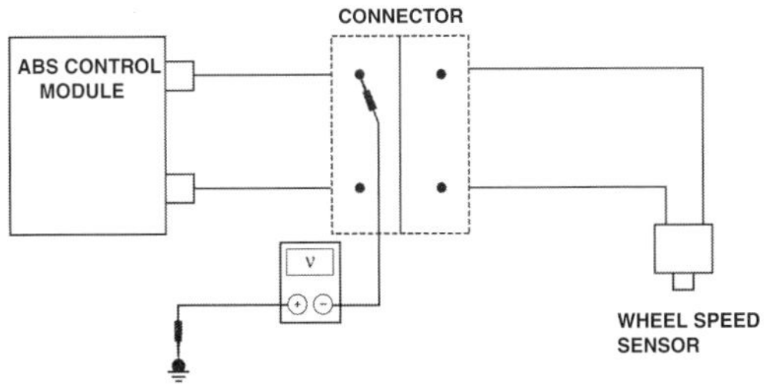

Figure 12-17. With the key ON, check for voltage on the supply wire. (Copyright DaimlerChrysler Corporation. Used with permission)

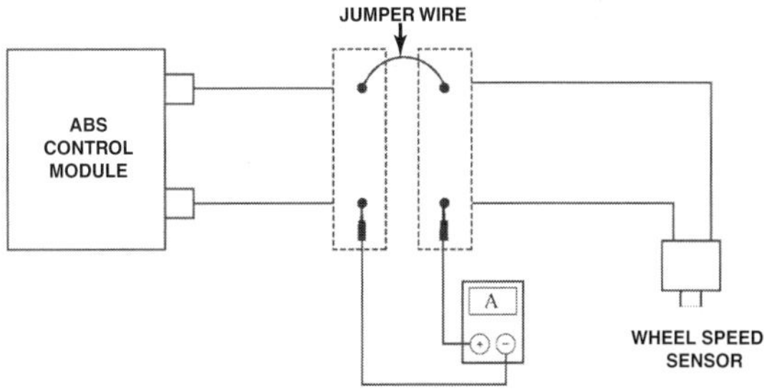

Figure 12-18. Using a jumper wire and an ammeter, measure the sensor signal current. (Copyright DaimlerChrysler Corporation. Used with permission)

Wheel Speed Sensor Replacement

Wheel speed sensors are fragile and you must handle them with care, especially on installation. Avoid any type of rapping to force the sensor into place; this can fracture the pickup magnet. On some vehicles, the left rear, left front, right front, and right rear wheel sensors may appear identical, but in fact are slightly different. These are a set, and individual sensors are not interchangeable. Installing a sensor in the wrong location will affect ABS function.

Coat steel wheel sensor housings with an anticorrosive high-temperature lubricant, such as synthetic grease or silicone brake grease, before installation, figure 12-20. Be sure the lubricant is designed to withstand the high demands of a brake system; do not use ordinary chassis grease. Avoid getting any

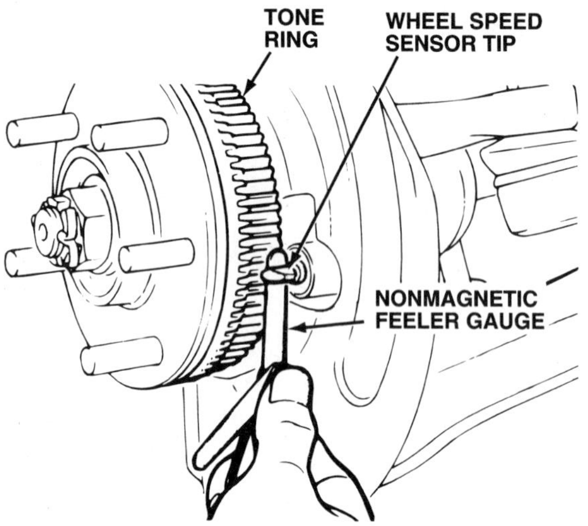

Figure 12-19. Use a nonmagnetic brass or plastic feeler gauge to check wheel speed sensor gap.

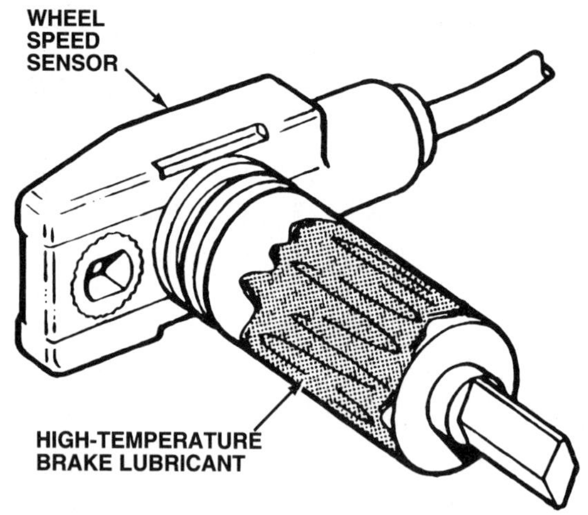

Figure 12-20. Coating the sides of a steel wheel speed sensor with an approved high-temperature lubricant will ease installation.

lubricant on the sensing portion of the assembly; this can result in an erroneous signal to the ABS control module.

GENERAL BLEEDING PROCEDURES

Perform regular preventive maintenance to protect the hydraulic ABS components by replacing the brake fluid at least once every two years. Changing the brake fluid every time you service the brakes will keep the system free from contaminates such as water and corrosion. Use only the brake fluid recommended by the vehicle manufacturer. ABS applications usually use DOT 3 or DOT 4 brake fluid—*never use DOT 5* silicone brake fluid.

You can manually bleed most vehicles with ABS in the manner you would for a conventional brake system. Procedures for using power bleeding equipment are usually the same as well. Be aware: You cannot use power bleeding equipment on some systems. Generally, special procedures are required if there is any air in the master cylinder or in the ABS hydraulic modulator. These may require you to either open the bleed screws on the modulator, or use a scan tool to cycle the ABS solenoids or motors. You can find instructions for bleeding specific systems in Chapter 13 of this manual.

13
ABS Diagnostic and Service Procedures

OBJECTIVES

Upon completion and review of this chapter, you will be able to:

- Identify ABS systems and component locations.
- Access ABS onboard diagnostic information.
- Flash and read ABS diagnostic trouble codes on the warning lamp where applicable.
- Retrieve ABS diagnostic trouble codes, or error messages, with a scan tool where applicable.
- Isolate the suspect circuit based on trouble code information.
- Perform ABS functional tests.
- Repair the cause of a code setting condition.
- Clear ABS codes from memory.
- Perform a hydraulic pressure test.
- Bleed any replacement hydraulic modulator or actuator assembly used for ABS.
- Bleed the brake hydraulic system.

INTRODUCTION

This chapter details ABS diagnostic routines and service procedures for a variety of popular systems. Although most vehicle manufacturers offer ABS as either standard or optional equipment, there is only a handful of brake manufacturers that supply the ABS for these vehicles. Information in this chapter is alphabetically organized by ABS manufacturer.

Although the same basic system may be used by a number of vehicle manufacturers, each ABS application is custom-tailored to meet the specific needs of the vehicle on which it is installed. Therefore, it is important to have accurate service information before you begin working. Information presented here is general in nature and is not to be substituted for factory specifications and procedures.

BENDIX ANTILOCK BRAKE SYSTEMS

Currently, there are six Bendix ABS systems in use. Five of these, Bendix 6, 9, 10, LC4, and ABX-4, are used exclusively by Chrysler. The Mecatronic II system, which incorporates both antilock braking and traction control, was introduced on the 1995 Ford Contour and Mercury Mystique. All are four-wheel systems, and share other common characteristics as well. The common features, discussed here, apply to all systems unless otherwise noted. A discussion of individual systems follows.

Bendix ABS systems have self-diagnostic capabilities. The control module, commonly known as the controller antilock brake or CAB, sets a diagnostic trouble code (DTC) if it detects a fault in the system. Bendix systems do not flash DTC information on the instrument panel warning lamp. The only function of the lamp is to alert the driver of a failure. Therefore, a scan tool must be used to access onboard diagnostics, read trouble codes, and perform functional tests.

With the exception of the Bendix 9 system, the CAB stores codes in nonvolatile memory, and clearing memory is a scan tool function. However, memory automatically clears if a fault does not repeat within a specific time frame, generally 50 ignition cycles.

Two instrument panel warning lamps, an amber ABS lamp and a red BRAKE lamp, alert the driver of a malfunction on all Chrysler applications. The Mecatronic II system has the familiar ABS lamp along with a traction control system (TCS) warning lamp. On all systems, both lamps should illuminate as a bulb check when the ignition switch is first turned on. The lamps stay on as the system performs a self-test of the electronic circuits. The circuit check should take less than three seconds, and the lamps will switch off provided there are no faults present.

Bendix 9 Diagnostics

The Bendix 9 system, used on the 1989–91 Jeep Cherokee and Wagoneer, is a three-channel integral system.

Accumulator pressure must be relieved prior to performing any brake work. Relieve accumulator pressure by firmly pumping the brake pedal 25 to 40 times while the ignition switch is off.

The CAB monitors all system inputs while driving. Should a fault occur, the system logs a DTC and illuminates one or both warning lamps. The warning lamp remains on as long as the fault is present, or for the duration of the ignition cycle. The ABS system is deactivated whenever the ABS lamp is illuminated, but normal braking is still available. The red BRAKE warning lamp signals a loss of hydraulic pressure or power assist, and is an indicator that the brakes may be unable to stop the vehicle. Normally, there will be enough residual accumulator pressure for about 15 to 20 power-assisted stops should the pump fail.

Accessing Codes

A scan tool must be used to access trouble codes. In addition to retrieving codes, you can also use the scan tool to perform a series of electrical checks on the ABS system. The system communicates through the 6-pin, L-shaped ABS data link connector (DLC) located in the engine compartment. Be aware, the ABS DLC is the same shape as the one used for engine testing. Look for the ABS connector on the passenger side of the engine compartment, figure 13-1.

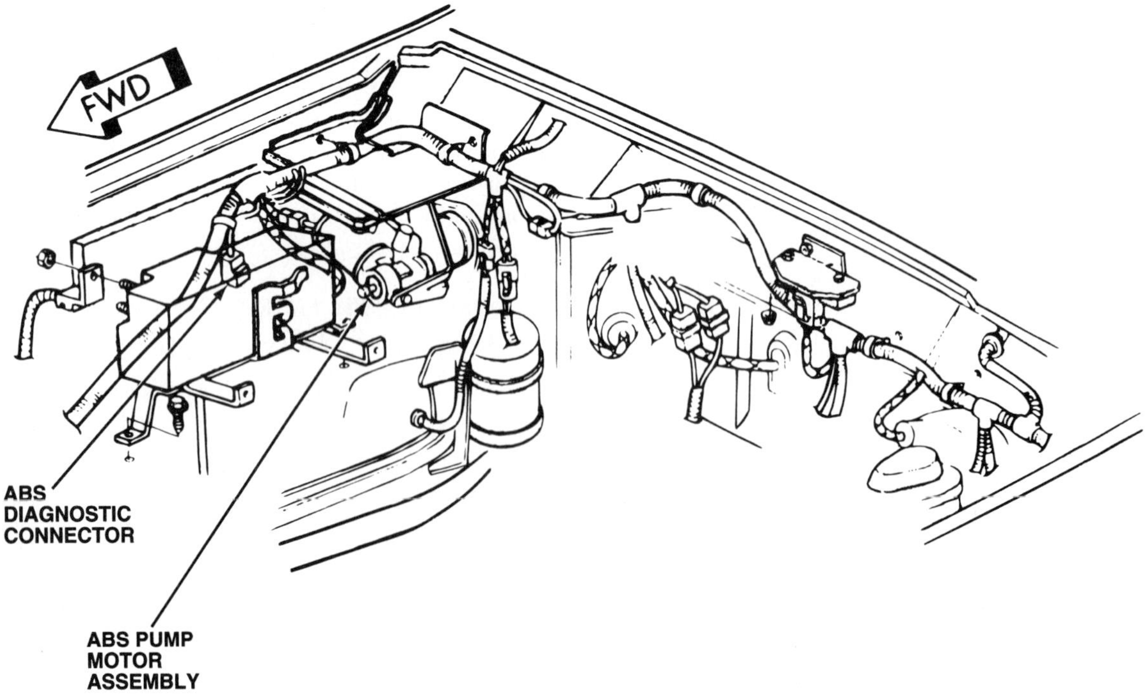

Figure 13-1. The Bendix 9 test connector looks the same as the engine test connector, but is located on the passenger side of the engine compartment.

ABS Diagnostic and Service Procedures

If a failure or problem occurs during testing, the scan tool displays a three-digit numerical DTC to indicate the problem circuit. Record and clear any codes that appear on the initial test, then road test the vehicle to see if faults recur. To clear codes, remove the ABS BAT fuse from the fuse panel, or disconnect the battery for at least 10 seconds. Be aware that disconnecting the battery will clear other stored data such as radio station presets and power seat settings.

DTC structure is unique to the Bendix 9 system, and definitions appear as in figure 13-2. The scan tool can also be used to monitor serial data, including activity from the wheel speed sensors, ABS solenoids, and the pump motor.

False Codes

False trouble codes are a common problem on Bendix 9 systems. Certain driving conditions can fool the CAB into believing a fault has occurred, when in fact there is nothing wrong. In two-wheel drive mode, should the wheels slip on ice, water, mud, snow, or gravel when accelerating from a stop, the system may interpret the slip as a faulty signal from the wheel speed sensors. This causes the ABS warning lamp to come on and a DTC to set. Other conditions that may cause a false code include deceleration on a steep grade or operating the vehicle with the transfer case in four-wheel low range. A marginally low brake fluid level may trigger the red BRAKE warning lamp during hard deceleration or when driving on an incline. Driving the vehicle at speeds over two to four miles per hour with the parking brake set can also result in a DTC. Do not assume you are dealing with false codes. Always perform a complete system check to rule out the possibility of a real problem.

You may encounter a different type of communications problem on some 1989–90 Cherokee models. The original CAB (P/N 56004028) may have been replaced by a later 1991 version (P/N 56004948). The two modules appear identical but communicate differently. As a result, the scan tool may display erroneous information. To resolve, first verify which CAB is installed; the unit mounts under the rear seat on most applications. When dealing with the newer CAB on an older system, connect a jump wire between terminals 3 and 4 on the back side of the diagnostic test connector. Now, connect the scan tool and it should display the correct data.

Bendix 9 Service

The following service procedures are provided as a general reference only. Always refer to the appropriate factory service manual before making repairs.

Brake Fluid Fill Procedure

To obtain an accurate fluid level reading, it is important to follow a special fluid fill procedure. This ensures that both accumulators are properly filled. Check fluid level as follows:

1. Fill the reservoir to the full mark.
2. Start the engine, then pump the brake pedal until the booster pump/motor turns on.
3. Stop pumping the brakes and wait until the pump/motor shuts off.
4. Recheck the fluid level and top off as needed.

Bleeding Procedure

You can bleed the brakes either manually or with pressure-bleeding equipment. However, the entire brake system, including the accumulators, pump, and master cylinder, must be bled. Bleed the accumulator, pump, and master cylinder simultaneously by opening the brake lines on the side of the modulator one at time, figure 13-3. Have an assistant hold steady pressure on the brake pedal during the procedure. Always perform this step first, before bleeding at the wheels.

With the ignition switch off, pump the brake pedal to relieve accumulator pressure. The ignition can remain off during the entire bleeding procedure. Bleed in the following sequence.

- Modulator
- Right rear

DTC	INDICATED FAULT
800	No voltage at ECM
801	No serial data from ECM
802	No parking brake signal
803	Warning lamps inoperative
804	Amber ABS warning lamp inoperative
805	Differential pressure fault
806	Boost pressure fault
807	Low accumulator pressure
808	Pressure modulator fault
809	Self-test failure
810	Solenoid under voltage
811	Relay fault
812	Pump/motor fault
813	Stoplight circuit fault
814	Low fluid
815	RR wheel speed sensor
816	LR wheel speed sensor
817	RF wheel speed sensor
818	LF wheel speed sensor
819	Open circuit at diagnostic connector

Figure 13-2. Bendix 9 diagnostic trouble codes.

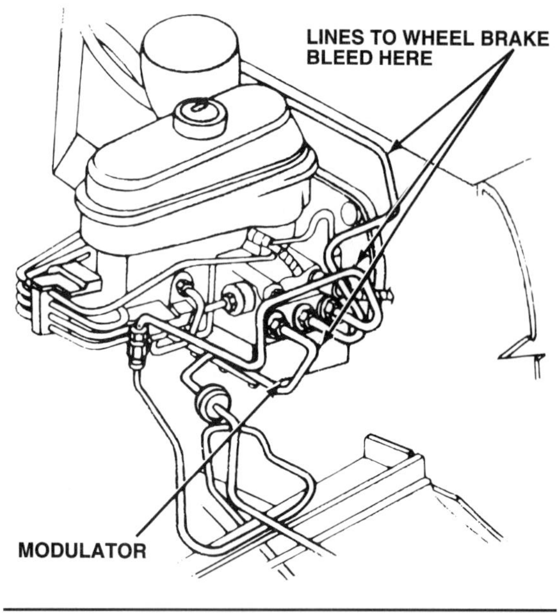

Figure 13-3. Bleed air from the accumulators, pump, and master cylinder by opening the wheel line connections at the modulator.

- Left rear
- Right front
- Left front.

Bendix 10 Diagnostics

Bendix 10 is a three-channel integral system used on 1990–93 Chrysler cars and 1991–92 minivans. Unlike Bendix 9, Bendix 10 retains trouble codes in nonvolatile memory, and features more comprehensive self-diagnostic information.

Following the bulb check on initial startup, the system performs additional self-tests. As soon as vehicle speed reaches three miles per hour, the CAB cycles each of the modulator solenoid valves to check their operation. This test automatically cancels should the driver apply the brakes.

System malfunctions are classified as latching faults or nonlatching faults. Latching faults are serious problems that can prevent proper function of the ABS system. When a latching fault occurs, the ABS disables itself, records a DTC, and switches the ABS warning lamp on to alert the driver. The ABS lamp remains on, and the system inoperative until the ignition is switched off.

A nonlatching fault is a less serious problem, and ABS remains operational. Nonlatching faults include low boost pressure, low accumulator pressure, and low system voltage. When the CAB detects a fault, it alerts the driver by illuminating one, or both, warning lamps. Which lamp illuminates depends upon the nature of the fault. The lamp remains on as long as the condition causing the fault exists. In most cases, a DTC will set.

Accessing Codes

A scan tool must be used to access trouble codes. Rather than numerical codes, Bendix 10 system malfunctions are displayed as "error messages" on the scan tool, figure 13-4. The test connector on Bendix 10 applications is located inside the passenger compartment, under the dash, to the left of the steering column. Look for a 6-pin, blue-colored connector. To access error messages and other diagnostic information, follow the specific instructions of the scan tool manufacturer.

Bendix 10 Service

Special precautions and procedures must be followed when performing service work on any integral ABS system. Always relieve residual pressure from the accumulator by pumping the brake pedal 20 to 40 times with the ignition off *before* opening any fluid lines. Accurate specifications and service instructions are equally important. Refer to the appropriate factory shop manual when making repairs.

Bleeding Procedure

Other than depressurizing the accumulator, bleeding Bendix 10 hydraulics does not require any special procedures. You can bleed the system either with pressure equipment or manually. Bleed at the wheels in the following sequence:

- Left rear
- Right rear
- Left front
- Right front.

Bendix 6 Diagnostics

Bendix 6, a three-channel nonintegral system, is used on 1991–93 Chrysler cars. Diagnostic information and self-test strategies are similar to those of the Bendix 10 system. After the bulb check, the CAB cycles the modulator valves and pump motor as a self-test once the vehicle is in motion. If the vehicle is not driven within three minutes of switching the ignition on, the CAB cycles the pump motor, but does not perform the modulator valve test.

Accessing Codes

As on the Bendix 10 system, a scan tool must be used to access error messages. Diagnostic error messages displayed on the scan tool are identical to those of the Bendix 10 system, figure 13-4, and indicate both latching and nonlatching faults. The blue, 6-pin DLC located under the fuse box access cover to the left of the steering column is also the same.

ABS Diagnostic and Service Procedures

ERROR MESSAGE	ABS MIL	BRAKE MIL	FAULT TYPE
Controller Antilock Brake (CAB)	ON	OFF	Latching
Modulator fault	ON	OFF	Latching
Solenoid under voltage	ON	OFF	Nonlatching
Low fluid/parking brake	ON[1]	ON	Nonlatching
ABS system relay	ON	OFF	Latching
Wheel speed sensor	ON	OFF	Latching
Boost pressure	ON[2]	ON	Nonlatching
Accumulator pressure low	ON	ON	Nonlatching
Excessive decay	ON	OFF	Nonlatching
Primary/Delta pressure	ON	OFF	Nonlatching

1. The brake lamp illuminates immediately, and the ABS lamp lights when speed reaches 3 mph.
2. Both lamps illuminate when the brakes are applied.

Figure 13-4. Bendix 6 and 10 scan tool error messages.

Bendix 6 Service

Since Bendix 6 is a nonintegral system, many routine service procedures are identical to those used for vehicles without ABS. However, the ABS system contains delicate electronic components that must be handled with care to avoid future failures. Always follow the recommended practices outlined in the factory service manual.

Bleeding Procedure

If the modulator has not been removed or exposed to air, the individual brake circuits can be bled conventionally using manual or pressure-bleeding techniques in the following sequence:

- Right rear
- Left rear
- Right front
- Left front.

When replacing the modulator, or if open brake lines allow air into the modulator, you must follow a special procedure. Use your scan tool to activate system valves in a specific sequence as you open bleed screws to purge air from the modulator, then bleed at the wheels. Bleed the modulator as follows:

1. Remove the battery, battery tray, and acid shield to access the four bleed screws on top of the modulator assembly, figure 13-5.
2. Reconnect the battery to the vehicle using jumper cables.
3. Connect the scan tool to the diagnostic connector.
4. Install a hose onto the secondary sump bleed screw (lower left screw) and place the open end into a suitable container. Pressurize the brake system using pressure-bleeding equipment, or have an assistant pump, then apply steady pressure on the brake pedal. Once the system is under pressure, open the bleed screw.
5. Use the scan tool to enter the ABS test mode and select the function that actuates the valves. Energize the left front build/decay valve first. Switch the valve off once clear brake fluid flows from the bleed valve. Next, actuate the right front build/decay valve and bleed until the fluid flow is clear.

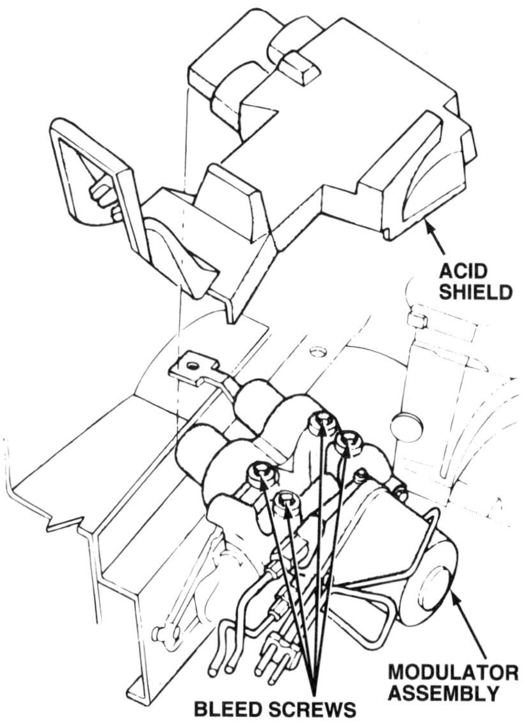

Figure 13-5. Remove the battery to gain clear access to the bleed screws on top of the Bendix 6 modulator.

6. The primary sump bleed screw (lower right) is bled next. Install the hose, open the bleed screw and bleed using the scan tool. Actuate the right front build/decay valve first, then the left front build/decay valve. Bleed both valves until clear fluid flows, then tighten the bleed screw.
7. Bleed the primary accumulator bleed (upper right) next. Attach the hose and open the bleed screw. Then, use the scan tool to actuate valves in the following sequence:
   - Right front isolation valve
   - Left rear isolation valve
   - Right front build/decay valve.

   Bleed each valve until you get a good, air-free flow of brake fluid. Then, tighten the bleed screw.
8. The last step is to bleed the secondary accumulator (upper left) bleed screw. With the hose in place and the bleed screw open, use the scan tool to actuate valves in the following order:
   - Left front isolation valve
   - Right rear isolation valve
   - Left front build/decay valve.

   Tighten the bleed screw and switch off the valve once you get a good flow of clear fluid.

   Finish the job by conventionally bleeding the brake lines at the wheels in the order given above.

Bendix LC4 Diagnostics

LC4 is a nonintegral, four-channel ABS system that made its debut on an assortment of 1994 Chrysler vehicles. Following the bulb check, the modulator solenoid valves and the pump motor are activated briefly as a self-test when vehicle speed reaches seven mph. If the vehicle is not driven within three minutes, the solenoid test is canceled, but the pump/motor is energized. Once vehicle speed is above eight mph, input from the wheel speed sensors is monitored continuously.

Accessing Codes

A scan tool must be used to access error messages. As with Bendix 10 and 6, the scan tool displays both latching and nonlatching error messages. However, LC4 transmits a different set of messages, figure 13-6. The scan tool connects to the now-familiar 6-pin connector located behind the fuse panel cover.

Bendix LC4 Service

You must follow specific procedures when bleeding the hydraulics and performing other repairs on a Bendix LC4 system. The bleeding procedure is detailed below. Follow instructions provided by the vehicle manufacturer when performing any other repair work.

ERROR MESSAGE	FAULT TYPE
ABS warning lamp circuit	Nonlatching
ABS warning lamp diode circuit	Nonlatching
Controller Antilock Brakes (CAB)	Latching
Excess decay	Nonlatching
LF wheel speed sensor	Latching
RF wheel speed sensor	Latching
LR wheel speed sensor	Latching
RR wheel speed sensor	Latching
LF wheel speed sensor continuity	Latching
RF wheel speed sensor continuity	Latching
LR wheel speed sensor continuity	Latching
RR wheel speed sensor continuity	Latching
Modulator circuit	Latching
Pump/motor circuit	Latching
Solenoid under voltage	Nonlatching

Figure 13-6. Error message for the Bendix LC4 and ABX-4 systems.

Bleeding Procedure

LC4 systems are manually bled following a special two-step procedure that requires a scan tool. *Pressure bleeding equipment CANNOT be used*, as it does not generate enough pressure to remove all air from the system.

Manually bleed at the wheels in the following sequence:

- Right rear
- Left front
- Left rear
- Right front.

Next, bleed the modulator. Gain clear access to the hydraulic modulator by removing the battery, battery tray, and acid shield, figure 13-7. Connect your scan tool, and bleed the modulator valves in the following sequence:

1. Primary check valve
2. Secondary check valve
3. Primary sump valve
4. Primary accumulator valve
5. Secondary sump valve
6. Secondary accumulator valve.

Bleed the primary and secondary check valves without energizing any of the solenoids. Attach a length of hose to the primary bleed screw, and place the other end in a clear container partially filled with brake fluid. Have an assistant pump the brake pedal several times, then maintain pressure on the pedal. Open the bleed screw at least one full turn, then tighten it when the pedal reaches the end of its travel. Repeat until the discharge fluid is free of air. Bleed the secondary check valve in the same manner.

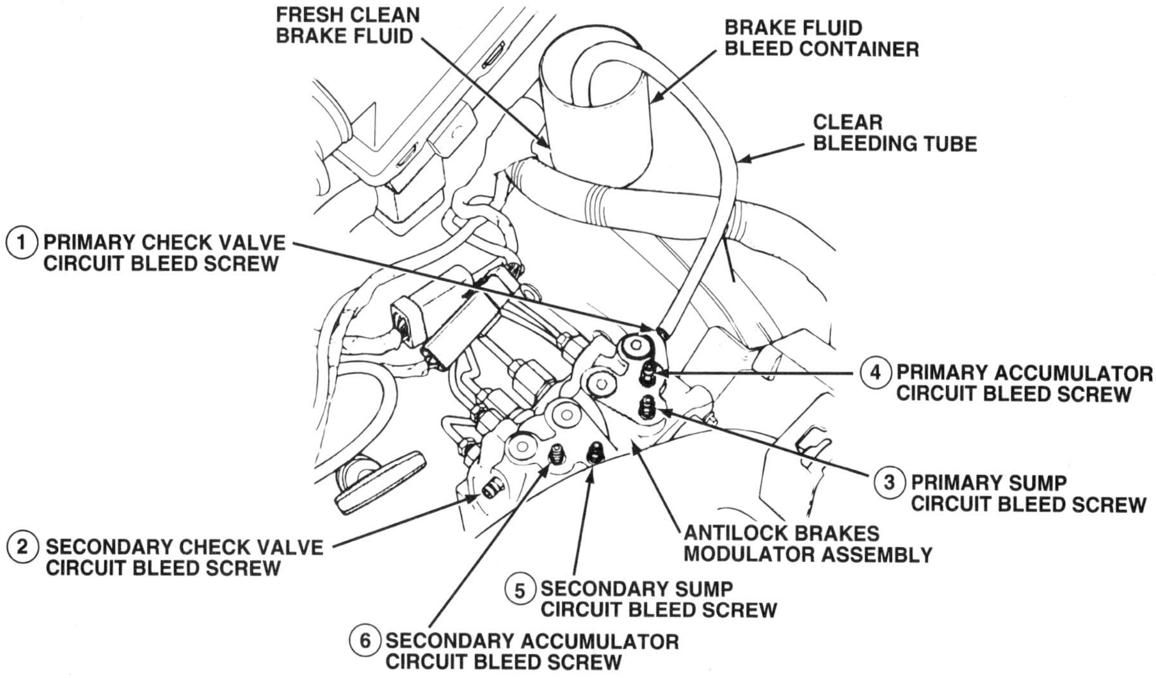

ABS Diagnostic and Service Procedures

Figure 13-7. There are six bleed points on the Bendix LC4 modulator assembly.

Use the scan tool to energize solenoids for bleeding the primary sump, secondary sump, and accumulator valves. In the Bleed ABS Mode, the scan tool alternately energizes the selected solenoid for five seconds. Valves must be bled in the above stated order following the instructions given below. Have your assistant pump the brake pedal several times, then maintain pressure. Open the bleed screw at least one turn, then use the scan tool to activate the solenoid.

When bleeding the primary and secondary sump valves, continue cycling the solenoid and applying pedal pressure until there are no bubbles visible in the fluid. Repeat as often as needed to clear the circuit of air. Use the scan tool to cycle the right front and left rear ABS solenoids when bleeding the primary sump valve. Energize the left front and right rear ABS solenoids when bleeding the secondary sump valve.

Both the primary and secondary accumulator valves are bled in the same manner. However, an additional step is required. After bleeding with the solenoids energized, the circuit is bled again without the solenoids energized. Pump and hold the brake pedal, then open the bleed valve. Repeat unitl the fluid is free of air. Cycle solenoids with the scan tool in similar fashion as used for the sump valves. Bleed the primary accumulator valve while cycling the right front and left rear ABS solenoids. Cycle the left front and right rear ABS solenoids to bleed the secondary accumulator valve.

Remember, all valves must be bled in exact sequence: primary check valve, secondary check valve, primary sump valve, primary accumulator valve, secondary sump valve, and secondary accumulator valve.

Bendix ABX-4 Diagnostics

ABX-4, a nonintegral, four-channel system first introduced on the 1995 Dodge and Plymouth Neon, is similar in design and function to the LC4 system. Once the initial startup self-test is performed, the CAB continuously monitors the ABS solenoids and wheel speed sensors for any faults that might occur. Failures are classified as either latching or nonlatching.

Accessing Codes

ABX-4 vehicles are OBD II compliant, and ABS diagnostic information is accessed by connecting the scan tool to the standard 16-pin DLC, figure 13-8. Bendix ABX-4 error messages are the same as those for Bendix LC4, figure 13-6.

Bendix ABX-4 Service

Most routine service procedures are identical, or similar to those used for vehicles without ABS. However, certain precautions must be observed. It is important to have accurate factory service information on hand.

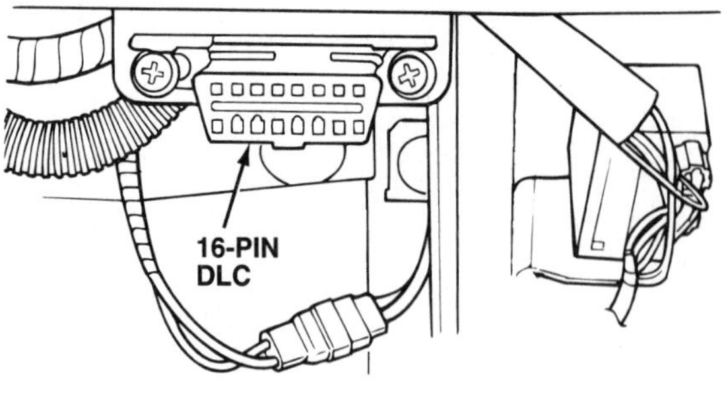

Figure 13-8. Electronically access ABX-4 systems through the standard OBD II 16-pin connector.

Bleeding Procedure

Unless air has been allowed to enter the modulator, the brake system can be bled manually or with pressure equipment following standard procedures. Bleed in the following sequence:

- Left rear
- Right front
- Right rear
- Left front.

If air has entered the hydraulic modulator, first bleed the brakes at the wheels, then, using a scan tool, bleed the modulator. Select the "Bleed ABS" mode on the scan tool. Apply the brake pedal firmly, then use the scan tool to activate and run the "Bleed ABS" routine. In this mode, the pump is energized and the ABS solenoids cycle. This circulates brake fluid through the modulator to flush any trapped air out of the modulator and toward the wheels.

Finish the job by bleeding the brakes at the wheels again. Repeat the "Bleed ABS" scan tool procedure a second time should a soft pedal indicate that air is still in the system.

Bendix Mecatronic and Mecatronic II Diagnostics

The Bendix Mecatronic control module on the Ford Contour and Mercury Mystique monitors antilock brake system (ABS) components. Vehicles with Mecatronic II have both ABS and traction control systems (TCS); the controller monitors both systems. If either the ABS or traction control warning lamp remains on following the bulb check, or comes on while driving, a fault that requires further diagnosis is indicated. Should the controller detect a fault in either system, it disables both until repairs are made.

Accessing Codes

A scan tool is used to access codes on both Mecatronic systems. On 1995 vehicles, there is a two-pin diagnostic connector located in the engine compartment near

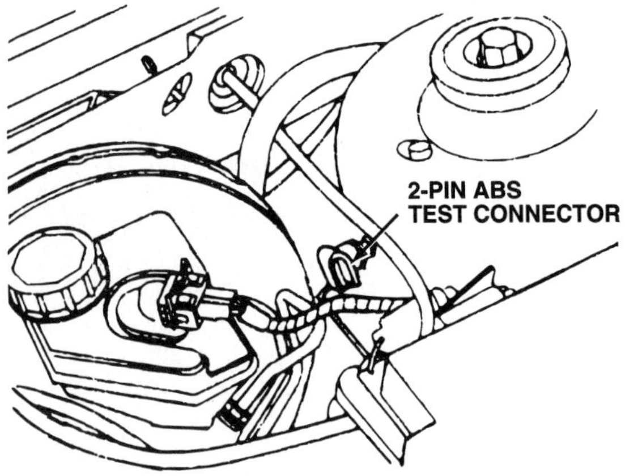

Figure 13-9. A 2-pin test connector for the Bendix Mecatronic system used by Ford is located near the left front strut tower.

the left strut tower, figure 13-9. On 1996 and later models, the scan tool connects to the standard OBD II 16-pin connector under the dash, figure 13-8.

The scan tool displays information as a five-digit, alphanumeric diagnostic trouble code, in compliance with OBD II specifications, figure 13-10.

Bendix Mecatronic Service

Observe the following precautions when working on the Mecatronic system:

- Never disconnect a wheel speed sensor while the ignition switch is on.
- Never use a 12-volt test light on the ABS circuitry.
- Never short or arc any wiring in the ABS circuitry.
- Never rotate or spin the wheels while the ignition is on, because a false wheel speed sensor code might set.

Bleeding Procedure

The hydraulic system can be bled manually or with pressure-bleeding equipment. Bleed at the wheels in this sequence:

- Right rear
- Left front
- Left rear
- Right front.

BOSCH ANTILOCK BRAKE SYSTEMS

The use of Bosch ABS is widespread, and Bosch manufactures a variety of both integral and nonintegral systems. Latest versions incorporate traction control and ABS into a single system. Bosch ABS is used on domestic, European, and Japanese vehicles.

ABS Diagnostic and Service Procedures

DTC	INDICATED FAULT
C1012, C1013	RF ABS solenoid valve
C1026, C1027, C1028	LF ABS solenoid valve
C1056, C1057, C1058	RR ABS solenoid valve
C1071, C1072, C1073	LR ABS solenoid valve
C1081, C1082, C1083	Incorrect system voltage
C1084	Reference (B+) voltage high or low
C1085	Incorrect system voltage
C1090	Either rear wheel speed sensor
C1095	Pump motor
C1101	RF ABS solenoid valve
C1110, C1120	Reference (B+) voltage high or low
C1137	Power circuit interrupted
C1138	Controller programming failure
C1146, C1147, C1148, C1149, C1150, C1152, C1153	RF wheel speed sensor
C1156, C1157, C1158, C1159, C1160, C1162, C1163	LF wheel speed sensor
C1166, C1167, C1168, C1169, C1170, C1172, C1173	RR wheel speed sensor
C1176, C1177, C1178, C1179, C1180, C1182, C1183	LR wheel speed sensor
C1401, C1402, C1403	RF TCS solenoid valve
C1411, C1412, C1413	LF TCS solenoid valve
C1414	ABS/TCS control module
C1491, C1492, C1493	Traction assist motor
C1495	TCS throttle cable position sensor

Figure 13-10. Bendix Mecatronic five-digit diagnostic trouble codes comply with OBD II standards.

DTC	INDICATED FAULT
1	LF wheel circuit valve
5	LF wheel speed sensor
2	RF wheel circuit valve
6	RF wheel speed sensor
3	RR wheel circuit valve
7	RR wheel speed sensor
4	LR wheel circuit valve
8	LR wheel speed sensor
9	LF and RR wheel speed sensor circuits
10	RF and LR wheel speed sensor circuits
11	Replenishing valve
12	Valve relay
13	Circuit failure
14	Piston travel switches
15	Stoplight switch
16	Control module

Figure 13-11. Bosch 3 diagnostic trouble codes for all Chrysler applications.

Bosch 3 Diagnostics

Bosch 3 is an integral, four-wheel, four-channel system used primarily by the Chrysler Corporation. Two versions of Bosch 3 were also used by General Motors on the Cadillac Allanté. All versions have self-diagnostic capabilities and record a retrievable diagnostic trouble code (DTC) should a failure occur.

On these systems, a second self-test is performed following the bulb check. This test sequence runs as the vehicle is driven, and begins when vehicle speed reaches three to four mph. Known as the built-in test equipment (BITE) check, the test activates all four of the ABS solenoid valves and the replenishing valve in the hydraulic unit to check their operation. During the test, a series of rapid clicks may be heard as components energize, and some feedback may be felt through the brake pedal. These conditions are normal and do not indicate a problem. Should the self-test reveal a fault, the control module records a DTC, illuminates the ABS warning lamp, and disables the system. The control module also continuously monitors input from each of the four wheel speed sensors while the care is in operation.

Accessing Chrysler Codes

Chrysler applications display DTC information by flashing the BRAKE warning lamp when the system is placed in the diagnostic mode. Make sure the parking brake is fully released before attempting to retrieve codes. To activate the code display, switch the ignition on without starting the engine, then depress and hold the brake pedal. After five seconds, the red BRAKE warning lamp, not the amber ABS lamp, begins to flash a code message. Count the number of times the lamp flashes, then refer to the code chart, figure 13-11, for

All Bosch systems have an amber ABS warning lamp on the instrument cluster. The warning lamp should come on momentarily as the ignition switches on, then extinguish after about three seconds. A lamp that fails to light when the ignition switches on, or a lamp that remains lit following the bulb check, indicates a failure. Check the bulb and circuit if the lamp fails to light. Should the self-diagnostic program detect a fault, the lamp may remain on after the bulb check, or come on during vehicle operation. In most instances, ABS is disabled when the warning lamp is illuminated.

Additional self-diagnostic features vary by system, as well as make and model. These are explained in the sections that follow. The first step is to make sure the warning lamp operates when you switch the ignition on.

DTC	INDICATED FAULT
1	LF brake circuit solenoid valve
2	RF brake circuit solenoid valve
3	RR brake circuit solenoid valve
4	LR brake circuit solenoid valve
5	LF wheel speed sensor
6	RF wheel speed sensor
7	RR wheel speed sensor
8	LR wheel speed sensor
9	Diagonal wheel speed sensor fault
10	Diagonal wheel speed sensor fault
11	Replenishing valve
12	Solenoid valve relay
13	Hydraulic unit plausibility switches[1]
14	Hydraulic unit plausibility switches[1]
15	Hydraulic unit plausibility switches[1]
16	ABS control module problem

1. These codes set if the brake light, piston travel, and control pressure switches are not activated in the proper sequence while braking.

Figure 13-12. Bosch 3 diagnostic trouble codes for Cadillac Allanté through 1989.

DTC	INDICATED FAULT
12	Start diagnostic mode or no faults
21	RF wheel speed sensor
25	LF wheel speed sensor
31	RR wheel speed sensor
35	LR wheel speed sensor
41	RF ABS solenoid valve
43	Traction control plunger disconnected
44	RF traction control valve
45	LF ABS solenoid valve
48	LF traction control valve
51	RR ABS solenoid valve
55	LR ABS solenoid valve
62	Replenishing valve
63	Solenoid relay valve
64	Plausibility switches in hydraulic unit
65	Plausibility switches in hydraulic unit
66	Plausibility switches in hydraulic unit
71	ABS control module error

Figure 13-13. Bosch 3 diagnostic trouble codes for Cadillac Allanté from 1990 through 1992.

further diagnosis. If the brake pedal remains depressed, the code display repeats after about 10 seconds.

The control module generates only one DTC at a time. Switching the ignition off clears the code. If multiple faults are present, you must repair the cause of the first code before the system will generate any additional codes.

Accessing Cadillac Allanté Codes
On the Cadillac Allanté, you can retrieve codes from memory and display them as flashes of the red BRAKE warning lamp using the control panel for the climate control system. The driver information center (DIC) screen prompts you as you manipulate the controls to access the system.

Cadillac uses two versions of Bosch 3 ABS on the Allanté. Although similar, the procedure to access codes, and the codes themselves, are different. Code definitions for the original system, used through the 1989 model year, appear in figure 13-12. For 1990, the retrieval procedure was revised slightly and the code list was expanded, figure 13-13.

The 1990 and later Allanté system incorporates traction control. These vehicles have a traction control (TRAC CNTRL) warning lamp and a combined ABS and BRAKE warning lamp. The TRAC CNTRL lamp illuminates when the system activates or when a system fault exists. In addition, the DIC displays messages to alert the driver when there is a problem. The ABS control module transmits information to the body control module (BCM), and the BCM controls the DIC. The BCM also serves as the electronic link between the ABS module and the engine control module. This link allows the system to maintain traction by reducing engine power output when necessary.

The DIC may display the following messages:

- ANTILOCK DISABLED—This indicates an ABS fault is present. The red BRAKE warning lamp lights and ABS disables. If the BRAKE lamp comes on without the message, there is a brake hydraulic problem, not an ABS malfunction.
- TRACTION DISABLED—This indicates a fault exists in the traction control portion of the Bosch 3 system.
- BRAKE FLUID LOW—This indicates a low fluid level as determined by the master cylinder reservoir fluid level sensor.
- TRACTION DISABLED MINI-SPARE—This indicates the electrical connector for the mini-spare tire is open. When the connector is open, the controller assumes the spare is installed on one of the wheels and disables traction control. Smaller diameter mini-spares rotate faster than normal tires. The controller interprets the increased wheel speed as wheelspin and will attempt to make corrections if the electrical connector isn't disconnected.
- USE LESS ACCELERATOR—This indicates the traction control system is actively trying to reduce engine power to maintain traction and the driver is not releasing the accelerator pedal.

ABS Diagnostic and Service Procedures

- TRACTION DISABLED SYSTEM OVER HEATED—The traction control system has an internal timer that discontinues active braking to prevent the brakes from overheating. Traction control is disabled after 30 seconds of continuous braking.
- ANTILOCK OK—This indicates there were no ABS faults detected during the initial self-tests.
- TRACTION OK—This indicates there were no traction control faults detected during the initial self-tests.

Accessing Codes on 1989 and Earlier Models

With the ignition key on and the parking brake fully released, enter the onboard diagnostics program using the climate control panel as follows:

1. Simultaneously press the "OFF" and "WARMER" buttons, figure 13-14. This signals the BCM to enter the diagnostic mode. Hold the buttons down until the system begins its segment check, about five seconds.
2. Following the segment check, the screen displays engine codes (prefixed by an "E"), then body codes (prefixed by a "B"), followed by lighting codes (prefixed by an "L").
3. After the code display, a prompt asks if you want to perform any additional diagnostic checks. Press the "LO" button to bypass each selection when the panel reads ECM?, BCM?, and LIGHTING?.
4. When the "ANTILOCK BRAKES?" option appears onscreen, press the "HI" button to select.
5. When the "KEEP BRAKE DEPRESSED" message appears, press and hold the brake pedal to activate diagnostic mode. After about five seconds, the display reads "COUNT LAMP FLASHES" and the red BRAKE warning lamp flashes codes. Count flashes and record the DTC.
6. To exit the diagnostic mode, press the "RESET" button on the climate control panel or turn the ignition off.

On these early systems, codes can be retrieved only one at a time. Priority is given to the code with the lowest numerical value. In addition, the controller erases any remaining codes whenever the ignition is switched off.

Accessing Codes on 1990 and Later Models

To retrieve codes on a late-model Allanté with ABS and traction control, switch the ignition on and fully release the parking brake. Then, manipulate the climate control panel as follows:

1. Enter the service mode by simultaneously pressing the "OFF" and "WARMER" buttons, figure 13-14. Hold both buttons down until the segment check begins.

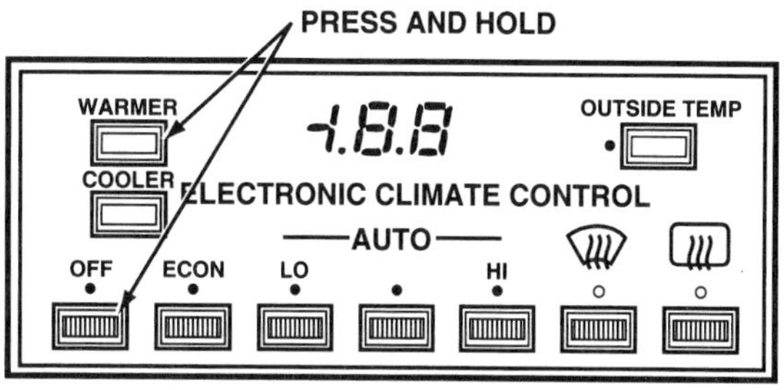

Figure 13-14. Simultaneously press the "OFF" and "WARMER" buttons on the climate control panel to enter the diagnostic mode.

2. After the segment check, about five seconds, codes from the engine and body controllers display on the DIC screen. Codes display in the following order: engine (E) codes, body (B) codes, lighting (L) codes, and restraint (R) codes. Most codes revealed here have no effect on ABS functions. However, codes E069, B421, B480, and B483 do. Watch for these codes and record them if they appear.
3. After the code display, a DIC prompt asks if you want to perform any additional diagnostic checks. Press the "LO" button to bypass each selection until the panel reads ABS/TCS fault codes.
4. With the ABS/TCS message displayed, install a jump wire between terminals "A" and "H" of the ALDL connector.
5. With the jump wire installed, ABS codes display as flashes of the red BRAKE warning lamp. The sequence will always begin with code 12; any additional codes will follow. Each code flashes three times. The system stores multiple codes, and the code display continues to repeat itself as long as the jump wire is in place.
6. Remove the jump wire to exit the diagnostic mode, and press the "RESET" button to exit the service mode.

On these later systems, you must clear codes from memory after repairs are made by interrupting power to the controller. Remove the 20-amp BRAKE fuse for 10 seconds or disconnect the battery. Controller memory also clears automatically if the condition that set the code does not reappear within 50 ignition cycles.

Bosch 3 Service

Bosch has a special service tool for testing the Bosch 3 system. The tester attaches to the ABS control module wiring harness to check wheel speed sensors, solenoid valves, and the replenishing valve, brake switch, piston travel switch, and control pressure switch. The tester also monitors the operation of the pump/motor.

A high-pressure hydraulic gauge along with the Bosch tester is used to monitor pump/motor and accumulator pressures as they build. A DVOM and breakout box are required to perform individual circuit checks.

Bleeding Procedure

Bleed the hydraulic system manually or with pressure-bleeding equipment. First, switch off the ignition and relieve accumulator pressure by pumping the pedal 25 to 40 times. No special procedures are required to bleed the brake lines at the wheels; the proper sequence is:

- Left rear
- Right rear
- Left front
- Right front.

To bleed the master cylinder/booster, relieve accumulator pressure and top off the fluid reservoir. Next, connect a transparent hose to the bleed screw on the right side of the hydraulic assembly and place the other end of the hose in a clear container. Open the bleed screw ½ to ¾ turn and switch on the ignition. This will start and run the pump/motor to force fluid into the container. Allow the pump to run until the fluid flowing through the hose is free of air bubbles.

Bosch 2 Diagnostics

The Bosch 2 controller on many older applications has limited self-diagnostic capabilities. Although it cannot generate trouble codes, it can detect a variety of faults that interfere with safe ABS operation. A newer Bosch 2 controller, used on certain Lexus, Mazda, Nissan, and Toyota models, does generate diagnostic trouble codes.

If the ABS control module fails to power up when the ignition is turned on, an "ABS diode" provides backup power for the warning lamp circuit. The diode provides an alternate ground path through the solenoid relay when no voltage is available to the controller. This allows the warning lamp to remain on and alert the driver that the ABS is inoperative. Loss of controller power may result from a faulty relay, wiring problems, or an open fuse.

The initial ABS self-test looks for any internal controller faults, as well as problems in the solenoid relay circuit. If the self-test detects a problem, the ABS lamp remains on following the bulb check and the system disables itself.

Once per ignition cycle, the system performs a self-test when vehicle speed reaches three to seven mph. The controller briefly activates the solenoid valves in the modulator assembly and energizes the return pump during the test.

During normal operation, the controller continuously monitors the wheel speed sensors, battery voltage, circuit voltages, and relays. The lateral acceleration switch, used on the Corvette, is monitored as well. In the event of a failure, the ABS lamp illuminates and the system disables. Certain failures set a diagnostic trouble code on some applications.

Bosch 2 Diagnostic Tester

Bosch supplies a special service tool for diagnosing Bosch 2 systems that do not generate trouble codes. However, this tool is not absolutely necessary as all testing, with the exception of cycling the ABS solenoids, can be performed using a DVOM and a breakout box.

The Bosch tester is used in conjunction with a high-impedance digital multimeter, and installs at the 35-pin harness connector of the ABS control module. The number and type of tests available vary by make and model. For example, 10 different tests are available for BMW applications, 11 for Mercedes-Benz, and up to 22 for Porsche.

Be sure the ignition is switched off before opening the ABS control module connector to attach the tester or a breakout box. Failure to do so can damage the module.

Unlike a scan tool, the Bosch ABS tester does not communicate with the ABS module. It simply cycles through a series of step-by-step circuit checks and solenoid tests to verify the operation of system components. The following tests are used by Mercedes-Benz:

- *Test 1*—Main relay and valve relay.
- *Test 2*—Supply voltage.
- *Test 3*—Valve relay.
- *Test 4*—Hydraulic control unit diode. Readings should be between 0.4 volt and 1.5 volts.
- *Test 5*—Wheel speed sensor internal resistance. Typical values range from 600 to 2300 ohms. Specifications vary by model.
- *Test 6*—Wheel speed sensor insulation resistance. Readings should be greater than 20,000 ohms.
- *Test 7*—Wheel speed sensor input signal. With the ignition on, rotate wheels by hand to generate a signal. Readings should be 0.1 volt or greater.
- *Test 8*—Modulator solenoid valve internal resistance. Specifications vary, but most are in the 0.7 to 2.3 ohm range.
- *Test 9*—Solenoid hold pressure check. With a solenoid in hold or isolation mode, brake application at the affected wheel is prevented.
- *Test 10*—Solenoid release pressure check. Energizing a solenoid relieves pressure at the affected wheel to release that brake when the pedal is ap-

ABS Diagnostic and Service Procedures

plied. The return pump should switch on during this step.
- *Test 11*—Brake pedal switch and overvoltage protection relay checks.

Accessing Lexus Codes

Lexus models with Bosch 2 ABS have the ability to record diagnostic trouble codes in the event of a malfunction. When the system detects a fault, a DTC records, the ANTILOCK lamp lights to warn the driver, and ABS operation disables. In diagnostic mode, the controller recalls codes from memory and displays them by flashing the ANTILOCK lamp.

Separate the two halves of the service connector, located in the engine compartment, while the ignition is on, figure 13-15. Next, enter diagnostic mode by installing a jump wire between terminals Tc and E1 of either the total diagnostic communication link (TDCL) connector, or the check connector. Both connectors are 17-pin designs. Which one is used depends on model application, figure 13-16.

All codes are two digits and display in ascending numerical sequence as flashes of the ANTILOCK lamp. The display begins with the first digit of the numerically lowest code. Following a 1.5-second pause, the second digit flashes on the lamp, figure 13-17. With multiple codes in memory, the ANTILOCK lamp remains off for 4.5 seconds between code displays. An ANTILOCK lamp that remains on continuously indicates an internal problem with the ABS control module. If there are no codes in memory, the ANTILOCK lamp flashes continuously four times per second after an initial 2-second pause.

On some models, additional diagnostic checks and information may be available by grounding other terminals of the TDLC. Consult the appropriate factory service manual for details.

To clear codes after repairs, enter diagnostic mode and pump the brake pedal eight or more times within 3 seconds.

Accessing Nissan Codes

The Nissan Bosch 2 system, used on the Maxima, 240SX, and Stanza, has limited self-diagnostic capability. In the event of a failure, the ABS warning lamp lights to alert the driver. At the same time, an LED mounted in the case of the ABS control module begins flashing a code message. The control module is located in the trunk, figure 13-18.

Be aware, the control module can generate only one code at a time, and the fault must be currently present. Unless the problem that set the code exists at the time of testing, all record of the failure is lost when the ignition is switched off. Therefore, if the ABS lamp is on, read the code from the LED *before* you switch off the ignition.

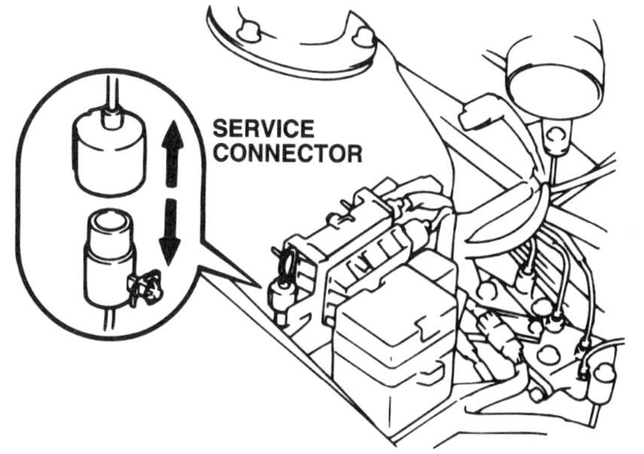

Figure 13-15. Locate and separate the two halves of the service connector.

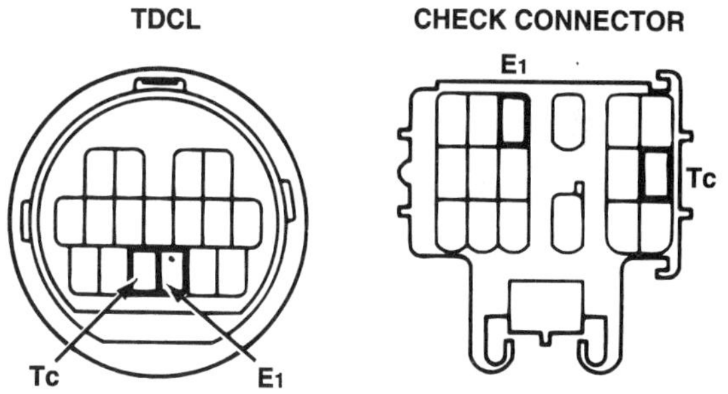

Figure 13-16. Locate either the TDCL or the check connector, and install a jump wire between terminals Tc and E1.

DTC	INDICATED FAULT
11	ABS solenoid relay circuit open
12	ABS solenoid relay circuit shorted
13	Pump motor relay circuit open
14	Pump motor relay circuit shorted
21	RF ABS solenoid
22	LF ABS solenoid
23	RR ABS solenoid
24	LR ABS solenoid
31	RF wheel speed sensor
32	LF wheel speed sensor
33	RR wheel speed sensor
34	LR wheel speed sensor
35	LF or RR wheel speed sensor
36	RF or LR wheel speed sensor
37	Wrong rear axle hubs on both sides
41	System voltage low (below 9.5 volts)
42	System voltage high (over 16.2 volts)
51	Pump motor circuit

Figure 13-17. Lexus and Toyota Bosch 2 diagnostic trouble codes.

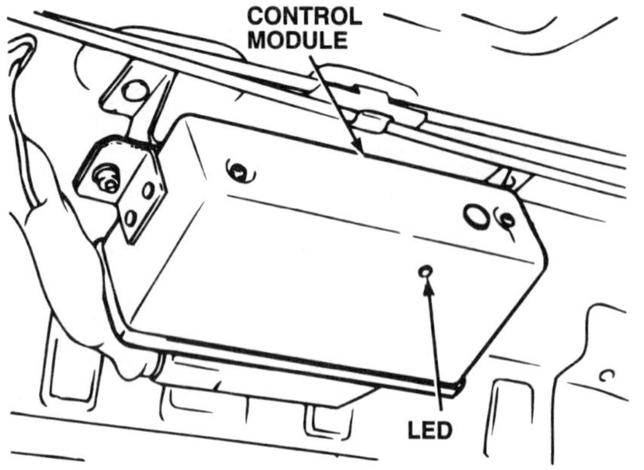

Figure 13-18. An LED on the ABS control module, located in the trunk, flashes trouble codes on Nissan vehicles.

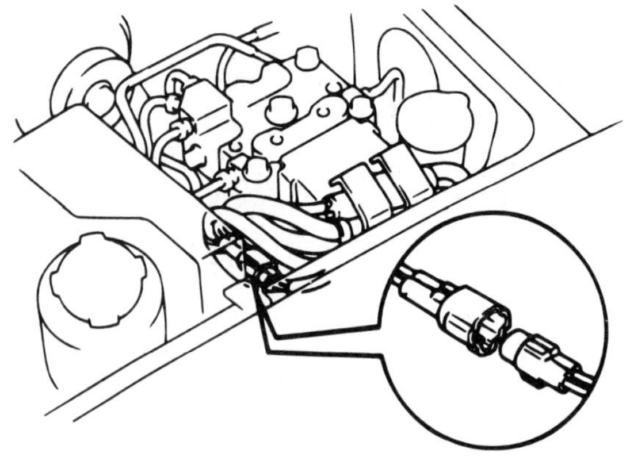

Figure 13-20. On a Toyota Camry, locate and open the check connector to enter the diagnostic mode.

DTC	INDICATED FAULT
1	LF ABS solenoid
2	RF ABS solenoid
3	RR ABS solenoid
4	LR ABS solenoid
5	LF wheel speed sensor
6	RF wheel speed sensor
7	RR wheel speed sensor
8	LR wheel speed sensor
9	Pump motor circuit
10	Solenoid valve circuit
16	ABS control module

Figure 13-19. Nissan Bosch 2 diagnostic trouble codes.

Interpret LED codes according to the accompanying diagnostic chart, figure 13-19. An LED that remains on remains on without flashing indicates an internal control module problem. Suspect a loss of power or ground at the module if the instrument cluster ABS lamp is on and the LED on the module is off.

Accessing Toyota Codes

The Toyota Bosch 2 system, used on the Toyota Camry, Celica, Cressida, and Supra, has self-diagnostic capabilities and will store trouble codes. All Toyota models display two-digit codes as a series of flashes on the instrument cluster warning lamp. Interpreting flash codes, code definitions, and code-clearing procedures are identical to those for Lexus. Refer to the preceding Lexus section. However, procedures for retrieving codes vary by model application.

Camry

To recall codes, switch the ignition on and disconnect the check connector. The connector is located near the modulator assembly, figure 13-20.

An additional diagnostic mode is available for checking the wheel speed sensors on Camry models. Results are displayed as special codes on the cluster warning lamp. Further diagnostic information may also be available; check the appropriate service manual.

To test, switch the ignition off and disconnect the check connector. Then, switch the ignition on and pump the brake pedal four to six times within two seconds to activate the test. The warning lamp should flash four times a second, indicating that the special wheel speed sensor diagnostic mode is active. In this mode, the controller checks the output signal of the speed sensors as the vehicle is driven in a straight line at 2.5 to 3.7 mph. Stop the vehicle and the warning lamp displays any additional codes for the speed sensors. The lamp flashes four times per second if no faults are present. The following special codes are used:

- 71 RF speed sensor, low voltage
- 72 LF speed sensor, low voltage
- 73 RR speed sensor, low voltage
- 74 LR speed sensor, low voltage
- 75 RF speed sensor, abnormal signal
- 76 LF speed sensor, abnormal signal
- 77 RR speed sensor, abnormal signal
- 78 LR speed sensor, abnormal signal.

If an abnormal or erratic signal is indicated, inspect the wheel speed sensor and sensor ring for damage. Look for road debris buildup, broken or missing sensor ring teeth, poor electrical connections, or damaged wiring.

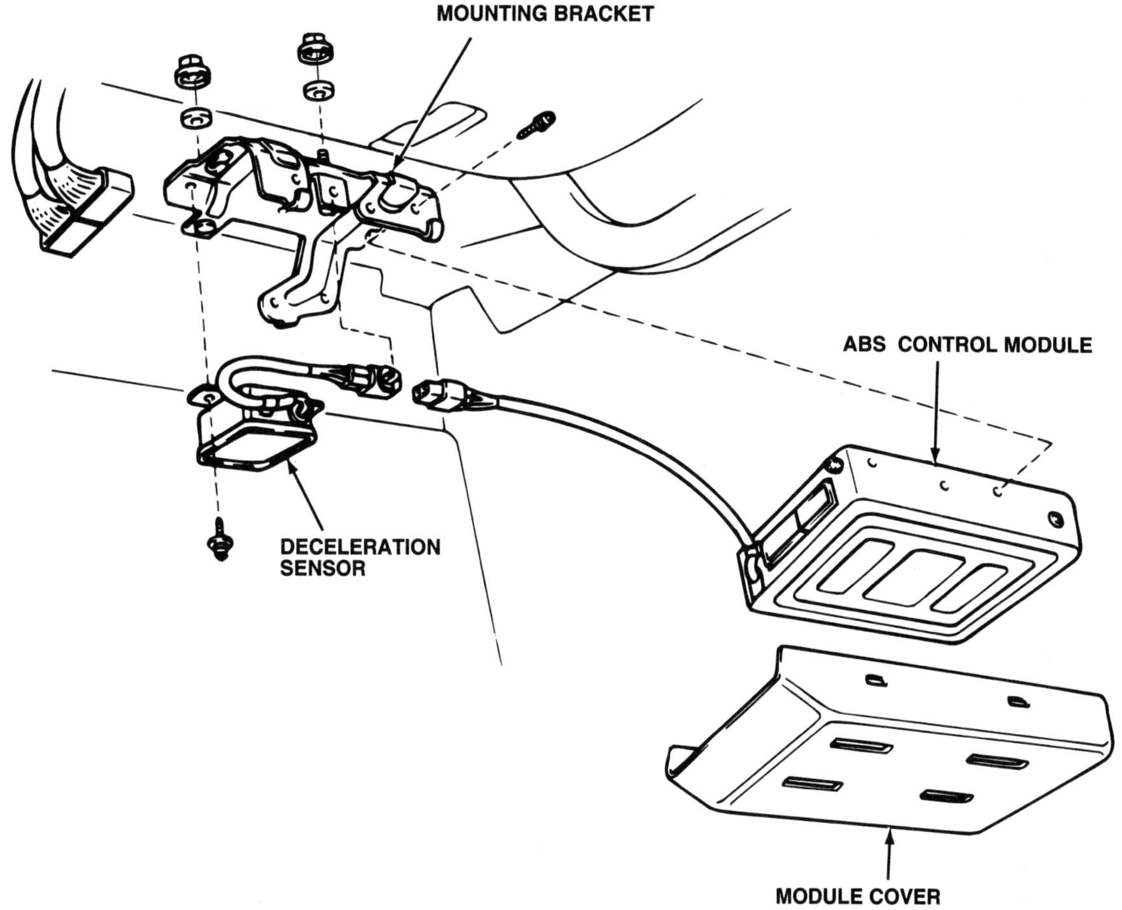

ABS Diagnostic and Service Procedures

Figure 13-21. A special test mode is available for checking the operation of the deceleration sensor on All-Trac Camry models.

Another special diagnostic mode is available for checking the deceleration sensor on All-Trac (all-wheel-drive) Camry models. The sensor, a mercury switch, mounts near the ABS module in the trunk and reacts to the additional load created by deceleration and acceleration, figure 13-21. When active, the sensor modifies the antilock brake programming during hard braking to compensate for changes in suspension loading. To engage the test mode, ground the terminals of the two-pin troubleshooting connector located next to the hydraulic modulator. Set the parking brake, depress the brake pedal, and start the engine to begin the code display. The ABS warning lamp flashes once per second in this mode. Raising the rear of the vehicle 33 inches off the ground should trigger the sensor and cause the warning lamp to stop flashing. You can also test by driving the vehicle at a specific speed and stopping suddenly. At 12.4 mph, the warning lamp should stop flashing and stay on steadily. If the sensor is functioning correctly, a sudden stop causes the lamp to flash at a rate of seven times per second.

Celica

Switch the ignition on and enter diagnostic mode by separating the service connector located near the ABS module. Read codes from the instrument cluster warning lamp. Similar to Camry, Celica models have special diagnostic modes for speed sensor testing on front-wheel-drive cars, and deceleration sensor testing on All-Trac versions.

For speed sensor mode, install a jump wire between terminals Tc and E1 of the check connector located near the master cylinder, figure 13-16. With the parking brake set and the engine running, the warning lamp flashes four times a second when the test is active. Drive to a speed of 2.5 to 3.7 mph, then brake to a stop. Codes display as previously described for the Camry.

Use a three-way jump wire, or two jump wires, to trigger the deceleration sensor mode on the All-Trac Celica. Terminal E1 of the check connector is the common connection. Install jump wires from E1 to terminal Tc and terminal Ts, figure 13-22. Test as described for Camry.

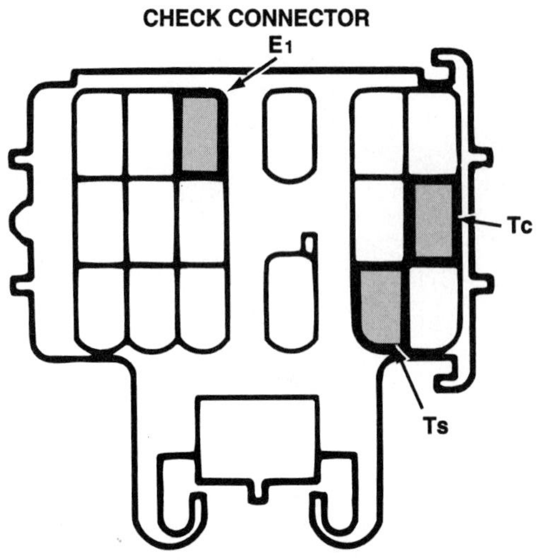

Figure 13-22. Activate the deceleration sensor test by jumping terminals Tc and Ts to terminal E1 on the check connector.

Cressida and Supra

To enter ABS diagnostics, switch the ignition on, and unplug the check connector mounted near the modulator assembly. Cressida models require installing a jump wire between terminals Tc and E1 of the TDCL to recall codes. Read codes as previously described.

The Cressida also has a speed sensor diagnostic mode. Enter by jumping terminals Tc and E1 of the TDCL with the ignition off. Activate and test as described for other Toyota models.

A special service tool is available for checking the modulator solenoids on Celica, Cressida, and Supra models.

Bosch 2 Service

Because Bosch 2 ABS is used on a variety of vehicles from a number of different manufacturers, it is important to follow the precise instructions for the vehicle being serviced. Refer to the appropriate factory service manual for vehicle specific procedures. The following information is provided as a general reference only.

Bleeding Procedure

Perform bleeding manually or with a power bleeder for all Bosch 2 ABS applications. Procedures are the same as for vehicles without ABS. In general, follow standard bleeding sequence by starting with the wheel that is farthest from the master cylinder.

To bleed the brakes on a Corvette, GM recommends raising the front of the car until the rear caliper bleed screws are in the 12 o'clock position. This prevents air from being trapped in the rear brake calipers.

Bosch 2E, 2U, 2S Micro, and ABS/ASR Diagnostics

Bosch 2E, 2U, and 2S Micro are all nonintegral systems that are essentially variants of the Bosch 2 system. Bosch ABS/ASR is a combination antilock brake and automatic slip regulation (ASR) system used on the Chevrolet Corvette and various Cadillac models. Self-diagnostic capabilities of these systems include checks on the controller, ABS solenoids, wheel speed sensors, pump motor and relay, and wiring harnesses. In addition, ABS/ASR performs a self-test on the lateral acceleration sensor and throttle position sensor.

The controller monitors all system inputs while driving, and performs an automatic self-test every time the engine starts. As with Bosch 2, the controller cycles the solenoids, relays, and pump motor to check their operation when vehicle speed reaches about four mph. The ABS warning lamp comes on, a DTC sets, and ABS disables if the controller senses a malfunction.

Intermittent problems, such as low system voltage and poor electrical connections, may cause the warning lamp to flicker on and off.

If voltage is not available to the control module, or the controller ground is weak, the ABS warning lamp will illuminate due to reverse current flow through the ABS warning lamp diode.

Preliminary System Checks

Prior to checking the system for codes, perform a preliminary inspection:

- Confirm that the warning lamps illuminate when the ignition switches on, and go out once the engine starts. A lamp that remains on indicates a hard, or current, fault.
- If the warning lamps fail to illuminate, check all system fuses, including the ones for the instrument cluster and ABS diode.
- Check the BRAKE warning light by turning the ignition on and applying the parking brake.
- Check the pump motor and solenoid relays to ensure that they are firmly seated and making good contact.
- Check for good contact at the 35-pin connector for the ABS controller.
- Be sure the brake fluid is at the proper level.

If no obvious problems are found during the preliminary inspection, proceed with onboard diagnostics.

Accessing Codes

You can manually access codes on General Motors vehicles with Bosch 2U and 2S Micro systems, but not on

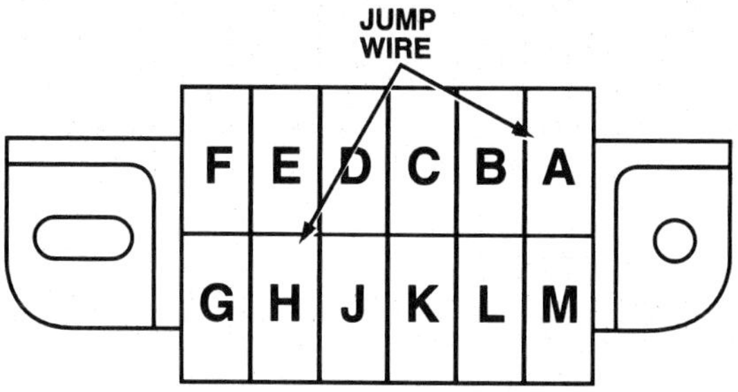

ABS Diagnostic and Service Procedures

Figure 13-23. To access codes on General Motors vehicles with Bosch 2U and 2S Micro systems, install a jump wire between ALDL terminals H and A.

DTC	INDICATED FAULT
11	LF wheel speed sensor
12	RF wheel speed sensor
13	LR wheel speed sensor
14	RR wheel speed sensor
15	Sensor fault
21	G-Force sensor
22	Stoplight switch circuit
41	LF ABS solenoid
42	RF ABS solenoid
43	Rear ABS solenoid
51	ABS solenoid valve relay
52	Motor relay
56	Control module

Figure 13-24. Diagnostic trouble codes for General Motors vehicles with Bosch 2 variations, except those with automatic slip regulation (ASR).

vehicles equipped with ABS/ASR. A scan tool must be used to retrieve codes from an ABS/ASR system. To manually retrieve Bosch 2U and 2S Micro codes:

1. Use a jump wire to connect ALDL pin "H" to pin "A" (ground), then switch the ignition on, figure 13-23.
2. Codes display as flashes on the ABS warning lamp. The display begins with a code 12, followed by any remaining ABS codes. Each code flashes three times. The system can store a maximum of three codes.

This technique reveals if certain fault codes are in memory, but it cannot reveal all possible codes. A scan tool must be used to retrieve some hard codes. The scan tool can also access other diagnostic information available from the system.

Hard codes cannot be erased by cycling the ignition; they can be cleared only with a scan tool. Codes remain in memory for 50 to 100 ignition cycles, depending on the application. If the fault that set the code does not recur during that time, the code erases automatically.

Scan Tool Diagnosis

In addition to accessing codes, a scan tool can perform various system tests. These system, or functional, tests are part of the onboard diagnostic program of the controller. However, the scan tool software must be capable of transmitting input commands to initiate the tests. Available functional tests include:

- A data test mode that continuously monitors wheel speed sensor and brake switch status.
- A snapshot mode for capturing ABS data before and after a problem occurs. The data can then be reviewed later to help diagnose the problem.
- A test mode for checking the operation of the ABS solenoid valves in the modulator. Tests are available for checking pressure release in each circuit, pressure hold in each circuit, and a cycling test that runs the pump briefly and cycles each ABS solenoid.

In a release test, a solenoid is energized to open. The wheel should turn freely when spun by hand even while brake pedal pressure is maintained. In a hold test, the solenoid is energized to close off the brake circuit. Applying the brakes should have no effect on the wheel in the circuit being tested.

The 1992 Corvette has an additional test mode, called "TPS Learn." This mode recalibrates the ABS/ASR controller if the throttle position sensor or throttle body has been removed. This calibration is necessary to reestablish the correct idle voltage for throttle reduction during ASR operation.

Connecting a scan tool suspends operation of a Bosch 2U, 2S Micro, or ABS/ASR system by switching off the solenoid relay. The ABS warning lamp illuminates and remains on until you disconnect the scan tool.

Attach the scan tool to the ALDL connector while the ignition is off. Switch the ignition on to check for codes and perform functional tests. Refer to the appropriate diagnostic chart in a factory shop manual to troubleshoot codes, figure 13-24. If more than one code is present, troubleshoot in order, starting with the lowest number code. After completing repairs, use the scan tool to clear codes.

Bosch ABS/ASR Diagnostics

Bosch ABS/ASR has been used on Chevrolet Corvette since 1992, and on selected Cadillac models since 1993. Although these systems are capable of flashing codes, diagnosis with the factory scan tool is the method preferred by General Motors. Because code retrieval and diagnostic procedures vary by year and model, they are not detailed here. Consult the appropriate factory service manual for troubleshooting these systems.

Bosch 2E, 2U, 2S Micro, and ABS/ASR Service

Service procedures vary according to application, so always refer to the appropriate shop manual for exact details of the vehicle being repaired. The following procedures are provided as a general reference only.

Bleeding Procedures

On all Bosch 2 variants, bleeding can be done either manually or with pressure-bleeding equipment.

For Dodge, Plymouth, and Mitsubishi vehicles with Bosch 2E systems, the recommended bleeding sequence is:

- Right rear
- Left front
- Left rear
- Right front.

The recommended bleeding sequence for General Motors rear-wheel-drive vehicles with Bosch 2U and Bosch ABS/ASR systems is:

- Right rear
- Left rear
- Right front
- Left front.

On a 1992 or later Corvette, always bleed the prime pipe on the master cylinder before bleeding at the wheels.

Use the following sequence to bleed the brakes on front-wheel-drive General Motors vehicles that have a Bosch 2 variant system (2U or 2S):

- Left front
- Right front
- Left rear
- Right rear.

A separate sequence is used for the 1991 and earlier Corvette. To prevent air from being trapped in the rear calipers, raise the front of the car so that the rear bleed screws are in the 12 o'clock position. Bleed in the following sequence:

- Right front
- Right rear
- Left rear
- Left front.

Bosch 5, Bosch 5.3, Bosch 5.7, and Delco/Bosch Diagnostics and Service

The Bosch 5 series includes Bosch 5, Bosch 5.3, Bosch 5.7, and the Delco/Bosch hybrid systems. Some applications include traction control. On Mercedes and others, Bosch 5.7 systems may also include acceleration slip regulation (ASR), brake assist system (BAS), electronic stability control (ESP), or electronic traction support (ETS); all are types of traction control systems.

Accessing Codes

Use a scan tool to access trouble codes. DTCs for the Bosch 5 system are displayed as two-digit numbers; see figure 13-25 for an example. Bosch 5.3, Bosch 5.7, and Delco/Bosch DTCs are OBD II compliant, displayed as a letter followed by a four-digit number. For example, C1232 is the Delco/Bosch DTC that indicates an open or short in the left front wheel sensor circuit.

DTCs vary from vehicle to vehicle and year to year. On systems with added features (traction control, brake assist, etc.), it is especially important to refer to the appropriate factory service information for DTCs and troubleshooting procedures.

Bosch 5 Bleeding Procedures

All Bosch 5 series systems can be bled using manual methods or pressure equipment. Refer to the appropriate factory service manual for procedures. Bosch 5 systems (but *not* Bosch 5.3 or Delco/Bosch), can be bled using a scan tool and auto-bleed procedure. This method operates the valves and pump, allowing air to be purged from the secondary circuits, which are closed off during normal bleeding. The auto-bleed sequence should be used if a secondary circuit has been opened or if the brake pressure modulator has been replaced.

Bosch 5.7 systems that include enhanced feature content (ASR, BAS, etc.) may require the use of a scan tool and special procedures to bleed the system, especially if the hydraulic actuator has been replaced. The procedure for the Mercedes C230/280 with ASR is typical.

To bleed the system on the Mercedes C230/280 (with/ASR V):

1. Connect a pressure bleeder according to the bleeder instructions.
    a. The bleeding sequence is RR, LR, RF, LF.
    b. Bleed each caliper in sequence until there is no air at the calipers.
2. Connect the scan tool to the data link connector under the dash. Turn the ignition switch to the RUN position.
    a. Initiate the bleeding routine on the scan tool and follow the onscreen instructions.

ABS Diagnostic and Service Procedures

DTC	INDICATED FAULT
21	RF wheel speed sensor (vehicle in motion)
23	RF wheel speed sensor (ignition on)
25	LF wheel speed sensor (vehicle in motion)
27	LF wheel speed sensor (ignition on)
28	Wheel speed sensor circuit frequency malfunction
31	RR wheel speed sensor (vehicle in motion)
33	RR wheel speed sensor (ignition on)
35	LR wheel speed sensor (vehicle in motion)
37	LR wheel speed sensor (ignition on)
41	RF ABS inlet valve solenoid
42	RF ABS outlet valve solenoid
45	LF ABS inlet valve solenoid
46	LF ABS outlet valve solenoid
47	ASV prime line solenoid
48	USV pilot valve solenoid
51	RR ABS inlet valve solenoid
52	RR ABS outlet valve solenoid
55	LR ABS inlet valve solenoid
56	LR ABS outlet solenoid valve
58	Traction control module internal malfunction
61	Modulator valve pump motor
62	RPM signal
63	Modulator valve power supply
64	Throttle position sensor
65	Throttle adjuster circuit
66	Throttle adjuster control
67	Throttle position sensor comparison
71	ABS control module internal malfunction
72	Serial data link
73	Spark retard monitor
75	Lateral acceleration sensor circuit
76	Lateral accelerometer signal out of range

Figure 13-25. 1995 Corvette with Bosch 5 ABS diagnostic trouble codes.

DTC	Related Circuits
C0035 - C0051	Wheel speed sensors
C0060 - C0095	Inlet and outlet solenoids
C0110	Pump motor relay
C0121	Solenoid valve power supply relay
C0161	Stop lamp switch
C0245	Speed sensor deviation, side to side or front to rear
C0129 or C0267	Fluid level sensor
C0550	Control module microprocessor fault
C0896	System voltage below 9.4 v or above 16.9 v
U1000 and U1255	Class 2 communications fault, no communication
U1300, U1301, U1305	Class 2 communication, voltage fault

Figure 13-26. Typical diagnostic trouble codes for Bosch 8.0 ABS.

b. After bleeding, make sure that no bubbles appear in the return line to the reservoir.
c. If bubbles are present, wait two minutes and repeat the process.
3. Check for any DTCs that may have been set during the procedure and clear them, if any. Turn the ignition off.

Bosch 8.0 Diagnostics and Service

Introduced on the Saturn Ion in 2003, the Bosch 8.0 antilock system is similar in operation and service to the Bosch 5 series. Bosch 8.0 includes, in addition to ABS, dynamic rear proportioning (DRP) and traction control system (TCS).

Accessing Codes
A scan tool must be used to view trouble codes. The DTCs are OBD II complaint and appear as five-digit codes, figure 13-26. DTCs may be different from manufacturer to manufacturer, so always consult a shop manual or other service information.

The Bosch 8.0 system has an enhanced diagnostic capability. The enhanced diagnostics system can store the last three DTCs to occur, with the following enhancements:

- The number of drive cycles since the DTC last occurred.
- The number of times the DTC occurred since the DTC was last cleared.
- The most recent DTC will display first. This DTC will also display a snapshot of various data values from the time the DTC set.

This information can help in troubleshooting a vehicle with an intermittent ABS concern.

Bosch 8.0 Bleeding Procedures
Bosch 8.0 ABS is bled in the conventional manner, manually or with a pressure bleeder. Use only DOT 3 brake fluid in this system. A scan tool is required if the hydraulic assembly has been changed, extreme loss of brake fluid has occurred, or air gets into the modulator assembly.

1. Using foot pressure or a pressure bleeder, bleed the calipers. The bleeding sequence is: RR, LF, LR, RF.
   a. If brake pedal feel and height are OK, the procedure is complete.
   b. If the pedal is soft or air is suspected in the modulator, perform the automated bleed procedure, step 2.

2. The automated bleed procedure cycles the modulator solenoids and pump to allow air trapped in the modulator to move outward to the calipers.
   a. Install the scan turn on the scan tool. Under ABS "Special Functions," select "Automated Bleed" to begin the process. Follow the instructions on the scan tool screen.
   b. Since this process moves air from the modulator to the calipers, step 1 will have to be repeated.
3. Clear any DTCs that may have been set during this process.

DELPHI CHASSIS (DELCO) ANTILOCK BRAKE SYSTEMS

Delphi Chassis ABS includes the Delco Powermaster III, Delco (Delphi) ABS-VI, and the Delphi DBC 7 series systems. Powermaster III and ABS-VI have been used on a variety of General Motors vehicles from 1989 through 2001, depending on model. For the 1994 model year, ABS-VI was modified to include traction control functions on some applications. Beginning in 1999, the Delphi DBC 7 series was phased in as a replacement for the ABS-VI system.

All Delco systems have an amber ABS warning lamp on the instrument cluster. The lamp illuminates for a bulb check when the ignition first switches on, and the system performs a self-test. On some applications, the warning lamp may remain on for up to 30 seconds as the system recharges the accumulator. If the self-test reveals a fault in any of the monitored circuits, the lamp remains on after the 30-second test period.

A serious system failure causes the ABS lamp to light continuously. These failures generally relate to the front wheel circuits and affect the integrity of the system. In response, the system may either partially or totally disable ABS and record a DTC.

When the controller detects a less-serious failure; the ABS warning lamp flashes intermittently. These failures do not impair system performance and ABS remains operational. However, immediate attention is required to prevent further damage.

Delco Powermaster III Diagnostics

The Powermaster III self-test strategy includes a check of the system power supply, control functions, and pump motor. The controller transmits test signals to the various components and monitors their response.

Accessing Codes

The only method of retrieving Powermaster III trouble codes is by using a scan tool with compatible software.

Before checking for codes, inspect for obvious problems such as low brake fluid level, worn or damaged isolator bushings on the Powermaster III assembly, fluid leaks around the unit, or damaged wheel speed sensor tone rings and wiring. To access diagnostic information, connect the scan tool to the ALDL connector. Figure 13-27 lists available trouble codes and their definitions.

In addition to retrieving codes, the scan tool can provide other diagnostic information and initiate various functional tests. The ABS control module transmits a data stream to the scan tool, Figure 13-28. Scan tool functional tests include:

- *Brake pressure readings*—The scan tool can display accumulator pressure to verify both pump operation and the ability of the accumulator to hold pressure. If the red BRAKE warning lamp is lit, and the system reads less than 1800 psi (12,411 kPa), examine the system further. If system pressure is 1800 psi (12,411 kPa), or higher, look for a faulty fluid level sensor or parking brake switch.
- *Basic ABS function test*—This procedure energizes the ABS hold and release solenoids for each brake circuit. When energized, each pair of solenoids should release the appropriate brake. While depressing the brake pedal, you should be able to rotate the wheel with little or no drag.
- *Hold function check*—This test checks the ABS hold solenoids. Spin a wheel by hand, energize the applicable hold solenoid, and depress the brake pedal. The wheel should rotate freely for six seconds before the brakes stop it. Should the wheel stop in less than six seconds, the brake pedal sink to the floor, or the pump motor run excessively, suspect a faulty solenoid.
- *Boost pressure check and pump run time*—This test reveals the rate at which the pump motor can pressurize the accumulator, how well the accumulator holds pressure, and how well the pump cycles. With a fully discharged accumulator, the pump should pressurize the brake fluid for up to 40 seconds after reaching the maximum pressure of 2700 psi (18,617 kPa). Expect a properly operating pump to engage when the accumulator pressure drops below 2000 psi (13,790 kPa). Applying the brakes when the accumulator is fully charged should not cause the pump to operate until 50 seconds have expired. If it comes on sooner, the initial charge in the accumulator may be low. The pressure should be above 600 psi (4137 kPa).
- *ABS snapshot mode*—This feature captures data stream information to help isolate intermittent problems that occur only while driving.
- *History codes*—This feature displays the order in which the last five codes were set.

ABS Diagnostic and Service Procedures

DTC	INDICATED FAULT	DTC	INDICATED FAULT
A001	ABS warning lamp open or shorted to ground	A028	Rear hold solenoid energized too long
		A030	Two wheel speed sensor circuits open
A002	ABS warning lamp shorted to power	A031	Pump motor feedback circuit open
A003	ABS diode or ground circuit open	A032	Hydraulic leak or brake switch open
A004	Enable relay or solenoid fault	A033	Brake switch open
A005	Front enable relay coil open	A034	Brake switch shorted
A006	Front enable relay shorted to power	A035	Pump motor running too long
A007	Rear enable relay coil open	A036	Pump motor not running
A008	Rear enable relay shorted to power	A037	Front enable relay coil shorted to ground
A009	RF hold solenoid open or shorted to ground	A038	Rear enable relay coil shorted to ground
A010	LF hold solenoid open or shorted to ground	A039	Front enable relay contacts open or shorted to power
A011	Rear hold solenoid open or shorted to ground	A040	Rear enable relay contacts shorted to power
A012	RF release solenoid open or shorted to ground	A041	Brake switch circuit open
A013	LF release solenoid open or shorted to ground	A042	Low brake pressure circuit open
		A043	Low system voltage, below 9.7 volts
A014	Rear release solenoid open or shorted to ground	A044	RF wheel speed sensor reads 0 mph
		A045	LF wheel speed sensor reads 0 mph
A015	One or more front solenoids shorted to power	A047	Rear wheel speed sensor reads 0 mph
		A048	RF wheel speed sensor excessive acceleration
A016	One or both rear solenoids shorted to power	A049	LF wheel speed sensor excessive acceleration
A017	RF hold solenoid shorted to power		
A018	LF hold solenoid shorted to power	A050	RR wheel speed sensor excessive acceleration
A019	Rear hold solenoid shorted to power		
A020	RF release solenoid shorted to power	A051	LR wheel speed sensor excessive acceleration
A021	LF release solenoid shorted to power		
A022	Rear release solenoid shorted to power	A052	ABS control module calibration error
		A054	Rear enable relay coil circuit open
A023	RF release solenoid energized too long	A055	ABS control module internal voltage fault
A024	LF release solenoid energized too long	A056	Brake switch open or hydraulic leak
		A059	Low brake pressure during ABS stop
A025	Rear release solenoid energized too long	A060	ABS control module internal fault
		A062	Accumulator charge low
A026	RF hold solenoid energized too long	A063	Both rear wheel speed sensor circuits open
A027	LF hold solenoid energized too long		

Figure 13-27. Delco Powermaster III diagnostic trouble codes.

Delco Powermaster III Service

The Powermaster III ABS system is an integral system with a high-pressure accumulator. Before opening any hydraulic lines, replacing hydraulic components, or performing any brake repairs, switch the ignition off and depress the brake pedal 25 to 40 times to relieve accumulator pressure.

Pressure Testing

Use a high-pressure brake gauge to check the operation of the pump motor, accumulator, and pressure switch. To use the gauge:

1. Relieve accumulator pressure.
2. Remove the accumulator and install the pressure gauge and adapter in its place. Screw the accumulator into the other end of the adapter, Figure 13-29. Torque all fittings according to specifications to prevent fluid leaks.
3. Turn the ignition on. Pump pressure should rise quickly to at least 600 psi (4137 kPa). If the accumulator is not able to maintain this minimum charge, replace it.
4. Pressure should continue to build until it reaches 2700 psi (18,617 kPa). Then, the pump should

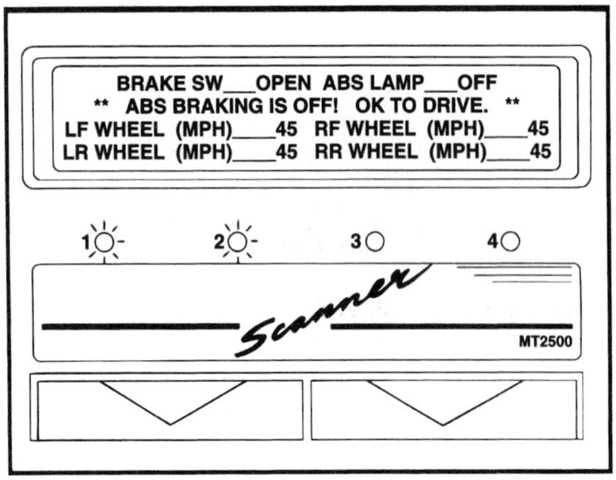

Figure 13-28. Typical Powermaster III data stream transmission displayed on a scan tool.

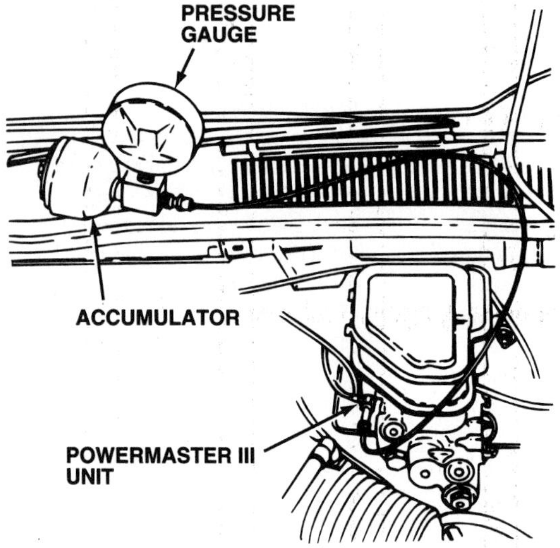

Figure 13-29. The pressure gauge installs inline between the accumulator and Powermaster III unit.

stop. A pressure switch failure is indicated if pressure exceeds 2900 psi (19,996 kPa). Check the circuitry and replace the pressure switch as needed.

5. When the pump stops operating at 2700 psi (18,617 kPa), expect the system to hold that pressure with the ignition switch off. Look for an internal leak if the system loses pressure gradually.
6. Turn the ignition switch on, then watch the pressure gauge as you slowly depress the brake pedal. The pump should engage when pressure drops below 2200 psi (15,169 kPa).
7. Turn the ignition switch off, relieve accumulator pressure, and remove the gauge.

Bleeding Procedure

Bleed the brakes using a special two-step procedure. Relieve accumulator pressure before you begin. Then, bleed the front brakes manually. Bleed the right front caliper first, then the left front.

Next, use accumulator pressure to bleed the rear brakes. You need the aid of an assistant to bleed the rear brakes. Turn the ignition switch on to recharge the accumulator. If the pump runs more than 60 seconds, turn the ignition off to prevent pump damage, and check for leaks or a low fluid level.

Bleed the rear circuits starting on the right side. Open the bleed valve as your assistant slowly depresses the brake pedal. Do not push the pedal to the end of its travel; doing so discharges the accumulator too quickly. The pump motor should engage during the bleeding procedure. With the pedal partially depressed, accumulator pressure forces fluid through the system to flush the rear brake line. After 15 seconds, close the bleed valve and release the brake pedal. Add fluid as needed, and repeat for the left rear brake.

If any air entered the Powermaster unit, purge it after bleeding the rear brake lines. The unit has two bleed screws; begin with the bleed screw closest to the engine. Switch the ignition on and apply light pressure to the brake pedal. Open the bleed screw and allow fluid to flow until it is clear, then close the bleed screw. Repeat the process for the second bleed screw.

After bleeding, switch the ignition off and relieve accumulator pressure. Wait about two minutes for the brake fluid to de-aerate, then top off using DOT 3 brake fluid.

The final step is to bleed the boost section. While applying moderate pressure on the brake pedal, switch the ignition on for three seconds, then switch it off. Repeat this ignition on, ignition off sequence a total of 10 times. Cycling the hold and release solenoids with a scan tool during this procedure can aid in releasing trapped air from the booster.

After two minutes, relieve accumulator pressure and top off the fluid level. Verify repairs by switching on the ignition to pressurize the accumulator and applying the brakes. The pedal should have a good, firm feel.

Delphi (Delco) ABS-VI Diagnostics

The Delco ABS-VI control module performs an initial self-test once vehicle speed exceeds three mph. During the self-test, the three system motors cycle on and off. The self-test delays if the brakes are applied. Once under way with self-test complete, the controller constantly monitors all system inputs.

As with Powermaster III, the amber ABS lamp either flashes or illuminates if the system detects a fault. In the event of a hydraulic failure, the red BRAKE lamp illuminates.

ABS Diagnostic and Service Procedures

Accessing Codes

You must use a scan tool to access or clear codes from memory on a Delco ABS-VI system. The system automatically erases codes that do not repeat within 50 ignition cycles of setting.

Six scan tool test modes are available for diagnosing the system. These include:

- *Data List*—Displays serial data for the wheel speed sensors, vehicle speed sensor, system voltage, warning lamp, brake switch, solenoids, motors, expansion spring brakes, enable relay, and other input and output devices.
- *Code History*—Displays the number of times the ignition switch has been cycled since a fault occurred and a DTC set. The system also displays the number of DTC occurrences.
- *Trouble Codes*—Retrieves and clears both current codes and history codes.
- *ABS Snapshot*—Records the serial data stream and is useful when diagnosing intermittent ABS problems that occur only while driving.
- *ABS Tests*—Includes a variety of functional tests for checking sensors, actuators, and subsystems.
- *Motor Rehome*—Commands hydraulic modulator motors to reposition in preparation for bleeding the system.

When checking for codes, first look for current codes, then history codes. A current code represents a failure that is present at the time of testing. These are generally easy to troubleshoot because the conditions that set the code are present on the current ignition cycle. History codes represent a failure that occurred in the past, but the conditions that set the code are no longer present. These problems can be difficult to isolate because the failure is not occurring on the current ignition cycle. Figure 13-30 defines the available trouble codes. Refer to the appropriate

DTC	INDICATED FAULT	DTC	INDICATED FAULT
11	ABS MIL open or shorted to ground	54	Rear channel in release too long
13	ABS MIL shorted power	55	Motor driver circuit interface fault
14	Switched battery circuit open	56	LF motor circuit open
15	Switched battery circuit shorted to power	57	LF motor circuit shorted to ground
16	Enable relay coil circuit open	58	LF motor circuit shorted to power
17	Enable relay coil shorted to ground	61	RF motor circuit open
18	Enable relay coil shorted to power	62	RF motor circuit shorted to ground
21	LF wheel speed sensor reads 0 mph	63	RF motor circuit shorted to power
22	RF wheel speed sensor reads 0 mph	64	Rear motor circuit open
23	LR wheel speed sensor reads 0 mph	65	Rear motor circuit shorted to ground
24	RR wheel speed sensor reads 0 mph	66	Rear motor circuit shorted to power
25	LF wheel speed sensor acceleration fault	67	LF release circuit open or grounded
		68	LF release circuit shorted to power
26	RF wheel speed sensor acceleration fault	71	RF release circuit open or grounded
		72	RF release circuit shorted to power
27	LR wheel speed sensor acceleration fault	76	LF solenoid circuit open or shorted to power
28	RR wheel speed sensor acceleration	77	LF solenoid circuit grounded
31	Two wheel speed sensors read 0 mph	78	RF solenoid circuit open or shorted to power
36	System voltage low		
37	System voltage high	81	RF solenoid circuit grounded
38	LF motor not holding	82	ABS control module calibration fault
41	RF motor not holding	86	Red BRAKE warning lamp on
42	Rear motor not holding	87	Red BRAKE warning lamp circuit open
44	LF motor frozen	88	Red BRAKE warning lamp circuit shorted to power
45	RF motor frozen		
46	Rear motor frozen	91	Brake switch open during normal stop
47	LF motor circuit current low	92	Brake switch open during ABS stop
48	RF motor circuit current low	93	Brake switch open during initial self-test
51	Rear motor circuit current low	94	Brake switch always closed
52	LF channel in release too long	95	Brake switch stoplight circuit open
53	RF channel in release too long	96	Stop light circuits or grounds open

Figure 13-30. Delco VI diagnostic trouble codes.

diagnostic flowchart in the service manual for troubleshooting. Generally, diagnosis begins with the lowest numbered code, then works in ascending order if more than one DTC is present.

When dealing with history codes or intermittent problems, try to re-create the conditions that set the code. You may be able to force a code to set by using the scan tool to perform a hydraulic modulator test. This procedure is available in the ABS Test mode. An alternative is to drive the vehicle with the scan tool connected and in snapshot mode.

Delphi (Delco) ABS-VI Service

A scan tool is required to perform a number of service procedures and to conduct system functional tests. The ABS functional tests provide:

- The ability to manually control each of the three hydraulic modulator motors, the two isolation solenoids, the enable relay, and the expansion spring brakes
- The ability to perform a voltage load test to check for high resistance in the power feed circuits
- The ability to test the warning lamps and their circuitry
- The ability to reverse each motor in the hydraulic modulator to check operation and to relieve gear tension prior to modulator removal.

Observe standard safety precautions, and follow factory service manual instructions when performing repairs.

Bleeding Procedure

Before bleeding the brake system, repair any code-setting conditions and clear codes from memory.

To bleed the system, the front and rear modulator displacement pistons must be in their topmost position to unseat their check balls. This can be done manually, but it is easier using a scan tool. From the ABS Test menu, select either the manual control or motor rehome option to reposition the modulator assembly motors.

Bleed the modulator by first attaching a length of clear tubing to the rear bleed screw, and submerging the opposite end of the tubing in a container partially filled with brake fluid, figure 13-31. Open the bleed screw and apply light pedal pressure. Close the bleeder screw when the pedal reaches the bottom of its travel. Repeat until the fluid flowing from the tube is free of air bubbles. Next, bleed the front bleed screw on the modulator in a similar fashion.

Finish by bleeding the brake lines at the wheels. This can be done manually or with pressure equipment. Use the following sequence:

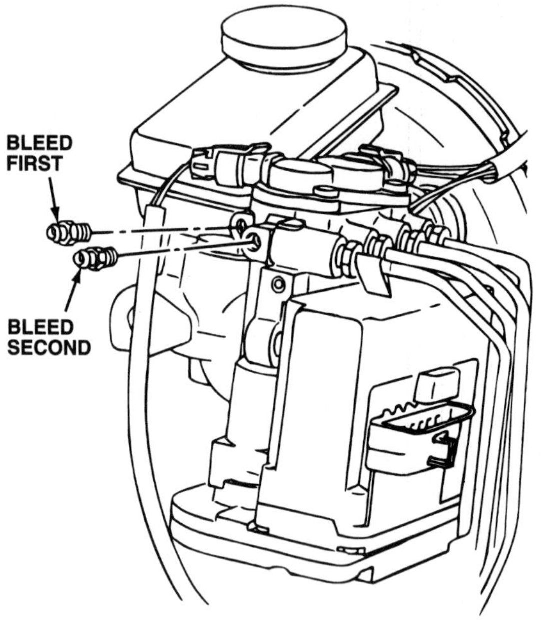

Figure 13-31. First bleed the rear bleed screw, then the front one on a Delco VI hydraulic modulator.

- Right rear
- Left rear
- Right front
- Left front.

To bleed without a scan tool, start the engine and allow it to run for at least 10 seconds. Do not touch the brake pedal while the engine is running. Switch the ignition off, then start and run the engine for a second time. Now, switch the ignition off and bleed the modulator and brake lines as previously described.

Delphi DBC 7 Series ABS Diagnostics and Service

Delphi DBC 7 series ABS is similar in operation to the Bosch 5.7 and 8.0 systems. DBC 7 ABS is used on General Motors vehicles beginning in 1999, with DBC 7.2 introduced in 2003 on some vehicles. Additional functions of the DBC 7 controller are:

- Dynamic rear proportioning (DRP)
- Variable effort steering (VES)
- Tire inflation monitoring system (TIMS)
- Enhanced traction system (ETS)
- Traction control system (TCS).

DBC 7.2 ABS adds engine drag control (EDC) and vehicle stability enhancement system (VSES).

Accessing Trouble Codes

Diagnostic trouble codes (DTCs) are read using a scan tool. As can be seen from the above additional func-

ABS Diagnostic and Service Procedures

tions, the DTC list is quite extensive. Refer to the manufacturer's service information for code details. The codes are similar to the five-digit code system as previously described in the section on Bosch 8.0 ABS.

Delphi 7 Series Bleeding Proceedure
Delphi 7 series ABS is bled in the same manner as described under Bosch 8.0 ABS. To summarize, the calipers are bled first and then the ABS modulator is bled, using an automatic bleed function, using the scan tool.

KELSEY-HAYES ANTILOCK BRAKE SYSTEMS

Kelsey-Hayes manufactures a variety of ABS systems. Designed for light truck and utility vehicle applications, Kelsey-Hayes ABS can be found on Chrysler, Ford, General Motors, Isuzu, Nissan, Mazda, and Suzuki vehicles. All Kelsey-Hayes systems are nonintegral, and work in conjunction with a standard master cylinder and power booster. There are two basic designs:

- Rear-wheel-only systems
- Four-wheel systems.

An instrument cluster warning lamp is used to alert the driver of a system malfunction. The warning lamp, or malfunction indicator lamp (MIL), may be either amber or red. When the ignition is first switched on, the MIL momentarily comes on as a bulb check. A MIL that remains on following the bulb check indicates problems that require additional diagnosis, as does a MIL that lights up or flashes while driving the vehicle.

Kelsey-Hayes EBC2 Diagnostics

Kelsey-Hayes EBC2, a nonintegral, one-channel, rear-wheel-only system, is used on Dodge, Ford, General Motors, Isuzu, Mazda, Nissan, and Suzuki light trucks and vans. The primary purpose of EBC2 is to maintain stability under braking whether the truck or van is empty or fully loaded.

Ford refers to Kelsey-Hayes EBC2 as RABS, for rear antilock brake system. Nissan uses the same name, but abbreviates it R-ABS. Dodge, General Motors, Isuzu, and Suzuki all use the acronym RWAL, for rear wheel antilock. Mazda simply calls it rear-wheel ABS. Basically, these systems are all the same regardless of application and the name assigned by the vehicle manufacturer.

Kelsey-Hayes EBC2 has self-diagnostic capabilities, and sets a diagnostic trouble code (DTC) and illuminates the MIL if the control module detects a malfunction in the system. However, self-diagnostics are limited, as the system can store only one DTC at a time. Dodge, Ford, Isuzu, Mazda, and Nissan applications use a dedicated ANTILOCK or ABS warning lamp to alert the driver to a failure. On General Motors and Suzuki vehicles, the same BRAKE warning lamp used to indicate hydraulic failures and parking brake application is used as the ABS MIL. In addition to setting a DTC, the system also disables antilock braking should a fault occur.

If the MIL is illuminated on a General Motors or Suzuki vehicle, first eliminate potential problems in the parking brake and hydraulic system before considering the ABS. If the MIL is on and the parking brake off, note the intensity of the warning lamp. Then, apply the parking brake as you watch the MIL. The lamp should become noticeably brighter as the parking brake applies and current is routed through a more direct path to ground. If there is no change in the brightness of the MIL, suspect a problem in the parking brake circuit. To eliminate the possibility of a hydraulic failure, unplug the electrical connector to the combination valve located near the master cylinder. If the lamp is on due to a hydraulic problem, it will go out when you unplug the combination valve. If the MIL remains on, there is an ABS problem.

Accessing Codes
Kelsey-Hayes EBC2 displays codes from memory by flashing the MIL when placed in diagnostic mode. Keep in mind, the system can store only one DTC at a time. In the event of multiple failures, the first code to set is the first code to display. To check for multiple codes, locate and repair the cause of the first DTC, clear codes from memory, then check for additional codes. You may need to drive the vehicle and reset the code.

Code definitions are similar, or identical, for all manufacturers, figure 13-32. However, each manufacturer has a unique method for entering the diagnostic mode. Interpreting the flash display can vary as well. Details for each vehicle manufacturer follow in alphabetical order.

Dodge
With the ignition switch on and the MIL illuminated, momentarily ground the diagnostic test connector located near the ABS control module, figure 13-33. Disconnect the test connector ground once the code display begins.

The MIL will pulse a single long flash to indicate the beginning of the code sequence. The code display follows as a series of short flashes. The display continues to repeat itself until you switch the ignition off. Count all MIL flashes; the initial long flash is part of the code. For example, a long flash followed by five short flashes would be a code six. Be aware, the MIL may begin flashing in the middle of a code sequence. Wait until you see a definite long flash before you begin your count.

DTC	INDICATED FAULT	APPLICATION
2	Isolation valve circuit open	A
3	Dump valve circuit open	A
4	Valve switch grounded or closed	A
5	Dump valve, excessive actuation	A
6	Speed sensor signal erratic	A
7	Isolation valve circuit shorted	A
8	Dump valve circuit shorted	A
9	Speed sensor circuit open	A
10	Speed sensor circuit shorted	D,F,I,M,N
10	Backup lamp switch circuit	G,S
11	Stop lamp switch circuit	D,F,I,M,S
13	Control module failure	A
13	Control module speed circuit failure	D,F,G,I,M,N
14	Control module program failure	D,F,G,I,M,N
15	Control module RAM failure	D,F,G,I,M,N

APPLICATIONS:
A = All, D = Dodge, F = Ford, G = General Motors,
I = Isuzu, M = Mazda, N = Nissan, S = Suzuki

Figure 13-32. Kelsey-Hayes ECB2 diagnostic trouble codes.

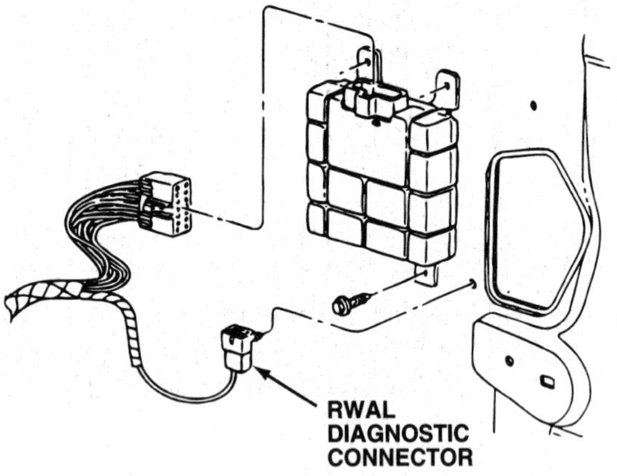

Figure 13-33. On Dodge trucks, look for the diagnostic connector near the ABS control module.

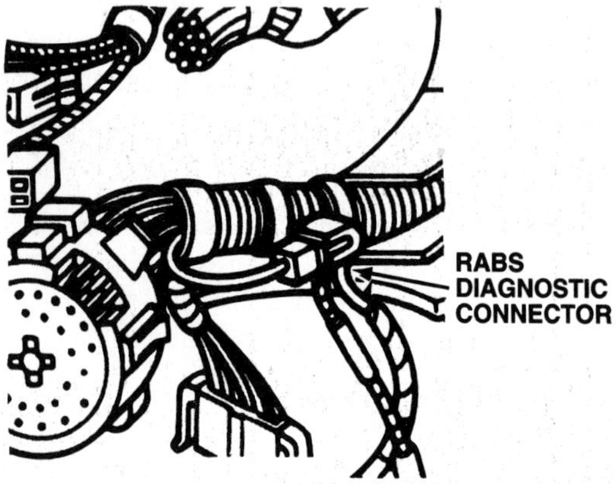

Figure 13-34. Ford trucks have a single-pin test connector inside the cab on the main harness. Look for a black/orange wire.

Most Dodge codes are retained in nonvolatile memory, so power to the controller must be interrupted to clear them. Disconnect either the battery or the ABS control module connector for about 10 seconds to clear memory.

Ford
To check codes on a Ford, install a jump wire to ground the RABS diagnostic test connector. Remove the jump wire after about one second to display codes on the MIL. The location of the test connector varies by model. All connectors are inside the passenger compartment. Look along the harnesses for a single pin connector on a black/orange wire, figure 13-34. On F-Series pickups and Bronco, the connector attaches to the instrument panel wiring harness near the parking brake pedal. On E-series vans, the test connector is near the brake control module harness connector near the parking brake mechanism. For Explorer, Ranger, Aerostar, and Bronco II models, the test connector is on the main wiring harness behind the 53-pin connector.

As with Dodge, the MIL displays codes as a series of short flashes separated by a single long flash, and the long flash is part of the code. The MIL may begin flashing in the middle of a code, so wait until you see a long flash and begin your count with the next short flash.

Ford RABS does not retain codes in nonvolatile memory, so there is no procedure for clearing them. Simply switch off the ignition and the code automatically clears.

General Motors
To flash ABS codes on General Motors vehicles, ground pin "H" of the ALDL connector. Once you install a jump wire between pins "A" and "H" of the ALDL, the MIL displays codes after a 20-second pause. Refer to figure 13-23.

The code displays as one long flash followed by a series of short flashes. Count all flashes, including the long one, to determine the code. Since the code repeats, you have several opportunities to confirm your count.

Codes are cleared manually by removing the ABS fuse or disconnecting the battery. A special code clearing procedure is used for 3500 Series heavy duty trucks; refer to the appropriate service manual.

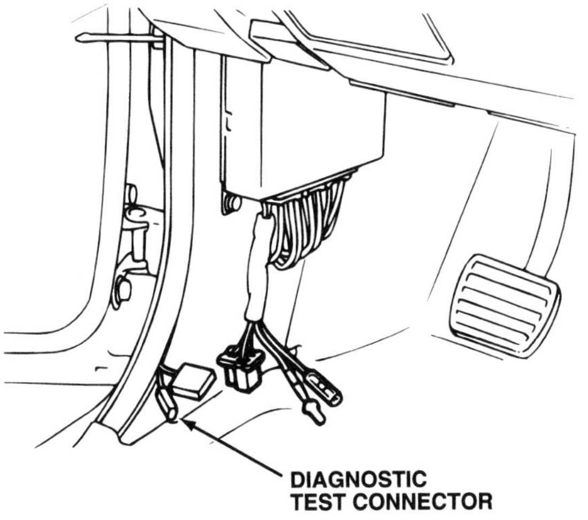

ABS Diagnostic and Service Procedures

Figure 13-35. On Izuzu trucks, remove the driver's side kick panel to access the diagnostic test connector.

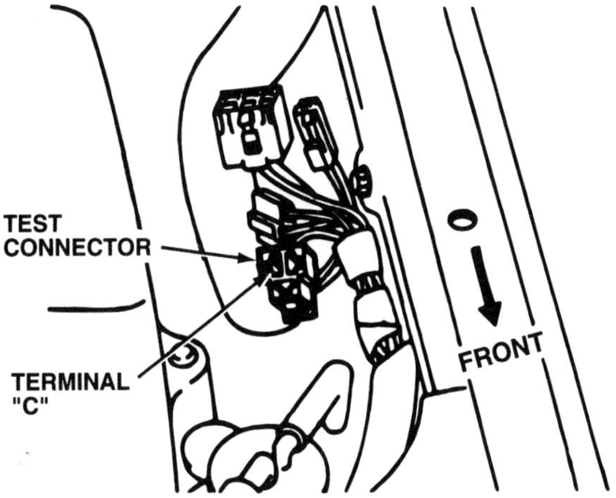

Figure 13-36. Access Mazda codes by grounding terminal C, the gray/white wire, of the three-pin test connector in the engine compartment.

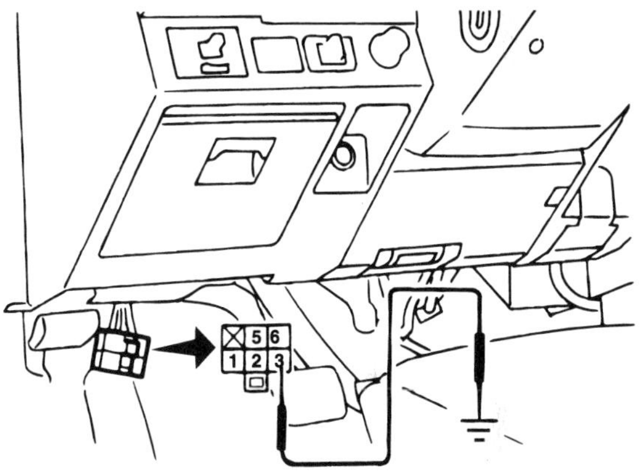

Figure 13-37. Nissan uses a six-pin test connector located under the dash. Jump terminal 3 to ground to display codes on the MIL.

A scan tool may also be used to retrieve and clear codes. The scan tool connects to the ALDL and allows functional testing of ABS solenoid valves, speed sensors and the brake switch. A scan tool is the only way to access codes on vehicles manufactured after August 1994.

In August 1990, General Motors modified the ABS control module software to convert codes 6, 9, and 10 into soft codes. These illuminate the MIL only when the fault is present. If the fault is intermittent, the software extinguishes the MIL with the next ignition cycle. Because the MIL will not flash soft codes, you must retrieve them with a scan tool. In addition, grounding pin "H" on the ALDL to display hard codes permanently erases any soft codes from memory.

Isuzu
To enter diagnostic mode on an Isuzu, momentarily ground the diagnostic test lead located on the left side kick panel, figure 13-35. The code display begins with a long flash of the MIL. Count the long flash plus any short flashes that follow to determine the code. Codes automatically clear when the ignition is switched off.

Mazda
Mazda uses a three-pin test connector located in the engine compartment, generally near the master cylinder, to access the code display. Locate the test connector and install a jump wire into terminal "C" with the gray/white wire, figure 13-36. Momentarily touch the opposite end of the jump wire to a good chassis ground to enter the diagnostic mode and display codes on the MIL.

Mazda codes also display with one long flash and a series of short flashes. Count all of the short flashes plus the long flash to identify the code.

Nissan
Nissan recommends driving the vehicle to precondition it prior to accessing trouble codes. Be sure to select 2WD range when working on a 4WD truck. The drive should include at least one minute of speeds over 25 miles an hour.

With the engine running, connect a jump wire between terminal 3 of the under-dash check connector and a good chassis ground, figure 13-37. Count the number of times the MIL flashes to determine the code.

Suzuki
To access self-diagnostics on a Suzuki, locate the monitor coupler connector that is near the fuse panel, figure 13-38. With the ignition switch on and the parking brake set, install a jump wire between terminals 3 and 5 of the monitor coupler. Leave the jump wire in

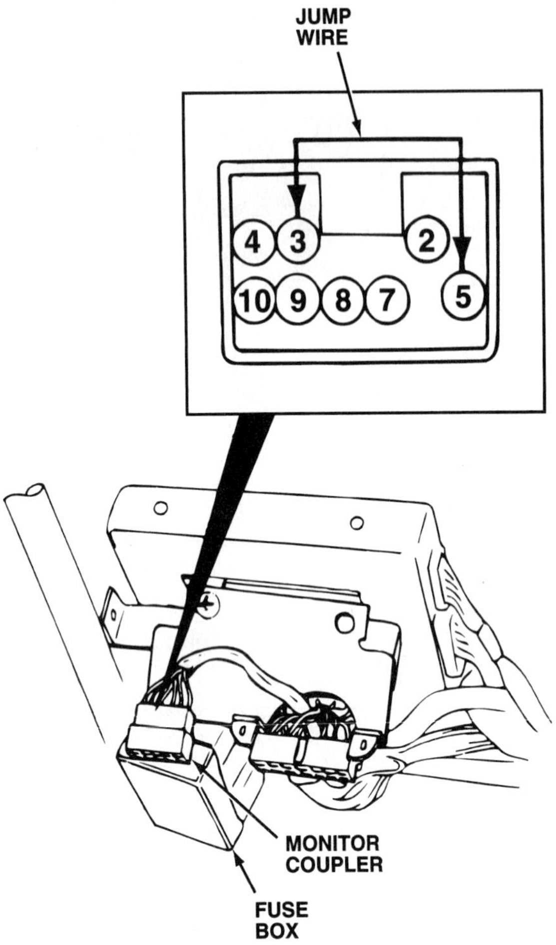

Figure 13-38. On a Suzuki, locate the monitor coupler connector near the fusebox and jump pin 3 to pin 5 to display codes.

place for two seconds, then remove it. Release the parking brake to begin the code display.

Codes display as a series of short flashes followed by a long flash on the BRAKE light. Count all flashes to determine the code. Switching the ignition off clears codes from memory.

False Codes

False codes are a fairly common problem with Kelsey-Hayes EBC2 systems. For example, when there are no codes in memory and the MIL is not illuminated, attempting to enter the diagnostic mode causes a false code 9 to set.

Early General Motors systems had several false code problems. On trucks with manual transmissions, switching the ignition off with the brakes applied and the vehicle still moving can set a false code 7, but only when the heater blower switch is set on high. This situation was corrected for the 1991 model year by an internal program modification. In addition, a revised brake pedal switch was released in 1990 to eliminate the problem of a false code 10.

Kelsey-Hayes EBC2 Service

Because EBC2 is a nonintegral, add-on system, most brake service operations are similar to those for standard brake systems. However, EBC2 does create some unique concerns.

Speed Sensor Contamination

Vehicle speed is calculated from the signal of a magnetic pickup sensor on either the differential or transmission. As a result of normal wear, the magnetic sensor can attract metallic debris that circulates in the lubricant and results in an erratic signal. The control module may interpret this as the rear wheels locking up, and responds by releasing hydraulic apply pressure to the rear brakes. Symptoms include clicking noises, a sinking brake pedal, and a DTC for the speed sensor.

To correct the problem, remove and inspect the speed sensor. Wipe any debris off of the sensor and change the lubricant in the differential or transmission. Refill using the specific fluid recommended by the manufacturer.

Low Brake Pedal

A brake pedal that gradually sinks to the floor is generally an indication of a worn master cylinder. However, with Kelsey-Hayes EBC2, the problem may be caused by an accumulation of dirt in the ABS modulator valve. If the accumulation is heavy enough, it can prevent the dump valve from fully seating and allow pressure to bleed past the valve.

To isolate the problem, disconnect the steel brake line that supplies the rear brakes from the master cylinder. Have an assistant depress the brake pedal about an inch to purge air from the outlet port, then cap the port with a plug and tighten it. Be sure to maintain pedal pressure to prevent damaging the primary cup as it moves across the vent port in the master cylinder. Release the pedal, then test by applying the brakes. Hold pressure on the pedal. If it continues to sink with the plug in place, the master cylinder is at fault and needs replacing. If the pedal holds firm, the problem is either in the rear brake circuit or in the ABS control valve.

To pinpoint the problem, block off the outlet port at the ABS control valve and check pedal feel as before. If the pedal now has a firm feel and does not sink, the problem is most likely caused by rear wheel cylinder leak. If the pedal continues to sink, the ABS dump valve is not seating and the ABS control valve assembly must be replaced.

Bleeding Procedure

You can bleed the brakes manually or with pressure bleeding equipment. Proper bleeding sequence varies

ABS Diagnostic and Service Procedures

by manufacturer, so check the appropriate service manual for the correct procedure. On most applications, the combination valve must be held open when pressure bleeding the system.

It may be necessary to bleed the modulator if any air has entered the lines. Bleed the modulator first, then bleed at the wheels, and complete the job by bleeding the modulator once again. Some older applications provide a modulator bleed screw, while newer ones do not. Loosen a brake line at the modulator to vent air from the modulator if no bleed screw is provided.

Kelsey-Hayes EBC4 Diagnostics

Kelsey-Hayes EBC4, a nonintegral, four-wheel, three-channel system used on General Motors light trucks, is more commonly known as 4WAL. The self-diagnostic capabilities of the 4WAL system surpass that of the EBC2 system by including more available codes, the ability to store multiple codes with enhanced display capability, and a more comprehensive self-test program.

On startup, the system performs two self-tests to check system integrity, then continuously monitors all system inputs while the vehicle is in operation. During the first self-test, the control module looks for opens and shorts on the controlled circuits. The second self-test activates once vehicle speed exceeds eight mph. At this point, the control module cycles the solenoids, relays, and pump motor to check their operation. Applying the brake delays the self-test.

The 4WAL system sets diagnostic trouble codes for both hard (current) failures, and soft (intermittent) failures. With either type of failure, the amber ABS warning lamp illuminates, a DTC sets, and ABS disables. Should a fault occur in the amber ABS MIL circuit, the red BRAKE warning lamp functions in its place. With a soft code, the MIL remains on as long as the key is on. With a hard code, the MIL comes on whenever the ignition is on, and will not extinguish until the cause of the fault is repaired. All codes remain in memory until you clear them.

Preliminary System Checks

Begin diagnosis with a preliminary visual inspection. Check for:

- The amber ABS and red BRAKE warning lamps to come on during the bulb check
- Blown fuses, including instrument cluster fuses if both warning lamps fail to illuminate
- Circuit faults if one lamp fails to illuminate
- Indicated faults, a MIL that remains on after the engine starts indicates a hard fault. A MIL that goes out indicates either no faults or an intermittent problem.

- BRAKE warning lamp operation by applying the parking brake with the ignition on. The light should come on with the parking brake applied, and go out when the brake is released.
- Good wiring connections at the modulator, wheel sensors, and other components
- Proper brake fluid level in the master cylinder reservoir.

Continue diagnosis by checking for codes in memory.

Accessing Codes

Place the 4WAL system in the diagnostic mode manually or with a scan tool. In manual mode, the amber MIL flashes to display codes. When using a scan tool, codes display numerically on the scan tool screen.

Manual Code Display

To enter diagnostic mode, install a jump wire between pin "A" and pin "H" of the ALDL connector, then switch the ignition on. The system displays codes by flashing the amber ABS warning lamp.

The two-digit codes display on the MIL in groups of flashes. The first group represents the first digit of the code, followed by a brief pause, then a second group of flashes to represent the second digit of the same DTC. Each set of two groups represents a complete DTC, which is followed by a longer pause. To identify codes, count the number of flashes, and keep track of the pause length. For example, code 12 would appear as a flash, brief pause, flash, flash, long pause. Each code repeats three times before the MIL display switches to the next code. Refer to a code chart to interpret results, figure 13-39. The red BRAKE warning lamp flashes codes if there is a problem in the amber ABS warning lamp circuit.

The display always begins with one of four specific codes. These indicate that the system is functional, and in self-diagnostic mode. Which code begins the display depends upon test conditions:

- Code 12, brakes not applied in 2WD mode
- Code 13, brakes applied in 2WD mode
- Code 14, brakes not applied in 4WD mode
- Code 15, brakes applied in 4WD mode.

These normal system codes allow you to quickly check the operation of the brake and 4WD switches without having to use a scan tool. After the initial code, any additional codes in memory display in numerically ascending order.

Scan Tool Procedure

The most accurate means of diagnosing Kelsey-Hayes 4WAL ABS is with a scan tool. For optimum results, the scan tool software must allow bidirectional communications with the controller. Bidirectional communication

DTC	INDICATED FAULT	DTC	INDICATED FAULT
12	System normal (brake not applied, 2WD range)	43	RF isolation valve, circuit shorted
13	System normal (brake applied, 2WD range)	44	RF modulation valve, circuit shorted
14	System normal (brake not applied, 4WD range)	45	LF isolation valve, circuit open
15	Normal (brake applied, 4WD range)	46	LF modulation valve, circuit open
21	RF wheel speed sensor, intermittent open	47	LF isolation valve, circuit shorted
22	RF wheel speed sensor, loss of signal	48	LF modulation valve, circuit shorted
23	RF wheel speed sensor, erratic signal	51	Rear isolation valve, circuit open
25	LF wheel speed sensor, intermittent open	52	Rear modulation valve, circuit open
26	LF wheel speed sensor, loss of signal	53	Rear isolation valve, circuit shorted
27	LF wheel speed sensor, erratic signal	54	Rear modulation valve, circuit shorted
28	Wheel speed sensor, erratic signal drop out	61	RF reset switch, circuit open
29	Wheel speed sensors, simultaneous loss of all 4 signals	62	LF reset switch, circuit open
31	RR wheel speed sensor, intermittent open	63	Rear reset switch, circuit open
32	RR wheel speed sensor, loss of signal	65	Pump motor relay, circuit open
33	RR wheel speed sensor, erratic signal	66	Pump motor relay, circuit shorted
35	LR wheel speed sensor, intermittent open	67	Pump motor, circuit open
36	LR wheel speed sensor, loss of signal	68	Pump motor is in a stalled condition
37	LR wheel speed sensor, erratic signal	71	Control module, RAM error
38	Wheel speed sensors indicate inconsistent speeds	72	Control module, ROM error
41	RF isolation valve, circuit open	73	Control module, internal circuit error
42	RF modulation valve, circuit open	74	Control module, excessive isolation time
		81	Brake switch circuit in continuous operation
		86	ANTILOCK warning lamp, circuit shorted
		88	BRAKE warning lamp, circuit shorted

Figure 13-39. Kelsey-Hayes EBC4 (4WAL) diagnostic trouble codes.

allows the technician, using the scan tool, to activate ABS solenoids, relays and the motor/pump to check operation. In addition to retrieving codes, the following tests can be performed with the scan tool:

- Check voltages at the ALDL connector.
- Display wheel speed sensor output for each sensor.
- Perform functional tests on the hydraulic modulator.
- Capture "snapshot" data during a test drive.

The scan tool also reveals the number of drive cycles since an intermittent fault occured and set a code. A drive cycle records when the vehicle exceeds a certain speed, usually eight mph, after startup.

Connect the scan tool to the ALDL connector; switch the ignition on; then, select trouble codes from the scanner program menu. The scan tool displays all codes, current and historical, that are recorded in memory.

If there is more than one code, troubleshoot in order, beginning with the lowest number first. Refer to the appropriate diagnostic chart in a shop manual for instructions on how to proceed. A DVOM and breakout box may be required to perform circuit checks on the system.

Clearing Codes

You can clear codes from memory either manually or with a scan tool. When using a scan tool, follow instructions provided by the tool manufacturer. Use the following procedure to clear codes manually:

1. Switch the ignition on.
2. Install a jump wire between ALDL terminals "A" and "H."
3. After two seconds, remove the jump wire.
4. After one second, reinstall the jump wire.
5. Again, remove the jump wire after two seconds.

This erases any hard codes and the MIL should switch off. To clear soft codes, switch the ignition off for approximately five seconds once the cause of the problem has been repaired.

Kelsey-Hayes EBC4 Service

Most service procedures for Kelsey-Hayes EBC4 are similar to those for vehicles without ABS. However, you must follow special bleeding procedures to ensure that all air is removed from the system.

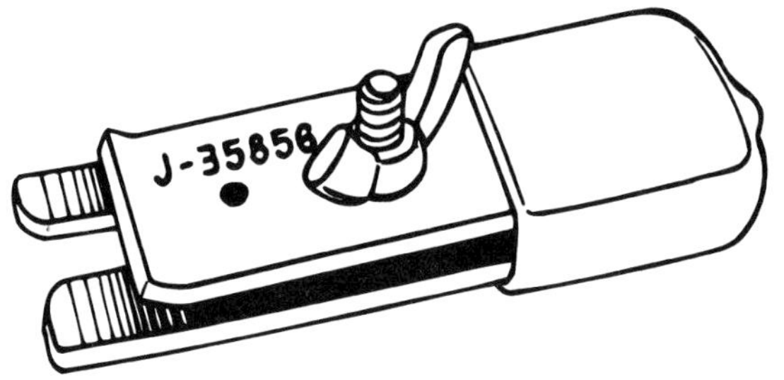

ABS Diagnostic and Service Procedures

Figure 13-40. Special bleed valve tools are required when bleeding the EBC4 modulator.

Bleeding Procedure

Bleed the hydraulic system manually or use power bleeding equipment. If no air has entered the modulator, use standard techniques to bleed the brakes at the wheels. The recommended bleeding sequence for most applications is:

- Right rear
- Left rear
- Right front
- Left front.

If air has entered the modulator as a result of master cylinder replacement, modulator replacement, or any other service work, bleed using the special procedure described below.

Modulator Bleeding

You need three special bleed valve tools (GM P/N J-35856) to bleed the modulator, figure 13-40. Always bleed the modulator first, before bleeding the system at the wheels.

To begin, switch the ignition off, pump the brake pedal several times to relieve pressure from the booster, and top off the master cylinder reservoir. Then, proceed as follows:

1. Install two of the bleed valve tools on the modulator high-pressure accumulators, figure 13-41.
2. Install the third tool on the combination valve.
3. Loosen the two internal modulator bleed screws about ¼ to ½ turn, figure 13-42.
4. Pressurize the system either by depressing the brake pedal or with pressure or vacuum bleeding equipment.
5. Open each bleed screw on the front of the modulator one at time for about 10 seconds. Close the bleed screws snugly, but do not overtighten.
6. Next, bleed the brake lines at the wheels in the sequence given above.

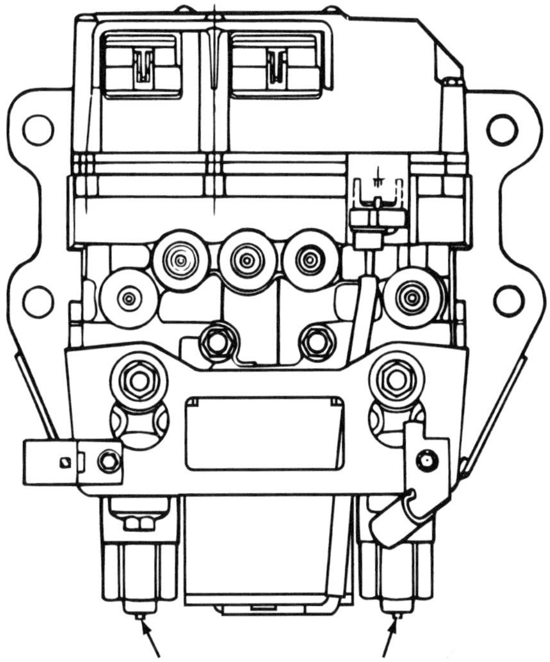

Figure 13-41. Two of the tools install on the high-pressure accumulator bleed valves.

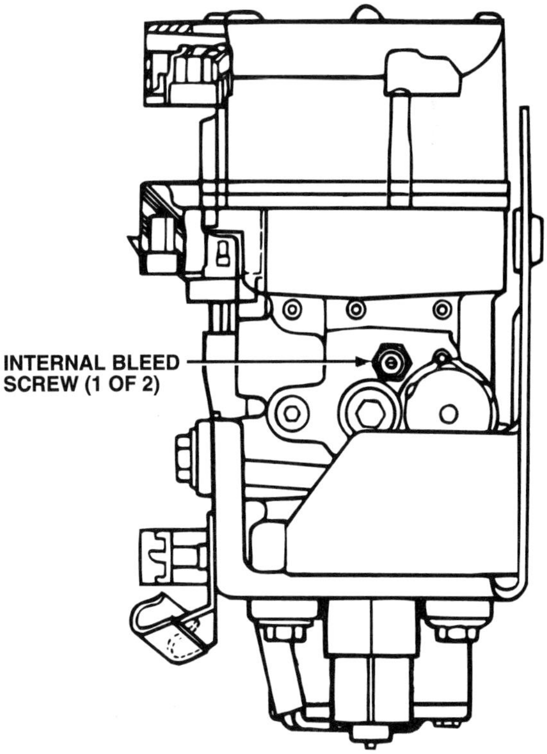

Figure 13-42. Loosen the two internal bleed screws on the hydraulic control unit.

Test the brake pedal. If it is not firm, repeat the above sequence, or use the scan tool to bleed air from the modulator. With the scan tool:

1. Firmly depress the brake pedal.
2. Select and activate the functional test that runs the modulator pump and operates the ABS solenoids. Maintain firm pedal pressure while the test is active.
3. Repeat step 2 three times.
4. Finish off by bleeding at the wheels to remove air that was forced into the lines from the modulator.

Apply the brake pedal to confirm that it has a good, solid feel. If the pedal is soft or spongy, repeat the above scan tool procedure until all air is removed.

Kelsey-Hayes EBC5H Diagnostics

Kelsey-Hayes EBC5H is a nonintegral, four-wheel, three-channel system used on some 1993 and later Dodge trucks. EBC5H is rather unique because it is a combination of two separate systems regulated by a single ABS control module. A standard ECB2 provides antilock brake function for the rear axle, while an additional two-wheel system prevents wheel lockup at the front axle during heavy braking, figure 13-43.

Kelsey-Hayes EBCH5 conducts a self-test to check the main relay, pump motor, and solenoids once vehicle speed reaches eight mph, and continuously monitors the system when the vehicle is in operation. In the event of a failure, the amber MIL illuminates, the system disables ABS, and a DTC sets. In addition, the control module has an external "watchdog" circuit that disables the ABS system should the control module fail internally.

Begin your diagnosis with a preliminary inspection. Confirm that the MIL is functional. Look for signs of damage and hydraulic leakage. Verify that all electrical connections are clean and tight. Make sure the master cylinder reservoir is filled to the correct level. Also, check the power supply and ground circuits to the control module.

The EBC5H system does not flash trouble codes on the MIL, so a scan tool must be used to access memory. The scan tool connects to a six-pin ABS data link connector located under the instrument panel below the steering column, figure 13-44. Depending on application, the test connector shell is light blue or black in color.

To successfully access EBC5H diagnostics, you need a Chrysler DRB scan tool. Rather than display numerical codes, the Chrysler scan tool displays error messages. Error messages reveal the affected circuit, and often the specific nature of the fault. The scan tool can monitor the serial data stream while the vehicle is being driven, and also conduct functional tests.

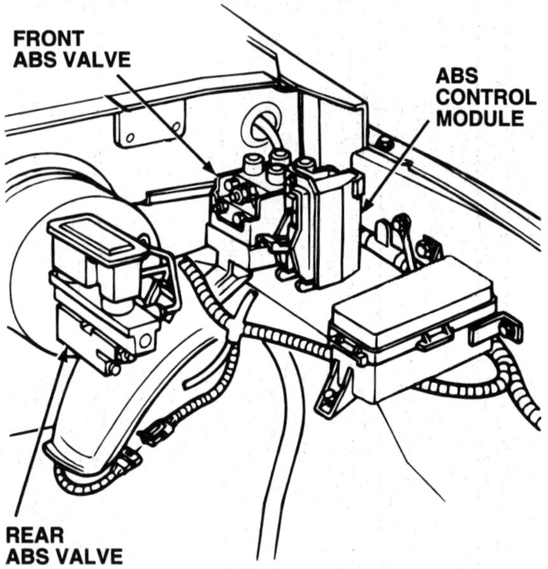

Figure 13-43. The Kelsey-Hayes EBC5H system has two separate valve assemblies, one for the front wheels and another for the rear wheels.

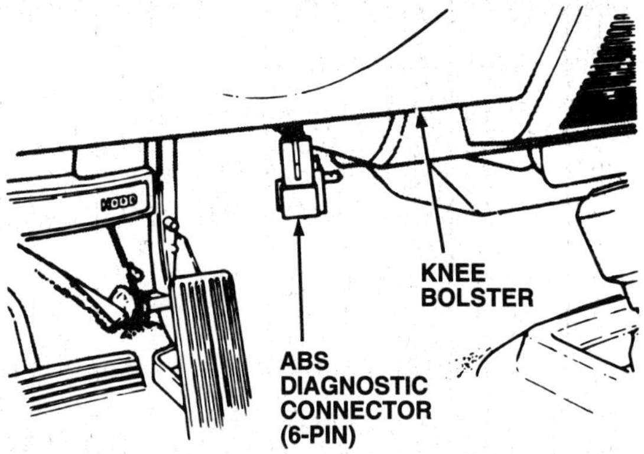

Figure 13-44. To read Kelsey-Hayes EBC5H codes, connect a scan tool to the six-pin diagnostic connector under the dash.

Kelsey-Hayes EBC 310/325 Diagnosis and Service

The Kelsey-Hayes EBC 310 ABS is used on 1995 to 1999 General Motors midsize and full-size trucks. From 1999 to 2000, EBC 310 was gradually replaced by the EBC 325 system. Both of these are functionally similar to the EBC 4 system that they replaced, with some added features. See the *Classroom Manual* for more details.

Accessing Codes

One major difference between EBC 4 and EBC 310/325 is that codes can no longer be read using the flashing ABS lamp. A scan tool must be used to retrieve DTCs on these systems. The presence of the standard OBD II

ABS Diagnostic and Service Procedures

16-pin data connector indicates that the vehicle ABS does *not* have blink codes capability. The codes will be similar to those already discussed under the Delphi DBC 7 antilock system.

Bleeding Procedure

The procedure requires two technicians; the brakes and modulator are bled using foot pressure. Follow these steps:

1. Beginning at the right rear wheel, install a clear hose on the bleeder screw. Put the end of the hose in a container partially filled with brake fluid.
2. Open the bleeder screw about one turn.
3. Slowly depress the brake pedal to the floor. With the pedal depressed, close the bleeder screw.
4. Release the brake pedal and wait 10 to 15 seconds. Make sure the reservoir does not run out of fluid.
5. Repeat until there is no air seen in the clear hose.
6. Repeat steps 2 through 5 on the other wheels, LR, RF, LF, until there is no air at any wheel.
7. Install and power up the scan tool.
8. Press the brake pedal firmly and run the scan tool automated bleed procedure. Follow the instructions on the scan tool.
9. Finally, repeat steps 1 through 6, bleeding all the wheels to remove any air that may have been released from the modulator.
10. This procedure may have to be repeated more than once to obtain a high, firm pedal.

Kelsey-Hayes EBC410 Diagnostics

Kelsey-Hayes EBC410, a nonintegral, four-wheel, four-channel system used on the Ford Windstar, has advanced self-diagnostic capabilities. The ABS control module records codes for on-demand (hard) and continuous (soft) failures. The system features bidirectional communications to perform functional tests using a scan tool.

Accessing Codes

The Windstar is an OBD II compliant vehicle and diagnostic information is accessed from the standard 16-pin DLC located in the passenger compartment. The sole purpose of the amber ABS warning lamp on the instrument cluster is to alert the driver of a system malfunction. A scan tool must be used to retrieve diagnostic information and to clear codes after repairs are made.

To access codes, connect the scan tool to the DLC and switch on the ignition. Use the scan tool to enter ABS diagnostics and recall codes from memory. A "System Pass" message indicates there are no codes in memory. Code structure follows the five-character OBD II format, figure 13-45. Refer to the service manual and follow the appropriate pinpoint chart to troubleshoot specific codes. Most diagnostic sequences require the use of a breakout box and a DVOM for performing circuit checks.

Kelsey-Hayes EBC410 Service

Since this is a nonintegral system, most service operations are performed as they would be on a similar system without ABS. Take care when removing and replacing brake rotors to avoid damaging the toothed tone ring for the wheel speed sensor. Check for proper clearance and alignment of the sensor and tone ring, and tighten fateners to their specified torque to avoid distortion.

Bleeding Procedure

The hydraulic system can be bled either manually or with pressure equipment. No special procedures are required unless air has entered the ABS valve assembly. To bleed at the wheels, follow standard procedure by bleeding the longest hydraulic circuit first, then work your way to the shortest circuit.

Bleeding the ABS valve assembly requires the use of a scan tool. You also need the help of an assistant. To begin, manually bleed the brakes at the wheels in the following sequence:

- Left front
- Right front
- Left rear
- Right rear.

Once the wheels are bled, start the engine and depress the brake pedal to the halfway point of its travel. Select and activate "ABS service bleed" from the functional test menu on the scan tool. With the test active, have your assistant open the left front bleed valve until the pedal bottoms out, then close the valve. Release the pedal and repeat the process a minimum of seven times. Bleed the right front wheel in the same manner. Repeat the process once again for both front wheels. Finish the job by bleeding the rear circuits in similar fashion.

Kelsey-Hayes (TRW) EBC 430 Diagnosis and Service

The TRW EBC 430 ABS (formerly Kelsey-Hayes) system is used on some General Motors full-size pickups and sports utility vehicles beginning in 2003. It is a four-wheel system with enhanced feature content that includes dynamic rear proportioning (DRP), traction control system (TCS), and vehicle stability enhancement system (VSES). See the *Classroom Manual* for more information.

Accessing Codes

A scan tool is required to service and access codes on the EBC 430 antilock system. These vehicles are

DTC	INDICATED FAULT	DTC	INDICATED FAULT
B1342	ABS control module	C1212	RF dump valve
C1095	Pump motor seized or circuit shorted	C1214	RF isolation valve
C1096	Pump motor circuit open	C1216	RF isolation valve
C1113	Power relay internal short or drive circuit	C1220	Amber MIL (ABS)
		C1222	Wheel speed differential error
C1115	Power relay contacts shorted	C1225	Red MIL (BRAKE) shorted to power
C1145	RF wheel speed sensor static test failure	C1226	Red MIL (BRAKE) shorted to ground
		C1233	LF wheel speed sensor inconsistent signal
C1148	RF wheel speed sensor erratic signal		
C1155	LF wheel speed sensor static test failure	C1234	RF wheel speed sensor inconsistent signal
C1158	LF wheel speed sensor erratic signal	C1235	RR wheel speed sensor inconsistent signal
C1165	RR wheel speed sensor static test failure	C1236	LR wheel speed sensor inconsistent signal
C1168	RR wheel speed sensor erratic signal		
C1175	LR wheel speed sensor static test failure	C1242	LR dump valve
		C1244	LR dump valve
C1178	LR wheel speed sensor erratic signal	C1246	RR dump valve
C1184	ABS system timeout	C1248	RR dump valve
C1185	Power relay circuit open	C1250	LR isolation valve
C1194	LF dump valve	C1252	LR isolation valve
C1196	LF dump valve	C1254	RR isolation valve
C1198	LF isolation valve	C1256	RR isolation valve
C1200	LF isolation valve	C1265	Red MIL (BRAKE) relay shorted
C1210	RF dump valve		

Figure 13-45. Kelsey-Hayes EBC410 diagnostic trouble codes.

OBD II compliant, so the 16-pin connector under the dash is used to attach the scan tool. The codes are similar to the Delphi DBC 7 system but with an extended list of DTCs.

EBC 430 DTCs will be a five-digit code beginning with the letter C. For example, DTC C0238 will set if the electronic brake control module (EBCM) detects that the speed of one wheel is more or less than 10 percent of the other wheels. This may occur if the owner has installed mismatched tire sizes.

Because the EBCM works in conjunction with the powertrain control module (PCM), the technician should also look for DTCs in the PCM when servicing any ABS-related concern. The PCM and the EBCM work together during any VSES event. If the scan tool shows DTCs beginning with "P," these are PCM DTCs and they must be corrected *before* diagnosing any EBCM DTCs.

Bleeding Procedure

Bleeding vehicles that use the EBC 430 antilock system is the same as just described under "Kelsey-Hayes EBC 310/325 Diagnosis and Service."

NIPPONDENSO ANTILOCK BRAKE SYSTEMS

Nippondenso ABS is used on a variety of Asian imports including Subaru, Toyota, Honda, and Acura. These systems may also be referred as *Denso* ABS in some service information. System operation is similar to Bosch 2, Bosch 5, and Bosch 5.3. Please refer to these sections for general bleeding instructions, but it is a good idea to also refer to the service manual for the vehicle being serviced.

Nippondenso 2L ABS

Used on some Subaru models and others from 1990 to 1997, this system can be compared to Bosch 2 ABS.

Accessing Codes

Codes are accessed by flashing the ABS warning light. Locate the diagnostic connector under the driver's side of the instrument panel, figure 13-46. With the ignition key OFF, plug one of the diagnostic terminals into cavity "L." The codes will flash, beginning with "11" indicating the start of codes, followed by any DTC that

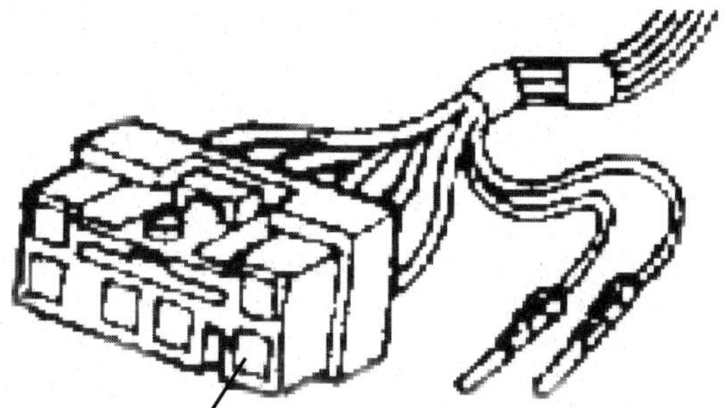

ABS Diagnostic and Service Procedures

Figure 13-46. The Subaru ABS diagnostic connector is located on the driver's side of the vehicle.

the unit may have stored. See the relevant service information or shop manual for a code list.

Nippondenso 5.3 ABS

Nippondenso and Denso 5.3 may be found on various Asian vehicles beginning in 1996. These are similar in operation to the Bosch 5 and 5.3 systems described earlier.

Accessing Codes

Retrieving codes from Denso 5.3 systems varies from vehicle to vehicle. On Subaru models up to 1997, codes may be accessed as described above. Starting in 1997, a scan tool attached to the OBD II connector may also be used. On Toyota and Lexus models, refer to the "Bosch 2 Diagnostics" or "Toyota ABS" sections in this chapter for code reading.

NOTE: Most current models will require use of a scan tool at the OBD II connector to read DTCs.

Nippondenso Variants

Some Honda and Acura 1987 to 1997 vehicles used a common design ABS that was named Nippondenso, Sumitomo, or Nissin, depending on the manufacturer.

Accessing Codes

Codes may be read on these systems by a light-emitting diode (LED) on the ABS ECU or by the ABS warning light. Early models (up to 1993) use an LED located under an inspection cover on the control module. To read codes:

1. Locate the LED on the ECU.
2. Turn ON the ignition (engine off).
3. Wait 10 seconds and the LED will flash any stored codes.

If the ECU does not have LEDs, look for a two-wire (not three-wire) diagnostic connector behind the right kick panel.

1. Connect a jumper wire across the two terminals.
2. Turn the key on (engine off) and wait 10 seconds.
3. The ABS warning light will flash any DTCs.

SUMITOMO ANTILOCK BRAKE SYSTEMS

Sumitomo manufactures two nonintegral, four-wheel antilock brake systems: Sumitomo I, a three-channel system, and Sumitomo II, a four-channel system. Sumitomo I is used by Honda for its entire product line, including the Acura Division. Sumitomo I is also used by Mazda on the RX7 through the 1991 model year, and on 626 and MX6 models built prior to March 1991. Beginning in March, Mazda upgraded to the four-channel Sumitomo II system for 626 and MX6 applications. The Ford Probe also uses Sumitomo ABS, with system applications identical to those of the Mazda MX6.

Sumitomo Diagnostics

Sumitomo antilock brake systems perform a warning lamp bulb check when the ignition is first switched on. Simultaneously, the control module conducts a self-test to check for circuit faults. If a failure exists, the warning lamp remains on, a trouble code is recorded, and the system disables itself.

Notice, an illuminated MIL does not necessarily indicate a problem with the ABS. The following conditions may cause the MIL to light:

- ABS pump running more than two minutes
- Driving the vehicle more than 30 seconds with the parking brake on
- Spinning drive wheels for longer than 20 seconds
- Erratic wheel speed sensor signals because of extremely rough road
- Low battery voltage
- Improper tire size
- Different traction characteristics on tires sharing the same axle.

If you suspect that one of the above-mentioned situations caused the MIL to illuminate, simply cycle the ignition off and back on again. The MIL should extinguish and remain out, providing there are no codes in memory. If the MIL comes back on, there is a problem and further troubleshooting measures are required.

Accessing Honda and Acura Codes

Sumitomo systems on Honda and Acura vehicles use one of two methods to display diagnostic trouble codes. The first flashes the MIL when the system is in diagnostic mode. The second illuminates the warning lamp, then uses an LED on the side of the ABS control module to flash codes. Both systems can only store up to three codes at a time.

To isolate the source of a problem, Honda supplies a special service tool (Honda P/N 07HAJ-SG0010A) for testing the ABS on its cars. The tool attaches to a six-pin diagnostic test connector located inside the passenger compartment. Connector location varies by model; look under the passenger seat, or behind the inspection cover on the passenger side of the console. The test tool can simulate wheel speed sensor voltages to check the operation of each brake circuit, as well as test the speed sensor and perform a modulator solenoid leak test. In addition, the tool can be used to cycle the solenoids to help bleed air from the hydraulic circuits in the modulator.

MIL Code Retrieval
To begin, locate the two-pin ABS service connector that is under the glove box, behind the passenger side kick panel, or behind the front cover of the center console, figure 13-47. Be careful not to confuse the ABS connector with the three-pronged data link connector. With the ignition switch off, install a jump wire between the two pins of the test connector. Switch the ignition on, and the MIL displays codes after a 10-second pause.

The MIL flashes the first digit of the first code, pauses for one second, then flashes the second digit of the same code. When multiple codes are in memory, a five-second pause, one brief flash, and another five-second pause separate them, figure 13-48. If you miscount the number of flashes, switch the ignition off and back on to restart the procedure. Figure 13-49 defines available codes; follow factory procedure to locate and repair the cause of the problem.

To clear codes, switch the ignition off and remove the ABS fuse from the fuse panel. Wait at least three seconds, then reinstall the fuse. Recheck for codes to be sure memory is clear, then test drive the vehicle to see if any codes return.

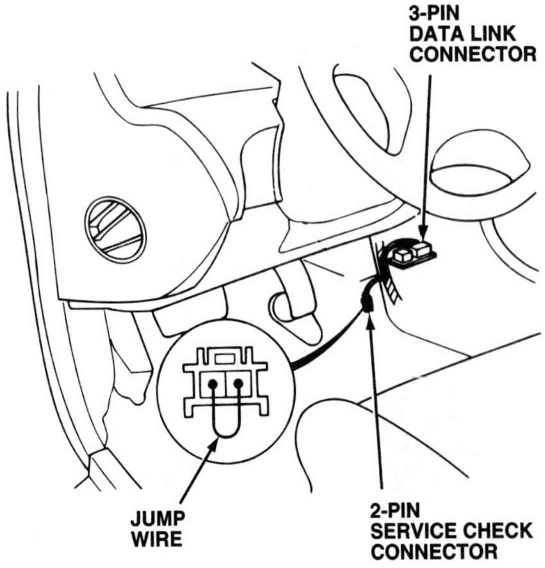

LED Code Retrieval
Remove the inspection cover to expose the ABS control module and view the LED display. On Hondas, the control module is below the dash. Look for the inspection cover on the passenger side of the console, figure 13-50. Four-door Acura models have the control module in the trunk. Acura Coupes store the control module next to the rear seat behind a trim panel. To retrieve codes, simply switch the ignition on without starting the engine. The LED flashes codes after a 10-second pause.

On the LED display, the first and second digits of a code are separated by a one-second pause. Multiple codes are separated by a five-second pause followed by a single flash and another five-second pause. The LED system offers more detailed information than the MIL system, and more codes are available, figure 13-51.

To clear the codes, switch the ignition off and remove the ABS power supply fuse for at least three seconds. Cycle the key back on to make sure codes are clear, then reinstall the inspection cover.

Accessing Mazda and Ford Probe Codes
Both Sumitomo systems used by Mazda, and on the Ford Probe, store multiple hard and soft trouble codes. The ABS control module can record codes for up to 32 separate failures.

Perform a bulb check to make sure the ABS warning lamp is functioning. How the MIL reacts following the bulb check can help you determine what type of code you are dealing with. A soft code causes the lamp to flash when the ignition switch is on, and a hard code causes the MIL to light continuously.

You need a jump wire and an analog voltmeter to read codes. Access the system through the four-pin ABS check connector that attaches to the wiring harness near the ABS control module. The control module is under the driver's seat, so you may have to remove the seat to expose the check connector. From this point, procedures vary slightly for the two systems.

Sumitomo I Trouble Codes
Although Sumitomo I stores multiple codes, you can display them only one at a time. After reading the ini-

Figure 13-47. Honda and Acura with Sumitomo systems that display codes on the MIL use a two-pin service check connector for diagnostic access.

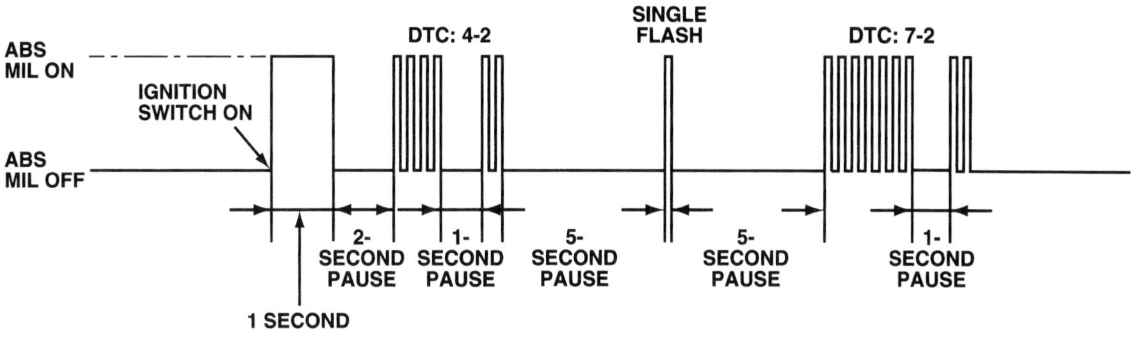

ABS Diagnostic and Service Procedures

Figure 13-48. Reading a Sumitomo multiple code display on a Honda or Acura MIL.

DTC	INDICATED FAULT
10	Pump motor over running
12	Pump motor circuit
13	High-pressure leakage
14	Pressure switch circuit
18	Accumulator gas leakage
21	Parking brake switch circuit
31	RF wheel speed sensor tone ring
32	LF wheel speed sensor tone ring
34	Rear wheel speed sensor (either) tone ring
41	RF wheel speed sensor signal
42	LF wheel speed sensor signal
44	RR wheel speed sensor signal
48	LR wheel speed sensor signal
50	Front wheel speed sensor (either) modulation
54	RR wheel speed sensor modulation
58	LR wheel speed sensor modulation
60	Fail-safe relay (either) open or short
61	Front fail-safe relay open or short
64	Rear fail-safe relay open or short
71	RF solenoid circuit open
72	LF solenoid circuit open
74	Rear solenoid (either) circuit open

Figure 13-49. Honda and Acura MIL display diagnostic trouble codes.

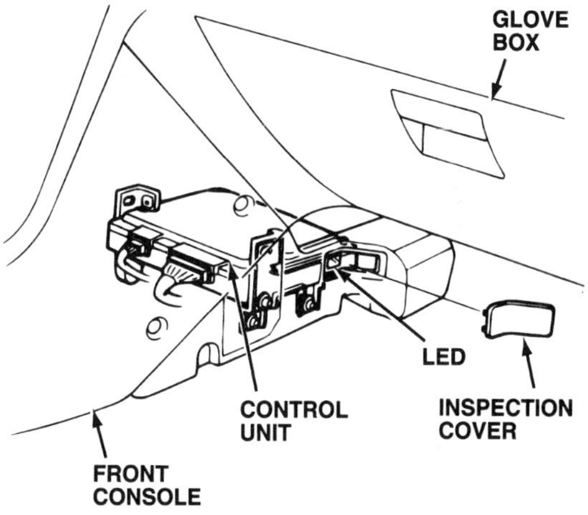

Figure 13-50. Remove the inspection cover to access the control module on Honda models that display codes on an LED.

tial code, repair the fault and clear the code from memory. Then, repeat the process to check for additional codes and repair as necessary. Continue the process until all codes setting conditions have been repaired and there are no further codes in memory.

Locate the check connector and install a jump wire between the terminal with a black wire and the terminal with a green/black wire, figure 13-52. Next, start the engine and observe the MIL. The lamp should either illuminate constantly, or begin to flash. If the MIL flashes, count the number of flashes. Then, connect the voltmeter to obtain more detailed information.

With the voltmeter set to read in the 0- to 20-volt range, connect the positive meter lead to the check connector terminal with the green/red wire, figure 13-53. Attach the negative meter lead to a reliable chasis ground. The voltmeter needle will sweep from 0 volt to about 12 volts and back to zero. Count the number of needle sweeps to determine the specific code, and refer to a diagnostic chart, figure 13-54.

Sumitomo I codes can be erased only one at a time. Install a jump wire between the check connector terminal with a green/red wire and the terminal with a green/black wire. Switch the ignition on without starting the engine and the MIL will light. Wait one to two seconds, switch the ignition off, and disconnect the jump wire from the green/red terminal.

Verify that the initial code is erased by starting the engine. The MIL should light momentarily, then go out. If the MIL remains on, there are additional codes in memory. Repeat the procedure to read and clear any additional codes one at a time.

DTC 1st DIGIT	DTC 2nd DIGIT	INDICATED FAULT	DTC 1st DIGIT	DTC 2nd DIGIT	INDICATED FAULT
1	0	Hydraulic-controlled component failure	8	3	RF solenoid circuit open, both sides
2	0	Parking brake switch circuit	8	4	LF solenoid circuit open, inlet side
3	1	Front fail-safe relay failure	8	8	LF solenoid circuit open, outlet side
3	2	Rear fail-safe relay failure	8	12	LF solenoid circuit open, both sides
3	13	RF wheel speed sensor tone ring	8	15	Front fail-safe relays misconnected
3	14	LF wheel speed sensor tone ring	9	0	Rear solenoid circuit open, inlet side
3	15	Rear wheel speed sensor (either) tone ring	10	0	Rear solenoid circuit open, outlet side
			11	0	Rear solenoid circuit open, both sides
4	4	RR wheel speed sensor modulation	11	3	RF and rear solenoid circuits open
4	8	LR wheel speed sensor modulation	11	12	LF and rear solenoid circuits open
4	12	Both rear wheel speed sensors modulation	11	15	All three solenoid circuits open
5	1	RF wheel speed sensor circuit	12	1	RF solenoid circuit shorted, inlet side
5	2	LF wheel speed sensor circuit	12	2	RF solenoid circuit shorted, outlet side
5	4	RR wheel speed sensor circuit	12	3	RF solenoid circuit shorted, both sides
5	8	LR wheel speed sensor circuit	12	4	LF solenoid circuit shorted, inlet side
6	1	RF wheel speed sensor circuit	12	8	LF solenoid circuit shorted, outlet side
6	2	LF wheel speed sensor circuit	12	12	LF solenoid circuit shorted, both sides
6	4	RR wheel speed sensor circuit	12	15	Both front solenoid circuits shorted
6	8	LR wheel speed sensor circuit	13	0	Rear solenoid circuit shorted, inlet side
7	1	RF wheel speed sensor circuit	14	0	Rear solenoid circuit shorted, outlet side
7	2	LF wheel speed sensor circuit	15	0	Rear solenoid circuit shorted, both sides
7	4	RR wheel speed sensor circuit			
7	8	LR wheel speed sensor circuit			
8	1	RF solenoid circuit open, inlet side	15	3	RF and rear solenoid circuits shorted
8	2	RF solenoid circuit open, outlet side	15	12	LF and rear solenoid circuits shorted

Figure 13-51. Honda and Acura LED display diagnostic trouble codes.

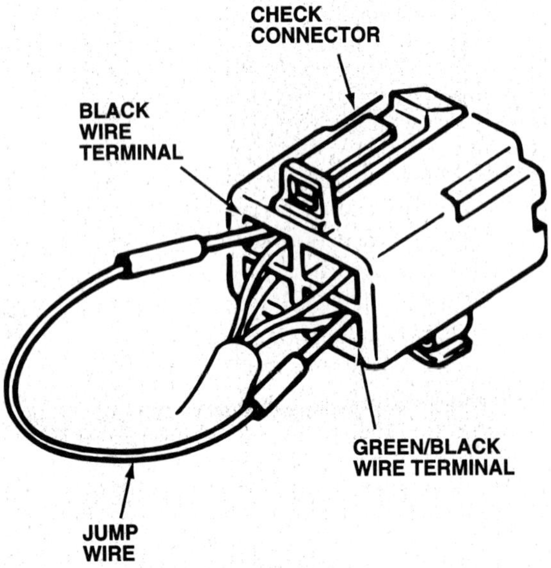

Figure 13-52. To begin diagnostics on Mazda Sumitomo I applications, jump the black wire on the check connector to the green/black wire.

Sumitomo II Trouble Codes

Sumitomo II also displays codes as a combination of analog voltmeter needle sweeps and flashes of the MIL. You can also read codes with a scan tool if you have compatible software. Improvements to the system include a simplified code-clearing procedure, a different method of displaying codes, and revised code numbering.

If the MIL is on, display codes by installing a jump wire between the check connector terminals with a black wire and a green/black wire. Switch the ignition on and the MIL lights continuously if a hard code is present. If a soft code is present, the MIL flashes. Use a scan tool, or install an analog voltmeter as with Sumitomo I, to read codes.

Voltmeter connections vary. The negative lead always goes to a good chassis ground while the positive lead goes to the self-test output terminal. The self-test terminal can be either a green/red wire or an orange/blue wire at the test connector. Check the service manual for the specific model you are working on. On some models, you can access codes from an underhood test connector, figure 13-55.

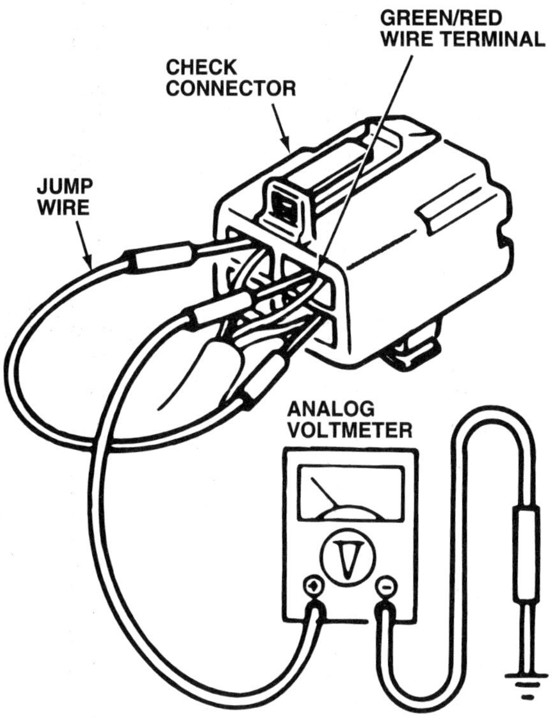

ABS Diagnostic and Service Procedures

Figure 13-53. Connect an analog voltmeter to the green/red wire of the check connector and to a good ground.

With a properly connected voltmeter, the needle will sweep a two-digit code message. All codes display one after the other, so have a pad of paper handy to write them down. The voltmeter needle sweeps the first digit of a code, pauses for 1.6 seconds, then sweeps the second digit of the code. Each DTC is separated by a four-second pause.

Refer to a code chart, figure 13-56, and follow the factory troubleshooting procedures to locate and repair indicated problems. To clear memory, depress the brake pedal 10 times at intervals of less than one second when the system is in diagnostic mode. All codes clear simultaneously.

Sumitomo ABS Service

All Sumitomo systems are nonintegral, so most service procedures are the same as brake systems without antilock brakes. Carefully inspect wheel speed sensor tone rings and wiring harnesses for damage whenever performing brake service. Always observe standard safety procedures.

Bleeding Procedure
Bleed the hydraulic system either manually or with pressure-bleeding equipment. Sumitomo systems are the diagonal-split type and must be bled in this sequence:

- Left rear
- Right front
- Right rear
- Left front.

TEVES ANTILOCK BRAKE SYSTEMS

Teves builds antilock brake systems that are used by a number of vehicle manufacturers on a variety of models. Teves Mark II is an integral, four-wheel, three-channel system used from the late 1980s to the early 1990s by Chrysler, Ford, General Motors, Peugeot, and Saab. The four-channel, nonintegral Mark IV system is used by Chrysler, Ford, General Motors, and Volkswagen. The Mark 20 system is used on DaimlerChrysler, Jaguar, Volkswagen, and other vehicles beginning in 1997. It is a three- or four-channel, nonintegral system, depending on application. Traction control is also available with this system. Continental Teves Mark 25 and Mark 60 ABS, introduced in 2003, is used on some European models, including Volkswagen and Jaguar.

An amber MIL for the ABS alerts the driver to system failures and should illuminate as a bulb check when the ignition is first switched on. A warning lamp that remains on after a few seconds indicates a problem, as does an MIL that lights up while driving. The ABS control module deactivates antilock braking when it detects a problem.

Teves Mark II Diagnostics

If the ABS control module detects a fault, the MIL remains on following the bulb check. Some, but not all, versions of Mark II set a retrievable diagnostic trouble code when a fault occurs. Be aware, a discharged accumulator causes the ABS MIL to light until sufficient pressure builds up. Usually, this will not take more than 30 seconds. A parking brake that is not fully released, low pressure on a hydraulic brake circuit, or a malfunctioning brake pressure switch can also cause the MIL to illuminate. Eliminate hydraulic problems by pressure testing before looking for problems in the electronic circuits.

Pressure Checks
The Teves Mark II pump should be able to maintain 1500 to 2610 psi (10,343 to 17,996 kPa) of accumulator pressure. Suspect a faulty pump when both the ABS and brake MIL are illuminated, and power assist is unavailable.

As a first step, verify that the pump is operating. Relieve accumulator pressure by pumping the brake pedal 25 to 40 times with the ignition switch off. Switch the ignition on and listen for the pump. It should operate

MIL CONDITION	VOLTMETER SWEEPS	INDICATED FAULT
One flash	1	RF wheel speed sensor
One flash	2	LF wheel speed sensor
One flash	3	Rear wheel speed sensor
One flash	4	RF wheel speed sensor tone ring
One flash	5	LF wheel speed sensor tone ring
One flash	6	RR wheel speed sensor tone ring
One flash	7	LR wheel speed sensor tone ring
On continuous	1	Modulator or harness problem
4 flashes	1	Modulator or harness problem
On or flashing	2, 3, 4	Relay or modulator problem
On or flashing	5	Modulator or ABS controller
On or flashing	6	ABS controller
On continuous	None	ABS controller or low voltage

Figure 13-54. Mazda Sumitomo I diagnostic trouble codes.

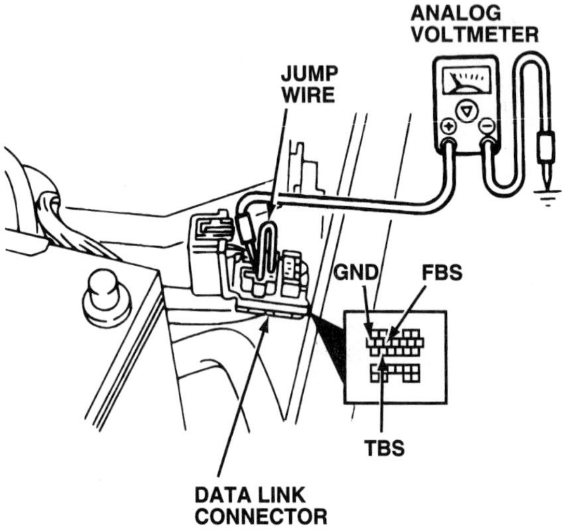

Figure 13-55. Accessing codes on a Ford Probe with Sumitomo II ABS.

DTC	INDICATED FAULT
11	RF wheel speed sensor
12	LF wheel speed sensor
13	RR wheel speed sensor
14	LR wheel speed sensor
15	Any wheel speed sensor
22	Modulator or wiring harness
51	Fail-safe relay
53	Pump motor or motor relay
61	ABS controller

Note: While reading codes from the voltmeter, hard codes will light the MIL continuously; soft codes will pulse the MIL simultaneously with the voltmeter needle sweeps.

Figure 13-56. Sumitomo II diagnostic trouble codes.

for about 30 seconds as it builds pressure, then switch off. If motor noise is absent, check for signal voltage at the pump connector and for high resistance across the ground connection. If you find low voltage or no voltage at the pump, check the pump relay.

If the pump runs, use a high-pressure gauge to check accumulator pressure, figure 13-57. Relieve accumulator pressure before installing the pressure gauge. With the gauge installed, switch the ignition on. Pressure should rise quickly to between 580 and 1160 psi (3999 and 7998 kPa), then continue to climb slowly to at least 2500 psi (17,238 kPa).

Leave the ignition on and pump the brake pedal until the pump motor engages. Allow the pump to run until it cycles off, then switch the ignition off. After three minutes, take a pressure gauge reading. Take a second pressure reading after five more minutes. Accumulator pressure loss should be less than 20 psi (138 kPa) between the two readings. Excessive pressure loss can be due to leakage in the pump or the master cylinder/booster assembly.

To check for pump leakage, switch the ignition on and let the pump run for one minute. Then, switch the ignition off, disconnect the return hose from the fluid reservoir, and plug the reservoir outlet. Place the free end of the hose into a container and keep an eye on it for the next five minutes. If any fluid flows through the hose, the pump is leaking. If no fluid flows from the hose, suspect a faulty master cylinder/booster assembly.

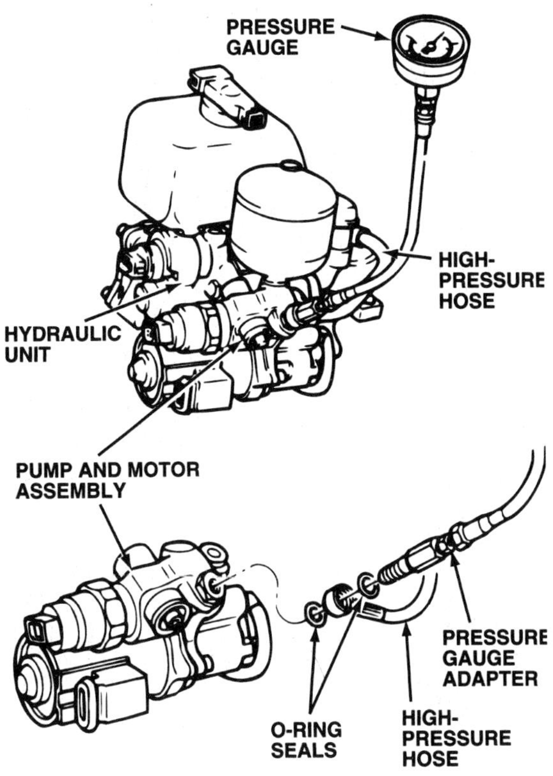

ABS Diagnostic and Service Procedures

Figure 13-57. Gauge installation for pressure checking the Teves Mark II system.

Accessing Codes

On some Teves Mark II applications, the MIL flashes codes when you ground one of the terminals of the diagnostic connector. However, it is quicker and more accurate to retrieve codes with a scan tool. Specific procedures vary by manufacturer.

Be aware, the ABS control module cannot store, simultaneously, more than one code with the same first digit. For example, assume the system set a DTC 23 at startup and then set a DTC 24 while driving. You will be able to retrieve only DTC 24, the last code set with a first digit of 2. However, the module can store multiple codes as long as the first digits are different. The second digit does not matter, so you could see codes 23, 33, and 43 at the same time. To ensure that you retrieve all codes, repair the cause of any initial codes, then clear memory and check for codes to reset. To clear codes, simply drive the vehicle faster than 25 mph.

Ford uses a dedicated six-pin ABS diagnostic connector identical in shape to the one used for engine self-tests. Location of the connector varies by model. Refer to a service manual to be sure you have the proper connector. Ground the self-test output terminal of the connector to place the system in diagnostic mode.

On 1986 and 1987 General Motors vehicles, diagnose faults by noting which MIL (ABS or BRAKE) is lit during a specific driving condition. Interpret results using a "light sequence chart," figure 13-58. The chart shows which tests to perform using a DVOM and breakout box. On 1988 to 1990 General Motors vehicles, you can flash codes on the MIL using the 12-pin ALDL connector.

For 1988 General Motors vehicles, install a jump wire from ALDL pin G to ground, pin A. On 1989 and 1990 vehicles, ground pin H of the ALDL connector. Switch the ignition on and the MIL flashes codes. A three-second pause separates the two digits of a code, and a single long flash indicates the end of DTC transmission. If there are no codes in memory, the MIL illuminates for four seconds and then switches off.

Mark II systems flash only one code at a time on the MIL. Refer to a code chart, figure 13-59, to isolate and repair the problem. Clear the code by driving the vehicle, then check for any additional codes.

Teves Mark II Service

The brake fluid level in the master cylinder reservoir rises as the accumulator discharges and returns fluid to the reservoir. Therefore, it is important to fully charge the accumulator before checking or adjusting the fluid level. Switch the ignition on and pump the brake pedal until the pump motor begins to run. Wait for the pump motor to cycle off, then check the level.

Always discharge accumulator pressure before opening any hydraulic lines. Discharge by pumping the brake pedal at least 20 times with the ignition switch off. There should be a noticeable change in pedal feel as pressure dissipates.

Bleeding Procedure

The Teves Mark II ABS used on some Ford and General Motors vehicles has a front/rear split hydraulic system. As explained in the *Classroom Manual,* the front brakes are applied by a dual master cylinder, while the rear brakes are applied directly by pressure in the boost chamber of the hydraulic power booster. The front wheels can be bled as in a normal brake system, manually or with a pressure bleeder. The rear brakes, however, may be bled using a pressure bleeder or the accumulator pressure of the booster. To successfully bleed the rear brake circuits manually, the accumulator must be fully charged.

The front brakes can be manually bled either with or without the assist of accumulator pressure. When using accumulator pressure, open each bleed valve in 10-second intervals while applying pressure to the brake pedal. The pump motor will occasionally energize during bleeding to maintain adequate system pressure. Do

SEQUENCE NUMBER	LAMP SEQUENCE	SYMPTOM DESCRIPTION	PERFORM TEST
1	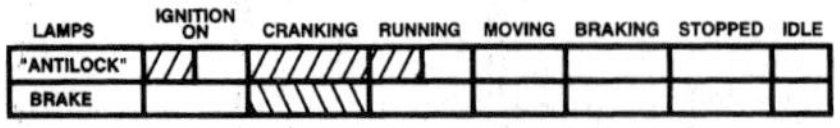	NORMAL LAMP SEQUENCE WITH -EXCESSIVE PEDAL TRAVEL OR SPONGY PEDAL -ANTILOCK BRAKING OPERATION OR VALVE CYCLING DURING NORMAL STOPS ON DRY PAVEMENT -POOR VEHICLE TRACKING DURING ANTILOCK BRAKING	H C D
2	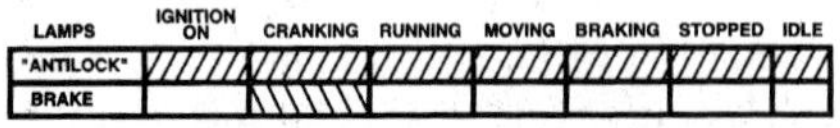	CONTINUOUS "ANTILOCK" LAMP NORMAL "BRAKE" LAMP	A
3	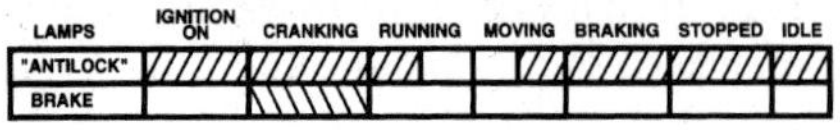	"ANTILOCK" LAMP COMES ON AFTER VEHICLE STARTS MOVING NORMAL BRAKE LAMP	C
4	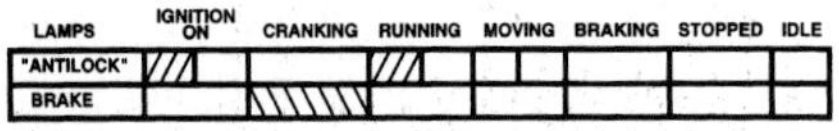	NO "ANTILOCK" LAMP WHILE CRANKING NORMAL "BRAKE" LAMP	E
5	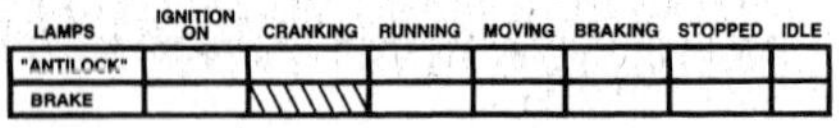	NO "ANTILOCK" LAMP NORMAL "BRAKE" LAMP	F
6	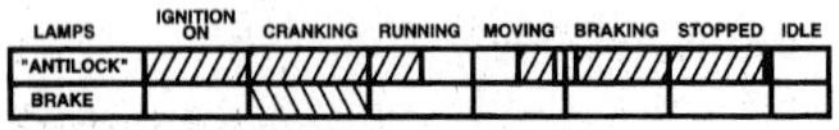	INTERMITTENT "ANTILOCK" LAMP WHILE DRIVING NORMAL "BRAKE" LAMP	G
7	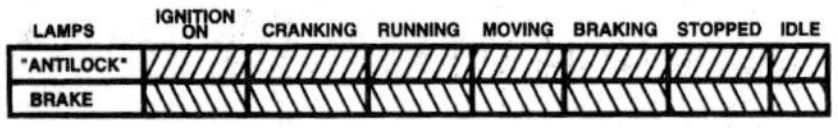	CONTINUOUS "ANTILOCK" LAMP CONTINUOUS "BRAKE" LAMP	B
8	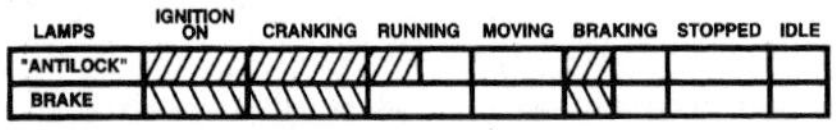	"ANTILOCK" AND "BRAKE" LAMPS COME ON WHILE BRAKING	B
9	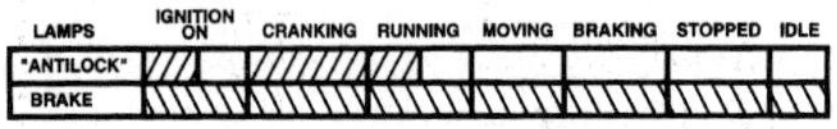	NORMAL "ANTILOCK" LAMP CONTINUOUS "BRAKE" LAMP	B
10	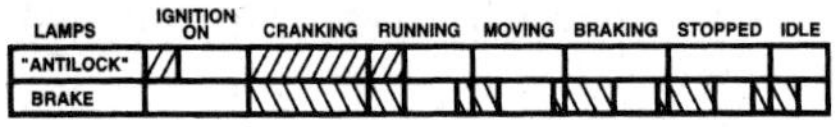	NORMAL OR CONTINUOUS "ANTILOCK" LAMP FLASHING "BRAKE" LAMP	B

Figure 13-58. A typical light sequence chart for Teves Mark II diagnosis on 1986–87 General Motors vehicles.

not allow the pump to run for more than one minute at a time; this can overheat and damage the unit. Bleed at the wheels in the following order

- Right front
- Left front
- Right rear
- Left rear.

After bleeding the front wheels, switch the ignition on and pump the brake pedal several times. This removes air from the modulator and allows the accumulator to fully charge so you can bleed the rear wheels.

Ford recommends bleeding the rear brakes with a pressure bleeder. The procedure is essentially the same as described in Chapter 3 with the following special considerations:

1. Charge the pressure bleeder to 35 psi (240 kPa).
2. When bleeding the brakes, open one rear bleeder screw for 10 seconds, close it, then open the bleeder screw at the opposite wheel for the same length of time. Alternate in this manner until the fluid from both bleeders is free of air bubbles.
3. When bleeding is completed, check the fluid level in the reservoir.

Bleeding the rear brakes of a Teves Mark II antilock brake system using accumulator pressure requires a bleeder screw wrench, approximately two feet of clear,

ABS Diagnostic and Service Procedures

DTC	INDICATED FAULT	DTC	INDICATED FAULT
11	ABS control module electrical circuit	45	LF plus one other wheel sensor signal missing
12	ABS control module	46	RF plus one other wheel sensor signal missing
21	Main valve electrical circuit	47	Both rear wheel speed signals missing
22	LF inlet valve electrical circuit	48	Three wheel speed signals missing
23	LF outlet valve electrical circuit	51	LF outlet valve, no dynamic response
24	RF inlet valve electrical circuit	52	RF outlet valve, no dynamic response
25	RF outlet valve electrical circuit	53	RR outlet valve, no dynamic response
26	Rear inlet valve electrical circuit	54	LR outlet valve, no dynamic response
27	Rear outlet valve electrical circuit	55	LF wheel sensor signal error
31	LF wheel sensor electrical circuit	56	RF wheel sensor signal error
32	RF wheel sensor electrical circuit	57	RR wheel sensor signal error
33	RR wheel sensor electrical circuit	58	LR wheel sensor signal error
34	LR wheel sensor electrical circuit	61	Low fluid level or low pressure indicator
35	LF wheel sensor electrical circuit	71	LF wheel sensor not responding to outlet valve
36	RF wheel sensor electrical circuit	72	RF wheel sensor not responding to outlet valve
37	RR wheel sensor electrical circuit	73	RR wheel sensor not responding to outlet valve
38	LR wheel sensor electrical circuit	74	LR wheel sensor not responding to outlet valve
41	LF wheel sensor electrical circuit	75	LF wheel sensor signal error
42	RF wheel sensor electrical circuit	76	RF wheel sensor signal error
43	RR wheel sensor electrical circuit	77	RR wheel sensor signal error
44	LR wheel sensor electrical circuit	78	LR wheel sensor signal error

Figure 13-59. Teves Mark II diagnostic trouble codes.

plastic hose with an inside diameter small enough to fit snugly over the bleeder screws, and a clear jar partially filled with clean brake fluid. To bleed the rear brakes using accumulator pressure:

1. Turn the ignition switch ON. Depress the brake pedal repeatedly until the electrohydraulic pump motor starts. The pump motor will stop when the accumulator is charged.
2. Slip the plastic hose over the bleeder screw of the right rear caliper and submerge the end of the tube in the jar of brake fluid.
3. With the ignition switch still in the ON position, have an assistant lightly depress and hold the brake pedal.
4. Alternately open the rear bleeder screws for 10 seconds at a time until the fluid coming from the bleeders is free of air bubbles. Open the bleeder screws slowly and carefully because the accumulator provides much higher pressure than is available from a pressure bleeder.
5. When bleeding is completed, check the fluid level in the reservoir.

Pump Priming Procedure

A pump or master cylinder/modulator assembly that has just been installed may not be able to prime itself. To prime the pump, turn the ignition off and connect a standard diaphragm-type pressure bleeder to the master cylinder. Use only DOT 3 brake fluid. Charge the pressure bleeder to 20 to 30 psi (138 to 207 kPa), open the valve to pressurize the reservoir, and switch the ignition on. The pump should prime itself within 30 seconds. After removing the pressure bleeder, bring the fluid level in the reservoir to the full mark by siphoning off any excess fluid.

Teves Mark IV Diagnostics

Teves Mark IV is a nonintegral, four-channel system. On some, but not all, applications it is combined with a traction control system. Vehicles with traction control have a warning lamp for ABS and a separate lamp for traction control.

When the ignition switches on, Mark IV performs an MIL bulb check while it simultaneously checks for electrical faults by briefly cycling the ABS solenoids. On models with traction control, these solenoids cycle as well. Once vehicle speed reaches 5 to 10 mph, the system performs a second self-test by energizing the pump motor. If a problem exists, a DTC is set, both ABS and traction control disable, and both warning lamps illuminate.

The control module stores codes in nonvolatile memory, and you must use a scan tool to erase them. If an intermittent failure does not recur within 50 ignition cycles, that code automatically clears. Hydraulic unit or controller failures set permanent codes that can be cleared only with a scan tool, even if the problem is intermittent.

Once the MIL comes on, it remains on for the duration of the ignition cycle. An open fluid level switch, DTC 61, is the only exception. With DTC 61, the warning lamps remain on only as long as the open switch condition exists. However, the code remains in memory after the MIL switches off.

Preliminary System Checks

When diagnosing an ABS fault on the Mark IV system, begin with a preliminary inspection as you look for obvious problems:

- Confirm MIL operation during the bulb check.
- Check system fuses, including those for the instrument cluster, if both warning lamps fail to illuminate. Check wiring connections and the bulb if only one MIL fails to come on.
- A hard fault is present if the amber ABS lamp remains on. If the MIL goes out, the problem is either intermittent or not ABS related.
- Apply the parking brake to check the red BRAKE lamp; it should come on, then go out when you release the brake.
- Check the condition of all system wiring harnesses.
- Check for good wiring connections at the brake pedal switch, ABS modulator, the 55-pin connector at the control module, and at the wheel speed sensors.
- Be sure the brake fluid is at the proper level.

If no obvious problems are found, access the onboard diagnostics to check for codes in memory.

Accessing Codes

The Mark IV system requires a scan tool to access diagnostics and retrieve codes. Procedures vary slightly by vehicle manufacturer. Be sure you have compatible scan tool software for the specific vehicle being tested.

The procedures detailed here provide basic, general information only. For accurate diagnosis, you must follow the specific troubleshooting procedures in the appropriate factory service manual.

Chrysler

The only way to access onboard diagnostic information on Chrysler vehicles is with the Chrysler DRB scan tool, figure 13-60. The DRB connects to the six-pin CCD bus data link connector located in the passenger compartment.

The DRB screen displays an error message, rather than a numeric code, when there are faults in memory.

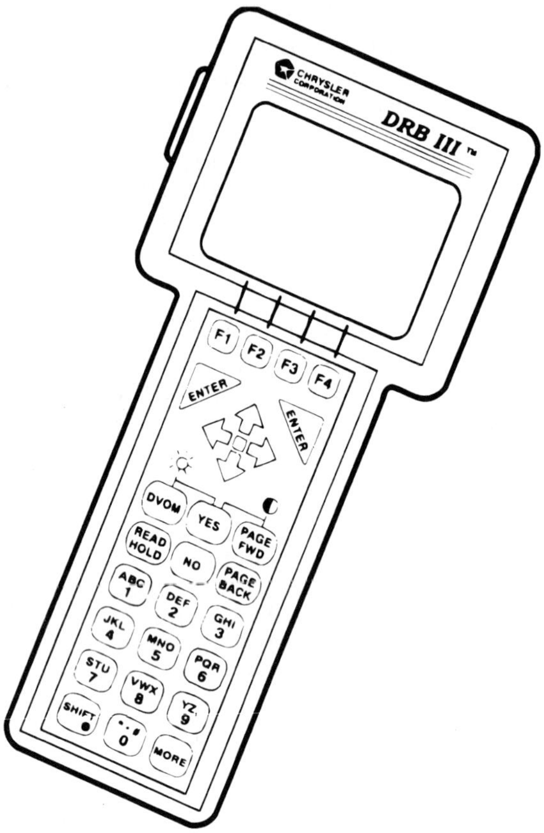

Figure 13-60. A DRB scan tool must be used to access Teves Mark IV diagnostics on Chrysler vehicles.

Write down any error messages received and use the scan tool to clear codes. Next, cycle the ignition off and back on to see if any error messages reappear. Messages that repeat at this time indicate hard faults.

To check for intermittent failures, try to re-create code-setting conditions by test driving the vehicle. Be sure to perform several ABS-assisted stops during your road test. Follow up by retrieving codes from memory once again. Any error messages that appear now indicate intermittent, or soft code, problems.

In general, error messages should be serviced in the order in which they appear on the screen. Always repair the cause of any hard faults first, before servicing soft faults.

Ford

On Ford vehicles, you can retrieve codes using a Ford STAR tester, or any scan tool with compatible software. Access the system through a dedicated six-pin ABS test connector. Be aware, the ABS test connector is the same shape as the connector used for engine testing, figure 13-61. Connector location varies by model; it may be in the engine compartment, passenger com-

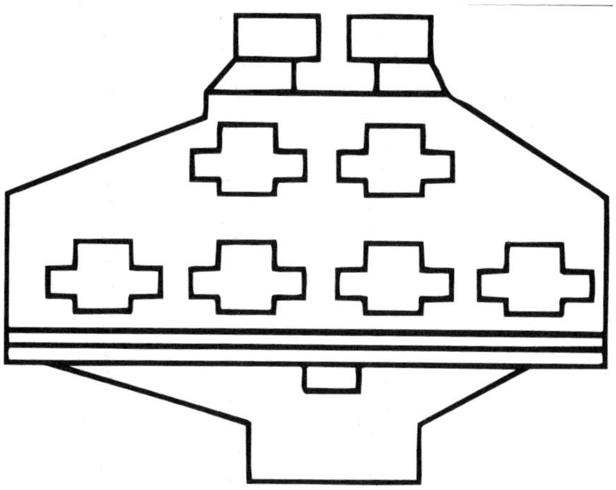

ABS Diagnostic and Service Procedures

Figure 13-61. The Ford Teves Mark IV test connector is the same shape as the connector used for engine testing. Do not confuse them.

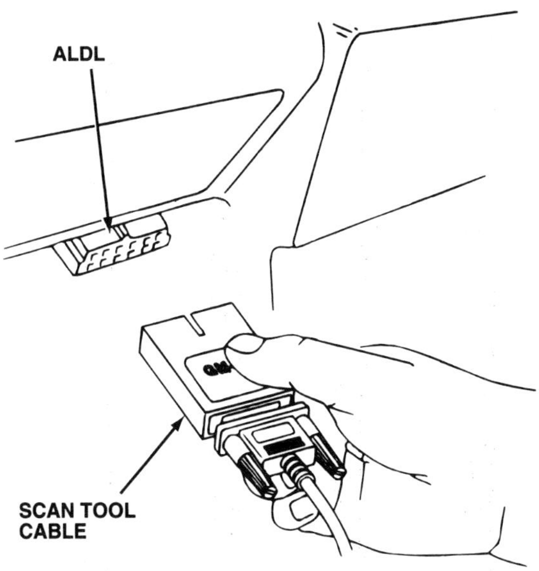

Figure 13-62. Connect your scan tool to the ALDL connector to access General Motors Teves Mark IV systems.

partment, or trunk. Check the appropriate service manual for the exact location.

With the scan tool connected and the system in diagnostic mode, the control module runs through a self-test program. All codes in memory display. However, the self-test does take time and you can expect about 15-second intervals between individual codes that come up on the screen. Follow Ford pinpoint test procedures to isolate and repair the cause of any faults.

Ford assigns a high priority to all 20-series codes. These indicate hydraulic control unit problems and must be given immediate attention. When a 20-series code is present, no other codes are available until the cause of the priority code is repaired. Following repairs, run the self-test once again to check for additional codes. Ignore 20-series codes that repeat on the retest if you have already made repairs. With traction control systems, isolation valve codes 18 and 19 override other codes in the same manner as 20-series codes.

Once repairs are made, clear codes from memory by driving the vehicle at speeds over 25 mph. The control module automatically clears its own memory if no additional faults occur. Code clearing takes place only after the entire ABS self-test sequence has completed. Switching the ignition off during the self-test interrupts the program. Run the self-test again, and allow it to complete. Then, drive the vehicle to clear codes.

General Motors

To retrieve fault codes on General Motors applications, connect a compatible scan tool to the ALDL connector and switch the ignition on, figure 13-62. Placing the system in diagnostic mode disables antilock braking. Although the vehicle can be driven, the control module cannot detect faults or set codes while the scan tool is in use.

Use factory troubleshooting procedures to isolate and repair the cause of any hard faults. An MIL that remains on following the initial key on self-test indicates a hard fault. After repairs, clear codes and drive the vehicle to see if any additional faults occur. Attempt to duplicate operating conditions that may have set history, or intermittent, codes.

Keep in mind, code troubleshooting charts are designed for hard faults only. Refer to the symptom diagnostic guide in the appropriate service manual to determine the cause of a soft code problem.

Clear codes using the scan tool. Test drive the vehicle and perform several ABS-assisted stops to verify operation.

Teves Mark IV Service

With any ABS, isolating the source of faults often requires the use of a breakout box and a DVOM. Always refer to a shop manual for exact procedures and specifications.

When you suspect a failure in a Teves Mark IV modulator assembly, you can quickly check the resistance of the solenoids using a DVOM. Most applications should test at the following resistances:

- Decay solenoid valves   3 to 6 ohms
- Build solenoid valves   5 to 8 ohms
- Traction control isolation solenoid valves   5 to 8 ohms

Service the modulator assembly as a unit and replace it if any of the solenoids test outside specifications.

You can also perform a quick check on the wheel speed sensors with your DVOM. Open the harness connector and check resistance; expect readings to be between 800 and 1400 ohms. Make sure the tone ring is in good condition and free of any accumulated debris before replacing an out-of-specification sensor.

Because Teves Mark IV is a nonintegral system, brake service procedures are similar to systems without ABS. Be careful not to damage wheel speed sensors and tone rings when removing and replacing brake drums and rotors.

Bleeding Procedure

Manual or pressure-bleeding equipment can be used to bleed the hydraulic circuits. Use standard procedures to bleed the brakes at the wheels. Bleeding sequence varies by manufacturer; check the appropriate service manual.

When replacing the hydraulic modulator, or if air has entered the unit, you need to energize the pump motor and cycle the solenoids to remove the trapped air from the assembly. Ford provides a special harness adapter (P/N T90P-50-ALA) that attaches to the 55-pin ABS module connector to accomplish this task. On Chrysler and General Motors applications, a scan tool functional test is available to run the pump motor and cycle the solenoids.

Teves Mark 20/25 Diagnostics and Service

Teves Mark 20 is a nonintegral antilock brake system used on 1997 and later Jeeps and Chrysler cars. Some applications are equipped with the Low-Speed Traction Control System (LTCS). Use a scan tool to retrieve DTCs. Refer to the appropriate factory service manual for troubleshooting procedures.

Diagnosis begins with a preliminary check of the system. This includes a visual inspection and a road test. Make sure that the battery and charging system are functioning properly. Check the following:

- Electrical connectors at the ABS controller and hydraulic unit
- Electrical connectors at the wheel speed sensors, figure 13-63.
- Any hydraulic leaks must be repaired first.
- Tires must be the proper size and inflated properly.

During the road test, observe the operation of the red brake warning light and the amber ABS warning light. Both lights should come on when the vehicle is started and then go off. A red warning light that stays

Figure 13-63. Check the connectors of the wheel speed sensors (1). (Copyright DaimlerChrysler Corporation. Used with permission)

on indicated a problem with the base brakes. Repair any base brake problems before working on the ABS.

1. Drive the vehicle at least 12 mph.
    a. If the ABS warning light does not come on, proceed to step 2.
    b. If the ABS warning light comes on, check for DTCs.
2. Drive to a speed of at least 40 mph and then bring the vehicle to a complete stop. Accelerate again to at least 25 mph. Check again to see if the ABS warning light comes on. If so, retrieve any DTCs.

Accessing Codes

Use a scan tool to retrieve DTCs. The scan tool attaches to the OBD II connector under the dash. Before attaching the scan tool, make sure that the brake lights operate properly. If not, repair the brake lights before accessing DTCs.

Bleeding Procedure

Vehicles using Teves Mark 20/25 ABS are bled in the normal manner; first the base brakes are bled and then the ABS unit. The base brakes can be bled manually or with a pressure bleeder. Bleeding the ABS hydraulic unit requires the use of a scan tool. On Daimler-Chrysler vehicles (FWD), the bleeding sequence is LR, RF, RR, LF.

After bleeding the base brakes, bleed the ABS hydraulic modulator.

1. Connect the scan tool to the data link connector (DLC) under the dash. Check for DTCs; if there are any, clear them before proceeding.
2. Follow the scan tool instructions to bleed the modulator. This operates the pump and solenoids to release any air trapped in the modulator.
3. After bleeding the modulator, bleed the base brakes again.
4. Repeat the whole procedure until a firm pedal is obtained.

ABS Diagnostic and Service Procedures

NOTE: The base brakes must always be bled both before and after bleeding the hydraulic modulator.

TOYOTA ANTILOCK BRAKE SYSTEMS

Toyota manufactures its own nonintegral, single-channel, rear-wheel-only antilock brake system. Toyota rear-wheel ABS has been used on 1990 through 1995 trucks, the 1993 and 1994 T100, and the 1990 through 1993 4Runner.

Toyota has also used three different four-wheel ABS designs. Bosch and Nippondenso systems were used in earlier models. By 1997, all models except the Land Cruiser used a Toyota system with three or four channels and two solenoids per channel.

The Toyota ABS control module monitors the system during vehicle operation, and records codes in the event of a failure. An amber ABS or REAR ANTILOCK warning lamp alerts the driver whenever a malfunction occurs.

When you switch on the ignition, the warning light should illuminate as a bulb check. After several seconds, the MIL switches off if there are no codes in memory. The control module on later models performs a system self-test whenever the ignition is switched on. Early model systems perform the self-test when vehicle speed exceeds four mph.

Toyota ABS Diagnostics

Begin your diagnosis with a preliminary inspection. Check the condition of all system wiring harnesses and verify that connectors are clean and tight. Look for signs of fluid leaks and any mechanical conditions that may cause or contribute to the problem. Check open circuit battery voltage. The battery must supply 10 to 14 volts for the electronic control system to operate properly.

Repair any problems encountered in the preliminary inspection, then check for trouble codes in memory.

Accessing Codes

Once the system is in diagnostic mode, codes are displayed by flashing the MIL. The method of entering diagnostic mode varies from model to model, so be sure to consult the appropriate service manual for specific details. Some early models require a combination of parking brake and service brake operation to enter diagnostic mode. To access codes on most models, locate the data link connector 1 (DLC 1), usually mounted alongside the fuse box, and remove its cover. If there is a short pin between two of the terminals, remove it, figure 13-64. On models without a short pin, separate

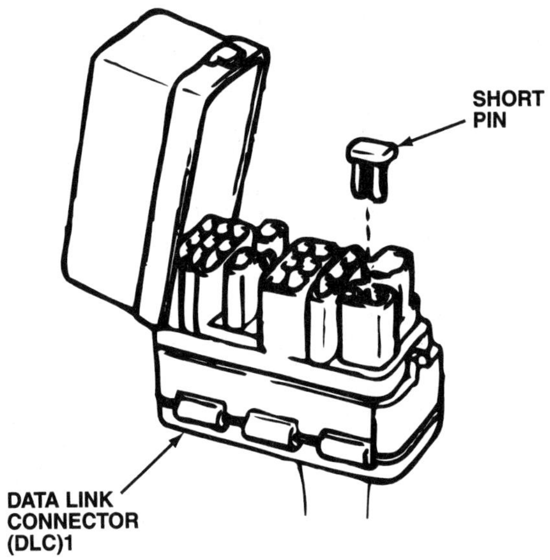

Figure 13-64. On later Toyota models, pull the short pin out of the service connector to begin diagnosis.

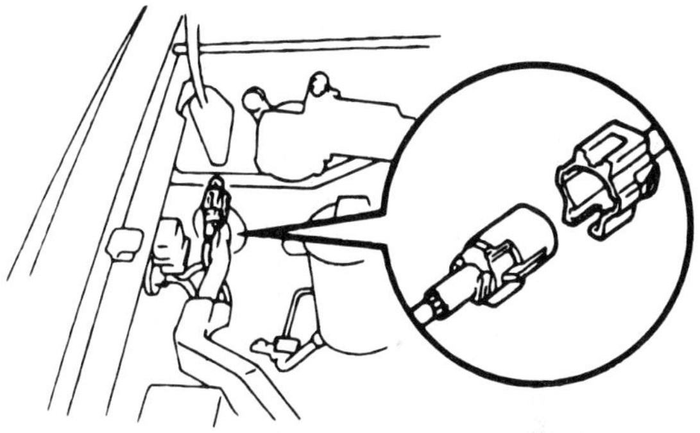

Figure 13-65. On early Toyota models, disconnect the service connector while the ignition is on to begin diagnosis.

the two halves of the service connector (under the hood next to the ABS solenoid relay, figure 13-65). Next, install a jumper wire between terminals Tc and E1, figure 13-66 or figure 13-67. Switch the ignition on. This places the system in diagnostic mode. If no codes are stored, the MIL will begin flashing two times per second after a two-second pause. If codes are stored, the MIL begins flashing them after a four-second pause.

All diagnostic trouble codes are two digits. The MIL flashes the first digit, pauses for 1.5 seconds, then flashes the second digit. In the event of multiple codes, a 2.5-second pause separates each code as they display in numerically ascending order. The MIL pauses four seconds at the end of the code list, then repeats the display beginning with the lowest-value DTC. When there are no codes in memory, the MIL flashes continuously twice per second.

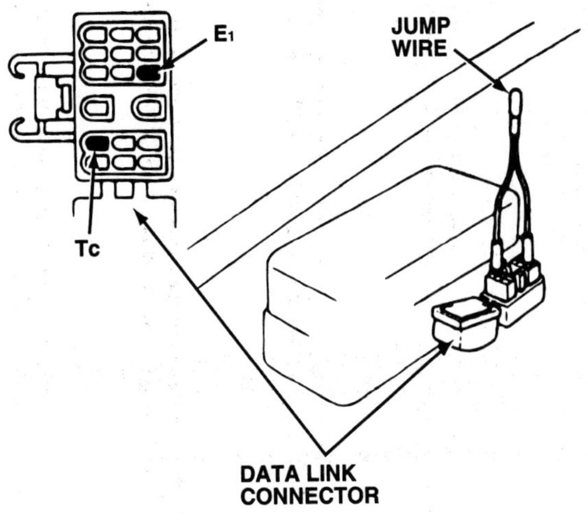

Figure 13-66. On early Toyota models, install a jump wire between terminals Tc and E1 of the data link connector to display codes.

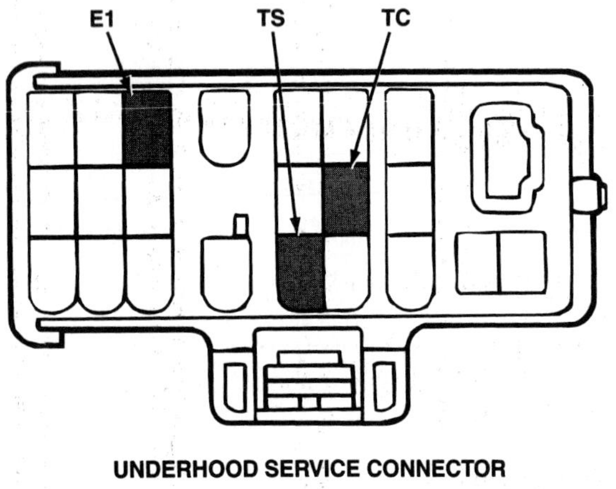

Figure 13-67. On later Toyota models, jump terminals Tc and E1 to display codes; jump terminals Ts and E1 for additional tests.

Use a code chart to interpret results, figure 13-68. Be aware, a constantly illuminated MIL in diagnostic mode is an indication of an internal ABS control module failure. Before replacing the control module, check both the power and ground circuits to the unit, and make certain all other ABS components are functioning properly.

Clearing codes is simple on most Toyota systems. Pump the brake pedal at least eight times within three seconds while the system is in diagnostic mode. As memory clears, the MIL begins flashing twice per second to indicate there are no further codes. Remove the jump wire from DLC 1 and the MIL should switch off. Remember to reconnect the service connector or reinstall the short pin.

Diagnostic Checks

The Toyota onboard diagnostic system also allows functional tests of the wheel speed sensors and the deceleration sensor. The following procedures produce additional codes to provide more detailed information. Perform these tests when a code check indicates a problem in the wheel speed or deceleration circuits. ANTILOCK braking is disabled during testing.

Speed and Deceleration Sensor Checks

Speed sensor tests involve driving the vehicle at a set speed, in a straight line, while in diagnostic mode. The vehicle is braked while you watch the MIL, then the vehicle is driven up to a second, higher speed. Speeds and braking sequences vary; consult the appropriate service manual for specifics. The MIL will begin flashing either a system normal code (twice per second), or up to eight special codes. Codes are two digits and display similar to other codes, figure 13-69. After repairs, clear codes using the same technique as previously described. Test drive the vehicle, then check for codes to verify that repairs are successful. The MIL should blink a normal code.

The deceleration sensor on all vehicles except the 1996 RAV4 can be tested statically or dynamically (with a road test). Begin a static test by placing the vehicle in diagnostic mode as described earlier. Next, connect a jumper wire between terminals Ts and E1 in DLC-1. You will need to jack up the front, then the rear of the vehicle to a specified height; consult the appropriate service manual for the specifications. Block the wheels so the vehicle can't roll, and start the engine. With the engine idling, slowly jack up the rear end to the specified height and watch the ABS light. It should blink four times per second, indicating a normal system. Lower the rear end of the vehicle and jack up the front end to the specified height. Again, the MIL should blink four times per second. If it doesn't, check the service manual to make sure the deceleration sensor is correctly installed. If the sensor is installed correctly, it is defective and must be replaced.

To perform the dynamic test of the deceleration sensor on all vehicles except the 1996 RAV4, begin by placing the vehicle in diagnostic mode as described earlier. Connect a jumper wire between terminals Ts and E1 in DLC-1. The MIL should flash at four times per second. Drive the vehicle in a straight line at 12 mph, then press the brake pedal lightly. The MIL should continue to flash at four times per second. Brake again from 12 mph, once moderately hard, once hard. The MIL should glow while the brakes are applied. If the light doesn't perform as described, check the service manual to make sure the deceleration sensor is correctly installed. If the sensor is installed correctly, it is defective: replace it.

ABS Diagnostic and Service Procedures

CODE	ABS WARNING LIGHT BLINKING PATTERN		DIAGNOSIS
11	ON/OFF ⎍⎍	BE3831	OPEN CIRCUIT IN ABS CONTROL (SOLENOID) RELAY CIRCUIT
12	ON/OFF ⎍⎍⎍	BE3831	SHORT CIRCUIT IN ABS CONTROL (SOLENOID) RELAY CIRCUIT
13	ON/OFF ⎍⎍⎍⎍	BE3831	OPEN CIRCUIT IN ABS CONTROL (MOTOR) RELAY CIRCUIT
14	ON/OFF ⎍⎍⎍⎍⎍	BE3831	SHORT CIRCUIT IN ABS CONTROL (MOTOR) RELAY CIRCUIT
21	ON/OFF ⎍⎍⎍_⎍	BE3832	OPEN OR SHORT CIRCUIT IN 3-POSITION SOLENOID CIRCUIT FOR RIGHT FRONT WHEEL
22	ON/OFF ⎍⎍⎍_⎍⎍	BE3832	OPEN OR SHORT CIRCUIT IN 3-POSITION SOLENOID CIRCUIT FOR LEFT FRONT WHEEL
23	ON/OFF ⎍⎍⎍_⎍⎍⎍	BE3832	OPEN OR SHORT CIRCUIT IN 3-POSITION SOLENOID CIRCUIT FOR RIGHT REAR WHEEL
24	ON/OFF ⎍⎍⎍_⎍⎍⎍⎍	BE3832	OPEN OR SHORT CIRCUIT IN 3-POSITION SOLENOID CIRCUIT FOR LEFT REAR WHEEL
31	ON/OFF ⎍⎍⎍⎍_⎍	BE3833	RIGHT FRONT WHEEL SPEED SENSOR SIGNAL MALFUNCTION
32	ON/OFF ⎍⎍⎍⎍_⎍⎍	BE3833	LEFT FRONT WHEEL SPEED SENSOR SIGNAL MALFUNCTION
33	ON/OFF ⎍⎍⎍⎍_⎍⎍⎍	BE3833	RIGHT REAR WHEEL SPEED SENSOR SIGNAL MALFUNCTION
34	ON/OFF ⎍⎍⎍⎍_⎍⎍⎍⎍	BE3832	LEFT REAR WHEEL SPEED SENSOR SIGNAL MALFUNCTION
35	ON/OFF ⎍⎍⎍⎍_⎍⎍⎍⎍⎍	BE3833	OPEN CIRCUIT IN LEFT FRONT OR RIGHT REAR SPEED SENSOR CIRCUIT
36	ON/OFF ⎍⎍⎍⎍_⎍⎍⎍⎍⎍⎍	BE3833	OPEN CIRCUIT IN RIGHT FRONT OR LEFT REAR SPEED SENSOR CIRCUIT
37	ON/OFF ⎍⎍⎍⎍_⎍⎍⎍⎍⎍⎍⎍	BE3833	FAULTY REAR SPEED SENSOR ROTOR
41	ON/OFF ⎍⎍⎍⎍⎍_⎍	BE3834	LOW BATTERY POSITIVE VOLTAGE OR ABNORMALLY HIGH BATTERY POSITIVE VOLTAGE
51	ON/OFF ⎍⎍⎍⎍⎍⎍_⎍	BE3836	PUMP MOTOR IS LOCKED OPEN IN PUMP MOTOR GROUND
ALWAYS ON	ON/OFF ⎍		MALFUNCTION IN ECU

Figure 13-68. Toyota ABS diagnostic trouble codes.

The 1996 RAV4 uses a semiconductor pressure-sensor-type deceleration sensor. Testing this design requires removing the sensor from the vehicle and powering it with three 1.5-volt batteries, then measuring voltage at the sensor terminals while the sensor is tilted or held horizontal. Consult the appropriate service manuals for details.

Additional diagnostic information is available if you have a Toyota handheld tester, or an equivalent scan tool. To check the ABS solenoid in the hydraulic actuator on rear ABS, use a scan tool and harness adapter, or the Toyota special tester. The scan tool or tester connects to the modulator and relay harness, so you can manually cycle the ABS solenoid. If the vehicle has a data link connector 2 (DLC-2) under the instrument panel, you can read codes using a scan tool rather than the MIL. Use a DVOM to check circuits and components. Expect to see about 580 to 700 ohms of resistance across a speed sensor, and about 80 ohms on the solenoid relay.

Toyota ABS Service

Routine service operations are the same as they would be for a Toyota vehicle without ABS.

Bleeding Procedure

Toyota recommends that you manually bleed the brakes beginning with the longest circuit. If brake lines were separated from the master cylinder, start the bleeding process at the master cylinder before

CODE NO.	DIAGNOSIS	TROUBLE AREA
71	LOW OUTPUT VOLTAGE OF RIGHT FRONT SPEED SENSOR	• RIGHT FRONT SPEED SENSOR • SENSOR INSTALLATION
72	LOW OUTPUT VOLTAGE OF LEFT FRONT SPEED SENSOR	• LEFT FRONT SPEED SENSOR • SENSOR INSTALLATION
73	LOW OUTPUT VOLTAGE OF RIGHT REAR SPEED SENSOR	• RIGHT REAR SPEED SENSOR • SENSOR INSTALLATION
74	LOW OUTPUT VOLTAGE OF LEFT REAR SPEED SENSOR	• LEFT REAR SPEED SENSOR • SENSOR INSTALLATION
75	ABNORMAL CHANGE IN OUTPUT VOLTAGE OF RIGHT FRONT SPEED SENSOR	• RIGHT FRONT SPEED SENSOR ROTOR
76	ABNORMAL CHANGE IN OUTPUT VOLTAGE OF LEFT FRONT SPEED SENSOR	• LEFT FRONT SPEED SENSOR ROTOR
77	ABNORMAL CHANGE IN OUTPUT VOLTAGE OF RIGHT REAR SPEED SENSOR	• RIGHT REAR SPEED SENSOR ROTOR
78	ABNORMAL CHANGE IN OUTPUT VOLTAGE OF LEFT REAR SPEED SENSOR	• LEFT REAR SPEED SENSOR ROTOR

Figure 13-69. Toyota ABS additional trouble codes.

bleeding the wheels. Special steps must be taken to bleed the system if any air has become trapped in the hydraulic actuator.

Hydraulic Actuator

The hydraulic actuator in rear-wheel ABS is driven by power-steering-pump pressure. When the actuator is removed or replaced, both the power steering and brake sides of the unit must be bled. A Toyota special tester, or a scan tool capable of toggling the solenoid, is required to bleed the hydraulic actuator.

Check and correct the fluid levels in the power-steering-pump reservoir and the brake fluid reservoir. Be sure to use the proper fluid. Next, bleed the brakes at the wheels twice. Bleed all wheels the first time with the engine running and a second time with the engine off. Then, bleed the actuator as follows:

1. Start and run the engine at idle, below 1000 rpm, as you turn the steering wheel from lock to lock several times. Then, switch the engine off.
2. Connect a clear hose to the bleed screw on top of the steering gear. Restart the engine and turn the steering wheel from lock to lock again several times; then, center the steering.
3. Loosen the bleed screw to allow power steering pump pressure to force fluid through the hose. When the fluid flow is free of air bubbles, tighten the bleed screw.
4. If the power steering fluid level rises or foams, repeat steps 1 through 3.
5. Shut the engine off, and follow equipment manufacturer directions to connect the scan tool or Toyota tester to the hydraulic actuator unit.
6. Start and run the engine at idle. Select the "air bleed" mode on the tool while applying firm pressure on the brake pedal. Releasing the brake pedal while energizing the solenoid can cause master cylinder damage. Toggle the solenoid on and off five times within three seconds.

To finish the job, switch the engine off, disconnect your test tools, and reconnect the ABS hydraulic actuator and relay. Check the brake and power-steering-fluid levels, and top off with appropriate fluids as needed.

14
Brake-Related Suspension Service

OBJECTIVES

Upon completion and review of this chapter, you will be able to:

- Perform bearing noise tests.
- Perform bearing feel tests.
- Diagnose bearing condition from a grease seal inspection.
- Check bearing axial play.
- Clean, inspect, and lubricate bearings.
- Replace tapered roller bearings, cups, and seals.
- Adjust tapered roller bearings.
- Replace sealed bearings on front or rear axles.
- Replace bearings and seals on solid rear axles.
- Install a wheel and tire with the proper lug nut torque and tightening sequence.
- Inspect a tire and wheel.
- Check tire and wheel runout.
- Correct tire and wheel runout.
- Inspect suspension.
- Inspect ball joints.

INTRODUCTION

The wheel bearings, tires and wheels, and vehicle chassis all affect braking performance to one degree or another. The wheel bearings support the brake drums and rotors. If the wheel bearings are not in good condition and adjusted properly, they can increase brake wear and vibration, reduce the stability of the vehicle while braking, and result in seal damage that can contaminate the brake linings with grease or axle lubricant. The tire and wheel assemblies form the friction link between the brake system and the road, so any problem in this area upsets traction and, therefore, braking power and balance. The vehicle chassis ties all these elements together, and unless it is in good condition, the car may pull under braking.

This chapter is not a comprehensive guide to wheel bearing, tire and wheel, and chassis service; it deals only with those areas that are encountered in the course of diagnosing brake problems or repairing the brake system. The bearing service section covers diagnosis, basic bearing service, and replacement procedures for the major types of wheel bearings and their seals. The tire and wheel service section covers installation, inspection, and checking procedures for radial and lateral runout. The chassis service section covers the basic inspection procedures for major chassis components.

TYPES OF WHEEL BEARINGS

As discussed in the *Classroom Manual*, three types of bearings are used as wheel bearings on automobiles: straight roller bearings, ball bearings, and tapered roller bearings. These bearings are used in three different ways to support the wheels, and each design requires somewhat different service procedures. The sections below describe the three basic styles of wheel bearings.

Adjustable Dual-Wheel Bearings

The most common wheel bearing design is adjustable dual bearings, figure 14-1. This layout is used on non-driven wheels at both the front and rear axles. With this design, the inner bearing is always somewhat larger than the outer bearing because it supports the additional loads created by inertia and weight shift during cornering. All modern vehicles with adjustable dual-wheel bearings use tapered roller bearings; however, some older cars have ball bearings instead.

Adjustable dual-wheel bearings require inspection, adjustment, and lubrication approximately every 30,000 miles (40,000 km) under normal driving conditions, and every 15,000 miles (20,000 km) in severe service. Consult the manufacturer's maintenance schedule to determine the exact intervals for the vehicle you are servicing. These bearings should also be serviced if they are removed in the course of brake work or other vehicle repairs.

Sealed Wheel Bearings

The second type of wheel bearing is the sealed, non-adjustable, double-row bearing assembly found on the front wheels of most FWD cars, figure 14-2 and figure 14-3. A similar bearing assembly is used on some non-

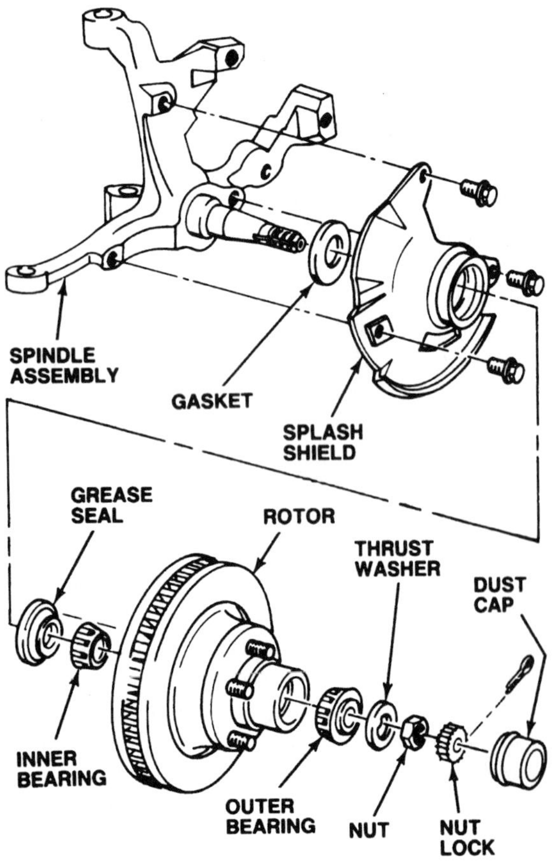

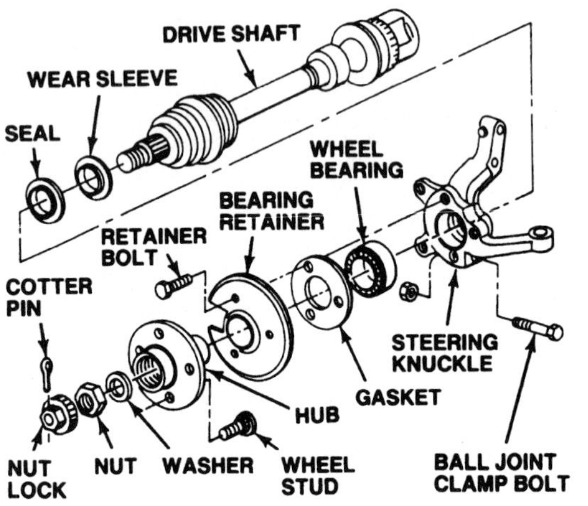

Figure 14-2. A sealed wheel bearing assembly, used on some FWD vehicles.

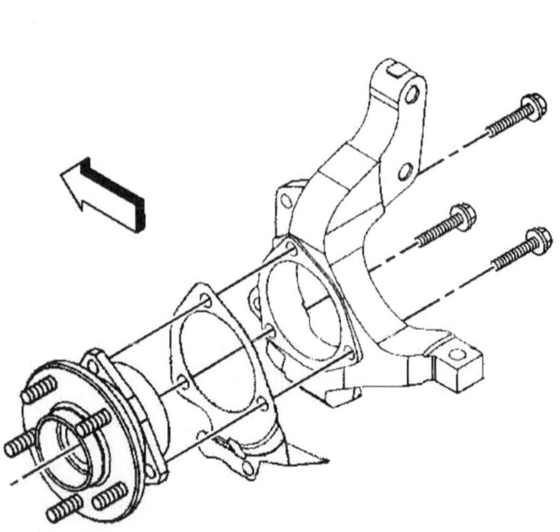

Figure 14-1. A typical adjustable dual-wheel bearing assembly with tapered roller bearings.

Figure 14-3. This sealed bearing and hub assembly is replaced as a unit. (Courtesy of General Motors Corporation, Service and Parts Operations)

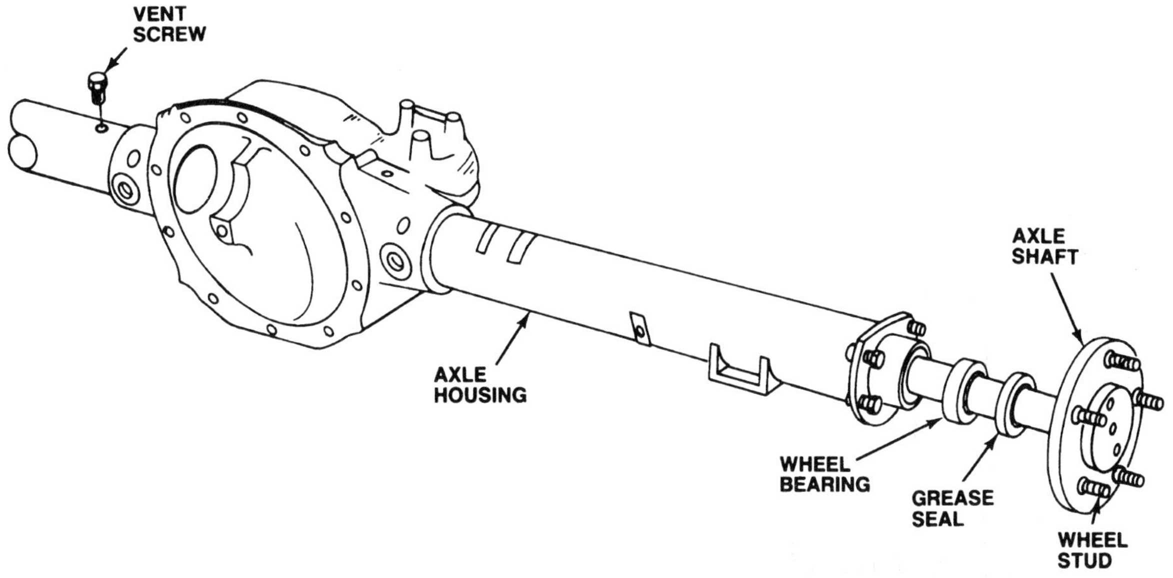

Brake-Related Suspension Service

Figure 14-4. A solid rear axle with straight roller wheel bearings.

driven axles as well. Both bearings in this design have the same fairly large size. Large bearings are necessary because they are close together, and the loads created by supporting the axle are therefore somewhat greater. Originally, most sealed bearing units used dual ball bearings; however, some newer cars have sealed bearings with dual-tapered roller bearings. Sealed bearings require no periodic maintenance, and must be replaced when they become worn.

Solid-Axle Wheel Bearings

The third type of wheel bearing is the single bearing used on vehicles with a solid rear axle. This type of wheel bearing, located near the outer end of the axle, can be either a straight roller bearing or a ball bearing. Straight roller bearings, figure 14-4, are pressed into the axle housing and use the axle shaft as the inner bearing race. The axle is retained in the housing by a C-lock that fits into a groove in the end of the shaft inside the differential. The axle lubricant also lubricates the wheel bearing, and a seal at the end of the housing keeps the lubricant inside the axle.

Ball bearings used on solid axles are generally pressed onto the axle shaft, figure 14-5, and the axle is held in place by a retainer plate that fits over the bearing and bolts to the axle housing. The retainer plate is usually secured by the same bolts that hold the brake backing plate in place. The ball bearings used on solid rear axles are either sealed units, or are unsealed and packed with bearing grease; rear axle ball bearings are not lubricated by the axle lubricant. An inner seal in the

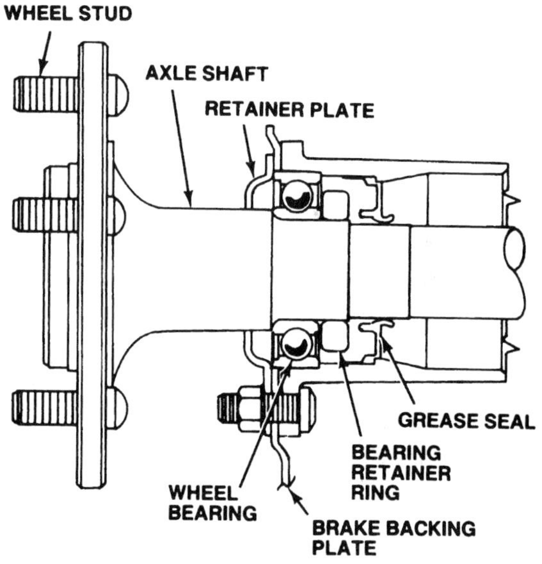

Figure 14-5. A solid rear axle with ball bearing wheel bearings.

axle housing prevents axle lubricant from coming into contact with the bearing, and in some cases, an outer seal in the retainer plate prevents the bearing grease from escaping and contaminating the brake linings.

Like sealed wheel bearing assemblies, solid-axle wheel bearings do not require periodic maintenance. They are only serviced when they become worn, or are removed in the course of brake work or other repairs.

WHEEL BEARING DIAGNOSIS

Worn or misadjusted wheel bearings can cause a number of brake problems. For example, loose or worn bearings allow brake drum and rotor runout that can lead to increased lining wear and excessive brake pedal travel. Loose bearings also make tire and wheel imbalance more noticeable, and at the front of the vehicle, bearing problems allow the wheel alignment to vary; both conditions cause instability during braking. At either axle, loose or worn bearings can lead to leaking wheel seals that allow grease or axle lubricant to contaminate the brake linings.

There are four signs that indicate a wheel bearing needs to be serviced: noise, roughness, grease seal leakage, and excessive axial play. These symptoms usually appear in various combinations, depending on the severity of the problem and the type of bearing used. The sections below describe the symptoms in greater detail, and explain the procedures used to isolate bad wheel bearings.

Bearing Noise Tests

Wheel bearings rarely fail all at once; instead, the rolling surfaces deteriorate slowly and become rough. As the bearing rotates, this roughness causes a growling sound that is the most common symptom of a wheel bearing problem. As wear becomes worse, the sound grows louder and louder until the vehicle owner brings the car in for service.

It is usually not too difficult to tell whether a bearing noise is coming from the front or rear axle, although it is harder in some cases than in others. However, deciding on which side of the car a bad bearing is located can be very difficult. There are two tests that use noise to help isolate a bad bearing; one is done on the road, the other is done in the shop.

Bearing Noise Road Test
The most common method used to isolate a bad wheel bearing is a road test. To road test a vehicle with a bearing noise, find a wide street or large parking lot where there is plenty of room to safely manuever. Drive at approximately 20 mph (30 kph), and swerve back and forth to alternately load and unload the bearings on each side of the vehicle. As you swerve to the right, the left-side bearings are put under greater load; as you swerve to the left, the right-side bearings are put under greater load. As you do this, listen for changes in the level of bearing noise. Unless there are bad bearings on both sides of the vehicle, the noise is usually much louder when turning in one direction than in the other.

The results of this test are interpreted in different ways, depending on the type of wheel bearings on the vehicle. With adjustable dual-wheel bearings where the inner bearing carries a larger part of the total load and creates a louder noise when it fails, the bearing noise will increase when the side of the vehicle with the defective bearing is loaded. For example, if the left-side inner bearing is bad, bearing noise will increase when the vehicle is steered to the right. If the right-side bearing is bad, bearing noise will increase when the vehicle is steered to the left.

Double-row sealed bearing noises are interpreted the same way as those from adjustable dual bearings, providing one of the inner bearings is bad. However, if an outer bearing is defective, the results will be reversed; the noise will increase when the side of the vehicle opposite the bad bearing is loaded. For example, if the outer bearing on the right side is bad, the noise will increase when the vehicle swerves to the right. This can create confusing test results, and one or more of the additional tests described below will be required to isolate a badly sealed bearing.

If a solid rear axle has ball bearings, the noise will increase when the side of the vehicle with the bad bearing is more heavily loaded. The same is true of a solid axle with straight roller bearings; however, a road test may not be conclusive in these cases because straight roller bearings do not support axial loads, and therefore the noises they make are not as greatly affected by side-to-side weight shifts. One or more of the additional tests described below will be required to isolate a bad straight roller bearing.

Bearing Noise Shop Test
If a suspect wheel bearing is on a driven axle, and the vehicle does not have a limited-slip differential, you can use the engine to spin the wheels individually in the shop to help locate the problem. The bad bearing will generally make more noise when it is spun. This test can also be inconclusive, however, because the wheels are unloaded, which reduces bearing noise somewhat. At the same time, the differential side gears are spinning, which increases the amount of background noise.

This test requires that you run the vehicle in gear while it is raised off the ground in the shop. For safety reasons, this is best done with the car on a hoist, although jack stands are acceptable. In either case, use extreme care and make sure the vehicle is properly supported so it cannot move in any way during the test. To check wheel bearing noise with the vehicle in the shop:

1. Raise the vehicle so the wheels clear the floor by about two inches, then support it so that the suspension is in approximately the same position as when the vehicle is resting on the

Brake-Related Suspension Service

ground. If the wheels are allowed to hang free, additional drivetrain noises will be created that interfere with bearing diagnosis. And, on FWD cars, the constant velocity (CV) joints may be damaged.
2. Block the wheels on one side of the driven axle so they cannot turn.
3. Have an assistant start the engine, place the vehicle in gear, and accelerate the vehicle until approximately 20 mph (30 kph) shows on the speedometer with the vehicle in high gear. With one driven wheel blocked, the opposite wheel will then rotate at a speed equivalent to about 40 mph (65 kph); do not exceed this limit or drivetrain damage may result.
4. Listen for bearing noise at the spinning wheel.
5. Stop the engine, block the wheel you just listened to so it cannot rotate, then repeat steps 3 and 4 at the opposite wheel.

Bearing Feel Tests

The same wear that causes bearing noise can also be felt as a roughness if the wheel is rotated with the vehicle supported off the ground. If the tests above are inconclusive, or the suspect bearing is not on a driven axle, raise and properly support the vehicle, then rotate the wheels by hand to check bearing condition. Feel for roughness in the bearing as it turns, and listen for a low-frequency rumbling noise. Compare the results on opposite sides of the vehicle to determine where the problem lies.

Bearing Grease Seal Tests

Another sign that a wheel bearing needs attention is leakage from the grease seal, figure 14-6. This is especially true of adjustable dual bearings and solid rear axle bearings. Grease or axle lubricant leaking from the seal can be a sign that excessive bearing play has caused seal damage. Also, once a seal begins to leak, brake dust and other contaminants can enter to harm the bearing. Always replace leaking grease seals to prevent contamination of the brake linings, and at the same time, service the wheel bearings.

Bearing Axial Play Tests

The final indication of wheel bearings that are worn or need adjustment is excessive axial play. If inward and outward movement of the bearing hub or axle exceeds specifications, the bearings must be serviced. Checking the axial play is the only means of determining the condition of sealed, double-row bearing assemblies; however, axial play cannot be used to

Figure 14-6. A leaking grease seal can indicate a bad wheel bearing.

check straight roller bearings in solid rear axles. Straight roller bearings do not support axial loads, so excessive side play does not indicate bearing condition, although it may indicate a worn C-lock or retaining groove in the axle.

The most common method used to check axial play on vehicles with adjustable dual-wheel bearings is by hand. With the vehicle raised and properly supported, grasp the top and bottom of the tire and attempt to wobble it back and forth and in and out. You should feel little or no axial play by hand. Experience will give you a better idea of how much play is normal. If play is excessive, service the bearings.

A more accurate way to check bearing axial play is to use a dial indicator. This method must be used to check sealed wheel bearing assemblies unless the bearing is so badly worn that movement is apparent in the hand test above. To check axial play with a dial indicator:

1. Raise and properly support the vehicle, then remove the wheel.
2. If the bearings to be checked are on a wheel equipped with a disc brake, use one of the methods described in Chapter 8 to push the caliper pistons into their bores just far enough that the brake pads do not drag against the rotor. It is not necessary to bottom the pistons in their bores.
3. Mount a dial indicator on the suspension, figure 14-7, and position the plunger against the edge of the bearing hub.

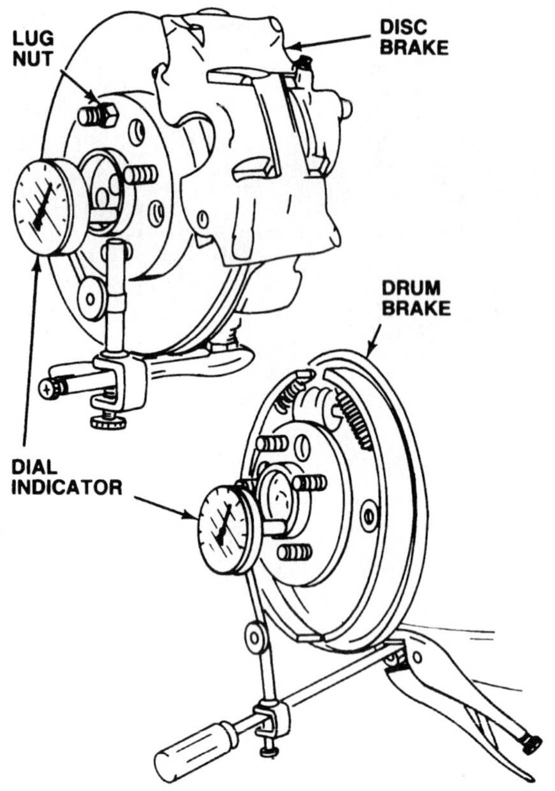

Figure 14-7. Using a dial indicator to check wheel bearing axial play.

4. Push the hub inward toward the suspension until it will move no farther, then zero the indicator dial.
5. Pull the hub outward, away from the suspension until it will move no farther. The reading on the indicator dial is the bearing axial play.

Adjustable dual-wheel bearings (tapered roller bearings) are generally allowed between .001″ and .005″ (.025 and .127 mm) axial play. A tapered roller bearing with less than .001″ (.025 mm) axial play will wear rapidly, and one with more than .005″ (.127 mm) axial play allows excessive drum or rotor runout. Though it is possible to only adjust loose bearings, the best policy is to always remove, clean, inspect, and repack the bearings unless you know they were recently serviced and are in good condition.

Sealed wheel bearing assemblies with ball bearings, or the single ball bearings used in solid rear axles, are allowed only a very small amount of axial play, usually a maximum of .002″ (.05 mm). Sealed bearing assemblies with tapered roller bearings are allowed up to .005″ (.125 mm) play like their adjustable counterparts. Always consult the factory shop manual to get the proper specifications for the vehicle being serviced. If the axial play of a sealed bearing, or a rear axle ball bearing, exceeds the amount allowed by the vehicle manufacturer, replace the bearing.

BASIC WHEEL BEARING SERVICE

Wheel bearings are removed for four reasons: they are diagnosed as being bad, they require repacking as part of routine maintenance, they must be removed so a leaking grease seal can be replaced, or they must be removed so other vehicle repairs can be made. The procedure to remove and reinstall a wheel bearing varies with the type of bearing used, and detailed instructions for this job are given later in the chapter. However, in each case, the procedure is basically the same whether the bearing is being replaced or simply repacked.

Except for sealed bearings, all wheel bearings share a number of common service procedures that should be performed whenever the bearing is removed for any reason. The sections below provide some general bearing service tips, and describe how to clean wheel bearings, inspect them for wear and damage, and pack them with grease.

General Bearing Replacement Tips

When you replace an unsealed wheel bearing, leave the new part in its package until you are ready to install it; the special wrappings are designed to keep the bearing clean and rust free. Before you touch a new bearing, wash your hands and dip your fingers in clean motor oil. This ensures that the acids on your fingers will not harm the bearing.

Whenever you replace a tapered roller or ball bearing that has a separate outer race, you must replace the race as well. Even though an old outer race may appear to be in perfect condition, it has been subjected to the same stress and metal fatigue as the old bearing. An old race also has a certain wear pattern from running against the old bearing. If you install a new bearing in an old race, it will not fit properly, and premature bearing wear and failure will result.

Whenever you service any type of wheel bearing, install new grease seals. Seals wear with age just like bearings, and are often damaged during bearing removal. A new seal keeps grease or axle lubricant off the brake linings and in the bearing or axle where it belongs. At the same time, a new seal keeps out the dirt, water, and brake dust that can shorten a bearing or axle's service life.

Wheel Bearing Cleaning

When an unsealed wheel bearing is removed, wipe away as much old grease as possible using dry rags or paper towels; inspect the grease on the towels for metal

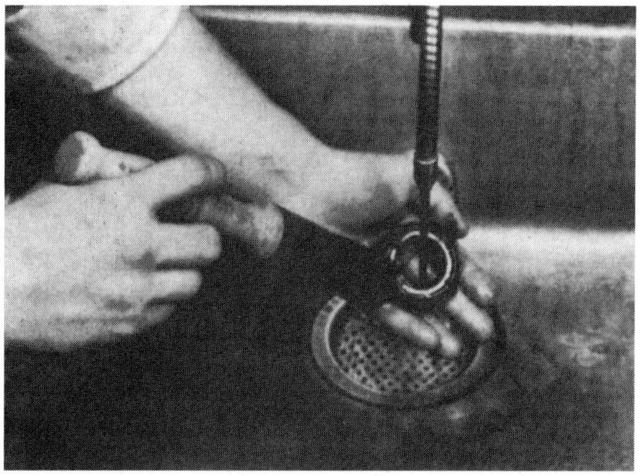

Brake-Related Suspension Service

Figure 14-8. Wash unsealed wheel bearings in clean solvent.

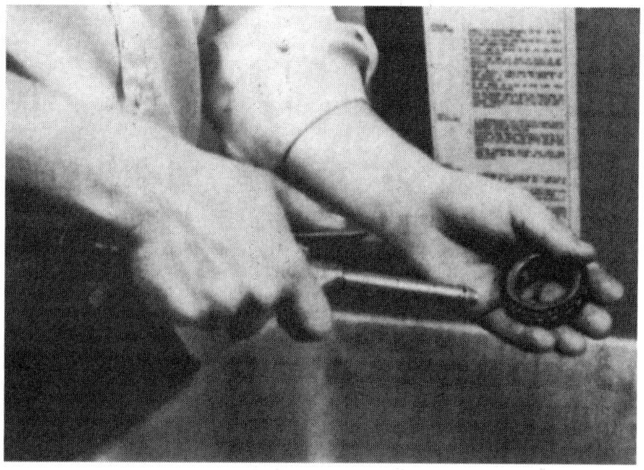

Figure 14-9. Use compressed air to dry wheel bearings.

chips or other indications of bearing wear or damage. Next, clean the bearing in a parts washer using clean petroleum-based solvent. A long-bristled brush is helpful to flush out hard-to-reach grit, figure 14-8. Wash each bearing individually, and keep bearings with detachable outer races separated so you can replace them in the same races from which they were removed. Clean unsealed rear axle ball bearings while they are still on the axle.

Once all of the old grease has been washed out, flush the bearings with a non-petroleum-based brake cleaning fluid; this removes any traces of oil and solvent that can contaminate the new grease and lead to premature bearing failure. Finally, hold the bearings by their cages and dry them with clean, unlubricated compressed air. Direct the air through the bearing so it travels across the balls or rollers from side to side, figure 14-9. Do not spin a bearing with air while drying it. The bearing is not properly lubricated at this time, and spinning it at high speed can cause rapid wear and damage. In addition, if the air pressure or bearing speed is great enough, the balls or rollers may fly out of the cage, causing personal injury and property damage.

Wheel Bearing Inspection

Once the bearings are clean and dry, inspect them for the problems shown in figure 14-10 (page 322). Although the illustration depicts tapered roller bearings, most of the same problems occur with straight roller and ball bearings as well. To inspect a bearing, rotate it carefully in a good light so the complete surface of each ball, roller, and race can be fully checked. If any problems are apparent, or you have a question about its condition, replace the bearing. Never reuse a suspect bearing to save money. Like the brake system, the wheel bearings are a high liability area. An accident caused by a wheel bearing failure can result in personal injury, property damage, and a lawsuit.

Wheel Bearing Greases

Greases are made from oils that are thickened so the lubricant will cling to the surfaces where it is needed. As their name implies, wheel bearing greases are used to lubricate wheel bearings—although there are some wheel bearing greases that also make good chassis lubricants; these products are called multi-purpose greases. Greases are classified in two ways, by their National Lubricating Grease Institute (NLGI) number, and by the type of thickening agent used.

The NLGI number designates the viscosity or consistency of a grease; the higher the number, the thicker the grease. The NLGI number is only a means of comparison, it is not a measure of quality or performance. Virtually all wheel bearing greases have an NLGI #2 consistency number.

Greases are thickened with several substances including calcium, sodium, and lithium. The type and amount of thickening agent determine the melting point, appearance, texture, and water resistance of a grease. Today, most manufacturers recommend wheel bearing grease made with a lithium-based thickener because these greases have a high melting point and offer superior water resistance.

Wheel bearing greases also contain additives that improve their performance. Sulphonates or amines are used to inhibit corrosion, and solid lubricants such as molybdenum disulphide (MS_2) improve the anti-seize properties of a grease. To increase the load-carrying ability of a grease under extreme pressure, sulphurized fatty oils are sometimes added. Always use grease that meets the vehicle manufacturer's specifications when you repack wheel bearings.

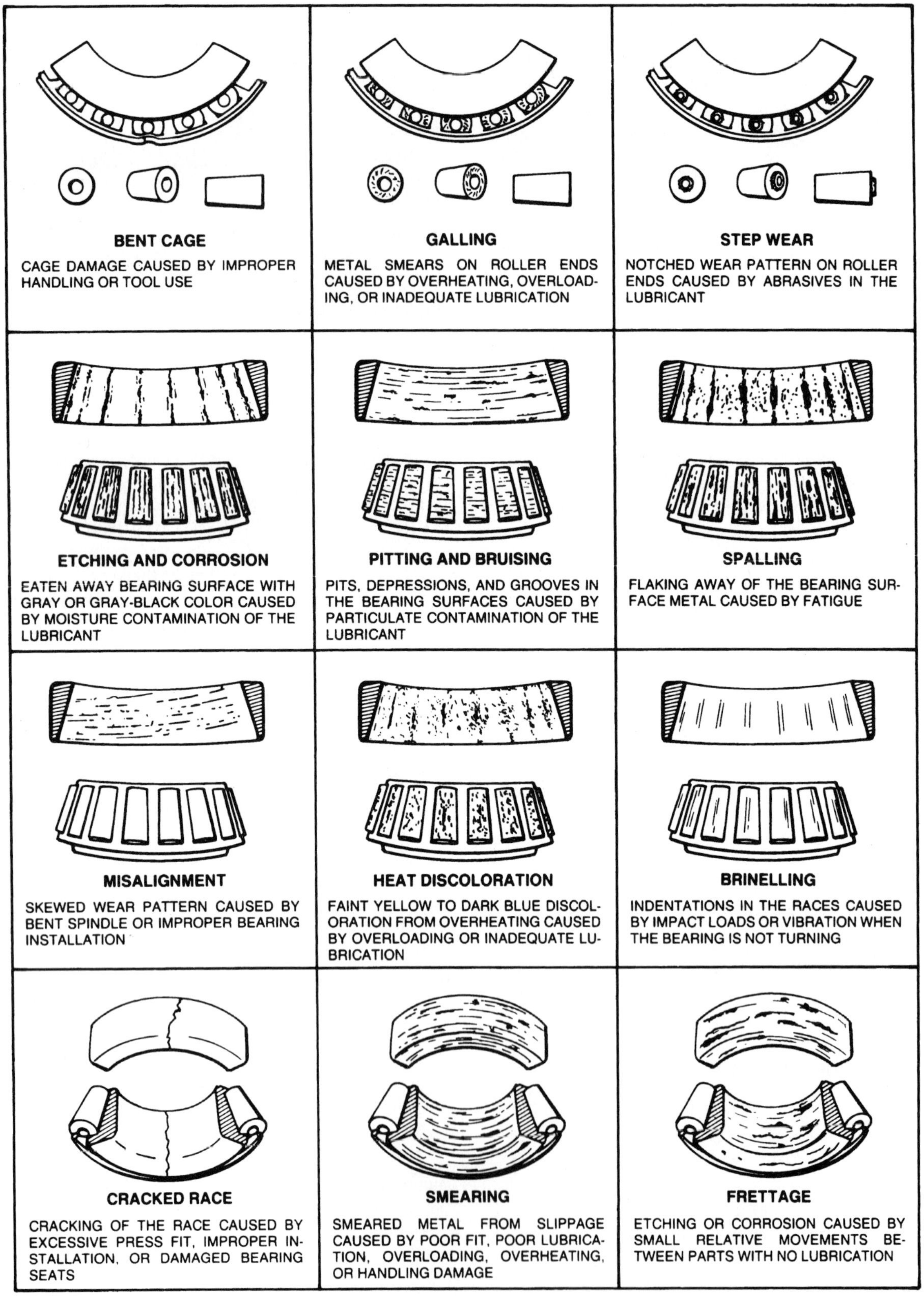

BENT CAGE CAGE DAMAGE CAUSED BY IMPROPER HANDLING OR TOOL USE	**GALLING** METAL SMEARS ON ROLLER ENDS CAUSED BY OVERHEATING, OVERLOADING, OR INADEQUATE LUBRICATION	**STEP WEAR** NOTCHED WEAR PATTERN ON ROLLER ENDS CAUSED BY ABRASIVES IN THE LUBRICANT
ETCHING AND CORROSION EATEN AWAY BEARING SURFACE WITH GRAY OR GRAY-BLACK COLOR CAUSED BY MOISTURE CONTAMINATION OF THE LUBRICANT	**PITTING AND BRUISING** PITS, DEPRESSIONS, AND GROOVES IN THE BEARING SURFACES CAUSED BY PARTICULATE CONTAMINATION OF THE LUBRICANT	**SPALLING** FLAKING AWAY OF THE BEARING SURFACE METAL CAUSED BY FATIGUE
MISALIGNMENT SKEWED WEAR PATTERN CAUSED BY BENT SPINDLE OR IMPROPER BEARING INSTALLATION	**HEAT DISCOLORATION** FAINT YELLOW TO DARK BLUE DISCOLORATION FROM OVERHEATING CAUSED BY OVERLOADING OR INADEQUATE LUBRICATION	**BRINELLING** INDENTATIONS IN THE RACES CAUSED BY IMPACT LOADS OR VIBRATION WHEN THE BEARING IS NOT TURNING
CRACKED RACE CRACKING OF THE RACE CAUSED BY EXCESSIVE PRESS FIT, IMPROPER INSTALLATION, OR DAMAGED BEARING SEATS	**SMEARING** SMEARED METAL FROM SLIPPAGE CAUSED BY POOR FIT, POOR LUBRICATION, OVERLOADING, OVERHEATING, OR HANDLING DAMAGE	**FRETTAGE** ETCHING OR CORROSION CAUSED BY SMALL RELATIVE MOVEMENTS BETWEEN PARTS WITH NO LUBRICATION

Figure 14-10. A wheel bearing inspection chart.

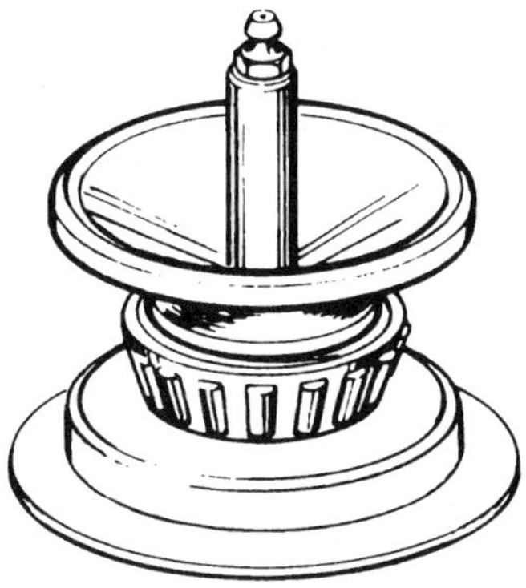

Brake-Related Suspension Service

Figure 14-11. Bearing packers do an excellent job of lubricating wheel bearings.

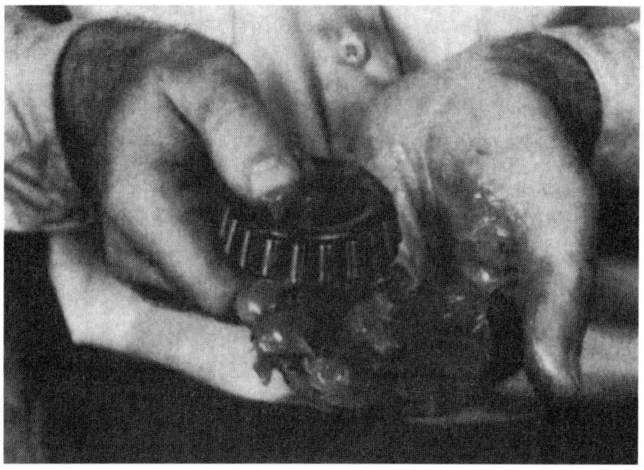

Figure 14-12. You can pack wheel bearings by hand.

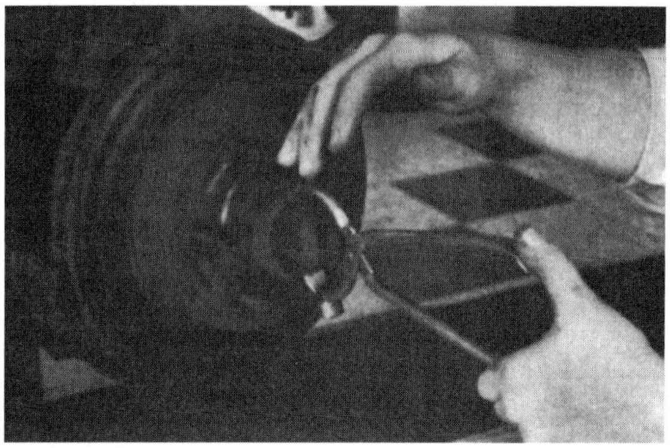

Figure 14-13. To prevent damage, use a special tool to remove the dust cap.

Wheel Bearing Lubrication

Whenever you pack a new or used wheel bearing with grease, it is extremely important that you use the type of grease recommended by the vehicle manufacturer. All wheel bearing greases consist of oils that have been given a heavy consistency through the addition of a thickening agent. However, several different thickening agents are used, and most do not mix. *Always* clean away every trace of old grease before you repack a wheel bearing, and *never* add new grease to old, or bearing damage may result.

When you pack a wheel bearing, work the grease into the cage and races, and between the balls or rollers, so that no air spaces remain. The most effective and efficient way to do this is to use a bearing packer, figure 14-11. These devices use air or hydraulic pressure to force new grease through the entire bearing in one quick operation.

If a bearing packer is unavailable, you can pack wheel bearings by hand, although this method is slower and messier. To hand-pack a tapered roller bearing, fill your palm with grease, place the large end of the bearing down, then draw the bearing across your palm, forcing grease into the cage and rollers until it oozes out the opposite side, figure 14-12. Repeat this process all around the bearing until it is completely filled with grease. Finish by spreading a medium coating of grease around the outside of the bearing. When you pack a ball bearing by hand, work the grease in from both sides until the space between the inner and outer races is completely filled with grease.

ADJUSTABLE DUAL-WHEEL BEARING SERVICE

Virtually all modern vehicles with adjustable dual-wheel bearings use tapered roller bearings, so only that type is dealt with in the procedure below. Except for removing and installing the bearing races, the procedure is basically the same whether tapered roller bearings are being replaced or simply repacked. The procedure is also the same whether the bearings are fitted in a brake drum hub or a brake rotor hub.

To service a set of adjustable dual-wheel bearings:

1. Raise and properly support the vehicle so the wheels with the bearings to be serviced hang free, then remove the wheels.
2. If the axle is equipped with disc brakes, remove the brake caliper and anchor plate as needed so the rotor can be removed from the axle (see Chapter 8).
3. Pull the dust cap from the center of the hub to expose the adjusting nut, figure 14-13.
4. Loosen the adjusting nut and back it off approximately ½ inch (13 mm). On most cars, the nut is secured by a castellated nut lock and cotter pin; remove the pin and nut lock, then unscrew the nut. Some imported cars have a split nut with a

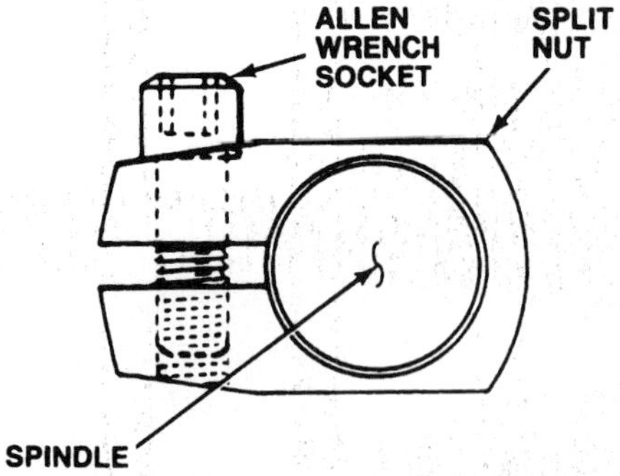

Figure 14-14. A split wheel bearing adjusting nut is used on some imported cars.

Figure 14-15. Remove the outer wheel bearing and related parts.

Figure 14-16. A puller may be required to remove a drum or rotor.

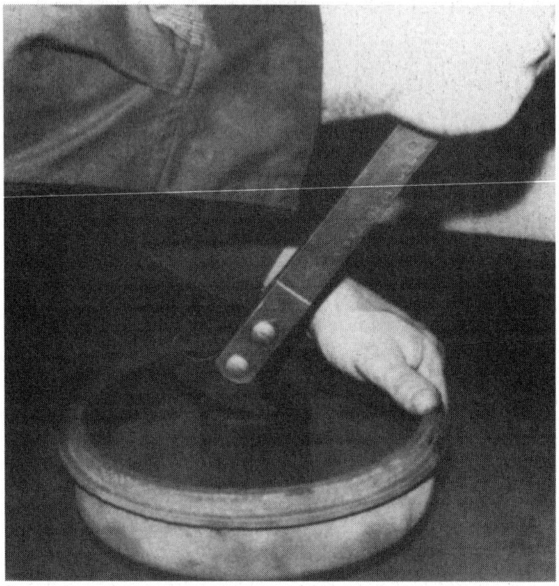

Figure 14-17. A seal puller speeds seal removal.

pinch bolt, figure 14-14; loosen the bolt, then unscrew the nut.
5. Pull the drum or rotor outward to free the thrust washer and outer wheel bearing, then push the drum or rotor inward on the spindle.
6. Remove the adjusting nut, thrust washer, and outer wheel bearing from the hub, figure 14-15, and set them aside.
7. Pull the drum or rotor outward and slide it off the spindle, taking care not to drag the inner wheel bearing across the adjusting nut threads. To remove some brake drums, you may have to loosen the brake adjustment as described in Chapter 7.
8. If the inner wheel bearing sticks on the spindle and makes the drum or rotor difficult to remove, use a puller or slide hammer to remove the drum or rotor, figure 14-16. Once the drum or rotor is off the axle, use a puller or a pair of pry bars to carefully remove the inner bearing and grease seal.
9. Support the drum or rotor on the workbench and remove the grease seal. This can be done in two ways:
    a. Hook the claw of a seal puller under the metal retaining ring of the seal, and lever the seal out, figure 14-17; a large screwdriver can also be used to pry out the seal.
    b. Position a nonmetallic drift about ¾ inch (19 mm) in diameter through the outer bearing opening so it contacts the inner race of the inner bearing, figure 14-18. Strike the drift with a hammer until the bearing and seal are driven from the hub.
10. Clean and inspect the bearings and bearing races as described earlier. Also clean the inside of the drum or rotor hub.
11. If a new bearing must be installed, remove the old race from the drum or rotor hub. This can be done in two ways:
    a. Use a special bearing race puller, figure 14-19.
    b. Insert a metal drift through the hub and position it against the backside of the race; use a

Brake-Related Suspension Service

Figure 14-18. Use a drift to remove onto inner wheel bearing and grease seal.

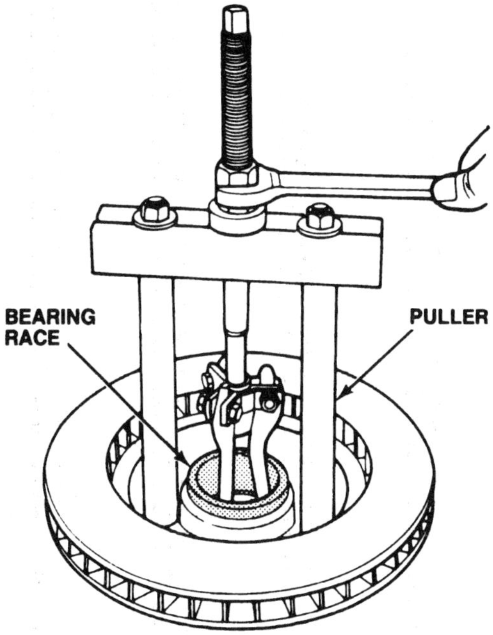

Figure 14-19. A wheel bearing race puller.

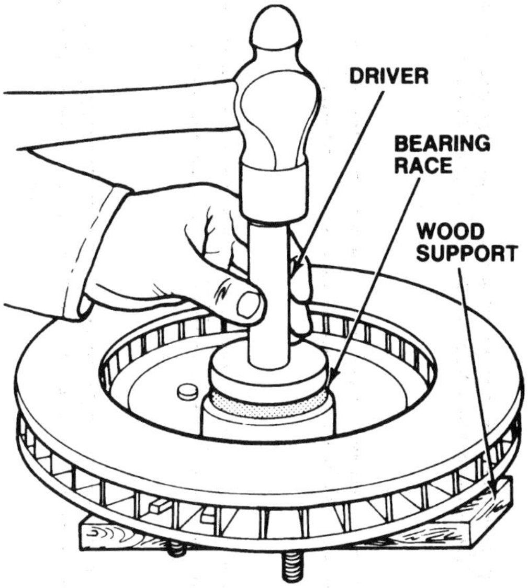

Figure 14-20. Installing a bearing race with a driver.

Figure 14-21. Install the grease seal into the hub over the inner bearing.

drift that is softer than the hub metal to prevent damage. Strike the drift with a hammer while moving it around the race to drive the race from the hub.

12. Use a bearing race driver or a suitably sized socket to install the new race in the drum or rotor hub, figure 14-20. The tool should only contact the outer edge of the race. Drive the race until it is fully seated; the pitch of the sound made when striking the driver will change when the bearing is seated.
13. Clean and inspect the spindle for rust, nicks, and scratches. Remove any blemishes with fine sandpaper, and make sure the inner races of both bearings slip easily over the spindle. If the spindle is badly scored or cracked in any way, it must be replaced.
14. Lightly coat the spindle with grease. This prevents rust and allows the inner bearing races to creep slightly so wear is distributed evenly around the bearings.
15. Pack the wheel bearings with grease as described earlier.
16. Place the drum or rotor outer side down on the workbench, then coat the inside of the hub with grease to prevent rust.
17. Put a medium coating of grease on the inner bearing race; place the inner bearing in the race.
18. Install the grease seal with a seal driver, figure 14-21, then put a light coating of grease on the seal lip.

Figure 14-22. Install the drum or rotor on the spindle.

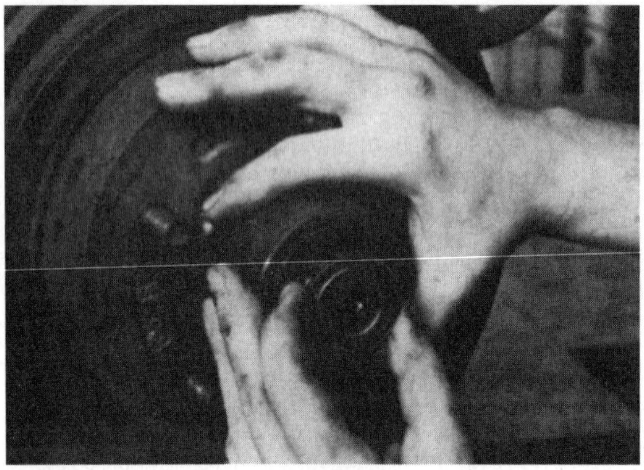

Figure 14-23. Install the outer bearing into the hub.

19. Turn the drum or rotor over and put a medium coating of grease on the outer bearing race.
20. Install the drum or rotor onto the spindle, figure 14-22, taking care to keep it centered so the inner bearing or outer bearing race does not drag on the adjusting nut threads.
21. Install the outer bearing into the hub, figure 14-23, place the thrust washer over it, and install the adjusting nut finger-tight.
22. Adjust the wheel bearings as described below.
23. If the axle is equipped with disc brakes, install the anchor plate and brake caliper as described in Chapter 8. If the axle has drum brakes, and the brake adjustment was loosened in step 7 or 22, adjust the brakes as described in Chapter 7.
24. Install the wheel and tighten the lug nuts to the correct torque in the proper sequence.

Tapered Roller Bearing Adjustment

Tapered roller wheel bearings require adjustment whenever you service them. Before you adjust the bearings, make sure the adjusting nut turns freely on

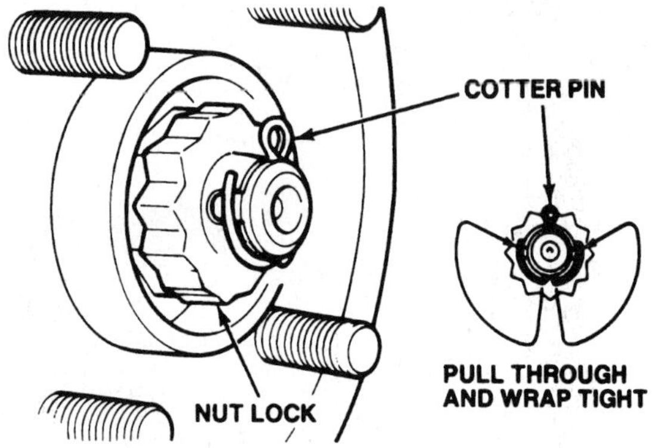

Figure 14-24. A properly secured wheel bearing adjusting nut.

the spindle threads. If the nut does not turns easily by hand, remove any nicks or burrs from the spindle threads with a thread file. If the adjusting nut still binds, run a tap through it or replace the nut.

There are three ways to adjust tapered roller bearings: by hand, with a torque wrench, or using a dial indicator. *Always use the adjusting method recommended by the vehicle manufacturer.* Once you set the proper axial play, lock the adjusting nut in place, and install the dust cap with a plastic hammer. If the adjusting nut is secured with a cotter pin, place the nut lock over the adjusting nut so the slots in the lock align with the cotter pin hole in the spindle. Insert a new cotter pin through the hole, and wrap the tabs around the nut lock, figure 14-24. If the car is equipped with a split adjusting nut, hold it in position with a suitably sized wrench, and tighten the pinch bolt to the torque specified by the vehicle manufacturer.

Hand Adjustment

To adjust the wheel bearings by hand, rotate the wheel and snug up the adjusting nut with a wrench to seat the bearings. As you continue to rotate the wheel, back off the adjusting nut ¼ to ½ turn or until it is just loose, then tighten the nut with your fingers to a snug fit. Lock the adjusting nut in place.

Torque Wrench Adjustment

To adjust the wheel bearings with a torque wrench, rotate the wheel while torquing the adjusting nut to the value specified by the manufacturer, typically 12 to 25 ft-lb (15 to 35 Nm). This will seat the bearings. Back off the adjusting nut ⅓ to ½ turn, then retighten it as specified by the manufacturer, usually 10 to 15 in-lb (1 to 1.5 Nm). On a Ford vehicle, lock the adjusting nut in place at this setting. On GM, Toyota, and many others, *loosen* the nut slightly, until the cotter pin can be inserted. A correctly adjusted bearing will have from .001″ to .004″ (.025 to .120 mm) end play.

Brake-Related Suspension Service

Figure 14-25. A dial indicator allows precise wheel bearing adjustment.

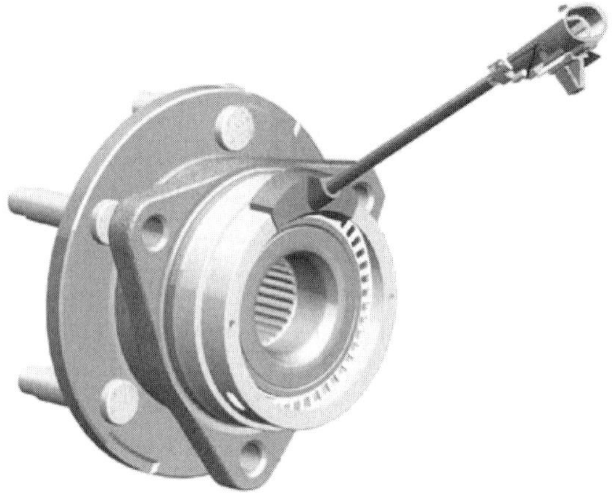

Figure 14-26. The wheel/hub assembly may also contain the ABS wheel speed sensor. (Courtesy of General Motors Corporation, Service and Parts Operations)

Figure 14-27. A wheel bearing retaining nut with a crimped collar.

Dial Indicator Adjustment

To adjust the wheel bearings with a dial indicator, rotate the wheel and torque the adjusting nut to 12 to 25 ft-lb (15 to 35 Nm). Back off the adjusting nut ¼ to ½ turn, or until it is just loose, then tighten the nut with your fingers to a snug fit. Mount a dial indicator on the drum or rotor and position the plunger against the end of the spindle, figure 14-25. Move the drum or rotor in and out to measure the axial play, and turn the adjusting nut as needed to obtain the clearance specified by the vehicle manufacturer, typically between .001″ and .005″ (.025 to .127 mm) end play. Lock the adjusting nut in place.

SEALED WHEEL BEARING REPLACEMENT

Sealed, double-row wheel bearings are common on many of today's vehicles, both on cars and light trucks. As shown in figure 14-2, earlier applications of this type of wheel bearing had the bearing as a separate component of the front or rear knuckle/hub assembly. This requires the removal and disassembly of the steering knuckle to replace the bearing.

Beginning in the early 1990s, General Motors and then others began using a hub and bearing assembly that is serviced as a complete unit, figure 14-26. The assembly will often also contain the ABS wheel speed sensor. This single-unit, bolt-on assembly simplifies replacement.

Front Axle Sealed Bearing Replacement

Replacing the sealed wheel bearing on a front-drive-axle vehicle is more involved than replacing the newer, one-piece hub/bearing assembly. The bearing is replaced as a separate component on many domestic and imported FWD models. On most vehicles, the steering knuckle must be removed before the wheel bearing can be replaced. In some cases, special tools may be available to remove the hub and bearing with the knuckle still on the car.

Always refer to the manufacturer's service information before starting the job. The general procedure is summarized here:

1. Remove the cotter pin from the axle nut. If the nut has a crimped collar, figure 14-27, uncrimp it with a small punch and hammer.
2. With the brakes applied, loosen but do not remove the axle nut using a breaker bar and socket. Do not use an impact wrench for this because the shocks it delivers can damage the CV joint.
3. Raise and properly support the vehicle. Remove the wheel.

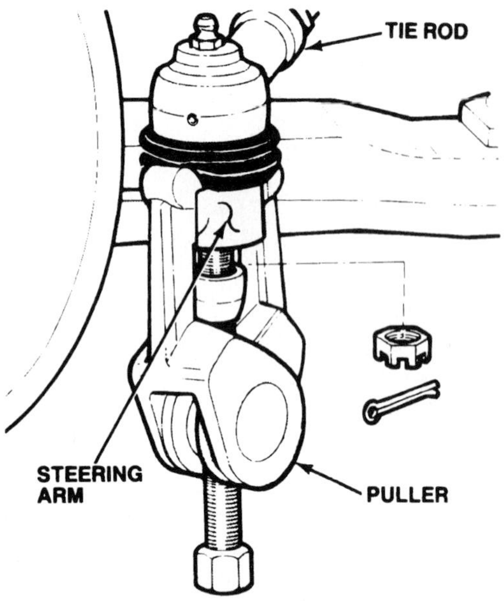

Figure 14-28. Use a puller to separate the tie rod from the steering arm.

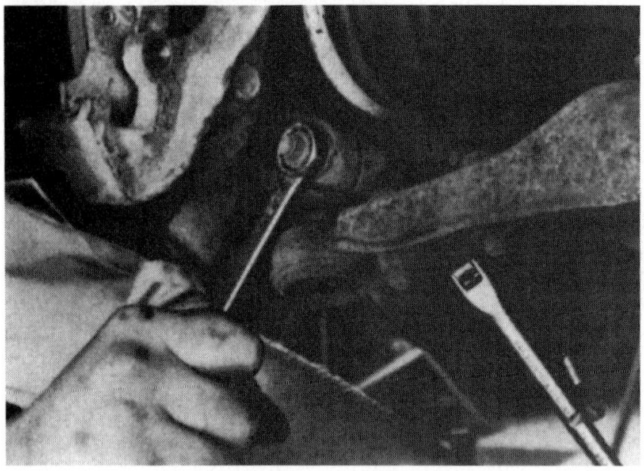

Figure 14-29. Loosen the ball joint stud clamp bolt to detach the lower control arm.

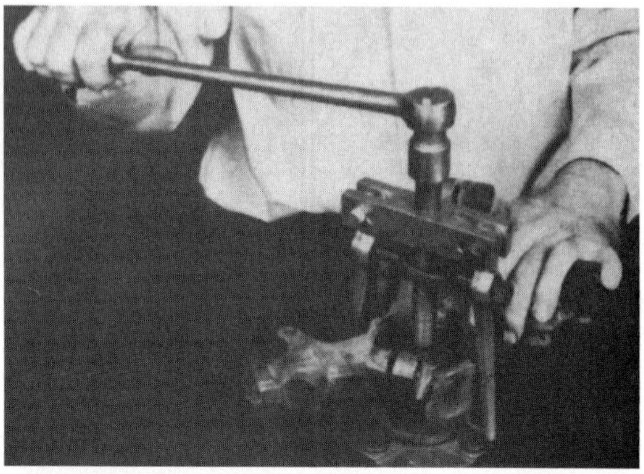

Figure 14-30. Remove the hub with a puller.

Figure 14-31. Use a press to remove the bearing assembly from the steering knuckle.

4. Remove the brake caliper and rotor.
5. Remove the axle nut and washer.
6. Remove the nut securing the tie rod end and use a puller to remove the tie rod from the steering arm, figure 14-28.
7. Disconnect the lower ball joint from the steering knuckle, figure 14-29.
8. Disconnect the knuckle from the strut. If the strut bolts are used to set the alignment, mark their position first.
9. While pushing the CV axle out from the hub, remove the knuckle/hub assembly. Use a puller if necessary.
10. Remove the hub from the bearing using a press, drift, or puller, figure 14-30.
11. Remove the bearing seal (if used) and the bearing retainer. This may be a bolted-on plate or a large snap ring.
12. Use a press to press out the bearing, figure 14-31.
13. Clean the bore of the steering knuckle and smooth away any nicks or burrs with a file or sandpaper.
14. Press the new bearing into the steering knuckle, figure 14-32. Apply pressure only to the outer bearing race.
15. Support the inner bearing race and press the hub into the bearing assembly, figure 14-33.
16. Install the bearing retainer plate or snap ring. Install the new seal, if used, figure 14-34.
17. Clean the splines of the CV axle and the inner hub bore. Align the axle and hub splines and slide the axle into the hub. At the same time, slide the lower ball joint mounting into position.
18. Reinstall the tie rod end, strut bolts, and lower ball joint nut or bolt.

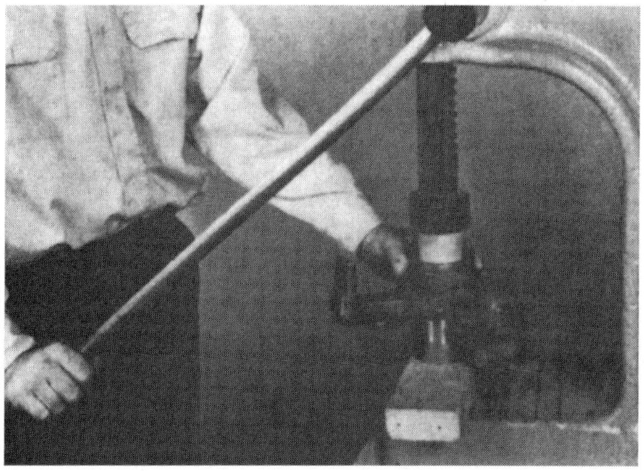

Brake-Related Suspension Service

Figure 14-32. Use a press to install the new bearing assembly.

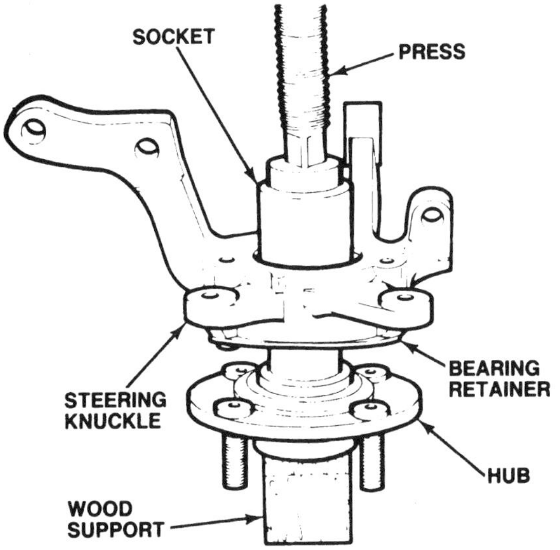

Figure 14-33. Use a press to install the hub into the wheel bearing assembly.

19. Install and tighten the axle washer and nut until it is fully seated.
20. Reinstall the dust shield, rotor, and brake caliper.
21. While an assistant holds the brakes, torque the axle nut to specifications, figure 14-35. This will be very tight, typically from 130 to 240 ft-lb (176 to 325 Nm).
22. Install the cotter pin or crimp the nut retaining collar using a blunt chisel.
23. Install the wheel and lower the vehicle.

Rear Axle Sealed Bearing Replacement

This design combines the bearings with the wheel hub assembly, figure 14-36, which makes replacement a relatively simple job. To replace one of these bearing/hub assemblies:

1. Raise and properly support the vehicle, then remove the wheel with the defective bearing.
2. If the axle is equipped with disc brakes, remove the caliper as described in Chapter 8.

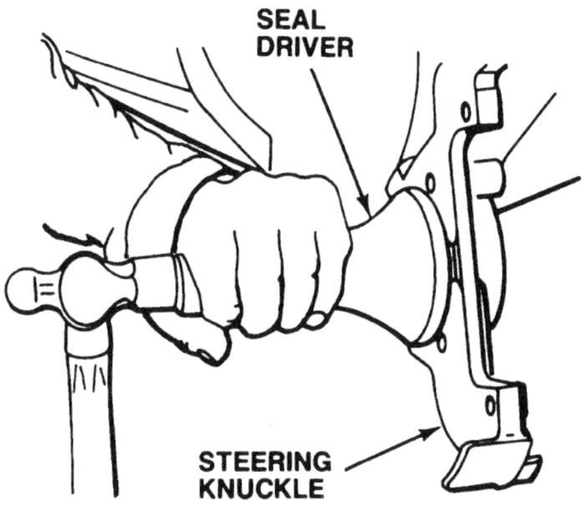

Figure 14-34. Use a driver to install a new dust seal.

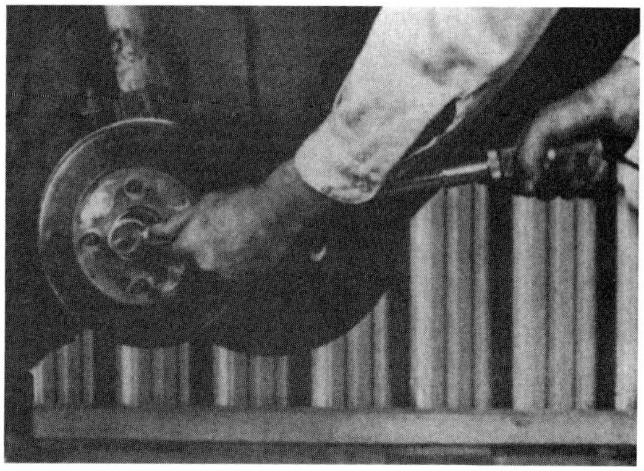

Figure 14-35. Torque the hub nut before you lower the car.

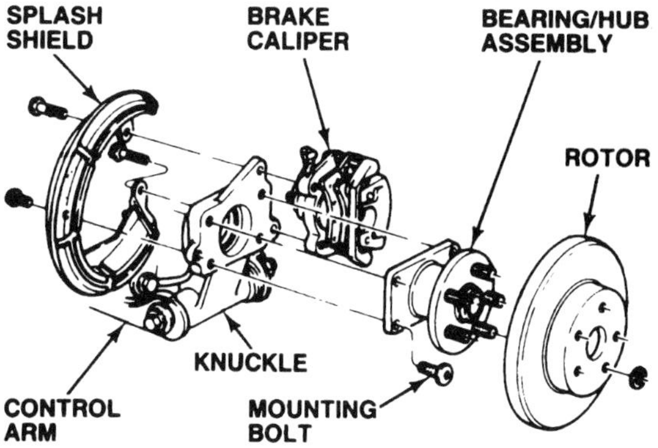

Figure 14-36. A rear-wheel sealed bearing/hub assembly.

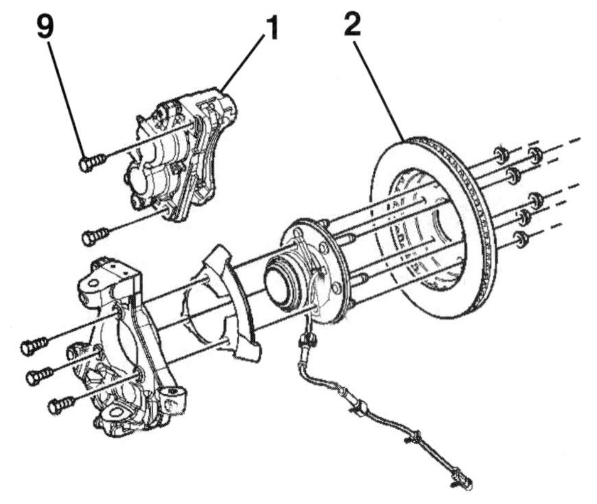

Figure 14-37. Remove the caliper bolts (9), the caliper (1), and the rotor (2). (Courtesy of General Motors Corporation, Service and Parts Operations)

3. Remove and discard any speed nuts, retaining bolts, or screws, then remove the brake drum or rotor from the hub.
4. Remove the four bearing/hub retaining bolts and the assembly.
5. Install the new bearing/hub assembly, and tighten the four retaining bolts to the torque specified by the vehicle manufacturer.
6. Position the brake drum or rotor over the wheel studs.
7. If the axle is equipped with disc brakes, install the brake caliper as described in Chapter 8.

Front Axle Bearing/Hub Assembly Replacement

Many late-model automobiles and light trucks use a sealed bearing and hub assembly, both on the front and rear of the vehicle. Replacement of these hub assemblies is not as difficult as the earlier separate bearing replacement.

As always, refer to the manufacturer's service information for details. The general procedure to replace a front bearing/hub assembly is:

1. Raise and support the vehicle at a comfortable working height.
2. Remove the wheel.
3. Remove the brake caliper and rotor, figure 14-37.
4. Remove the wheel speed sensor (if equipped) and move it out of the way.
5. Remove the bearing/hub assembly mounting bolts, figure 14-38.
6. Remove the hub assembly and splash shield.
7. Clean or replace the O-ring seal, if equipped.

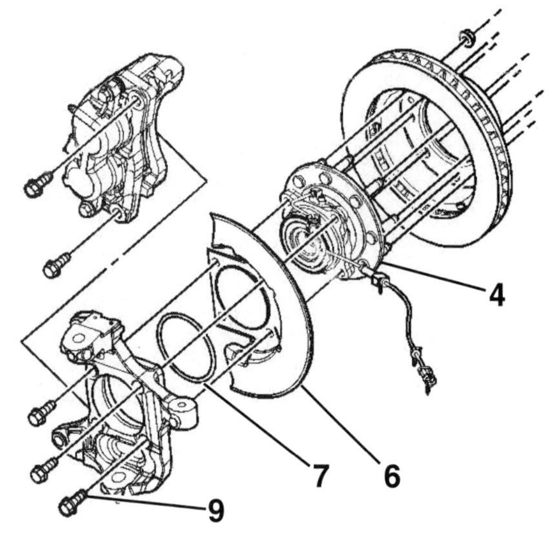

Figure 14-38. Remove the mounting bolts (9) and lift off the hub/bearing assembly (4) and the splash shield (6). Replace the O-ring (7) if needed. (Courtesy of General Motors Corporation, Service and Parts Operations)

8. Lightly grease the steering knuckle bore. Install the new hub assembly.
9. Install the splash shield and mounting bolts. Torque to 130 ft-lb (180 Nm).
10. Install the wheel speed sensor.
11. Install the brake rotor, caliper, and wheel.
12. Lower the vehicle.

SOLID AXLE WHEEL BEARING SERVICE

One of the most common reasons for removing the wheel bearings from a solid rear axle is to replace leaking grease seals that have allowed axle lubricant to contaminate the brake linings. However, before you undertake this job, first check the axle vent on top of the axle housing, figure 14-4. If the vent is plugged, heat can cause a pressure buildup inside the housing that will force lubricant past the seals even if they are in perfect condition. If the vent is not obstructed, replace the leaking seals.

As discussed at the beginning of this chapter, there are two ways axle shafts are retained in solid rear axle housings: axles that ride on straight roller bearings have C-locks; axles that ride on ball bearings have retainer plates. Because the two types require different service procedures, determine which type of axle you are servicing before you begin work.

To ready the vehicle with either type of axle for bearing service, raise and properly support the vehicle, then remove the wheels. Next, remove the brake drums

Brake-Related Suspension Service

or brake calipers and rotors. Drum removal information is covered in Chapter 7, and brake caliper removal is covered in Chapter 8.

Bearing and Seal Service—C-Lock Axles

To service the wheel bearing and grease seal on a solid rear axle retained by a C-lock:

1. Clean any dirt from around the differential cover, then remove the cover and drain the axle lubricant into a suitable drain pan.
2. Rotate the differential carrier until the pinion shaft lock bolt is accessible, then remove the lock bolt and pinion shaft, figure 14-39.
3. Without rotating the axle, push it toward the center of the car until the C-lock clears the counterbore in the differential side gear; remove the C-lock from its groove, figure 14-40.
4. Return the axle to its original position, and replace the pinion shaft and lock bolt to hold the differential carrier pinion gears in position.
5. Pull the axle straight out of the housing by hand, making sure it does not drag on the wheel bearing and cause damage.
6. Pry the seal from the axle housing with a seal puller or large screwdriver, figure 14-41.
7. Use a slide hammer to remove the bearing from the axle housing, figure 14-42.
8. Clean the axle and inspect the surface where the bearing and seal ride. It should be smooth; dull gray in color; and free of any pitting, indentations, scratches, or flaking metal. If any damage is present, replace both the axle and bearing.
9. Clean and inspect the bearing as described earlier. Replace the bearing if any problems are present.
10. Clean the axle housing bore where the bearing and seal fit, and check for damage.
11. Lubricate the outside of the bearing with wheel bearing grease, then align the bearing squarely with the opening in the axle housing. Drive the bearing into place with a suitably sized socket or bearing driver, figure 14-43, that contacts only the outer race of the bearing. The pitch of the sound made when striking the driver will change when the bearing is seated.
12. Install a new grease seal into the axle housing with a seal driver, figure 14-44.
13. Lubricate the bearing rollers, seal lip, and axle sealing surface with axle lubricant, then carefully slide the axle into the housing. Do not allow the splines on the axle to damage the seal or bearing during installation. It may be necessary to rotate the axle slightly to align its splines with those in the differential side gear.

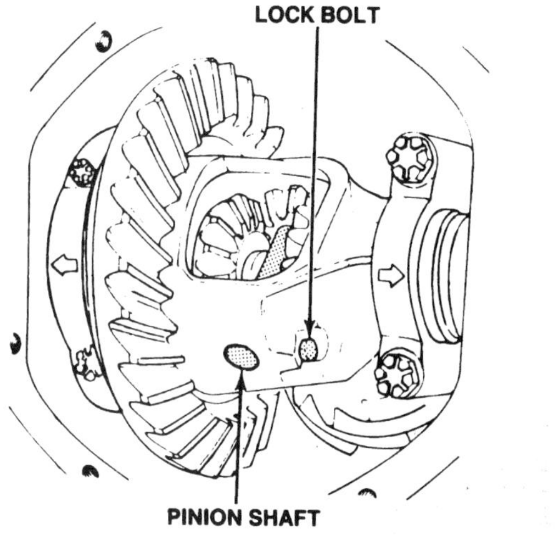

Figure 14-39. To remove a C-lock, first remove the pinion shaft and lock bolt.

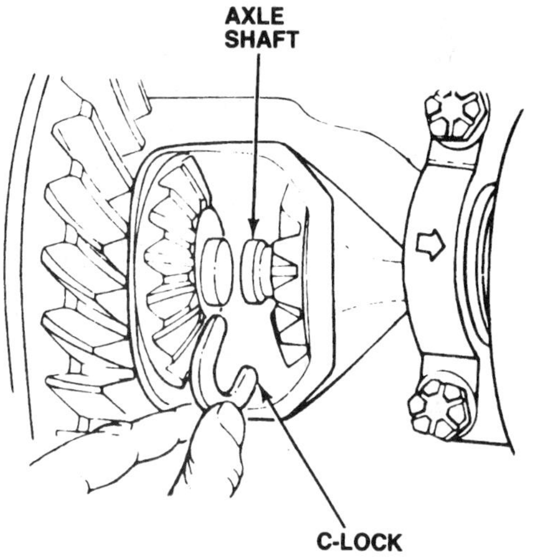

Figure 14-40. Remove the C-lock from its groove in the axle.

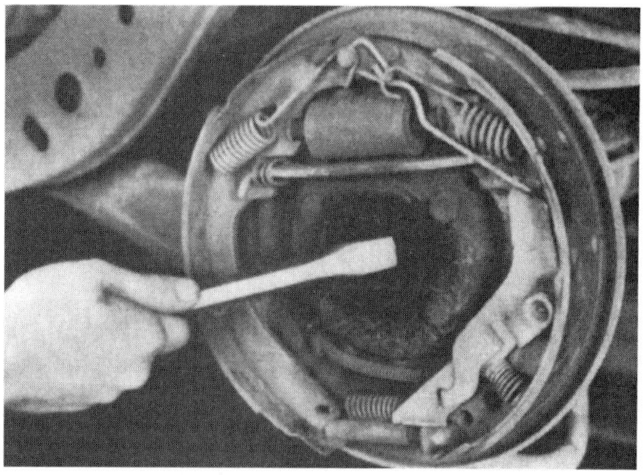

Figure 14-41. Remove the seal from the axle housing.

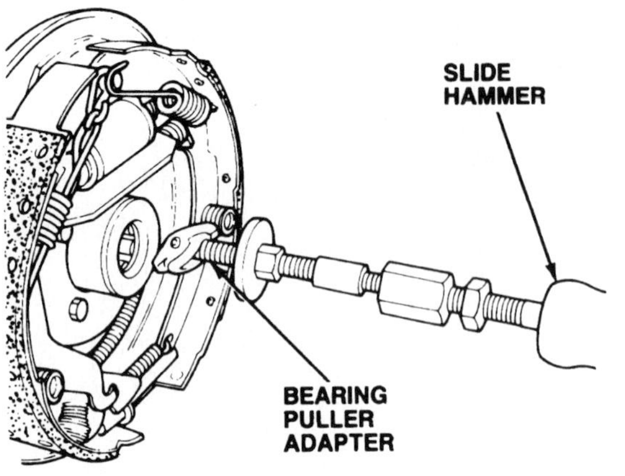

Figure 14-42. Use a slide hammer to pull the bearing out of the axle housing.

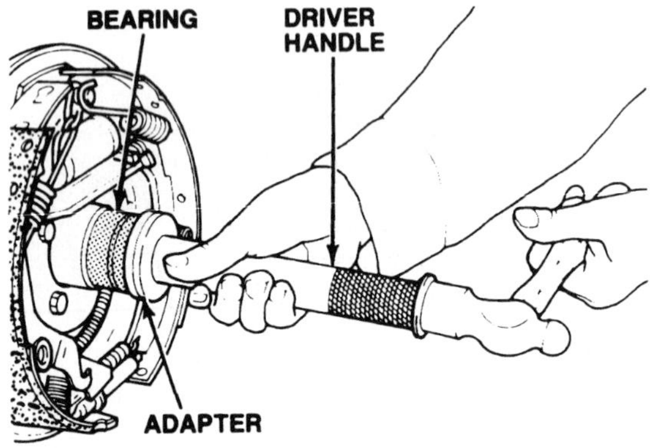

Figure 14-43. Install the new bearing with a bearing driver.

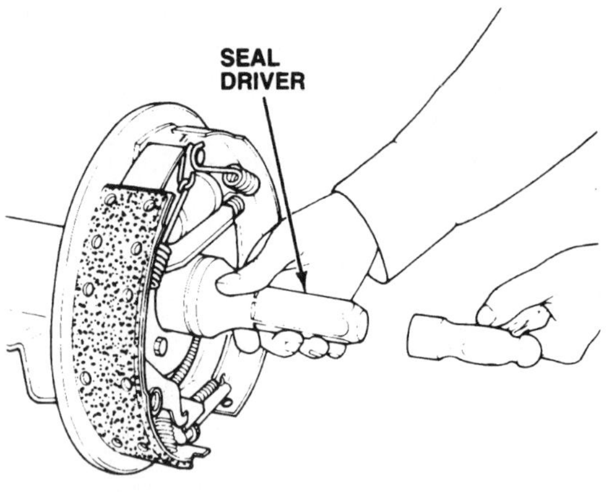

Figure 14-44. Drive the grease seal into the axle housing.

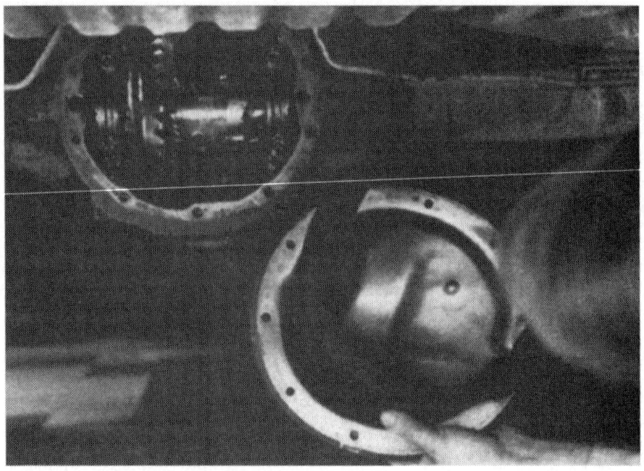

Figure 14-45. Use a new gasket when you install the differential cover.

14. Remove the lock bolt and pinion shaft from the differential carrier, and push the axle inward until the C-lock groove clears the counterbore in the differential side gear. Do not rotate the axle during this operation or the differential carrier pinion gears may be dislodged, making reassembly more difficult.
15. Insert the C-lock into the groove in the inner end of the axle, then pull the axle outward to seat the C-lock in the counterbore of the differential side gear.
16. Install the pinion shaft and lock bolt, then tighten the lock bolt to the torque specified by the vehicle manufacturer.
17. Install the differential cover using a new gasket or silicone sealer as specified by the vehicle manufacturer, figure 14-45.
18. With the axle in its normal operating position, fill the differential to the bottom edge of the fill hole with the lubricant specified by the vehicle manufacturer.

Bearing and Seal Service—Retainer Plate Axles

On most solid rear axles where the wheel bearing and grease seal are secured by a retainer plate, service the bearing and seal as follows:

1. Remove the nuts that hold the retainer plate to the backing plate, figure 14-46.
2. Slide the retainer plate off of the studs, then reinstall two of the nuts finger-tight to keep the brake backing plate in place.
3. Use a puller or slide hammer to remove the axle shaft and bearing from the axle housing, figure 14-47.
4. Remove the seal from the axle housing.
5. Clean the axle housing bore where the bearing and seal fit, and check for damage.
6. If the wheel bearing is unsealed, clean and inspect it as described earlier. If the bearing is sealed, turn it by hand to feel for roughness, lis-

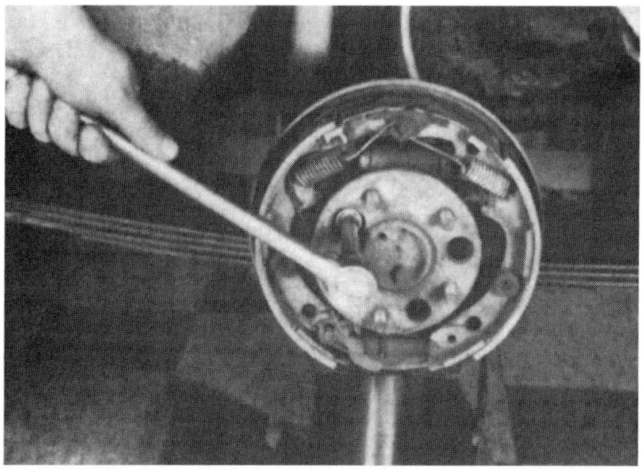

Brake-Related Suspension Service

Figure 14-46. You can unscrew retainer plate nuts through a hole in the axle flange.

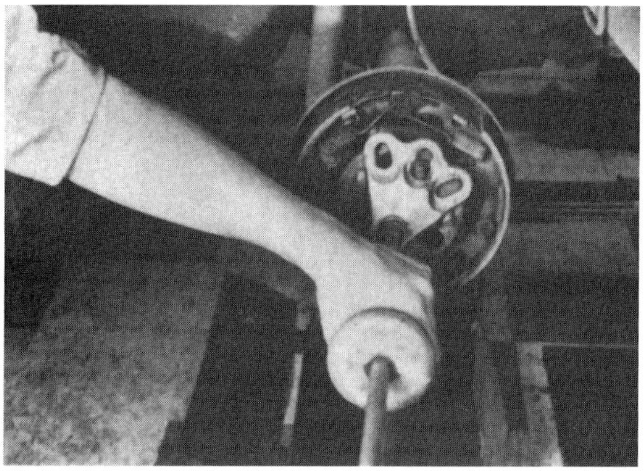

Figure 14-47. Pull the axle from the housing with a slide hammer.

Figure 14-48. One way to free a bearing retaining ring is to notch it with a chisel.

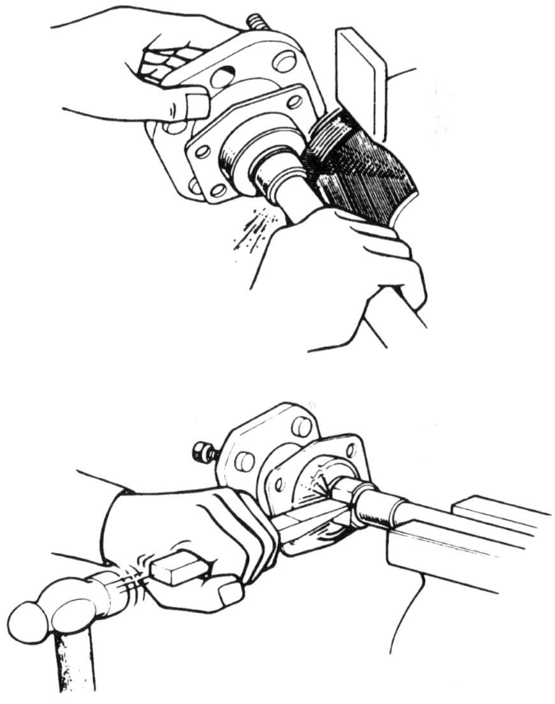

Figure 14-49. Stubborn bearing retaining rings must be ground and cut away.

ten for noise, and make sure the metal side plates are not dented. Replace the bearing if a problem is apparent, or you have any question about the bearing's condition.

7. If the bearing must be replaced, remove the retaining ring that secures it on the axle. Depending on the hardness of the ring and how tightly it fits, use one of these methods, being sure to wear safety glasses to protect your eyes:
   a. Mount the axle in a vise, and use a hammer and chisel to notch the retaining ring in several places around its outer edge, figure 14-48. The ring may loosen enough to remove it from the axle.
   b. Use a grinder to cut away the ring almost to the axle, figure 14-49, then use a hammer and chisel to split the ring and remove it from the axle. Take care not to damage the axle in any way.
8. Using a bearing splitter or other adapter that contacts the *inner* race, press the old bearing off the axle. Never attempt to remove a wheel bearing by pressing against the outer race; the bearing may come apart and cause an injury.
9. Remove the retainer plate and inspect the area on the axle where the bearing and seal make contact; it should be smooth and have a dull gray appearance. Replace the axle if it is rough or worn.
10. Clean all traces of the old gasket from the retainer plate and the brake backing plate. If the retainer plate contains an outer seal, install a new seal and lubricate the seal lip with wheel bearing

Figure 14-50. Press the new bearing into position on the axle.

grease. Replace the retainer plate and a new gasket on the axle.

11. If the new wheel bearing is unsealed, pack it with grease as described earlier.
12. Press the new wheel bearing onto the axle, figure 14-50. Apply pressure only to the inner race of the bearing.
13. Press a new bearing retaining ring onto the axle. Never attempt to press a bearing *and* retaining ring onto the axle at the same time.
14. Install a new seal into the axle housing with a seal driver, and lightly lubricate the lip of the seal with axle lubricant.
15. Carefully slide the axle into the housing so as not to damage the seal. Rotate the axle as necessary to align its splines with those in the differential side gear.
16. Gently tap the end of the axle with a hammer until the bearing is fully seated in the axle housing.
17. Remove the two nuts holding the backing plate in place, then slide the retainer plate onto the axle housing studs.
18. Install the retainer plate nuts, and tighten them to the torque specified by the vehicle manufacturer.

TIRE AND WHEEL SERVICE

The effectiveness of even the best brake repairs can be reduced if there are tire and wheel problems that reduce traction. In some cases, problems associated with tire and wheel service can directly affect the friction developed between the brake drum or rotor and the brake linings. The sections below describe how to properly install the tire and wheel assemblies, how to visually inspect tires and wheel assemblies, how to visually inspect tires and wheels for problems that may affect braking, and how to measure tire and wheel runout.

Tire and Wheel Installation

Although the job of installing a tire and wheel assembly on the car may seem relatively simple, unless certain procedures are strictly observed, braking problems may result. The two main areas of concern are the lug nut or bolt torque and the sequence in which the lug nuts or bolts are tightened. If you overtighten lug nuts and bolts, tighten them unevenly, or tighten them in the wrong sequence, you can distort the wheel, the hub, and the brake drum or rotor. This distortion causes runout and results in a pulsating brake pedal, reduced traction, uneven drum or rotor wear, and poor contact between the drum or rotor and the brake linings. In addition, if you overtighten the lug nuts or bolts too much, the car owner may be unable to remove them with the vehicle lug wrench in the event of a flat tire.

Always use an accurate torque wrench to tighten the lug nuts and bolts to the torque specified by the vehicle manufacturer, figure 14-51. This figure can be found in the owner's manual, the shop manual, and in publications from tire companies and other aftermarket firms that provide specifications to the service industry. Although an impact wrench is useful for removing lug nuts and bolts, never use such a wrench to install a wheel because the torque it applies cannot be accurately controlled.

In addition to the proper tightening torque, it is also important that you tighten lug nuts or bolts in the proper sequence, figure 14-52. As with the proper torque, this helps prevent distortion. All sequences are essentially criss-cross patterns in which you tighten the nuts or bolts alternating from one side of the wheel to the other.

To properly install a tire and wheel assembly, make sure the mounting surfaces on both the wheel and vehicle are clean; remove any dirt, rust, or corrosion with a wire brush. Install the wheel straight onto the car, taking care not to drag it across the wheel stud threads, then install all of the lug nuts or bolts. Do not use any type of lubricant on the wheel studs or lug bolts unless specifically instructed to do so by the vehicle manufacturer. Tighten the nuts or bolts by hand with a wrench until they are snug, then tighten each nut or bolt in the proper sequence to approximately half the specified torque. Go through the sequence once more, and bring the nuts or bolts to their final tightness.

Tire and Wheel Inspection

As discussed in the *Classroom Manual,* tires that are improperly inflated, excessively worn, or mismatched in some manner are all possible causes of braking problems. Bent, cracked, or otherwise damaged wheels can also affect braking performance. The para-

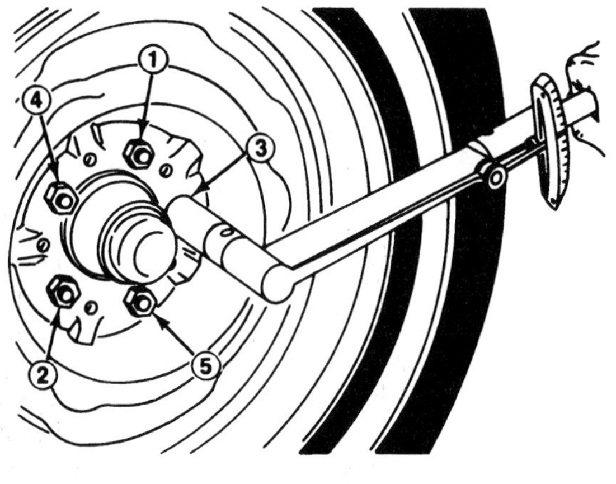

Brake-Related Suspension Service

Figure 14-51. Use a torque wrench to tighten lug nuts or bolts.

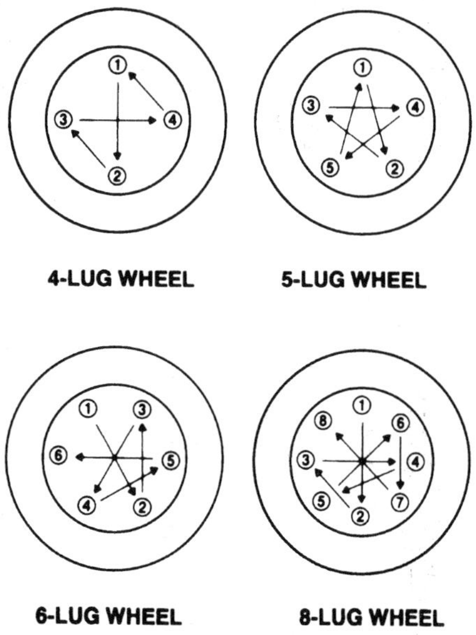

Figure 14-52. Proper lug nut tightening sequences.

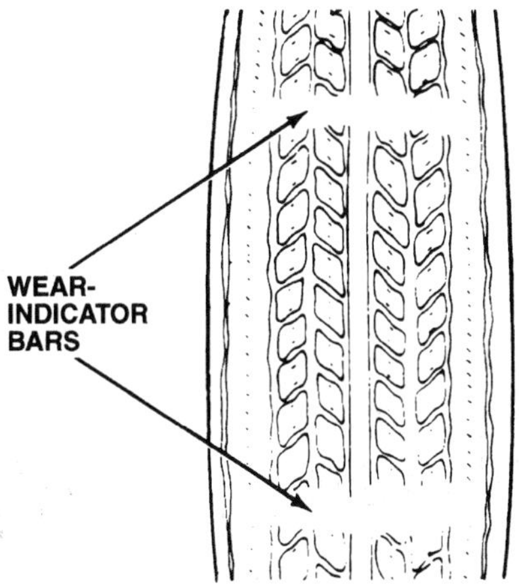

Figure 14-53. The wear indicators on this tire are showing.

graphs below describe the checks and inspections used to identify these problems.

Tire Inflation

Improper inflation is a common tire problem, and many studies show that over half the vehicles on the road have incorrectly inflated tires at any given time. Inflation pressures higher or lower than those specified by the vehicle manufacturer decrease the tire contact patch with the road and reduce braking traction and stability.

Use an accurate high-quality gauge to check the pressure in each tire. If necessary, adjust the pressure to the figure specified by the vehicle manufacturer.

Most cars have a sticker in the glove box or on the driver's door jamb that gives the recommended tire pressures for the size of tires that came on the vehicle. These pressures generally apply to similarly sized replacement tires as well. However, you should never inflate a tire beyond the maximum pressure molded into its sidewall.

Tire pressures often vary, depending on the load the vehicle carries and speed at which the car is driven; heavier loads and faster speeds require higher tire inflation pressures. Be sure to set the pressures to a level appropriate for your customer's driving conditions.

Tire Wear

Tire wear can affect braking in two ways. On dry roads, worn tires actually offer greater braking traction because tread squirm is reduced and there may be more rubber on the road. However, on wet pavement, worn tires have reduced braking traction because they have a much greater tendency to hydroplane. When you check tire wear to trace a brake pull, look primarily for uneven amounts of wear from side to side on an axle.

All modern tires are equipped with tread wear indicator bars that show when only about $1/16$ inch (1.5 mm) of tread is left. The bars appear as bald strips approximately $1/2$ inch (13 mm) wide that run across the tire, figure 14-53. Replace a tire when the wear indicators appear in two or more adjacent tread grooves, if there is localized balding, or if cord is visible at any point.

Mismatched Tires

In order to have even braking power at each wheel, all four tires should be the same type and size unless otherwise specified by the vehicle manufacturer. If the tires differ in their construction (radial, bias-belted, bias-ply), section width (155, 165, etc.), aspect ratio (60, 70, etc.), or diameter (13, 14, etc.), they will have different traction characteristics. This upsets brake balance if the difference is between the front and rear axles, or can cause a brake pull if the difference is between tires on the same axle.

If you have eliminated all other possible causes of a brake balance or pull problem, and suspect that the tires may be contributing to the difficulty, check the size designations molded into the tire sidewalls. If tires of different types or sizes have been mixed, replace them with tires that match the vehicle manufacturer's recommendations.

Tire and Wheel Size and ABS

Not only do mismatched tires and/or wheels affect braking, they also can cause problems with the vehicle's ABS. The vehicle ABS electronic brake control module (EBCM) is programmed with the vehicle tire and wheel size when built. Any variation from the factory calibration may be seen as a wheel speed sensor fault.

Aftermarket wheels and tires that are a different size from original equipment also will change the operation of the ABS in addition to speedometer readings and transmission shift points. If tire and wheel sizes are changed, the EBCM must be reprogrammed with the new tire size.

Wheel Damage

Mild forms of wheel damage, such as a slightly bent rim, may only cause the tire to lose air pressure. More dramatic damage reduces braking traction by causing runout that makes the wheel difficult or impossible to balance. In addition, an impact that causes such damage will usually affect wheel alignment as well. Cracked or badly rusted wheels are especially dangerous because they can fail entirely under the stress of heavy braking.

Inspect all wheels for bent or distorted rims, cracks, and rust or corrosion. If the amount of distortion is minor, you may have to use a dial indicator to check for wheel runout as described in the next section. Replace any wheel that is cracked or badly rusted. Bent or distorted steel wheels can sometimes be straightened by a wheel repair specialist if the damage is not too severe. Alloy wheels, however, cannot be repaired and must be replaced if they are damaged in any way.

TIRE AND WHEEL RUNOUT

Tire and wheel assemblies suffer two kinds of runout, radial and lateral. Radial runout is when the assembly is out of round; this reveals itself as an irregular up and down motion. Lateral runout is when the assembly does not run true from side to side; this reveals itself as an oscillation or wobble. Because it cannot be balanced properly, a tire and wheel assembly with excessive runout does not maintain smooth contact with the road, which upsets braking traction. Tire and wheel runout is most often felt as a vibration in the car body, or a shimmy in the steering wheel.

Checking Tire and Wheel Runout

Runout of the tire and wheel assembly is usually caused by the tire only, the wheel only, or a combination of the two. In rare instances, the vehicle hub may have runout as well. When you check for runout, check at the tire first because this gives you the combined runout of the entire assembly. If runout at the tire is acceptable, there is no need to check further. However, if runout at the tire is excessive, you should then check the wheel runout to determine which part of the assembly is causing the problem.

Before you measure tire and wheel runout, take the following steps to prevent false readings. First, make sure the wheel bearings are properly adjusted; loose bearings increase the amount of runout. Some technicians prefer to check runout with the tire and wheel assembly mounted on a computer wheel balancer because this eliminates wheel bearing play as a factor in the measurement.

Second, make sure the lug nuts or bolts are properly torqued. As discussed earlier in the chapter, overtightened lug nuts or bolts distort the hubs and wheels, and makes it impossible to get an accurate runout reading.

Finally, drive the car for several miles to warm the tires to operating temperature. When a vehicle is parked for any length of time, the cords in the flattened portion of the tire where it contacts the road take a set. Unless the tire is warmed up, the cord set will cause runout during the test. Immediately after you drive the car, raise and properly support it to prevent the tires from taking a new set.

It is easiest to check tire and wheel runout with a special dial indicator made for this purpose, figure 14-54. This tool has a small roller on the end of its plunger that makes it less likely to drag or catch on the tire or wheel. Check for radial runout of the tire and wheel assembly first because it is a more common source of problems, then check for lateral runout.

Radial Runout Test

1. Raise and properly support the vehicle so the tire and wheel to be checked spin freely.
2. Position the plunger of the dial indicator against a center tire tread, figure 14-55.
3. Rotate the tire until the lowest reading shows on the indicator dial; then zero the dial. Ignore any

Brake-Related Suspension Service

Figure 14-54. A dial indicator designed to check tire runout.

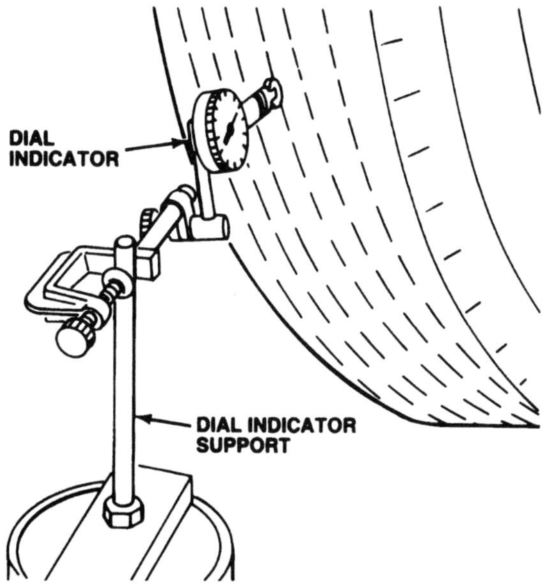

Figure 14-55. Check tire radial runout with the dial indicator against a center tread.

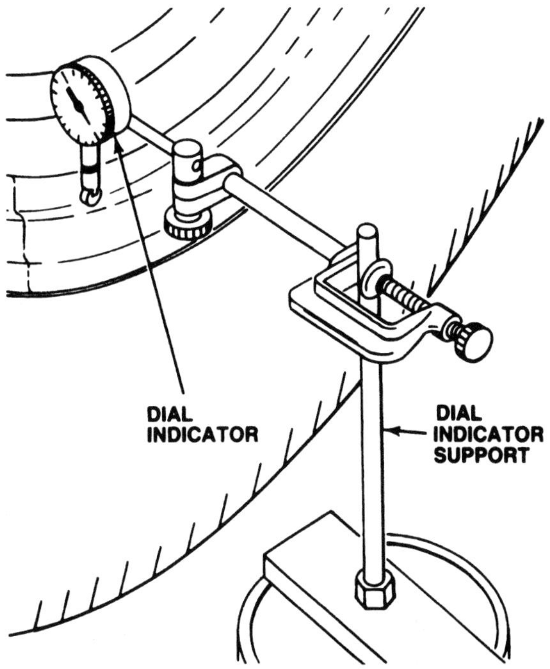

Figure 14-56. Check wheel radial runout with the dial indicator against a horizontal surface.

sudden changes in reading caused by irregularities in the tread.

4. Rotate the tire until the highest reading shows on the indicator dial; this is the total radial runout of the tire and wheel assembly.
   a. If the total radial runout is less than .060″ (1.5 mm), check the lateral runout as described in the next section.
   b. If the total radial runout is greater than .060″ (1.5 mm), continue with step 5 to check the wheel runout.
5. Position the plunger of the dial indicator against the inside of the wheel rim, figure 14-56.
6. Rotate the wheel until the lowest reading shows on the indicator dial, then zero the dial. Ignore any sudden changes in reading caused by irregularities in the wheel surface.
7. Rotate the wheel until the highest reading shows on the indicator dial; this is the total radial runout of the wheel. The runout should be less than .040″ (1.00 mm) for a steel wheel or .030″ (.75 mm) for an alloy wheel.
   a. If the wheel radial runout is within specifications, attempt to correct the total radial runout by match-mounting the tire on the rim as described below. If this is unsuccessful, replace the tire.
   b. If the wheel radial runout is outside specifications, attempt to correct it by repositioning the wheel on the hub as described below. If this is unsuccessful, replace the wheel.

Lateral Runout Test

1. Position the plunger of the dial indicator against a smooth portion of the tire sidewall, figure 14-57.
2. Rotate the wheel until the lowest reading shows on the indicator dial, then zero the dial. Ignore any sudden changes in reading caused by irregularities in the sidewall.
3. Rotate the wheel until the highest reading shows on the indicator dial; this is the total lateral runout of the tire and wheel assembly.

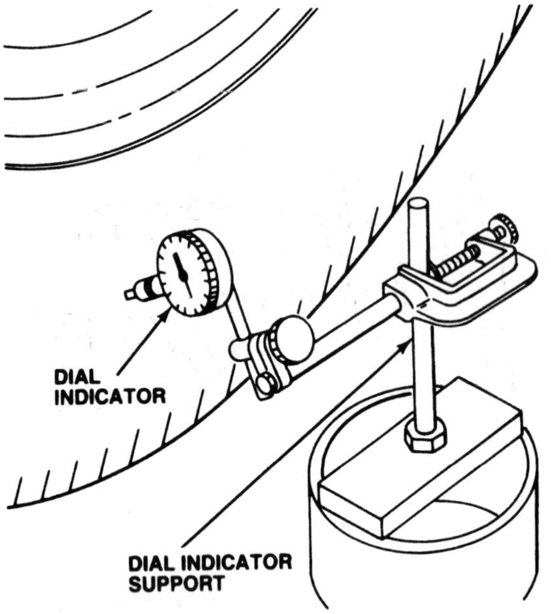

Figure 14-57. Check tire lateral runout with the dial indicator against the sidewall.

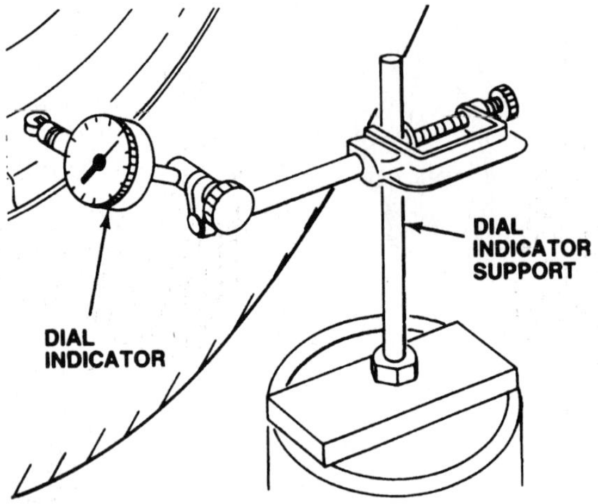

Figure 14-58. Check wheel lateral runout with the dial indicator against a vertical surface.

    a. If the total lateral runout is less than .080″ (2.00 mm), tire and wheel runout is not a problem.

    b. If the total lateral runout is greater than .080″ (2.00 mm), continue with step 4 to check the wheel runout.

4. Position the plunger of the dial indicator against the side of the wheel rim, figure 14-58.
5. Rotate the wheel until the lowest reading shows on the indicator dial, then zero the dial. Ignore any sudden changes in reading caused by irregularities in the wheel surface.
6. Rotate the wheel until the highest reading shows on the indicator dial; this is the total lateral runout of the wheel. The runout should be less than .045″ (1.15 mm) for a steel wheel or .030″ (.75 mm) for an alloy wheel.

    a. If the wheel lateral runout is within specifications, attempt to correct the total lateral runout by match-mounting the tire on the rim as described below. If this is unsuccessful, replace the tire.

    b. If the wheel lateral runout is outside specifications, attempt to correct it by repositioning the wheel on the hub as described below. If this is unsuccessful, replace the wheel.

Correcting Tire and Wheel Runout

If the runout of a tire and wheel assembly is not within specifications, there are four ways you can correct it: reposition the wheel on the hub, match-mount the tire on the wheel, replace the tire, or replace the wheel. As instructed in the procedures above, you should always attempt to reposition the wheel or match-mount the tire before you replace the tire or wheel.

Repositioning the wheel on the hub can correct runout if a stack up of manufacturing tolerances is contributing to the problem. If you install the wheel in a new position, the tolerances may offset one another and reduce the runout to an acceptable figure. To do this, unbolt the wheel, rotate it two studs over from its original position, and remount it making sure you tighten the lug nuts or bolts to the correct torque in the proper sequence. Recheck for radial and lateral runout as described above.

Match-mounting the tire on the wheel can also correct for runout if the high spots of the tire and wheel are aligned. To do this, break the bead of the tire loose from the rim, and reposition the tire 180 degrees from its original position. Recheck for radial and lateral runout as described above.

CHASSIS SERVICE

Chassis problems that affect braking usually result in a pull toward one side when the brakes are applied. This can be caused by damaged or worn suspension components, or by incorrect wheel alignment. If the brakes, tires, and wheels are all in good condition but a pull under braking persists, inspect the suspension and replace any defective parts you may find. Then, put the car on an alignment rack and adjust the suspension to the vehicle manufacturer's specifications.

Brake-Related Suspension Service

Suspension Inspection

You can make a partial check of the suspension while the car is still on the ground. Examine the car at rest, and look for any obvious leanings that may indicate a broken spring or spring mount, or a weak and sagging spring. If you suspect a problem, check the vehicle ride height against the specifications in the shop manual to make sure the car is level.

Next, raise and properly support the vehicle, then inspect the shock absorbers, tie-rod ends, and ball joints. Check the shock absorbers or struts for large amounts of oil leakage that indicate a blown seal; a small amount of seepage is considered normal. Also check for broken or loose shock absorbers or strut mounts.

Check the tie-rod ends for looseness and wear that results in radial and axial play. To test a tie-rod end for radial play, grasp the tire and turn it sharply from side to side while watching for play. To test a tie-rod end for axial play, grasp the tie rod next to the tie-rod end, and attempt to move the rod up and down while watching for play. Replace any tie-rod end that has detectable play.

Ball joints suffer the most wear of any suspension component, and are therefore the most likely to contribute to a braking problem. A worn ball joint allows the spindle to continually change position as the load on the wheel changes. This directly affects wheel alignment, and the stability of the car under braking.

Wear-indicator Ball Joints

Many newer cars are equipped with wear-indicator ball joints. You check the wear on these ball joints while the weight of the vehicle is resting on the wheels. On Chrysler cars, grasp the ball joint grease fitting and attempt to wiggle it, figure 14-59; replace the joint if any movement occurs. On Ford and General Motors cars, check the position of the ball joint grease fitting, figure 14-60. Replace the joint if the fitting boss is flush with, or extends below, the ball joint cover.

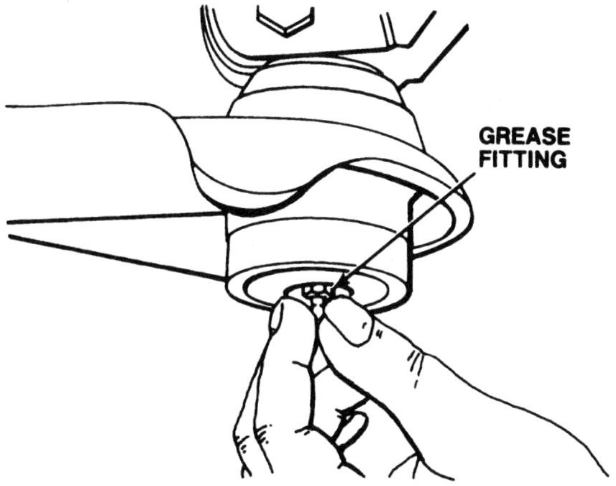

Ball Joints Without Wear Indicators

On cars that do not have wear-indicator ball joints, you check the wear of the joints with the weight of the vehicle off the wheels. Typically, the wear will be concentrated in the load-carrying ball joint, figure 14-61, that supports the weight of the car. If necessary, adjust the wheel bearings before you check the ball joints so you do not mistake bearing play for ball joint wear.

To check the ball joints, raise the car with a floor jack at the appropriate point shown in figure 14-61; this removes tension from the load-carrying ball joint so it will be free to move. Grasp the top and bottom of

Figure 14-59. Checking a Chrysler wear-indicator ball joint.

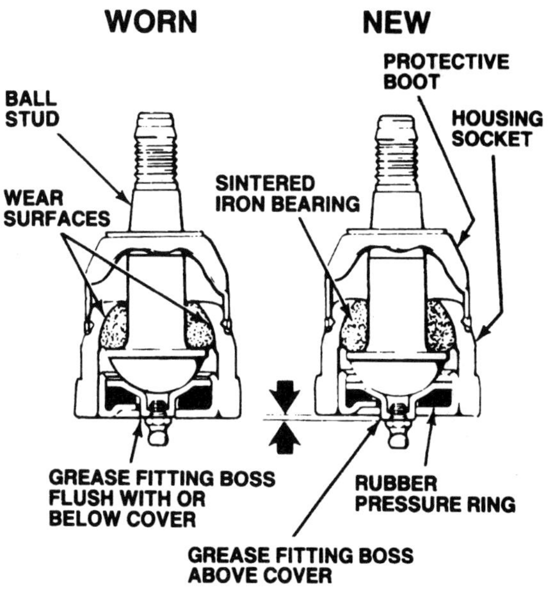

Figure 14-60. Grease fitting position indicates the condition of Ford and GM wear-indicator ball joints.

the tire, and rock it in and out while watching for radial play in the ball joints. Next, place a pry bar under the tire and lever it up and down while looking for axial play in the ball joints. Replace the load-carrying ball joint if its radial or axial play exceeds the specifications. Replace non-load-carrying ball joints if any play is detectable.

Alignment Inspection

While you inspect the suspension as described above, you should also look for any signs of accident damage that may have bent the chassis and upset the wheel

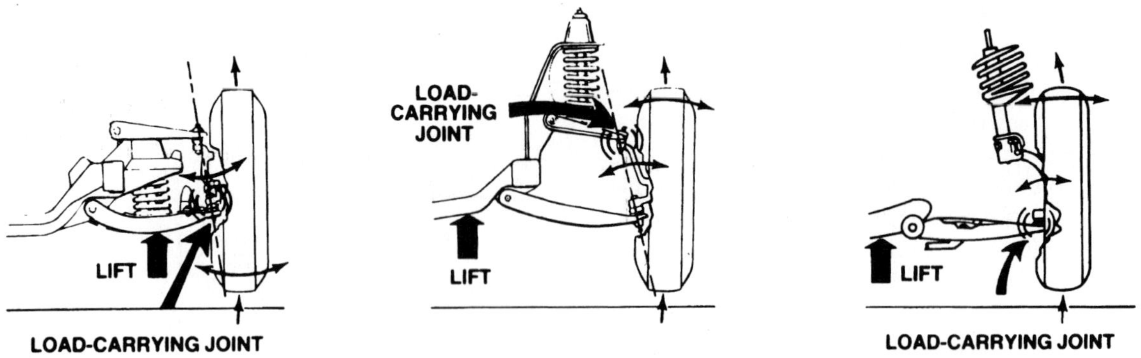

Figure 14-61. Support the suspension as shown to relieve tension on the load-carrying ball joint.

alignment. Once you have replaced any damaged or worn parts, put the vehicle on an alignment rack and check the alignment. Pay special attention to the caster variation from one side of the car to the other.

A brake pull is most likely to occur if the caster is negative at one front wheel and positive on the other. This can occur even with new parts set to specifications. For example, if the manufacturer specifies a maximum one-degree caster variation between the wheels, you could have ½ degree negative caster at one wheel and ½ degree positive caster at the other. Never align a front end so there is positive caster at one wheel and negative caster at the other.